Action &
Self-Development

Jochen Brandtstädter
Richard M. Lerner
Editors

Action &
Self-Development

Theory
and
Research
Through
the
Life
Span

Sage Publications, Inc.
International Educational and Professional Publisher
Thousand Oaks ▪ London ▪ New Delhi

For information:

 Sage Publications, Inc.
2455 Teller Road
Thousand Oaks, California 91320
E-mail: order@sagepub.com

Sage Publications Ltd.
6 Bonhill Street
London EC2A 4PU
United Kingdom

Sage Publications India Pvt. Ltd.
M-32 Market
Greater Kailash I
New Delhi 110 048 India

Printed in the United States of America

Library of Congress Cataloging-in-Publication Data

Main entry under title:

Action and self-development: Theory and research through the
life span / edited by Jochen Brandtstädter and Richard M. Lerner.
    p.   cm.
    Includes bibliographical references (p.   ) and index.
    ISBN 0-7619-1543-5 (acid-free paper)
    1. Intentionality. 2. Action theory. 3. Maturation (Psychology)
I. Brandtstädter, Jochen. II. Lerner, Richard M.
    BF619.5
    155.2'5—dc21   99-6325

This book is printed on acid-free paper.

99 00 01 02 03 10 9 8 7 6 5 4 3 2 1

Acquiring Editor:	Jim Brace-Thompson
Editorial Assistant:	Anna Howland
Production Editor:	Astrid Virding
Editorial Assistant:	Nevair Kabakian
Designer/Typesetter:	Janelle LeMaster

CONTENTS

INTRODUCTION

Development, Action, and Intentionality

Jochen Brandtstädter
Richard M. Lerner

The notion of intentional self-development presented in this volume epitomizes a theoretical stance that has become increasingly influential in developmental research and theory. At the core of this notion is the proposition that individuals are both the products and active producers of their ontogeny and personal development over the life span. Through action, and through experiencing the effects and limitations of goal-related activities, we construe representations and internal working models of ourselves and of the physical, social, and symbolic environments in which we are situated. These representations in turn guide and motivate activities through which we shape the further course of personal development. It follows that we cannot adequately understand human ontogeny over the life span, including the processes of aging, without considering the ways in which individuals, in cognition, action, and social interaction, construe their personal development. Intentionality, and the "intentional world"

(Shweder, 1990) in which intentional activity is embedded, thus becomes an indispensable explanatory category for developmental research. The chapters collected in this volume cover the different themes and strands of an action perspective on development that have emerged in recent years, and they provide an indication of the promise that this perspective holds as a central paradigm for developmental research.

The basic proposition that human individuals actively contribute to shaping their development has never been controversial among developmental researchers, of course. Indeed, the formative role of action and interaction in human ontogeny has been explicitly stressed in most paradigms (see Chapman, 1984). Traditional views, however, have tended to conceive of developmental change as an outcome or by-product, rather than as a target area, of goal-related activity, and thus have missed the basic logic of human development as a self-referential process that both creates and is formed by intentionality and action (see Brandtstädter, 1984; Lerner, 1982).

There are several reasons for this apparent neglect. Some of them certainly have their roots in epistemological complications of the concepts of action and intentionality. As human activities in general, actions related to the control of personal development are situated simultaneously in social and physical as well as mental and symbolic contexts; the question of how these contexts or levels of discourse are linked or can be theoretically integrated leads right into the heart of the mind/body problem (e.g., Greve, 1994; Searle, 1983). Can action explanations be framed according to the causal explanatory scheme? How can we hope to find lawful regularities of action and development, given the fact that we, as intentional actors, reflect upon these regularities and thus may act on them in order to change or destroy them? Would an action perspective on human development not necessarily involve a disavowal of the classical nomothetical ideal of developmental research, which aims at universality and lawful connectedness? These are important but controversial questions, and any attempt to settle them in short compass here would be preposterous (for discussion, see, e.g., Brandtstädter, 1985, 1998; Dannefer, 1989). Suffice it to express our conviction that we apparently must transcend (or deconstruct) traditional dichotomies that have split our worldviews—such as "causes versus reasons," "freedom versus determinism," and "nature versus culture"—in order to gain a comprehensive perspective on human development. "Avoid all splits" (Overton, 1998b) appears to be a fitting motto and guiding methodological principle for this view.

Today, resentments against notions of action and intentionality have faded away. Action-theoretical concepts have made strong inroads into nearly all fields of human and social science (for examples, see Lenk, 1981; Lerner, 1998a). Developmental researchers, impressed by the plasticity and contextual variation of development in most functional domains, have come to recognize that observed ontogenetic patterns reflect cultural and personal agency (see Baltes, 1987; Brandtstädter, 1984; Brim & Kagan, 1980; Bruner, 1990; Eckensberger & Meacham, 1984; Emde & Harmon, 1984; Gergen, 1980; Gollin, 1981; Gottlieb, 1991; Lerner, 1998b; Lerner & Busch-Rossnagel, 1981; Magnusson, 1995; Silbereisen, Eyferth, & Rudinger, 1987; Valsiner, 1987; Wozniak & Fischer, 1993; see also in this volume Lerner & Walls, Chapter 1; Brandtstädter, Chapter 2). Constructs such as "life tasks," "identity goals," "personal projects," "life planning," "possible selves," "life themes," and "compensation," which belong to the conceptual sphere of action theory, have imported notions of intentionality to the developmental domain and have become vantage points of innovative theorizing and research (e.g., Bäckman & Dixon, 1992; Cantor & Fleeson, 1991; Emmons, 1989; Little, 1989; Markus & Ruvolo, 1989; Pulkkinen & Rönkä, 1994; see also in this volume Brunstein, Schultheiss, & Maier, Chapter 6; Little, Chapter 7; Smith, Chapter 8; Gollwitzer, Bayer, Scherer, & Seifert, Chapter 10; Oettingen, Chapter 11; Freund, Li, & Baltes, Chapter 14).

As implied above, intentionality and intentional action are not only driving forces of human ontogeny, but also ontogenetic products (e.g., Brandtstädter, 1998; Bullock, 1991; Higgins, 1988; Oppenheimer & Valsiner, 1991; see also in this volume Brandtstädter, Chapter 2; Mascolo, Fischer, & Neimeyer, Chapter 5; Skinner, Chapter 16). It is only when both sides of this circular relationship are heeded that the central contours of a new developmental paradigm emerge. From early transactions with the environment, and by inauguration into social networks of knowledge and practice, children form the primordial representations of self and personal development from which the processes of intentional self-development evolve. These lines of development eventually merge in the formation of the knowledge systems, identity goals, and self-regulatory skills that are basic to intentional self-development. Typically, the skills and intentional contents involved in self-regulation become more articulate in adolescence and early adulthood, that is, during a transitional period when developmental tasks of identity formation and of an autonomous, self-reliant life planning become salient concerns.

The emergence of processes of intentional self-development marks a dialectic shift in the relation between action and development. To the extent that development gradually forms intentionality and the self, intentional action comes to form development. This is a shift only in emphasis, however; the beliefs, values, and goals that guide activities of intentional self-development remain subject to change along historical and ontogenetic dimensions of time. Normative self-definitions are filled with new meanings in response to role expectations and developmental tasks that confront individuals as they move across the life cycle, and personal ambitions are continually adjusted to age-related alterations in physical, material, and temporal resources of action. Indeed, negotiating a balance between available resources and developmental goals appears to be a basic task of intentional self-development, which becomes particularly salient in contexts of aging (see in this volume Heckhausen & Schulz, Chapter 3; Brandtstädter, Wentura, & Rothermund, Chapter 13; Freund et al., Chapter 14).

The diversity of goals, projects, and life designs that may guide the reflexive monitoring of behavior and development cannot be captured in an exhaustive taxonomy; on a more abstract level, however, we may discern two overarching themes of intentional self-development: self-efficiency and self-cultivation. These themes do not denote developmental outcomes that could be achieved through a finite sequence of instrumental steps, but rather constitute basic motivational tendencies that underlie all self-referent and self-regulatory actions, and that take different expressions in different sociocultural contexts and different phases of the life course. Both themes involve the capacity and readiness to act and reflect upon oneself and to make one's own behavior and development the object of evaluation and intervention.

Self-cultivation, on the one hand, comprises all self-regulatory actions and processes through which we try to bring ourselves and our lives into a form that conforms with normative standards or ideals. As a historical aside, it may be noted that the earliest notions of life-span development were largely synonymous with self-perfection and self-cultivation (e.g., Tetens, 1777). Activities of self-cultivation may reflect notions of virtue and competence, aesthetic ideals, moral or ethical maxims, or socially shared notions of a "good life"; they involve visions of development or conduct that we admire or respect and that influence our choice of developmental paths within culturally preformed opportunity structures.

In the course of their ontogeny, individuals develop not only intentionality, but also intentions about intentions; that is, they can form intentions to have, or not to have, particular intentions. It should be noted at this juncture, however, that our capacity to originate or control our own mental states intentionally is not without limits. This holds not only for pathological cases, but in general: Although we can to some extent strategically control attention and thought, we cannot choose or change our beliefs and preferences by mere act of fiat. Action theorists increasingly recognize that an intentional system that would need to originate intentionally its own intentions would not be able to act at all, for logical as well as functional reasons (see Baumeister, Heatherton, & Tice, 1994; Brandtstädter, 1998; Gilbert, 1993). Nevertheless, it is obvious that self-regulatory processes hinge crucially on the capacity to form, and enact, "second-order volitions" (Frankfurt, 1971); the normative standards of rationality and morality that we embody in our behavior and development generally operate on this metaintentional level.

The theme of *self-efficiency,* on the other hand, points to the basic fact that we generally strive to expand our action resources and developmental potentials, to defend them against losses and constraints, and to economize the use of resources so that there remain reserves to enrich our developmental prospects. Generally speaking, self-efficiency becomes a dominant motivational concern wherever individuals approach performance limits or "production possibility frontiers," to put it in economic terms (see Brandtstädter & Wentura, 1995).

From a developmental point of view, the transition to later life constitutes a paradigm case. The curtailment of physical, social, and temporal action reserves that typically accompanies the processes of aging puts pressure on the optimization and optimal allocation of functional resources, as well as on the selection and accommodation of goals and ambitions (see in this volume Heckhausen & Schulz, Chapter 3; Brandtstädter et al., Chapter 13; Freund et al., Chapter 14). The themes of self-efficiency and self-cultivation merge in what Rawls (1971) has termed the "Aristotelian principle," that is, in the tendency to select and create environments where one's capacities and competencies can be used and expressed on their highest and most differentiated levels; this tendency constitutes a fundamental motivational vector of intentional self-development (see also Bandura, 1991; Brim, 1992).

From a social-historical point of view, it should be noted that issues related to self-management and compensation of deficits gain particular weight under conditions of cultural acceleration, globalization, and pluralization of life forms. The necessity of adjusting life policies to rapidly changing role structures and task environments has led to a gradual blurring of normative "timetables" for individuals' organization of life and development; development has increasingly become a "reflexive project" (Giddens, 1991, p. 145) requiring individualized choice and planful competence. In addition, developmental settings under conditions of modernity have placed increasing emphasis on the efficient use and allocation of temporal, physical, and psychological resources, thus forcing individuals to take active, self-monitoring, and optimizing attitudes toward their own behavior and development. While opening new options for intentional self-development across the life span, these historical trends also involve developmental hazards. The maintenance of a sense of personal continuity and control and the creation of meaningful identity projects under conditions of uncertainty, change, and risk have become developmental tasks in themselves (see Sennett, 1998).

These preliminary considerations should not be read to imply that humans are the sole or omnipotent producers of their development. Like any other human activity, intentional self-development is structured by the interaction of biological, social, and cultural forces. Although these constraints are in turn to a large extent structured by human action and interaction, they are not throughout mentally represented by individual actors, and they partly transcend personal control (see Giddens, 1979). Thus elements of autonomy and of heteronomy are closely intertwined in intentional self-development (see Dannefer, Chapter 4, this volume); this holds all the more as intentional activities throughout involve nonintentional and subintentional mechanisms (see Bargh & Barndollar, 1996; Brandtstädter, 1998). Furthermore, due to the bounded rationality of human actors and the partial intransparency of the external and "internal" contexts of action, life histories are always a mixture of controllable and uncontrollable elements. Over the life course, some desired goals and developmental outcomes are accomplished, others remain unachieved or drift outside the individual's span of control, which itself is subject to developmental change and modifications across the life cycle (see in this volume Fung, Abeles, & Carstensen, Chapter 12; Skinner, Chapter 16).

Notions of self-regulation and personal control over development thus converge with a growing emphasis in developmental psychology on the malleability, contextual embeddedness, and sociohistorical specificity of developmental patterns; at the same time, these ideas provide scope to integrate biological and evolutionary points of view. Among the biological and evolutionary factors that enforce, and at the same time make possible, intentional self-regulation, the great openness and plasticity of human development must be mentioned as of primary importance (see Lerner, 1984, 1998b). Anthropologists and biologists have recognized that culture, and the functional potentials to create culture and cultivate personal development, to a large extent compensates for a lack of adaptive specialization in the human species (e.g., Geertz, 1973; see also in this volume Brandtstädter, Chapter 2; Heckhausen & Schulz, Chapter 3). Biology does not impose rigid constraints on development, but rather establishes norms of reaction that involve a range of developmental outcomes over a range of environmental conditions (see Gould, 1981). Epigenetic environmental influences, however, are structured and temporally organized through interactions of the developing individual with his or her environment. Phenotypic and genotypic conditions are thus linked in a circular, co-constructive relation; the influence and expression of genetic factors in ontogeny are interactively moderated, as well as mediated, by activities through which individuals select and construct their developmental ecology (see Gottlieb, 1997; Gottlieb, Wahlsten, & Lickliter, 1998). In this view, traditional splits between "nature" and "culture," as well as attempts to establish a causal priority between these categories, are rendered obsolete (e.g., Overton, 1998a; Tooby & Cosmides, 1992; see also Lerner & Walls, Chapter 1, this volume).

As noted above, concepts of action and intentionality cannot be isolated from the sociocultural forces that structure goal-related human activity. The notion of intentional self-development integrates personal and contextual views on personal development and braids together action-theoretical, developmental, cultural, and historical perspectives. In fact, the concepts of intentionality, development, and culture presuppose one another; we cannot explicate one of these terms without referring to the other two. As Boesch (1991) has put it, cultures "develop, change, *and* remain constant as a result of individual actions and interactions" (p. 31); this holds even if the action results are not completely desired or anticipated, and certainly do not form a coherent intentional plan. Cultural systems maintain, reproduce, and reform themselves across historical time not only by imposing constraints on action, but also by providing tools and compensatory devices that expand personal action spaces. The self-reproductive or "autopoietic" functions (see Dupuy & Varela, 1992) of sociocultural systems also involve the control of human ontogeny over the life span.

Across all areas and throughout all phases of the human life course, developmental processes are shaped and canalized by culturally preformed arrangements of stimulation and information as well as by institutionalized beliefs about optimal development and successful aging. Activities of intentional self-development form part of, and in fact mediate, the cultural regulation of development, although individual actors may play an unwitting part in this process. It is through transaction with their social and cultural environment that individuals form personal conceptions of possible and desired developmental courses, as well as acquire the knowledge and means to implement them. Sociocultural demands and expectations about development, of course, often conflict with personal goals and developmental potentials. Such conflicts, and the ways in which they are personally negotiated, are important forces in both cultural evolution and personal development, as they motivate individuals to create a "personal culture" (Heidmets, 1985) that may partly diverge from culturally scripted patterns of the life course.

Developmental researchers not only analyze, explain, and predict development, they also put ideas about development into the heads of developing individuals. Some of these ideas may encourage them to take a proactive stance with regard to their own development and aging; others may undermine such an active and engaged attitude. The contributions collected in this volume speak clearly for the former option. They remind us, as scientists and developing individuals, that our theoretical ideas also shape and inform our lives and personal development. Thus, in effect, our theories become part of the antecedent conditions of the processes that they attempt to explain.

ACKNOWLEDGMENTS

We would like to close this introduction by expressing our appreciation for the support we have received from many quarters during the conceptualization and implementation of this volume. Our first thanks are due to the authors who have joined us in exploring the interfaces among action, intentionality, and development, and who share our fascination for this particular theoretical perspective. We appreciate their splendid contributions as well as their responsiveness to our editorial wishes. We also wish to express our gratitude to Sage Publications, and in particular to our editor at Sage, Jim Brace-Thompson, for support and advice. A number of people have helped us in the task of preparing this volume for publication; above all, we should pay tribute to Brigitte Goerigk-Seitz (Trier) and Sofia T.

Romero (Boston) for their skillful assistance in editing the chapters. This volume was completed while Jochen Brandtstädter was a Fellow at the Center for Advanced Study in the Behavioral Sciences (Stanford); the financial support by the German-American Academic Council is gratefully acknowledged. Richard M. Lerner's work was supported in part by a grant from the William T. Grant Foundation, which he gratefully acknowledges.

REFERENCES

Bäckman, L., & Dixon, R. A. (1992). Psychological compensation: A theoretical framework. *Psychological Bulletin, 112*, 259-283.

Baltes, P. B. (1987). Theoretical propositions of life-span developmental psychology: On the dynamics between growth and decline. *Developmental Psychology, 23*, 611-626.

Bandura, A. (1991). Self-regulation of motivation through anticipatory and self-reactive mechanisms. In R. Dienstbier (Ed.), *Nebraska Symposium on Motivation: Vol. 38. Perspectives on motivation* (pp. 69-164). Lincoln: University of Nebraska Press.

Bargh, J. A., & Barndollar, K. (1996). Automaticity in action: The unconscious as repository of chronic goals and motives. In P. M. Gollwitzer & J. A. Bargh (Eds.), *The psychology of action: Linking cognition and motivation to behavior* (pp. 457-481). New York: Guilford.

Baumeister, R. F., Heatherton, T. F., & Tice, D. M. (1994). *Losing control: How and why people fail at self-regulation.* San Diego, CA: Academic Press.

Boesch, E. E. (1991). *Symbolic action theory in cultural psychology.* Berlin: Springer.

Brandtstädter, J. (1984). Personal and social control over development: Some implications of an action perspective in life-span developmental psychology. In P. B. Baltes & O. G. Brim, Jr. (Eds.), *Life-span development and behavior* (Vol. 6, pp. 1-32). New York: Academic Press.

Brandtstädter, J. (1985). Individual development in social action contexts: Problems of explanation. In J. R. Nesselroade & A. von Eye (Eds.), *Individual development and social change: Explanatory analysis* (pp. 243-264). New York: Academic Press.

Brandtstädter, J. (1998). Action perspectives on human development. In W. Damon (Series Ed.) & R. M. Lerner (Vol. Ed.), *Handbook of child psychology: Vol. 1. Theoretical models of human development* (5th ed., pp. 807-863). New York: John Wiley.

Brandtstädter, J., & Wentura, D. (1995). Adjustment to shifting possibility frontiers in later life: Complementary adaptive modes. In R. A. Dixon & L. Bäckman (Eds.), *Compensating for psychological deficits and declines: Managing losses and promoting gains* (pp. 83-106). Mahwah, NJ: Lawrence Erlbaum.

Brim, G. (1992). *Ambition: How we manage success and failure throughout our lives.* New York: Basic Books.

Brim, O. G., Jr., & Kagan, J. (Eds.). (1980). *Constancy and change in human development.* Cambridge, MA: Harvard University Press.

Bruner, J. S. (1990). Culture and human development: A new look. *Human Development, 33,* 344-355.

Bullock, M. (Ed.). (1991). *The development of intentional action: Cognitive, motivational, and interactive processes.* Basel: Karger.

Cantor, N., & Fleeson, W. (1991). Life tasks and self-regulatory processes. In M. L. Maehr & P. R. Pintrich (Eds.), *Advances in motivation and achievement* (Vol. 7, pp. 327-369). Greenwich, CT: JAI.

Chapman, M. (Ed.). (1984). Intentional action as a paradigm for developmental psychology: A symposium. *Human Development, 27,* 113-144.

Dannefer, D. (1989). Human action and its place in theories of aging. *Journal of Aging Studies, 3,* 1-20.

Dupuy, J.-P., & Varela, F. J. (1992). Understanding origins: An introduction. In F. J. Varela & J.-P. Dupuy (Eds.), *Understanding origins: Contemporary views on the origin of life, mind, and society* (pp. 1-25). Dordrecht, Netherlands: Kluwer.

Eckensberger, L. H., & Meacham, J. A. (1984). The essentials of action theory: A framework for discussion. *Human Development, 27,* 166-172.

Emde, R. N., & Harmon, R. J. (Eds.). (1984). *Continuities and discontinuities in development.* New York: Plenum.

Emmons, R. A. (1989). The personal striving approach to personality. In L. A. Pervin (Ed.), *Goal concepts in personality and social psychology* (pp. 87-126). Hillsdale, NJ: Lawrence Erlbaum.

Frankfurt, H. G. (1971). Freedom of the will and the concept of a person. *Journal of Philosophy, 68,* 5-20.

Geertz, C. (1973). *The interpretation of cultures: Selected essays.* New York: Basic Books.

Gergen, K. J. (1980). The emerging crisis in life-span developmental theory. In P. B. Baltes & O. G. Brim, Jr. (Eds.), *Life-span development and behavior* (Vol. 3, pp. 31-63). New York: Academic Press.

Giddens, A. (1979). *Central problems in social theory: Action, structure, and contradiction in social analysis.* London: Macmillan.

Giddens, A. (1991). *Modernity and self-identity: Self and society in the late modern age.* Stanford, CA: Stanford University Press.

Gilbert, D. T. (1993). The assent of man: Mental representation and the control of belief. In D. M. Wegner & J. W. Pennebaker (Eds.), *Handbook of mental control* (pp. 57-87). Englewood Cliffs, NJ: Prentice Hall.

Gollin, E. S. (Ed.). (1981). *Developmental plasticity: Behavioral and biological aspects of variations in development.* New York: Academic Press.

Gottlieb, G. (1991). Epigenetic systems view of human development. *Developmental Psychology, 27,* 33-34.

Gottlieb, G. (1997). *Synthesizing nature-nurture: Prenatal roots of instinctive behavior.* Mahwah, NJ: Lawrence Erlbaum.

Gottlieb, G., Wahlsten, D., & Lickliter, R. (1998). The significance of biology for human development: A developmental psychobiological systems view. In W. Damon (Series Ed.) and R. M. Lerner (Vol. Ed.), *Handbook of child psychology: Vol. 1. Theoretical models of human development* (5th ed., pp. 233-273). New York: John Wiley.

Gould, S. J. (1981). *The mismeasure of man.* New York: W. W. Norton.

Greve, W. (1994). *Handlungsklärung.* Göttingen, Germany: Hogrefe.

Heidmets, M. (1985). Environment as the mediator of human relationships: Historical and ontogenetic aspects. In T. Gärling & J. Valsiner (Eds.), *Children within environments: Toward a psychology of accident prevention* (pp. 217-227). New York: Plenum.

Higgins, E. T. (1988). Development of self-regulatory and self-evaluative processes: Costs, benefits, and trade-offs. In M. R. Gunnar & L. A. Sroufe (Eds.), *Minnesota Symposium on Child Psychology: Vol. 23. Self processes in development* (pp. 125-165). Minneapolis: University of Minnesota Press.

Lenk, H. (1981). Interpretative action constructs. In J. Agassi & R. S. Cohen (Eds.), *Scientific philosophy today* (pp. 151-157). Dordrecht, Netherlands: Reidel.

Lerner, R. M. (1982). Children and adolescents as producers of their own development. *Developmental Review, 2,* 342-370.

Lerner, R. M. (1984). *On the nature of human plasticity.* Cambridge: Cambridge University Press.

Lerner, R. M. (Ed.). (1998a). *Theoretical models of human development* (Vol. 1 of *Handbook of child psychology,* 5th ed.; W. Damon, Series Ed.). New York: John Wiley.

Lerner, R. M. (1998b). Theories of human development: Contemporary perspectives. In W. Damon (Series Ed.) & R. M. Lerner (Vol. Ed.), *Handbook of child psychology: Vol. 1. Theoretical models of human development* (5th ed., pp. 1-24). New York: John Wiley.

Lerner, R. M., & Busch-Rossnagel, N. A. (Eds.). (1981). *Individuals as producers of their development: A life-span perspective.* New York: Academic Press.

Little, B. R. (1989). Personal projects analyses: Trivial pursuits, magnificent obsessions and the search for coherence. In D. M. Buss & N. Cantor (Eds.), *Personality psychology: Recent trends and emerging directions* (pp. 15-31). New York: Springer.

Magnusson, D. (1995). Individual development: A holistic, integrated model. In P. Moen, G. H. Elder, Jr., & K. Luscher (Eds.), *Examining lives in context: Perspectives on the ecology of human development* (pp. 19-60). Washington, DC: American Psychological Association.

Markus, H., & Ruvolo, A. (1989). Possible selves: Personalized representations of goals. In L. A. Pervin (Ed.), *Goal concepts in personality and social psychology* (pp. 211-241). Hillsdale, NJ: Lawrence Erlbaum.

Oppenheimer, L., & Valsiner, J. (Eds.). (1991). *The origins of action: Interdisciplinary and international perspectives.* New York: Springer.

Overton, W. F. (1998a). Developmental psychology: Philosophy, concepts, and methods. In W. Damon (Series Ed.) & R. M. Lerner (Vol. Ed.), *Handbook of child psychology: Vol. 1. Theoretical models of human development* (5th ed., pp. 107-188). New York: John Wiley.

Overton, W. F. (1998b). Relational-developmental theory: A psychology perspective. In D. Görlitz, J. H. Harloff, J. Valsiner, & G. Mey (Eds.), *Children, cities, and psychological theories: Developing relationships* (pp. 315-335). Berlin: Walter de Gruyter.

Pulkkinen, L., & Rönkä, A. (1994). Personal control over development. *Developmental Psychology, 30,* 260-271.

Rawls, J. (1971). *A theory of justice.* Cambridge: Cambridge University Press.

Searle, J. R. (1983). *Intentionality: An essay in the philosophy of mind.* New York: Cambridge University Press.

Sennett, D. (1998). *The corrosion of character.* New York: W. W. Norton.

Shweder, R. A. (1990). Cultural psychology: What is it? In J. W. Stigler, R. A. Shweder, & G. Herdt (Eds.), *Cultural psychology: Essays on comparative human development* (pp. 1-43). Cambridge: Cambridge University Press.

Silbereisen, R. K., Eyferth, K., & Rudinger, G. (Eds.). (1987). *Development as action in context.* New York: Springer.

Tetens, J. (1777). *Philosophische Versuche über die menschliche Natur und ihre Entwicklung.* Leipzig: M. G. Weidmanns Erben und Reich.

Tooby, J., & Cosmides, L. (1992). The psychological foundations of culture. In J. H. Barkow, L. Cosmides, & J. Tooby (Eds.), *The adapted mind: Evolutionary psychology and the generation of culture* (pp. 19-139). New York: Oxford University Press.

Valsiner, J. (1987). *Culture and the development of children's action.* New York: John Wiley.

Wozniak, R. H., & Fischer, K. W. (Eds.). (1993). *Development in context: Acting and thinking in specific environments.* Hillsdale, NJ: Lawrence Erlbaum.

Part I

DEVELOPMENT AS A PERSONAL AND SOCIAL CONSTRUCTION

1

REVISITING *INDIVIDUALS AS PRODUCERS OF THEIR DEVELOPMENT*

From Dynamic Interactionism to Developmental Systems

Richard M. Lerner
Ted Walls

The nature-nurture issue was resolved in the mid-1950s, at least insofar as the field of human development is concerned. Introductory psychology and child development textbooks still cast the study of nature and nurture in the form of what Anastasi (1958) terms the "Which one?" or "How much of each?" questions (e.g., Feldman, 1998; Gray, 1998; Lahey, 1998; Meyers, 1998; Papalia, Olds, & Feldman, 1998). In addition, sociobiologists (e.g., Rushton, 1987) and behavioral geneticists (e.g., Rowe, 1994) continue to make concerted efforts to keep intellectually alive a failed conception of nature as split from nurture (see Overton, 1998). Nevertheless, Anastasi's paper, as well as earlier ones by Schneirla (1956, 1957) and Lehrman (1953) and contemporaneous scholarship by Kuo (1967, 1976) that would become well-known only in subsequent decades, explained that *nature* and *nurture* are terms that pertain to components of a fully integrated (Gollin, 1981), "fused" (Tobach & Greenberg, 1984), coactional (Gottlieb, 1997), or dynamic interactional (Lerner, 1978, 1979) system. Thus, to Anastasi, Schneirla, Lehrman, and others with their theoretical orientation—Tobach, Greenberg, Gollin, Gottlieb, and Kuo, for instance—conceptions that split, and methodologies that purported to study, nature as distinct from nurture, maturation as independent from experience, or organism as apart from the environment were inherently flawed, counterfactual, and counterproductive.

Indeed, Schneirla (1957) illustrated the dynamic nature of the link between sources of development—that is, the reciprocal and inextricable influence of one source upon others—by explaining that across ontogeny organisms influenced the context that was influencing them. In a passage in his chapter in Harris's classic volume *The Concept of Development* (1957), Schneirla (1957, pp. 86-89) describes the role of circular functions and self-stimulation across the life span. Through the individual actions organisms take in and on their environment, including their social/interpersonal environment, and through the actions others take in reaction to their interindividually distinct actions and characteristics, organisms influence a source of their own development: That is, they influence their context (e.g., the microsystem; Bronfenbrenner, 1979). The feedback (e.g., the stimulation) from others that accrues to the organism as a consequence of its individuality constitutes a ubiquitous circular function between organism and environment. This circular function provides a key instance of the fusion of nature and nurture; it illustrates the levels of organization that are integrated in the coactional living system that constitutes human development (Gottlieb, 1997). Moreover, the idea of circular functions in ontogeny promotes a focus on the relational characteristics—the features of the connections between individual and context—that structure this system.

Simply, then, within the perspective forwarded by Schneirla (1956), levels of organization in human life—spanning the inner biological through the sociocultural and historical (e.g., see Baltes, 1987; Bronfenbrenner, 1979; Elder, 1998; Riegel, 1975, 1976a, 1976b)—are fully integrated in the structure and function of human behavior and development. Thus individuals, through the network of coactions within this integrated ecology—that is, through the relations between their actions on this context and the actions of the context on them—are active agents in their own development. People, as a consequence of their individuality, and through their activities and actions, are producers of their own development.

THE GENESIS OF ATTEMPTS TO UNDERSTAND THE ROLE OF INDIVIDUALS IN THEIR OWN DEVELOPMENT

Science is an appropriately conservative institution. The knowledge base should not be revised without thorough attention to issues of reliability and validity of evidence. Accordingly, paradigms—systematic ways of understanding the character of the phenomena of a field, of interpreting and integrating evidence—are not easily disregarded or dropped from the repertoire of intellectual commerce (see Kuhn, 1970). Thus from the mid-1950s to the mid-1970s the perspective of Schneirla and others was seen as an important but not necessarily predominant theoretical focus within the study of development. The "paradigm" represented by Schneirla and his colleagues required additional empirical support, especially for the study of *human* development, before it could become a "revolutionary" force in the field and "overthrow" the predominance of mechanistic and reductionist theories—paradigms that split nature from nurture and emphasized either environmental or biological (genetic) mechanisms (Cairns, 1998; Dixon & Lerner, 1999; Overton, 1998).

By the mid- to late 1970s, however, such a paradigm shift was evident. Accounts of human development that emphasized *action*—that is, (a) the action of individuals on contexts; (b) the action of contexts on individuals; and, most important, (c) the relation, or coaction (Gottlieb, 1991, 1997), between a and b—began to fill the literature of human development. Examples include the publications emanating from the West Virginia University Life-Span Development conference series (e.g., Baltes & Schaie, 1973; Goulet & Baltes, 1970; Nesselroade & Reese, 1973). Indeed, by the end of the 1970s and the beginning of the 1980s, the perspective championed at West Virginia University had spread to other institutions (e.g., Penn State University, through the arrival there of Paul B. Baltes and John R. Nesselroade; and at the University of Southern California, through the arrival of K. Warner Schaie). For instance, two volumes that were produced at Penn State used this integrated-levels, action perspective to understand child-family relations across the life span (Lerner & Spanier, 1978) and more general instances of person-context relations across life (Lerner & Busch-Rossnagel, 1981a).

Development, seen from a perspective that emphasized systematic coactions across multiple, integrated levels—that is, that emphasized developmental systems (Ford & Lerner, 1992; Lerner, 1998b; Thelen & Smith, 1998)—was studied with an array of change-sensitive measures, designs, and data-analytic tools. These investigations were conducted by teams of scholars from diverse disciplines who worked collaboratively to understand the individual-context relational bases of continuity and change, of plasticity, across the life span (e.g., Baltes & Baltes, 1980; Baltes, Reese, & Lipsitt, 1980; Baltes, Reese, & Nesselroade, 1977; Brim & Kagan, 1980; Elder, 1979, 1980; Featherman, 1983; Hetherington, Lerner, & Perlmutter, 1988; R. M. Lerner, 1984; Nesselroade & Baltes, 1979; Nesselroade & von Eye, 1985; Riley, 1979; Sørensen, Weinert, & Sherrod, 1986).

By the mid- to late 1990s, the theoretical orientation framing this scholarship had become predominant in the study of human development. For instance, in at least 17 of the 19 chapters of Volume 1 of the fifth edition of the *Handbook of Child Psychology,* a volume titled *Theoretical Models of Human Development* (Lerner, 1998a), authors forward perspectives consonant with the "family" of ideas associated with developmental systems thinking.

The substantive development of the ideas associated with developmental systems thinking can be traced in many ways (e.g., see Cairns, 1998; Dixon & Lerner, 1999; Ford & Lerner, 1992; Gottlieb, 1992, 1997; Sameroff, 1983; Thelen & Smith, 1994). These histories reflect a synthesis of continuity and discontinuity in ideas that mirrors the multilevel, coactional syntheses depicted within developmental systems thinking. Accordingly, to illustrate the developmental character of developmental systems thinking and to provide some ideas about the possible futures of scholarship predicated on these ideas, we will recount the evolution of one instance of this perspective: developmental contextualism (e.g., Lerner, 1979, 1987, 1991, 1995, 1996, 1998b; Lerner & Kauffman, 1985, 1986).

Across the more than 20 years that have been devoted to the elaboration of this member of the developmental systems theoretical "family," there have been several important revisions/refinements in the ideas associated with this position. For example, early in the development of developmental contextual thinking, it became clear that the notion of circular functions was mute in regard to the nature of the feedback an organism would receive (e.g., its positive or negative valence) from others as a consequence of the organism's individuality. Accordingly, borrowing from the insights of Thomas and Chess (1977; Chess & Thomas, 1984; Thomas, Chess, Birch, Hertzig, & Korn, 1963) in the study of temperamental individuality, the "goodness of fit" model was developed to account for the character of the feedback involved in circular functions and to predict later developmental sequelae arising from the quality of organism-context fit (e.g., J. V. Lerner, 1984; Lerner & Lerner, 1983, 1989). Characteristics of organism individuality that fit (matched, or were congruent with) behavioral, cognitive, or physical demands (or presses) of the context were predicted to be associated with positive exchanges between the organism and its context; the positive valence of these circular functions was expected to be associated with healthy/positive development.

Across the changes that were incorporated into developmental contextual theory, there was one key constant: the focus on relational actions. There was a continual focus on the relations between (a) the actions of the person on the context and (b) the actions of the context on the person. In other words, the focus on the individual as a producer of his or her own development remained constant in the evolution of the thinking associated with developmental contextualism.

Accordingly, to review this evolution and to discuss its likely future course, we will contrast the ideas found in two watershed publications pertinent to this perspective. First, we will discuss the ideas about developmental contextualism found in the opening chapter of Lerner and Busch-Rossnagel's 1981 edited volume, *Individuals as Producers of Their Development*. We will then contrast the ideas presented by Lerner and Busch-Rossnagel (1981b), and by the colleagues contributing to their volume, with the perspective about developmental contextualism presented by Lerner (1998b) in his introductory chapter to Volume 1 of the 1998 *Handbook of Child Psychology*. Here, too, we will review both the ideas presented by Lerner and the other conceptions in the volume that are pertinent to our understanding of contemporary features of developmental systems thinking.

LERNER AND BUSCH-ROSSNAGEL ON "INDIVIDUALS AS PRODUCERS OF THEIR DEVELOPMENT"

Writing at the beginning of the 1980s, Lerner and Busch-Rossnagel (1981b) drew upon then-current interest in Klaus Riegel's dialectical model of human development and upon the then-burgeoning life-span view of human development to explain the role of organism and contextual coactions in the construction of the course of development. As Riegel (1976a) explained, the dialectical model involves a commitment to the study of "ceaseless flux," of actions and changes, and to a concern with short-term (e.g., situational) changes, long-term (e.g., individual and cultural) changes, and *especially* the interrelation between the two. Thus ceaseless, interrelated changes in actions are the core ideas in the paradigm promoted by Riegel.

These ideas were also basic to the contextual paradigm of Pepper (1942). From this view, "every behavior and incident in the world is a historic event," and "change and novelty are accepted as fundamental" (Hultsch & Hickey, 1978, p. 79). The basic facts of existence are "complexes or contexts" (Pepper, 1942, p. 142), where "the real historic event, the event in its actuality, is when it is going on now, the dynamic dramatic active event" (p. 232), and where "the relations involved in a historic event are inexhaustible, and a set of contextualistic categories does not so much determine the nature of our world as lead one to appreciate fair samples of the world's events" (p. 237). Thus constant change of the "now" (the event) and the total interrelation of this event are the basic ideas of Pepper's contextual paradigm. Riegel (1975, 1976a, 1976b), then, along with Pepper (1942), promoted interest in the developmental implications of active organisms' being engaged in relations with their active context.

Riegel's ideas meshed with the then-emerging life-span view of human development. By stressing that there is change across life, and that it involves variables from several levels of analysis, Riegel presented ideas that were compatible with the multidisciplinary, empirical, and conceptual activity found in "life-span developmental psychology" or the "life-span view of human development" (Baltes, 1979a, 1979b; Baltes et al., 1980). From this perspective, the potential for developmental change is seen to be present across all of life; the human life course is held to be potentially multidirectional and necessarily multidimensional (Baltes & Nesselroade, 1973). In addition, the sources of the potentially continual changes across life are seen to involve actions among the inner-biological and outer-ecological levels of the context within which the organism is embedded. Indeed, although their ideas constituted an orientation toward the study of development and not a specific theory of development, it is clear that life-span developmentalists were disposed to a reciprocal model of organism-context action. As Baltes (1979b) indicated:

> Lifespan developmental psychologists emphasize *contextualistic-dialectic* paradigms of development (Datan & Reese, 1977; Lerner, Skinner, & Sorell, 1980; Riegel, 1976a) rather than the use of "mechanistic" or "organismic" ones more typical of child development work. There are two primary rationales for this preference. One is, of course, evident also in current child development work. As development unfolds, it becomes more and more apparent that individuals act on the environment and produce novel behavior outcomes, thereby making the active and selective nature of human beings of paramount importance. Furthermore, the recognition of the interplay between age-graded, history graded, and non-normative life events suggests a contextualistic and dialectical conception of development. This dialectic is further accentuated by the fact that individual development is the reflection of multiple forces which are not always in synergism, or convergence, nor do they always permit the delineation of a specific set of endstates. (p. 2)

In short, the development of life-span developmental psychology in the 1970s led to a multidisciplinary view of human development, one suggesting that individual changes across life are both products and producers of the multiple levels of context within which the person is embedded. Simply, individuals, in action with their changing context, were seen to provide a basis of their own development.

The purpose of the Lerner and Busch-Rossnagel (1981a) book was to explore the conceptual, methodological, and empirical implications of the idea that individuals are producers of their development, both at specific portions of the life span and for selected processes across the life span. Moreover, the centrality of this concept for an understanding of developmental processes was illustrated by the inclusion of chapters written by scholars who used distinct theoretical perspectives. For instance, cognitive developmental (Fein, 1981; Labouvie-Vief, 1981; Liben, 1981), cognitive social learning (Jones & Haney, 1981; Worell, 1981), and psychodynamic (Haan, 1981; Rodeheaver & Datan, 1981) orientations were represented. In addition, conceptions derived from contextual (Busch-Rossnagel, 1981; Sorrell & Nowak, 1981; Super & Harkness, 1981; Thomas & Chess, 1981; Tobach, 1981), dialectic (Meacham, 1981), and human ecological (Belsky & Tolan, 1981) perspectives were forwarded. This pluralism of theoretical perspectives was enhanced by the inclusion of chapters by authors trained in the psychological subdisciplines of clinical, comparative, developmental, and anthropological psychology and the disciplines of special education, cultural anthropology, and psychiatry. Moreover, chapters evaluated the "individuals as producers" notion within successive portions of life: infancy (Belsky & Tolan, 1981), childhood (Liben, 1981), adolescence and young adulthood (Haan, 1981), adulthood (Rodeheaver & Datan, 1981), and the aged years (Labouvie-Vief, 1981). Other chapters considered variables and/or processes that, across the life span, may provide a basis for the person's contribution to his or her own development. The roles of temperament (Thomas & Chess, 1981), characteristics of the physical setting of development (Fein, 1981), physical handicaps (Busch-Rossnagel, 1981), sex (Worell, 1981), race (Jones & Haney, 1981), and physical attractiveness (Sorell & Nowak, 1981) were discussed.

Accordingly, the Lerner and Busch-Rossnagel (1981a) book illustrated the idea that individuals are producers of their development by drawing on conceptual and empirical work that had bases in several disciplines. Lerner and Busch-Rossnagel (1981b) argued that this scholarship was linked superordinately to two key concepts associated with the model of development that was then labeled as *contextual-dialectic* or dynamical interactional but today is framed as *developmental contextualism* (Lerner, 1996, 1998b; Lerner & Kauffman, 1985). These ideas are *constant change* of all levels of analysis and *embeddedness* of each level with all others—that changes in one level may promote changes in all levels. The concept of constant change denotes that there is no complete uniformity or constancy. Rather than change being a to-be-explained phenomenon, a perturbation in a stable system, it is a given (Overton, 1978); thus the task of the scientist is to describe, explain, and optimize the parameter and trajectory of processes (i.e., variables that show time-related change in their quantity and/or quality).

The second concept is thus raised. It stresses the interrelation of all levels of analysis. Because phenomena are not seen as static, but rather as change processes, and any change process occurs within a similarly (i.e., constantly) changing world (of processes), any target change must be conceptualized in the context of the other changes within which it is embedded. Thus change will continue constantly as a consequence of this embeddedness.

Lerner and Busch-Rossnagel (1981b) argued that conceptualizations of human development associated with the concepts of embeddedness and constant change speak of the joining of multiple change processes (e.g., see Lerner, 1978, 1979; Meacham, 1976, 1977; Riegel, 1975). Whereas a personological explanation of human development is therefore seen as quite limited from this perspective (Baltes et al., 1980), this view does not mean *only* that the individual's ontogeny must be understood as linked to his or her family and society. In addition, it means that the inner and outer syntheses that compose the human condition have to be integrated as well; biological and cultural change—or, in other words, biocultural, historical, or evolutionary changes—must be understood (Baltes et al., 1980; Bronfenbrenner & Ceci, 1994; Lerner, 1978; Lewontin & Levins, 1978; Schneirla, 1957; Tobach, 1981; Tobach & Schneirla, 1968).

Thus the idea of embeddedness, that any level of analysis is reciprocally related to all others, leads to the idea that human biology is both a producer and a product of social and cultural change. This view contrasts with those of other scholars who, in writing about the relation between biological and social change, stress either that the former is primarily the unidirectional shaper of the latter (e.g., Rowe, 1994; Rushton, 1988; Wilson, 1975) or that the two are relatively independent (Campbell, 1975). Lerner and Busch-Rossnagel's (1981b) position was that any level of analysis may be understood in the context of the distal biocultural and more proximal ontogenetic changes of which it is a part (Tobach, 1981), and that the idea of "one level in isolation" as the "prime mover" of change is not a useful one.

Moreover, the idea of embeddedness, in relation to the constant change assumption of contextualism, leads to another key idea about the character of human development. If change on multiple, interrelated levels of analysis characterizes the human life span, then neither specific ontogenetic end states (Baltes, 1979b) nor totally uniform features of development at any portion of ontogeny characterize the life course. Instead, the human life span is characterized by the *potential* for plasticity (i.e., systematic intraindividual change; Baltes & Baltes, 1980; R. M. Lerner, 1984; Schneirla, 1957; Tobach & Schneirla, 1968) as well as by the potential for interindividual differences in such change.

In short, the ideas of constant change and embeddedness, summarized by the term *dynamic interactionism,* led to ideas stressing both the plastic and the social natures of biological and psychological developments. Lerner and Busch-Rossnagel (1981b) saw these ideas as having strong implications for the understanding of evolution, of ontogeny, and thus of organism-environment relations. Lerner and Busch-Rossnagel drew on several lines of evidence (from evolutionary biology through sociology and cultural anthropology) in support of the importance of the concepts of constant change and embeddedness for understanding the role of individual-context coactions in human development (see also R. M. Lerner, 1984). These lines were linked, however, by the view that human development is an outcome of interdependent biological, psychological, and sociocultural changes (e.g., Lewontin & Levins, 1978; Schneirla, 1957; Tobach & Schneirla, 1968).

Given this relation, Lerner and Busch-Rossnagel (1981b) argued that processes linking the person to the group have been selected for in evolution and that the task of human developmentalists was to understand what processes, across ontogeny, integrate the individual in his or her context. In fact, as illustrated by the chapters in their volume, re-inforcement processes, cognitive developmental processes, and social rela-tional processes, such as attachment and dependency, may *all* be involved. Indeed, because of the link between individual adaptation and social functioning, the group is necessary for the individual's survival, and, in turn, the group needs the individual, and a singular individual at that. The individual is necessary for the group's survival (e.g., to populate it and perpetuate the techniques it has used for survival). That is, as Brim and Kagan (1980) have put the issue, "Society must transform the raw material of individual biology into persons suitable for the activities and require-ments of society" (p. 19).

In sum, Lerner and Busch-Rossnagel's (1981b) chapter presented key features of a conceptualization of development derived from a dynamic interactional (now a developmental contextual) theory: plasticity, the social nature of human development, and—centrally—the role of individuals as producers of their development. Yet, despite the multidisciplinary concep-tual and empirical support for these ideas, Lerner and Busch-Rossnagel thought it most prudent and appropriate to characterize their presentation as more of a prospectus for theory building than a detailing of the particulars of a finished system. They saw their ideas more as a promise about the potential of interdisciplinary integration than as an instance of its realized assets. They believed that in order for the promise to be fulfilled, traditional intra- and interdisciplinary boundaries would have to be tran-scended.

Were they? The publication of the fifth edition of the *Handbook of Child Psychology* and of Lerner's introductory chapter to that volume provides a means by which we can gauge whether progress has occurred in devel-opmental contextual thinking over the subsequent two decades, whether its use as a model of development and as an instance of developmental systems thinking has been enhanced, and whether the promissory note of 1981 has been repaid at least in part.

LERNER'S "THEORIES OF HUMAN DEVELOPMENT: CONTEMPORARY PERSPECTIVES"

As evidenced by the chapters that follow his introductory chapter in Volume 1 of the *Handbook of Child Psychology,* Lerner (1998b) argues that the cutting edge of contemporary developmental theory is represented by conceptions of process, of how structures function and how functions are structured over time. Thus, as reflected in the *Handbook,* in most contemporary theories of human development the person is not biologized, psychologized, or sociologized. Rather, the individual is "systemized"; that is, his or her development is embedded within an integrated matrix of variables derived from multiple levels of organization. Development is conceptualized as deriving from the dynamic relations among the variables within this multitiered matrix. To the extent that the chapters in Lerner's (1998a) edited volume represent the state of the art in developmental theory at the end of the 1990s, one may conclude that the Lerner and Busch-Rossnagel promissory note has been paid: The individual, in dynamic interactions on and by his or her context is at the core of the relations of the developmental system during ontogenetic change.

How did this happen? What are the features of, or emphases in, the theories represented in Lerner's (1998a) volume that allow theoreticians to take positions consistent with developmental systems thinking, as represented in developmental contextualism? The theories represented in Lerner's volume use the polarities that have engaged developmental theory in the past (e.g., nature/nurture, individual/society, biology/culture; Lerner, 1976, 1986), but not to "split" depictions of developmental processes along conceptually implausible and empirically counterfactual lines (Gollin, 1981; Gottlieb, 1997; Overton, 1998) or to force counterproductive choices between false opposites. Rather, these issues are used to offer insight into the integrations that exist among the multiple levels of organization involved in human development. These theoretical positions are certainly more complex than their one-sided predecessors; however, they are also more nuanced, more flexible, more balanced, and less susceptible to extravagant, or even absurd, claims (for instance, that "nature," split from "nurture," can shape the course of human development; that there is a gene for altruism, militarism, intelligence, or even television watching; or that when the social context is demonstrated to affect development the influence can be reduced to a genetic one; e.g., Hamburger, 1957; Lorenz,

1966; Plomin, 1986; Plomin, Corley, DeFries, & Faulker, 1990; Rowe, 1994; Rushton, 1987, 1988).

The mechanistic and atomistic views of the past had by 1998 been replaced, then, by theoretical models that stress the dynamic synthesis of multiple levels of analysis, a perspective consonant with the viewpoint articulated by Lerner and Busch-Rossnagel (1981b) and having its roots in action-theoretical accounts of human development (Brandtstädter, 1984, 1985) *and* in systems theories of biological development (Cairns, 1998; Gottlieb, 1992; Kuo, 1930, 1967, 1976; Schneirla, 1956, 1957; von Bertalanffy, 1933). In other words, development, understood as a property of systemic change in the multiple and integrated levels of organization (ranging from biology to culture and history) constituting human life and its ecology—or a *developmental systems perspective*—was by 1998 seen as the overarching conceptual frame associated with contemporary theoretical models in the field of human development.

Accordingly, the power of the theories found in the Lerner (1998a) volume lies in the multilevel and, hence, multidimensional design criteria they impose on concepts (and research) pertinent to any content area about, or dimension of, the person. More specifically, this power of the developmental systems ideas forwarded in the theories found in the Lerner (1998a) volume is constituted by four interrelated, and in fact "fused" (Tobach & Greenberg, 1984), conceptual themes, themes consonant with the ideas of constant change, embeddedness, and plasticity discussed by Lerner and Busch-Rossnagel (1981b). These four themes are (a) change and relative plasticity, (b) relationism and the integration of levels of organization, (c) historical embeddedness and temporality, and (d) the limits of generalizability, diversity, and individual differences. To begin to demonstrate the continuity between the ideas forwarded by Lerner and Busch-Rossnagel (1981b) and those noted by Lerner (1998b) to characterize the key themes in the major theoretical models of development extant in 1998, we focus first on the theme of plasticity.

Relative Plasticity and Change

The theories presented in Lerner's (1998a) edited volume stress that the focus of developmental understanding must be on (systematic) change (see Brandtstädter, 1998; Bronfenbrenner & Morris, 1998; Csikszentmihalyi & Rathunde, 1998; Fischer & Bidell, 1998; Gardner, 1998; Gottlieb, Wahlsten, & Lickliter, 1998; Magnusson & Stattin, 1998; Overton, 1998;

Thelen & Smith, 1998; Wapner & Demick, 1998; see also Ford & Lerner, 1992; Sameroff, 1983). This focus is required because of the belief that the potential for change exists across (a) the life span and (b) the multiple levels of organization that constitute the ecology of human development (e.g., see Baltes, Lindenberger, & Staudinger, 1998; Bronfenbrenner & Morris, 1998; Elder, 1998; Shweder et al., 1998; see also Baltes, 1987). Although it is also assumed that systematic change is not limitless (e.g., it is constrained by both past developments and contemporary ecological, or contextual, conditions), the theories presented by Lerner's (1998a) contributors stress that *relative plasticity* exists across life (see Baltes et al., 1998; Brandtstädter, 1998; Keil, 1998; Overton, 1998; Spelke & Newport, 1998; see also R. M. Lerner, 1984).

There are important implications of relative plasticity for an understanding of the range of intraindividual variation that can exist over ontogeny (see Fisher, Jackson, & Villarruel, 1998) and, in turn, for the application of developmental science. For instance, the presence of relative plasticity legitimates a proactive search across the life span for characteristics of people and of their contexts that, together, can influence the design of policies and programs promoting positive development (Birkel, Lerner, & Smyer, 1989; Fisher & Lerner, 1994; Lerner & Hood, 1986). For example, the plasticity of intellectual development, which is a feature of a systems view of mental functioning (e.g., see Fischer & Bidell, 1998; Gardner, 1998; Keil, 1998), provides legitimation for educational policies and school- and community-based programs aimed at enhancing cognitive and social cognitive development (Dryfoos, 1994; Villarruel & Lerner, 1994); such implications for the design of policies and programs stand in marked contrast to those associated with mechanistic, genetic reductionist theories that suggest that genetic inheritance constrains intellectual development among particular minority and/or low-income groups (Herrnstein, 1973; Herrnstein & Murray, 1994; Jensen, 1969, 1980; Rushton, 1987, 1988).

Accordingly, from the developmental systems perspective found in the chapters in Lerner's (1998a) edited volume (see also Gottlieb, 1992; Lerner, 1984, 1991; Tobach, 1981; Tobach & Greenberg, 1984), the study of plasticity—whether directed to analysis of inter- or intraspecies differences—always involves the scrutiny of the history of dynamic organism-context interactions or, in more general terms, of the fused or systemic relations between nature and nurture. Thus plasticity is not a product of nature (e.g., of genes in general or, more specifically, of a purported genetic program). In turn, plasticity is not a product of nurture (e.g., a specific learning regimen, reinforcement program, or sequence of stimulation). Rather, the level of plasticity attained by an animal over the course of its life is an outcome of the *temporally changing and dynamic relation* of nature and nurture (Elder, 1998; Ford & Lerner, 1992; Lerner, 1984, 1991). In short, as emphasized by Lerner and Busch-Rossnagel (1981b), plasticity is, then, a key feature of the process of development.

The theoretical and empirical evidence available by 1998 buttressed this position. To illustrate, Gottlieb (1992, 1997) stresses the bidirectionality of influences among the levels of organization involved in development. He indicates that individual development involves the emergence of new structural and functional properties and competencies at all levels of analysis (e.g., molecular, subcellular, cellular, organismic) of a developmental system, including the organism-environment one. These emergent characteristics derive from *horizontal* coactions involving intralevel relationships (e.g., gene-gene, cell-cell, tissue-tissue, or organism-organism) and from *vertical* coactions involving interlevel relationships (e.g., gene-cytoplasm, cell-tissue, or behavioral activity-nervous system) (Gottlieb, 1992, 1997). These horizontal and vertical coactions are reciprocal, in that influences occur in any direction—from one "component" to another within a level, from lower-level to higher-level components, and/or from higher-level to lower-level components within the developmental system (Gottlieb, 1992, 1997). From this perspective the causes of development are the *relationships* among components, and not the components themselves (Gottlieb, 1992, 1997; Lerner, 1991; Overton, 1998).

For example, the emergence of menarche is a result of vertical coactions involving biology, culture, physical features of the ecology, and the socioeconomic resources (related, for instance, to available technology, nutrition, and medical care) of the society within which the young female is embedded. For instance, among youth of African ancestry living in Cuba the median age of menarche is 12.4 years, whereas the median ages of menarche for girls of corresponding ancestry living in Uganda, in South Africa, and in New Guinea are 13.4 years, 15.0 years, and 18.8 years, respectively (Katchadourian, 1977). These differences have been associated with variations in the nutritional and medical resources available to young girls in the nations in question; better nutrition and medical care are linked to lower age of menarche (Tanner, 1991).

Similarly, differences in age of menarche within the same nation are often seen between young females from urban areas and those from poor rural areas, with those from the former settings having lower ages of menarche as a consequence of their advantaged socioeconomic situation. For example, in Romania the average age of menarche is 13.5 years in towns and 14.6 in villages, and corresponding urban-rural differences have been found in nations of the former Soviet Union (13.0 years and 14.3 years, respectively) and in India (12.8 and 14.2 years, respectively) (Tanner, 1970, 1991). Moreover, in Hong Kong, the average ages of menarche of girls from rich, average income, and poor families are 12.5 years, 12.8 years, and 13.3 years, respectively (Tanner, 1970, 1991).

Clearly, then, the distinction between the developmental systems view of plasticity and the genetic determination/genetic program conception of this feature of development (e.g., Brauth, Hall, & Dooling, 1991; Wilson, 1975) is not just a matter of semantics or of emphasis. To the contrary, the distinction pertains to important logical and empirical issues. In regard to the former issues, the linear and mechanistic view of the genetic determination/programming of plasticity is unfalsifiable. The genetic program that purportedly causes the plasticity of behavior is indexed only by the behavior involved in the manifestation of plasticity. The presence of the behavior is, then, taken as evidence of the genetic program, *and* variation in the behavior is taken as an indication of the degree of "appropriate environmental stimulation" (Brauth et al., 1991, p. 3) and *not* as information pertinent to the assumption of the presence of a causal genetic program. Thus, although behavior is the only evidence used to index this viewpoint, there is no behavioral evidence that can lead to the rejection of the belief in the presence of a genetic program for plasticity.

Nevertheless, and in regard to empirical issues, there is abundant evidence within the field of molecular genetics that the "fact" of a genetic program proposed by Brauth et al. (1991) is, in actuality, a counterfactual assertion. Indeed, molecular genetics provides evidence that the entire view of genetic activity represented by genetic determinists is mistaken. For example, molecular geneticist Mae-Wan Ho (1984) indicates:

> Forever exorcised from our collective consciousness is any remaining illusion of development as a genetic programme involving the readout of the DNA "master" tape by the cellular "slave" machinery. On the contrary, it is the cellular machinery which imposes control over the genes. . . . The classical view of the ultraconservative genome—the unmoved mover of development—is completely turned around. Not only is there no master tape to be read out automatically, but the "tape" itself can get variously chopped,

rearranged, transposed, and amplified in different cells at different times. (p. 285)

Similarly, molecular and cell biologist R. C. Strohman (1993) notes:

> Many experimental biologists outside the biomedical-industrial complex are just now coming (back) to grips with the facts of epigenesis, with the profound mystery that developmental biology is, with the poverty of gene programs as an explanatory device, and with a crisis defined by the realization that an increasingly deficient theory of developmental genetics is the only theory currently available. The question remains: If biologists are starting to learn this lesson, will the psychologists be far behind? (p. 150)

Certainly, some psychologists have incorporated this "lesson" into their theory and research (e.g., Gottlieb, 1992, 1997; Tobach, 1981; Tobach & Greenberg, 1984) and, as a consequence, have reached conclusions about the systems nature of development in general and of the processes involved in plasticity in particular.

In essence, then, the "genetic program" view of plasticity represented by Brauth et al. (1991) and by other advocates of a genetic primacy perspective, such as behavior geneticists (e.g., Plomin, 1986; Plomin et al., 1990; Rowe, 1994) and human sociobiologists (e.g., Belsky, Steinberg, & Draper, 1991; Freedman, 1979; MacDonald, 1994; Rushton, 1987, 1988), is quite distinct from the "developmental process/systems" view forwarded by, among others, Schneirla, Hebb, Tobach, Gottlieb, and Greenberg. Moreover, the genetic program view is not supported by the current literature in molecular genetics (Ho, 1984; Strohman, 1993). Indeed, as Gottlieb (1992) has observed, "The ultimate aim of dissolving the nature-nurture dichotomy will be achieved only through the establishment of a fully developmental theory of the phenotype from gene to organism" (p. vii). In other words, transcending the nature-nurture dichotomy requires a stress on the relations among integrated levels of organization (Overton, 1998; Schneirla, 1957; Tobach, 1981).

Relationism and the Integration of Levels of Organization

As Lerner (1998b) notes, the theories presented by the contributors to his edited volume stress that the bases for change, and for both plasticity and constraints in development, lie in the relations that exist among the multiple levels of organization that constitute the substance of human life (see Baltes et al., 1998; Brandtstädter, 1998; Bronfenbrenner & Morris, 1998; Cairns, 1998; Csikszentmihalyi & Rathunde, 1998; Elder, 1998; Fischer & Bidell, 1998; Fisher et al., 1998; Gardner, 1998; Gottlieb et al., 1998; Magnusson & Stattin, 1998; Overton, 1998; Shweder et al., 1998; Thelen & Smith, 1998; Valsiner, 1998; Wapner & Demick, 1998; see also Ford & Lerner, 1992; Schneirla, 1957; Tobach, 1981). As Lerner and Busch-Rossnagel's (1981a) contributors specified, these levels range from the inner-biological through the individual/psychological and the proximal social relational (e.g., involving dyads, peer groups, and nuclear families), to the sociocultural level (including key macroinstitutions such as educational, public policy, governmental, and economic systems) and the natural and designed physical ecologies of human development (Bronfenbrenner, 1979; Bronfenbrenner & Morris, 1998; Riegel, 1975). These tiers are structurally and functionally integrated, and thus a systems view of the levels involved in human development is required (Ford & Lerner, 1992; Sameroff, 1983; Smith & Thelen, 1993; Thelen & Smith, 1994; Wapner, 1993). The developmental contextualism forwarded by Lerner and Busch-Rossnagel is one instance of such a viewpoint (Lerner, 1986, 1991, 1995, 1996).

Such a developmental systems perspective promotes a *relational* unit of analysis as a prerequisite of developmental analysis (see Brandtstädter, 1998; Bronfenbrenner & Morris, 1998; Csikszentmihalyi & Rathunde, 1998; Elder, 1998; Fisher et al., 1998; Gottlieb et al., 1998; Magnusson & Stattin, 1998; Overton, 1998; see also Lerner, 1991): Variables associated with any level of organization exist (are structured) in relation to variables from other levels; the qualitative and quantitative dimensions of the function of any variable are shaped as well by the relations that variable has with variables from other levels. Unilevel units of analysis (or the components of, or elements in, a relation) are not an adequate target for developmental analysis; rather, the relation itself—the interlevel linkage—should be the focus of such analysis (Fisher et al., 1998; Lerner, 1991; Riegel, 1975). Thus variables from different levels—for instance, heredity and environment—are seen as coequal influences in the development of behavior.

To illustrate, a girl may have genes that in one set of circumstances would be associated with her beginning her menstrual cycle quite early, say at about 10 years of age; yet, as noted earlier, the nutrition and health care she receives will influence whether her cycle begins at that time, later, or perhaps even earlier (Katchadourian, 1977). In turn, the environment may "promote" more or less of a behavior and/or may afford one or another characteristic, depending on the specific biological characteristics of the people living in the environment (Tanner, 1991). Excellent nutrition and health care may maximize the possible height of members of groups of people who are of hereditarily shorter stature than the average person (e.g., members of pygmy tribes); however, no known diet or medical intervention will increase the typically occurring heights of members of this group to levels found, say, in groups having hereditarily tall stature (Katchadourian, 1977).

Thus genes and environment always constrain each other. However, their mutual influence means that these constraints are flexible, not absolute. The fusion of heredity and environment, as conceived of within a perspective emphasizing developmental systems, means there is a resulting mutuality of influence between these two levels of organization; in addition, there is a mutuality of flexibility in the constraints they impose on behavior and development. This fusion means there is relative plasticity in human behavior and development. However, the range of behaviors that can occur in an individual's life is certainly not infinite or limitless (Lerner, 1984). Females do not, as a group, normatively begin their menstrual cycles (that is, do not experience menarche) at 5 years of age; and pygmies, as a group, do not normatively have an average adult height of 6 feet. However, the concept of relative plasticity means that the number of distinct characteristics any one individual can show is quite large given the fusion of heredity and environment. A girl's menarche can begin, within normal limits, anywhere between the 9th and 17th years (Katchadourian, 1977; Tanner, 1991); the average adult height of any group can vary widely; and individuals' intelligence, personalities, and motivations can show enormous degrees of variation (Plomin, 1986).

In short, integrated, interlevel changes constitute the process of developmental change within a developmental systems perspective. If the course of human development is the product of the processes involved in the "fusions" (or "dynamic interactions"; Lerner, 1978, 1979, 1984) among integrative levels, then the processes of development are more plastic than has often previously been believed (see Brim & Kagan, 1980).

Historical Embeddedness and Temporality

The relational units of analysis of concern in the theories presented in Lerner's (1998a) edited volume are understood as change units (see Bronfenbrenner & Morris, 1998; Magnusson & Stattin, 1998; Thelen & Smith, 1998; see also Lerner, 1991). The change component of these units derives from the idea that all of the levels of organization involved in human development are embedded in history—that is, they are integrated with historical change (see Baltes et al., 1998; Cairns, 1998; Elder, 1998; Overton, 1998; Shweder et al., 1998; Valsiner, 1998; see also Elder, 1980; Elder, Modell, & Parke, 1993).

Relationism and integration mean that no level of organization functions as a consequence of its own, isolated activity (see Brandtstädter, 1998; Gottlieb et al., 1998; Thelen & Smith, 1998; Wapner & Demick, 1998; see also Gottlieb, 1992, 1997; Tobach, 1981; Tobach & Schneirla, 1968). Each level functions as a consequence of its fusion (its structural integration) with other levels (Gottlieb et al., 1998; Tobach & Greenberg, 1984). History—change over time—is incessant and continuous, and it is a level of organization that is fused with all other levels. This linkage means that change is a necessary, an inevitable, feature of variables from all levels of organization (see Baltes et al., 1998; Overton, 1998; Wapner & Demick, 1998; see also Baltes, 1987; R. M. Lerner, 1984); in addition, this linkage means that the structure, as well as the function, of variables changes over time.

An illustration of the temporality of developmental change is found in secular trends in child and adolescent physical and physiological maturation (Garn, 1980; Katchadourian, 1977; Tanner, 1991). Since 1900, children of preschool age have been taller on an average of 1.0 centimeter and heavier on an average of 0.5 kilogram per decade (Katchadourian, 1977). In turn, changes in height and weight occurring during the adolescent growth spurt have involved gains of 2.5 centimeters and 2.5 kilograms, respectively (Katchadourian, 1977; Tanner, 1991). In addition, there has been a historical trend downward in the average age of menarche. Among European samples there was a decrease of about 4 months per decade in age of menarche from about 1840 to about 1950 (Tanner, 1962, 1991). This rate seems to have slowed down, but it has not stopped (Marshall & Tanner, 1986; Tanner, 1991). Within American samples, however, the decline in age of menarche seems to have stopped about 1940. Since that time, the expected (mean) age of menarche among European American samples has been 12.5 years. The most dramatic secular trend has been evidenced in Japan, where from the immediate post-World War II years until about 1975, there was a decline of 11 months a decade in the average age of menarche (Marshall & Tanner, 1986). These temporal changes in the biological maturation of youth are linked to historical improvements in health and nutrition in their respective nations, variation in turn associated with socioeconomic and technological changes in their societies. Simply, biological structure and function and societal structure and function are linked systemically across history.

Indeed, at the biological level of organization one prime set of structural changes across history is subsumed under the concept of evolution (see Cairns, 1998; Gardner, 1998; Gottlieb et al., 1998; Keil, 1998; Overton, 1998; see also Gould, 1977; Lewontin, 1981; Lewontin, Rose, & Kamin, 1984); of course, the concept of evolution can be applied also to functional changes (Darwin, 1872; Gottlieb, 1992). In turn, at more macro levels of organization many of the historically linked changes in social and cultural institutions or products are evaluated in the context of discussions of the concept of progress (Nisbet, 1980).

In sum, because historical change is continuous, temporality is infused in all levels of organization (Elder, 1998; Elder et al., 1993). Accordingly, the temporality involved in contemporary theories of human development necessitates change-sensitive measures of structure and function *and* change-sensitive (i.e., longitudinal) designs (Baltes et al., 1977; Brim & Kagan, 1980; Bronfenbrenner & Morris, 1998; Fisher et al., 1998; Overton, 1998). The key question vis-à-vis temporality in such research is not whether change occurs; rather, the question is whether the changes that do occur make a difference for a given developmental outcome (Lerner et al., 1980).

Given that the study of these changes will involve appraisal of both quantitative and qualitative features of change, which may occur at multiple levels of organization, researchers need to use both quantitative and qualitative data collection and analysis methods, methods associated with the range of disciplines having specialized expertise at the multiple levels of organization at which either quantitative or qualitative change can occur (Shweder et al., 1998). In essence, then, the concepts of historical embeddedness and temporality indicate that a program of developmental research adequate to address the relational, integrated, embedded, and temporal changes involved in human life must involve multiple occasions, methods, levels, variables, and cohorts (Baltes, 1987; Lerner, 1986, 1991; Schaie & Strother, 1968).

The Limits of Generalizability, Diversity, and Individual Differences

The temporality of the changing relations among levels of organization means that changes that are seen within one historical period (or time of measurement), and/or with one set of instances of variables from the multiple levels of the ecology of human development, may not be seen at other points in time (see Bronfenbrenner & Morris, 1998; Cairns, 1998; Elder, 1998; Valsiner, 1998; see also Baltes et al., 1977; Bronfenbrenner, 1979). What is seen in one data set may be only an instance of what does or what could exist. Accordingly, contemporary theories focus on diversity—of people, of relations, of settings, and of times of measurement (see Baltes et al., 1998; Bronfenbrenner & Morris, 1998; Fischer & Bidell, 1998; Fisher et al., 1998; Overton, 1998; Wapner & Demick, 1998; see also Lerner, 1991, 1995, 1996).

Individual differences within and across all levels of organization are seen as having core substantive significance for the understanding of human development (Lerner, 1991, 1995, 1996; see also Freund, Li, & Baltes, Chapter 14, this volume). Diversity is the exemplary illustration of the presence of relative plasticity in human development (Fisher et al., 1998; R. M. Lerner, 1984). Diversity is also the best evidence that exists of the potential for change in the states and conditions of human life (Brim & Kagan, 1980).

Moreover, just as contributors to Lerner and Busch-Rossnagel's (1981a) volume argued, some of Lerner's (1998a) contributors stress that the individual structural and functional characteristics of a person constitute an important source of his or her development (see Brandtstädter, 1998; Csikszentmihalyi & Rathunde, 1998; see also Brandtstädter, 1985; Lerner, 1982). Moreover, the changing match, congruence, or goodness of fit between the developmental characteristics of the person and of his or her context are seen to provide a basis for consonance or dissonance in the ecological milieu of the person; the dynamic nature of this interaction is held to constitute a source of variation in positive and negative outcomes of developmental change (see Baltes et al., 1998; Fischer & Bidell, 1998).

Additional support for these person-context relational ideas is found in several studies of American adolescents. Pubertal maturation alters negatively the nature of the social interactions between youth and their parents; for example, at the height of pubertal change more conflict and greater emotional distance are seen (e.g., Hill, Holmbeck, Marlow, Green, & Lynch, 1985a, 1985b; Holmbeck & Hill, 1991; Steinberg, 1987, 1990; Steinberg & Hill, 1978). However, although there are important data from European samples supporting the dynamic interactional linkage between pubertal change and psychosocial functioning (e.g., Magnusson & Stattin, 1998; Stattin & Magnusson, 1990), most findings about this puberty-context association have been derived in large part from research with homogeneous European American samples of adolescents and their families (Brooks-Gunn & Reiter, 1990).

Accordingly, when diversity is introduced into the database used for understanding the links between pubertal change and adolescent-parent relationships, a much more complicated—and richer and more interesting—pattern is evident. Among samples of Latino (primarily Mexican American) boys and their families, pubertal maturation brings youth *closer* to their parents (Molina & Chassin, 1996). Puberty among these Latino youth is associated with greater parental social support and less intergenerational conflict than is the case either for correspondingly mature European American samples (where the completely opposite effect of puberty on family relations is seen) or for Latino youth prior to or after their maturation. In turn, the influences of early maturation on Swedish girls' norm-breaking behaviors depends on the ages of the peers with whom they interact; that is, early-maturing girls with same-age peers break fewer rules than do early-maturing girls with older peers (Stattin & Magnusson, 1990).

In essence, then, we must understand racial/ethnic, cultural, and developmental diversity systemically in order to appreciate the nature and variation that exists within and across time in human behavior and development. In other words, individual differences arise inevitably from the action of the development system; in turn, they move the system in ways that elaborate diversity further. Also, these dynamic interactions create, and promote a focus in developmental scholarship on, individual differences—of people and of settings—*and* changes in both of these types of differences and in the relations among them (i.e., in person-context relations). Understanding and study of these temporal dimensions of dynamic interactions is critical, not only for theoretical precision but for the advancement of research and application in human development. This assertion leads us to some concluding comments.

CONCLUSIONS AND IMPLICATIONS

The ideas presented in Lerner and Busch-Rossnagel's (1981a) edited volume derived from the comparative scholarship that had resolved the nature-nurture dichotomy in favor of relational, developmental systems thinking (e.g., Gottlieb, 1992, 1997; Schneirla, 1956, 1957; Tobach, 1981). Not only did the ideas in Lerner and Busch-Rossnagel's book reflect this past, they presaged the themes found in the theories of human development presented in Lerner's (1998a) recent volume of the *Handbook of Child Psychology* and summarized by Lerner (1998b) in his introduction to that book: systematic change and relative plasticity, relationism and integration, embeddedness and temporality, and generalizability limits and diversity. As projected by Lerner and Busch-Rossnagel, the ideas associated with these conceptual themes have now, at the end of the 1990s, become very much intertwined facets of a common and predominant theoretical core: They form the corpus of a superordinate developmental systems view of human development (see Bronfenbrenner & Morris, 1998; Fischer & Bidell, 1998; Gardner, 1998; Gottlieb et al., 1998; Magnusson & Stattin, 1998; Thelen & Smith, 1998; Wapner & Demick, 1998; see also Ford & Lerner, 1992), one that elaborates on Lerner and Busch-Rossnagel's ideas of constant change and embeddedness, that derives from the integrated coactions between the individual and his or her multilevel context, and that provides an agenda for capitalizing on the relative plasticity of human development to foster applications (e.g., preventive interventions) promoting positive development (Lerner, 1984, 1995).

Although clearly associated with the earlier Lerner and Busch-Rossnagel work, the ideas associated with developmental systems theories, such as developmental contextualism in Lerner (1998b)—and the rich biological and psychosocial literatures that provide empirical support for this conception (Gottlieb, 1992, 1997; Lerner, 1998a)—have extended the scope and utility of the perspective provided in the Lerner and Busch-Rossnagel volume, creating a powerful frame for research and application in human development. This frame embraces the role of the individual, of his or her actions on the context; it also stresses the fused influence of the context on his or her further individuality.

In sum, the developmental systems perspective represented in the ideas of Lerner (1998b) and Lerner and Busch-Rossnagel (1981a, 1981b) involves the study of active people providing a source across the life span of their individual developmental trajectories; this development occurs through the dynamic interactions people experience with the specific characteristics of the changing contexts within which they are embedded (Brandtstädter, 1998; see also Chapter 2, this volume). This stress on the dynamic relation between the individual and his or her context indicates that a synthesis of perspectives from multiple disciplines is needed if we are to understand the multilevel (e.g., person, family, and community) integrations involved in human development. As a result, to understand the basic process of human development—the process of change involved in the relations between individually distinct people and their diverse contexts—researchers must conduct both descriptive and explanatory investigations within the actual ecology of people's lives.

This research should no longer make a priori assumptions about the existence of generic developmental laws or the primacy of such laws in providing the key information about the life of a given person or group. Simply, integrated multidisciplinary and developmental research devoted to the study of diversity and context must be moved to the fore of scholarly concern. Our goal must be to understand how the individually different actions of diverse people, and the actions of their similarly diverse contexts on them, combine—coact—to foster the unique developmental trajectories involved in human life.

REFERENCES

Anastasi, A. (1958). Heredity, environment, and the question, "how?" *Psychological Review, 65,* 197-208.

Baltes, P. B. (1979a). Life-span developmental psychology: Some converging observations on history and theory. In P. B. Baltes & O. G. Brim, Jr. (Eds.), *Life-span development and behavior* (Vol. 2, pp. 255-279). New York: Academic Press.

Baltes, P. B. (1979b, Summer). On the potential and limits of child development: Life-span developmental perspectives. *Newsletter of the Society for Research in Child Development,* pp. 1-4.

Baltes, P. B. (1987). Theoretical propositions of life-span developmental psychology: On the dynamics between growth and decline. *Developmental Psychology, 23,* 611-626.

Baltes, P. B., & Baltes, M. M. (1980). Plasticity and variability in psychological aging: Methodological and theoretical issues. In G. E. Gurski (Ed.), *Determining the effects of aging on the central nervous system* (pp. 41-66). Berlin: Schering.

Baltes, P. B., Lindenberger, U., & Staudinger, U. M. (1998). Life-span theory in developmental psychology. In W. Damon (Series Ed.) & R. M. Lerner (Vol. Ed.), *Handbook of child psychology: Vol. 1. Theoretical models of human development* (5th ed., pp. 1029-1143). New York: John Wiley.

Baltes, P. B., & Nesselroade, J. R. (1973). The developmental analysis of individual differences on multiple measures. In J. R. Nesselroade & H. W. Reese (Eds.), *Life-span developmental psychology: Introduction to research methodological issues* (pp. 219-251). New York: Academic Press.

Baltes, P. B., Reese, H. W., & Lipsitt, L. P. (1980). Life-span developmental psychology. *Annual Review of Psychology, 31,* 65-110.

Baltes, P. B., Reese, H. W., & Nesselroade, J. R. (1977). *Life-span developmental psychology: Introduction to research methods.* Monterey, CA: Brooks/Cole.

Baltes, P. B., & Schaie, K. W. (Eds.). (1973). *Life-span developmental psychology: Personality and socialization.* New York: Academic Press.

Belsky, J., Steinberg, L., & Draper, P. (1991). Childhood experience, interpersonal development, and reproductive strategy: An evolutionary theory of socialization. *Child Development, 62,* 647-670.

Belsky, J., & Tolan, W. J. (1981). Infants as producers of their own development: An ecological analysis. In R. M. Lerner & N. A. Busch-Rossnagel (Eds.), *Individuals as producers of their development: A life-span perspective* (pp. 87-116). New York: Academic Press.

Birkel, R., Lerner, R. M., & Smyer, M. A. (1989). Applied developmental psychology as an implementation of a life-span view of human development. *Journal of Applied Developmental Psychology, 10,* 425-445.

Brandtstädter, J. (1984). Personal and social control over development: Some implications of an action perspective in life-span developmental psychology. In P. B. Baltes & O. G. Brim, Jr. (Eds.), *Life-span development and behavior* (Vol. 6, pp. 1-32). New York: Academic Press.

Brandtstädter, J. (1985). Individual development in social action contexts: Problems of explanation. In J. R. Nesselroade & A. von Eye (Eds.), *Individual development and social change: Explanatory analysis* (pp. 243-264). New York: Academic Press.

Brandtstädter, J. (1998). Action perspectives on human development. In W. Damon (Series Ed.) & R. M. Lerner (Vol. Ed.), *Handbook of child psychology: Vol. 1. Theoretical models of human development* (5th ed., pp. 807-863). New York: John Wiley.

Brauth, S. E., Hall, W. S., & Dooling, R. J. (Eds.). (1991). *Plasticity of development.* Cambridge: MIT Press.

Brim, O. G., Jr., & Kagan, J. (Eds.). (1980). *Constancy and change in human development.* Cambridge, MA: Harvard University Press.

Bronfenbrenner, U. (1979). *The ecology of human development*. Cambridge, MA: Harvard University Press.

Bronfenbrenner, U., & Ceci, S. J. (1994). Nature-nurture reconceptualized: A biological model. *Psychological Review, 101*, 568-586.

Bronfenbrenner, U., & Morris, P. A. (1998). The ecology of developmental processes. In W. Damon (Series Ed.) & R. M. Lerner (Vol. Ed.), *Handbook of child psychology: Vol. 1. Theoretical models of human development* (5th ed., pp. 993-1028). New York: John Wiley.

Brooks-Gunn, J., & Reiter, E. O. (1990). The role of pubertal processes in the early adolescent transition. In S. Feldman & G. Elliott (Eds.), *At the threshold: The developing adolescent* (pp. 16-53). Cambridge, MA: Harvard University Press.

Busch-Rossnagel, N. A. (1981). Where is the handicap in disability? The contextual impact of physical disability. In R. M. Lerner & N. A. Busch-Rossnagel (Eds.), *Individuals as producers of their development: A life-span perspective* (pp. 281-312). New York: Academic Press.

Cairns, R. B. (1998). The making of developmental psychology. In W. Damon (Series Ed.) & R. M. Lerner (Vol. Ed.), *Handbook of child psychology: Vol. 1. Theoretical models of human development* (5th ed., pp. 25-105). New York: John Wiley.

Campbell, D. T. (1975). On the conflicts between biological and social evolution and between psychology and moral tradition. *American Psychologist, 30*, 1103-1126.

Chess, S., & Thomas, A. (1984). *The origins and evolution of behavior disorders: Infancy to early adult life*. New York: Brunner/Mazel.

Csikszentmihalyi, M., & Rathunde, K. (1998). The development of the person: An experiential perspective on the ontogenesis of psychological complexity. In W. Damon (Series Ed.) & R. M. Lerner (Vol. Ed.), *Handbook of child psychology: Vol. 1. Theoretical models of human development* (5th ed., pp. 635-684). New York: John Wiley.

Darwin, C. (1872). *The expression of emotion in men and animals*. London: J. Murray.

Datan, N., & Reese, H. W. (Eds.). (1977). *Life-span developmental psychology: Dialectical perspectives on experimental research*. New York: Academic Press.

Dixon, R. A., & Lerner, R. M. (1999). A history of systems in developmental psychology. In M. H. Bornstein & M. E. Lamb (Ed.), *Developmental psychology: An advanced textbook* (pp. 3-45). Hillsdale, NJ: Lawrence Erlbaum.

Dryfoos, J. G. (1994). *Full service schools: A revolution in health and social services of children, youth and families*. San Francisco: Jossey-Bass.

Elder, G. H., Jr. (1979). Historical change in life patterns and personality. In P. B. Baltes & O. G. Brim, Jr. (Eds.), *Life-span development and behavior* (Vol. 2. pp. 117-159). New York: Academic Press.

Elder, G. H., Jr. (1980). Adolescence in historical perspective. In J. Adelson (Ed.), *Handbooks of adolescent psychology* (pp. 3-46). New York: John Wiley.

Elder, G. H., Jr. (1998). The life course and human development. In W. Damon (Series Ed.) & R. M. Lerner (Vol. Ed.), *Handbook of child psychology: Vol. 1.*

Theoretical models of human development (5th ed., pp. 939-991). New York: John Wiley.

Elder, G. H., Jr., Modell, J., & Parke, R. D. (Eds.). (1993). *Children in time and place: Developmental and historical insights.* New York: Cambridge University Press.

Featherman, D. L. (1983). Life-span perspectives in social science research. In P. B. Baltes & O. G. Brim, Jr. (Eds.), *Life-span development and behavior* (Vol. 5, pp. 1-57). New York: Academic Press.

Fein, G. G. (1981). The physical environment: Stimulation or evocation. In R. M. Lerner & N. A. Busch-Rossnagel (Eds.), *Individuals as producers of their development: A life-span perspective* (pp. 257-279). New York: Academic Press.

Feldman, R. (1998). *Understanding psychology* (5th ed.). New York: McGraw-Hill.

Fischer, K. W., & Bidell, T. (1998). Dynamic development of psychological structures in action and thought. In W. Damon (Series Ed.) & R. M. Lerner (Vol. Ed.), *Handbook of child psychology: Vol. 1. Theoretical models of human development* (5th ed.). New York: John Wiley.

Fisher, C. B., Jackson, J. F., & Villarruel, F. A. (1998). The study of African American and Latin American children and youth. In W. Damon (Series Ed.) & R. M. Lerner (Vol. Ed.), *Handbook of child psychology: Vol. 1. Theoretical models of human development* (5th ed., pp. 1145-1207). New York: John Wiley.

Fisher, C. B., & Lerner, R. M. (Eds.). (1994). *Applied developmental psychology.* New York: McGraw-Hill.

Ford, D. H., & Lerner, R. M. (1992). *Developmental systems theory: An integrative approach.* Newbury Park, CA: Sage.

Freedman, D. G. (1979). *Human sociobiology: A holistic approach.* New York: Free Press.

Gardner, H. E. (1998). Extraordinary cognitive achievements (ECA): A symbol systems approach. In W. Damon (Series Ed.) & R. M. Lerner (Vol. Ed.), *Handbook of child psychology: Vol. 1. Theoretical models of human development* (5th ed., pp. 415-466). New York: John Wiley.

Garn, S. M. (1980). Continuities and change in maturational timing. In O. G. Brim, Jr., & J. Kagan (Eds.), *Constancy and change in human development* (pp. 113-162). Cambridge, MA: Harvard University Press.

Gollin, E. S. (1981). Development and plasticity. In E. S. Gollin (Ed.), *Developmental plasticity: Behavioral and biological aspects of variations in development* (pp. 231-251). New York: Academic Press.

Gottlieb, G. (1991). The experiential canalization of behavioral development: Theory. *Developmental Psychology, 27,* 4-13.

Gottlieb, G. (1992). *Individual development and evolution: The genesis of novel behavior.* New York: Oxford University Press.

Gottlieb, G. (1997). *Synthesizing nature and nurture.* Thousand Oaks, CA: Sage.

Gottlieb, G., Wahlsten, D., & Lickliter, R. (1998). The significance of biology for human development: A developmental psychobiological systems view. In W. Damon (Series Ed.) & R. M. Lerner (Vol. Ed.), *Handbook of child psychology: Vol. 1.*

Theoretical models of human development (5th ed., pp. 233-273). New York: John Wiley.

Gould, S. J. (1977). *Ontogeny and phylogeny.* Cambridge, MA: Belknap.

Goulet, L. R., & Baltes, P. B. (Eds.). (1970). *Life-span developmental psychology: Research and theory.* New York: Academic Press.

Gray, P. (1998). *Psychology* (2nd ed.). New York: Worth.

Haan, N. (1981). Adolescents and young adults as producers of their development. In R. M. Lerner & N. A. Busch-Rossnagel (Eds.), *Individuals as producers of their development: A life-span perspective* (pp. 155-182). New York: Academic Press.

Hamburger, V. (1957). The concept of development in biology. In D. B. Harris (Ed.), *The concept of development* (pp. 49-58). Minneapolis: University of Minnesota Press.

Harris, D. B. (1957). (Ed.). *The concept of development.* Minneapolis: University of Minnesota Press.

Herrnstein, R. J. (1973). *IQ and the meritocracy.* Boston: Little, Brown.

Herrnstein, R. J., & Murray, C. (1994). *The bell curve: Intelligence and class structure in American life.* New York: Free Press.

Hetherington, E. M., Lerner, R. M., & Perlmutter, M. (Eds.). (1988). *Child development in life-span perspective.* Hillsdale, NJ: Lawrence Erlbaum.

Hill, J. P., Holmbeck, G. N., Marlow, L., Green, T. M., & Lynch, M. E. (1985a). Menarcheal status and parent-child relations in families of seventh-grade girls. *Journal of Youth and Adolescence, 14,* 301-316.

Hill, J. P., Holmbeck, G. N., Marlow, L., Green, T. M., & Lynch, M. E. (1985b). Pubertal status and parent-child relations in families of seventh-grade boys. *Journal of Early Adolescence, 5,* 31-44.

Ho, M.-W. (1984). Environment and heredity in development and evolution. In M.-W. Ho & P. T. Saunders (Eds.), *Beyond neo-Darwinism: An introduction to the new evolutionary paradigm* (pp. 267-289). London: Academic Press.

Holmbeck, G. N., & Hill, J. P. (1991). Conflictive engagement, positive affect, and menarche in families with seventh-grade girls. *Child Development, 62,* 1030-1048.

Hultsch, D. F., & Hickey, T. (1978). External validity in the study of human development: Theoretical and methodological issues. *Human Development, 21,* 76-91.

Jensen, A. R. (1969). How much can we boost IQ and scholastic achievement? *Harvard Educational Review, 39,* 1-123.

Jensen, A. R. (1980). *Bias in mental testing.* New York: Free Press.

Jones, R. T., & Haney, J. I. (1981). A body-behavior conceptualization of a somatopsychological problem: Race. In R. M. Lerner & N. A. Busch-Rossnagel (Eds.), *Individuals as producers of their development: A life-span perspective* (pp. 349-388). New York: Academic Press.

Katchadourian, H. (1977). *The biology of adolescence.* San Francisco: W. H. Freeman.

Keil, F. C. (1998). Cognitive science and the origins of thought and knowledge. In W. Damon (Series Ed.) & R. M. Lerner (Vol. Ed.), *Handbook of child psychology: Vol. 1. Theoretical models of human development* (5th ed., pp. 341-413). New York: John Wiley.

Kuo, Z.-Y. (1930). The genesis of the cat's response to the rat. *Journal of Comparative Psychology, 11,* 1-35.

Kuo, Z.-Y. (1967). *The dynamics of behavior development.* New York: Random House.

Kuo, Z.-Y. (1976). *The dynamics of behavior development: An epigenetic view.* New York: Plenum.

Kuhn, T. S. (1970). *The structure of scientific revolutions* (2nd ed.). Chicago: University of Chicago Press.

Labouvie-Vief, G. (1981). Proactive and reactive aspects of constructivism: Growth and aging in life-span perspective. In R. M. Lerner & N. A. Busch-Rossnagel (Eds.), *Individuals as producers of their development: A life-span perspective* (pp. 197-230). New York: Academic Press.

Lahey, B. (1998). *Psychology: An introduction* (6th ed.). New York: McGraw-Hill.

Lehrman, D. S. (1953). A critique of Konrad Lorenz's theory of instinctive behavior. *Quarterly Review of Biology, 28,* 337-363.

Lerner, J. V. (1984). The import of temperament for psychosocial functioning: Tests of a "goodness of fit" model. *Merrill-Palmer Quarterly, 30,* 177-188.

Lerner, R. M. (1976). *Concepts and theories of human development.* Reading, MA: Addison-Wesley.

Lerner, R. M. (1978). Nature, nurture, and dynamic interactionism. *Human Development, 21,* 1-20.

Lerner, R. M. (1979). The life-span view of human development: The sample case of aging. *Contemporary Psychology, 24,* 1008-1009.

Lerner, R. M. (1982). Children and adolescents as producers of their own development. *Developmental Review, 2,* 342-370.

Lerner, R. M. (1984). *On the nature of human plasticity.* New York: Cambridge University Press.

Lerner, R. M. (1986). *Concepts and theories of human development* (2nd ed.). New York: Random House.

Lerner, R. M. (1987). A life-span perspective for early adolescence. In R. M. Lerner & T. T. Foch (Eds.), *Biological-psychosocial interactions in early adolescence: A life-span perspective* (pp. 9-34). Hillsdale, NJ: Lawrence Erlbaum.

Lerner, R. M. (1991). Changing organism-context relations as the basic process of development: A developmental-contextual perspective. *Developmental Psychology, 27,* 27-32.

Lerner, R. M. (1995). *America's youth in crisis: Challenges and options for programs and policies.* Thousand Oaks, CA: Sage.

Lerner, R. M. (1996). Relative plasticity, integration, temporality, and diversity in human development: A developmental contextual perspective about theory, process, and method. *Developmental Psychology, 32,* 781-786.

Lerner, R. M. (Ed.). (1998a). *Theoretical models of human development* (Vol. 1 of *Handbook of child psychology,* 5th ed.; W. Damon, Series Ed.). New York: John Wiley.

Lerner, R. M. (1998b). Theories of human development. In W. Damon (Series Ed.) & R. M. Lerner (Vol. Ed.), *Handbook of child psychology: Vol. 1. Theoretical models of human development* (5th ed., pp. 1-24). New York: John Wiley.

Lerner, R. M., & Busch-Rossnagel, N. A. (Eds.). (1981a). *Individuals as producers of their development: A life-span perspective.* New York: Academic Press.

Lerner, R. M., & Busch-Rossnagel, N. A. (1981b). Individuals as producers of their development: Conceptual and empirical bases. In R. M. Lerner & N. A. Busch-Rossnagel (Eds.), *Individuals as producers of their development: A life-span perspective* (pp. 1-36). New York: Academic Press.

Lerner, R. M., & Hood, K. E. (1986). Plasticity in development: Concepts and issues for intervention. *Journal of Applied Developmental Psychology, 7,* 139-152.

Lerner, R. M., & Kauffman, M. B. (1985). The concept of development in contextualism. *Developmental Review, 5,* 309-333.

Lerner, R. M., & Kauffman, M. B. (1986). On the metatheoretical relativism of analyses of metatheoretical analyses: A critique of Kendler's comments. *Developmental Review, 6,* 96-106.

Lerner, R. M., & Lerner, J. V. (1983). Temperament-intelligence reciprocities in early childhood: A contextual model. In M. Lewis (Ed.), *Origins of intelligence: Infancy and early childhood* (pp. 399-421). New York: Plenum.

Lerner, R. M., & Lerner, J. V. (1989). Organismic and social contextual bases of development: The sample case of early adolescence. In W. Damon (Ed.), *Child development today and tomorrow* (pp. 69-85). San Francisco: Jossey-Bass.

Lerner, R. M., Skinner, E. A., & Sorell, G. T. (1980). Methodological implications of contextual/dialectic theories of development. *Human Development, 23,* 225-235.

Lerner, R. M., & Spanier, G. B. (Eds.). (1978). *Child influences on marital and family interaction: A life-span perspective.* New York: Academic Press.

Lewontin, R. C. (1981). On constraints and adaptation. *Behavioral and Brain Sciences, 4,* 244-245.

Lewontin, R. C., Rose, S., & Kamin, L. J. (1984). *Not in our genes: Biology, ideology, and human nature.* New York: Pantheon.

Lewontin, R. C., & Levins, R. (1978). Evolution. In *Encyclopedia Einaudi* (Vol. 5). Turin, Italy: Einaudi.

Liben, L. S. (1981). Individuals' contributions to their own development during childhood: A Piagetian perspective. In R. M. Lerner & N. A. Busch-Rossnagel (Eds.), *Individuals as producers of their development: A life-span perspective* (pp. 117-153). New York: Academic Press.

Lorenz, K. (1966). *On aggression.* New York: Harcourt, Brace & World.

MacDonald, K. (1994). *A people that shall dwell alone: Judaism as an evolutionary group strategy.* Westport, CT: Greenwood.

Magnusson, D., & Stattin, H. (1998). Person-context interaction theories. In W. Damon (Series Ed.) & R. M. Lerner (Vol. Ed.), *Handbook of child psychology: Vol. 1. Theoretical models of human development* (5th ed., pp. 685-759). New York: John Wiley.

Marshall, W. A., & Tanner, J. M. (1986). Puberty. In F. Falkner & J. M. Tanner (Eds.), *Human growth* (2nd ed., Vol. 2, pp. 171-209). New York: Plenum.

Meacham, J. A. (1976). Continuing the dialogue: Dialectics and remembering. *Human Development, 19,* 304-309.

Meacham, J. A. (1977). A transactional model of remembering. In N. Datan & H. W. Reese (Eds.), *Life-span developmental psychology: Dialectical perspectives on experimental research.* (pp. 261-283). New York: Academic Press.

Meacham, J. A. (1981). Political values, conceptual models, and research. In R. M. Lerner & N. A. Busch-Rossnagel (Eds.), *Individuals as producers of their development: A life-span perspective* (pp. 447-474). New York: Academic Press.

Meyers, D. G. (1998). *Exploring psychology* (4th ed.). New York: Worth.

Molina, B. S. G., & Chassin, L. (1996). The parent-adolescent relationship at puberty: Hispanic ethnicity and parent alcoholism as moderators. *Developmental Psychology, 32,* 675-686.

Nesselroade, J. R., & Baltes, P. B. (Eds.). (1979). *Longitudinal research in the study of behavior and development.* New York: Academic Press.

Nesselroade, J. R., & Reese, H. W. (Eds.). (1973). *Life-span developmental psychology: Introduction to research methodological issues.* New York: Academic Press.

Nesselroade, J. R., & von Eye, A. (Eds.). (1985). *Individual development and social change: Explanatory analysis.* New York: Academic Press.

Nisbet, R. A. (1980). *History of the idea of progress.* New York: Basic Books.

Overton, W. F. (1978). Klaus Riegel: Theoretical contribution to concepts of stability and change. *Human Development, 21,* 360-363.

Overton, W. F. (1998). Developmental psychology: Philosophy, concepts, and methods. In W. Damon (Series Ed.) & R. M. Lerner (Vol. Ed.), *Handbook of child psychology: Vol. 1. Theoretical models of human development* (5th ed., pp. 107-188). New York: John Wiley.

Papalia, D., Olds, S. W., & Feldman, R. F. (1998). *A child's world* (8th ed.). New York: McGraw-Hill.

Pepper, S. C. (1942). *World hypotheses: A study in evidence.* Berkeley: University of California Press.

Plomin, R. (1986). *Development, genetics, and psychology.* Hillsdale, NJ: Lawrence Erlbaum.

Plomin, R., Corley, R., DeFries, J. C., & Faulker, D. W. (1990). Individual differences in television viewing in early childhood: Nature as well as nurture. *Psychological Science, 1,* 371-377.

Riegel, K. F. (1975). Toward a dialectical theory of development. *Human Development, 18,* 50-64.

Riegel, K. F. (1976a). The dialectics of human development. *American Psychologist, 31,* 689-700.

Riegel, K. F. (1976b). From traits and equilibrium toward developmental dialectics. In W. J. Arnold (Eds.), *Nebraska Symposium on Motivation: Vol. 23. Conceptual foundations of psychology* (pp. 348-408). Lincoln: University of Nebraska Press.

Riley, M. W. (Ed.). (1979). *Aging from birth to death.* Washington, DC: American Association for the Advancement of Science.

Rodeheaver, D., & Datan, N. (1981). Making it: The dialectics of middle age. In R. M. Lerner & N. A. Busch-Rossnagel (Eds.), *Individuals as producers of their development: A life-span perspective* (pp. 183-196). New York: Academic Press.

Rowe, D. C. (1994). *The limits of family influence: Genes, experience, and behavior.* New York: Guilford.

Rushton, J. P. (1987). An evolutionary theory of health, longevity, and personality: Sociobiology and r/K reproductive strategies. *Psychological Reports, 60,* 539-549.

Rushton, J. P. (1988). Do r/K reproductive strategies apply to human differences? *Social Biology, 35,* 337-340.

Sameroff, A. J. (1983). Developmental systems: Contexts and evolution. In P. H. Mussen (Series Ed.) & W. Kessen (Vol. Ed.), *Handbook of child psychology: Vol. 1. History, theory, and methods* (4th ed., pp. 237-294). New York: John Wiley.

Schaie, K. W., & Strother, C. R. (1968). A cross-sequential study of age changes in cognitive behavior. *Psychological Bulletin, 70,* 671-680.

Schneirla, T. C. (1956). Interrelationships of the innate and the acquired in instinctive behavior. In P. P. Grasse (Ed.), *L'instinct dans le conportement des animaux et de l'homme* (pp. 387-452). Paris: Mason et Cie.

Schneirla, T. C. (1957). The concept of development in comparative psychology. In D. B. Harris (Ed.), *The concept of development* (pp. 78-108). Minneapolis: University of Minnesota.

Shweder, R. A., Goodnow, J., Hatano, G., Kessel, F., LeVine, R. A., Markus, H., & Miller, P. (1998). The cultural psychology of development. In W. Damon (Series Ed.) & R. M. Lerner (Vol. Ed.), *Handbook of child psychology: Vol. 1. Theoretical models of human development* (5th ed., pp. 865-937). New York: John Wiley.

Smith, L. B., & Thelen, E. (Eds.). (1993). *A dynamic systems approach to development: Applications.* Cambridge: MIT Press.

Sorell, G. T., & Nowak, C. A. (1981). The role of physical attractiveness as a contributor to individual development. In R. M. Lerner & N. A. Busch-Rossnagel (Eds.), *Individuals as producers of their development: A life-span perspective* (pp. 389-446). New York: Academic Press.

Sørensen, A. B., Weinert, F. E., & Sherrod, L. R. (Eds.). (1986). *Human development and the life course: Multidisciplinary perspectives.* Hillsdale, NJ: Lawrence Erlbaum.

Spelke, E. S., & Newport, E. L. (1998). Nativism, empiricism, and the development of knowledge. In W. Damon (Series Ed.) & R. M. Lerner (Vol. Ed.), *Handbook of child psychology: Vol. 1. Theoretical models of human development* (5th ed., pp. 275-340). New York: John Wiley.

Stattin, H., & Magnusson, D. (1990). *Pubertal maturation in female development.* Hillsdale, NJ: Lawrence Erlbaum.

Steinberg, L. (1987). The impact of puberty on family relations: Effects of pubertal status and pubertal timing. *Developmental Psychology, 23,* 833-840.

Steinberg, L. (1990). Autonomy, conflict, and harmony in the family relationship. In S. S. Feldman & G. R. Elliott (Eds.), *At the threshold: The developing adolescent* (pp. 255-276). Cambridge, MA: Harvard University Press.

Steinberg, L., & Hill, J. P. (1978). Patterns of family interaction as a function of age, the onset of puberty, and formal thinking. *Developmental Psychology, 14,* 683-684.

Strohman, R. C. (1993). Organism and experience [Review of the book *Final solutions,* by R. M. Lerner]. *Journal of Applied Developmental Psychology, 14,* 147-151.

Super, C. M., & Harkness, S. (1981). Figure, ground, and gestalt: The cultural context of the active individual. In R. M. Lerner & N. A. Busch-Rossnagel (Eds.), *Individuals as producers of their development: A life-span perspective* (pp. 69-86). New York: Academic Press.

Tanner, J. M. (1962). *Growth at adolescence.* Springfield, IL: Charles C Thomas.

Tanner, J. M. (1970). Physical growth. In P. H. Mussen (Ed.), *Carmichael's manual of child psychology* (Vol. 1, pp. 77-155). New York: John Wiley.

Tanner, J. M. (1991). Menarche, secular trend in age of. In R. M. Lerner, A. C. Petersen, & J. Brooks-Gunn (Ed.), *Encyclopedia of adolescence* (pp. 637-641). New York: Garland.

Thelen, E., & Smith, L. B. (1994). *A dynamic systems approach to the development of cognition and action.* Cambridge: MIT Press.

Thelen, E., & Smith, L. B. (1998). Dynamic systems theories. In W. Damon (Series Ed.) & R. M. Lerner (Vol. Ed.), *Handbook of child psychology: Vol. 1. Theoretical models of human development* (5th ed., pp. 563-633). New York: John Wiley.

Thomas, A., & Chess, S. (1977). *Temperament and development.* New York: Brunner/Mazel.

Thomas, A., & Chess, S. (1981). The role of temperament in the contributions of individuals to their development. In R. M. Lerner & N. A. Busch-Rossnagel (Eds.), *Individuals as producers of their development: A life-span perspective* (pp. 231-255). New York: Academic Press.

Thomas, A., Chess, S., Birch, H. G., Hertzig, M. E., & Korn, S. (1963). *Behavioral individuality in early childhood.* New York: New York University.

Tobach, E. (1981). Evolutionary aspects of the activity of the organism and its development. In R. M. Lerner & N. A. Busch-Rossnagel (Eds.), *Individuals as producers of their development: A life-span perspective* (pp. 37-68). New York: Academic Press.

Tobach, E., & Greenberg, G. (1984). The significance of T. C. Schneirla's contribution to the concept of levels of integration. In G. Greenberg & E. Tobach (Eds.), *Behavioral evolution and integrative levels* (pp. 1-7). Hillsdale, NJ: Lawrence Erlbaum.

Tobach, E., & Schneirla, T. C. (1968). The biopsychology of social behavior of animals. In R. E. Cooke & S. Levin (Eds.), *Biologic basis of pediatric practice* (pp. 68-82). New York: McGraw-Hill.

Valsiner, J. (1998). The development of the concept of development: Historical and epistemological perspectives. In W. Damon (Series Ed.) & R. M. Lerner (Vol. Ed.), *Handbook of child psychology: Vol. 1. Theoretical models of human development* (5th ed., pp. 189-232). New York: John Wiley.

Villarruel, F. A., & Lerner, R. M. (Eds.). (1994). *Promoting community-based programs for socialization and learning.* San Francisco: Jossey-Bass.

von Bertalanffy, L. (1933). *Modern theories of development.* London: Oxford University.

Wapner, S. (1993). Parental development: A holistic, developmental system-oriented perspective. In J. Demick, K. Bursik, & R. DiBiase (Eds.), *Parental development* (pp. 3-37). Hillsdale, NJ: Lawrence Erlbaum.

Wapner, S., & Demick, J. (1998). Developmental analysis: A holistic, developmental, systems-oriented perspective. In W. Damon (Series Ed.) & R. M. Lerner (Vol. Ed.), *Handbook of child psychology: Vol. 1. Theoretical models of human development* (5th ed., pp. 761-805). New York: John Wiley.

Wilson, E. O. (1975). *Sociobiology: The new synthesis.* Cambridge, MA: Harvard University Press.

Worell, J. (1981). Life-span sex roles: Development, continuity, and change. In R. M. Lerner & N. A. Busch-Rossnagel (Eds.), *Individuals as producers of their development: A life-span perspective* (pp. 313-347). New York: Academic Press.

2

THE SELF IN ACTION AND DEVELOPMENT

Cultural, Biosocial, and Ontogenetic Bases of Intentional Self-Development

Jochen Brandtstädter

The view that individuals are not only products but also producers of their development is not a novel one. Organismic, interactionist, and social-constructivist paradigms have emphasized the formative role of person-environment transactions and the constructive functions of cultural tools and symbols in human ontogeny (e.g., Piaget, 1976; Valsiner, 1989; Vygotsky, 1978), and thus have contributed to the installment of human activity and interaction as the central locus of development in cultural contexts. These traditional accounts, however, have tended to conceive of ontogenetic change as a result or by-product rather than as an intentional target area of action. Thus they have largely disregarded a basic dimension of human development, namely, the fact that the individual, and the adult in particular, takes an active and creative stance toward his or her personal development. In the course of their ontogeny, individuals form mental representations of what they can or should be or become, and these representations feed into the ways in which they interpret, organize, and evaluate their actual and future development. The notion of intentional self-development, on which this volume centers, embraces this theoretical perspective. At the core of this concept is the assumption that we cannot go far in understanding development over the life span without considering the self-reflective and self-regulative processes that, in a reciprocal way, link developmental change to the ways in which individuals, in mentation and purposeful action, construe their development over the life span.

An action-theoretical stance on human development ties in with broader perspectives in the human and social sciences that have gained momentum over the past few years. In the social sciences, for example, theoretical views that consider personal action and development merely as expressions of impersonal societal and sociohistorical forces no longer hold the sway they once held; although the possibility of reducing holistic explanatory accounts to individualistic ones is a matter of continuing dispute, there is increasing consensus that holistic or structuralist stances must be complemented by accounts that show how social facts issue from individual actions (see Elster, 1989; Jackson & Pettit, 1992). In the developmental sciences, researchers have become sensitized to the fact that developmental patterns cannot be registered in terms of invariant laws and universal nomological principles; rather, they reflect cultural and personal agentivity (see Brandtstädter, 1984, 1997; Brim & Kagan, 1980; Chapman & Skinner, 1985; Dannefer, 1989; Eckensberger & Meacham, 1984; Lerner, 1984; Lerner & Busch-Rossnagel, 1981). Although we must avoid the fallacy of equating the lack of evidence for invariance and lawful connectivity with evidence for the lack of these factors in human ontogeny or with positive evidence of a "limitless" plasticity and malleability in human development, it appears that developmental regularities can often be explained in a way that shows how human agents have constructed, or could destruct, them (Brandtstädter, 1998). In biology, anthropology, and developmental genetics, there is growing recognition that the self-regulatory potentials of humans are intrinsically linked to their phylogenetic and evolutionary design, and increasing attention has been paid to the mediating role of action systems in the developmental expression of genetic differences (see Lewontin, 1982; Odling-Smee, 1994; Plomin, 1994). Such theoretical convergences suggest that action-theoretical concepts provide a link for synthesizing notions of intentional self-development with cultural and biological perspectives on development.

Action, intention, and culture are interdefined concepts. Actions, as opposed to nonactional forms of behavior, are enacted intentions; when describing, explaining, and predicting actions, we try to infer these intentions and to show how they are linked with the beliefs and preferences that the actors hold with regard to themselves and the world. Actions are, in a functional, structural, as well as developmental sense, linked to a given sociocultural and sociohistorical context. For one, human action is situated in cultural "fields of action" (Boesch, 1991), that is, within a social and cultural matrix of affordances and constraints. Furthermore, actions, and the mental representations that guide and regulate intentional activity, are tied to the symbol systems, institutions, and linguistic structures that constitute and integrate cultures. Sociocultural systems maintain themselves, and are continually reconstituted, through the action and interaction of human actors (Dannefer & Perlmutter, 1990), and in particular through those specific activities through which individuals give form, purpose, and meaning to their lives and personal development.

Nonetheless, we should be aware of some limitations of an "intentional stance" (Dennett, 1987) as an explanatory framework. For one, action outcomes are mediated by contextual and causal structures that are partly or completely intransparent to the actors; it is a characteristic of human action under constraints of "bounded rationality" (Simon, 1983) that the effects of action often do not coincide with the actor's intentions. Undesired and unexpected side effects of action, and attempts to cope with them, are a driving force in human ontogeny, as well as in cultural evolution (e.g., Giddens, 1984). Uncontrolled and unpredicted events constitute the dramatic ingredient in biographical narratives; human biographies are histories of actions "plus trouble" (Bruner, 1990b). Individuals of course differ with respect to the influence that they ascribe themselves in the regulation of their personal development; constructs of perceived control and self-efficacy refer to such differences (e.g., Bandura, 1986; Skinner, 1995).

When we turn to the formation of intentions and volitions, the limits of intentionalist accounts are perhaps even more evident. We are not entirely free to decide upon which experiences will please us, and we cannot voluntarily choose or change our preferences or beliefs, although we may try to come to have particular mental states (see Gilbert, 1993; Honderich, 1988). Non- or subintentional mechanisms are also involved in the processes through which individuals dissolve attachments and disengage from prior goals and commitments; such processes are obviously of great importance in intentional self-development (see, e.g., Brandtstädter & Greve, 1994; see also Brandtstädter, Wentura, & Rothermund, Chapter 13, this volume). With some notable exceptions (e.g., Bargh, 1996), psychological theories of action have generally given short shrift to the heteronomous (subintentional or nonintentional) mechanisms in action and action regulation, which presumably reflect features of the basic evolutionary architecture of the human mind (see Tooby & Cosmides, 1992). Apparently, any notion of intentional self-development that disregards those factors in development and action that are beyond intentional control would be seriously biased.

Although humans may not be free throughout to choose or change their wants, beliefs, or desires, they have evolved the unique capacity to take an evaluative, critical stance toward them, and to form metaintentions or "second-order volitions" (Frankfurt, 1971). In other words, we can form the intention to have particular desires, intentions, or beliefs. The capacity to enact such secondary volitions, and to empower them with sufficient strength to override "primary" action tendencies, is addressed in such traditional virtue concepts as "willpower" and "self-discipline" as well as in psychological concepts of self-regulation and self-management (e.g., see Baumeister, Heatherton, & Tice, 1994; Karoly, 1993). Obviously, these metavolitional capacities constitute an important aspect of intentional self-development.

The mental processes and capacities that undergird activities of intentional self-development are themselves developmental outcomes. Signs of intentionality emerge very early in development (see Papousek & Papousek, 1989), but the early forms of intentional activity of course do not implicate mental representations of personal development, and they are not directed toward particular developmental tasks or goals. In early childhood, intentionality is first superimposed by external agents, in particular by the parents or caretakers who try to influence and shape the child's behavior and development according to some implicit agenda. This mode of control is exemplified by the purposeful arrangement of "zones of promoted development" and "zones of free movement" (Valsiner, 1987) and by the child's gradual inauguration into cultural techniques and practices (learning through apprenticeship; Rogoff, 1995). In a more indirect sense, intentionality is also imposed on individual development by the symbolic and material tools that are provided in cultural contexts, as far as these tools embody institutionalized problem solutions, enforce particular forms of appropriate use, and become integrated into the regulation of action (e.g., Vygotsky, 1978; Wertsch, 1984).

CULTURAL FOUNDATIONS AND FUNCTIONS OF INTENTIONAL SELF-DEVELOPMENT

Activities of intentional self-development form part of the processes through which cultures organize and reproduce themselves. Comparable to living organisms, sociocultural systems do not simply exist over time, but have to permanently create and re-create the conditions that warrant their permanence and continuity; they thus exhibit features of "autopoiesis" (Maturana & Varela, 1980). However, stability and change in cultural structures and institutions do not reflect inherent homeostatic or self-organizing automatisms, but result from the imposition of constraints and normative standards on action, interaction, and development.

Standardization and Institutionalization of Developmental Processes

The sociocultural control of ontogeny involves all phases and functional domains of development. Cultural systems organize developmental change through the fostering and institutionalizing of the acquisition of cultural tools and techniques, through resource allocation, as well as through age-graded normative expectancies and "developmental tasks" (Havighurst, 1974; see also Flammer & Avramakis, 1992; Nurmi, 1993). Within this field of affordances and constraints, an individual selects and shapes his or her own developmental ecology, thereby gradually creating a "personal culture" (Heidmets, 1985) that reflects the individualized way in which the developing person negotiates cultural demands and expectancies.

The structure of developmentally relevant cultural constraints and affordances constitutes what may be called a "cultural script" (Hagestad, 1991) of the life course. From a functional point of view, this script synchronizes and coordinates developmental and role transitions in various life domains (education, occupation, family), thereby promoting coordination and organizational simplification in educational, economic, and industrial contexts (see Chudacoff, 1989). Life-course scripts may vary across demographic factors such as gender and socioeconomic level; political and economic factors, as well as changes in age stratification, have further impacts on social representations of what constitutes a "normal" life course (e.g., Settersten & Mayer, 1997).

Cultural scripts of the life course blend prescriptive and descriptive elements. What is "normal" in a descriptive, statistical sense often reflects the directive influence of social norms, values, and customs. On the other hand, simple statistical regularities can gain normative force because they often serve as benchmarks for self-evaluation. Although developmental tasks and normative expectancies are not explicitly codified throughout, people have similar views concerning what "people in general" expect from persons of given ages (see Fallo-Mitchell & Ryff, 1982; Hagestad & Neugarten, 1985). Adults of all age groups share normative expectancies concerning the temporal patterning of life transitions for their peer group as well as for other cohorts; however, it appears that such expectancies are more homogeneous, and conform more strongly with presumed public expectancies, among older individuals (e.g., Heckhausen, 1990). Given the lack of pertinent longitudinal analyses, it remains open whether these findings reflect genuine ontogenetic age-graded change or result from generational differences. The latter interpretation receives some support from a historical trend toward a liberalization of age norms that has emerged during the past few decades. Although current notions of a "deinstitutionalization" (e.g., Held, 1986) of the life course may overstate the case, it is obvious that accelerated cultural change and an increasing global interconnectedness of societal and economic processes enforce an increased adaptive flexibility and openness of cultural life-course scripts. Regarding processes of intentional development, these historical trends promote an individuation and flexibility of personal life designs. The ascent of developmental paradigms that emphasize the variability and malleability of developmental patterns may be seen as a correlated phenomenon. The other side of the coin, however, is that images about future life become more fuzzy and planning about life becomes more difficult and demanding under conditions of accelerated culture change.

Cultural norms can have directive force in development only insofar as they correspond to personal action resources and developmental capacities. Normative expectancies about development—whether personal or collective—generally entail assumptions about developmental sequences and contingencies; in particular, they entail beliefs concerning the typical age or age range at which a person becomes capable, or incapable, of successfully accomplishing particular tasks. For example, Nydegger (1986) has shown that subjective age norms concerning fatherhood imply assumptions as to which competencies are important for this social role and how these competencies develop. Implicit developmental assumptions define obligations and responsibilities; by the same token, they also can boost or dampen responsibility attributions. According to the semantic rules of moral discourse, persons should not be held responsible for events that are beyond their control; this—together with stereotyped age expectancies— presumably explains why people tend to react more leniently to awkward or inefficient behavior in elderly persons than they do when observing similar behaviors in younger adults (see Banziger, 1987).

From an action-theoretical point of view, the question arises of how sociocultural tasks and expectations are integrated into the processes of intentional self-development. Cognitive, psychoanalytic, and social-constructivist approaches commonly use the explanatory notions of interiorization, internalization, and identification. By interiorizing, and identifying with, the norms and reality constructions of their social environments, individuals construe the "self-guides" (Higgins, 1988) and personal standards that serve as reference points in the control and evaluation of personal development. Social systems promote this developmental process by linking norm-conforming and norm-deviant behaviors with motivationally relevant contingencies, as well as by institutionalizing stories that rationalize normative expectations. Notions of "internalization" and "interiorization," however, may be misleading as far as they connote the simple transmission or translation of external demands into an "intrapsychic" code. Rather, social norms and demands are interpreted and enacted in a constructive, idiosyncratic way that reflects differences and changes in competencies and developmental achievements (see Lawrence & Valsiner, 1993).

Developmental tasks and normative age expectancies reflect socially shared representations of "normal" or desirable patterns of development over the life course. By forming an orienting framework for interactions and interpersonal expectancies, these representations can turn into self-fulfilling prophecies (see Green, 1981). As intimated above, social representations of "normal" biographies are interlinked with schematic assumptions of the presumptive causes underlying a divergence from the normative pattern. These explanatory schemata also generate inferences about the presumptive personality profiles of individuals who have not accomplished developmental tasks or role transitions according to culturally scripted timetables; "deviant" individuals may appear as irresponsible, incompetent, lazy, maybe also as unconventional or particularly talented, depending on the considered domains and on the assumed degree of personal control within them. Obviously, such schematic attributions can affect self-evaluations and self-corrective efforts, although negative attributions may be neutralized to some extent through particular defensive strategies (e.g., the individual may adjust normative expectations post hoc to factual features of his or her own biography; see Kalicki, 1995).

Regulative and Constitutive Rules in Action and Development

Human actions are not only shaped and regulated by external or internalized rules and belief systems; they are in a stronger sense *constituted* by sociocultural rules, institutions, and language games. The distinction between regulative and constitutive rules of action (see D'Andrade, 1984; Searle, 1968) is of great importance for a deeper understanding of the cultural foundations of intentional self-development (see Brandtstädter, 1988). *Regulative* rules, such as customs, moral prescriptions, developmental tasks, and personal maxims, specify a desired course of behavior or development for particular target groups and contexts ("One should not turn up the volume of one's radio to the point that it disturbs the neighbors"; "As an adult one ought to have formed clear concepts of one's professional future"). Individuals can of course deviate from such rules. *Constitutive* rules, by contrast, prescribe how something must be formed or construed in order to count as a legitimate exemplar of some conceptual category. Just as one can checkmate somebody only within the rules of the game of chess, one can greet someone, promise something, or marry somebody only within the framework of sociocultural rules and institutions that constitute the structure and meaning of such actions. Constitutive rules cannot be transgressed, at least not in the sense in which regulative rules can be. When one moves pieces on a chessboard in ways that do not conform with the rules of the game, one is no longer playing chess. Similarly, acts such as promising something or marrying somebody presuppose an institutional context that determines what kinds of behavior or behavioral interactions in what kinds of circumstances constitute the respective types of act; only a person familiar with the corresponding constitutive rules can identify a given behavior in a given situation as a particular action. Constitutive rules may be fuzzy, and there may even be cases where it is impossible to write down the criteria that are common to all instantiations of a generic category (Rosch, 1977). This notwithstanding, actions gain their particular meanings only within a particular texture of rules, conventions, and linguistic structures. Thus new types of acts and social facts may emerge in the course of cultural change, whereas others may vanish together with the institutions to which they are inseparably linked (see also D'Andrade, 1984).

Obviously, then, processes of self-regulation, intentional self-development, and identity construction are intimately linked to the linguistic structures or, to use Wittgenstein's (1968) term, to the "language games" that prevail in a given social and historical context. The concepts we use in describing and evaluating behavioral and developmental phenomena are interrelated within semantic networks that define patterns of "co-predicable" attributes (Keil, 1986). When ascribing particular traits to a person, we imply a disposition to behave in particular ways in particular types of situations: To be "honest" implies to be disposed to tell the truth and to react with feelings of shame, guilt, or indignation upon encountering dishonest behavior in others or oneself; to be "altruistic" implies a readiness to sacrifice some personal advantage to the benefit of another person as well as the ability to recognize when others need help. Similarly, concepts denoting particular emotional states entail particular types of cognitions and emotional tendencies: To be "worried" implies doubts about personal capabilities to avert some impending adversity; feelings of "guilt" seem to imply a perceived violation of normative expectancies as well as a tendency of atonement; and so on (see Brandtstädter, 1984).

Such implicative structures are individually represented in cognitive scripts and inferential schemata, which form the semantic basis on which processes of self-observation, self-evaluation, and self-monitoring operate. From this point of view, education, socialization, and intentional self-development may generally be seen as organized attempts to bring our behavior, development, and self into forms that justify the ascription of specific attributes, specifically of those attributes that have positive social or personal valence (such as particular competencies or virtues). The symbolic and semiotic structures that prevail in a linguistic community also impose order on ontogenetic sequences. For example, if the notion of competent moral judgment conceptually entails the competent use of moral concepts such as guilt or responsibility, which in turn entails the cognitive capacity to assess the motives or intentions of other persons, then moral competence—as far as this disposition is validly measured—will not emerge prior to the acquisition of this particular social cognitive capacity. Empirical deviations from these "predictions" are excluded not by some causal law, but by conceptual rules. These rules guide not only the processes of developmental control on the cultural and personal level, but also the construction of the measurement procedures and observational instruments that we use for gauging developmental outcomes. These considerations also afford new perspectives for the understanding of "developmental universals" (for a more detailed discussion, see Brandtstädter, 1987).

EVOLUTIONARY PREDICAMENTS
REGARDING INTENTIONAL SELF-DEVELOPMENT

Although the cultural and personal meanings that constitute intentional activity have no "echo" in the physical and causal processes that subserve this activity (see Davidson, 1980; Searle, 1984), we have to recognize that actions and intentions reflect not only the formative influence of cultures, but likewise the architecture of the human mind as it has phylogenetically evolved. Cultures may be considered as a "set of prosthetic devices by which human beings can exceed or even redefine the 'natural limits' of human functioning" (Bruner, 1990a, p. 21; see also Lewontin, 1981). However, humans would not be able to make use of cultural tools and affordances without being endowed and predisposed to do so by their evolutionary design.

As already intimated above, a basic evolutionary feature that makes possible—and at the same time enforces—cultural and personal control of ontogeny is the great plasticity and openness of development (see Gollin, 1981; Lerner, 1984). These features of human ontogeny imply adaptive potentials as well as vulnerabilities, and they have concomitantly evolved with mechanisms to cope with the latter. The capacities to create, maintain, and enact culture, and to plot the "trajectory of . . . life on the societal map" (Berger, Berger, & Kellner, 1967, p. 67), are rooted in this coevolutionary process. Generally, developmental plasticity is already implicated in the notion of culture, as far as this notion connotes the cultivation of some process that is open to modification and optimization. The human organism is not tied through preformed adaptive automatisms to narrowly confined environmental segments; the plasticity of human development brings with it both the potential to adapt to a wide range of environmental variations and the necessity to create and use cultural instruments and institutions that compensate for the lack of adaptive specializations. The human mind is equipped with the means and developmental potential to accomplish these adaptive tasks. Human actors have a unique capacity to extract order from the flux of experiences and to form mental models of self and environment that allow for the representation and mental simulation of action-outcome contingencies. This adaptive flexibility is further potentiated by the human capacity to acquire and use language. Language provides the individual with the symbolic means to represent and control the behavior of others as well as his or her own behavior, to export his or her own thinking into a public space, and to transmit problem solutions through space and time (see Luria, 1979; Markl, 1997). The excessive growth of the telencephalic parts of the hominid brain, the prolonged phase of physiological growth and vulnerability, and the emergence of family structures that organize nutrition, stimulation, and information for the developing organism during a markedly extended period of protection and care form a synergistic complex of evolutionary factors that make enculturation and self-cultivation possible as well as indispensable in human ontogeny (see Bruner, 1990b; Gould, 1977; Lerner, 1984). We are thus geared by evolution to "complete or finish ourselves through culture" (Geertz, 1973, p. 49), or, as Gehlen (1988) has pointedly put it, culture has become the "second nature" of humankind.

From these anthropological perspectives, the notions of action and intentional self-development gain pivotal importance for an understanding of human development in culturally structured environments. When considering genetic and environmental influences as driving forces of development, we must differentiate such notions to account for the fact that developmental ecologies are individually and culturally shaped in order to accomplish particular developmental goals (see Lewontin, 1982). As already intimated, the environment that mediates and modulates the genetic control of development is to a large extent patterned by the selective and constructive activities of the developing individuals (see Odling-Smee, 1994; Plomin, 1994; Scarr & McCartney, 1983). Phenotypes and their environments are thus related in a coevolutionary and co-constructive process; organisms create external structures that are integral to their functioning and development and accordingly may be considered "extensions" of their phenotypes (Dawkins, 1982).

The notion of extended phenotypes is typically illustrated using processes of habitat construction in the animal kingdom, such as the spider's web and the beaver's dam, but it applies as well to the activities through which humans construct, stabilize, and change their relationships with their developmentally relevant environments. As intimated above, the individual's developmental ecology, as well as his or her integral history of life, reflects and codetermines the expression of genotypic effects in development from birth to death. As evidence from adopted twin studies suggests, genetic similarities between individuals can manifest themselves even in biographical similarities, and even in biographical events that are under personal control and reflect intentional choice (e.g., Plomin, Lichtenstein, Pedersen, McClearn, & Nesselroade, 1990).

In spite of obvious similarities, the activities that mediate the extension of phenotypes in animals and humans of course differ in important respects. For example, the spider does not follow a cognitively represented goal or plan when building a web; in particular, one would not assume that it "could have done otherwise." By contrast, the activities through which humans create and extend their phenotypes—and their selves—into their personalized ways of life and development are to a considerable extent intentional and, as such, related to conscious self-representations.[1]

THE SELF IN INTENTIONAL SELF-DEVELOPMENT

Intentional self-development obviously implicates the "self" as a locus of personal agency and as a target of self-referent activity. It should be noted that activities of intentional self-development are self-related in a double sense: First, they are reflexive in a simple grammatical sense—that is, they are directed back on the agents themselves (in ways that, as we will see below, are already instantiated in more primitive biological systems). Second, they are reflexive in a cognitive sense: They are actualizations of the agent's Self in a capital-S sense, that is, of the mental representations that individuals construe of themselves and their past, present, and future personal development. A variety of compound constructs have been advanced to capture the multifaceted ways in which human actors reflect upon and control themselves: "self-awareness," "self-monitoring," "strategic self-presentation," "self-handicapping," "self-affirmation," "self-verification," "compensatory self-inflation," and more (see Duval & Wicklund,

1972; Greenberg & Pyszczynski, 1985; Jones & Pittman, 1982; Snyder & Campbell, 1982; Steele, 1988; Swann, 1983; see also Markus & Wurf, 1987). The two meanings of self-referentiality distinguished above are often confounded in these notions; this is a source of confusion that we should avoid when reflecting on the role of the self in intentional self-development.

A primordial sense of self or selfishness is already implied in the basic autopoietic activities that are fundamental to the self-reproduction and self-maintenance of any living organism. As Dennett (1990) notes:

> The original distinction between self and other is a deep biological principle; one might say it is the deepest principle, for biology begins in self-preservation—in the emergence of entities (the simplest replicators) who resisted destruction and decay. . . . As soon as something gets into the business of self-preservation, boundaries become important. . . . this distinction between everything on the *inside* of a closed boundary and everything in the *external world*, is at the heart of all biological processes. (pp. 6-7; see also Dennett, 1991, p. 174)

A self in this minimal, functional sense is instantiated in any biological system that controls, selects, and transforms its environment in ways that are functional for its development and self-maintenance. As already hinted, the boundaries that separate self from nonself may well extend beyond the organism, and may encompass those aspects of the biotic and abiotic environment that the organism integrates into its autopoietic activity: "You are what you control and care for" (Dennett, 1990, p. 10). Organic systems comprise component systems that in turn constitute "environments" for each other, which the individual systems transform and control for "selfish purposes"; a central functional entity that coordinates and integrates the activities of the constituents is not necessarily implied. Likewise, the activity of individual organisms may be integrated into larger systems of social action and interaction. Again, the functioning of such larger social systems does not necessarily presuppose a central, coordinating "self," and the "purposes" or adaptive functions that can be ascribed to a system as a whole need not be represented on lower system levels (human actors, how- ever, can integrate a "system perspective" into their intentional activity).

These considerations point to important similarities between subhuman and human autopoietic activities. To gain a view of the role of the "self" in human self-regulation and intentional self-development, however, we have to go beyond these basic similarities. In self-regulatory and self-corrective action, we make ourselves—our behavior and development—the object of goal-related activities; we are guided herein by mental representations of how we are, could be, or should be (or become). These representations develop and change through ontogeny; they are intrinsically linked to cultural language games and reality constructions and are influenced by self-referential feedback that individuals receive through transactions with their physical and social environments. The self, as it is enacted in activities of self-regulation and intentional self-development, manifests itself in the reflective, evaluative, and active stance that we take toward ourselves and our development.

Activities of intentional self-development not only presuppose self-representations, but are integrally involved in construing personal continuity and identity over the life span (see Brandtstädter & Greve, 1994; Markus & Herzog, 1991). The self is often conceptualized as a system of self-referential cognitive schemata that are involved in the regulation of thought and action and provide an orientational framework for life planning and personal development (e.g., Markus & Wurf, 1987). Many of our self-referential cognitions are, however, patently irrelevant to our personal identities. If asked to characterize ourselves, we usually refer to particular classes of self-descriptors. Rather than mentioning, for instance, "I had an omelette for breakfast" or "I was at the barber's yesterday," we use descriptors such as socially valued attributes, family and work roles, habits, and hobbies to characterize ourselves (e.g., McCrae & Costa, 1988). The self that we express, defend, and actualize in activities of intentional self-regulation is not just the totality of self-referent cognitions, but comprises mainly those attributes that describe and distinguish us in subjectively essential ways and thus are constitutive to our identity.

Obviously, the range of attributes through which, taken separately or in combination, individuals may define their identities is very broad and may encompass particular skills or habits, features of bodily appearance, ethnicity, gender, biographical particulars, and so on. By the same token, there can be "multiple" identities that are actualized in different situations or life periods, and that may not form a coherent structure, but are connected only by the fact that they refer to the same individual (see Higgins, van Hook, & Dorfman, 1988). A conceptual self, in the sense outlined above, apparently is basic to, and seems to coevolve ontogenetically with, those particular kinds of intentional activities through which individuals try to shape their development and give a particular form to their lives.

THE DEVELOPMENT OF INTENTIONAL SELF-DEVELOPMENT: SOME PRELIMINARY OBSERVATIONS

Making oneself and one's own development the target of observation, evaluation, and control, and integrating into this process the perspectives of other individuals as well as socially shared normative representations of the life course, presupposes particular competencies that gradually emerge in cognitive, linguistic, and sociomoral development. To cast the antecedents of intentional self-regulation in an ontogenetic perspective, four general lines of development may be considered that originate in the primordial epistemic separation between self and nonself during early sensorimotor development (see Kegan, 1983):

1. The emergent capacity to recognize action-outcome contingencies, to coordinate representations of one's own behaviors and external effects, and to anticipate action-contingent events
2. The development of a semantically structured self-concept that represents the self in an objectified sense as an entity having stable and distinctive characteristics, and that also reflects the social metaperspective of other individuals
3. The development of self-regulatory capacities, including the acquisition of "metavolitional" skills to evaluate, control, and correct one's own actions, intentions, and mental processes
4. The integration of these self-processes into an identity structure that provides an orienting framework for life planning and the choice and definition of life tasks, and also includes strategies and mechanisms to secure and protect personal continuity across the life span

In the interest of tractability, I will specify these lines of development in terms of the emergence of different "selves," distinguishing among an *intentional* self, a *conceptual* self, a *self-monitoring* self, a *self-actualizing* self, and a *self-maintaining* self. Although these distinctions partly reflect an ontogenetic ordering, they do not constitute a rigid, stagelike sequence, but rather refer to facets of self-development that are intertwined and overlap to a certain extent.

Origins of an Intentional Self

Intentionality is manifested in behaviors that obviously aim at producing or evoking some positively valued consequence. Intentional goal orientations can particularly be inferred when multiple means are used to reach the same end. Intentional behavior presupposes the capacity to recognize and mentally represent behavior-outcome contingencies and to form anticipatory schemata that guide the selection of means to particular ends. Early signs of intentionality indicating a growing capacity to recognize regular behavior-outcome contingencies, to form anticipatory schemata, and to instrumentalize contextual contingencies can already be observed in the first months of life.

In an operant-conditioning paradigm, 8-week-old children can learn simple instrumental behaviors to produce some interesting effect; however, they display signs of anger as well as a reactant increase of effort when the contingency is disrupted during an extinction phase (Lewis, 1990). At about 4 months, infants become capable of forming a differentiated and coordinated representation of their own behavior and its effects in the nonsocial and social environment (e.g., between the sensory representation of the mother's facial expressions and the proprioceptive representation of their own vocalizations); the integration of these representations in goal-directed action is manifested in the initiation of motor play, nonverbal requests for assistance, and the like (e.g., Papousek & Papousek, 1989). Sensitive and responsive parents as well as contextual factors such as the degree of fit between the child's skill level and task environments foster the development of internal "working models" from which a sense of agentivity and efficacy can grow (see Case, 1991; Lamb & Easterbrooks, 1981; Skinner, 1995). The capacity to recognize, encode, and instrumentally utilize behavior-outcome contingencies evolves in tandem with symbolic capacities during the first 2 years of life. Further progress along these lines is crucially related to the acquisition of language, which not only serves as a symbolic means to represent potential outcomes and meanings of action, but also as an instrument to express and execute one's own intentions.

The Emergence of a Conceptual Self

A crucial feature of language development is the acquisition of semantic rules that guide the ascription of attributes to oneself or others. Around the age of 3, children have acquired primordial notions of appropriateness and competence and begin to evaluate their behavior and themselves in such terms (e.g., Kagan, 1984). The capacity to represent social standards of behavior, and to adjust one's own behavior and thought to such standards, coincides with the emergence of self-evaluative emotions such as shame, guilt, and embarrassment. These developments herald the gradual acquisition of "self-guides" (Higgins, 1988), which are of course revised and expanded during further cognitive and sociomoral development.

Closely tied to the development of linguistic and symbolic competence is the capacity to reflect upon the mental states of other individuals. The emergence of a "theory of mind" (e.g., Lewis & Mitchell, 1994) lends a new dimension to intentional action and self-regulation, with children now becoming able to form inferences about thoughts and motives of other individuals and to integrate them strategically into their own goal-related activity. They now are in a position to appraise themselves from perspectives other than their own and to evaluate their behavior not only in terms of expected outcomes, but also with respect to what those behaviors mean and signify within a social context. Reflecting on the expressive or symbolic valence of actions becomes increasingly important in action regulation and self-evaluation; a specific course of action may be selected not only because it evokes particular reactions from the environment, but because it exhibits features that allow the actor to be described as a particular type of person (Brandtstädter, Gräser, & Mazomeit, 1990).

On this basis, the child begins to think of him- or herself in terms of a dispositional self (see Higgins, 1988). The notion of an "invariant" or core self that warrants identity and self-continuity over time seems to originate on the level of concrete-operational thinking concomitantly with the capacity to grasp physical invariances. The child now begins to represent him- or herself in terms of dispositions that are stable, transsituationally consistent, and central to the child's identity as a person (see Brandtstädter, 1998; Harter, 1983; Higgins, 1988). These developments set the stage for self-system processes that aim at the actualization, maintenance, and defense of self-definitions. Such processes are integral to activities of intentional self-development through adulthood and later life.

The Self-Monitoring Self

Self-monitoring and intentional self-regulation operate through subfunctions of self-observation, self-evaluation, and self-corrective action. As intimated above, these functions are tied to language development and the emergence of self-referent semantic structures. Self-referent speech is a powerful means of self-regulation (e.g., Zivin, 1979); it supports the maintenance of intentions by buffering them against distractive influences and helps the individual to transcend the proximal stimulus environment by focusing on distal outcomes and symbolic meanings of actions. Self-regulatory potentials are further empowered by the child's growing capacity to take a reflective stance toward his or her own mental states, and by the emergence of metacognitive strategies in middle childhood that are intentionally used to control attention, motivation, emotion, and memory (see Diaz, Neal, & Amaya-Williams, 1991; Flavell, Speer, Green, & August, 1981; Kopp, 1989).

Generally, self-regulative intentions—"second-order volitions" in the sense noted earlier—are mediated by symbolic and conceptual representations; depending on how one's own behaviors are interpreted and semantically categorized, self-corrective tendencies may be activated or dampened (see Bandura, 1989). It should be noted at this juncture that standards of conduct are typically linked to higher-level acts or principles (e.g., being polite) rather than to concrete behaviors that may instantiate these acts in particular contexts (e.g., offering refreshments to guests; see Baumeister et al., 1994). Controlling and adjusting one's behavior in accordance with general desired attributes in a contextually sensitive way presupposes a generalized understanding of how these attributes are instantiated in different contexts. Already by middle childhood, self-evaluative concepts and standards are represented with sufficient complexity in episodic and semantic memory that children can explicitly describe prototypical situations in which, for example, they would feel proud or ashamed of themselves (see Harter, 1983). To evaluate one's past and future development in terms of general self-ideals, however, requires a capacity to contrast hypothetical factual and possible developmental courses, which presupposes a formal-operational level of thinking (Selman, 1980). Self-evaluative concepts have an open texture; they may take on partly new meanings during the course of cognitive and sociomoral development and may be linked to different goals and normative expectancies as the individual passes through an age-graded system of cultural tasks.

The Self-Actualizing Self

The gradual emergence and integration of the intentional, symbolic, and self-monitoring functions of the self-system set the stage for a profound shift in the relationship between development and intentional action, in that self-system processes now increasingly become a driving force of developmental change. Most adult individuals have formed some anticipatory schemata of the general contours of their lives; they have more or less elaborated images of what they would like (and dislike) to be or become, and what they might be likely or capable of becoming. Representations of "actual," "desired," "ought," "possible," and "counterfactual" selves thus feed into the ways in which individuals interpret, evaluate, plan, and control their lives and personal development (see Brandtstädter, 1998; Higgins, 1996; Markus & Wurf, 1987). Together with generalized beliefs about development, these self-representations determine how the individual negotiates sociocultural developmental tasks and guide the choice and implementation of "life tasks" (Cantor & Fleeson, 1991), "personal projects" (Little, 1989), or "identity goals" (Gollwitzer, 1987). To the degree that personal development becomes the target of intentional action, it becomes an expression and extension of the self.

The goals, beliefs, and self-images that drive intentional self-development remain at the same time subject to developmental change. Although the "core" of personal identity may remain fairly invariant over time, different self-attributes may become salient in different role contexts and in different phases of the life cycle. Furthermore, choice and specification of goals and life tasks crucially depend on the personal and contextual resources available for implementing them. Individuals differ with regard to their perceived degree of control over their personal lives and development, and these dispositional differences affect not only self-regulatory intentions, but individuals' emotional appraisals of their personal lives and development (Brandtstädter, Krampen, & Greve, 1987). Apart from such dispositional factors, ontogenetic or age-related changes in action potentials and developmental reserves occurring across the life span can force persons to adjust their goals and priorities of intentional self-development. Identity goals and life tasks are selected and implemented within a field of forces that is itself developmentally open, and that at the same time influences, and is influenced by, intentional self-development.

The Self-Maintaining Self

With advancing age, preserving action resources and counteracting developmental losses may become dominant concerns in themselves as the basic vectors of intentional self-development shift from expansion or self-actualization toward the maintenance and defense of established self-definitions (see Baltes & Carstensen, 1996; Brandtstädter, Wentura, & Greve, 1993). Researchers have noted, sometimes with amazement, the stability of self-definitions over time and the remarkable resilience of the aging self against experiences of loss (e.g., Costa & McCrae, 1994; Staudinger, Marsiske, & Baltes, 1995). Rather than being a static phenomenon, this stability is achieved at a molar level through self-maintaining processes that tend to coadjust and integrate desired, actual, and potential selves in ways that promote self-worth and personal continuity (see Brandtstädter & Greve, 1994; Markus & Herzog, 1991).

Self-continuity hinges in particular on three basic types of protective processes. To remove a mismatch between factual and desired developmental outcomes, individuals can try actively to modify their situations or themselves; this adaptive mode is exemplified by instrumental efforts to prevent or actively compensate for developmental loss, to reshape social relationship patterns, and to strategically select contexts where losses are less relevant or salient (see Bäckman & Dixon, 1992; Carstensen, 1993). Second, individuals may remove the mismatch by accommodating their goals, aspirations, and self-evaluative standards to current circumstances; disengagement from—and downgrading of—barren goals and the positive reappraisal of initially aversive losses are examples of this second adaptive mode (see Klinger, 1987). Goals and developmental tasks tend to be selected according to a principle of manageable difficulty (Brim, 1992); the narrowing of physical, temporal, and social resources of action in later life thus enforces a continuous readjustment of goals to the feasible set of developmental options. In fact, the flexibility to adjust plans and goals to such changes is apparently of central importance for individuals' securing personal continuity and maintaining a positive view of self and personal development in later life (see Brandtstädter & Wentura, 1994; see also Brandtstädter et al., Chapter 13, this volume). Third, individuals may "immunize" the core of their identity by negotiating self-referent feedback in ways that neutralize experiences of loss and leave preferred and strongly entrenched self-definitions unscathed. Although only the first of these modes involves self-regulatory activity in the intentional sense of the term, it is obvious that self-development across the life span essentially hinges on the interplay among these adaptive or self-protective modes (for a fuller discussion of this theoretical view, see Brandtstädter & Greve, 1994; see also Brandtstädter et al., Chapter 13, this volume).

SUMMARY

Development over the life span is a history that combines controllable and uncontrollable elements and that, from a personal point of view, involves gain and loss. As purposeful agents, individuals try to optimize their developmental prospects and to achieve and maintain a favorable balance of developmental gains and losses over the course of their lives. Human ontogeny over the life span, including the processes of aging, cannot be adequately understood without attention to the reciprocal relations that link developmental changes to the ways in which individuals, cognitively and actively, construe their personal development.

The notion of intentional development braids together developmental, cultural, and action-theoretical perspectives. Cultural systems maintain and re-create themselves through the regulation and control of development across the life span; activities of intentional self-development are integrated into this basic process. By transaction with their social and cultural contexts, individuals construe personal representations of possible and desired developmental courses and acquire the knowledge and means to implement them. Through activities of intentional development, the personal biography becomes, as it were, an extension of the individual's self. These activities evolve from, and to some extent replace, external regulations of development, but they remain related to, and in fact mediate, the process of cultural control of development.

Among the biological and evolutionary predicaments that enforce—and at the same time make possible—the intentional self-regulation of development is the great openness and plasticity of development. Biologists and anthropologists have suggested that the adaptive and functional potentials necessary for creating culture and cultivating personal development to a large extent compensate for the lack of adaptive specialization in the human species. Even the influence of genetic factors in ontogeny is mediated by the activities through which individuals select and construct their developmental ecology and personal culture. Notions of self-regulation and personal control over development thus converge with a growing theoretical emphasis on the malleability, contextual embeddedness, and sociohistorical specificity of developmental patterns, without excluding biological points of view.

Activities of intentional self-development are themselves ontogenetic results. From early transactions with the environment, and by inauguration into social networks of knowledge and practice, children form the primordial concepts of self and personal development from which the processes of intentional self-development gradually emerge. The emergence of processes of intentional self-development marks, as it were, a dialectic shift in the relation between action and development. As development forms action and intentionality, intentional action gradually comes to form development. This is a shift, however, only in emphasis; the beliefs, values, and goals that guide and regulate activities of intentional self-development remain subject to developmental change. As individuals move through their life cycles, they continuously revise and reinterpret the goals and plans they adopt for themselves in response to this previous history, as well as in response to changes in competencies, motives, and external demands.

NOTE

1. Although these differences are immensely important, they should perhaps not be overstressed. As we have seen, intentional action is subserved and permeated by processes that are beyond personal control. Thus it may be difficult to separate clearly those "instinctual" behavioral programs that have "meaning" and "purpose" only in a derived or metaphorical sense from reflexive, intentional forms of activity (see Dennett, 1987), even if the categorical distinction between personal agency and subpersonal behavioral automatisms remains of greatest importance from functional as well as moral points of view.

REFERENCES

Bäckman, L., & Dixon, R. A. (1992). Psychological compensation: A theoretical framework. *Psychological Bulletin, 112,* 259-283.

Baltes, M. M., & Carstensen, L. L. (1996). The process of successful ageing. *Ageing and Society, 16,* 397-442.

Bandura, A. (1986). *Social foundations of thought and action: A social cognitive theory.* Englewood Cliffs, NJ: Prentice Hall.

Bandura, A. (1989). Self-regulation of motivation and action through internal standards and goal systems. In L. A. Pervin (Ed.), *Goal concepts in personality and social psychology* (pp. 19-85). Hillsdale, NJ: Lawrence Erlbaum.

Banziger, G. (1987). Contemporary social psychology and aging: Issues of attribution in a life-span perspective. In R. P. Abeles (Ed.), *Life-span perspectives and social psychology* (pp. 85-102). Hillsdale, NJ: Lawrence Erlbaum.

Bargh, J. A. (1996). Automaticity in social psychology. In E. T. Higgins & A. W. Kruglanski (Eds.), *Social psychology: Handbook of basic principles* (pp. 169-183). New York: Guilford.

Baumeister, R. F., Heatherton, T. F., & Tice, D. M. (1994). *Losing control: How and why people fail at self-regulation.* San Diego, CA: Academic Press.

Berger, P. L., Berger, B., & Kellner, H. (1967). *The homeless mind: Modernization and unconsciousness.* New York: Random House.

Boesch, E. E. (1991). *Symbolic action theory in cultural psychology.* Berlin: Springer.

Brandtstädter, J. (1984). Personal and social control over development: Some implications of an action perspective in life-span developmental psychology. In P. B. Baltes & O. G. Brim, Jr. (Eds.), *Life-span development and behavior* (Vol. 6, pp. 1-32). New York: Academic Press.

Brandtstädter, J. (1987). On certainty and universality in human development: Developmental psychology between apriorism and empiricism. In M. Chapman & R. A. Dixon (Eds.), *Meaning and the growth of understanding: Wittgenstein's significance for developmental psychology* (pp. 69-84). Berlin: Springer.

Brandtstädter, J. (1988). Continuity, change and context in human development. In P. Bieri & B. Harshav (Eds.), Interpretation in context in science and culture [Special issue]. *Poetics Today, 9,* 187-204.

Brandtstädter, J. (1997). Action, culture, and development: Points of convergence. *Culture and Psychology, 3,* 335-352.

Brandtstädter, J. (1998). Action perspectives on human development. In W. Damon (Series Ed.) & R. M. Lerner (Vol. Ed.), *Handbook of child psychology: Vol. 1. Theoretical models of human development* (5th ed., pp. 807-863). New York: John Wiley.

Brandtstädter, J., Gräser, H., & Mazomeit, A. (1990). *Expressive Valenz und Selbstbildkonsistenz von Handlungen: Untersuchungen im Altersbereich von 7-11 Jahren* (Berichte aus der Arbeitsgruppe "Entwicklung und Handeln" No. 32). Trier: Universität Trier.

Brandtstädter, J., & Greve, W. (1994). The aging self: Stabilizing and protective processes. *Developmental Review, 14,* 52-80.

Brandtstädter, J., Krampen, G., & Greve, W. (1987). Personal control over development: Effects on the perception and emotional evaluation of personal development in adulthood. *International Journal of Behavioral Development, 10,* 99-120.

Brandtstädter, J., & Wentura, D. (1994). Veränderungen der Zeit- und Zukunftsperspektive im Übergang zum höheren Erwachsenenalter: entwicklungspsychologische und differentielle Aspekte. *Zeitschrift für Entwicklungspsychologie und Pädagogische Psychologie, 26,* 2-21.

Brandtstädter, J., Wentura, D., & Greve, W. (1993). Adaptive resources of the aging self: Outlines of an emergent perspective. *International Journal of Behavioral Development, 16,* 323-349.

Brim, G. (1992). *Ambition: How we manage success and failure throughout our lives.* New York: Basic Books.

Brim, O. G., Jr., & Kagan, J. (1980). Constancy and change: A view of the issues. In O. G. Brim, Jr., & J. Kagan (Eds.), *Constancy and change in human development* (pp. 1-25). Cambridge, MA: Harvard University Press.

Bruner, J. S. (1990a). *Acts of meaning.* Cambridge, MA: Harvard University Press.

Bruner, J. S. (1990b). Culture and human development: A new look. *Human Development, 33,* 344-355.

Cantor, N., & Fleeson, W. (1991). Life tasks and self-regulatory processes. In M. L. Maehr & P. R. Pintrich (Eds.), *Advances in motivation and achievement* (Vol. 7, pp. 327-369). Greenwich, CT: JAI.

Carstensen, L. L. (1993). Motivation for social contact across the life-span: A theory of socioemotional selectivity. In J. E. Jacobs (Ed.), *Nebraska Symposium on Motivation: Vol. 40. Developmental perspectives on motivation* (pp. 209-254). Lincoln: University of Nebraska Press.

Case, R. (1991). Stages in the development of the young child's first sense of self. *Developmental Review, 11,* 210-230.

Chapman, M., & Skinner, E. A. (1985). Action in development—development in action. In M. Frese & J. Sabini (Eds.), *Goal-directed behavior: The concept of action in psychology* (pp. 199-213). Hillsdale, NJ: Lawrence Erlbaum.

Chudacoff, H. P. (1989). *How old are you? Age consciousness in American culture.* Princeton, NJ: Princeton University Press.

Costa, P. T., & McCrae, R. R. (1994). Set like plaster? Evidence for the stability of adult personality. In T. F. Heatherton & J. L. Weinberger (Eds.), *Can personality change?* (pp. 21-40). Washington, DC: American Psychological Association.

D'Andrade, R. G. (1984). Cultural meaning systems. In R. A. Shweder & R. A. LeVine (Eds.), *Culture theory: Essays on mind, self, and emotion* (pp. 88-119). Cambridge: Cambridge University Press.

Dannefer, D. (1989). Human action and its place in theories of aging. *Journal of Aging Studies, 3,* 1-20.

Dannefer, D., & Perlmutter, M. (1990). Development as a multidimensional process: Individual and social constituents. *Human Development, 33,* 108-137.

Davidson, D. (1980). *Essays on actions and events.* Oxford: Clarendon.

Dawkins, R. (1982). *The extended phenotype: The gene as the unit of selection.* Oxford: Oxford University Press.

Dennett, D. C. (1987). *The intentional stance.* Cambridge: MIT Press.

Dennett, D. C. (1990). *The origins of selves* (Report no. 14). Bielefeld, Germany: University of Bielefeld, Center for Interdisciplinary Research, Research Group on "Mind and Brain."

Dennett, D. C. (1991). *Consciousness explained.* Boston: Little, Brown.

Diaz, R. M., Neal, L. J., & Amaya-Williams, M. (1991). The social origins of self-regulation. In L. Moll (Ed.), *Vygotsky and education* (pp. 127-154). London: Cambridge University Press.

Duval, S., & Wicklund, R. A. (1972). *A theory of objective self-awareness.* New York: Academic Press.

Eckensberger, L. H., & Meacham, J. A. (1984). The essentials of action theory: A framework for discussion. *Human Development, 27,* 166-172.

Elster, J. (1989). *Nuts and bolts for the social sciences.* New York: Cambridge University Press.

Fallo-Mitchell, L., & Ryff, C. (1982). Preferred timing of female life events. *Research on Aging, 4,* 249-267.

Flammer, A., & Avramakis, J. (1992). Developmental tasks: Where do they come from? In M. von Cranach, W. Doise, & G. Mugny (Eds.), *Social representations and the social bases of knowledge* (pp. 56-63). Lewinston: Hogrefe & Huwer.

Flavell, J. H., Speer, J. R., Green, F. L., & August, D. L. (1981). The development of comprehension monitoring and knowledge about communication. *Monographs of the Society for Research and Child Development, 46* (Serial No. 192).

Frankfurt, H. G. (1971). Freedom of the will and the concept of a person. *Journal of Philosophy, 68,* 5-20.

Geertz, C. (1973). *The interpretation of cultures: Selected essays.* New York: Basic Books.

Gehlen, A. (1988). *Man, his nature and place in the world.* New York: Columbia University Press.

Giddens, A. (1984). *The constitution of society.* Berkeley: University of California Press.

Gilbert, D. T. (1993). The assent of man: Mental representation and the control of belief. In D. M. Wegner & J. W. Pennebaker (Eds.), *Handbook of mental control* (pp. 57-87). Englewood Cliffs, NJ: Prentice Hall.

Gollin, E. S. (1981). Development and plasticity. In E. S. Gollin (Ed.), *Developmental plasticity: Behavioral and biological aspects of variations in development* (pp. 231-251). New York: Academic Press.

Gollwitzer, P. M. (1987). Suchen, Finden und Festigen der eigenen Identität: unstillbare Zielintentionen. In H. Heckhausen, P. M. Gollwitzer, & F. E. Weinert (Eds.), *Jenseits des Rubikon: Der Wille in den Sozialwissenschaften* (pp. 176-189). Berlin: Springer.

Gould, S. J. (1977). *Ontogeny and phylogeny.* Cambridge, MA: Belknap.

Green, S. K. (1981). Attitudes and perceptions about the elderly: Current and future perspectives. *International Journal of Aging and Human Development, 13,* 99-119.

Greenberg, J., & Pyszczynski, T. (1985). Compensatory self-inflation: A response to the threat to self regard of public failure. *Journal of Personality and Social Psychology, 49,* 273-280.

Hagestad, G. O. (1991). Trends and dilemmas in life course research: An international perspective. In W. R. Heinz (Ed.), *Theoretical advances in life course research* (pp. 23-57). Weinheim, Germany: Deutscher Studien Verlag.

Hagestad, G. O., & Neugarten, B. L. (1985). Age and the life course. In R. H. Binstock & E. Shanas (Eds.), *Handbook of aging and the social sciences* (pp. 38-61). New York: Van Nostrand.

Harter, S. (1983). Developmental perspectives on the self-system. In P. H. Mussen (Series Ed.) & E. M. Hetherington (Vol. Ed.), *Handbook of child psychology: Vol. 4. Socialization, personality, and social development* (4th ed., pp. 275-385). New York: John Wiley.

Havighurst, R. J. (1974). *Developmental tasks and education* (3rd ed.). New York: McKay.

Heckhausen, J. (1990). Erwerb und Funktion normativer Vorstellungen über den Lebenslauf. *Kölner Zeitschrift für Soziologie und Sozialpsychologie, 31,* 251-373.

Heidmets, M. (1985). Environment as the mediator of human relationships: Historical and ontogenetic aspects. In T. Gärling & J. Valsiner (Eds.), *Children within environments. Toward a psychology of accident prevention* (pp. 217-227). New York: Plenum.

Held, T. (1986). Institutionalization and deinstitutionalization of the life course. *Human Development, 29,* 157-162.

Higgins, E. T. (1988). Development of self-regulatory and self-evaluative processes: Costs, benefits, and trade-offs. In M. R. Gunnar & L. A. Sroufe (Eds.), *Minnesota Symposium on Child Psychology: Vol. 23. Self processes in development* (pp. 125-165). Minneapolis: University of Minnesota Press.

Higgins, E. T. (1996). Ideals, oughts, and regulatory focus: Affect and motivation form distinct pains and pleasures. In P. M. Gollwitzer & J. A. Bargh (Eds.), *The psychology of action: Linking cognition and motivation to behavior* (pp. 91-114). New York: Guilford.

Higgins, E. T., van Hook, E., & Dorfman, D. (1988). Do self-attributes form a cognitive structure? *Social Cognition, 6,* 177-207.

Honderich, T. (1988). *A theory of determinism: The mind, neuroscience, and life-hopes.* Oxford: Clarendon.

Jackson, F., & Pettit, P. (1992). Structural explanation in social theory. In D. Charles & K. Lennon (Eds.), *Reduction, explanation, and realism* (pp. 97-131). Oxford: Clarendon.

Jones, E. E., & Pittman, T. S. (1982). Toward a general theory of strategic self-presentation. In J. Suls (Ed.), *Psychological perspectives on the self* (Vol. 1, pp. 231-262). Hillsdale, NJ: Lawrence Erlbaum.

Kagan, J. (1984). *The nature of the child.* New York: Basic Books.

Kalicki, B. (1995). *Die Normalbiographie als psychologisches Regulativ. Zum subjektiven Bedeutungsgehalt von Lebensereignissen, die vom normalbiographischen Zeitmuster abweichen.* Unpublished doctoral dissertation, University of Trier, Trier, Germany.

Karoly, P. (1993). Mechanisms of self-regulation: A systems view. *Annual Review of Psychology, 44,* 23-52.

Kegan, R. (1983). A neo-Piagetian approach to object relations. In B. Lec & G. G. Noam (Eds.), *Developmental approaches to the self* (pp. 267-307). New York: Plenum.

Keil, F. C. (1986). On the structure-dependent nature of stages of cognitive development. In I. Levin (Ed.), *Stage and structure: Reopening the debate* (pp. 144-163). Norwood, NJ: Ablex.

Klinger, E. (1987). Current concerns and disengagement from incentives. In F. Halisch & J. Kuhl (Eds.), *Motivation, intention, and volition* (pp. 337-347). Berlin: Springer.

Kopp, C. B. (1989). Regulation of distress and negative emotions: A developmental view. *Developmental Psychology, 25,* 343-354.

Lamb, M. E., & Easterbrooks, M. A. (1981). Individual differences in parental sensitivity: Some thoughts about origins, components, and consequences. In M. E. Lamb & R. L. Sherrod (Eds.), *Infant social cognition: Empirical and theoretical considerations* (pp. 127-153). Hillsdale, NJ: Lawrence Erlbaum.

Lawrence, J. A., & Valsiner, J. (1993). Conceptual roots of internalization: From transmission to transformation. *Human Development, 36,* 150-167.

Lerner, R. M. (1984). *On the nature of human plasticity.* Cambridge: Cambridge University Press.

Lerner, R. M., & Busch-Rossnagel, N. A. (Eds.). (1981). *Individuals as producers of their development: A life-span perspective.* New York: Academic Press.

Lewis, C., & Mitchell, P. (Eds.). (1994). *Children's early understanding of mind: Origins and development.* Howe, UK: Lawrence Erlbaum.

Lewis, M. (1990). The development of intentionality and the role of consciousness. *Psychological Inquiry, 1,* 231-247.

Lewontin, R. C. (1981). On constraints and adaptation. *Behavioral and Brain Sciences, 4,* 244-245.

Lewontin, R. C. (1982). Organism and environment. In H. C. Plotkin (Ed.), *Learning, development and culture* (pp. 151-170). Chichester: John Wiley.

Little, B. R. (1989). Personal projects analyses: Trivial pursuits, magnificent obsessions and the search for coherence. In D. M. Buss & N. Cantor (Eds.), *Personality psychology: Recent trends and emerging directions* (pp. 15-31). New York: Springer.

Luria, A. D. (1979). *The making of mind.* Cambridge, MA: Harvard University Press.

Markl, H. (1997). Language and the evolution of the human mind. *European Review, 5,* 1-21.

Markus, H. R., & Herzog, A. R. (1991). The role of the self-concept in aging. *Annual Review of Gerontology and Geriatrics, 11,* 111-143.

Markus, H. R., & Wurf, E. (1987). The dynamic self-concept: A social psychological perspective. *Annual Review of Psychology, 38,* 299-337.

Maturana, H., & Varela, F. (1980). *Autopoiesis and cognition: The realization of the living.* Boston: D. Reidel.

McCrae, R. R., & Costa, P. T. (1988). Age, personality, and the spontaneous self-concept. *Journals of Gerontology: Social Sciences, 43,* 177-185.

Nurmi, J.-E. (1993). Adolescent development in an age-graded context: The role of personal beliefs, goals, and strategies in the tackling of developmental tasks and standards. *International Journal of Behavioral Development, 16,* 169-189.

Nydegger, C. (1986). Timetables and implicit theory. *American Behavioral Scientist, 29,* 710-729.

Odling-Smee, F. J. (1994). Niche construction: Evolution and culture. In T. Ingold (Ed.), *Companion encyclopedia of anthropology: Humanity, culture, and social life* (pp. 162-196). London: Routledge.

Papousek, M., & Papousek, H. (1989). Stimmliche Kommunikation im frühen Säuglingsalter als Wegbereiter der Sprachentwicklung. In H. Keller (Ed.), *Handbuch der Kleinkindforschung* (pp. 465-489). Berlin: Springer.

Piaget, J. (1976). *The grasp of consciousness: Action and concept in the young child.* Cambridge, MA: Harvard University Press.

Plomin, R. (1994). *Genetics and experience: The interplay between nature and nurture.* Thousand Oaks, CA: Sage.

Plomin, R., Lichtenstein, P., Pedersen, N. L., McClearn, G. E., & Nesselroade, J. R. (1990). Genetic influence on life events during the last half of the life span. *Psychology and Aging, 5,* 25-30.

Rogoff, B. (1995). Observing sociocultural activity on three planes: Participatory appropriation, guided participation, and apprenticeship. In J. V. Wertsch, P. del Rio, & A. Alvarez (Eds.), *Sociocultural studies of mind* (pp. 139-164). Cambridge: Cambridge University Press.

Rosch, E. (1977). Human categorization. In N. Warren (Ed.), *Studies in cross-cultural psychology* (pp. 1-49). New York: Academic Press.

Scarr, S., & McCartney, K. (1983). How people make their own environments: A theory of genotype-environment effects. *Child Development, 54,* 424-435.

Searle, J. R. (1968). *Speech acts.* London: Cambridge University Press.

Searle, J. R. (1984). *Minds, brains, and science.* Cambridge, MA: Harvard University Press.

Selman, R. (1980). *The growth of interpersonal understanding.* New York: Academic Press.

Settersten, R. A., Jr., & Mayer, K. U. (1997). The measurement of age, age structuring, and the life course. *Annual Review of Sociology, 23,* 233-261.

Simon, H. A. (1983). *Reason in human affairs.* Oxford: Basil Blackwell.

Skinner, E. A. (1995). *Perceived control, motivation, and coping.* Thousand Oaks, CA: Sage.

Snyder, M., & Campbell, B. H. (1982). Self-monitoring: The self in action. In J. Suls (Ed.), *Psychological perspectives on the self* (Vol. 1, pp. 185-208). Hillsdale, NJ: Lawrence Erlbaum.

Staudinger, U. M., Marsiske, M., & Baltes, P. B. (1995). Resilience and reserve capacity in later adulthood: Potentials and limits of development across the life span. In D. Cicchetti & D. Cohen (Eds.), *Developmental psychopathology: Vol. 2. Risk, disorder, and adaptation* (pp. 801-847). New York: John Wiley.

Steele, C. M. (1988). The psychology of self-affirmation: Sustaining the integrity of the self. In L. Berkowitz (Ed.), *Advances in experimental social psychology: Vol. 21. Social psychological studies of the self: Perspectives and programs* (pp. 261-302). New York: Academic Press.

Swann, W. B. (1983). Self-verification: Bringing the social reality in harmony with the self. In J. Suls & A. G. Greenwald (Eds.), *Psychological perspectives on the self* (Vol. 2, pp. 33-66). Hillsdale, NJ: Lawrence Erlbaum.

Tooby, J., & Cosmides, L. (1992). The psychological foundations of culture. In J. H. Barkow, L. Cosmides, & J. Tooby (Eds.), *The adapted mind: Evolutionary psychology and the generation of culture* (pp. 19-136). New York: Oxford University Press.

Valsiner, J. (1987). *Culture and the development of children's action.* New York: John Wiley.

Valsiner, J. (1989). *Human development and culture.* Lexington, MA: D. C. Heath.

Vygotsky, L. S. (1978). *Mind in society: The development of higher psychological processes* (M. Cole, V. John-Steiner, S. Scribner, & E. Souberman, Eds.). Cambridge, MA: Harvard University Press.

Wertsch, J. V. (1984). The zone of proximal development: Some conceptual issues. In B. Rogoff & J. V. Wertsch (Eds.), *Children's learning in the zone of proximal development* (pp. 7-18). San Francisco: Jossey-Bass.

Wittgenstein, L. (1968). *Philosophical investigations* (3rd ed.). New York: Macmillan.

Zivin, G. E. (1979). *The development of self-regulation through private speech.* New York: John Wiley.

3

SELECTIVITY IN LIFE-SPAN DEVELOPMENT

Biological and Societal Canalizations and Individuals' Developmental Goals

Jutta Heckhausen
Richard Schulz

In recent years we have proposed a life-span theory of control that starts from the assumption of two fundamental challenges to the regulation of behavior and ontogenetic change in particular (Heckhausen, 1999; Heckhausen & Schulz, 1993, 1995; Schulz & Heckhausen, 1996). These two

AUTHORS' NOTE: This chapter owes much to the first author's 1-year fellowship at the Center for Advanced Study in the Behavioral Sciences, Stanford (John D. and Catherine T. MacArthur Foundation, Grant 8900078), and to her involvement in a Center project group on "culture, mind, and biology" together with William Durham, Shinobu Kitayama, Hazel R. Markus, Paul Rozin, and Richard Shweder. The first author is especially grateful for many conversations with Paul Rozin about biological theories and phenomena in evolution and development, which introduced her into a new and fascinating field of intellectual endeavor and also enlightened her thinking about psychological development in humans.

fundamental challenges are the regulation of selectivity and the compensation of failure and loss. Our life-span theory specifies two types of control behavior, primary and secondary control, that the individual can employ, jointly and in a refined distribution of regulatory tasks, to master the challenges of developmental selectivity and failure compensation (regarding our model of optimization by primary and secondary control, or OPS model, see Heckhausen, 1999; Heckhausen, Schulz, & Wrosch, 1998).

In this chapter we focus on the issue of selectivity in developmental regulation across the human life span. The basic position we put forward here is that life-span developmental selectivity is jointly produced by biological and societal canalization of developmental pathways and the individual's efforts to influence and come to terms with his or her unfolding development and life course. Moreover, we propose that the specifically realized interactions of the three influencing systems—biology, society, and individual—tend to form optimally efficient regulatory higher-order systems. In such optimized higher-order systems, regulatory mechanisms of the three systems together make positive trade-offs, so that (relatively) stable systems contain minimized conflicts among biology, society, and individual and also entail minimized overdetermination by the three systems. Optimized systems of developmental regulation can vary with regard to the respective profiles of relative influence of biology, society, and individual. However, we propose that this variability of higher-order regulatory systems is constrained to a limited repertoire of optimizable systems as a function of human phylogeny and history, in a manner analogous to the way individual life courses are constrained by "constrained developmental pathways" (Heckhausen & Schulz, 1993).

Finally, we discuss in this chapter a model of the individual's contribution to developmental regulation in modern industrial societies, with their elaborate systems of labor division, corresponding social strata, and structures of social mobility. According to this model, individual developmental regulation is organized around age-graded and sequential action cycles in pursuing developmental goals, their activation and deactivation, according to age-graded opportunities and constraints.

FUNDAMENTAL REQUIREMENTS OF HUMAN BEHAVIOR AND DEVELOPMENT

Within the phylogeny of mammals, a biological stratum characterized by open behavioral programs (Mayr, 1974), *Homo sapiens* has evolved as a species with unprecedented variability and flexibility in the regulation of behavior and ontogeny. With few exceptions, human behavior is not regulated by preprogrammed stimulus-response patterns but entails the potential for adaptation to a variety of ecologies and stimulus constellations, in terms of both concurrently available behavioral options and—even more important for ontogenetic change—the acquisition of new behavioral patterns. This holds and is even accentuated when one views the evolution of the human mind from a perspective of evolved domain-specific behavioral and cognitive modules (Cosmides & Tooby, 1987, 1994; Fodor, 1983; Gigerenzer, 1991) that are open to ecological and cultural variations (e.g., Tooby & Cosmides, 1992). In the course of human phylogeny such evolved mental modules may have escaped domain-specific encapsulation (see Fodor's original conception of encapsulated modules, 1983) and thus provided the building blocks of human intellectual capacities and behavioral adaptiveness (on "cognitive fluidity," see Mithen, 1996; on "accessibility" of "adaptive specializations," see Rozin, 1976).

Humans have evolved with the ability to adapt flexibly to a great range of environmental conditions, and in particular with the ability to generate new patterns of behavior. Piaget (1967) conceptualizes this process as a breakage of instinctual control that gives way to more flexible regulations of behavior and mental processes. Thus, when one takes into account human ontogenetic potential and its evolved openness to experience and enculturation, the scope of variability and adaptive flexibility in human behavior is further enhanced. Indeed, this great potential for variability, plasticity, and adaptivity in human ontogeny is a cornerstone of life-span developmental theories (Baltes, 1987; Baltes, Lindenberger, & Staudinger, 1998; Brandtstädter, 1997, 1998; Ford & Lerner, 1992; Lerner, 1984). The combination of genetic and environmental factors can thus generate an immense, albeit not infinite, spectrum of potential developmental pathways (on "relative plasticity," see Ford & Lerner, 1992). This variability in behavior and development is as much a product of evolution as the more narrowly constrained behavioral systems of other species (e.g., Wilson, 1980).

However, the relative dearth of biologically based predetermination of behavior gives rise to a high regulatory requirement on the part of the human individual and the social community. The sociocultural community and the individual along with the biological predispositions jointly fulfill two major regulatory requirements: the management of selectivity and the compensation for failure and loss (Heckhausen, 1999). An overall adaptive and thus reasonably stable higher-order system of regulation needs to control behavior such that resources are invested in an organized and focused way and that failure experiences lead to improvement rather than to deterioration of behavioral means. It is these requirements for regulation that set the stage for the phenomena we address in this chapter. In particular, we address the requirements of developmental selectivity and the ways in which biological and societal opportunities and constraints provide adaptive challenges in terms of "constrained developmental pathways" (Heckhausen & Schulz, 1993) for the individual's attempts to coproduce his or her own development.

Selectivity

The great variability and flexibility of human behavior and development are advantages in terms of enhanced adaptive potential. However, the organism needs to organize his or her resource investment by making choices and focusing resources accordingly. Thus life-span development theory inherently raises questions of how individuals decide which domains or goals to select and how they remain focused on the domains or goals they have chosen. Therefore, the notion of selection or selectivity has been emphasized in various life-span developmental conceptions, such as in Baltes and Baltes's prototheoretical model of selective optimization with compensation (see Baltes & Baltes, 1990; Freund & Baltes, in press; Marsiske, Lang, Baltes, & Baltes, 1995) and Carstensen's (1993, 1998) socioemotional selectivity model.

The requirements of behavioral and developmental selectivity are twofold: First, the organism must make a *choice* among behavioral options or goals; second, once it has made a choice, the organism has to invest its resources in a selectively *focused* way on the chosen action path or developmental pathway (Heckhausen, 1999).

The *choice* aspect of selectivity is the classic domain of motivational psychology, with its emphasis on evaluative and expectancy aspects of goal choices. A case in point is the student selecting a subject for a graduate project. Such a choice will be informed by the student's subjective interest and anticipated enjoyment of the work, the longer-term gratifications the student expects the project to have for his or her professional career, the amount of difficulty and controllability posed by study of the subject, and the student's perceived personal agency (for a detailed review of expectancy-value models of motivation, see Heckhausen, 1989/1991).

This example also illustrates how the regulation of choices becomes even more salient and consequential when considered from an ontogenetic perspective. Across the life span, different choices of developmental paths result in a great diversity of life-course developmental tracks. People become butchers, generals, steelworkers, professors, or doctors; they marry or stay single, have children or not, divorce and remarry; develop conservative, liberal, or radical political views; and so on. The long-term effects of choosing a particular life-course option are amplified with the passage of time. Alternative paths move further and further out of reach as the individual invests resources exclusively in promoting the chosen life path. Moreover, time is a scarce and irretrievable resource, which renders investment in inappropriate life goals a highly prohibitive enterprise. Such nonadaptive investments prevent the individual from pursuing and realizing more suitable goals, and, what makes matters worse, the costs accumulate ever more with time spent on the wrong choice of path. This holds particularly for long-term goals such as professional careers and family building, which consume an entire lifetime and therefore are, at least in the given domain of functioning, exclusive enterprises. Therefore, the choice of goals has to be monitored in view of life-span-encompassing and domain-overarching criteria of adaptiveness on the higher-order regulatory level of optimization (see the discussion of principles of developmental optimization below).

The *focus* aspect of selectivity refers to the focused investment of resources in a chosen goal. An individual can successfully implement his or her goal choice only by focusing resources on the chosen activity. Resources include behavioral investments (e.g., activity extended over time, effort), motivational and volitional commitment (e.g., resisting conflicting temptations and distractions), emotional resources (e.g., affective balance, self-esteem), and external support (e.g., others' help). We will see below how the management of these four types of resource investments is reflected in different strategies of control. At this point, it seems important to emphasize the inclusion of motivational/volitional focus in our model. This aspect of focused investment in a chosen goal corresponds to modern motivational theories and their renewed interest in phenomena of volitional commitment (Heckhausen, 1989/1991; Heckhausen & Kuhl, 1985; Kuhl, 1983, 1984). Once the individual has chosen a particular goal or course of action, he or she must protect that choice against competing action tendencies, especially when, during the course of action (or development, for that matter), unexpected obstacles arise.[1]

Compensation of Failure and Loss

The second fundamental requirement of behavioral and developmental regulation is the compensation of failure and loss. Again, this characteristic of human life-span development has led to important theoretical models, such as Baltes and Baltes's (1990; Marsiske et al., 1995) model of selective optimization with compensation and Salthouse's (1985, 1991) cognitive aging model that incorporates a compensatory process. The model of optimization in primary and secondary control (Heckhausen, 1999; Heckhausen & Schulz, 1993; Heckhausen, Schulz, & Wrosch, 1998; Schulz & Heckhausen, 1996) identifies two control strategies to cope with the compensatory requirements: compensatory primary control, which involves the recruitment of help, technical aids, and unusual means; and compensatory secondary control, which is directed at protecting motivational and emotional resources (hopefulness and self-esteem) from being depleted by failure experiences (see the discussion of the OPS model below).

This requirement to compensate failure and loss is also a result of the great variability and flexibility of human behavior. The human potential to learn and acquire new skills has great adaptive value. However, it also exposes the individual to experiences of failure in the process of acquisition, especially at intermediary levels of difficulty, when learning potential is maximized but so is the likelihood of failure experiences that are diagnostic of the individual's ability (see the review in Heckhausen, 1989/1991). These failure experiences bear a twofold danger to the individual's potential for action: frustration and negative effects on self-esteem, a key element of motivational resources. Frustration is a negative affective experience that withdraws the individual's attention from goal striving. Moreover, repeated frustrations might well deplete the individual's future motivation to try the goal activity again. Moreover, repeated failure experiences tend to undermine the individual's perceived competence and even feelings of general self-worth, and these in turn are essential ingredients of successful goal striving.

Across the life span, negative effects of wrong choices accumulate, and therefore a greater need to compensate for mistakes arises. In addition, due to.aging-related declines in various domains of functioning, the elderly are especially failure-prone, and therefore need mechanisms to balance the risk of frustration and loss of self-worth even more than do people at other ages. Empirical support for this assumption is increasing. For example, older adults are more prepared to adapt their goals flexibly to objective conditions (Brandtstädter & Renner, 1992; Brandtstädter & Wentura, 1995; Heckhausen, 1997). Moreover, older adults tend to view their own developmental changes in psychological attributes more favorably than those of most other old adults (Heckhausen & Krueger, 1993), and if they are problem stricken in a given domain (e.g., health, finances, loneliness), their psychological well-being is improved by their viewing age peers as suffering even more in that domain (Heckhausen & Brim, 1997).

Summary and Implications

The necessity of managing selectivity and compensation of failure results from the vast behavioral and ontogenetic potential in human behavior. In the context of life-span development, both requirements are enhanced in their salience and consequences. The management of selectivity comprises two aspects: the choice of behavioral options and the focusing of behavioral resources. The consequences of both choice and focus of behavior are amplified in the context of ontogenetic change across the life course. Experiences of failure and loss are inevitable and frequent in human behavior, and thus need to be compensated for. Compensation addresses two consequences of failure experiences: the frustration of goal intentions and negative effects on self-perception in terms of competence. Experiences of failure and loss have enhanced consequences in the context of development throughout the life span and become more prevalent toward the end of life. Accordingly, the need to compensate for failure and loss is present throughout the life span, but it is enhanced at older ages.

It is important to note that the individual faces fundamental choices for certain life-course developmental pathways infrequently and only at certain critical junctures (Geulen, 1981), such as when choosing an occupation or making a commitment to a long-term relationship. It is characteristic for human developmental regulation that biological and sociostructural constraints reduce the number of such choice situations. We discuss the principles and mechanisms that constitute these biological and sociostructural canalizations in the next two sections.

MODELS OF CANALIZATION
IN DEVELOPMENTAL BIOLOGY

In this section we consider processes of developmental canalization that arise from the universal changes associated with biological maturation and aging. In addition, we discuss biological conceptions of canalization in ontogenesis as models for explaining universal characteristics in developmental change. The phenomena addressed are those of selective focus in developmental change. How does development run along certain pathways rather than produce arbitrary change? The regulatory load for channeling behavioral and motivational resources into certain paths does not have to be carried by the individual alone. Biological processes of maturation and aging and the social structure of the life course provide an adaptive scaffold of age-graded opportunities and constraints.

Biological influences on development are typically expressed in age-related and relatively universal patterns of change, which include maturational processes as well as aging-related decline. Modern evolutionary biology and behavioral biology assert that genetic influences on development—far from being simply determinants of change—are mediated by relevant exogenous conditions for the expression of genetic programs of development (Gottlieb, 1991; Plomin, 1986). Genetically controlled patterns of biological development are most pronounced during childhood, adolescence, and early adulthood, but they also extend far beyond childhood into adulthood and old age. These genetically controlled biological change patterns mold and channel development into certain paths. However, the biologically based "canalization" of development weakens at ages beyond childhood (McCall, 1979). Increasingly at older ages, evolutionary genetic influences become less functionally adapted, because at ages beyond reproduction genetically determined characteristics are less subject to the processes of evolutionary selection for inclusive fitness (Charlesworth, 1990; Finch, 1990; Rose, 1991; Williams, 1957).

It is important to note that evolution not only favors adaptive behavior, but may, as a secondary effect of adaptive selection, promote the spread of dysfunctional characteristics in a population. For reasons of anatomical structure (e.g., inherently related features in anatomy) or genetic transmission (e.g., physical linkage of genetic information), maladaptive characteristics may accompany selection processes (Gould, 1977; see also the metaphor of the "spandrels of San Marco" in Gould & Lewontin, 1979). Typically this happens when the benefits of adaptive characteristics outweigh the costs of maladaptive characteristics for inclusive fitness.

In the context of laying out his theory of coevolution of genes and culture, Durham (1991) reports a case in point regarding the differential prevalence of sickle-cell anemia in different but neighboring West African populations. Durham shows that a gene that is adaptive in conferring resistance to malaria in the heterozygote state is nonadaptive, even lethal, when it causes sickle-cell anemia (in the homozygote state). This state of affairs favors a higher prevalence of sickle-cell anemia in populations inhabiting areas with a high risk for malaria infection (due to forest clearing and seasonal accumulation of open ponds that allow for mosquito breeding). The punch line of this example in the context of Durham's theory of gene-culture coevolution is that the agricultural custom of clearing the forest—thus creating opportunities for open water puddles and thereby mosquito breeding grounds—is the ultimate reason for the generation of a selective advantage of the sickle-cell-anemia-prone but malaria-resistant gene cluster. In this way, a cultural activity (agriculturally motivated clearings in the forest) has directly influenced the gene pool of local populations.

Negative side effects of selective adaptations are especially relevant for the biology of aging (see overviews in Baltes et al., 1998; Crews, 1993; Finch, 1990) because selective fitness is mostly determined by prereproductive and reproductive characteristics rather than by postreproductive late-onset characteristics. Given that selective adaptations are focused on the life span before and around reproduction, late-onset malfunctions and disease will not be eliminated from the genetic pool. In a species with costly and extended prereproductive phases and high mortality rates in young adults—true for the early hominids—late-onset nonadaptive characteristics might well accumulate (Charlesworth, 1990; Finch, 1990; Rose, 1991; Williams, 1957). Thus evolutionary selection in humans most likely has favored various nonadaptive late-life-onset side products of early-onset adaptive characteristics. Such old-age genetic calamities can be brought about by a variety of mechanisms. One such mechanism is captured by the concept of "antagonistic pleiotropy" (Williams, 1957) or the "counterpart theory of aging" (Baltes & Graf, 1996; Birren, 1988; Yates & Benton, 1995), which proposes that the long-term effects of developmental growth in early life are detrimental in old age. A case in point is the gene selected for the physiological process of bone growth in childhood, which produces arteriosclerosis in old age (a hypothetical example offered by Williams, 1957). Another particularly destructive mechanism disfavoring old age may be the coupling of late-onset disease with adaptive characteristics in early life. Thus, in a way similar to that in which sickle-cell anemia is genetically coded along with malaria resistance, some important resilience factor relevant for early life (e.g., resilience against life-threatening infectious diseases) may, for instance, have the side effect of rendering an individual vulnerable for Alzheimer's disease in old age. Such a systematic mechanism could be expected to produce high prevalence rates of Alzheimer's in old age, as have actually been found in very old populations (about 50% of adults over 90 years of age; see Helmchen et al., 1996).

Life-span trajectories of age-related decreases in evolutionary selection pressure have also been discussed for the realm of psychological functioning (Baltes & Graf, 1996; Baltes et al., 1998). Thus biological aging brings about major restrictions in capacities, declines in physiological and psychological functioning, and vulnerability to disease. All of these present major challenges for the regulation of human behavior and development by the cultural system, societal institutions, and the individual. The sociocultural construction of old age by the society and the individual is, therefore, presented with increasing requirements at higher age levels in adulthood so as to bridge the widening gap between biological resources and sociocultural expectations associated with old age (see Baltes et al., 1998, regarding "age-related increase in need for culture").

In general, the biological resources for physical and mental capacities follow an inverted U-shaped trajectory across the life span. During childhood and adolescence, the individual's motor and mental capacities develop and mature from complete helplessness and dependence on adult caregivers to advanced functioning in a rich assortment of domains. During childhood, maturation of motor skills and the nervous system produces an ordered sequence of developmental attainments in the sense that new abilities (walking, counting, writing) typically are expected and expressed as soon as they move into the range of the individual's developmental capacity ("zone of proximal development"; Vygotsky, 1978; see also Brown, 1982).

However, depending on the cultural system and its construction of the life span, developmental attainments may be delayed relative to their maturational availability. An example is the case of reproduction, which in most societies is delayed to some point after sexual maturity has been reached. Biological change and aging in particular also mark the inverse phenomenon, that certain capacities of the organism become unavailable at higher ages. Again the prototypical case is reproduction, which is severely constrained for women after age 40, due to rapidly declining productivity of the ovaries. We will return to this issue below in our discussion of the model of developmental deadlines.

Sometime during adulthood, functioning in each of these domains peaks, plateaus, and thereafter declines (Lehman, 1953; Simonton, 1995). A case in point is neuronal functioning in terms of receptivity to neurotransmitters, which starts to show significant decreases by midlife and progressive losses up to 40% by the ninth decade of life (see the review in Finch, 1986, 1990). Another prototypical case is fertility in women, and to a lesser degree in men, which shows a biologically determined age trajectory from maximum functioning in young adulthood to minimal functioning in midlife. Age-related trajectories of maturation and aging in vital biological systems, such as the immune response (Miller, 1990) and cardiovascular and pulmonary functioning (Lakatta, 1990), lead to increasing risks for functional decline and disease at higher ages in adulthood and particularly in old age. Other salient trajectories of increase, peak, and decline can be identified in those domains of functioning that the individual has selected as top priority, because they are most sensitive to reductions of reserve capacity, which is known to decrease from midlife to old age (Schaie & Hertzog, 1983). This is shown in activity-specific age trajectories of peak performance—for instance, in superathletic performance (Ericsson, 1990; Schulz & Curnow, 1988), expert mnemonics (Kliegl & Baltes, 1987), and with regard to late-life dementia being predicted by performance speed in highly trained intelligence tasks (Baltes, Kühl, & Sowarka, 1992).

Health as the basic biological resource of the individual starts to become more vulnerable during late midlife. In advanced age, individuals become increasingly susceptible to various diseases, chronic conditions, disabilities, and life-threatening illnesses (Brock, Guralnick, & Brody, 1990). At the upper limits of the life span, the majority of individuals will develop frailty and multiple chronic illnesses, eventually leading to death (Schneider & Rowe, 1990).

Given the inverted U-shaped trajectory of biological resources, the individual first increases and then decreases physical capacities to obtain important goals in life. This implies that during childhood and adolescence certain goals that were hard or impossible to obtain earlier (e.g., climbing stairs, learning to write) become accessible and even prescribed as developmental tasks (Havighurst, 1973). Conversely, during midlife and increasingly in old age, certain goals become harder to obtain (e.g., running at competitive speeds with younger adults) and thus have to be either given up or pursued with increased effort so as to compensate for the physical constraints. These age-graded changes in opportunities and abilities to pursue certain developmental goals constitute "constrained pathways" (Heckhausen & Schulz, 1993) that guide individuals in their efforts to shape and regulate their own development and life course.

A particularly fruitful model of constrained pathways from developmental biology refers to the process of developmental canalization (Alberch,

1980; Gottlieb, 1991; Oster & Alberch, 1982; Waddington, 1957). Developmental processes are canalized into restricted paths and thus produce a limited and discrete set of outcomes rather than a continuous and random variation of outcomes. Developmental canalization organizes the combination of different characteristics, so that certain types as opposed to arbitrary and form-exhaustive structures can result. Processes of canalization apply to numerous phenomena both in the evolution of species and in the development of individual organisms. In fact, the concept of epigenetic regulation is at the interface of evolution and development in that "morphological phyletic evolution is seen as the product of ontogenetic changes in timing and rates" (Alberch, 1980, p. 660).

An example is the morphogenesis of skin organs, which can lead to feathers, scales, hair, or skin glands (Oster & Alberch, 1982). After some initial stages of epithelia development that are uniform across the diverse outcomes, morphogenesis branches into two different pathways for feathers and scales on the one hand and hair and skin glands on the other; these are later differentiated further. Similarly, the morphogenesis of limbs, with their highly specialized cells and structures, involves a dedication of initially undifferentiated cells (muscle, bone, and so on) to ever more specific functions and forms. The dedication of a given cell and thus the entry into an epigenetic pathway depends on the cell's neighboring tissue. Transplanting cells to new sites leads to a redirection of morphological development unless the specialization has already happened and the cell "is well on its way," in which case deviant structures such as limbs with multiple forearms will result.

Developmental canalization involves a set of key characteristics. First, developmental constraints and predispositions make possible a small set of outcomes out of an essentially infinite range of possible outcomes. Second, at the start of the developmental process, comparatively small and often minute (e.g., regionalization of cell tissue in early embryonic development) differences may get amplified into qualitatively different and thus discrete outcomes. Third, development along the epigenetic path is buffered against disturbances. There is a very strong tendency for normal development to occur. Fourth, the preceding three characteristics of epigenesis taken together imply that genes and permissive environments do not directly determine development. Development starts out as a stochastic process, and increasingly along the pathway generates a life of its own. And fifth, the developmental pathways are shaped by genes, permissive environments, and also behavior. Behavior itself can be part of this constraining context to development (Gottlieb, 1991). Gottlieb (1991) has proposed a systems perspective on canalization according to which canalization processes occur not only at the genetic level, but at all levels of the developing organism, including genetic expression, neural activity, behavior, and experience in the environment. The typical or usual experience of an organism promotes species-typical behavior and also favors species-typical over species-atypical experiences (environment, stimulation). Thus canalization is a function of the constellation of many factors (genetic, physiological, behavioral, and environmental). It is plausible that a limited set of combinations of individual behavior, sociocultural system, and biological maturation and aging could represent functional systems of influences to promote adaptive developmental trajectories across the life span.

MODELS OF STRUCTURAL CONSTRAINTS IN LIFE-COURSE SOCIOLOGY

An analogous line of argument regarding the relative flexibility of human behavior and its consequences for regulation holds for the role of sociostructural and age-normative constraints. Social structure and its age-graded and age-sequential organization as well as social norms about the timing and sequencing of life-course transitions provide an adaptive scaffold for the individual's attempts to regulate his or her own development. This reasoning has strong roots in social anthropology as well as in life-course sociological research.

Theories of sociological anthropology argue that the relatively weak biologically based predetermination in human behavior constitutes a fundamental anthropological universal (Berger & Luckmann, 1967; Claessens, 1968; Gehlen, 1958; see reviews in Esser, 1993; Huinink, 1995). However, it is this insufficiency that also furnishes an openness to the world (*Weltoffenheit*), an ability to act, and a readiness to develop. But this advantage comes at a cost, the cost of regulatory challenge. The individual needs a social scaffold and social reassurance to regulate his or her behavior. Humans are thus dependent on social institutions for behavioral regulation.

While emphasizing the adaptive implications of the great variability and flexibility in human behavior, Claessens (1968) asserts that these advantages need to be supported by the regulatory impact of social groups. Being part of a social group releases some of the regulatory load and provides reassurance to the individual about his or her own behavior by way of group approval. Modern cultural anthropologists argue more specifically that social conventions become transformed into institutionalized ways of thinking (Douglas, 1986). When it comes to implicitly regulating individuals' behavior, institutional ways of thinking are superior to explicit social conventions because conventions as pragmatic rules for social interactions are too transparent and therefore vulnerable to conflicts of interest between social agents. In contrast, institutionalized ways of thinking are powerful shapers of individuals' beliefs because they appear to be grounded in nature itself. From the individual's perspective, institutionalized ways of thinking "turn individual thought over to an automatic pilot," and for society "there is a saving of energy from institutional coding and inertia" (Douglas, 1986, p. 63). Berger and Luckmann's (1967) notion of social constructions of reality follows a similar logic in that social constructions provide both societal stability and predictability as well as subjective certainty about a mutually habitualized, and thereby institutionalized, foundation of individual action.

In the consideration of life-course developmental patterns, one characteristic of societies is particularly relevant for both the opportunity structure and the social constructions of reality: the degree of social mobility available in a given social structure. Societies at different times in history as well as concurrently differ greatly with regard to the opportunities and risks they provide for individuals to move upward or downward in social rank. In feudalistic times, most individuals were fixed at the social rank of their parents. This changed gradually with the rise of industrialization in the increasingly influential cities of medieval Europe. A radical increase in social mobility both between generations and within generations came with the rise of manufacturing and industrial production. Today, however, and in spite of the much-cited phenomenon of globalization, social mobility patterns are far from uniform across the industrial nations. There are impressive differences both in terms of overall life-span encompassing social mobility and in terms of postadolescent, or post-early-adulthood, mobility. Permeability of occupational careers, as one key aspect of social mobility, is, for instance, much greater in the United States, with its potential for midlife career changes, than in Germany, where occupational career tracks are usually set by late adolescence (Hamilton, 1994). Accordingly, the individual faces greater or lesser challenges in terms of both avoiding the risk of being downgraded and realizing chances for moving up the social ladder. Social constructions of what it means to lead a

successful life would have to reflect these constrained or expanded opportunities for producing successful life courses. Examples are found in values
and belief systems that emphasize either individual achievement and merit
or social adjustment and duty.

In most human societies, the life course is composed of age segments or
age categories that stratify the society into age groups (Riley, 1986) and
also involve age norms for important life events and role transitions.
Regarding the regulation of individuals' behavior directed at the life course
and development, two types of sociocultural influences need to be considered. One is the social structure of the life course, with its age-chronological
and age-sequential constraints, such as laws for child and adolescent
welfare (*Jugendschutz*), prescribed entry and exit ages for the educational
system, and retirement laws. The other pertains to age-normative conceptions about age timing that are internalized and shared by the members of
a given community and thereby contribute to the notion of good and bad
timing of life events and transitions—the "social clock" (Hagestad &
Neugarten, 1985; Kohli & Meyer, 1986). We propose that these two
sources of constraining influences form a historically dynamic system of
regulation (see also Heckhausen, 1990, 1999). We will first consider the
sociostructural constraints of life-course patterns, and then discuss the
historical dynamic and role of age-normative conceptions about development and the life course held by individual members of a given society.

Sociostructural Constraints of Life-Course Patterns

Externally institutionalized age-chronological constraints are constituted by entry, exit, and transition times institutionalized in legislation and
state as well as private organizations' promotion rules (e.g., Mayer, 1986;
Mayer & Müller, 1986). Such social institutional constraints provide
time-ordered opportunity structures for certain life-course events and thus
form part of the "sociostructural scaffolding" of life-course development.
Specifically, this implies that for any given life event there is an age range
with optimal opportunities. In contrast, individuals at "off-time" ages face
nonfacilitative opportunity structures and even obstacles. Consider, for
instance, the availability of student grants for individuals at different ages
or in different life-course periods. In most European countries it is much
easier to obtain a study grant at the age of 20, before one has started an
occupational career, than at the age of 45, after one has worked in an
occupation for 25 years. The same holds for the availability of summer

jobs, cheap accommodations, and so forth. Society provides an opportunity structure to study for the 20-year-old, but not for the 45- or 60-year-old. This means that the "off-time" student has to invest many more personal resources to compensate for the lack of sociostructural support.

Another kind of externally institutionalized life-course constraint is the age-sequential structure of life-course events and developmental change, which restrains the repertoire of potential sequences. Age-sequential constraints provide order and predictability to individuals' life courses, both for individuals' and societal planning. Instead of fanning out in arbitrarily meandering life paths, life courses are typically channeled into sequential patterns or biographical tracks (e.g., Geulen, 1981). As individuals try to attain certain life-course outcomes, they are channeled through sequentially organized patterns of opportunities and constraints (Sørensen, 1986), guided by prescriptions for sequencing and spacing of life events and transitions (Hogan, 1981; Marini, 1984; Mayer & Huinink, 1990). For example, after completing occupational training one can obtain an entry-level job, followed by the first promotion, and so on. Similar to chronological constraints, these sequential constraints are generated by multiple sources, such as the state and its laws (such as laws dealing with equality in job opportunities based on qualification only).

Age-sequential constraints can come into play through segregated biographical paths, segregated labor markets, and social networks (Blossfeld & Mayer, 1988; Featherman & Lerner, 1985; Geulen, 1981; Kohli & Meyer, 1986; Mayer, 1986). Such constraints foster selectivity and can thus be conceived of as "canalization" of life courses.

From a critical perspective, these constraints are conceived as differential and socially unjust allocations of resources to individuals of different social classes (Mayer & Carroll, 1987), gender (Mayer, Allmendinger, & Huinink, 1991), and race or ethnicity (Jencks, 1992) that result in unequal opportunities for social mobility (Dannefer, 1987). The greater the investments along the constrained developmental pathways, the greater the accumulated effect of canalization. Further along a life-course track, an individual has optimized his or her investment of material, behavioral, and motivational resources, and thus has less flexibility to switch to another pathway.

In sociology this phenomenon has been studied as the sequentially enhanced effect of differential allocations of social resources over the life course (Dannefer, 1988; Merton, 1968). In a study on advantages and disadvantages in scientists' career patterns, Merton (1968, 1973) identified lifetime-sequential cumulations of resources, a phenomenon he labeled the "Matthew effect," from the gospel of Matthew: "To he who hath, shall more be given, and to he who hath not, shall be taken away, even that which he hath" (as cited in Dannefer & Sell, 1988, p. 4). Dannefer (1987; Dannefer & Sell, 1988) has proposed applying the notion of the Matthew effect to a wider range of life-course phenomena reflecting "aged heterogeneity." In this more general application of the concept, the Matthew effect denotes the fanning out of life-course careers across the life span that is based on initial social inequality. Recent research on lifetime accumulation of personal resources has provided empirical support for the idea that interindividual divergence increases across the life span (e.g., Henretta & Campbell, 1976; Maddox & Douglas, 1974; Rosenbaum, 1984; Schaie, 1989; Walberg & Tsai, 1983).

We take a nonevaluative perspective on this issue and focus on identifying the function of the combined system of societal institutions and individuals' conceptions about the life course that helps regulate individual life courses. Across history, we propose, this system is calibrated such that the individual members of society can psychologically manage their life courses (avoidance of volition or planning overload) while the life-course patterns remain reasonably predictable on the societal level so as to safeguard social stability. We now turn to a discussion of the role of age-normative conceptions about the life course shared by members of a given society.

Age-Normative Conceptions About the Life Course

The idea of a historically dynamic system of developmental regulation is inspired by Norbert Elias's (1969) analysis of the process of civilization in Western societies. Along with many of his contemporary sociologists, cultural anthropologists, and historians, Elias was fascinated by the question of what makes people comply with certain rules of social conduct in a given society if these rules are not enforced by direct sanctions of social institutions. How do individual members of society become "civilized" into conforming to commonly shared rules, and how does this process relate to the evolution and change of social institutions? Elias answers these questions by showing, with reference to various domains of behavior (e.g., table manners, control of aggression, patterns of cosleeping), that external enforcement by way of the suppressive institutions of the feudalistic social system was gradually, over centuries, transformed into rules and norms of conduct and behavior that were internalized by individuals. To the extent that the individual members of society accepted such norms as guidelines for their own behavior, the external suppressive institutions became obsolete. The regulation of behavior and affect came to appear natural and inevitable (see also Parsons, 1951; and Douglas, 1986, on "institutionalized ways of thinking").

In a similar way, modern regulation of life-course patterns may have come under increasing control of internalized age norms and conceptions about proper sequencing of developmental transitions (Heckhausen, 1990, 1999). Such a conception would help resolve the apparent paradox found in the weakening institutionalization of the life course (Dannefer, 1989; Held, 1986; Neugarten, 1979; Rindfuss, Swicegood, & Rosenfeld, 1987) while normative life-course patterns with constrained age timing of life events and transitions still prevail in the general population (Hogan, 1981; Marini, 1984; Modell, Furstenberg, & Hershberg, 1976; Modell, Furstenberg, & Strong, 1978; Uhlenberg, 1974). It is important to note that even when social institutions were partially dissolved in the course of World War II and the Great Depression, the age timing of life transitions (e.g., graduation from school, marriage) did not change (Blossfeld, 1987, 1988), and neither did age-normative conceptions about the age timing of these life events (Modell, 1980). Blossfeld (1987, 1988) investigated the age timing of transitions in education during the post-World War II period in Germany and found stable age timing of transitions even during a period when the societal system had collapsed. Modell (1980) has reported similar findings regarding the age timing of marriage in the United States during the 1930s and 1940s. Modell shows that normative conceptions about the ideal age timing of marriage remained constant even when people were forced to delay marriage because of the Great Depression or to marry earlier because of World War II. Thus it seems that age-normative conceptions are inert and powerful regulators of developmental and life-course timing, even (or especially) when externally institutionalized constraints are weakened.

How do normative conceptions about development and the life course gain influence over individuals' attempts to influence their own development? Some life-course sociologists have proposed that people's age-normative conceptions about the life course are merely epiphenomenal to sociostructural systems of age grading, in that they only reflect statistically dominant behavioral patterns that may have been socialized and modeled to the individual (Marini, 1984; Mayer, 1987, 1996; Riley, 1986). Proponents of this approach have argued against the view that age-normative conceptions are constitutive for homogeneity and variability in populations' life-course patterns (e.g., Marini, 1984) and have also opposed the conceptualizing of age-normative beliefs of individuals as social norms, because such beliefs lack two fundamental characteristics of social norms: They are not behavioral prescriptions in the sense of "ought" rules, and they do not elicit social sanctions in the case of transgressions.

However, from the point of view of social psychology and the sociology of knowledge, age-normative conceptions about development and the life course may serve as guiding images that regulate behavior. Their committing force may result precisely from the fact that they are *not* enforced by external institutional control but rather are internalized and thereby naturalized as social frames of reference (see also the distinction between social control and socialization drawn by Parsons, 1951).

In accordance with Kelley's (1967) model, an explanatory need arises once an individual departs from what is perceived as the norm ("consensus"). Typically, the reasons for norm discrepancies are attributed to the individual's disposition. In a study on social perceptions of on-time and off-time characteristics of middle-aged adults, Krueger, Heckhausen, and Hundertmark (1995) showed that off-time developmental attainments elicited surprise and more extreme judgments of the personal characteristics of the target persons.

Thus the internalization of age norms by individual members of a society has much more far-reaching implications than if these norms were merely a passive reflection of statistical age norms. Age-normative conceptions provide social frames of reference and, as such, produce age-graded aspirations in the pursuit of developmental goals for individual agents. An individual's failure to attain these aspirations and goals has negative consequences for self-evaluation. In this way, age-normative conceptions acquire a psychological control over life courses that their counterparts in the realm of social institutions may have lost to some degree: They do have the status of ought rules, and failing to abide by them results in sanctions.

THE INDIVIDUAL AS A COPRODUCER OF DEVELOPMENT: DEVELOPMENTAL GOALS AS ORGANIZERS OF DEVELOPMENTAL REGULATION

What is the role of the individual in optimizing selectivity in life-span development? Based on what we have said in the previous two sections on the developmental and life-course pathways carved out by biological and sociostructural constraints, one might argue that few degrees of freedom are left for the individual to coproduce developmental change and life-course patterns. And in a sense this is true. Indeed, individuals' influences are constrained, but they are constrained adaptively, in that the age-graded structure of opportunities provided by biology and social system scaffolds the individual's attempts to shape his or her own development (Heck-hausen, 1999). The age-graded constraints lend predictability to what would otherwise appear to the individual as a world of ubiquitous affor-dances, without order in time and space. The joint influences of develop-mental biology (maturation and aging) and social structure provide age-timed windows for individual choice and action, and shepherd along the individual's volition to stay on a chosen developmental pathway.

To be sure, the degree to which biological and social ecologies of devel-opment are constraining is not universal; it varies across historical time and cultures, even within fairly similar societies such as the United States and Germany. In addition, radical sociohistorical transitions or crises such as the Great Depression (e.g., Elder, 1974; Elder & Caspi, 1990) and German reunification (Heckhausen, 1994, 1998) can weaken the effects of pre-viously stable sociostructural constraints. Accordingly, more or less leeway —with accompanying chances and risks—is given to individual agents to coproduce their own lives. Thus the influence of individual initiative on life-course outcomes is extended, and with it the effects of interindividual differences in action-related beliefs (Diewald, Huinink, & Heckhausen, 1996; Huinink, Diewald, & Heckhausen, 1996) and other relevant per-sonality characteristics on developmental outcomes are amplified.

One potentially highly relevant personality factor in this context involves individual profiles of relative importance for key motive systems, such as the motive systems for achievement, affiliation, and power. At the level of the individual organism, this requirement of selectivity is probably best served by domain-specific emotions and motivational systems (Schneider, 1996; Schneider & Dittrich, 1990; see also Schulz & Heckhausen, 1997). They provide incentives to strive for and set priorities between potentially conflicting domains (e.g., work as favored by a strong achievement orien-tation, family as favored by a strong affiliation orientation). Over and beyond the opportunity structure in a given developmental ecology, such individual preference profiles across major motive systems help to channel individuals' activities along chosen developmental paths. Such individual preference profiles may also allow the individual the deviate from age-normative developmental patterns, but at the cost of unusually high investments in a given goal, so that "swimming against the stream" of age-graded opportunity structures is rendered successful (Heckhausen, 1989). However, such cases of deviant life courses are the exception and bear high risks of failure, because they do not make optimal use of biologically and societally provided opportunity structures and have to come up against constraints. In the typical case, the key to a successful development across the life span is the fit that the individual achieves in his or her life course with the biologically and sociostructurally determined opportunities at any given age.

Three Principles of Developmental Optimization

Individuals can achieve optimal fit between their efforts to regulate their own development and age-graded opportunities by choosing the goals they strive for carefully, in accordance with certain principles. The careful choosing of developmental goals is what we call, in the context of the OPS model, *optimization* (Heckhausen, 1999; Heckhausen & Schulz, 1993; Schulz & Heckhausen, 1996). Developmental optimization is guided by three principles: age appropriateness, management of positive and negative trade-offs, and maintenance of diversity.

The first principle of optimization, age appropriateness, implies that the individual selects his or her developmental goals to strive for when the opportunities provided by the biological resources and the societal support systems (e.g., education, parental, or state support) are at their maximum. In this way, age-appropriate goal selection is in agreement with Ford and Lerner's (1992) conception of "individual's behavior as the means of fusing the influences of biology and context on development" (pp. 80 ff.). The notion that opportunities for certain developmental attainments are age structured and reach maxima at certain ages during the life span converges with the concept of developmental tasks (Havighurst, 1952, 1953). Age-appropriate goal selections not only maximize access to relevant resources for goal attainment, they minimize the regulatory burden for volition. Pursuing age-typical developmental goals means that age peers strive for similar goals and thus, by way of social facilitation (modeling, common concern), help to keep the goal in focus. By selecting age-appropriate goals, the individual can orchestrate goal investment in a sequential manner, rather than strive for multiple goals simultaneously—although sometimes overlap may be difficult to avoid. A particularly helpful feature of the opportunity structure in this regard is the shifting point from advantageous to disadvantageous opportunities, the developmental deadline (we return to this topic below). Developmental deadlines provide salient age-time markers for shifting developmental investment from one goal to another, depending on favorable versus unfavorable opportunities.

The second principle of developmental optimization addresses the issue of positive and negative trade-offs between domains of functioning and between short- and long-term implications of goal investment. Investing behavioral and motivational resources for a given developmental goal often has consequences far beyond the domain immediately involved. For one thing, investments in one domain always imply that the resources invested cannot be used for other domains at the same time. Thus excessively focused goal investments, such as the pursuit of a career as a world-class athlete, may be devastating for fundamentally important domains that compete for resources, such as education and occupational training (Schulz & Heckhausen, 1996). A moderate negative trade-off for other domains is unavoidable for any pursuit of developmental goals. However, the costs have to be taken into account and excess damage to other domains and long-term development must be prevented. Positive trade-offs of striving for developmental goals typically ensue when the goals involve general-purpose abilities. An example is education in terms of basic abilities and skills, such as reading, writing, algebra, and languages. It is hardly surprising that this principle of developmental optimization is not left to the individual but institutionalized in modern educational systems. It has become part of the societal canalization of developmental growth.

The third principle of developmental optimization pertains to the issue of diversity of developmental potential. Analogously to phylogenesis and the process of evolution, ontogenesis and developmental growth require variability. Change in general cannot occur without its raw material, the availability of multiple options and pathways. Too narrow developmental pathways with excess specializations leave the individual highly vulnerable. Any change in the opportunity structure pertaining to the chosen narrow path can curtail further development and leave the individual without options to switch developmental investments to or to compensate.

Whereas developmental optimization in terms of adaptive goal selection fulfills the fundamental regulatory requirement of selectivity, the principle of maintaining diversity embedded in optimization protects the individual from excessive narrowing down of developmental pathways. Although selectivity in resource investment is necessary, it has the potential of becoming dysfunctional if pushed to the extreme.

An example of a domain where continuous selectivity throughout the life course may become dysfunctional is social relations. According to the widely respected theory of socioemotional selectivity (Carstensen, 1993), the shift from informational to socioemotional needs that occurs with increasing age throughout adulthood motivates individuals to narrow down their social networks cumulatively to exclude less close social partners to the benefit of very close social partners (see also Lang & Carstensen, 1994). It seems, however, that if such a process of lifelong winnowing out is not balanced by periods of diversification, the individual might end up with too few social partners to satisfy even the most select need for close emotional relations in old age. Most individuals at late adolescence or early adulthood start out with a pool of social contacts who to a large extent become irrelevant and nonadaptive for later phases of the life span. Precisely because individuals often select social partners to suit the needs of the developmental phases they are in, there is no reason to assume that contacts established earlier in life have a longer-term likelihood to be adaptive than contacts formed later in life, unless we talk about family relations—between individuals and members of their own families of origin, or between individuals and their partners and/or children—which are likely to emerge relatively early in life and stay with us for most of our lives.

We propose that cycles of diversification and contraction of social networks occur during developmental segments of the life course, such as during college time, work life, and retirement. Thus at the beginning of a new period in life (e.g., school-to-college transition) an individual will expand his or her social network. Then, in the course of the developmental period, the individual will structure his or her social network in terms of closeness (i.e., differentiating into closer and less close social partners) and start the winnowing-out process. Finally, toward the end of the developmental period, when the "social ending" (Carstensen, 1993) draws near, the individual will narrow down the social network to the close and dear.

Optimization in Primary and Secondary Control

Given the selection of appropriate developmental goals as described in the section on optimization above, the individual can employ a set of

TABLE 3.1   OPS Model: Optimization in Primary and Secondary Control

Optimization
adaptive goal selection: long-term and age-appropriate goals
management of positive and negative trade-offs for other life domains and future life course
maintenance of diversity, avoidance of dead ends

Selective primary control	Selective secondary control
investment of effort, ability	enhancement of goal value
investment of time	devaluation of competing goals
acquisition of new skills	enhancement of control perception
fighting of difficulties	anticipation of positive consequences of goal attainment
Compensatory primary control	Compensatory secondary control
recruitment of others' help	goal disengagement (sour grapes)
seeking of others' advice	self-protective attributions
use of technical aids	self-protective social comparison
employment of unusual means	self-protective intraindividual comparison

SOURCE: Adapted from Heckhausen (1999).

control strategies to strive for and disengage from goals. Table 3.1 informs about the four types of control strategies, along with the three principles of optimization, as proposed in the OPS model (Heckhausen, 1999; Heckhausen & Schulz, 1993; Schulz & Heckhausen, 1996).

First, we distinguish between primary and secondary control strategies. Primary control strategies are directed at the external world and serve to bring about effects in the environment. Secondary control strategies, by contrast, are directed to the internal world of the individual and serve to focus and protect the motivational resources for primary control.

Specifically, we differentiate four control strategies (see Table 3.1): *Selective primary control* involves the investment of behavioral resources such as time, effort, and skills to achieve effects directly in the environment. *Compensatory primary control* comes into play when internal resources are insufficient and external means are recruited, such as other people's help and advice, technical aids, or unusual action. *Selective secondary control* refers to the focusing of motivational resources to goal pursuit by means of volitional self-commitment, such as enhanced perceptions of goal value, devaluation of alternative and competing goals, and boosted perceptions of control for goal achievement. Finally, *compensatory secondary control* protects the individual's motivational and emotional resources after experiences of failure and loss, and involves such strategies as goal disengagement, goal substitution, self-protective attribution, and strategic downward social comparisons.

Strategies adaptive for goal striving are selective primary, compensatory primary, and selective secondary control. Goal disengagement and long-term protection of motivational resources are promoted by compensatory secondary control strategies.

Action Cycles of Developmental Goal Pursuit: An Action-Phase Model of Developmental Regulation

Throughout the life course, the individual encounters changes in opportunities for attaining various developmental goals. During phases of increasing opportunities, developmental goals become activated. As opportunities decline, an individual who has not yet realized a given goal will have to invest increased effort to attain the goal before opportunities vanish. The point at which opportunities have declined so much that goal attainment becomes unlikely can be called a *developmental deadline*.

Figure 3.1 displays an action-phase model of developmental regulation. The model builds on Heinz Heckhausen's (1989/1991; Heckhausen & Gollwitzer, 1986) "Rubicon model" of action phases, which distinguishes predecisional phases of action, which are characterized by deliberations of goal selection before the decisional Rubicon is crossed, from postdecisional phases of action, when the individual has committed to a goal and is volitionally focused and biased toward it. We have extended the Rubicon model of action phases to include a postaction transition from predeadline goal engagement to postdeadline goal disengagement. According to the respective functions of goal engagement to disengagement, appropriate control strategies are expected to be dominant. Thus, during the urgent predeadline phase of goal striving, selective primary, selective secondary, and compensatory primary control strategies will be intensified. In contrast, these three types of control strategies are expected to be deactivated once the deadline is passed. Postdeadline processing after failure to reach the goal is characterized by compensatory secondary control processes such as goal disengagement, goal substitution, self-protective social comparisons, and causal attribution.

We investigated this action-phase model of developmental regulation around deadlines for two paradigmatic developmental goals. The first is the developmental goal of parenting, which for women is subject to the

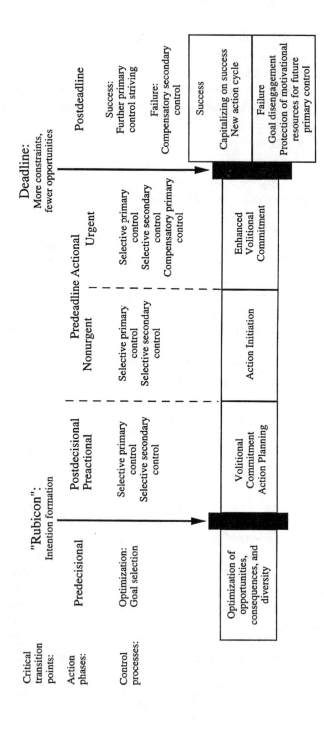

Figure 3.1. Action-phase model of developmental regulation
SOURCE: Adapted from Heckhausen (1999).

so-called biological clock. We found clear patterns of predeadline goal selection, endorsements of control strategies, and biased cognitive processing (Heckhausen, Schulz, & Wrosch, 1998; Heckhausen, Wrosch, & Fleeson, 1998). Predeadline women without children report more child- and family-related goals, value selective primary and selective secondary control more highly, and show greater incidental recall of positive aspects of having a child. Postdeadline childless women, by contrast, report more goals directed at self-development or at improving the social network; they value compensatory secondary control strategies more and evidence lower incidental recall of positive aspects of having a child.

The second paradigm for deadline-dependent goal striving pertains to the partnership domain (Wrosch, 1999; Wrosch & Heckhausen, in press a, in press b). Men and women in early (20 to 35 years) and late (50 to 60 years) adulthood who were recently separated from their partners versus those who had recently committed to a new partner were asked about developmental goals and control strategies, and performed an incidental memory task on partnership-related positive and negative attributes. In accordance with the model of developmental regulation around deadlines, younger separated adults more frequently reported the goal of forming a new partnership. Interestingly, newly committed older adults were highly invested in their new partnerships, even more so than younger freshly committed adults. Young adults in general favored selective primary control and selective secondary control more than older separated adults. Older separated adults more frequently preferred compensatory secondary control strategies. Finally, older separated adults recalled a greater proportion of negative attributes about partnerships than did younger separated or older committed adults.

Thus we have consistent evidence from different life domains that individuals' attempts to regulate their own development are organized in action cycles of goal engagement and disengagement around developmental deadlines.

CONCLUSION

One of the fundamental regulatory requirements for life-span development is selectivity. Individuals need to select certain pathways and goals out of an array of possible options. Once they make their choices, they must invest their behavioral and motivational resources in a focused manner. Mechanisms and systems of selectivity are a key component of developmental and evolutionary biology, and may be best described in Waddington's (1957) model of epigenetic landscape. Small, continuous, and chance-based differences in the beginning of a change process lead to substantial differences and discrete outcomes in the end. Societal structuring of the life course, chronological timing, and sequential organization of normative life events and transitions function in an analogous manner to the constrained pathways provided by the biology of development. Thus, in the course of maturation and aging, and by way of societally organized life-course transitions, individuals' developmental pathways are canalized. Within these canalized pathways, individuals hold manageable degrees of freedom to regulate their own life courses and developmental change. Individuals' contribution to developmental regulation across the life span is organized by cycles of engagement for and disengagement from developmental goals. The onset of goal engagement is given by the emergence of opportunities for goal attainment during a given lifetime window. Striving for goal achievement becomes urgent when opportunities become more scarce. Finally, goal disengagement processes and self-protection strategies need to be activated when developmental deadlines have been passed without goal attainment. Thus biological and societal canalizations help to organized cycles of engagement for developmental goals along the lifetime axis, and thus function as adaptive scaffolds for life-span development.

NOTE

1. Of course, such volitional commitment can become maladaptive when costs of the chosen action course become prohibitive. In such cases, the phenomenon of adaptive regret comes into play (see also Heckhausen, 1999, in press).

REFERENCES

Alberch, P. (1980). Ontogenesis and morphological diversification. *American Zoologist, 20,* 653-667.

Baltes, M. M., Kühl, K.-P., & Sowarka, D. (1992). Testing for limits of cognitive reserve capacity: A promising strategy for early diagnosis of dementia? *Journals of Gerontology: Psychological Sciences, 47B,* 165-167.

Baltes, P. B. (1987). Theoretical propositions of life-span developmental psychology: On the dynamics between growth and decline. *Developmental Psychology, 23,* 611-626.

Baltes, P. B., & Baltes, M. M. (Eds.). (1990). *Successful aging: Perspectives from the behavioral sciences.* Cambridge: Cambridge University Press.

Baltes, P. B., & Graf, P. (1996). Psychological aspects of aging: Facts and frontiers. In D. Magnusson, B. Winblad, & L.-G. Nilsson (Eds.), *The lifespan development of individuals: Behavioral, neurobiological, and psychosocial perspectives: A synthesis* (pp. 427-459). New York: Cambridge University Press.

Baltes, P. B., Lindenberger, U., & Staudinger, U. M. (1998). Life-span theory in developmental psychology. In W. Damon (Series Ed.) & R. M. Lerner (Vol. Ed.), *Handbook of child psychology: Vol. 1. Theoretical models of human development* (5th ed., pp. 1029-1143). New York: John Wiley.

Berger, P. L., & Luckmann, T. (1967). *The social construction of reality: A treatise in the sociology of knowledge.* Garden City, NY: Doubleday.

Birren, J. E. (1988). A contribution to the theory of the psychology of aging: As a counterpart of development. In J. E. Birren & V. L. Bengtson (Eds.), *Emergent theories of aging* (pp. 153-176). New York: Springer.

Blossfeld, H.-P. (1987). Labor market entry and the sexual segregation of careers in the Federal Republic of Germany. *American Journal of Sociology, 93,* 89-118.

Blossfeld, H.-P. (1988). Sensible Phasen im Bildungsverlauf–Eine Längsschnittana-lyse über die Prägung von Bildungskarrieren durch den gesellschaftlichen Wandel [Critical phases in educational careers: A longitudinal analysis about the impact of societal change on educational careers]. *Zeitschrift für Pädagogik, 34,* 45-63.

Blossfeld, H.-P., & Mayer, K. U. (1988). Labor market segmentation in the Federal Republic of Germany: An empirical study of segmentation theories from a life course perspective. *European Sociological Review, 4,* 123-140.

Brandtstädter, J. (1997). Action, culture, and development: Points of convergence. *Culture and Psychology, 3,* 335-352.

Brandtstädter, J. (1998). Action perspectives on human development. In W. Damon (Series Ed.) & R. M. Lerner (Vol. Ed.), *Handbook of child psychology: Vol. 1. Theoretical models of human development* (5th ed., pp. 807-863). New York: John Wiley.

Brandtstädter, J., & Renner, G. (1992). Coping with discrepancies between aspirations and achievements in adult development: A dual-process model. In L. Montada, S.-H. Filipp, & R. M. Lerner (Eds.), *Life crises and experiences of loss in adulthood* (pp. 301-319). Hillsdale, NJ: Lawrence Erlbaum.

Brandtstädter, J., & Wentura, D. (1995). Adjustment to shifting possibility frontiers in later life: Complementary adaptive modes. In R. A. Dixon & L. Bäckman (Eds.), *Compensating for psychological deficits and declines: Managing losses and promoting gains* (pp. 83-106). Hillsdale, NJ: Lawrence Erlbaum.

Brock, D. B., Guralnick, J. M., & Brody, J. A. (1990). Demography and epidemiology of aging in the United States. In E. L. Schneider & J. W. Rowe (Eds.), *Handbook of the biology of aging* (3rd ed., pp. 3-23). New York: Academic Press.

Brown, A. (1982). Learning and development: The problem of compatibility, access, and induction. *Human Development, 25,* 89-115.

Carstensen, L. L. (1993). Motivation for social contact across the life-span: A theory of socioemotional selectivity. In J. E. Jacobs (Ed.), *Nebraska Symposium on Motivation: Vol. 40. Developmental perspectives on motivation* (pp. 209-254). Lincoln: University of Nebraska Press.

Carstensen, L. L. (1998). A life-span approach to social motivation. In J. Heckhausen & C. S. Dweck (Eds.), *Motivation and self-regulation across the life span* (pp. 341-364). New York: Cambridge University Press.

Charlesworth, B. (1990). Natural selection and life history patterns. In D. E. Harrison (Ed.), *Genetic effects on aging* (Vol. 2). Caldwell, NJ: Telford.

Claessens, D. (1968). *Instinkt, Psyche, Geltung: Bestimmungsfaktoren menschlichen Verhaltens. Eine soziologische Anthropologie* [Instinct, psyche, status-determining factors in human behavior: A sociological anthropology]. Cologne, Germany: Westdeutscher Verlag.

Cosmides, L., & Tooby, J. (1987). From evolution to behavior: Evolutionary psychology as the missing link. In J. Dupré (Ed.), *The latest on the best: Essays on evolution and optimality* (pp. 277-306). Cambridge: Cambridge University Press.

Cosmides, L., & Tooby, J. (1994). Origins of domain-specificity: The evolution of functional organization. In L. A. Hirschfeld & S. A. Gelman (Eds.), *Mapping the mind: Domain specificity in cognition and culture* (pp. 85-116). Cambridge: Cambridge University Press.

Crews, D. E. (1993). Biological anthropology and human aging: Some current directions in aging research. *American Review of Anthropology, 22,* 395-423.

Dannefer, D. (1987). Aging as intracohort differentiation: Accentuation, the Matthew effect, and the life course. *Sociological Forum, 2,* 211-236.

Dannefer, D. (1988). Differential gerontology and the stratified life course: Conceptual and methodological issues. In G. L. Maddox & M. P. Lawton (Eds.), *Annual review of gerontology and geriatrics* (Vol. 8, pp. 3-36). New York: Springer.

Dannefer, D. (1989). Human action and its place in theories of aging. *Journal of Aging Studies, 3,* 1-20.

Dannefer, D., & Sell, R. R. (1988). Age structure, the life course, and "aged heterogeneity": Prospects for research and theory. *Comprehensive Gerontology, 2,* 1-10.

Diewald, M., Huinink, J., & Heckhausen, J. (1996). Lebensverläufe und individuelle Entwicklung im gesellschaftlichen Umbruch: Kohortenschicksale und Kontrollverhalten in Ostdeutschland nach der Wende [Life courses and individual development during societal transformation: Cohort differences and control behavior in East Germany after reunification]. *Kölner Zeitschrift für Soziologie und Sozialpsychologie, 48,* 219-248.

Douglas, M. (1986). *How institutions think.* Syracuse, NY: Syracuse University Press.

Durham, W. H. (1991). *Coevolution: Genes, culture, and human diversity.* Stanford, CA: Stanford University Press.

Elder, G. H., Jr. (1974). *Children of the Great Depression.* Chicago: University of Chicago Press.

Elder, G. H., Jr., & Caspi, A. (1990). Studying lives in a changing society: Sociological and personological explorations. In A. Rabin, R. Zucker, R. Emmons, & S. Frank (Eds.), *Studying persons and lives* (pp. 201-247). New York: Springer.

Elias, N. (1969). *Über den Prozess der Zivilisation: Soziogenetische und psychogenetische Untersuchungen* [On the process of civilization: Sociogenetic and psychogenetic investigations]. Bern, Switzerland: Francke Verlag.

Ericsson, K. A. (1990). Peak performance and age: An examination of peak performance in sports. In P. B. Baltes & M. M. Baltes (Eds.), *Successful aging: Perspectives from the behavioral sciences* (pp. 164-196). Cambridge: Cambridge University Press.

Esser, H. (1993). *Soziologie.* Frankfurt: Campus Verlag.

Featherman, D. L., & Lerner, R. M. (1985). Ontogenesis and sociogenesis: Problematics for theory and research about development and socialization across the life span. *American Sociological Review, 50,* 659-679.

Finch, C. E. (1986). Issues in the analysis of interrelationships between the individual and the environment during aging. In A. B. Sørensen, F. E. Weinert, & L. R. Sherrod (Eds.), *Human development and the life course: Multidisciplinary perspectives* (pp. 17-29). Hillsdale, NJ: Lawrence Erlbaum.

Finch, C. E. (1990). *Longevity, senescence, and the genome.* Chicago: University of Chicago Press.

Fodor, J. (1983). *The modularity of mind.* Cambridge: MIT Press.

Ford, D. H., & Lerner, R. M. (1992). *Developmental systems theory: An integrative approach.* Newbury Park, CA: Sage.

Freund, A. M., & Baltes, P. B. (in press). The orchestration of selection, optimization, and compensation: An action-theoretical conceptualization of a theory of developmental regulation. In W. J. Perrig & A. Grob (Eds.), *Control of human behavior, mental processes and consciousness.* Mahwah, NJ: Lawrence Erlbaum.

Gehlen, A. (1958). *Der Mensch. Seine Natur und seine Stellung in der Welt* [The human being: His nature and status in the world]. Bonn, Germany: Athenäum.

Geulen, D. (1981). Zur Konzeptionalisierung sozialisationstheoretischer Entwicklungsmodelle [Conceptualizing developmental models in socialization theory]. In J. Matthes (Ed.), *Lebenswelt und soziale Probleme. Verhandlungen des 20. Deutschen Soziologentages* (pp. 537-556). Frankfurt: Campus.

Gigerenzer, G. (1991). From tools to theories: A heuristic of discovery in cognitive psychology. *Psychological Review, 98,* 254-267.

Gottlieb, G. (1991). Experiential canalization of behavioral development: Theory. *Developmental Psychology, 27,* 4-13.

Gould, S. J. (1977). *Ontogeny and phylogeny.* Cambridge, MA: Belknap.

Gould, S. J., & Lewontin, R. C. (1979). The spandrels of San Marco and the Panglossian paradigm: A critique of the adaptionist programme. *Proceedings of the Royal Society of London, B, 205,* 581-598.

Hagestad, G. O., & Neugarten, B. L. (1985). Age and the life course. In R. H. Binstock & E. Shanas (Eds.), *Handbook of aging and the social sciences* (pp. 35-61). New York: Van Nostrand Reinhold.

Hamilton, S. F. (1994). Employment prospects as motivation for school achievement: Links and gaps between school and work in seven countries. In R. K. Silbereisen & E. Todt (Eds.), *Adolescence in context: The interplay of family, school, peers, and work in adjustment* (pp. 267-303). New York: Springer.

Havighurst, R. J. (1952). *Developmental tasks and education.* New York: David McKay.

Havighurst, R. J. (1953). *Human development and education.* London: Longman.

Havighurst, R. J. (1973). History of developmental psychology: Socialization and personality development through the life span. In P. B. Baltes & K. W. Schaie (Eds.), *Life-span developmental psychology: Personality and socialization* (pp. 3-24). New York: Academic Press.

Heckhausen, H. (1991). *Motivation and action* (P. K. Leppmann, Trans.). New York: Springer. (Original work published 1989)

Heckhausen, H., & Gollwitzer, P. M. (1986). Information processing before and after the formation of an intent. In F. Klix & H. Hagendorf (Eds.), *In memoriam Hermann Ebbinghaus: Symposium on the structure and function of human memory* (pp. 1071-1082). Amsterdam: Elsevier.

Heckhausen, H., & Kuhl, J. (1985). From wishes to action: The dead ends and short cuts on the long way to action. In M. Frese & J. Sabini (Eds.), *Goal-directed behavior: The concept of action in psychology* (pp. 134-159). Hillsdale, NJ: Lawrence Erlbaum.

Heckhausen, J. (1989). Normatives Entwicklungswissen als Bezugsrahmen zur (Re)Konstruktion der eigenen Biographie [Normative conceptions about development as a frame of reference for (re)constructing one's own biography]. In P. Alheit & E. Hoerning (Eds.), *Biographisches Wissen: Beiträge zu einer Theorie lebensgeschichtlicher Erfahrung* (pp. 202-282). Frankfurt: Campus.

Heckhausen, J. (1990). Erwerb und Funktion normativer Vorstellungen über den Lebenslauf: Ein entwicklungspsychologischer Beitrag zur sozio-psychischen Konstruktion von Biographien [Acquisition and function of normative conceptions about the life course: A developmental psychology approach to the sociopsychological construction of biographies]. *Kölner Zeitschrift für Soziologie und Sozialpsychologie, 31,* 351-373.

Heckhausen, J. (1994). Entwicklungsziele und Kontrollüberzeugungen Ost- und Westberliner Erwachsener [Developmental goals and control beliefs in East and West Berlin adults]. In G. Trommsdorff (Ed.), *Psychologische Aspekte des soziopolitischen Wandels in Ostdeutschland* (pp. 124-133). Berlin: Walter de Gruyter.

Heckhausen, J. (1997). Developmental regulation across adulthood: Primary and secondary control of age-related challenges. *Developmental Psychology, 33,* 176-187.

Heckhausen, J. (1999). *Developmental regulation in adulthood: Age-normative and sociostructural constraints as adaptive challenges.* New York: Cambridge University Press.

Heckhausen, J. (in press). Wo hängen die süßen Trauben? Entwicklungs und motivations-psychologische überlegungen zur Funktionalität des Bereuens [Where are the sweet grapes? Developmental and motivational perspectives on the function of regret.]. *Psychologische Rundschau.*

Heckhausen, J., & Brim, O. G. (1997). Perceived problems for self and others: Self-protection by social downgrading throughout adulthood. *Psychology and Aging, 12,* 610-619.

Heckhausen, J., & Krueger, J. (1993). Developmental expectations for the self and "most other people": Age-grading in three functions of social comparison. *Developmental Psychology, 29,* 539-548.

Heckhausen, J., & Schulz, R. (1993). Optimisation by selection and compensation: Balancing primary and secondary control in life-span development. *International Journal of Behavioral Development, 16,* 287-303.

Heckhausen, J., & Schulz, R. (1995). A life-span theory of control. *Psychological Review, 102,* 284-304.

Heckhausen, J., Schulz, R., & Wrosch, C. (1998). *Developmental regulation in adulthood: Optimization in primary and secondary control.* Berlin: Max Planck Institute for Human Development.

Heckhausen, J., Wrosch, C., & Fleeson, W. (1998). *Developmental regulation before and after a developmental deadline: The sample case of "biological clock" for child-bearing.* Manuscript submitted for publication.

Held, T. (1986). Institutionalization and deinstitutionalization of the life course. *Human Development, 29,* 157-162.

Helmchen, H., Baltes, M. M., Geiselmann, B., Kanowski, S., Linden, M., Reischies, F., & Wilms, H.-U. (1996). Psychische Erkrankungen im Alter. In K. U. Mayer & P. B. Baltes (Eds.), *Die Berliner Altersstudie* (pp. 185-219). Berlin: Akademie Verlag.

Henretta, J. C., & Campbell, R. T. (1976). Status attainment and status maintenance: A study of stratification in old age. *American Sociological Review, 41,* 981-992.

Hogan, D. (1981). *Transitions and the life course.* New York: Academic Press.

Huinink, J. (1995). *Warum noch Familie? Zur Attraktivität von Partnerschaft und Elternschaft in unserer Gesellschaft* [Why family today? On the attractiveness of partnership and parenthood in our society]. Frankfurt am Main: Campus.

Huinink, J., Diewald, M., & Heckhausen, J. (1996). Veränderungen im Erwerbsverlauf nach 1989 und ihr Zusammenhang mit Kontrollüberzeugungen und Kontrollstrategien [Changes in employment patterns after 1989 and their relation to control beliefs and control strategies]. In M. Diewald & K. U. Mayer (Eds.), *Zwischenbilanz der Wiedervereinigung: Mobilität im Transformationsprozeß* (pp. 251-267). Leverkusen, Germany: Leske & Budrich.

Jencks, C. (1992). *Rethinking social policy: Race, poverty, and the underclass.* Cambridge, MA: Harvard University Press.

Kelley, H. H. (1967). Attribution theory in social psychology. In D. Levine (Ed.), *Nebraska Symposium on Motivation* (Vol. 15, pp. 192-238). Lincoln: University of Nebraska Press.

Kliegl, R., & Baltes, P. B. (1987). Theory-guided analysis of mechanisms of development and aging through testing-the-limits and research on expertise. In C. Schooler & K. W. Schaie (Eds.), *Cognitive functioning and social structure over the life course* (pp. 95-119). Norwood, NJ: Ablex.

Kohli, M., & Meyer, J. W. (1986). Social structure and social construction of life stages. *Human Development, 29,* 145-180.

Krueger, J., Heckhausen, J., & Hundertmark, J. (1995). Perceiving middle-aged adults: Effects of stereotype-congruent and incongruent information. *Journals of Gerontology: Psychological Sciences, 50B,* 82-93.

Kuhl, J. (1983). *Motivation, Konflikt und Handlungskontrolle* [Motivation, conflict, and action control]. Berlin: Springer.

Kuhl, J. (1984). Motivational aspects of achievement motivation and learned helplessness: Toward a comprehensive theory of action control. In B. A. Maher & W. B. Maher (Eds.), *Progress in experimental personality research* (Vol. 13, pp. 99-171). New York: Academic Press.

Lakatta, E. G. (1990). Heart and circulation. In E. L. Schneider & J. W. Rowe (Eds.), *Handbook of the biology of aging* (3rd ed., pp. 181-216). New York: Academic Press.

Lang, F. R., & Carstensen, L. L. (1994). Close emotional relationships in late life: Further support for proactive aging in the social domain. *Psychology and Aging, 9,* 1-10.

Lehman, H. C. (1953). *Age and achievement.* Princeton, NJ: Princeton University Press.

Lerner, R. M. (1984). *On the nature of human plasticity.* New York: Cambridge University Press.

Maddox, G. L., & Douglas, E. (1974). Aging and individual differences: A longitudinal analysis of social, psychological, and physiological indicators. *Journal of Gerontology, 29,* 555-563.

Marini, M. M. (1984). Age and sequencing norms in the transition to adulthood. *Social Forces, 63,* 229-244.

Marsiske, M., Lang, F. R., Baltes, P. B., & Baltes, M. M. (1995). Selective optimization with compensation: Life-span perspectives on successful human development. In R. A. Dixon & L. Bäckman (Eds.), *Compensating for psychological deficits and declines: Managing losses and promoting gains* (pp. 35-79). Mahwah, NJ: Lawrence Erlbaum.

Mayer, K. U. (1986). Structural constraints on the life course. *Human Development, 29,* 163-170.

Mayer, K. U. (1987). Lebenslaufforschung [Life course research]. In W. Voges (Ed.), *Methoden der Biographie- und Lebenslaufforschung* (pp. 51-73). Opladen, Germany: Leske & Budrich.

Mayer, K. U. (1996). Lebensverläufe und gesellschaftlicher Wandel—eine Theoriekritik und eine Analyse zum Zusammenhang von Bildungs- und Geburtenentwicklung. In J. Behrens & W. Voges (Eds.), *Kritische übergänge: Statuspassagen und Institutionalisierung* (pp. 43-72). Frankfurt: Campus.

Mayer, K. U., Allmendinger, J., & Huinink, J. (1991). *Vom Regen in die Traufe: Frauen zwischen Beruf und Familie* [From the pan into the fire: Women between occupation and family]. Frankfurt: Campus.

Mayer, K. U., & Carroll, G. R. (1987). Jobs and classes: Structural constraints on career mobility. *European Sociological Review, 3,* 14-38.

Mayer, K. U., & Huinink, J. (1990). Age, period, and cohort in the study of the life course: A comparison of classical A-P-C-analysis with event history analysis or farewell to Lexis? In D. Magnusson & L. R. Bergman (Eds.), *Data quality in longitudinal research* (pp. 211-232). Cambridge: Cambridge University Press.

Mayer, K. U., & Müller, W. (1986). The state and the structure of the life course. In A. B. Sørensen, F. E. Weinert, & L. R. Sherrod (Eds.), *Human development and the life course: Multidisciplinary perspectives* (pp. 217-245). Hillsdale, NJ: Lawrence Erlbaum.

Mayr, E. (1974). Behavior programs and evolutionary strategies. *American Scientist, 62,* 650-659.

McCall, R. B. (1979). Individual differences in the pattern of habituation at 5 and 10 months of age. *Developmental Psychology, 15,* 558-568.

Merton, R. K. (1968). The Matthew effect in science: The reward and communication systems of science. *Science, 199,* 55-63.

Merton, R. K. (1973). *The sociology of science: Theoretical and empirical investigations.* Chicago: University of Chicago Press.

Miller, R. A. (1990). Aging and the immune response. In E. L. Schneider & J. W. Rowe (Eds.), *Handbook of the biology of aging* (3rd ed., pp. 157-180). New York: Academic Press.

Mithen, S. (1996). *The prehistory of the mind: A search for the origins of art, religion and science.* London: Thames & Hudson.

Modell, J. (1980). Normative aspects of American marriage timing since World War II. *Journal of Family History, 5,* 210-234.

Modell, J., Furstenberg, F. F., Jr., & Hershberg, T. (1976). Social change and transitions to adulthood in historical perspective. *Journal of Family History, 1,* 7-32.

Modell, J., Furstenberg, F. F., Jr., & Strong, D. (1978). The timing of marriage in the transition to adulthood: Continuity and change, 1860-1975. *American Journal of Sociology, 84,* 120-150.

Neugarten, B. L. (1979). Time, age, and the life cycle. *American Journal of Psychiatry, 136,* 887-894.

Oster, G., & Alberch, P. (1982). Evolution and bifurcation of developmental programs. *Evolution, 36,* 444-459.

Parsons, T. (1951). *The social system.* London: Routledge & Kegan Paul.

Piaget, J. (1967). *Biologie und Erkenntnis: Über die Beziehung zwischen organischen Regulationen und kognitiven Prozessen* [Biology and insight: On the relationship between organic regulation and cognitive processes]. Tübingen, Germany: Fischer.

Plomin, R. (1986). *Development, genetics, and psychology*. Hillsdale, NJ: Lawrence Erlbaum.

Riley, M. W. (1986). Overview and highlights of a sociological perspective. In A. B. Sørensen, F. E. Weinert, & L. R. Sherrod (Eds.), *Human development and the life course: Multidisciplinary perspectives* (pp. 153-175). Hillsdale, NJ: Lawrence Erlbaum.

Rindfuss, R. R., Swicegood, C. G., & Rosenfeld, R. A. (1987). Disorder in the life course: How common and does it matter? *American Sociological Review, 52,* 785-801.

Rose, M. (1991). *Evolutionary biology of aging*. New York: Oxford University Press.

Rosenbaum, J. E. (1984). *Career mobility in a corporate hierarchy*. New York: Academic Press.

Rozin, P. (1976). The evolution of intelligence and access to the cognitive unconscious. In J. M. Sprague & A. N. Epstein (Eds.), *Progress in psychobiology and physiological psychology* (pp. 245-277). New York: Academic Press.

Salthouse, T. A. (1985). *A theory of cognitive aging*. Amsterdam: North Holland.

Salthouse, T. A. (1991). Cognitive facets of aging well. *Generations, 15,* 35-38.

Schaie, K. W. (1989). Individual differences in rate of cognitive change in adulthood. In V. L. Bengtson & K. W. Schaie (Eds.), *The course of later life: Research and reflections* (pp. 65-85). New York: Springer.

Schaie, K. W., & Hertzog, C. (1983). Fourteen-year cohort-sequential analyses of adult intellectual development. *Developmental Psychology, 19,* 531-543.

Schneider, E. L., & Rowe, J. W. (Eds.). (1990). *Handbook of the biology of aging* (3rd ed.). New York: Academic Press.

Schneider, K. (1996). Intrinsisch (autotelisch) motiviertes Verhalten—dargestellt an den Beispielen des Neugierverhaltens sowie verwandter Verhaltenssysteme (Spielen und leistungsmotiviertes Handeln). In J. Kuhl & H. Heckhausen (Eds.), *Enzyklopädie der Psychologie: Motivation, Volition und Handlung* (pp. 119-152). Göttingen, Germany: Hogrefe.

Schneider, K., & Dittrich, W. (1990). Evolution und Funktion von Emotionen. In K. R. Scherer (Ed.), *Enzyklopädie der Psychologie: Psychologie der Emotion* (pp. 41-114). Göttingen, Germany: Hogrefe.

Schulz, R., & Curnow, C. (1988). Peak performance and age among superathletes: Track and field, swimming, baseball, tennis, and golf. *Journals of Gerontology: Psychological Sciences, 43B,* 113-120.

Schulz, R., & Heckhausen, J. (1996). A life-span model of successful aging. *American Psychologist, 51,* 702-714.

Schulz, R., & Heckhausen, J. (1997). Emotions and control: A life-span perspective. In M. P. Lawton & K. W. Schaie (Eds.), *Annual review of gerontology and geriatrics* (Vol. 17, pp. 185-205). New York: Springer.

Simonton, D. K. (1995). *Greatness: Who makes history and why.* New York: Guilford.

Sørensen, A. B. (1986). Social structure and mechanisms of life-course processes. In A. B. Sørensen, F. E. Weinert, & L. R. Sherrod (Eds.), *Human development and the life course: Multidisciplinary perspectives* (pp. 177-197). Hillsdale, NJ: Lawrence Erlbaum.

Tooby, J., & Cosmides, L. (1992). The psychological foundations of culture. In J. H. Barkow, L. Cosmides, & J. Tooby (Eds.), *The adapted mind: Evolutionary psychology and the generation of culture* (pp. 19-136). New York: Oxford University Press.

Uhlenberg, P. (1974). Cohort variations in family life cycle experiences of U.S. females. *Journal of Marriage and the Family, 36,* 284-292.

Vygotsky, L. S. (1978). *Mind in society: The development of higher psychological processes* (M. Cole, V. John-Steiner, S. Scribner, & E. Souberman, Eds.). Cambridge, MA: Harvard University Press.

Waddington, C. H. (1957). *The strategy of the genes.* London: Allen & Unwin.

Walberg, H. J., & Tsai, S.-L. (1983). Matthew effects in education. *American Educational Research Journal, 20,* 359-373.

Williams, G. C. (1957). Pleiotropy, natural selection, and the evolution of senescence. *Evolution, 11,* 398-411.

Wilson, E. O. (1980). *Sociobiology.* Cambridge, MA: Belknap.

Wrosch, C. (1999). *Entwicklungsfristen im Partnerschaftsbereich: Bezugsrahmen für Prozesse der Aktivierung und Deaktivierung von Entwicklungszielen* [Developmental deadlines in the partnership domain: Reference frame for activation and deactivation of developmental goals]. Berlin: Waxmann.

Wrosch, C., & Heckhausen, J. (in press a). Control processes before and after passing a developmental deadline: Activation and deactivation of intimate relationship goals. *Journal of Personality and Social Psychology.*

Wrosch, C., & Heckhausen, J. (in press b). Being on-time or off-time: Developmental deadlines for regulating one's own development. In A. N. Perret-Clermont, J. M. Barrelet, A. Flammer, D. Miéville, J. F. Perret, & W. Perrig (Eds.), *Mind and time.* Göttingen, Germany: Hogrefe & Huber.

Yates, E., & Benton, L. A. (1995). Biological senescence: Loss of integration and resilience. *Canadian Journal on Aging, 14,* 106-120.

4

FREEDOM ISN'T FREE

Power, Alienation, and the Consequences of Action

Dale Dannefer

INTENTIONAL ACTION: "REAL" AND "IDEAL"

The *reality* of intentional human action is that it is largely hyperhabituated, unreflective, and routinized, and that it reproduces existing structures, both personal and social. For the most part, human action has nothing to do with personal or relational change in any deliberate and planful sense and is alienated from its own consequences. Its efficacy, rationality, and volition are open to question.

This appraisal—inevitable when the matter is viewed from a social-constitutive perspective—is at considerable variance with the thematic terms in which action is often described in the social and behavioral sciences: agency, volition, rationality, planfulness, personally directed change, reflec-

AUTHOR'S NOTE: I am indebted to Elaine Dannefer, Lorraine Gianvecchio, and Paul Stein for their critical comments on an earlier draft of this chapter.

tiveness, control (Brandtstädter, 1984, 1998; Campbell, 1996; Chapman, 1984a, 1984b; Clausen, 1993; Eckensberger & Meacham, 1984; Elder, 1998; MacMurray, 1957). From a social-constitutive approach, such hopeful terms represent values, or *ideals*—desirable features of human development, but features the full realization of which is very much in doubt. They are *variables,* not constants.

My argument in this chapter proceeds through the possibly counterintuitive logic of focusing on the *consequences* of action. Human action is irreducibly *dialectical.* As employed here, this overworked word does not refer to "influence," "feedback," or "bidirectional interaction," but is used in its original sense of *mutual reconstitution* (see Baars, 1991; Hegel, 1977; Marx, 1967). As a moment in the dialectic of human development, the consequences of human action have received relatively little scrutiny. It is my contention, however, that the character of consequences must be grasped if the theoretical understanding of the significance of action in development is to advance. Any moment of a dialectical process constitutes a distinct developmental force in its own right. As I will show, this statement clearly applies to the consequences of intentional action.

The chapter is organized as follows: First, I define action from a social-constitutive perspective; I then present a general description of the consequences of action, followed by some principles for understanding the relation of human action and social systems; finally, I propose a general direction for reformulation of some problematic aspects of the concept of intentional action. I contend that this reformulation obviates theoretical problems in the discourse on action, such as the philosophically problematic aspects of viewing action as rational and volitional (see Brandtstädter, 1984, 1998; Chapman, 1984b; Dannefer, 1989).

ACTION DEFINED: EXTERNALIZED MEANING

From a social-constitutive approach, human action is defined as *subjectively meaningful and intentional conduct.* Human action *externalizes* the intentions of the consciousness of the human subject. This definition is indebted to the classical sociological tradition most often associated with Max Weber (1964) but also present in the work of other classical theorists such as Simmel (1908/1950), Marx (1967), and Mills (1940). It is consistent with interactionist (Blumer, 1969; Mead, 1934), phenomenological (Schütz, 1971), and critical (Broughton, 1987; Wexler, 1983) traditions, and with social theory generally (Berger & Luckmann, 1967; Giddens, 1984; Parsons, 1951).

The breadth of this definition indicates the pervasiveness of action in human experience. At the same time, it implies some clear boundaries: Human action cannot be equated with the action of the biological human organism. For example, "holding still" for the dentist is action, even though one's muscles and joints remain inert; on the other hand, dramatic physical movements do not necessarily qualify as action. The classic example is offered by Weber (1964, p. 113), who describes an accidental collision of two bicycles, which, despite the noticeable physical movement of both riders' bodies, does not count as action because the movement produced by the event entails no intention or meaning.

Because the *sources* of intentional action reside in the meanings held in consciousness, they are irreducibly social. Subjective meaning and intention are experienced and expressed in linguistic or other symbolic terms that are themselves necessarily social. If I intend to do something, I can explain to myself and to others what it is I intend to do, or, alternatively, I can intend *not* to tell others. Language is socially specific, of course, but the social sources of action are not limited to language, even when one includes its gestural and other nonverbal dimensions. Even those physiologically motivated activities requiring intentional human action (e.g., eating, elimination) involve internalized social practices, as human variations in taste, etiquette, and norms of privacy attest. Action is thus entirely a property of the self, and the self has its genesis in social interaction (Mead, 1934; Staudinger, 1996).

The parallel question of whether the *act* (as opposed to its sources) is always social is a matter of some debate in the social sciences (see Campbell, 1996; Dawe, 1978; Meacham, 1984). Although this debate need not be resolved in the context of the present argument, it is well to note some of the dimensions that define the issue. Consider, for example, the solitary actions of the artisan or the farmer who spends long days shaping metal or tilling the soil of remote grainfields, in complete social isolation. Despite the active solitude such activities entail, the experience is hardly nonsocial for several reasons. First, the inherent structure and meaning of the routines that organize these tasks are instances of institutionalized cultural practices. Second, unless the actor leads the existence of a completely isolated hermit who is the lone consumer of the products of his labor, he probably acts with the intent and anticipation of realizing an economic reward through exchanges with others. Finally, the products of the solitary work will generally be evaluated by others according to taken-for-granted cultural standards, and farmer and artisan are both well aware that this evaluation will inform the esteem in which others hold them. Thus neither the immediate physical presence of others nor any intent to communicate directly with others is required to give action decided social significance, a significance that has ramifications for how others view the actor, and for how the actor views her- or himself.

CONSEQUENCES OF ACTION: THE CO-CONSTITUTION OF SELF AND SOCIAL RELATIONS

The Constitution of Systems of Social Relations

It is necessary to begin the analysis of the consequences of action by examining its dynamics in the direct immediacy of a face-to-face interactional exchange. The foundation of all human action is social *inter*action, because it is only in interaction with others that the self develops in the first place, and there can be no intentional action (no matter how solitary) apart from the self (Mead, 1934; Vygotsky, 1978). But if interaction is central to the constitution of the actor, it is no less important to the constitution of society.[1]

The significance of the consequences of action and interaction in face-to-face situations cannot be overestimated: The externalization of intentions in action is the essential means through which social relationships, and ultimately society, are constituted (Baars, 1991; Berger & Luckmann, 1967; Dannefer & Perlmutter, 1990). Society is realized only through social interaction. This is, of course, a very different meaning of the term *reality construction* than the cognitive mapping of reality described by Piaget (1977) in his use of that phrase, because it entails a construction not in the mind, but in the world. It is a process that not only affects the actions of others, but also constitutes the systems of social relations in which action is embedded. *System* can be defined as sets of interrelated elements (which, depending on one's analytic purposes, may be actors, acts, roles, or nested subsystems, such as dyads within a five-person group).

Although this general point has been explicitly recognized within the discourse on intentional action (e.g., Brandtstädter, 1984, p. 115), its implications for theory have yet to be developed. Of course, an important thrust of action theory in development is the concept of individuals as producers (Lerner, 1982; Lerner & Busch-Rossnagel, 1981). From a social-constitutive perspective, this insight is important, but it reveals only a portion of an irreducibly broader dynamic. Self and systems of social relations are *co-constituted,* and it is not possible to apprehend *how* an actor "produces her development" apart from this process of co-constitution.[2] The co-constitution involves, for example, a contribution to the shaping of the social system that does not merely form the context for each actor's self-constitution, but is actually an integral, interactive force in that self-constitution.

The actor's own development is thus not the only product of her action; at the same time, the structure of social relations the actor inhabits is also, simultaneously, constituted through her actions. The family, the reference group, the grade school class, the bureaucracy, the tribe, the nation-state are all *products of action.* Without intentional human action, none of these systems could have been generated or can long be sustained. This coproduction of self and systems of social relations means that human action has considerably more potency and consequence than is implied by the concept of individuals as producers only of their own development. It also means that the actor comes to occupy a position in the system of social relations that is defined in certain ways (e.g., generous, threatening, possessing expert knowledge) that create expectations for the nature of relationships, for others as well as for the actor.

The Constitution of Self

The constitution of the self through action (see Lerner & Busch-Rossnagel, 1981) and in social interaction (e.g., Baars, 1991; Berger & Luckmann, 1967; Brandtstädter, 1998; Dannefer & Perlmutter, 1990; Gehlen, 1988; Mead, 1934) has been discussed extensively. Focusing on the consequences of action redirects theoretical attention to the process involved in self-production, however. A consequence of action in social systems is the actor's formation of a sense of identity and selfhood, not just as an actor, but as an objective component—a member, a role—of the system of social relations that his action is co-constituting.

This consequence thus entails the role of the self as object in relation to the self as agent, or, in Mead's (1934, pp. 173-176) classic discussion, the *me* in relation to the *I*. Taking the self as object means seeing the self as the actor imagines that others see her, as indicated by Mead's (1934) phrase "taking the role of the other" (pp. 152-159). This is a definitional characteristic of *having* a self. Having a self is to be able to reflect upon oneself, to stand outside of oneself, to converse with oneself. To varying degrees, humans engage in this recursive process whether acting in complete isolation or interacting with and constituting social relations with others. Thus the human actor's sense of her own position within the system of social relations that she is co-constructing is an integral moment—arguably the critical moment—in the dialectic of action (see Berger & Luckmann, 1967). It defines her sense of where she stands in relation to others, and it is in that relation that the actor continuously defines and redefines herself.

The Constitution of Reality

To say that action and interaction constitute social relations, and to say that society itself is thereby constituted, still does not enable a full appreciation of the consequences for individual development of this process. The actor's entire *sense of reality* comes from this social-constitutive process. What she finds *plausible*—from "factual" matters (e.g., the shape of the earth and the benefits of scrubbing before practicing surgery) to "judgment calls" (e.g., which of her work colleagues are to be liked or considered competent)—depends on the content of conversation with the others whom she trusts, even as it injects into that conversation her own action, that is, her externalization of her own subjectivity in communication. Such perceptions of reality need not be stable to provide a sense of stability in the world, so long as they remain temporally synchronized with the changing perceptions of significant others. The entire matrix of subjective perception and meaning that forms the ground from which intentional action springs is, therefore, always organized from within the particular symbolic apparatus of one's social world.

The force of such processes has been amply documented through experimental (Asch, 1952; Festinger, 1957; Gergen, 1980; Sherif & Sherif, 1953), historical (e.g., Ginzburg, 1987; Tuchman, 1978), and anthropological research. Indeed, it is because of the force of such relationships that anthropologists (and occasionally psychotherapists working solo; see Lindner, 1958) confront the very real "danger" of "going native" (Powdermaker, 1966; see also Geertz, 1973). In such a situation, the actor struggles to maintain her established sense of self while engaged in an alternative social system that confronts her with an alien, but compelling, version of reality. The particular difficulty that the anthropologist and clinician face is that the practice of their professional skills precludes them from aggressively asserting their own views of the world; their task is to remain unobtrusive and draw out the other. When one works in sustained isolation from others who share one's own culture or subculture, the plausibility of one's "culture of origin" may be severely eroded.[3]

ACTION AND THE SYSTEMS OF SOCIAL RELATIONS CONSTITUTED BY IT: SOME STRUCTURAL FEATURES OF THEIR INTERACTION

Self and social relations—action and structure—are not only co-constituted as the consequence of human action; they are also in constant interaction with each other. Efforts to systematize completely the character of that interaction lie well beyond the scope of the present argument; indeed, this task remains the central problem of social theory (see Giddens, 1979). Nevertheless, it is important to explicate some basic features of the relationship between actors and social systems. In this section, I present three interrelated features. First, *agentic asymmetry* refers to the relative force of social systems and other members of those systems relative to the force of the actor, revealing limits on agentic control over outcomes. Second, just as outcomes are not fully controlled, they cannot be fully anticipated; this circumstance confronts the actor with the likelihood of producing *unintended consequences* through her action. Third, if the consequences of action are not controlled and not anticipated, they may also go altogether unrecognized, which means that the actor is *alienated* from them.

Agentic Asymmetry

Any social system, from a family group to a large corporation, exists only through its reenactment through intentional human activity. It is not unusual to find this point introduced with assertions that the reciprocal influences of context and individual are bidirectional, and are at least implied to be equivalent. Context influences the individual, and the individual influences context (see Levinson, Darrow, Klein, Levinson, & McKee, 1978; Scarr & McCartney, 1983). Yet the influence of the action of any single human in producing such a system is always constrained by the actions of others and by the dynamics of social relations generated by interaction. This constraint does not necessarily take the form of a limitation, but may even amplify an individual's influence (as when a powerful member of a group sponsors a new member and instructs the group to listen to her because of her exceptional expertise). Yet the influence of the system on the actions or characteristics of actors is generally greater than the reverse (some dyads may constitute an exception; see Simmel, 1908/1950).

The actual magnitude of individual influence varies with the size of the system and the individual's position in the system. For example, intentional action carries a great deal of weight in one's family, especially (but not only) if one happens to be a parent. As actors share life in the same household over a period of time, the ongoing conversation that sustains their system of relationships is likely to reflect prominently the assertion of each member's personal concerns, agendas, and interests. This is true regardless of how pleasant or functional life in the household is, as illustrated by the following accounts offered by a 29-year-old married couple. First, the husband:

> I used to get mad and holler a lot. Or else I'd stay out late at night and get her worried about what I was doing. We had nothing but fights in those days because all she wanted to do was to take care of the baby, and she never had any time for me.

The wife:

> It felt like I was going crazy. There I was with a new baby and he was all the time nagging me for something or other. Instead of helping me out so I wouldn't be so tired, he'd just holler, or else he'd run out and stay out all night. Then he'd come home and expect me to be friendly and loving. Why should I? What was he doing for me? I didn't like being stuck with all those dirty diapers any more than he did, but *somebody* had to do it, and he sure wasn't. (quoted in Rubin, 1992, pp. 82-83)

Despite the unhappy result, the constitution of a specific couple relationship through the actions of both spouses is no less evident here than in the case of a couple who interact with insightful, consensual planning and sensitive, responsive communication. In either case, a powerful effect on the relationship is exerted by intentional action.

Consider a second account, taken from a study of airline stewardesses:

> A twenty-year-old flight attendant trainee sat with 122 others listening to a pilot speak in the auditorium of the Delta Airlines Stewardess Training Center. Even by modern American standards, and certainly by standards for women's work, she had landed an excellent job. . . .
>
> The young trainee sitting next to me wrote on her notepad, "Important to smile. Don't forget smile." The admonition came from the speaker in the front of the room, a crew-cut pilot in his early fifties, speaking in a Southern drawl: "Now girls, I want you to go out there and really SMILE. Your smile is your biggest ASSET. I want you to go out there and use it. Smile. REALLY smile. Really LAY IT ON." (Hochschild, 1983, pp. 3-4)

As a functioning social system, this training program depends on the intentional action of trainees no less than the instructor. Yet the possibility of a trainee actively reshaping the structure of the social system described in this account is scant. The system is designed to reward conformity to its own agenda and to remove efficiently those trainees who refuse to conform. Although some avenues of system influence logically remain available to any trainee who wishes to attempt system change (e.g., mobilizing other recruits to confront the system, or subversion), the very existence of Delta Airlines as a viable, ongoing concern is testimony to the improbability of such an event. The rewards for trainees are clear, and the behavior required to achieve those rewards is tightly regulated. The action of the trainees, therefore, is guided by their intention to bring their own skills in organization, self-presentation, physical coordination, and the like into line with Delta's requirements. The system is designed, in short, to ensure its own reproduction through channeling the intentional action of the trainees into serving the system's goals.

But a further point deserves to be introduced concerning this training process, which concerns the intraindividual *depth* of the planned structuring of action required by the corporate agenda. The trainee is being asked not just to learn the mechanics of stewardess work—safety protocols, stocking food and beverage carts, efficient serving routines, making change, dealing with passenger emergencies, and so on. With apparently equal urgency, she is also expected to discipline her self-presentation to indicate that she is *happy* to be doing her job—happy to be serving, happy to be interacting with passengers regardless of their behavior. In

Hochschild's (1983) terms, this is "emotional labor" and "management of the heart," and her data confirm the ready acceptance by trainees of this structuring of emotional response by the job. Although the organization by social and cultural forces of the emotional as well as cognitive depths of selfhood is hardly a remarkable point in the present context (Brandt-städter, 1984, 1998; Dannefer, in press; Dannefer & Perlmutter, 1990), its deliberate and effective manipulation on behalf of a powerful interest is worth pondering: Whose intentions are being realized in the smiles of flight attendants?

Before leaving the episode of the training school, it will also be useful to focus on the role of the instructor. Clearly, agentic asymmetry has a different meaning in his case; it is his job to project into the room the social reality of Delta and the social reality of this training experience. He accomplishes this with a skillfully scripted drama that includes the follow-ing elements: an auditorium structured with seating oriented to center stage, sound and lighting systems to adumbrate the speaker, and an authoritative persona delivering crisply packaged instructional content, which is confidently and matter-of-factly presented as "the truth." Relative to the trainees, the instructor's power is enormous: He begins and termi-nates the event and defines its meaning. Thus he renders viable and plausible the social system of the training class as an event, as well as the importance and legitimacy of the content. Clearly, he is the most powerful person in the room in terms of the effect of his inputs into the social system of the training class.

The matter appears slightly differently, however, if we ask the question of how the instructor's range of behavioral options compares with that of the trainees. Despite his power in this situation, he is—as any teacher knows—in many respects more constrained than the trainees. He has certain freedoms: He can decide, for example, when to crack a joke or how to deliver his lines, or whether to embarrass a whispering trainee; he can decide what examples to use, and possibly even the order in which he covers various topics. On the other hand, he cannot allow his own attention to wander, and he cannot take a nap. Very possibly, he cannot say what he really is thinking, or what he would like to say. He must focus his attention and intentions on the task of effectively conveying information and inspi-ration to the trainees. Indeed, despite his great power in the social system of the training session, the constraints on his intentionality and the resultant action are at least as great as those of the trainees, and for what are, in the final analysis, similar reasons. His own career is tied to the evaluation of his job performance by his superiors.

Paradoxically, for the most powerful individuals in social systems, such constraints on intentional action are felt to become even more intrusive:

> The new chief executive begins by watching—and controlling—virtually every aspect of his public behavior. He discovers he must ignore his personal interests for the public good. . . .
>
> Take Mitchell Fromstein [on assuming the CEO role at Manpower]: ". . . I tried to adopt the attitude that I was the company, and not me, not Mitch Fromstein. . . ."
>
> . . . stepping into the chief executive's shoes "means that you lose some sense of individuality," [Jim Risher, CEO of Exide Electronics] says. It's a complaint voiced by many, but not all, corporate leaders. (Wall Street Journal, 1989, pp. 86-87, 89)

The dilemmas expressed here imply that it is not just the system of social relations to which the actor has surrendered his being that constrains him, but his internalized view of himself as well. The force of the system of social relations that constrains the actor's intent includes the constraints imposed upon him by his own perception of the definition of his own role or place in the group as defined by its other members. The role exists outside of him, as an objective (that is, socially shared) reality to be confronted. Whether it is a definition he embraces or one from which he feels *distance* (for a brilliant analysis of role distance, see Goffman, 1961, pp. 85 ff.), it is a part of the system of social relations that constrains his possibilities for intentional action within the group.

In sum, the force of an individual's intentional action in constituting and sustaining a system of social relations varies according to such features of the social system in question as size, structure, and the individual's position within that system. Although action is potent and perhaps necessary to the viability of the overall system, the magnitude of its effect on the social system is less than that of the system upon the actor.

Unintended Consequences

A second principle concerns the relation of the intent of action to its consequences. Whether or not intentional acts eventuate in the realization of their author's *intent,* they are inherently multicausal (see Baltes, 1987) and have constitutive effects on social systems and/or the actor herself that are altogether unintended. The possibility of unintended effects of action has been acknowledged in discussions of action in development (e.g., Chapman, 1982) but has received little attention in comparison to the strong emphasis placed on planfulness and the realization of goals as part of deliberate self-development.[4] A comprehensive discussion of unintended consequences lies well beyond the scope of the present argument, but the dimensions of the theoretical problems such consequences pose for the analysis of human action may be suggested by a typology of three kinds of unintended consequences: unrealized goals, the generation of unintended dynamics in human interaction, and the unintended contribution by action to the functioning of larger social systems.

Unrealized Goals

Much intentional action entails a risk that its intended goal will not be realized, at least statistically; moreover, problems and failures in achieving goals provide much of the content of human drama, in literature and in reality. The universal human experience of failing to realize a goal (due to its inherent difficulty, extenuating circumstances, or the like) is logically the simplest form of unintended consequence. For many such intentions, known risks are of course quite high (I know that the probability of my making a 3-point basketball shot is less than 50%; I invest in pharmaceuticals hoping to double the investment rapidly, but realizing that the prospect of doing so is far from certain); alternatively, they may be contingent on the chances for success of others (e.g., in competitions or gaming). Of course, countless human mistakes, accidents, and so on, whether trivial or fatal, are based on this logically straightforward notion of a gap between the intention and the outcome of an act.

The Generation of Unintended
Interactional Dynamics

The work of family therapists, organizational consultants, and group facilitators is testimony to the force of the unintended but powerful dynamics generated in human interaction. Such dynamics often tend to become habituated components of action as well as institutionalized components of social systems, whether they remain within a fairly stable and homeostatically regulated range or tend to spiral out of control. Such an unintended dynamic is evident in the case of the couple quoted above (Rubin, 1992); this husband and wife describe a mutually reinforcing negative spiral resulting from reactions when each mate perceived a lack of support from the other. Indeed, at the time of their interview with Rubin, they had retrospectively developed a degree of insight into the self-reproducing tendency of their earlier conflictual dynamic.

The fact that an entire industry of "professional help" has proliferated to address such group processes should not be taken to imply that unintended consequences are necessarily negative. In principle, positive unintended consequences are similarly pervasive; an example is the contagiously pleasant neighbor, clerk, or uncle whose behavior illustrates the maxim "A smile can change someone's day." In many cases, such actors presumably smile and laugh to express their feelings, without knowing or intending to change the interactional dynamics of those around them. The fact that the sources of their positive affect can, no less than negative affect, be subjected to a causal analysis and debate (and may well be situational as well as personal in origin) does nothing to minimize the efficacy of the act in shaping the character of social relations. Indeed, one important effect of communicative acts generally is the creation and sustenance of social systems, as noted earlier; but the outcome of creating a viable social system is seldom an intent in the mind of the actor. This observation introduces the third type of unintended consequence.

The Functional Importance of the Unintended Consequences of Action for Social Systems

A classic example of the general principle that intentional action has unintended consequences for social systems is the act of sexual intercourse: Generally, a disjuncture may be said to exist between the *motivation* for copulation (which always entails intent on the part of at least one party) and a key human *consequence* of copulation, which is the physical reproduction of the species and hence the provision of actors to replenish existing social systems. Even when pregnancy is intended, it is generally fueled by some combination of passion and ideas about the desirability of rearing children (whether economically or sentimentally based) rather than by an intent to contribute to the survival of society. A classic principle of sociology concerns this analytic distinction between (a) the actor's meaning and purpose and (b) the social function of the act.

This general logic has been employed by functionalist analysts to attribute culture-maintaining functions to a vast range of empirical phenomena that do not have ready explanations. To employ one of Merton's (1968b) favorite examples, consider the intent of Hopi actors performing a ceremonial rain dance. From the view of Western science, the dance does not serve to produce rain; rather, its consequence (or "functional significance") lies elsewhere:

> Ceremonials may fulfil the latent function of reinforcing the group identity by providing a periodic occasion on which the scattered members of a group assemble to engage in a common activity. . . . such ceremonials are a means by which collective expression is afforded the sentiments which, in a further analysis, are found to be a basic source of group unity. (pp. 118-119)

Although such analyses can appear plausible, they risk the unwarranted legitimation of existing social arrangements. Functional analysis has been used to justify, for example, male dominance and the historically specific institution of domesticity (e.g., Parsons & Bales, 1955; see also Cott, 1977), the acquiescent character of the student role (Berger & Neuhaus, 1970; Parsons & Platt, 1973), arbitrary medical (Jones, 1981; Warren, 1987) and nursing (Gubrium, 1975; Kayser-Jones, 1990; Thomas, 1996) practices, and historically specific life-course or developmental stages (Cumming & Henry, 1961; Parsons, 1964; see also Dannefer, 1984; Lichtman, 1987; Riley, 1978).[5]

This theoretical problem has a special relevance for the consideration of intentional human action and its unintended consequences from a human development perspective: The logic that legitimates existing social arrangements often justifies, in the process, the "trapping" of actors in systems that are arbitrarily destructive of their opportunities and the frustrating of the actors' intent.

For example, consider the intent of the typical student in a U.S. public school. What is for the individual student a career process (e.g., of annual grade progression) and a means of social mobility has a "larger" meaning for the school system. For school system officials, matching the members of each cohort to an array of stratified classrooms and special programs is a central task. This intentional process of intragrade sorting and allocation (Dannefer & Perlmutter, 1990; Riley, Johnson, & Foner, 1972; Riley,

Kahn, & Foner, 1994) produces stratification within each school grade (Gubrium, Holstein, & Buckholdt, 1994; Oakes, 1985). In societies (such as the United States) that claim to have "open" educational opportunity systems, students and their parents often are unaware of the intentional stratifying effects of educational systems (Rosenbaum, 1976). Such systems often have strongly destructive consequences for individuals, even while the individuals' intentional actions reproduce the systems in which they participate (e.g., students who willingly attend low-track classes; Oakes, 1985; Smith, 1994).

Thus such system-level outcomes represent unintended consequences of the actions of students (and parents). Each student's intent is to "make it" and "get ahead," but his actions (along with those of his classmates) have the unintended consequence of reproducing a system designed to allocate access to resources and power unequally among them.

From a functionalist perspective, such stratifying processes (resulting in the systematic cumulation of advantage by some individuals in each cohort and disadvantage by others) are considered socially beneficial because, it is argued, they enable the efficient operation of the system as a whole, distributing not only rewards but the action and interaction opportunities of individuals in socially optimal ways. This is the theoretical point attached to Merton's (1968a) treatment of the "Matthew effect," which he views as unambiguously positive in defining social mechanisms for facilitating communication among a system's most talented members.

Whether or not one agrees with the desirability of social processes that systematically advantage some actors and disadvantage others (independent of the effort of the actor) or considers it an example of faulty, teleological logic (O'Connor, 1984), it is clear that such processes occur across the life course (Crystal & Waehrer, 1996; Dannefer, 1987, 1988; Dannefer & Sell, 1988; Gubrium, 1975; Hagestad, 1992; O'Rand, 1996; Rosenbaum, 1983).

The issue of unintended consequences of action thus inevitably raises the question of the perspective of the analyst. The description and evaluation of unintended consequences will appear different from the vantage points of different actors and observers. Indeed, whether or not a consequence is intended or unintended depends upon the vantage point of the actor (and sometimes analyst) in question. The divergence is sometimes extraordinary, as in the case of school tracking discussed above: Whereas the intentional actions of students are organized by the general and societally announced promise of education and the perceived need to do well in school, to learn, and to please parents, the *intentional actions* of the teachers, counselors, and administrators who make and oversee the process of allocating students to classes are governed, at least in part, by the logic of fitting students into a finite number of "slots" in classes of finite size. Because the resultant distribution of skills will map onto the existing market for postsecondary education and jobs, teachers and students are both, from a broader system perspective, unintentionally engaged in reproducing a stratified labor force. This example is thus characterized by a disjuncture between the intentions of various actors in this system who possess differential amounts of power and knowledge and discontinuity between the intent of action and the products of action. The disjuncture between the intent of action and the products of action brings into view alienation, the third structural feature of the relation of action and social systems.

Alienation

This chapter is organized by the overarching image of human beings as actors who, through their intentional actions, constitute both the worlds they inhabit and their own selfhood. It has been proposed that the path from intention to act to consequence is not linear, but dialectical: As consciousness is externalized into the world, it encounters asymmetric forces, ranging from physical and biological characteristics of nature to the interpretations (and misinterpretations) made of the individual's acts by others. Given the complex and multidirectional interaction of the host of such operative forces, it is not surprising that the unintended consequences of interaction may often be more forceful and enduring than those that are intended.

If the consequences of this action for others and for systems of social relations are unanticipated or even unrecognized, it takes nothing away from the intentionality of the moment of action. However, one of the most fundamental types of unintended consequences generally has to do with the actor herself, and that is the efficacy of her own agency in constituting both social relations as well as her own being.

In its most technically precise classical sense, *alienation* refers to the human agent's failure to recognize precisely this: that the products of human action—including the systems of social relations that we inhabit and the actor's own being and development—*are* the products of human action (Ollman, 1976).

This is not a pejorative or politicized assertion; it simply describes an existential feature of the anthropological condition of *Homo sapiens*: Humans are generally untrained to recognize either the social relations they construct or their own selves and identities as constituted through their own intentionality expressed in interaction with others. This applies in the conventional sense, as when a factory worker whose job it is to attach two parts to a metal gear case several hundred times an hour has no awareness of how the resultant transmission is used, even if it is a part of the washing machine in the basement of his house. Such a man can be said to be alienated from the products of his own actions, but so can the parents who subtly but continuously communicate that one child is a star while relentlessly scolding her sibling, without realizing that their actions are shaping the personalities of their children. The continuous process of social constitution through human action and interaction is largely "alienated" in this sense, because the consequences and products of action are generally unrecognized by the actors themselves.

ALIENATION, POWER, AND THE POSSIBILITIES OF CHOICE

If the argument constructed thus far can be accepted, it implies a fundamental reconceptualization of the theoretical stature of the principle features of action (rationality, planfulness, choicefulness, and so on), for it implies that their accomplishment is a possibility, but hardly a fait accompli; thus they necessarily are to be conceived as variables, and not as constants.

Consider, for instance, the dynamics of choice. I select choice as an example because it is perhaps the modal feature of action that appears across multiple definitions and multiple disciplines (e.g., Campbell, 1996; Chapman, 1984b; Eckensberger & Meacham, 1984; MacMurray, 1957; Parsons, 1951). For example, Eckensberger and Meacham (1984) state:

> It is essential to the action-theoretic perspective that [a] person has freely chosen one from among all these possible means. It is because of this free choice that we are able to characterize what the person is doing not merely as behavior but as action; and it is for the same reason alone that we can hold this person responsible for the consequences that follow from what he or she does. (p. 168)

Of course, choice also continues to be a problematic feature of action, both heuristically and philosophically (Brandtstädter, 1998; Chapman, 1984b; Dannefer, 1989; Dannefer & Perlmutter, 1990). Philosophers and social scientists still cannot agree, not only about whether or not human beings have "free will," but about whether or not it is possible to resolve the issue in any definitive way (Brandtstädter, 1998; see also Honderich, 1988; White, 1992). One can readily argue that—no matter how limited one's objective situation by coercive physical constraints, whether natural or human—consciousness irreducibly possesses an existential bedrock of voluntariness (absent disabling organic or chemical alteration to mental states). Indeed, having to act in contradictory situations that impose catch-22s is a staple of human drama; indeed, it is the basis of the moral dilemmas used in the study of such aspects of development as morality (e.g., Kohlberg, 1981; Smetana, 1995) and wisdom (Staudinger, 1996; Staudinger & Baltes, 1994).

From the vantage point of the argument that has just been sketched, arguments about the ontological nature of freedom are irrelevant. Consider the Delta trainee and the instructor. Whatever position one takes on the ontological status of volition, it is empirically the case that the intentional action of both of them is tightly scripted within fairly narrow tolerance limits, with strong negative sanctions for deviance (as noted earlier). One may say that they are *volitionally engaged* in the constitution of the training class and of Delta Airlines, even as they are constrained by what Durkheim (1964, pp. 14-31) calls the social facticity (*choseité*) of the situation as well as by the structure of career rewards and sanctions.[6]

But consider as a final brief example the experiences of a young Chinese teenager, as reported in *Business Week*:

> Hong Biu Yun is clearly exhausted as she sticks Mickey Mouse heads on to motorized toys at a factory in Shekou, China. One of twelve thousand mainland Chinese employed by Hong Kong's largest toymaker, Kader Enterprises Ltd., Hong works fourteen hours a day, seven days a week. . . . Recently, her hours grew even more oppressive: To meet the holiday demand . . . the girls at the Kader plant were ordered to put in one or two twenty-four hour shifts each month, with only two meal breaks per shift.
>
> Troubled by such abuses, Chinese government officials have pressured Kader to respect the law, but, in the words of a Kader executive in Hong Kong, Andy Lee, "We told them, this is the toy biz. If you don't allow us to do things our way, we'll close down our Chinese factories and move to Thailand." (Lee & Brady, 1988, pp. 46-47)

No less than the Delta student and instructor, Hong Biu Yun and Andy Lee are both engaged in intentional action. For Hong Biu Yun to remain at her station, performing the rapid, repetitive motions of assembly-line work, requires disciplined intentionality (even though the actions become quickly habituated); Andy Lee intends to be an effective spokesman for Kader. One can also readily argue that each of them is, at the level of existential bedrock, acting "voluntarily": Hong Biu Yun (whatever reprisals she may face from, e.g., parents or company thugs) is "free" to leave the assembly line and walk out the door. Andy Lee is constrained by the nature of his job to make threats to the government of China and (apparently) to explain to the media the "inevitability" and "necessity" of Kader's practices. Of course, he is also "free" to resign or to practice subversion within Kader, although to do so would entail clear costs for him, just as it would for Hong Biu Yun.

However, in any humanly meaningful sense, the claim that both Hong and Lee have freedom at some level is irrelevant to each person's *subjective experience of choicefulness* in her or his moment-by-moment, daily lived experience. Lee may himself sometimes work 14-hour days, especially if one counts as work the time spent in such activities as the racquetball game with a protégé or the gourmet business lunch. But how he arranges his time, and perhaps when and even whether to work such days, is largely at his own discretion. Comparing Lee and Hong to the Delta trainees, then, one can propose that the Delta trainees experience less discretion in the formation of their intentions and actions than does Andy Lee, and that Hong Biu Yun and the hundreds of millions of other young people in the Third World in her position have less discretion in the formation of their intentions and actions than do the Delta trainees.

Thus "freedom to choose"—whatever its presumed ontological status—varies materially among actors, and so it requires conceptualization as an ordinal variable rather than a constant. From this perspective, the unsolvable issue of the existential bedrock of human choice is rendered theoretically irrelevant. The key problem is the developmental implications of truly vast material differences in the lived experience of *choicefulness*.

Similarly, the association of intentional action with change as opposed to stability (see White, 1992, pp. 230-232), with a sense of personal control, with insight and innovation as opposed to habituated routines (see Langer, 1989), and with deliberate planfulness also can be fruitfully conceptualized as variables, although that enterprise must lie beyond the scope of the present chapter.

SUMMARY

I have proposed (a) that social relationships and social structures are the products, as well as the context, of human action; (b) that this circumstance implies that human agency has more potency than is generally acknowledged, including by the conventional individualistic conceptions of social and behavioral scientists; and (c) that a recognition of these principles unavoidably confronts the study of intentional action with the phenomena of power, unintended consequences, and alienation, and hence (d) requires a reconceptualization of intentional action in dialectical terms. It is my claim that, rather than complicating the analysis of action, this reassessment obviates difficult theoretical problems that are raised by some of the dimensions of action.

As an example of how this reconceptualization may proceed to the benefit of theory, I have presented an analysis of "choice" (or volition) in social-constitutive terms, showing that choice is best conceived neither as a dogmatically asserted feature of action nor as a philosophical problem, but as a variable to measure and an existential feature of experience to be enhanced, rather than an anthropological constant that becomes a quagmire of unsolvable dispute among behavioral and social scientists and philosophers.

The differentiation of these two aspects of action enables the clarification of other anomalous and seemingly paradoxical findings, such as the presumption that Western modernity has ushered in an era of unprecedented "individual freedom" (see Turner, 1976) even while the population becomes increasingly conformist along age-graded lines in life-course transitions and roles (see Dannefer, 1984; Dannefer & Uhlenberg, 1999; Hogan, 1981; Kohli, 1985; Modell, Furstenberg, & Strong, 1976; Uhlenberg, 1978). Such paradoxes find resolution in a more fundamental one, that human action is simultaneously potent and constrained.

Intentional action is thus seen as the sole source of, and the only force that can create, society and culture (although these results are often unintended and unrecognized) at the same time that the actor's "choicefulness" is substantially constrained. These two aspects of human agency—efficacy and volition—thus are essentially orthogonal and cannot be properly conceived as tandem or covarying definitional attributes of the phenomenon of action. Seen as a variable, freedom of choice is itself socially regulated and varies over the life course. Its more basic parameters are also modifiable, through critical reflection and deliberate intentional action. Meaningful changes in such parameters cannot occur at the individual level but involve deliberate effort (and often costly and painful struggle) at the social level, as social movements (e.g., for the abolition of slavery in the United States, for resisting political repression in Eastern Europe, or for women's rights) attest. The possibilities of one's individual choicefulness or freedom are therefore not independent of the same possibilities of other members of the social system in question.

This perspective brings into view a fresh set of research problems with direct implications for the study of intentional action as a potentially emancipatory moment of human development, such as how to conceptualize and measure existentially and developmentally crucial characteristics such as choicefulness, control, and rationality as variable terms. This task defines a potentially important agenda of research, an agenda that can only begin with a deconstruction of the construct of action and a recognition of action as situated in systems of its own creation. It also brings into view the unavoidable conclusion that research and theory are not only located within a broader system of human action, they also have consequences for politics and practice, whether ideological or emancipatory.

NOTES

1. Although I focus on interaction in this section, I use the terms *action* and *interaction* interchangeably.

2. Whether or not a person living as a completely isolated hermit for a long period of time constitutes an exception is an interesting question, but one that need not be resolved in the present context.

3. This general perspective on human activity as the source of definitions of reality (as well as social relations) is hardly new. It is indebted to classical work in social psychology and is well established in social theory and the sociology of knowledge (Berger & Luckmann, 1967). It has been applied to virtually every domain of human enterprise, including the activity and interaction of scientists in labs and at professional conferences (e.g., Keller, 1985; Knorr-Cetina, 1992; Latour & Woolgar, 1986) no less than to interaction among family members (Piotrkowski, 1979).

4. More generally, some of the most dramatic discoveries in the behavioral and social sciences have concerned instances in which the intended outcomes of action were overwhelmed by unexpected and unintended outcomes or "latent" outcomes. For example, the Hawthorne effect is an instance of an unintended effect that reacted directly upon the experimenters' ability to carry off their research as intended (e.g., Merton, 1968b; Roethlisberger & Dickson, 1939). As another example, consider the "pursuer-distancer" dynamic, in which an actor who presumably wants to intensify in some way his relationship with another actor leads

her to run farther and faster in the opposite direction as a consequence of his pursuing her (e.g., Satir, 1972), thereby endangering or destroying the relationship he is trying to build. Clearly, traces of this dynamic are evident in the relationship of the couple quoted above (Rubin, 1992).

5. Underlying this logic is an organismic model of society: If society is conceived as an organism composed of interdependent elements, its established institutions should all have contributions to make to its overall functioning. Although the application of the organismic paradigm to society has been extensive and is logically seductive, it is untenable as a paradigm for social system analysis and cannot be defended as more than a superficial analogy. It readily lends itself to tautologous and teleological excesses and can lead to uncritical acceptance of existing social arrangements because they are assumed to perform some "social function" (see Buckley, 1967; Giddens, 1984; Turner, 1976).

6. The very *presence* of these actors at the Delta Airlines Stewardess Training Center represents, as it is commonly said, a "choice" on their part: "No one was holding guns to their heads." Scrutiny of the actual alternative opportunities perceived to be available to these individuals—both trainees and instructor—would likely reveal that such glib assertions overlook the calculation of rewards and costs that make many such decisions "no-brainers" at the same time they are perceived by those who make them as the "lesser of evils."

REFERENCES

Asch, S. (1952). *Social psychology.* New York: Prentice Hall.

Baars, J. (1991). The challenge of critical gerontology: The problem of social constitution. *Journal of Aging Studies, 3,* 219-243.

Baltes, P. B. (1987). Theoretical propositions of life-span developmental psychology: On the dynamics between growth and decline. *Developmental Psychology, 23,* 611-696.

Berger, P. L., & Luckmann, T. (1967). *The social construction of reality: A treatise in the sociology of knowledge.* Garden City, NY: Doubleday.

Berger, P. L., & Neuhaus, R. J. (1970). *Movement and revolution.* Garden City, NY: Anchor.

Blumer, H. (1969). *Symbolic interactionism: Perspective and method.* Englewood Cliffs, NJ: Prentice Hall.

Brandtstädter, J. (1984). Action development and development through action. In M. Chapman (Ed.), Intentional action as a paradigm for development: A symposium. *Human Development, 27,* 113-118.

Brandtstädter, J. (1998). Action perspectives on human development. In W. Damon (Series Ed.) & R. M. Lerner (Vol. Ed.), *Handbook of child psychology: Vol. 1. Theoretical models of human development* (5th ed., pp. 807-863). New York: John Wiley.

Broughton, J. (Ed.). (1987). *Critical theories of psychological development.* New York: Plenum.

Buckley, W. (1967). *Sociology and modern systems theory.* Englewood Cliffs, NJ: Prentice Hall.

Campbell, C. (1996). *The myth of social action.* Cambridge: Cambridge University Press.

Chapman, M. (1982). Action and interaction: The study of social cognition in Germany and the United States. *Human Development, 24,* 295-302.

Chapman, M. (1984a). Conclusion: Action, intention and subjectivity. In M. Chapman (Ed.), Intentional action as a paradigm for development: A symposium. *Human Development, 27,* 142-144.

Chapman, M. (Ed.). (1984b). Intentional action as a paradigm for development: A symposium. *Human Development, 27,* 113-144.

Clausen, M. (1993). *American lives: Looking back at the children of the Great Depression.* New York: Free Press.

Cott, N. (1977). *Bonds of womanhood.* New Haven, CT: Yale University Press.

Crystal, S., & Waehrer, K. (1996). Later-life economic inequality in longitudinal perspective. *Journal of Gerontology, 51,* S307-S318.

Cumming, E., & Henry, W. E. (1961). *Growing old: The process of disengagement.* New York: Basic Books.

Dannefer, D. (1984). Adult development and social theory: A paradigmatic reappraisal. *American Sociological Review, 49,* 100-116.

Dannefer, D. (1987). Aging as intracohort differentiation: Accentuation, the Matthew effect, and the life course. *Sociological Forum, 2,* 211-236.

Dannefer, D. (1988). Differential gerontology and the stratified life course: Conceptual and methodological issues. In G. L. Maddox & M. P. Lawton (Eds.), *Annual review of gerontology and geriatrics* (Vol. 8, pp. 3-36). New York: Springer.

Dannefer, D. (1989). Human action and its place in theories of aging. *Journal of Aging Studies, 3,* 1-20.

Dannefer, D. (in press). Neoteny, naturalization, and other constituents of human development. In C. D. Ryff & V. Marshall (Eds.), *Self and society in aging processes.* New York: Springer.

Dannefer, D., & Perlmutter, M. (1990). Development as a multidimensional process: Individual and social constituents. *Human Development, 33,* 108-137.

Dannefer, D., & Sell, R. R. (1988). Age structure, the life course, and "aged heterogeneity": Prospects for research and theory. *Comprehensive Gerontology, 2,* 1-10.

Dannefer, D., & Uhlenberg, P. (1999). Paths of the life course: A typology. In V. L. Bengtson & K. W. Schaie (Eds.), *Handbook of theories of aging: In honor of Jim Birren.* New York: Springer.

Dawe, A. (1978). Theories of social action. In T. Bottomore & R. Nisbet (Eds.), *A history of sociological analysis* (pp. 362-417). New York: Basic Books.

Durkheim, E. (1964). *The rules of the sociological method* (S. S. Solovay & J. H. Mueller, Trans.; G. E. G. Catlin, Ed.). New York: Free Press.

Eckensberger, L. H., & Meacham, J. A. (1984). The essentials of action theory: A framework for discussion. *Human Development, 27,* 166-172.

Elder, G. H., Jr. (1998). The life course and human development. In W. Damon (Series Ed.) & R. M. Lerner (Vol. Ed.), *Handbook of child psychology: Vol. 1. Theoretical models of human development* (5th ed., pp. 939-991). New York: John Wiley.

Festinger, L. (1957). *A theory of cognitive dissonance.* Evanston, IL: Row, Peterson.

Geertz, C. (1973). *The interpretation of cultures: Selected essays.* New York: Basic Books.

Gehlen, A. (1988). *Man: His nature and place in the world.* New York: Columbia University Press.

Gergen, K. J. (1980). The emerging crisis in life-span developmental theory. In P. B. Baltes & O. G. Brim, Jr. (Eds.), *Life-span development and behavior* (Vol. 3, pp. 31-63). New York: Academic Press.

Giddens, A. (1979). *Central problems in social theory: Action, structure, and contradiction in social analysis.* Berkeley: University of California Press.

Giddens, A. (1984). *The constitution of society: Outline of the theory of structuration.* Berkeley: University of California Press.

Ginzburg, C. (1987). *The cheese and the worms: The cosmos of a sixteenth-century miller.* New York: Penguin.

Goffman, E. (1961). *Encounters.* Indianapolis: Bobbs-Merrill.

Gubrium, J. F. (1975). *Living and dying at Murray Manor.* New York: St. Martin's.

Gubrium, J. F., Holstein, J., & Buckholdt, D. R. (1994). *Constructing the life course.* Dix Hills, NY: General Hall.

Hagestad, G. (1992, November). *Aging in global perspective.* Plenary session presentation at the annual meeting of the Gerontological Society of America, Washington, DC.

Hegel, G. W. F. (1977). *The phenomenology of mind* (2nd ed.). New York: Allen & Unwin.

Hochschild, A. R. (1983). *The managed heart: Commercialization of human feeling.* Berkeley: University of California Press.

Hogan, D. (1981). *Transitions and social change.* New York: Academic Press.

Honderich, T. (1988). *A theory of determinism: The mind, neuroscience, and life-hopes.* Oxford: Clarendon.

Jones, J. H. (1981). *Bad blood: The Tuskegee syphilis experiments.* New York: Basic Books.

Kayser-Jones, J. S. (1990). *Old, alone and neglected: Care of the aged in Scotland and the United States.* Berkeley: University of California Press.

Keller, E. F. (1985). *Reflections on gender and science.* New Haven, CT: Yale University Press.

Knorr-Cetina, K. (1992). The couch, the cathedral, and the laboratory: On the relationships between experiment and laboratory in science. In A. Pickering (Ed.), *Science as practice and culture* (pp. 113-138). Chicago: University of Chicago Press.

Kohlberg, L. (1981). *The philosophy of moral development: Moral stages and ideas of justice.* San Francisco: Harper & Row.

Kohli, M. (1985). The world we forgot: A historical review of the life course. In V. W. Marshall (Ed.), *Later life: The social psychology of aging* (pp. 271-303). Beverly Hills, CA: Sage.

Langer, E. (1989). *Mindfulness.* Reading, MA: Addison-Wesley.

Latour, B., & Woolgar, S. (1986). *Laboratory life: The construction of scientific facts.* Princeton, NJ: Princeton University Press.

Lee, D., & Brady, R. (1988, October 31). Long hard days—at pennies an hour. *Business Week* (Industrial/Technology Ed.), *3077,* 46-47.

Lerner, R. M. (1982). Adolescents as producers of their own development. *Developmental Review, 2,* 342-370.

Lerner, R. M., & Busch-Rossnagel, N. A. (Eds.). (1981). *Individuals as producers of their development: A life-span perspective.* New York: Academic Press.

Levinson, D. J., Darrow, C. N., Klein, E. B., Levinson, M. H., & McKee, B. (1978). *The seasons of man's life.* New York: Alfred A. Knopf.

Lichtman, R. (1987). The illusion of maturation in an age of decline. In J. M. Broughton (Ed.), *Critical theories of psychological development* (pp. 127-148). New York: Plenum.

Lindner, R. (1958). *The fifty-minute hour: A collection of true psychoanalytic tales.* New York: Bantam.

MacMurray, J. (1957). *The self as agent.* London: Faber & Faber.

Marx, K. (1967). *Kapital* (Vol. 1). New York: International.

Meacham, J. A. (1984). The social basis of intentional action. In M. Chapman (Ed.), Intentional action as a paradigm for development: A symposium. *Human Development, 27,* 119-124.

Mead, G. H. (1934). *Mind, self, and society: From the standpoint of a social behaviorist* (C. W. Morris, Ed.). Chicago: University of Chicago Press.

Merton, R. K. (1968a). The Matthew effect in science: The reward and communications system of science. *Science, 199,* 55-63.

Merton, R. K. (1968b). *Social theory and social structure.* New York: Free Press.

Mills, C. W. (1940). Situated action and the vocabulary of motives. *American Sociological Review, 5,* 904-913.

Modell, J., Furstenberg, F., & Strong, D. (1976). Social change and transitions to adulthood in historical perspective. *Journal of Family History, 1,* 7-32.

Oakes, J. (1985). *Keeping track.* New Haven, CT: Yale University Press.

O'Connor, J. (1984). *Accumulation crisis.* New York: Basil Blackwell.

Ollman, B. (1976). *Alienation: Marx's conception of man in capitalist society.* Berkeley: University of California Press.

O'Rand, A. (1996). The precious and the precocious: The cumulation of disadvantage and advantage over the life course. *Gerontologist, 36,* 230-238.

Parsons, T. (1951). *The social system.* New York: Free Press.

Parsons, T. (1964). *Social structure and personality.* New York: Free Press.

130 DEVELOPMENT AS CONSTRUCTION

Parsons, T., & Bales, R. F. (1955). *Family, socialization, and interaction process.* Glencoe, IL: Free Press.

Parsons, T., & Platt, G. (1973). *The American university.* Cambridge, MA: Harvard University Press.

Piaget, J. (1977). *The equilibration of cognitive structures.* Chicago: University of Chicago Press.

Piotrkowski, C. (1979). *Work and the family system.* New York: Free Press.

Powdermaker, H. (1966). *Stranger and friend: The way of an anthropologist.* New York: W. W. Norton.

Riley, M. W. (1978). Aging, social change, and the power of ideas. *Daedalus, 107,* 39-52.

Riley, M. W., Johnson, M. E., & Foner, A. (1972). *Aging and society: Vol. 3. A sociology of age stratification.* New York: Russell Sage Foundation.

Riley, M. W., Kahn, R., & Foner, A. (1994). *Age and structural lag: Society's failure to provide meaningful opportunities in work, family, and leisure.* New York: Wiley-Interscience.

Roethlisberger, F. J., & Dickson, W. J. (1939). *Management and the worker.* Cambridge, MA: Harvard University Press.

Rosenbaum, J. (1976). *Making inequality: The hidden curriculum of high school tracking.* New York: John Wiley.

Rosenbaum, J. (1983). *Career mobility in a corporate hierarchy.* New York: Academic Press.

Rubin, L. (1992). *Worlds of pain: Life in the working-class family.* New York: Harper Colophon.

Satir, V. (1972). *People-making.* Palo Alto, CA: Science and Behavior Books.

Scarr, S., & McCartney, K. (1983). How people make their environments: A theory of genotype-environment effects. *Child Development, 54,* 424-435.

Schütz, A. (1971). *Collected papers: Vol. 1. The problem of social reality* (I. Schütz, Ed.). The Hague: Martinus Nijhoff.

Sherif, M., & Sherif, C. W. (1953). *Groups in harmony and tension.* New York: Harper.

Simmel, G. (1950). *The sociology of George Simmel* (K. H. Wolff, Ed. and Trans.). New York: Free Press. (Original work published 1908)

Smetana, J. (1995). Morality in context: Abstraction, ambiguities, and application. *Annals of Child Development, 10,* 83-130.

Smith, J. (1994). Does an extra year make any difference? The impact of early access to algebra on long-term gains in math assessment. *Educational Evaluation and Policy Analysis, 18,* 141-153.

Staudinger, U. M. (1996). Wisdom and the social-interactive foundation of the mind. In P. B. Baltes & U. M. Staudinger (Eds.), *Interactive minds: Life-span perspectives on the social foundation of cognition* (pp. 276-315). New York: Cambridge University Press.

Staudinger, U. M., & Baltes, P. B. (1994). Psychology of wisdom. In R. J. Sternberg (Ed.), *Encyclopedia of human intelligence* (Vol. 2, pp. 1143-1152). New York: Macmillan.

Thomas, W. H. (1996). *Life worth living: How someone you love can still enjoy life in a nursing home.* Boston: VanderWyk & Burnham.

Tuchman, B. (1978). *A distant mirror: The calamitous 14th century.* New York: Ballantine.

Turner, R. (1976). The real self: From institution to impulse. *American Journal of Sociology, 81,* 989-1016.

Uhlenberg, P. (1978). Changing configurations of the life course. In T. K. Hareven (Ed.), *Transitions: The family and the life course in historical perspective.* New York: Academic Press.

Vygotsky, L. S. (1978). *Mind in society: The development of higher psychological processes* (M. Cole, V. John-Steiner, S. Scribner, & E. Souberman, Eds.). Cambridge, MA: Harvard University Press.

Wall Street Journal. (1989). *The Wall Street Journal book of chief executive style: Amenities and customs of America's corporate elite.* New York: William Morrow.

Warren, C. A. (1987). *Madwives: Schizophrenic women in the 1950's.* New Brunswick, NJ: Rutgers University Press.

Weber, M. (1964). *The theory of social and economic organization* (A. M. Henderson & T. Parsons, Trans.). New York: Free Press.

Wexler, P. (1983). *Critical social psychology.* London: Routledge.

White, H. C. (1992). *Identity and control: A structural theory of action.* Princeton, NJ: Princeton University Press.

5

THE DYNAMIC CODEVELOPMENT OF INTENTIONALITY, SELF, AND SOCIAL RELATIONS

Michael F. Mascolo
Kurt W. Fischer
Robert A. Neimeyer

THE ORIGINS OF INTENTIONALITY AND THE DEVELOPMENT OF SELF

His father was a Scots-man, his mother of the African people, and this distinction between "man" and "people" was an important distinction, for one of them came off the boat as part of a horde, already demonized, mind blank to everything but human suffering, each face the same as the one next to it; the other came off the boat of his own volition, seeking to fulfill a destiny, a vision of himself he carried in his mind's eye. (Kincaid, 1996, p. 181)

In this passage, Kincaid (1996) alludes to the rich interplay among intentionality, self, and social relations. Her words suggest that an intentional agent is one who can act on "his own volition, seeking to fulfill a destiny,

133

a vision of himself he carrie[s] in his mind's eye." The concepts of intentionality and agency are central to any coherent conception of self. Without them, selves become reduced to things that can only be pushed or pulled instead of actors who can exert some control over their actions. However, although active in their agency, selves are never autonomous. In this passage, Kincaid alludes to the ways in which intentional agency is channelized by visions of the self that take shape and function within particular social and cultural relations. Thus any complete analysis of the developing capacity for intentional action must address ways in which intentionality and self codevelop in dynamic interactions that occur between embodied individuals within particular sociocultural contexts.

In this chapter, we examine these issues from the perspective of dynamic skill theory (Fischer, 1980; Fischer & Bidell, 1998; Mascolo & Fischer, 1998). We first examine current tensions in theory and research about the origins and development of intentionality in infancy. We then outline a dynamic skill theory model of the development of intentionality from infancy onward. From this view, the capacity for intentional action is best seen as a skill that begins to develop soon after birth and undergoes a series of qualitative and quantitative changes throughout ontogenesis. Intentional skills function as dynamic control structures through which individuals guide their actions and thoughts within particular social and physical contexts. Skill theory maintains that intentional skills develop as properties not of isolated individuals, but of persons in social contexts. As such, a skill analysis can provide a framework for resolving important tensions in the study of intentionality and self. After an analysis of developmental changes in intentional skills from infancy to adulthood, we present a case study that illustrates the ways in which self-representations in adults function as hierarchically organized intentional systems that emerge, develop, and function within affectively charged joint interactions with others.

CURRENT THEORY ON THE DEVELOPMENT
OF INTENTIONAL ACTION IN INFANCY

Theorists have erected a variety of theoretical frameworks for understanding intentionality and its development. Drawing upon Zeedyk (1996), one can classify approaches in terms of whether intentionality is defined in terms of (a) goal-directedness, (b) mutual intersubjectivity, or (c) object-directedness.

Intentionality as Goal-Directedness

Most theorists define intentionality in terms of goal-directedness, which consists of the capacity to regulate action in terms of a goal or internal representation. Within this view, theorists differ in whether they regard intentionality as an early- or late-developing skill (Zeedyk, 1996). Butterworth and Hopkins (1988) found that neonates often began to open their mouths before bringing their thumbs to their lips, an observation they interpret as evidence of primitive goal-directedness. Lewis, Alessandri, and Sullivan (1990) found that infants as young as 2 months detected a contingency between arm pulling and the onset of an audiovisual display. Infants evinced joy in the presence of the contingency and anger in its absence. Other theorists locate the onset of intentionality later in infancy. These include theorists who study the intention to communicate (Bates, Camaioni, & Volterra, 1979; Harding, 1982) and those who define intentionality in terms of the capacity to differentiate means from ends (Frye, 1990; Piaget, 1952/1963).

Piaget (1952/1963) is often considered to be a proponent of the late onset of intentionality. Although he holds that the capacity for intentional action builds on early forms of goal-directedness as manifested in primary and secondary reactions, Piaget maintains that it is not until about 8 months that infants become able to coordinate two secondary schemes into a means-ends relation. To illustrate, consider Piaget's observation of his 8-month-old daughter. After Jacqueline attempted to reach for a cigarette case, Piaget removed it and placed it between some crossed strings above her bassinet. After first failing to grasp the case, Jacqueline then pulled the strings, causing the case to fall. In this example, pulling the strings served as a means to obtain the unambiguous goal of grasping the case, a goal that was operative from the outset of the episode. Of course, for Piaget, the capacity for intentionality continues to develop, leading to the emergence of symbolic representations as guides to action around 18-24 months.

The Interpersonal Nature of Intentional Action

Theorists who assert the interpersonal nature of intentional activity fall into two categories (Zeedyk, 1996). Those in the first group maintain that infant intentionality itself has social origins (Kaye, 1982; Lock, 1980; Newson, 1979; Schaffer, 1984). These theorists suggest that infants are not born intentional beings but instead develop into intentional agents because socialization agents treat them from birth "as if" they were intentional from a very early age. For example, many of the utterances that mothers direct to young infants refer to the infants' desires, wishes, and preferences (Kaye, 1982; Kruper & Uzgiris, 1987; Snow, 1977). From this view, adults skillfully place their actions at the junctures of infants' preattuned behaviors in ways that produce apparently intentional and reciprocal exchange. Infants acquire the capacity for intentional action as they internalize social meanings that are initially external to them, a process similar to Vygotsky's (1981) analysis of the social origins of pointing.

Rather than holding that intentionality has social origins, a second group of theorists suggest that infants are intentional and intersubjective beings from birth onward (Brazelton, 1982; Stern, 1985; Trevarthen, 1978; Tronick, 1981). For example, Trevarthen and his colleagues hold that intentionality is manifested in children's early socioemotional exchanges with others, rather than in solitary actions on objects (see Murray & Trevarthen, 1986; Trevarthen, 1978, 1979, 1993; Trevarthen & Hubley, 1978). According to Trevarthen (1979), intentionality refers to "the capacity to originate coordinated acts that are directed to express a specific line of experience" (p. 120). Trevarthen proposes that young infants intentionally attempt to communicate feelings to others within affectively charged interactions with adults. The intersubjective capacity for intentional action undergoes developmental change (Trevarthen, 1979, 1993). By about 2 months, infants exhibit *primary intersubjectivity*, which involves face-to-face sharing of experiences for the sake of communication itself rather than for the relaying of information about a topic. By about 5 months, interest in social interaction wanes and infants begin to direct their actions to physical objects. By 9 months, infant-mother dyads exhibit *secondary intersubjectivity* (Trevarthen & Hubley, 1978), which involves the capacity to incorporate objects in joint and intentional exchanges. Thus, from this view, intentionality is seen as an interpersonal phenomenon that manifests itself first in intersubjective engagements and only later in individual and joint actions on objects.

Intention as Behavioral Object-Directedness

Vedeler (1991, 1994) has launched a critique of the commonly held assumption that intentionality consists of goal-directedness. To Vedeler, goal-directedness implies that physical behavior is under the control of some type of inner mental representation. To say that infant action is goal directed would therefore imply the infant's capacity to have some idea, however primitive, of what she or he wants at some point in the future, however near. To Vedeler, to the extent that goals require capacity to represent cognitively an absent state of affairs, their emergence must be *explained* rather than *presupposed* in development. Vedeler (1991) holds that actions are *not* fundamentally preceded by goals, but instead, "goals emerge through the deployment of actions" (p. 432). Drawing upon Merleau-Ponty (1942/1963) and others, Vedeler defines intentionality in its philosophical sense, that is, in terms of the *aboutness* or *object-directedness* of consciousness and behavior. Because all consciousness and behavior is necessarily directed at something, "intentionality is where the focus of attention and activity is" (p. 441). Defined in this way, intentional action need not require goal-directedness or any type of representational content; it simply consists of behavior that an infant controls or directs toward some physical or social object.

In a longitudinal study, Vedeler (1994) filmed everyday interactions between parents and infants ages 12 to 36 weeks. He measured the degree of intentionality of infant action in terms of a composite of the intensity of attention directed toward social or physical objects and the general behavioral coherence of an infant's directed actions. Defined in this way, and consistent with Trevarthen's expectations, infants displayed intentional behavior prior to 6 months of age. As Trevarthen predicted, 2- and 3-month-olds directed most of their behaviors toward social figures, whereas 4- and 8-month-olds directed their actions more often toward objects. Contrary to predictions of "as if" theorists, parent attribution of physical and social intentions to infants corresponded with the object- or social-directedness of infants' behavior. These results illustrate the merits of applying Vedeler's definition of intentionality.

Addressing Dichotomies in Current Thinking About Infant Intentionality

Controversy surrounding the origins of intentional action centers on (a) the point of emergence, (b) its interpersonal nature, and (c) the role of goals in intentional activity. Much of the controversy about the point at which intentional action emerges can be resolved simply through the adoption of a truly developmental approach. For example, many identify Piaget as an advocate for the late onset of intentionality at 8 months of age. However, Piaget holds that only one *form* of intentionality—the capacity to differentiate means from ends from the outset of acting—emerges around 8 months of age. Consistent with the claims of critics (Lewis, 1990), Piaget clearly identifies earlier forms of explicitly intentional action in the form of secondary schemes in infants as young as 2½ months of age and precursors to intentional action even at the stage of reflexes. Thus it is not helpful to ask about the *point* at which intentionality emerges; it is better to examine changes in the organization of goal-directed action as it occurs in different contexts and points in ontogenesis.

Second, cognitive approaches that define intentionality in terms of individual goals underrepresent the role of social context in activating, supporting, and actually putting together intentional action (Schaffer, 1984; Trevarthen, 1979; Uzgiris, 1990). However, in approaches that emphasize social embeddedness, intentionality seems to be defined simply in terms of the active involvement of children in communicative exchanges. We suggest that there is a need to specify more precisely the particular organization of what individual children actually control in the production of intentional acts, even as those acts are co-constructed in socioemotional interaction. Finally, although Vedeler is appropriately critical of the commonsense view that action is necessarily preceded by inner goals and representations, we suggest that he has overextended his case. In defining intentionality in terms of the capacity to control or direct attention toward objects, Vedeler does not specify a theory of what infants actually *do* when they control their attention and behavior. One might argue that *control* over action must occur relative to some type of goal or reference standard, even if such a standard involves reflexive or sensorimotor goals that are activated and jointly controlled by environmental events. The very concept of directed action implies some type of goal-directedness. The goals that mediate action need not be understood as inner mental representations that are separate from and prior to overt activity-on-objects.

In what follows, we elaborate a dynamic skill model of intentionality, self, and social relations in development (Fischer, 1980; Fischer & Bidell, 1998; Mascolo & Fischer, 1998, in press). From this view, intentional action proceeds as a type of developing skill. *Skill* here refers to the capacity to coordinate action, thought, and feeling within a given social context. Because skills are control structures, they are inherently goal directed. Further, because skills are properties of persons-in-social-contexts, intentional action is always under the joint control of the individual and the social environment. Skill theory provides a set of conceptual and methodological tools for charting major and fine-grained changes in the dynamic organization of intentional action within social contexts. Finally, skills are necessarily actions *on* something. The first skills are mediated by reflexive and sensorimotor goals that are activated by objects in the physical and social environment. There is no need to postulate complex mental representations that mediate primitive actions. Thus a theory of skill development can provide a framework from which to address current tensions in our understanding of the development of intentional action.

A DYNAMIC SKILL THEORY APPROACH TO THE DEVELOPMENT OF INTENTIONALITY AND AGENCY

According to dynamic skill theory (Fischer, 1980; Fischer & Bidell, 1998; Mascolo & Fischer, 1998; Mascolo, Pollack, & Fischer, 1997), individuals direct their actions through the formation of skills. A skill consists of a *control system* for organizing and directing one's behavior within a given context and behavioral domain. From this view, all controlled and self-relevant activity involves the regulation of behavior in terms of some type of reference standard or goal. For example, Carver and Scheier (1981, 1990) describe control systems in terms of a series of hierarchically embedded feedback loops, each of which operates in terms of a series of behavioral *standards* (Powers, 1973). From this view, a standard refers to any type of set point, reference value, goal, or point of comparison. Each negative feedback loop operates as a TOTE (test, operate, test, exit) unit (see Miller, Galanter, & Pribram, 1960). In so doing, each unit engages in a *test* to determine whether input to the system meets the currently operative reference standard. If a mismatch exists between the input and the standard, the system *operates*, or takes action. Feedback from action is thereupon and continuously *tested* against the operative reference standard and *exits* when the standard is finally met. In this way, the TOTE unit provides a metaphor that describes the structure of goal-directed action.

One can understand complex action in terms of the hierarchical organization of control systems. Within a hierarchically organized control system, the output from a superordinate or higher-level loop specifies the reference standard for the next lower subordinate level of loops (Carver & Scheier, 1981). For example, consider an adolescent who sets out to impress her family and friends with her superior athletic ability. At the most superordinate level, her behavior is governed by the principled self-standard or goal "demonstrate superior athletic ability." The control system works to meet this standard by invoking a series of lower-level feedback loops defined in terms of more local standards or goals. For example, at the next lower level of "scripted activity" the standard "play baseball" might be invoked. To meet this standard, the system invokes a standard governing a "subscript" for "batting." This subscript involves a series of component behaviors (approaching the plate, orienting to the pitcher, hitting an oncoming ball, and so on), many of which must be performed in a given sequence. At the level of "sequence," the system can invoke a standard such as "hitting an oncoming ball." This requires still lower-level standards governing relations among component acts (coordinating looking at the pitcher with anticipated movement of the bat), which requires still lower-level standards regulating the actual movement of the bat, the movement of arms through space, and eventually sensory feedback from associated muscle changes. Physical behavior is produced only at this lowest level, where sensory feedback from muscle movement is compared against standards that regulate muscular intensity. The output from lower-level loops is continuously forwarded to the next highest level of loops, and so on, and is eventually compared with the highest-level goals, informing the person of her success in presenting herself as a "superior athlete."

Within dynamic skill theory (Fischer, 1980), humans exert control over their behavior through the formation of multiple sets of dynamic control systems called *skills*. A skill is an individual's capacity to organize and direct action, thinking, and feeling within a given context and psychological domain. A skill consists of a set of actions performed on something. Further, a skill is always an action performed in a context, and is thus under the joint control of person and context. For example, when a batter is actually hitting a baseball, the trajectory of her swing is determined by her attempt to adjust her behavior to the oncoming path of the ball. In this way, the batter's intentional action is not autonomous. The actual swing is under the joint control of the batter and the environment, which includes not only the path of the oncoming ball, but the intentions and movements of the pitcher, the number of runners on base, whether or not the strategy calls for a "hit and run" play, and even the expectations of the audience members whom the batter is attempting to impress. A change in context can prompt change in the form and developmental level of behavior in profound ways.

Further, like Carver and Scheier's (1981) control systems, skills are hierarchically organized. Thus they organize lower-level component actions into higher-order actions and representations. It is through such hierarchies that individuals direct their behavior and thinking within given contexts. An individual's capacity to organize his or her behavior into skills within specified contexts and domains undergoes a series of qualitative and quantitative transformations in ontogenesis. According to dynamic skill theory, skills develop through four broad tiers of development (reflexes, sensorimotor actions, representations, and abstractions) and a series of four levels within each tier (single sets, mappings, systems, and systems of systems), the last level of which specifies the first level of the next broad tier of development. Further, skill theory (Fischer, 1980) provides ways to identify an indefinite number of steps between any given pair of levels. Higher-level skills result from the intercoordination of multiple lower-level skills into a single control structure. The various tiers and levels of skills are depicted in Table 5.1.

To understand the nature of developing skills, consider changes in the organization of skills throughout the sensorimotor tier of development. There are four levels of sensorimotor activity, the first of which emerges through the coordination of lower-level reflex systems (Fischer & Hogan, 1989). Beginning around 4 months of age, an infant can begin to coordinate multiple reflex systems into a single *sensorimotor action*. At this level, an infant can control a single, flexible action on a physical or social object. For example, he can skillfully use his hands to grasp a teddy bear lying on the bed beside him (without looking at it) or turn his head from side to side to actively look at a teddy bear sitting before him. Although an infant at this level can direct his hands toward a seen teddy bear or even adjust his hand in relation to the bear, full coordination of grasping and looking is made possible by the onset of *sensorimotor mappings* around 7-8 months of age. Sensorimotor mappings result from the coordination of two sensorimotor actions. At this level, a child can skillfully coordinate grasping and looking. Thus she can grasp a teddy bear in order to look at it or look at a bear in order to grasp it. *Sensorimotor systems* emerge beginning around 12-13 months, with the ability to coordinate two sensorimotor mappings. Whereas a younger infant could coordinate looking and grasping into a mapping relation, many 13-month-olds can examine a teddy bear skillfully through multiple coordinated acts of grasping and looking. Thus, in a single skill, an infant can explore different ways of grasping and looking at an object.

A new tier in development begins to emerge around 18-24 months, with the onset of the capacity to coordinate at least two sensorimotor systems into a system of sensorimotor systems, which is the equivalent of a *single*

TABLE 5.1 The Origins and Development of Intentional Action

Level	Developmental Tier				Example of Skill	Age
	Reflexive	Sensorimotor	Representations	Abstractions		
Rf1: single reflexes	[GRASP$_{ball}$]				**Single, simple species-specific action components whose goals are activated by events in environment.** With fixed posture, infant grasps a ball placed in hand; looks at ball moving in front of face.	3-4 weeks
Rf2: reflex mapping	[TURN$_{head}$ —— MOBILE$_{see}$]				**Coordination of two action components into means-end relation activated by context.** After discovering contingency, infant moves head to see a mobile move.	7-8 weeks
Rf3: reflex systems	$\begin{bmatrix} \text{see face} \\ \text{PARENT} \\ \text{hear voice} \end{bmatrix}$ ⟷ $\begin{bmatrix} \text{nod head} \\ \text{ACT} \\ \text{coo} \end{bmatrix}$				**Controlled coordination of subsets of action components activated by supporting context.** Looking at face and hearing voice evokes coordinated smiling, cooing, and nodding (greeting response).	10-11 weeks
Rf4/S1: system of reflex systems that are single sensorimotor actions	[LOOK$_{ball+}$] or [GRASP$_{ball}$]				**Coordination of reflex systems produces a flexible goal-directed sensorimotor act from the outset of a situation.** Infant effortfully attempts to grasp a seen ball, adjusts hand to minor movements in ball's trajectory.	15-17 weeks
S2: sensorimotor mappings	[LOOK$_{ball}$] $\xrightarrow{\text{in order to}}$ GRASP$_{ball}$ or [GRASP$_{ball}$] $\xrightarrow{\text{in order to}}$ LOOK$_{ball}$				**Coordination of two sensorimotor actions into a means-end relation.** Without having to discover a contingency by accident or through social support, infant grasps ball in order to look at it or looks at ball in order to grasp it.	7-8 months

S3a: sensorimotor systems	$$\begin{bmatrix} \text{up} \\ \text{MOVE RATTLE} \updownarrow \\ \text{down} \end{bmatrix} \begin{bmatrix} \text{top} \\ \text{SEE} \updownarrow \\ \text{bottom} \end{bmatrix}$$	**Intentional exploration through the sensorimotor coordination of multiple means-end relations.** Infant moves a rattle in different ways in order to explore different parts.	11-13 months
Sb4/Rp1: system of sensorimotor systems that are single representations	$$\begin{bmatrix} \text{doll at point 1} \\ \text{LOOK} \updownarrow \\ \text{doll at point 2} \end{bmatrix} \begin{bmatrix} \text{doll at point 1} \\ \text{GRASP} \updownarrow \\ \text{doll at point 2} \end{bmatrix}$$ $$\Longleftrightarrow$$ $$\begin{bmatrix} \text{leg 1} \\ \text{MOVE} \updownarrow \\ \text{leg 2} \end{bmatrix} \begin{bmatrix} \text{point 1} \\ \text{GO FORWARD} \updownarrow \\ \text{point 2} \end{bmatrix}$$ $$\equiv \begin{bmatrix} DOLL \\ \text{walk} \end{bmatrix}$$	**Coordination of action systems produces single concrete representations that function as primitive "plans."** Child can use one sensorimotor system to "plan," evoke, or direct another sensorimotor system. Child coordinates skills to manipulate doll and move it forward to represent an absent activity of the doll (walking). As such, child "plans" doll's activity.	18-24 months
Rp2: representational mappings	$$\begin{bmatrix} ME \xrightarrow{\text{just like}} YOU \\ \text{will run} \quad\quad \text{can run} \end{bmatrix}$$	**Comparative intentions involving coordination between representations.** Child uses relation between two representations (e.g., social comparison of valued acts) as an explicit guide to action. For example, on the beach a 4-year-old girl said, "I'm gonna run into the water just like the big girl did!" and then runs from the beach to the water.	3½-4 years
Rp3: representational systems	$$\begin{bmatrix} ME & \xrightarrow{\text{to be like}} & FRIEND \\ \text{wants glove} & & \text{has glove} \\ \text{do chores to buy} & & \text{is "cool"} \end{bmatrix}$$	**Planful coordination between two self-related mappings.** Child invokes a concrete intention-outcome plan in order to reach higher-order goal defined by social comparison. For example, "I want a baseball glove so I can be cool like Jerri, so I'll do extra chores to save money and buy it."	6-7 years

(continued)

TABLE 5.1 Continued

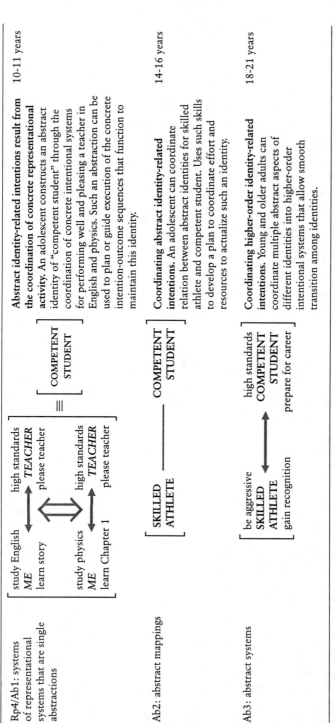

Rp4/Ab1: systems of representational systems that are single abstractions	study English *ME* learn story ⟺ study physics *ME* learn Chapter 1 ≡ high standards *TEACHER* please teacher high standards *TEACHER* please teacher ⎡ COMPETENT STUDENT ⎤	**Abstract identity-related intentions result from the coordination of concrete representational activity.** An adolescent constructs an abstract identity of "competent student" through the coordination of concrete intentional systems for performing well and pleasing a teacher in English and physics. Such an abstraction can be used to plan or guide execution of the concrete intention-outcome sequences that function to maintain this identity.	10-11 years
Ab2: abstract mappings	⎡ SKILLED ──── COMPETENT ATHLETE STUDENT ⎤	**Coordinating abstract identity-related intentions.** An adolescent can coordinate relation between abstract identities for skilled athlete and competent student. Uses such skills to develop a plan to coordinate effort and resources to actualize such an identity.	14-16 years
Ab3: abstract systems	⎡ be aggressive high standards SKILLED ←→ COMPETENT ATHLETE STUDENT gain recognition prepare for career ⎤	**Coordinating higher-order identity-related intentions.** Young and older adults can coordinate multiple abstract aspects of different identities into higher-order intentional systems that allow smooth transition among identities.	18-21 years

NOTE: In skill structures, each word or phrase denotes a skill component, with each large word designating a main component (set) and each adjacent smaller word or phrase designating a further specification or subset of the main component. Words in small plain letters designate reflexes (action components), words in boldface designate sensorimotor actions, words in italics designate representations, and words in large plain letters designate abstractions. Lines connecting sets designate relations forming a mapping, single-line arrows designate relations forming a system, and double-line arrows designate relations forming a system of systems. Ages of emergence specify modal times at which a level first appears, extrapolated from research with middle-class North American and European children. They may differ across individuals, cultures, and other social groups.

144

representation. In this way, the fourth level of the sensorimotor tier of development constitutes the first level of the representational tier. At this level, through the coordination of two sensorimotor systems, the child can use one sensorimotor system to stand for or evoke another sensorimotor system. This occurs in symbolic or pretend play, for example, when the child coordinates one sensorimotor system for looking and grasping a teddy bear with another for making the bear move forward. In this way, the child can use the movements of a teddy bear to represent an act of walking or talking. Single representations also occur in everyday speech, as when a child uses a simple declarative utterance (e.g., "bear walk") to communicate a representation of an event in the absence of that event's occurrence. This sequence illustrates the ways in which skills develop through a series of levels and tiers. Skills develop through the coordination of lower-level action systems to produce higher-order systems of action and thought within a given context. A parallel progression of levels from single sets, to mappings, systems, and systems of systems occurs throughout each broad tier of development (reflexes, sensorimotor, representations, abstractions), thus producing the 12 levels indicated in Table 5.1.

An important principle of skill theory is that individuals do not function at any single skill level or at any particular point in development. Instead, individuals function at a range of skill levels depending upon context, task, behavioral domain, emotional state, and a suite of other variables. For example, the social context in which a task is performed exerts a direct influence on an individual's level of performance in any given skilled activity. Skill theory differentiates between an individual's *optimal* and *functional* levels of skilled activity. An individual's optimal level of performance in a given domain consists of the upper limit of that person's skill. Most often, a person can achieve optimal-level performance in contexts that provide high levels of environmental support for the skill in question. Examples of high support can include a person's modeling of a target behavior before a child is asked to produce the behavior in question and the use of cultural tools (e.g., an abacus, calculator) or memory supports (e.g., suggested memory strategies). An individual's functional level is the level at which he or she performs in a given domain in everyday contexts in which high support is lacking. Many studies indicate that children perform at higher levels in the presence of contextual support than in contexts that provide low levels of support (Fischer, Bullock, Rotenberg, & Raya, 1993; Fischer & Kenny, 1986; Kitchener, Lynch, Fischer, & Wood, 1993; Rogoff, 1990; Vygotsky, 1978). For example, a 4-year-old who might ordinarily tell a story about nice or mean interactions at the level of single representations might function at the level of representational mappings if an adult were to model such a story for the child (Fischer et al., 1993). The difference between the child's functional and optimal levels in any given conceptual domain constitutes the *developmental range* for the skill in question.

Further, it is important to differentiate high- and low-support contexts from contexts that provide social scaffolding. High- and low-support contexts, as defined above, consist of environments that provide different degrees of support for behavior that an individual produces on his or her own, without the direct intervention of another person. *Scaffolding* refers to a process whereby another person directs, supports, or otherwise assists a child in carrying out a given activity (Rogoff, 1990). In contexts involving scaffolding, another person's behavior helps support, direct, or structure the child's behavior throughout the course of the task. Such scaffolding can take the form of verbal directions, emotional encouragement or support, or the actual performance of parts of the task for the child. For example, in helping a 15-month-old child manipulate a jack-in-the-box, a parent might hold the box and verbally direct the child to turn the handle. In this situation, the child's behavior occurs under the continuous direction of the parent, who also supports the child's behavior by performing a part of the task for the child (i.e., holding the box). Thus children are often capable of performing at higher developmental levels when working with other persons than when working alone. With development, children increasingly gain the capacity to coordinate and control for themselves those elements of task activity that had previously been controlled in conjunction with others in scaffolded and joint activity (Bidell & Fischer, 1996; Mascolo, Craig-Bray, & Neimeyer, 1997).

THE ORIGINS AND DEVELOPMENT OF INTENTIONAL ACTIVITY

To what do we refer when we speak of *intentionality*? Scholars and laypersons alike use this term to express a variety of meanings, including goal-directedness (conscious or nonconscious) (Lewis, 1990), the capacity to differentiate means from ends in actions (Piaget, 1952/1963), the ability to use mental representations as a guide for behavior (Olson, 1992), the capacity to represent one's intentions explicitly (Anscombe, 1959; Davidson, 1980), and the capacity to engage in thoughtful planning prior to action. From a developmental perspective, these different meanings reflect different levels of skill development, and thus different forms of intentional activity, and begin to appear at different points in development.

We define intentionality broadly as *the capacity to perform an action on purpose*. When acting intentionally, one performs a particular action *in order to* obtain a wanted state. In doing so, one must be able to control both the *means* of the act (the action itself) and the *end* of the action (i.e., be aware of a wanted state of affairs). This does not mean that the individual must be aware *that she has a goal*; she only needs to be aware of the relation between an action and a goal state—a wanted outcome, however primitive. Thus, at its most basic level, an *intention* refers to the awareness of a state of affairs toward which an action is directed. Like any skill, the capacity for intentional action develops gradually in ontogenesis and undergoes a series of developmental changes. From this view, intentional skills have their early origins in the first controlled actions, and thereafter undergo massive differentiation and hierarchic integration in development.

Table 5.1 provides a description of developmental changes in the structure of goal-directed and intentional action from birth through 21 years of age. Drawing on skill theory, the table shows that the first goal-directed actions emerge with the onset of single reflexes, beginning around 3-4 weeks of age. Using single reflexes (Step Rf1 in Table 5.1), a child can exert control over single action elements in contexts that directly support or activate those action elements. For example, a 1-month-old will grasp an object that is placed directly in his hands. To the extent that control systems operate with reference to some type of goal or reference standard (however primitive), we suggest that these first controlled reflexes are guided by *motor goals that are activated by the immediate environment*. Seen in this way, single reflexes are the first goal-directed acts. However, they are extremely limited; the "goals" that regulate them consist of simple sensori-motor reference standards that govern simple action sequences, rather than representations of future states. Further, infants can exert control over their actions only once they have been activated by the immediate context. Thus, at this early step, infants exert limited control over action elements (the means), but only when the motor goal has been activated by an environmental event.

An important step in the development of intentionality occurs when an infant gains the capacity to *control both the means and the ends* of simple reflexes in contexts that highly support such coordinations. A primitive form of means-end differentiation can be identified at the level of *reflex mappings,* which begin to emerge around 6 to 8 weeks of age (Step Rf2). At this level, in a supportive context, an infant can begin actively to coordinate one simple reflex with another. Simple intentional acts emerge as the infant uses one reflex as a means to obtain a simple outcome produced by another. Lewis et al.'s (1990) finding that 2-month-olds will engage in arm pulling in order to look at an audiovisual display is a case in point (see also Watson & Ramey, 1972)—an infant can use one reflex (a swipe of the arm) as a means to achieve a particular end (i.e., looking at the display). Lewis et al.'s finding that infants evinced anger and continued to engage in arm pulling after cessation of the arm pull-display contingency suggests that the infants' actions were clearly intentional in this context. Further, because the infants continued the arm pulling after the contingency had been terminated, it could not be the environmental feedback per se that activated the arm pulling (i.e., the on-line presence of the audiovisual display); it was activated by the continuation of the infants' goal of looking at the desired outcome, after they had discovered or were trained to detect the earlier contingency. Note that this early form of intentional behavior occurred within a highly structured context that approached the richness of contingent social interaction. With the onset of *reflex systems* at around 10-11 weeks of age (Step Rf3 in Table 5.1), infants can actively coordinate multiple action elements into an intention-outcome relation, again activated and supported by the immediate social context. Using reflex systems, within the context of ongoing social exchange, a child can use one set of coordinated reflexes (e.g., shaking her head and cooing) as a means to achieve a particular end (e.g., seeing a parent's smiling face and hearing his excited voice).

Early intentional reflex coordinations occur in the context of richly textured interactions and environments that provide immediate feedback. Such early intentions differ significantly from later intentional skills. Beginning around 4 months, infants can begin to coordinate two reflex systems to form a single flexible *sensorimotor action.* At this level (Step S1), an infant's goal-directed actions require less support and structure from the physical or social environment. For example, whereas 2-month-olds are capable of grasping when objects are placed in their hands, 4- and 5-month-olds can begin to reach for seen balls and can make rudimentary adjustments to accommodate changes in a ball's movement. Alternatively, these infants can actively trace the trajectory of a moving ball or move their hands to pursue objects lying next to them (without looking). Thus an infant's smoothly organized actions are goal directed from the outset of a situation and do not require direct activation and postural support from the social environment.

With the onset of *sensorimotor mappings* beginning around 7-8 months of age (Step S2), an infant can actively use one sensorimotor action as a means to achieve an outcome produced by another from the outset of a situation. For example, at the outset of acting, an infant can look at a ball *in order to* grasp it or can uncover an object *in order to* retrieve it. Further, as described by Piaget (1952/1963), at this level infants are capable of redeploying their intentional actions when obstacles are placed in their paths, thus showing clear and forward-seeking control over both the means and the ends of their sensorimotor actions. With the onset of *sensorimotor systems* at around 11-13 months (Step S3), intentional action can become increasingly flexible and fluid. For example, by coordinating multiple sensorimotor intention-outcome sequences, an infant can actively and intentionally explore a novel object. For example, an infant can move a rattle or teddy bear up and down to explore intentionally (through visual and manual coordination) its top and bottom.

Beginning around 18-24 months of age, intentional action becomes qualitatively transformed with the onset of *single representations*. At this level (Step S4/Rp1 in Table 5.1), children can begin to coordinate two sensorimotor systems to form a single representation. In so doing, they can use one sensorimotor system to evoke or stand for (represent) another sensorimotor system. For example, a child can coordinate a sensorimotor system for manipulating a doll with another for making it move forward to represent or symbolize the doll's walking. As such, the child's intentional action is mediated by her capacity to represent and evoke absent aspects of a situation. The child can begin to use representations as an intentional "plan" to make a doll walk or talk, or something similar. Note that, ontogenetically, the capacity to represent absent and future meanings develops through the coordination of goal-directed sensorimotor action systems. Thus context-embedded goal-directed action precedes representation in ontogenesis, and not vice versa. One need not invoke a sophisticated concept of representation to explain intentionality. The use of representations consists of a special form of intentionality in which actions are "planned" prior to execution.

With development, the capacity for planned, mediated intentional action undergoes extensive developmental change. With the onset of *representational mappings* (Step Rp2) at around 3½ to 4 years of age, children can coordinate the relationship between two representations. Children can understand two or more representations in terms of a variety of different relationships, including causality, part-whole, reciprocity, and temporality. The capacity for representational mappings enables the construction of more complex and controlled representational intentions and plans. For example, when she was 44 months old, Mica Kanner-Mascolo watched intently as older girls ran from the beach and jumped into the water. Mica exclaimed, "I'm gonna run into the water just like the big girl!" and thereafter excitedly ran into the water. Being somewhat wary of the water, she had not previously evinced this skill. Because Mica expressed her intention before she actually ran into the water, this example illustrates how complex comparative and self-referential mappings can function as intentional guides for future overt action.

Self-representations and intentions become more sophisticated and planful with the emergence of *representational systems* at around 6-7 years of age in contexts that support their production. Using representational systems, children can coordinate the relationship between at least two representational mappings. For example, comparing self to others, a child might wish to purchase a particular item (e.g., computer game, baseball glove) in order to be like valued playmates. Using representational systems, a child can coordinate this representational mapping with a concrete plan to obtain the object (e.g., perform extra chores to earn money in order to purchase the glove). The structure of this planful and concrete self-related intention is depicted in Step Rp3 in Table 5.1.

The next broad tier of skill development emerges around 10-11 years of age with the capacity to coordinate at least two representational systems into a *single abstraction* in high-support contexts. Using single abstractions, an adolescent can construct generalized and intangible goal-related representations (Step Rp4/Ab1). For example, an adolescent can construct an abstract goal-related representation of self by abstracting across what is common to two representational systems concerning self-related intention-outcome relations. For example, using single abstractions, a young adolescent might coordinate a concrete representational system related to studying hard in order to do well and please his teacher in an English class with another such system to work hard in order to get a high grade on a physics test. Generalizing across these concrete systems, an adolescent can construct an identity-related abstraction of the self as a *competent student*.[1] At the level of single abstractions, the adolescent's attempt to identify himself as a competent student would function as a higher-order goal or intention that would drive the instantiation of lower-level intention-outcome systems that define the concrete characteristics of a competent student (e.g., studying and performing well in an English and/or physics class).

With development, individuals can construct increasingly sophisticated self-intentions as they gain the capacity to coordinate abstractions into abstract mappings (Step Ab2) and abstract systems (Step Ab3). For example, beginning around ages 14-16, in high-support contexts, individuals can coordinate relations between two abstractions. For example, an adolescent can coordinate a generalized desire to be a *skilled athlete* with a competing goal to be a *competent student*. (Similar coordinations may occur later in life as individuals attempt to develop ways to coordinate their *careers* and their *family lives.*) To coordinate both of these generalized identities successfully, an adolescent might develop the goal of budgeting her time in order to realize the concrete intentions that subordinate each abstract identity (e.g., studying different texts in different ways to earn high grades in English and physics, working out with weights and running to develop different skills in field hockey and track). Beginning around 18-21 years, at the level of abstract systems, an individual can coordinate two such mappings into a still higher-order intentional system. For example, to plan out how one might simultaneously develop one's identity as both an athlete and a scholar, one might coordinate two related abstract aspects of being a skilled athlete with two related aspects of being a competent student. For example, in an attempt to live a full life, a young adult might wish to develop *aggressiveness* in different sports in order to gain *social recognition* as a skilled athlete, but devote time and effort to *meeting high academic standards* in order to prepare for *different possible careers*. Alternatively, an adult might work to develop an abstract plan to coordinate different abstract aspects of career (being successful in teaching and scholarship) with different aspects of family life (spending time with his spouse, nurturing his children).

Implications of a Skill Analysis of the Development of Intentionality

The foregoing developmental analysis has important implications for how we might address important problems in our attempts to understand the concept of intentional action, including issues related to divergent uses of the concept of intentionality and the roles of representation, social context, conscious awareness, and affect in intentional action.

The Roles of Thoughtfulness, Deliberation, and Planning in Intentional Action

It is often assumed that an action is intentional when it is guided by an internal representation of a desired event. In this sense, intentional activity is seen as a type of deliberation, planning, or "thinking before acting." Philosophers, for example, speak of the problem of "pure intention"—that is, the idea that it is possible to intend to do something without actually doing it (Davidson, 1980). Further, laypersons and scholars alike often speak as if actions are necessarily preceded by preplanned thoughts and intentions. From this view, intending would be seen as consisting of processes that are separate from action and that occur prior to it—the result of a cognitive process that exists behind action and directs it from within. However, it is not necessary to invoke a separate cognitive sphere to explain intentional action or even acts of "pure intending." According to dynamic skill theory, deliberation, planning, and representing are all skills that build upon and develop through the hierarchical coordination of lower-order component actions to form higher-order actions, representations, and abstractions (Mascolo & Fischer, in press). As such, representations build on actions, not vice versa. Once children gain the capacity to represent events independent of their on-line occurrence, they can use representations as guides to action. Further, to say that all action requires an intentional plan would imply an infinite regress, as to explain a thought or intention prior to any given action, one would need yet another intention, and then another to explain that intention, and so forth. Dynamic skill theory avoids these problems by making representation dependent upon action in ontogenesis, and not vice versa.

The Role of Social Context in the Production of Intentional Activity

A commonly used example of intentional action involves the simple act of lifting one's finger. One says, "I am going to lift my finger," and then does so. This idealized example gives the impression that intentional acts originate within individuals who consciously represent actions prior to their execution. However, most goal-directed and even intentional activity is neither autonomous nor reflective. Intentional activity takes place within social contexts that exert direct effects on ongoing behavior. From the standpoint of skill theory, any skill or intentional action is under the joint control of individual and context. For example, consider the finding that

2-month-old infants are capable of controlling simple intention-outcome relations (Step Rf2 in Table 5.1). We suggest that the operant procedures (Lewis et al., 1990; Watson & Ramey, 1972) used to promote such actions function as high-support contexts that precipitate and structure the emergence of such intentional acts. Such procedures target quite simple action elements and, through direct feedback, support the infant's coordination of action elements into means-end relations. In the absence of such support, infants otherwise capable of producing reflex mappings will not spontaneously organize them into intentional relations.

Such high levels of support are similar to the continuous flow of information that occurs between infants and adults during face-to-face communication. In general, face-to-face interaction occurs through continuous process communication in which both partners are active and continuously adjust their actions, goals, and intentions to the ongoing intentions and actions of the other (Fogel, 1993). In so doing, each partner's intentions and actions become a part of the very process that directs the other's behavior (Fischer et al., 1993). As a result, social interaction provides a high-support context that scaffolds and spurs optimal-level intentional behavior in social partners (Kaye, 1982; Rogoff, 1993). It is in these terms that we interpret assertions that reciprocal exchanges in gaze, facial expression, and vocalization between parents and infants constitute evidence of intentional behavior in young infants (Trevarthen, 1978, 1979, 1993; Vedeler, 1994; Zeedyk, 1996). Like the theorists who make these assertions, we agree that young infants are active and responsive social partners who are capable of intentional behavior in some contexts. However, in analyzing infant intentionality, there is a need to specify the limited and shifting nature of the particular intention-outcome relations that young infants are capable of controlling, as well as the specific interpersonal relations that give form to such actions. In this way, interpersonal exchanges function as high-support contexts that activate, scaffold, and support an infant's coordination of primitive intention-outcome relations.

The Question of Nonconscious Intentional Action

What is the role of conscious awareness in intentional activity? Is it possible for intentional action to proceed without awareness? If we define intentional activity as *performing an act on purpose,* then it follows that an individual must be aware of the purpose or anticipated outcome of an action in order for the action to be considered intentional. According to skill theory, persons build higher-order skills through the hierarchical coordination of lower-level systems of action. With development, subordinate control structures and action patterns become increasingly automatized and nonconscious. As such, at any given time, only the most immediately adaptive level of an ongoing skill hierarchy is conscious. Thus, within an active skill hierarchy, an action may be regarded as *goal directed* but not *intentional* if the goal that guides the action is not in the individual's mind during or preceding the act's production (Bargh, 1990). For example, during an automobile trip, a passenger expressed his amusement at the driver, one of the authors, who kept lifting his hand from the steering wheel every few minutes for no apparent reason. Surprised to learn that he was doing this, the driver began to attend to the movements of his hand. It soon became clear that every few minutes, the driver lifted his hand in order to look at the speedometer. The driver's hand lifting was clearly goal directed, but it was not directly intentional in the sense that he did not have the local goal state in mind when he performed the action.

The Role of Affect in Goal-Directed Behavior

Intentional behavior is activity that involves agentive control by individuals. Controlled behavior is often defined in contrast to affective or emotional behavior, which is often seen as uncontrolled or even disruptive. However, recent scholarship has underscored the organizing role of emotion in virtually all behavior. In asserting the interdependence of cognition and affect, recent scholarship implicates affect in the organization of virtually all behavior, including processes generally regarded as controlled, cognitive, and intentional (Fischer, Shaver, & Carnochan, 1990; Griffin & Mascolo, 1998; Kosslyn & Koenig, 1995). For example, recent theorists have proposed systems models of emotion that emphasize the dynamic interplay between affect and cognition (Fogel et al., 1992; Lewis & Douglas, 1998; Lewis, Sullivan, & Michalson, 1984; Mascolo, Harkins, & Harakal, in press). These theorists maintain that cognitive, affective, and motivational processes mutually regulate one another in the production of any given behavior. For example, Mascolo and Harkins (1998) suggest that affective processes often begin with the individual's motive-relevant appraisals of the relations between events and his or her goals, motives, and concerns (Frijda, 1986). Appraisals function to monitor all classes of event-related input and often proceed without conscious awareness. Affective reactions are generated when appraisals detect events that have implications for the person's goals, motives, and concerns. Once generated, affect sends continuous feedback that alerts and orients the individual to the importance of the very events that are under appraisal. In this way, appraisal and affect regulate each other (Brown & Kozak, 1998; Lewis, 1996; Lewis & Douglas, 1998; Mascolo & Harkins, 1998).

For example, under routine circumstances, individuals are often unaware of their actions while driving an automobile. However, an appraisal that a child has run into the path of one's car produces affect that not only selects this event for conscious attention but also orients one's actions accordingly. The organizing functions of affect, however, are not restricted to such dramatic events. Affect also alerts individuals to the appraised significance of everyday events. Affect and feeling play important roles in the selection of everyday goals, actions, and decisions, whether those behaviors include decisions about what movie to see, whether to avoid a phone call, what car to buy, or what to make for dinner (Brown & Kozak, 1998). Thus goal-directed activity is not simply a cognitive affair. Behavior is goal directed because certain outcomes are *desired* by the organism (Bargh, 1990; Lewis, 1990) and *selected* by affect (Brown & Kozak, 1998). By alerting individuals to the relevance of actions and events for desires and motives, affect plays an important role in the selection and organization of goal-directed and intentional behavior.

THE DYNAMIC CO-CONSTRUCTION AND DEPLOYMENT OF INTENTIONAL SELF-SYSTEMS AMONG ADULTS

Skills function as hierarchical control systems (Carver & Scheier, 1981) through which individuals regulate action, thought, and feeling. As control systems, skills are hierarchically organized, with higher-level structures (e.g., abstractions) regulating lower-level control structures (e.g., representations, overt sensorimotor activity) within given contexts. Thus, as individuals construct higher-order representations of self, co-constructed representations and images of self can function as superordinate reference standards that participate in the coregulation of action in social contexts. To illustrate the co-construction of novel self-representations and the skilled performances that instantiate them, we turn to an analysis of the microgenesis of higher-order self-representations as they develop among adults in psychotherapy (Mascolo, Craig-Bray, & Neimeyer, 1997).

Qualitative transformations in self-representation as a result of the construction of new, higher-order intentions can be illustrated by the (actual) case of Rick and Leah, who sought therapy at Leah's insistence after 19 years of marriage.[2] The six sessions of biweekly marital therapy that resulted provided a context for significant self-development for both partners, although for our purposes here, we will focus primarily on the elaboration of a substantially new self-representation on the part of Rick, who was the focus of Leah's initial complaints. Indeed, her dissatisfaction with their relationship had grown to the point of her quite seriously threatening divorce despite their long history and joint parenting of two children, ages 12 and 14. Leah's frustration and hopelessness, which reflected her appraisal of the discrepancy between her superordinate goal of maintaining a "close relationship" and her perception of the status of her marriage, thus provided the instigating affective context for change efforts on the part of both partners.

Rick opened the first session with a series of humorous diversions, prompting Leah to summarize their problem succinctly: Rick, she claimed, was "easy to get along with," but also very "controlling." Rick retorted tersely that "somebody had to make decisions in the house," triggering a discussion of their "19-year cycle" of failed attempts to find a more mutually satisfying way of being together. A litany of mutual complaints ensued, centering on Rick's near-total control of family finances and his "perfectionism" about housework, counterbalanced by Leah's "misman-agement" of money and her "sloppiness" about taking care of their mutual possessions. A particularly clear example of this dynamic was provided by their purchase of a used motor home the previous summer. Not only had Rick exercised repeated "veto power" over their consideration of several available vehicles, but he also dictatorially forbade the children and Leah to spend time in the motor home, out of an attempt to "protect his investment." This led to repeated arguments, both during the months of Rick's fastidious repair work on the vehicle and during the weeks of travel that followed. Each spouse, however, made some concessions to the other's outlook, with Rick acknowledging his "pickiness" and Leah owning her "clumsiness" in taking care of mobile home and house alike.

Figure 5.1 depicts a series of interpersonal skill diagrams that describe four coregulated moments in the therapeutic process (Mascolo, 1998; Mascolo & Harkins, 1998; Mascolo et al., in press). Drawing upon dynamic skill theory (Fischer, 1980; Fischer & Granott, 1995), inter-

personal skill diagrams not only provide representations of the structure
of an individual's skills and control structures as they operate within
specified contexts, they also provide representations of how the control
over each partner's actions, thoughts, and feelings is distributed (and thus
coregulated) between and among partners within interpersonal interactions. Thus each interpersonal skill diagram represents not only the
emergent structure of Rick's self-representations with the context specified,
but also the dynamic structure of the interpersonal interactions themselves.
Diagram I in Figure 5.1 provides a representation of the conflictual state
between Rick's and Leah's self-representations when they entered into
therapy. Rick's abstract, multileveled self-representation as "household
controller" regulated the execution of lower-level representational and
sensorimotor skills consistent with this abstraction (e.g., deciding to purchase a recreational vehicle). Rick's self-representation directly clashed
with Leah's higher-order desire to "have a close relationship," which itself
superordinated a series of embedded representational and sensorimotor
skill structures.

To engage the couple initially, the therapist therefore suggested that both
spouses perform some therapeutic "homework" of not only listing their
long- and short-term goals for their marriage, but also writing down their
"best guesses" as to their partner's goals. The responses to this initial task,
as evaluated at the second session, were revealing. Rick's long-and short-
term goals were specific and financial: to save for retirement and to save
for hunting equipment, respectively. Leah's were more abstract: to find
more "unstructured time" for them as a couple and to seek "financial
counseling." What was more revealing was Leah's ability to predict Rick's
goals, whereas he was clearly less accurate in formulating her long- and
short-term objectives, which he guessed would be house painting and
landscaping, respectively. This discrepancy prompted Leah to "feel very
sad" and fatalistic about the marriage, emotions that the therapist amplified
considerably in an empathic 15-minute "interview" with her conducted
spontaneously in the session in her husband's presence. This attention to
and amplification of affect, common in constructivist therapies (Neimeyer
& Mahoney, 1995; Neimeyer & Stewart, in press), functioned to provide
feedback to Rick regarding his wife's feelings and to orient him to the
affective importance of the issues under discussion (see Mascolo & Harkins, 1998). Leah usually shed tears only in private, and her tears during the
interview had just the intended effect. This therapeutic moment is depicted

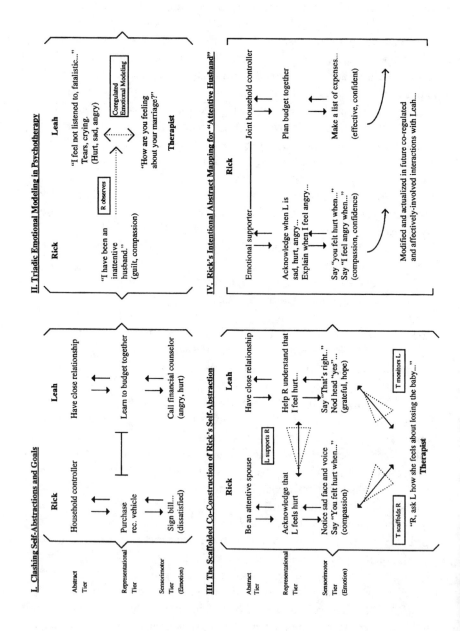

I. Clashing Self-Abstractions and Goals

II. Triadic Emotional Modeling in Psychotherapy

III. The Scaffolded Co-Construction of Rick's Self-Abstraction

IV. Rick's Intentional Abstract Mapping for "Attentive Husband"

Figure 5.1. Representing the Interpersonal and Personal Structures of Four Therapeutic Moments

NOTE: Diagrams I, II, and III in this figure (each in a set of pointed brackets) refer to interpersonal skill structures in actual therapeutic moments; Diagram IV is a skill diagram for a single individual (and so is enclosed in square brackets). The horizontal line with blunted ends in Diagram I indicates an instance of coregulated conflict within the dyad. The bidirectional arrows depicted in Diagram I (as well as in Diagrams III and IV) indicate the operation of hierarchical control structures (TOTE units) among multiple hierarchic tiers (i.e., among abstract, representational, and sensorimotor tiers of functioning). In Diagram II, the dotted bidirectional arrow refers to coregulated communication involving emotional modeling and speech that occurs between Leah and the therapist. The dotted unidirectional line represents Rick's observation of this modeling, in the absence of immediate coregulation. The triangulated bidirectional arrows in Diagram III indicate asymmetrical (scaffolded) coregulation in which one individual (indicated by the wide end of the dotted triangle) is regulating the actions of the other individual to a greater extent than vice versa. (Consequently, the scaffolded individual, indicated by the sharp end of the dotted triangle, is adjusting his or her actions to the scaffolding individual to a greater extent than vice versa.) Diagram IV represents an intentional abstract mapping for Rick. The single horizontal line represents a mapping relationship between the superordinate abstractions "emotional supporter" and "joint household controller." Emotions listed in parentheses indicate affective states that organize action within each immediate or anticipated coregulated exchange for all diagrams.

in Diagram II in Figure 5.1. Supported by feelings of compassion and guilt prompted by the empathic interview between Leah and the therapist, Rick was able to construct an initial representation of his inattentiveness in relation to his wife.

The third session of therapy saw a deepening of the "control" theme, as well as therapeutic scaffolding (Rogoff, 1990) for the emergence of the new skill of empathic listening on Rick's part. Leah began by declaring her need for an "apology" for the years during which Rick "called all the shots" in their relationship, dramatically documenting this complaint with the "very awful experience" of the stillbirth of their last baby nearly 10 years before. Following the loss of this baby, who was wanted by Leah but not by Rick, he had become "hypercontrolling and critical" about petty home repairs, while she grieved alone. Like the "interview" conducted in the previous session, this affectively powerful exchange focused Rick's attention on the extent to which he fell short of the standard of being an "attentive spouse," and his own tearful apology was accompanied by his declared intention to do better.

Seizing the moment, the therapist gently helped Rick articulate his objective to become more the type of husband his wife needed, and then coached him in representing this goal in concrete behaviors in that therapeutic moment. With his wife's trembling expectation as further encouragement, Rick was able to reflect her feelings about the death accurately as a precondition to sharing his own. This therapeutic moment is depicted in Diagram III in Figure 5.1. This jointly regulated and affectively charged intervention functioned to provide social support (by Leah) and direct scaffolding (by the therapist) for the co-construction and optimal performance of a new skill in Rick (giving attention to his wife's emotional life). Significantly, however, these representational and sensorimotor skills of empathic listening and self-disclosure not only emerged in response to high levels of environmental support, but also were realized and elaborated in Rick's developing abstract intention to become a more attentive spouse. In Carver and Scheier's (1990) terms, this new hierarchical self-structure established a set of subordinate control systems with increasingly specific reference standards (e.g., to respond appropriately to his wife's needs, as further instantiated in reflecting her feelings accurately in a given conversational turn). As the session closed, the therapist elicited feedback from Leah on her husband's successful performance of this complex skill, providing further affective support for his self-development.

The remaining three sessions of therapy consolidated the gains achieved in the first three. Further therapeutic scaffolding of new behaviors (e.g., in mutually drafting a budget and a process for deciding on future expenditures) helped Rick to implement concretely his intention to be a more attentive, considerate, and democratic spouse, and by the fifth session, Leah stated that she was "over the hump of bitterness." Noting that Rick's "consistent kindness over the last months" made her "feel comfortable giving back," Leah confessed that she appraised the change as a permanent one "despite herself." Diagram IV in Figure 5.1 provides a representation of Rick's newly developed self-representation as "attentive husband." At the level of abstract mappings, Rick was able to coordinate his abstract intention to provide emotional support to Leah with his abstract intention to share in household decisions. These abstract intentions directed the instantiation of lower-level representational and sensorimotor skills that actualized and modified these plans in future affectively charged, coregulated interchanges with Leah.

The couple and therapist spent the final session reviewing the fairly remarkable and rapid changes instituted by both partners, which had generalized to a host of new areas (collaborative "troubleshooting" of family problems, spontaneous "dates," and even improved sexual intimacy). Both Rick and Leah were surprised by the "mysteriousness" of the change—they were aware only of their intent to change, and could not quite recall how they had accomplished it. In response, the therapist explained that the "mysterious" quality of the change was a predictable result of the selectivity of awareness, as only their highest-level intentions (e.g., to be considerate) were conscious in a given encounter. Once routinized, the subordinate control systems and their associated behaviors (e.g., being sensitive to each other's implied feelings or explicitly sharing their own) became relatively nonconscious, while still subserving the higher-order goal. Moreover, the entire process of change represented a form of continuous process communication (Fogel, 1993) between the partners, during which each inevitably adjusted his or her own actions, goals, and intentions to those of the other. Whereas the therapist exercised some control over this process through supporting and scaffolding new skills on the part of both spouses, he was himself very much a participant in this system, whose actions were jointly controlled by his own intentions and by the affordances of the therapeutic situation itself. Ultimately, the emergence of Rick's new higher-order self-representation as an attentive spouse was one result of this process, a durable personal acquisition that was nonetheless jointly constructed in emotionally significant exchanges with his spouse and therapist.

TOWARD AN INTEGRATIVE ACCOUNT OF SELF AND INTENTIONALITY WITHIN SOCIAL RELATIONSHIPS

The concept of intentionality is central to any meaningful concept of self. Without it, the concept of person becomes reduced to that of a determined object, rather than that of an agent who can exert control over action. Dynamic skill theory provides a set of conceptual and methodological tools for understanding the concept of intentional action, for charting gross and fine-grained changes in its origin and development. Further, skill theory provides a framework for studying the codevelopment of intentionality and self as they are dynamically co-constructed over time in social contexts. As children develop the capacity to become aware of and represent the self in terms of social categories and images, the capacity for intentional action itself becomes transformed. With development, co-constructed and affectively charged representations and abstractions related to the self come to function as higher-order intentions that both shape and are shaped by ongoing interaction.

Thus one might suggest that an intentional agent is one who can act in accordance with "a vision of himself [that he carries] in his mind's eye" (Kincaid, 1996, p. 181). Nonetheless, as Kincaid cautions, individuals cannot be considered autonomous in their agency. We suggest that instead of being seen as bounded and autonomous agents, persons function as embedded and embodied agents. That is, human agents are *embedded* within sociocultural systems that frame the co-constructed "visions of self" that inform intentional action. Further, human actions are *embodied* to the extent that they are actualized in specific bodies and are accompanied by affective experiences that constrain, direct, and organize behavior. In this way, skill theory offers a framework for an integrative analysis of the codevelopment of intentionality, self, and social relations.

NOTES

1. The single abstraction "competent student" differs from what might be called *concrete generalizations* such as "good student," which children are able to construct at earlier levels of development (e.g., using complex representational

systems). Unlike concrete generalizations that require only a capacity to construct generalized categories of concrete characteristics of good students (e.g., "I can read"; "I know my addition tables"), using single abstractions, children are able to represent intangible aspects of academic competence (or some other abstract identity) and link them clearly to concrete instances.

2. All significant details of this case are faithful to the actual therapy, which was performed by the third author. However, we have followed the convention of fictionalizing all potentially identifying information to protect client confidentiality.

REFERENCES

Anscombe, G. E. M. (1959). *Intention*. Oxford: Basil Blackwell.

Bargh, J. A. (1990). Goal ≠ intent: Goal-directed thought and behavior are often unintentional. *Psychological Inquiry, 1*, 248-251.

Bates, E., Camaioni, L., & Volterra, V. (1979). Determining intentionality prior to and at the onset of speech. In E. Ochs & B. B. Schieffelin (Eds.), *Developmental pragmatics*. London: Academic Press.

Bidell, T., & Fischer, K. W. (1996). Between nature and nurture: The role of human agency in the epigenesis of intelligence. In R. J. Sternberg & E. Grigorenko (Eds.), *Intelligence: Heredity and environment* (pp. 193-242). New York: Cambridge University Press.

Brazelton, T. B. (1982). Joint regulation of neonate-parent behavior. In E. Z. Tronick (Ed.), *Social interchange in infancy: Affect, cognition and communication*. Baltimore: University Park Press.

Brown, T., & Kozak, A. (1998). Emotion and the possibility of psychologists entering into heaven. In M. F. Mascolo & S. Griffin (Eds.). *What develops in emotional development?* New York: Plenum.

Butterworth, G., & Hopkins, B. (1988). Hand-mouth coordination in the newborn baby. *British Journal of Developmental Psychology, 6*, 303-314.

Carver, C. S., & Scheier, M. F. (1981). *Attention and self-regulation: A control-theory approach to human behavior.* New York: Springer-Verlag.

Carver, C. S., & Scheier, M. F. (1990). Origins and functions of positive and negative affect: A control process view. *Psychological Review, 97*, 19-35.

Davidson, D. (1980). *Essays on actions and events.* Oxford: Clarendon.

Fischer, K. W. (1980). A theory of cognitive development: The control and construction of hierarchies of skills. *Psychological Review, 87*, 447-531.

Fischer, K. W., & Bidell, T. (1998). Dynamic development of psychological structures in action and thought. In W. Damon (Series Ed.) & R. M. Lerner (Vol. Ed.), *Handbook of child psychology: Vol. 1. Theoretical models of human development* (5th ed.). New York: John Wiley.

Fischer, K. W., Bullock, D. H., Rotenberg, E. J., & Raya, P. (1993). The dynamics of competence: How context contributes directly to skill. In R. Wozniak & K. W. Fischer (Eds.), *Development in context: Acting and thinking in specific environments* (pp. 93-117). Hillsdale, NJ: Lawrence Erlbaum.

Fischer, K. W., & Granott, N. (1995). Beyond one-dimensional change: Parallel, concurrent, socially distributed processes in learning and development. *Human Development, 38,* 302-314.

Fischer, K. W., & Hogan, A. E. (1989). The big picture in infant development: Levels and variations. In J. Lockman & N. Hazan (Eds.), *Action in social context: Perspectives on early development* (pp. 275-305). New York: Plenum.

Fischer, K. W., & Kenny, S. L. (1986). The environmental conditions for discontinuities in the development of abstractions. In R. Mines & K. Kitchener (Eds.), *Adult cognitive development: Methods and models* (pp. 57-75). New York: Praeger.

Fischer, K. W., Shaver, P. R., & Carnochan, P. (1990). How emotions develop and how they organize development. *Cognition and Emotion, 4,* 81-128.

Fogel, A. (1993). *Development through relationships: Origins of communication, self and culture.* Chicago: University of Chicago Press.

Fogel, A., Nwokah, E., Dedo, J. Y., Messinger, D., Dickson, K. L., Matusov, E., & Holt, S. A. (1992). Social process theory of emotion: A dynamic systems perspective. *Social Development, 1,* 122-142.

Frijda, N. H. (1986). *The emotions.* New York: Cambridge University Press.

Frye, D. (1990). The origins of intention in infancy. In D. Frye & C. Moore (Eds.), *Children's theories of mind: Mental states and social understanding.* Hillsdale, NJ: Lawrence Erlbaum.

Griffin, S., & Mascolo, M. F. (1998). The nature, development and functions of emotions. In M. F. Mascolo & S. Griffin (Eds.), *What develops in emotional development?* (pp. 3-27). New York: Plenum.

Harding, C. G. (1982). Development of the intention to communicate. *Human Development, 25,* 140-151.

Kaye, K. (1982). *The mental and social life of babies: How parents create persons.* London: Harvester.

Kincaid, J. (1996). *The autobiography of my mother.* New York: Farrar, Straus & Giroux.

Kitchener, K. S., Lynch, C. L., Fischer, K. W., & Wood, P. K. (1993). Developmental range of reflective judgment: The effect of contextual support and practice on developmental stage. *Developmental Psychology, 29,* 893-906.

Kosslyn, S. M., & Koenig, O. (1995). *Wet minds: The new cognitive neuroscience.* New York: Free Press.

Kruper, J. C., & Uzgiris, I. C. (1987). Fathers' and mothers' speech to young infants. *Journal of Psycholinguistic Research, 16,* 597-614.

Lewis, M. (1990). The development of intentionality and the role of consciousness. *Psychological Inquiry, 1,* 231-247.

Lewis, M., Alessandri, S., & Sullivan, M. W. (1990). Expectancy, loss of control and anger in young infants. *Developmental Psychology, 26,* 745-751.

Lewis, M., Sullivan, M. W., & Michalson, L. (1984). The cognitive-emotional fugue. In C. E. Izard, J. Kagan, & R. B. Zajonc (Eds.), *Emotions, cognition and behavior* (pp. 264-288). Cambridge: Cambridge University Press.

Lewis, M. D. (1996). Self-organising cognitive appraisals. *Cognition and Emotion*, *10*, 1-25.

Lewis, M. D., & Douglas, L. (1998). A dynamic systems approach to cognitive-emotion interactions in development. In M. F. Mascolo, & S. Griffin (Eds.). *What develops in emotional development?* (pp. 159-188). New York: Plenum.

Lock, A. (1980). *The guided reinvention of language.* London: Academic Press.

Mascolo, M. F. (1998). *Representing the dynamic structure of joint action, thought and feeling.* Unpublished manuscript.

Mascolo, M. F., Craig-Bray, L., & Neimeyer, R. A. (1997). The construction of meaning and action in development and psychotherapy: An epigenetic systems perspective. In G. J. Neimeyer & R. A. Neimeyer (Eds.), *Advances in personal construct psychology* (Vol. 4, pp. 3-37). Greenwich, CT: JAI.

Mascolo, M. F., & Fischer, K. W. (1998). The development of self through the coordination of component systems. In M. Ferrari & R. J. Sternberg (Eds.), *Self-awareness: Its nature and development* (pp. 332-384). New York: Guilford.

Mascolo, M. F., & Fischer, K. W. (in press). The development of representation as the coordination of component systems of action. In I. Sigel (Ed.), *Theoretical perspectives on the concept of representation.* Hillsdale, NJ: Lawrence Erlbaum.

Mascolo, M. F., & Harkins, D. (1998). Toward a component systems model of emotional development. In M. F. Mascolo & S. Griffin (Eds.), *What develops in emotional development?* (pp. 189-217). New York: Plenum.

Mascolo, M. F., Harkins, D., & Harakal, T. (in press). The dynamic construction of emotion: Varieties in anger. In M. D. Lewis & I. Grinka (Eds.), *Emotion, self-organization and development.* New York: Cambridge University Press.

Mascolo, M. F., Pollack, R., & Fischer, K. W. (1997). Keeping the constructor in development: An epigenetic systems approach. *Journal of Constructivist Psychology*, *10*, 25-49.

Merleau-Ponty, M. (1963). *The structure of behavior* (A. L. Fisher, Trans.). Boston: Beacon. (Original work published 1942)

Miller, G. A., Galanter, E., & Pribram, K. H. (1960). *Plans and the structure of behavior.* New York: Holt, Rinehart & Winston.

Murray, L., & Trevarthen, C. (1986). The infant's role in mother-infant communications. *Journal of Child Language, 13*, 15-29.

Neimeyer, R. A., & Mahoney, M. (1995). *Constructivism in psychotherapy.* Washington, DC: American Psychological Association.

Neimeyer, R. A., & Stewart, A. E. (in press). Constructivist and narrative psychotherapies. In C. R. Snyder & R. E. Ingram (Eds.), *Handbook of psychotherapy.* New York: John Wiley.

Newson, J. (1979). Intentional behavior in the young infant. In D. Shaffer & J. Dunn (Eds.), *The first year of life: Psychological and medical implications of early experience.* Chichester: John Wiley.

Olson, D. R. (1992). The development of representations: The origins of mental life. *Canadian Psychology, 34*, 293-306.

Piaget, J. (1963). *The origins of intelligence in children.* New York: W. W. Norton. (Original work published 1952)

Powers, W. T. (1973). *Behavior: The control of perception.* Chicago: Aldine.

Rogoff, B. (1990). *Apprenticeship in thinking.* New York: Oxford University Press.

Rogoff, B. (1993). Children's guided participation and participatory appropriation in sociocultural activity. In R. Wozniak & K. W. Fischer (Eds.), *Development in context: Acting and thinking in specific learning environments* (pp. 121-154). Hillsdale, NJ: Lawrence Erlbaum.

Schaffer, H. R. (1984). *The child's entry into a social world.* London: Academic Press.

Snow, C. E. (1977). The development of conversation between mothers and babies. *Journal of Child Language, 4,* 1-22.

Stern, C. (1985). *The interpersonal world of the infant.* New York: Basic Books.

Trevarthen, C. (1978). Modes of perceiving and modes of action. In H. L. Pick, Jr., & E. Saltzman (Eds.), *Modes of perceiving and processing information* (pp. 99-136). Cambridge: Cambridge University Press.

Trevarthen, C. (1979). Communication and cooperation in early infancy: A description of primary intersubjectivity. In M. Bullowa (Ed.), *Before speech: The beginning of interpersonal communication.* Cambridge: Cambridge University Press.

Trevarthen, C. (1993). The functions of motions in early infant communication and development. In J. Nadel & L. Camaioni (Eds.), *New perspectives in early communication development.* London: Routledge.

Trevarthen, C., & Hubley, P. (1978). Secondary intersubjectivity: Confidence, confiding, and acts of meaning in the first year. In A. Lock (Ed.), *Action, gesture, and symbol: The emergence of language.* New York: Academic Press.

Tronick, E. Z. (1981). Infant communication intent: The infant's reference to social interaction. In M. Stark (Ed.), *Language behavior in infancy and early childhood.* New York: Elsevier.

Uzgiris, I. C. (1990). Commentary on Lewis: How does intentional action develop? *Psychological Inquiry, 1,* 269-271.

Vedeler, D. (1991). Infant intentionality as object directedness: An alternative to representationalism. *Journal for the Theory of Social Behavior, 21,* 431-448.

Vedeler, D. (1994). Infant intentionality as object directedness: A method for observation. *Scandinavian Journal of Psychology, 35,* 343-366.

Vygotsky, L. S. (1978). *Mind in society: The development of higher psychological processes* (M. Cole, V. John-Steiner, S. Scribner, & E. Souberman, Eds.). Cambridge, MA: Harvard University Press.

Vygotsky, L. S. (1981). The genesis of higher mental functions. In J. V. Wertsch (Ed.), *The concept of activity in Soviet psychology* (pp. 144-188). Armonk, NY: M. E. Sharpe.

Watson, J. S., & Ramey, C. T. (1972). Reactions to response-contingent stimulation in early infancy. *Merrill-Palmer Quarterly, 18,* 219-227.

Zeedyk, M. S. (1996). Developmental accounts of intentionality: Toward integration. *Developmental Review, 16,* 416-461.

Part II

DESIGNING PERSONAL DEVELOPMENT

Goals, Plans, and Future Selves

6

THE PURSUIT OF PERSONAL GOALS

A Motivational Approach to Well-Being and Life Adjustment

Joachim C. Brunstein
Oliver C. Schultheiss
Günter W. Maier

Among personality researchers and social psychologists, there has been a resurgence of interest in the purposive, goal-seeking quality of human behavior in recent years (see Gollwitzer & Bargh, 1996; Martin & Tesser, 1996; Pervin, 1989). At the same time, as this volume clearly shows, developmental psychologists have started to focus on the course of human development from an action perspective, highlighting the importance of motivational concerns and life plans as they emerge from and shape the nature of person-environment transactions over the life span (see Brandtstädter, 1998). Inherent in this reawakened interest in the intentionality of human behavior is the notion that beyond the pressure of internal drives and environmental incentives, individuals are propelled by their capacity to determine their own activities through the setting and pursuit of future-oriented goals.

Our purpose in this chapter is to analyze how the pursuit of personal goals influences people's well-being and life adjustment during adulthood. We first focus on research suggesting that goal setting and striving play a central role in an individual's emotional life. Specifically, we argue that to achieve high levels of well-being, it is important for an individual to have both a strong sense of commitment to valued goals and a life situation that provides favorable conditions for the attainment of these goals. The core idea underlying this consideration is that high investments in the pursuit of personal goals do not necessarily produce happiness and elation. Rather, to achieve well-being and avoid distress, individuals also require access to social and environmental resources that they can use to materialize their commitments. To concretize this position, we consider the pursuit of personal goals in various social settings (e.g., in close relationships) and discuss the importance of receiving social support from others in the goal-achievement process. We furthermore propose that progress in the achievement of personal goals constitutes a necessary but not sufficient condition for high emotional well-being. Rather, we suggest that it is only when personal goals contribute to the satisfaction of basic motives that goal progress promotes experiences of positive well-being.

After outlining the importance of goals in the development and maintenance of subjective well-being and mental health, we consider the role of establishing meaningful goals in individuals' efforts to shape the course of their own development. In doing so, we take the position that goal seeking infuses the course of adult development with a sense of future orientation and self-directedness. We furthermore suggest that the construal of organized patterns of long- and short-term goals is fundamental for the individual's achievement of developmental continuity in life as well as the creation of variability and change over the life course. We also address alterations in goal priorities and goal orientations across the life span and finally propose that a flexible balance between establishing personally fulfilling goals and disengaging from obsolete concerns lies at the heart of the successful negotiation of life transitions. Before we consider these issues in more detail, however, we briefly summarize the basic premises underlying the concept of personal goals.

PERSONAL GOALS

Personal goals can be conceived of as future-oriented representations of what individuals are striving for in their current life situations and what they try to attain or avoid in various life domains (Brunstein, Dangelmayer, & Schultheiss, 1996; Brunstein & Maier, 1996). During the past two decades, the concept of personal goals has been described by different theorists in terms of different cognitive-motivational units of analysis, such as "current concerns" (Klinger, 1977), "personal projects" (Little, 1983), "personal strivings" (Emmons, 1986), and (individualized) "life tasks" (Cantor & Kihlstrom, 1987). These concepts have in common that people are seen as forward-looking, self-motivated beings who are capable of determining their own destinies by construing personally meaningful objectives and directing their activities toward the attainment of those objectives.

Personal-goal setting might best be understood in terms of a creative process that includes both a person's search for desired ends and goals and the construction of behavioral plans that serve as a means to the end of goal accomplishment (Nuttin, 1984). Both internal and external factors are involved in the construal of personal goals. In order to set goals that are both realistic and fulfilling, a person has to weigh his or her own values, interests, and needs against the tasks, demands, and affordances inherent in his or her sociocultural environment (Cantor, 1994). When people set their own goals, they elaborate the incentives provided by such motivational sources and personalize them in accordance with preexisting life plans. Thus goal setting is not just a product of internal and external constraints, but also implies an act of choice and self-commitment (Emmons & Kaiser, 1996).

Working on a set of self-generated goals infuses a person's activities in daily life with structure and personal meaning (Klinger, 1977). People frequently identify themselves with the goals they set and pursue (Nuttin, 1984) and invest considerable time and energy in the achievement of their commitments (Brunstein & Gollwitzer, 1996; Novacek & Lazarus, 1990). They translate their goals into behavioral plans and associated instrumental activities, selectively choose environments that facilitate goal enactment, monitor progress toward goal achievement, and modify their strategies and plans in response to goal-relevant feedback information. In this way, people are capable of regulating their own behavior in relationship to valued future states (Ford, 1987).

Individuals are frequently involved in a multitude of goals varying widely in terms of the level of generality of the intentions involved and the time range covered by different pursuits. However, there is a widespread belief among goal theorists that goals are organized in a hierarchical system ranging from overarching life goals to specific behavioral intentions (see Carver & Scheier, 1990). Situated right in the middle of this hypothetical system, personal goals occupy an intermediate position (Cantor & Zirkel, 1990). They can be concretized and broken down into patterned sequences of day-to-day activities, but can also be generalized and substantiated with reference to higher-order themes and meanings of life (Little, 1989; McGregor & Little, 1998).

Although people are not supposed to reflect on their goals continuously, but rather to focus their attention on the execution of goal-directed plans of action, it is assumed that personal goals are accessible to conscious awareness and can therefore be inferred from an individual's self-report. A mixed idiographic-nomothetic assessment technique is typically used to assess personal goals (see Klinger, Barta, & Maxeiner, 1981). Respondents are asked to describe the strivings, projects, and objectives they currently pursue and want to achieve in the future. Such self-reports of goals that persons feel involved in are inherently idiosyncratic. However, personal goals can also be assessed along a set of nomothetic variables, such as formal (e.g., goal importance or difficulty) and content-related goal attributes (e.g., motivational themes reflected in self-reported goals). In this way, interindividual differences in properties of personal goals are examined, on the basis of which assumptions about the relationship to other variables, such as individuals' subjective well-being, can be studied.

GOAL COMMITMENT AND GOAL ATTAINABILITY: THE BENEFITS AND COSTS OF GOAL STRIVING

During the past decade, several researchers have emphasized the importance of people's possessing a clear sense of goal directedness to achieve high levels of happiness and satisfaction with life (for a review, see Emmons, 1996). Active involvement in the pursuit of valued goals may promote individuals' well-being and mental health in at least the following three ways: First, personal-goal setting stimulates individuals to engage in a host of cognitive, interpersonal, and physical activities aimed at the achievement of desired objectives (Cross & Markus, 1991; Harlow & Cantor, 1996;

Holahan, 1988). Second, striving for personal goals gives structure to a person's life and infuses his or her activities with personal meaning (Baumeister, 1991; Erikson, Erikson, & Kivnick, 1986; Lazarus & De-Longis, 1983). Third, goals provide individuals with the cornerstones necessary for successful and self-determined development (Brandtstädter, 1984; Bühler & Massarik, 1968). In keeping with these arguments, several investigators have found that individuals who feel personally involved in the pursuit of goals indicate higher psychological well-being and display better health than do individuals who lack a sense of goal directedness in their lives (e.g., Emmons, 1986; Holahan, 1988; Robbins, Lee, & Wan, 1994; Wessman & Ricks, 1966).

However, striving for personal goals may also produce detrimental effects on individuals' well-being. For instance, Klinger (1977) points out that people typically experience unpleasant moods—and may even lapse into depressive episodes—if their pursuit of valued goals is blocked through hindrances and failures. Michalos (1980), too, posits that individuals who perceive gaps between their aspirations and their achievements tend to feel unhappy and dissatisfied with their lives. These positions imply that to understand the relationship between goal striving and well-being, it is important to take into account not only individuals' sense of involvement in the pursuit of personal goals, but also their appraisals concerning the attainability of personal goals.

Proceeding on this idea, Brunstein (1993) explored the importance of both individuals' commitment to personal goals and their evaluations of the attainability of personal goals as precursors of subjective well-being. The concept of goal commitment, on the one hand, denotes that a person has a strong sense of determination to pursue personal goals, is willing to invest effort in the accomplishment of goals, and feels some urgency about implementing his or her goals immediately. The concept of goal attainability, on the other hand, is used as a summary term specifying the extent to which a person perceives favorable or unfavorable conditions for the attainment of personal goals in his or her current life situation. High goal attainability indicates that a person has enough time and opportunity to work on goals, that he or she perceives the accomplishment of goals to be under his or her personal control, and that the person's goal-directed efforts are reliably assisted by social support from significant others.

To account for the development of change in people's well-being over time, Brunstein (1993) has suggested the following personal-goal model of subjective well-being (see Figure 6.1; information within dotted lines in

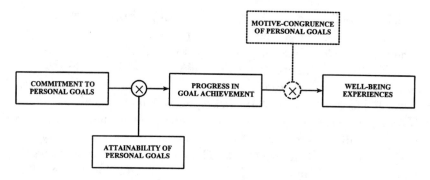

Figure 6.1. Personal-Goal Model of Subjective Well-Being

the figure will be explained below): Goal commitment and goal attainability both constitute distal predictors of well-being. However, each of these two goal variables serves a distinctive function in the prediction of well-being. The strength of goal commitment determines the extent to which well-being experiences depend on the pursuit of personal goals. Yet, although high commitment to personal goals guarantees strong effects of goal striving on subjective well-being, it does not determine the direction of those effects (i.e., whether well-being increases or decreases as a function of goal striving). Rather, the direction of change in subjective well-being depends on the person's appraisal of goal attainability. Favorable conditions, which are associated with a facilitation of goal attainment, are linked to increased well-being. In contrast, unfavorable conditions, which pose a threat to the accomplishment of valued goals, are associated with a decline in well-being. Note, however, that according to the logic underlying this model, experiences of well-being are sensitive to perceptions of goal attainability only to the extent to which individuals feel committed to the pursuit of personal goals.

Moreover, as illustrated in Figure 6.1, progress in goal achievement is assigned an intermediary role in the prediction of well-being. On the one hand, perceived progress toward goals is considered a proximate cause of well-being. Accordingly, well-being emotions and judgments of life satisfaction should largely evolve from an evaluative feedback system that monitors and reflects an individual's status concerning the advancement of his or her goals. On the other hand, high progress is expected to depend on the confluence of high levels of goal commitment with high levels of goal attainability. Accordingly, progress in goal achievement is conceived of as a mediating variable that accounts for the hypothesized effect of the interaction between commitment to and attainability of personal goals on people's subjective well-being.

To test the validity of this model, Brunstein (1993) carried out a semester-long research project with students. Based on a longitudinal design, data were collected at four testing periods. At the beginning of a new term (Time 1), participants were asked to describe their goals for the current semester and to rate them on a number of commitment and attainability scales. At intervals 4 weeks (Time 2), 10 weeks (Time 3), and 12 weeks (Time 4) after they had listed their goals, participants were asked to indicate both their current levels of well-being (i.e., elated and depressed moods as well as judgments of satisfaction with life as a whole) and their estimations of progress toward their goals. As expected, the interaction between goal commitment and goal attainability reliably predicted both progress in goal achievement and changes in subjective well-being during the course of the semester (see Figure 6.2). For students who felt strongly committed to their goals, favorable conditions to attain those goals led to high rates of progress that in turn translated into enhanced well-being. In contrast, poor conditions to attain personal goals were associated with impaired progress and predicted a decline in well-being, particularly among strongly committed students. In comparison, for students who lacked a sense of goal commitment, experiences of well-being were largely insensitive to variations in goal attainability.

Two additional studies lend further support to the model outlined in Figure 6.1. In one study (Brunstein, 1999), retired adults ranging in age from 60 to 80 years old reported their personal goals in five life areas (family, friends, finances, hobbies, health) and then rated their goals according to a number of attributes reflecting their sense of goal commitment and attainability. After age, income, health status, and social contacts with family members and friends were controlled for, high goal attainability was associated with better psychological adjustment, indicated by the predominance of pleasant moods, high life satisfaction, and positive views of aging. Moreover, only for highly committed elders did poor conditions to attain personal goals significantly relate to the prevalence of unpleasant moods, impaired life satisfaction, and negative attitudes toward aging.

In another study, Brunstein, Ganserer, Maier, and Heckhausen (1991) asked women who defined themselves as homemakers and mothers to report their current moods eight times on each of 7 consecutive days immediately after they had listed and rated their current goals and con-

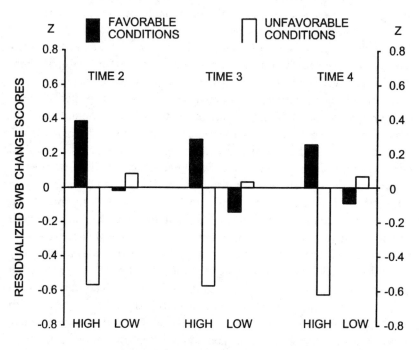

Figure 6.2. Residualized Change in Subjective Well-Being (SWB) Scores from Time 1 to Times 2, 3, and 4 in Subjects With High or Low Levels of Goal Commitment and With Favorable or Unfavorable Conditions to Attain Personal Goals (one *SD* unit above and below the means)

SOURCE: J. C. Brunstein, "Personal Goals and Subjective Well-Being: A Longitudinal Study," *Journal of Personality and Social Psychology, 65* (1993): 1066. Copyright 1993 by the American Psychological Association. Reprinted with permission.

cerns. In this study, ratings of positive and negative affect constituted two independent mood dimensions. Women who felt strongly committed to goals experienced a higher frequency of pleasant moods than did women who lacked a sense of goal commitment. In contrast, unpleasant moods prevailed among women who indicated poor conditions to implement their goals in everyday situations and therefore did not expect that they would be capable of fulfilling their aspirations.

In addition, Brunstein et al. (1991) found that women who experienced unfavorable conditions to work on and attain personal goals reported a greater number of symptoms of depression, as assessed by the Beck Depression Inventory (Beck & Beck, 1972), than did women who estimated their living conditions to be favorable for the attainment of personal goals. Similarly, in an analysis of the personal projects of undergraduates, Lecci, Karoly, Briggs, and Kuhn (1994) found that negative appraisals of goals in terms of low outcome expectancy and control, but high stress and difficulty, were significantly associated with symptoms of depression and anxiety. Röhrle, Hedke, and Leibold (1994) obtained similar results in a study designed to explore depressed patients' appraisals of personal projects and goals. Patients with reactive and unipolar depressions rated their goals as less controllable and more difficult and stressful than did nondepressed controls. Remarkably, in none of the aforementioned studies were high levels of depression significantly associated with a lack of involvement in the pursuit of personal goals. Thus, although depressed individuals do not appear to lack a sense of commitment to goals, they clearly indicate that they do not see a way of accomplishing their goals in their current life situations. Needless to say, although these results are in accord with Brunstein's (1993) predictive model of the effects of goal striving on people's emotional well-being, further research is needed to examine the causal direction underlying the relationship between blocked goals and depressive affect.

In sum, the findings described above advance the position that individuals who commit themselves to goals in the absence of favorable conditions are vulnerable to unpleasant mood states and syndromes of depression. In this situation, disengagement may constitute a healthy response to unduly stressful pursuits that permits individuals to reduce emotional distress and restore a sense of happiness (Klinger, 1975).

PERSONAL GOAL SUPPORT AND SOCIAL LIFE SATISFACTION

Among all goal-attainability variables assessed in Brunstein's (1993) study, support of personal goals by significant others turned out to be the most powerful predictor of students' emotional well-being and satisfaction with life. Similarly, Ruehlman and Wolchik (1988) found that interindividual differences in ratings of social support and hindrances as related to the pursuit of personal projects or goals significantly accounted for interindividual differences in students' experiences of well-being and distress. In a similar vein, Diener and Fujita (1995) report findings suggesting that social resources and networks promote mental health because they help people achieve personal strivings and goals.

Extending these findings, we have started to investigate the importance of goal-related social support in different types of interpersonal settings (Brunstein et al., 1996; Maier, 1996). In two studies, Brunstein et al. explored the role of receiving and giving goal support within the context of close relationships. These studies were carried out to examine how receiving and giving goal support from and to one's intimate partner relates to partners' relationship moods and dyadic adjustment. The principle guiding this research was that for individuals involved in highly interdependent relationships, perceptions of one's partner's supportive versus undermining actions exert a great deal of influence on the enactment of goals and thereby on the development of relationship satisfaction. In Study 1, students engaged in young relationships were asked to list two types of goals: goals pursued within a close relationship (*relationship goals*) and goals pursued outside a close relationship (*individual goals*). After participants had listed their goals, they were asked to rate each goal according to how much support (e.g., tangible assistance, appreciation, and encouragement) they received from their partners in the pursuit of that goal. Estimations of received support for relationship goals and estimations of received support for individual goals represented two independent goal dimensions. Each of these two dimensions uniquely contributed to the prediction of short-term changes in students' relationship moods over 1 month. Participants felt most satisfied with their relationships if they perceived their partners as promoting *both* the achievement of relationship goals and the achievement of individual goals. Moreover, for both types of goals, it was found that goal support received from partner was positively related to the enactment of goals. Mediational analyses revealed that variations in goal enactment largely accounted for the positive effect of personal-goal support on students' relationship satisfaction. These findings illustrate that even for individuals engaged in young, nonmarital relationships, receiving goal support from partners is crucial to both the implementation of goals and the development of relationship satisfaction.

Middle-aged partners married for many years participated in a second study (Brunstein et al., 1996, Study 2). In this investigation, respondents were asked to describe four types of goals: (a) their own most important relationship goal, (b) their own most important individual goal, (c) the putatively most important relationship goal of their partner, and (d) the putatively most important individual goal of their partner. Spousal support of relationship goals significantly contributed to husbands' and wives' marital satisfaction as assessed by the Dyadic Adjustment Scale (Spanier, 1976). Moreover, marital support of individual goals was a unique predictor of marital satisfaction for men, whereas interpersonal goal conflict—a dimension independent of marital goal support—was significantly associated with impaired satisfaction with marriage for women. Participants high in marital satisfaction also reported that they gave a lot of support to the goals they assumed their spouses to be pursuing. However, it was only among participants who correctly identified their spouses' most important goals that ratings of giving goal support predicted the marital satisfaction of their spouses. In contrast, for participants who were not able to identify their spouses' most important goals, ratings of giving goal support were independent of their spouses' satisfaction with marriage. These findings indicate that to promote the marital satisfaction of one's partner, it is important both that one is aware of the partner's particular goals and that one supports him or her in the pursuit of those goals.

Maier (1996) analyzed the role of personal-goal support within the context of organizational settings. Specifically, he investigated the importance for newcomers of receiving goal-related social support from coworkers and supervisors in newcomers' early career adjustment. Six months after they had entered a large organization, newcomers were asked to specify their personal career goals and to report how much support they received from their coworkers and supervisors in the pursuit of those goals. Among newcomers who felt personally committed to their career goals, those who received high goal support made substantial progress toward goal achievement and displayed a significant increase in job satisfaction 9 months after they had reported their goals. Conversely, a lack of goal-related social support at the workplace predicted a marked decline in job satisfaction, particularly among those newcomers who felt strongly determined to accomplish their career goals.

The aforementioned findings suggest that receiving goal support from significant others improves the attainability of personal goals and thereby promotes experiences of satisfaction within specific social settings. Notably, however, Harlow and Cantor (1994) report evidence suggesting that seeking goal support from others may occasionally produce detrimental effects on individuals' social life satisfaction. In a sample of students, Harlow and Cantor analyzed undesired side effects of seeking social reassurance from friends in response to negative academic events (e.g., doing badly on an exam). Students who were highly concerned with such setbacks and difficulties ("outcome-focused" students, in Harlow & Cantor's terminology) and addressed them in the company of friends felt increasingly dissatisfied with their social lives and did not further enjoy activities in interpersonal situations. According to Harlow and Cantor, these results indicate that although seeking reassurance from friends may consolidate the pursuit of stressful academic goals, a spillover of such concerns to the domain of interpersonal relationships may dramatically reduce individuals' social life satisfaction. Cantor and Blanton (1996) recently reported that there was another group of "mood-instrumental" students who employed a different strategy of using social support in response to academic difficulties: Unlike outcome-focused students, mood-instrumental students increased their engagement in enjoyable social activities and used the positive affect gained from socializing and leisure activities as a means of improving their mood for mastering academic challenges. These findings illustrate that in order to understand the influence of goal-related social support on people's social life satisfaction, it is necessary to take into account not only the social resources individuals may use to advance in the pursuit of their goals but also the different types of help-seeking strategies they choose when they try to overcome goal obstacles.

GOAL STRIVING AND NEED SATISFACTION

In a series of recent studies, we attempted to elaborate in greater detail how and why the pursuit and advancement of goals influences people's emotional well-being (Brunstein, Lautenschlager, Nawroth, Pöhlmann, & Schultheiss, 1995; Brunstein, Schultheiss, & Grässmann, 1998). In doing so, we speculated that striving for self-generated *explicit* goals may serve the function of satisfying *implicit* motives, which are generally assumed to be less accessible to a person's conscious awareness. Drawing on McClelland's (1985) work on motive dispositions, we conceived of motives as interindividual difference variables that determine the extent to which a person will get satisfaction from the pursuit and accomplishment of self-set goals. Thus, to return to and complete the description of the personal-goal model of well-being displayed in Figure 6.1, we assumed that the thematic congruence between motive dispositions and personal goals would play a central role in the prediction of people's affective experiences of well-being.

To examine this proposition, Brunstein et al. (1995) assessed both students' motive dispositions and their personal goals within two different striving areas: striving for *agency* (i.e., achievement and power) and striving for *communion* (i.e., affiliation and intimacy). Students' agentic and communal motives were assessed with a picture-story test akin to Murray's (1943) Thematic Apperception Test (TAT). Correspondingly, students' self-reported goals were content coded according to the extent to which they reflected agentic and communal concerns. Notably, and similar to findings reported by King (1995), TAT measures of motives were not significantly correlated with self-report measures of goals in either of the two striving areas (i.e., agency and communion). This result indicates that although people may be involved in goals corresponding to their motive dispositions, they also frequently commit themselves to goals that do not fit their motive dispositions. To explore the consequences of varying degrees of fit between individuals' motive dispositions and their personal goals, Brunstein et al. also administered a mood adjective checklist designed to tap students' current emotional well-being. Results were as follows: Striving for communal goals (see Figure 6.3A) was positively related to emotional well-being for communion-motivated students (i.e., students whose TAT need for communion was stronger than their TAT need for agency) but negatively related to emotional well-being for agency-motivated students (i.e., students whose TAT need for agency was stronger than their TAT need for communion). Conversely, agentic-goal striving (Figure 6.3B) was positively associated with emotional well-being for agency-motivated students but negatively associated with emotional well-being for communion-motivated students. This pattern of findings suggests that working on goals that correspond to one's motives leads to enhanced emotional well-being, whereas striving for goals that do not fit or that even contradict one's motives results in impaired emotional well-being.

Brunstein et al. (1998, Study 2) found further evidence for the notion that motives and goals interact with each other to determine people's well-being emotions. At the beginning of a new term, students were asked to report both agentic goals (e.g., striving for social influence and mastery experiences) and communal goals (e.g., striving for interpersonal closeness and friendly social contacts) that they intended to pursue during the current semester. Participants were also asked to appraise each goal listed in terms of their current sense of goal commitment and goal attainability. Students'

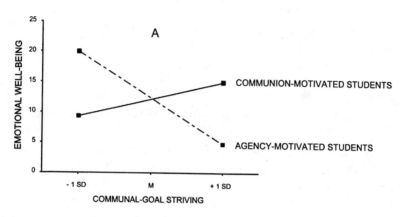

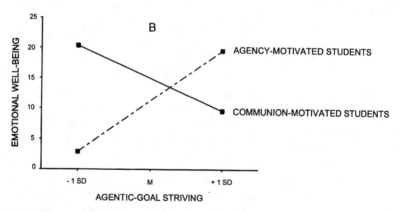

Figure 6.3. Emotional Well-Being as a Function of Type of Goal Striving: Regression Slopes for Agency-Motivated and Communion-Motivated Students

SOURCE: J. C. Brunstein, U. Lautenschlager, B. Nawroth, K. Pöhlmann, & O. Schultheiss, "Persönliche Anliegen, soziale Motive und emotionales Wohlbefinden" [Personal goals, social motives, and emotional well-being]. *Zeitschrift für Differentielle und Diagnostische Psychologie, 16* (1995): 7. Copyright 1995 by Verlag Hans Huber. Adapted with permission.

needs for agency (i.e., achievement and power motives) and communion (i.e., intimacy and affiliation motives) were assessed with a TAT-type picture-story test. With regard to motive-congruent goals (i.e., agentic goals for students with a predominant need for agency and communal goals for students with a predominant need for communion), this study yielded results similar to those obtained in Brunstein's (1993) study. In conjunction with favorable conditions to attain motive-congruent goals, high commitment to such goals predicted an increase in emotional well-being from the beginning to the end of the term. Yet a different result emerged from the analysis of motive-incongruent goals. For students who felt strongly committed to motive-incongruent goals (i.e., communal goals for students with a predominant need for agency and agentic goals for students with a predominant need for communion), emotional well-being decreased during the course of the semester. The key to the understanding of these findings turned out to be perceived progress in goal achievement, which had been assessed in this study several times during the semester. Whereas greater progress toward motive-incongruent goals did not result in enhanced well-being, greater progress toward motive-congruent goals did. Moreover, both commitment to and attainability of motive-congruent goals were positively related to progress in the achievement of these goals. In contrast, high commitment to motive-incongruent goals was associated with impaired progress toward motive-congruent goals and thus, as noted above, with decreased emotional well-being.

These findings are in keeping with the notion that motives operate as emotional weighting dispositions that moderate the extent to which the pursuit and accomplishment of personal goals are reflected in people's well-being emotions. More specifically, the data reported by Brunstein et al. (1998) suggest that it is only when personal goals qualify for the satisfaction of motives that experiences of progress translate into experiences of positive well-being. To achieve high levels of well-being, it is therefore important for people both to commit themselves to goals that correspond to their motives and to have life situations that promote the achievement of such motive-congruent goals. This precondition, however, is met as often as not, as the low correlations between TAT measures of motives and self-report measures of goals obtained in recent studies suggest. Moreover, the findings of the aforementioned study indicate that high investments in the pursuit of motive-incongruent goals may keep individuals from the accomplishment of motive-congruent goals and thereby result in a lack of need satisfaction, which in turn is expressed in feelings of frustration and dejection.

This interpretation is compatible with a two-system model of human motivation advocated by McClelland, Koestner, and Weinberger (1989). In this model, McClelland et al. differentiate a cognition-based motivational system that comprises the person's self-articulated goals, values, and self-concepts from an emotion-driven implicit motivational system consisting of the individual's general motives and needs. One major reason for the differences between as well as the independence of these two systems can be seen in the fact that their foundations are laid at different times in the course of an individual's development. Research findings indicate that the strength of an individual's motives is determined by emotional experiences in his or her early childhood that do not require language as a mediator (McClelland & Pilon, 1983). In contrast, the development of the explicit motivational system as a means of self-regulation vis-à-vis the demands and expectations of the sociocultural environment the individual grows up in necessitates the acquisition of language. Goals as long-term objectives the person sets for him- or herself emerge only during adolescence (see Brandtstädter, 1998) and hence are developmentally distant from the origin of motives. Moreover, because goals represent anticipated end states in the future and are dealt with within the language-based explicit motivational system, they do not have the capacity to appeal directly to the implicit motivational system, which is oriented toward immediate experiences in the present. As Schultheiss and Brunstein (1999) have found, it is only after the translation of goals into perceptionlike mental simulations that a person can decide on the basis of his or her subsequent emotional reactions whether a potential goal matches his or her motives and should therefore be pursued or ignored.

Thus congruence between an individual's motives and the goals to which he or she is committed is not preprogrammed ontogenetically, but rather represents a challenge that has to be mastered in the course of successful individual development. The results of the motive-goal studies reviewed above indicate that young adults, who represented most of the participants, have not yet achieved harmony between their motive dispositions and the goals they pursue in their everyday lives. This does not, however, preclude that they can learn at later stages of their development how to formulate and set their goals more prudently with regard to their capacity to satisfy their emotional needs.

CHANGES IN PERSONAL-GOAL COMMITMENTS ACROSS THE LIFE SPAN

Several researchers have investigated how personal goals change over the course of the life span. The primary focus of this research has been to explore age differences in the content of individuals' self-reported commitments. For instance, Nurmi (1992) asked 19- to 64-year-old adults to report their current life goals and then classified them according to a number of content categories, such as family, education, occupation, leisure activities, and health. This analysis revealed that young adults frequently mentioned goals related to education, family, self-development, and friends. Middle-aged adults were primarily concerned with occupational and material goals as well as with objectives related to their children's lives. Health, leisure activities, and world-related matters represented predominant topics reflected in the goals of older adults (for similar findings, see Cross & Markus, 1991; Heckhausen, 1997; Kuhlen & Johnson, 1952). As Nurmi notes, these findings indicate that the content of personal goals typically reflects the normative tasks and social constraints specifying for a given sociocultural community what seems to be desirable and acceptable at particular stages in the life span. However, although age-graded life tasks may provide a rough description of the goals people characteristically try to attain in certain life phases, they also leave much room for variation in the ways individuals adopt, transform, and appropriate prescribed tasks and societal expectations (Cantor, 1990).

Apart from assessing content-related goal attributes, Nurmi and his colleagues have also examined age differences in control beliefs and time perspectives associated with the pursuit of personal goals (see Nurmi, 1992; Nurmi, Pulliainen, & Salmela-Aro, 1992). Accordingly, Nurmi asked his participants to assess their personal goals according to (a) future-time perspective (i.e., the temporal extension of goal striving) and (b) internality of control (i.e., internal versus external control over goal-relevant outcomes). Notably, he found no significant age differences in the overall temporal extension associated with the pursuit of goals. For young adults, an extended future-time perspective was associated with goals related to family, education, and work. For middle-aged and older adults, an extended future-time perspective was associated with goals related to health and these adults' children's lives. Thus, as Nurmi notes, these findings illustrate that an extended future-time perspective is generally associated with goals people become interested in as they anticipate and go through certain periods of the life cycle. Moreover, Nurmi et al. (1992) found that the internality of goal-related control beliefs decreased with increasing adult age. To account for this finding, these researchers present an intriguing argument. As noted above, education and occupation represent topics frequently reflected in young adults' goals. In contrast, middle-aged and older adults are more frequently committed to goals related to their own health and their children's future lives. These latter goals, however, are generally associated with lower internality of control than are educational or work-related goals. Thus Nurmi et al. suggest that a decline in the internality of control beliefs during adulthood may largely be accounted for by age-related changes in people's preferred goals and the content of their motivational commitments.

Heckhausen (1997) proposes that older adults differ from younger adults not only in the extent to which they believe they are able to exert control over goal accomplishment, but also in the particular way in which they frame or consciously represent their commitments. According to Heckhausen, the goals of younger adults are primarily oriented toward "developmental gains" (e.g., the advancement of their occupational careers) and are therefore associated with efforts to approach positively valenced incentives. In comparison, Heckhausen notes, elders are more frequently concerned with "developmental losses" (e.g., declines in cognitive, physical, and social abilities) and therefore tend to frame their goals in terms of avoidance projects. In keeping with this notion, Heckhausen found that the proportion of loss-avoiding goals increased with adult age, whereas the number of gain-oriented goals was negatively correlated with age.

Ogilvie and Rose (1995) used a more extended taxonomy to classify people's goal orientations. Using the classification of operant learning contingencies, these researchers differentiated among four types of goals: striving for positively valenced future conditions (acquire-motivation goals), maintaining currently existing positive conditions (keep-motivation goals), avoiding negatively valenced future conditions (prevent-motivation goals), and getting rid of existing negative conditions (cure-motivation goals). By comparing the goals of three age groups (adolescents, middle-aged adults, and elders), Ogilvie and Rose found that the majority of goals listed by participants fit the acquire-motivation category. Yet the greatest proportion of acquire-motivation goals was reported by adolescents. Cure-motivation goals were most frequently mentioned by middle-aged adults, presumably reflecting that work- and family-related stressors and demands reach their peak in this age group. In contrast, keep-motivation goals prevailed among elders. This latter finding indicates that older adults—in contrast to middle-aged adults and adolescents—are more intensively concerned with the maintenance of what they have already achieved in life (see Reker, Peacock, & Wong, 1987). For all age groups, prevent-motivation goals represented the least frequently occurring goal category.

Keep-motivation and maintenance goals do not necessarily imply passivity or resignation in old age, as Rapkin and Fischer (1992) argue. On the contrary, these investigators found that elders who placed high priority on the maintenance of social values and roles (e.g., "keep up with old friendships") displayed lower depression and reported greater self-esteem than elders who expressed a desire to reduce their activities and wanted to disengage from social roles. Similarly, Holahan (1988) reports evidence suggesting that the maintenance of life goals is beneficial for older individuals. In this study, active engagement in life goals, such as striving for autonomy (e.g., maintaining one's independence and health), involvement (e.g., hobbies and self-development), and achievement (e.g., productive work and societal contributions), positively contributed both directly and indirectly, through activity participation, to the health and well-being of a 65- to 75-year-old subsample of Terman's Study of the Gifted.

The aforementioned findings suggest that although people's goal priorities and goal orientations shift across the life course, a sense of investment in the pursuit of personal goals appears to remain a significant source of satisfaction in late adulthood (for a related argument, see Baltes & Carstensen, 1996). Accordingly, it is important to identify factors that promote both goal setting and goal fulfillment in later life. Robbins et al. (1994) report evidence suggesting that the availability of social support represents such a goal-promoting factor. These researchers investigated the importance of "goal continuity," defined as the ability to establish and enact personal goals, as a precursor of early retirees' life adjustment. Perceived availability of social support (e.g., emotional support and tangible assistance) turned out to be positively related to participants' sense of goal continuity, which in turn was linked to increased leisure-time quality, emotional well-being, and optimism about life.

PERSONAL GOALS AND LIFE ADJUSTMENT

In the preceding passages, we have reported evidence for the notion that the pursuit and accomplishment of personal goals plays an important role in the development and maintenance of individuals' emotional well-being and satisfaction with life. Moreover, as reported above, a number of studies have shown that striving for meaningful objectives is crucial to people's mental health throughout all life phases. Notably, subjective accounts of

psychological and physical well-being have frequently been used to estimate individuals' overall life adjustment as well as to assess their adaptational success as they negotiate life transitions. In this section, we finally
discuss how both dynamic and structural properties of personal goals are
involved in individuals' development during adulthood.

Considering humans as self-motivated beings who set their own personal
goals implies the view that people actively produce discrepancies between
their status quo and desired future states and then mobilize efforts to reduce
these self-imposed discrepancies through instrumental activities expected
to bring about desired ends (Bandura, 1986). Personal-goal setting therefore involves both a disruption of a current state, which is no longer
preferred, and an orientation toward a desired future state, which has not
yet been achieved (Ford & Lerner, 1992). Even if individuals achieve the
goals they have been pursuing, goal striving does not end. Rather, people
may commit themselves to new challenges and thereby create further
discrepancies to be removed. In effect, this interplay between discrepancy-
producing (i.e., goal-setting) and discrepancy-reducing (i.e., goal-striving)
activities may provoke a host of change processes in the way people interact
with their environments, appraise their current life contexts, and try to
shape their daily lives (Lazarus & DeLongis, 1983). Individuals expand
their world- and self-related knowledge as they strive for personal goals,
acquire skills, and master the competencies they need to reach their goals,
transform their life situations to fit their aspirations, and shape their
relationships with others in accordance with the consequences they seek
to attain. Thus the pursuit of personal goals provides both directive and
energetic functions that enable individuals to exercise self-influence and
thereby become, as Lerner and Busch-Rossnagel (1981) put it, "producers
of their own development."

Yet, to highlight the role of personal goals in adult development, it is
important not only to consider motivational properties of goals but to
analyze how personal-goal systems unfold over time and change across
different phases of the life course. For this purpose, it might be quite fruitful
to differentiate between two types of change processes involved in the
development of goal systems: formative and transitional change processes.

Formative change processes involve the creation and elaboration of a
coherent pattern of personal goals within a hierarchically ordered system.
These change processes typically start to operate when a person adopts a
life goal and thereby establishes a superordinate purpose in his or her life.

Life goals frequently reflect the developmental tasks individuals seek to master (e.g., think of an adolescent who struggles for independence and autonomy; see Zirkel & Cantor, 1990) and the self-definitions they try to attain (e.g., think of a young adult who is preoccupied with the identity goal of becoming a responsive father or mother; see Gollwitzer, 1986) in various life phases. Although life goals are fueled with a sense of personal meaning, they constitute highly abstract qualities and therefore do not provide concrete guidelines for the planning and enactment of instrumental behavior. Rather, to implement and move further toward the attainment of life goals, individuals need to elaborate these goals and translate them into a set of more specific commitments. This elaboration occurs through differentiative and integrative processes, which are both involved in the formative development of personal-goal systems. As Sheldon and Emmons (1995) state, a goal system is differentiated to the extent to which a person generates and pursues a variety of distinctive concerns at a relatively low level of abstraction. The person achieves integration within such a system by skillfully linking goals at lower levels of the hierarchy to the achievement of higher-order aspirations.

Considering personal goals as constituents of a hierarchically organized motivational system has important implications for the conceptualization of continuity and change in a person's life (see Atchley, 1989). From a goal-system perspective, a sense of developmental continuity derives from the pursuit of overarching life goals that cannot be achieved at once but have to be realized step by step over extended periods. This persistent life-goal pursuit permits the individual to knit his or her past experiences, present concerns, and future prospects into a coherent biographical tapestry. Furthermore, life goals leave much room for variation in the specific way a person tries to materialize his or her superordinate commitments. At lower levels of the hierarchy, high flexibility is achieved through a person's engagement in the creation, enactment, and reconceptualization of behavior projects and activities that instantiate higher-order purposes within a given life context. Lower-order goals as well as the standards associated with them may change considerably as a person advances in a life-goal career (think, for instance, of a person who advances in his or her professional career from beginner to expert status) and adjusts his or her specific concerns to changing environmental opportunities (think, for instance, of a person who enters a new position). Yet neither success nor failure in accomplishing a subordinate objective leads to the relinquishment of a higher-order goal. Rather, there still remains a variety of tasks and pathways by which an individual may try to maintain a general goal and move further toward its attainment.

Whereas formative change processes promote the unfolding of a coherent pattern of goals within a hierarchically ordered system, *transitional change processes* involve a reprioritization of life goals and associated commitment patterns. We use the term *transitional* to denote that this reordering of goal priorities is integral to individuals' efforts to adapt to and cope with life transitions. Because transitional stages in life are associated with considerable changes in social role demands, behavioral opportunities, and resources available to an individual, they also require major shifts in life-goal investments. However, as Lazarus and DeLongis (1983) persuasively argue, such shifts are not simply a product of insight and rationality. Rather, transitional changes in personal-goal systems require individuals to commit themselves to new life goals *and* to disengage from long-standing aspirations that no longer can be attained (think, for instance, of a manager who has invested considerable energy in career-related goals for quite some time, but now faces retirement).

An individual who flexibly engages in each of these two activities (i.e., commitment and disengagement processes) during life transitions should be likely to adjust his or her goal priorities to the behavioral affordances and demands associated with the new life stage. This flexibility should in turn promote the person's adaptive success (see Brandtstädter & Renner, 1990). In contrast, within the framework presented here, maladaptive responses would be likely to occur when a person tries to resist a life transition, either by maintaining a set of obsolete pretransition goals or by failing to generate a set of posttransition goals that will fit the new life situation. This mismatch between goals and behavioral opportunities might lead to serious trouble in the former case as the individual continues to struggle for now unattainable goals; in the latter case, trouble might arise because the individual fails to instill a new sense of meaning in his or her life.

But how can a person smoothly traverse from one life phase to another? In her remarkable work on the role of goals in adaptation during adulthood, Lowenthal (1971) argues that adaptive responses to life transitions, such as leaving home, starting a family, the empty nest, and retirement, involve both an "expansion" of goals and associated activity patterns that fit the demands inherent in the new life situation and a "constriction" of goals and associated activity patterns that do not match the affordances provided by the advent of the new life situation. In the case of scheduled or normative life transitions, each of these behavioral reorientations (i.e., expansion and constriction) may be established proactively—that is, before a person actually undergoes a given life transition. An individual may anticipate change and establish posttransition goals in the pretransition period, and thereby implement a pattern of commitments that might fit the anticipated life situation better than the current one.

In effect, the anticipatory creation of posttransition goals may temporarily lead to a state of disequilibrium caused by the opposing forces of long-standing commitments and newly established concerns competing for common resources (e.g., time) in the pretransition phase (think, for instance, of a preretirement adult who pursues an increasing number of leisure goals but still feels behaviorally involved in his or her work role). This conflict, however, might be quite productive in the sense that active involvement in a new set of goals may weaken the strength of deep-seated commitments that will no longer be feasible, at least in their present form, in the posttransition phase. Moreover, pretransition conflicts between "old" and "new" goals can easily be resolved when the life transition actually occurs. In this situation, the person will be more capable of abandoning the old goals, which now have become a burden, and finally will be able to dedicate all of his or her time and effort to the pursuit of the new and more attractive goals. This will result in a new balance or equilibrium among personal goals, preferred activity patterns, and situational affordances. Hence a person who follows this roughly sketched model of negotiating a life transition should experience a gain rather than a loss of goal-related opportunities when she or he crosses the bridge between the old and the new life stage. All of this implies, however, that a person is both willing and able to anticipate and plan for a transitional stage in life and to integrate that transition into his or her own life-cycle perspective.

CONCLUSION

Our aim in this chapter has been to highlight the pivotal role the pursuit of personally meaningful goals plays in individuals' subjective well-being and life adjustment. We have emphasized the notion that to develop high levels of well-being and maintain mental health, individuals need to achieve a fit between the goals they feel committed to attaining and the opportunities and constraints inherent in their social environments. Moreover, we have pointed out that it is only when personal goals match a person's inner motives and needs that the advancement of goals translates into feelings of happiness and satisfaction. Finally, we have argued that continuity and change in personal-goal systems are both necessary for individuals to achieve a sense of developmental continuity as well as to master life transitions successfully.

REFERENCES

Atchley, R. C. (1989). A continuity theory of normal aging. *Gerontologist, 29,* 183-190.

Baltes, M., & Carstensen, L. L. (1996). The process of successful ageing. *Ageing and Society, 16,* 397-422.

Bandura, A. (1986). *Social foundations of thought and action: A social cognitive theory.* Englewood Cliffs, NJ: Prentice Hall.

Baumeister, R. F. (1991). *Meanings of life.* New York: Guilford.

Beck, A. T., & Beck, R. W. (1972). Screening depressed patients in family practice: A rapid technic. *Postgraduate Medicine, 52,* 81-85.

Brandtstädter, J. (1984). Personal and social control over development: Some implications of an action perspective in life-span developmental psychology. In P. B. Baltes & O. G. Brim, Jr. (Eds.), *Life-span development and behavior* (Vol. 6, pp. 1-32). New York: Academic Press.

Brandtstädter, J. (1998). Action perspectives on human development. In W. Damon (Series Ed.) & R. M. Lerner (Vol. Ed.), *Handbook of child psychology: Vol. 1. Theoretical models of human development* (5th ed., pp. 807-863). New York: John Wiley.

Brandtstädter, J., & Renner, G. (1990). Tenacious goal pursuit and flexible goal adjustment: Explication and age-related analysis of assimilative and accommodative strategies of coping. *Psychology and Aging, 5,* 58-67.

Brunstein, J. C. (1993). Personal goals and subjective well-being: A longitudinal study. *Journal of Personality and Social Psychology, 65,* 1061-1070.

Brunstein, J. C. (1999). Persönliche Ziele und subjektives Wohlbefinden bei älteren Menschen [Personal goals and subjective well-being among older adults]. *Zeitschrift für Differentielle und Diagnostische Psychologie, 20,* 58-71.

Brunstein, J. C., Dangelmayer, G., & Schultheiss, O. C. (1996). Personal goals and social support in close relationships: Effects on relationship mood and marital satisfaction. *Journal of Personality and Social Psychology, 71,* 1006-1019.

Brunstein, J. C., Ganserer, J., Maier, G. W., & Heckhausen, H. (1991). *Persönliche Anliegen in Alltagssituationen* [Personal goals in everyday situations] (Memorandum No. 82). University of Erlangen, Department of Psychology.

Brunstein, J. C., & Gollwitzer, P. M. (1996). Effects of failure on subsequent performance: The importance of self-defining goals. *Journal of Personality and Social Psychology, 70,* 395-407.

Brunstein, J. C., Lautenschlager, U., Nawroth, B., Pöhlmann, K., & Schultheiss, O. (1995). Persönliche Anliegen, soziale Motive und emotionales Wohlbefinden [Personal goals, social motives, and emotional well-being]. *Zeitschrift für Differentielle und Diagnostische Psychologie, 16,* 1-10.

Brunstein, J. C., & Maier, G. W. (1996). Persönliche Ziele: Ein Überblick zum Stand der Forschung [Personal goals: A state-of-the-art review]. *Psychologische Rundschau, 47,* 146-160.

Brunstein, J. C., Schultheiss, O. C., & Grässmann, R. (1998). Personal goals and emotional well-being: The moderating role of motive dispositions. *Journal of Personality and Social Psychology, 75,* 494-508.

Bühler, C., & Massarik, F. (Eds.). (1968). *The course of human life.* New York: Springer.

Cantor, N. (1990). From thought to behavior: "Having" and "doing" in the study of personality and cognition. *American Psychologist, 45,* 735-750.

Cantor, N. (1994). Life task problem solving: Situational affordances and personal needs. *Personality and Social Psychology Bulletin, 20,* 235-243.

Cantor, N., & Blanton, H. (1996). Effortful pursuit of personal goals in daily life. In P. M. Gollwitzer & J. A. Bargh (Eds.), *The psychology of action: Linking cognition and motivation to behavior* (pp. 338-359). New York: Guilford.

Cantor, N., & Kihlstrom, J. F. (1987). *Personality and social intelligence.* Englewood Cliffs, NJ: Prentice Hall.

Cantor, N., & Zirkel, S. (1990). Personality, cognition, and purposive behavior. In L. A. Pervin (Ed.), *Handbook of personality: Theory and research* (pp. 135-164). New York: Guilford.

Carver, C. S., & Scheier, M. F. (1990). Principles of self-regulation: Action and emotion. In E. T. Higgins & R. M. Sorrentino (Eds.), *Handbook of motivation and cognition: Vol. 2. Foundations of social behavior* (pp. 3-52). New York: Guilford.

Cross, S., & Markus, H. (1991). Possible selves across the life span. *Human Development, 34,* 230-255.

Diener, E., & Fujita, F. (1995). Resources, personal strivings, and subjective well-being: A nomothetic and idiographic approach. *Journal of Personality and Social Psychology, 68,* 926-935.

Emmons, R. A. (1986). Personal strivings: An approach to personality and subjective well-being. *Journal of Personality and Social Psychology, 51,* 1058-1068.

Emmons, R. A. (1996). Striving and feeling: Personal goals and subjective well-being. In P. M. Gollwitzer & J. A. Bargh (Eds.), *The psychology of action: Linking motivation and cognition to behavior* (pp. 313-337). New York: Guilford.

Emmons, R. A., & Kaiser, H. A. (1996). Goal orientation and emotional well-being: Linking goals and affect through the self. In L. L. Martin & A. Tesser (Eds.), *Striving and feeling: Interactions among goals, affect, and self-regulation* (pp. 79-98). Mahwah, NJ: Lawrence Erlbaum.

Erikson, E. H., Erikson, J. M., & Kivnick, H. Q. (1986). *Vital involvement in old age.* New York: W. W. Norton.

Ford, D. H. (1987). *Humans as self-constructing living systems: A developmental perspective on behavior and personality.* Hillsdale, NJ: Lawrence Erlbaum.

Ford, D. H., & Lerner, R. M. (1992). *Developmental systems theory: An integrative approach.* Newbury Park, CA: Sage.

Gollwitzer, P. M. (1986). Striving for specific identities: The social reality of self-symbolizing. In R. F. Baumeister (Ed.), *Public self and private self* (pp. 143-159). New York: Springer-Verlag.

Gollwitzer, P. M., & Bargh, J. A. (Eds.). (1996). *The psychology of action: Linking cognition and motivation to behavior.* New York: Guilford.

Harlow, R. E., & Cantor, N. (1994). Social pursuit of academics: Side effects and spillover of strategic reassurance seeking. *Journal of Personality and Social Psychology, 66,* 386-397.

Harlow, R. E., & Cantor, N. (1996). Still participating after all these years: A study of life task participation in later life. *Journal of Personality and Social Psychology, 71,* 1235-1249.

Heckhausen, J. (1997). Developmental regulation across adulthood: Primary and secondary control of age-related challenges. *Developmental Psychology, 33,* 176-187.

Holahan, C. K. (1988). Relation of life goals at age 70 to activity participation and health and psychological well-being among Terman's gifted men and women. *Psychology and Aging, 3,* 286-291.

King, L. A. (1995). Wishes, motives, goals, and personal memories: Relations of measures of human motivation. *Journal of Personality, 63,* 985-1007.

Klinger, E. (1975). Consequences of commitment to and disengagement from incentives. *Psychological Review, 82,* 1-25.

Klinger, E. (1977). *Meaning and void: Inner experience and the incentives in lives.* Minneapolis: University of Minnesota Press.

Klinger, E., Barta, S. G., & Maxeiner, M. E. (1981). Current concerns: Assessing therapeutically relevant motivation. In P. C. Kendall & S. D. Hollon (Eds.), *Assessment strategies for cognitive-behavioral interventions* (pp. 161-196). New York: Academic Press.

Kuhlen, R. G., & Johnson, G. H. (1952). Changes in goals with adult increasing age. *Journal of Consulting Psychology, 16,* 1-4.

Lazarus, R. S., & DeLongis, A. (1983). Psychological stress and coping in aging. *American Psychologist, 38,* 245-254.

Lecci, L., Karoly, P., Briggs, C., & Kuhn, K. (1994). Specificity and generality of motivational components in depression: A personal projects analysis. *Journal of Abnormal Psychology, 103,* 404-408.

Lerner, R. M., & Busch-Rossnagel, N. A. (Eds.). (1981). *Individuals as producers of their development: A life-span perspective.* New York: Academic Press.

Little, B. R. (1983). Personal projects: A rationale and method for investigation. *Environment and Behavior, 15,* 273-309.

Little, B. R. (1989). Personal projects analysis: Trivial pursuits, magnificent obsessions, and the search for coherence. In D. M. Buss & N. Cantor (Eds.),

Personality psychology: Recent trends and emerging directions (pp. 15-31). New York: Springer.

Lowenthal, M. F. (1971). Intentionality: Toward a framework for the study of adaptation in adulthood. *Aging and Human Development, 2,* 79-95.

Maier, G. W. (1996). *Persönliche Ziele im Unternehmen: Ergebnisse einer Längsschnittstudie bei Berufseinsteigern* [Personal goals at the workplace: A longitudinal study with a sample of newcomers]. Unpublished doctoral dissertation, University of Munich.

Martin, L. L., & Tesser, A. (Eds.). (1996). *Striving and feeling: Interactions among goals, affect, and self-regulation.* Mahwah, NJ: Lawrence Erlbaum.

McClelland, D. C. (1985). *Human motivation.* Glenview, IL: Scott, Foresman.

McClelland, D. C., Koestner, R., & Weinberger, J. (1989). How do self-attributed and implicit motives differ? *Psychological Review, 96,* 690-702.

McClelland, D. C., & Pilon, D. A. (1983). Sources of adult motivation in patterns of parent behavior in early childhood. *Journal of Personality and Social Psychology, 44,* 564-574.

McGregor, I., & Little, B. R. (1998). Personal projects, happiness, and meaning: On doing well and being yourself. *Journal of Personality and Social Psychology, 74,* 494-512.

Michalos, A. C. (1980). Satisfaction and happiness. *Social Indicators Research, 8,* 385-422.

Murray, H. A. (1943). *Thematic Apperception Test manual.* Cambridge, MA: Harvard University Press.

Novacek, J., & Lazarus, R. S. (1990). The structure of personal commitments. *Journal of Personality, 58,* 693-715.

Nurmi, J.-E. (1992). Age differences in adult life goals, concerns, and their temporal extension: A life course approach to future-oriented motivation. *International Journal of Behavioral Development, 15,* 487-508.

Nurmi, J.-E., Pulliainen, H., & Salmela-Aro, K. (1992). Age differences in adults' control beliefs related to life goals and concerns. *Psychology and Aging, 7,* 194-196.

Nuttin, J. (1984). *Motivation, planning, and action.* Hillsdale, NJ: Lawrence Erlbaum.

Ogilvie, D. M., & Rose, K. M. (1995). Self-with-other representations and a taxonomy of motives: Two approaches to study persons. *Journal of Personality, 63,* 643-679.

Pervin, L. A. (Ed.). (1989). *Goal concepts in personality and social psychology.* Hillsdale, NJ: Lawrence Erlbaum.

Rapkin, B. D., & Fischer, K. W. (1992). Framing the construct of life satisfaction in terms of older adults' personal goals. *Psychology and Aging, 7,* 138-149.

Reker, G. T., Peacock, E. J., & Wong, P. T. P. (1987). Meaning and purpose in life and well-being: A life-span perspective. *Journal of Gerontology, 42,* 44-49.

Robbins, S. B., Lee, R. M., & Wan, T. T. H. (1994). Goal continuity as a mediator of early retirement adjustment: Testing a multidimensional model. *Journal of Counseling Psychology, 41,* 18-26.

Röhrle, B., Hedke, J., & Leibold, S. (1994). Persönliche Projekte zur Herstellung und Pflege sozialer Beziehungen bei depressiven und nicht depressiven Personen [Social relationships as personal projects in depressives and non-depressives]. *Zeitschrift für Klinische Psychologie, 23,* 43-51.

Ruehlman, L. S., & Wolchik, S. A. (1988). Personal goals and interpersonal support and hindrance as factors in psychological distress and well-being. *Journal of Personality and Social Psychology, 55,* 293-301.

Schultheiss, O. C., & Brunstein, J. C. (1999). Goal imagery: Bridging the gap between implicit motives and explicit goals. *Journal of Personality, 67,* 1-38.

Sheldon, K. M., & Emmons, R. A. (1995). Comparing differentiation and integration within personal goal systems. *Personality and Individual Differences, 18,* 39-46.

Spanier, G. B. (1976). Measuring dyadic adjustment: New scales for assessing the quality of marriage and similar dyads. *Journal of Marriage and the Family, 38,* 15-28.

Wessman, A. E., & Ricks, D. F. (1966). *Mood and personality.* New York: Holt, Rinehart & Winston.

Zirkel, S., & Cantor, N. (1990). Personal construal of life tasks: Those who struggle for independence. *Journal of Personality and Social Psychology, 58,* 172-185.

7

PERSONAL PROJECTS AND SOCIAL ECOLOGY

Themes and Variations Across the Life Span

Brian R. Little

Jill is seething. She has had yet another blowup with her boss and is rehearsing her resignation speech as she stares out of her office tower window. Twenty-one stories below, and two miles to the southeast, Jack, a toddling tantrum in disposable diapers, is also having a bad day. Jill is surrounded by the pleasant amenities of a postmodern upscale office. Jack lives with his stepbrother and grandmother in a crowded apartment that

AUTHOR'S NOTE: This work was developed in close collaboration with my students, first at Oxford and, for the past two decades, in the Social Ecology Laboratory in the Department of Psychology at Carleton University. This chapter gives me the first chance to link our earliest work with our most recent research by examining self-development and personal action from several different, but converging, perspectives. My use of plural first-person pronouns at times in this chapter is not a stylistic convention; rather, it reflects a collegial conviction that this has been very much an interdependent enterprise. I wish to acknowledge the very helpful comments of the volume editors and the continuing support of the Social Sciences and Humanities Research Council of Canada.

could be regarded, at best, as decidedly downscale. Jill has not always been angry; Jack will be smiling again by 6 o'clock. Jack and Jill do not know each other, but by the end of this chapter they might just meet.

What is going on in these lives? What type of conceptual framework and analytic tools help us understand the daily pursuits and distinctive concerns of the Jacks and Jills of this world and of those who care for them, for better or for worse? This chapter explores recent advances in one such framework, a social ecological model of human development. Our research lies at the intersection of personality, social ecology, and developmental science, although in recent years it has expanded into domains rather remote from its psychological origins, ranging from taxonomic analysis to economic philosophy and public policy (Little, in press-b). In the next section, I introduce some of the core aspects of our conceptual, methodological, and empirical approach to human development drawn from three separate stages of our research program. I then discuss the most central concept in our research, *personal projects,* and how these extended sets of personally salient actions differ across the life span in their meaning, manageability, and support. The section that follows that discussion proposes three tiers for developmental science that parallel similar tiers in contemporary personality psychology (Little, 1996; McAdams, 1996)—a base level of stable traits or temperamental differences, a middle level of personal action constructs, and a third level of life stories. I will allude throughout the chapter to the lives of Jack and Jill and look at the interdependent natures of their lives, so that we can see more clearly why people can both climb hills and tumble down them together, sometimes by design and sometimes by default. I will also speculate on how people in the process of climbing hills and developing together can avoid breaking their crowns.

A SOCIAL ECOLOGICAL FRAMEWORK FOR DEVELOPMENTAL SCIENCE: FROM SPECIALIZATION THEORY TO PERSONAL PROJECTS

Specialization Theory

Our research program began as an attempt to integrate Kelly's (1955) personal construct theory and his view of humans as "lay scientists" with an ecological perspective on personality (Little, 1968, 1972, 1976). In essence, it attempted to link constructivist and contextualist approaches to human development (Little, in press-c). In contrast with perspectives on development that emphasized passive responding or the automatic unfolding of stages, Kelly saw humans of all ages as mounting and testing hypotheses called "personal constructs," and as revising these constructs in the light of experience. Although Kelly personally eschewed the label *cognitive,* his theory was decades ahead of its time in providing both a conceptual and a measurement framework for exploring humans as active, self-creating, and rather audacious creatures.

Although deeply Kellian in spirit, our early research expanded and modified the notion of humans as tacit scientists. We advanced the thesis that, if individuals are scientists, they are *selectively* scientific, displaying differential orientations toward and competencies with different ecological domains and objects. In short, humans are "specialists." The transactions between individuals and their contexts are characterized by *specialization loops* in which affective, cognitive, and behavioral features are mutually facilitating: The greater the affective orientation toward a domain, the greater the degree of cognitive differentiation and integration and the more frequently the individual is likely to engage in behavioral encounters within the domain. For example, specialization theory calls for greater attention to be paid to the nature of the environmental and contextual objects with which the developing individual has interactions. We posited persons and things as primary objects and showed that person orientation and thing orientation play important roles in how individuals create their own environments and influence their own developmental trajectories. We found that person specialists, relative to more thing-oriented individuals, scored high on measures of affective orientation toward others, had greater verbal complexity in their personal constructs about others, and attended more to the psychological and expressive features of others than to more superficial characteristics.

More important for the theme of this volume, person specialists were more emotionally expressive in terms of their facial cues in social interaction. This expressive feature of person specialists, we have argued, attracts more social interactions with others and generates a more complex and differentiated set of constructs about those encounters (Little, 1976). The context-engendering nature of specialized orientation serves both as a confirmation of the view of active agents creating their own environments and as a warning that such agency is selective and focused. Development is *channelized* both by the constructs that individuals develop in the course of specialized pursuits and by the affordances and constraints provided by the ecological niches and primary objects to which they are exposed (Little, 1972).

One of the most robust empirical findings in research on person-thing specialization is that measures of these selective orientations are orthogonal, generating a fourfold typology of specialized orientations that we have labeled *nonspecialists* (low on both), *person specialists, thing specialists,* and *generalists* (high on both). Although the distinctive features of these groups go beyond the confines of this chapter, the characteristics of the nonspecialists and the generalists will be shown to foreshadow some of the findings in contemporary research on goal pursuit and personal action. We have speculated that nonspecialists, because of the extent of ego-centered construing in their personal constructs, may be fairly regarded as being *self*-specialists, primarily concerned with trying to make sense of their own feelings and personalities. Generalists, on the other hand, have been shown to have the ability to shift flexibly between construing environmental objects in personalistic or physicalistic terms and are, as a result, more likely to be highly creative, flexible, and adaptable in their environmental encounters—they are more likely, in Kellian terms, to have higher degrees of freedom in their life trajectories than those who are more selectively attuned to persons, things, or self (Little, 1972, 1976).

It was a short step from studies of primary specialization and the mutually reinforcing components of specialization loops to the more general question of what the different "specialties" are, above and beyond primary specialization, in which individuals might engage and that would create different life paths at each stage of development. Here we suggested that, instead of relying exclusively on personal constructs as analytic units, we should consider specialists as being engaged in "personal projects"— extended sets of personally salient activities that, as a whole, characterized their specialized, distinctive, indeed unique, pursuits.

From Personal Constructs to Personal Projects:
Contextualizing the Assessment of Persons

I mentioned earlier that one of Kelly's distinctive contributions was the provision of a methodology through which his personal construct theory could be measured and tested. His repertory grid technique involves an elegant set of flexible probes examining the personal constructs through which individuals view their lives and, particularly, but not restrictively, other individuals. It contains techniques for eliciting constructs and for appraising such characteristics as individuals' hierarchical structures, implicative linkages, and resistance to change (Kelly, 1955).

Personal projects analysis (PPA), similarly, was designed to meet 12 measurement criteria that we felt were central to understanding the interplay of persons and contexts in life-course development (Little, 1983, 1989, in press-b). Recently, these criteria have been summarized under four assumptive themes: constructivism, contextualism, conativism, and consiliency (Little, in press-c). Below I provide a brief overview of these by weaving together the narratives of Jill, Jack, and the loved and not-so-loved ones with whom they negotiate the projects of their lives.

Constructivism refers to a set of criteria that have as their common theme the need to elicit information that is personally salient and evocative for the individual. PPA does this by asking individuals to generate a list of their personal projects. Jill may generate a list that includes "figure out why I keep getting blindsided by the Accounting Department," "help mom cope with Alzheimer's," and "be less sensitive to Eric's cynical management style." Although the toddler Jack needs to be well out of his diapers before he can complete a PPA, he figures mightily in the project systems of others. Take his stepbrother, Luke. Luke might list the projects "babysit Jack," "play B-ball with the guys," and "study history." These are idiosyncratically formulated sets of personal action. We believe that direct elicitation from individuals of their current concerns, tasks, projects, and goals is a credible and necessary starting place (although not necessarily the termination point) for the sensitive analysis of personal action. Although he may occasionally distort, misperceive, or "put us on," the project gospel according to Luke has privileged status if we want to understand his life and play a constructive role in enhancing its quality.

The second assumptive theme, *contextualism,* urges that measurement of personal projects must provide a vantage point for viewing the daily contextual elements of individuals' lives—eliciting, for example, information about the spatial, social, and temporal ecologies within which personal projects are embedded. We ask individuals to specify where and with whom they are engaged in project pursuits, and to describe the standing of each project on the timeline that extends from the intimation of the possibility of a project to its conclusion. We might, for example, notice that many of Jill's projects are work focused and at the inception stage rather than moving toward completion; Luke's appear to be more present focused and include a diversity of domains. Jack's grandmother, Ada, on the other hand, is largely consumed with thoughts of projects from her past. Another contextualist feature of PPA, to be given more attention below, is the use of ad hoc dimensions in studies where we are interested in appraisals of projects in particular contexts or ecosettings for which the standard dimensions would be insensitive. For example, among the ad hoc project dimensions used in developmentally focused studies in our own laboratory have been "support by spouse" among pregnant women, where the pregnancy was appraised as a personal project; "age you feel when engaged in this project" in a study of middle-aged men; and "extent to which your organization supports this project" in senior managers contemplating early retirement. With widows and widowers, Breed and Emmons (1996) used a dimension that tapped how much a respondent's deceased spouse would have likely supported the different projects engaged in by the surviving spouse. Each of these ad hoc dimensions, it should be noted, was a significant predictor of measures of well-being for the particular group in question. Chambers (1997) has completed the definitive compendium of the literally hundreds of ad hoc dimensions used in PPA to capture the contextual subtleties of people's pursuits.

The third assumptive theme undergirding PPA is a *conativist* emphasis: Personal projects are intentional, volitional acts. They are a set of coordinated acts about which people care; they are, in Brunerian terms, acts of meaning (Bruner, 1990; Little, 1993, 1998). We tap into the personal significance of projects by asking respondents to rate each of their projects on a set of appraisal dimensions (typically from 0 to 10) that have been chosen for their theoretical and applied significance (e.g., how enjoyable, under one's control, and stressful they are). The 17 standard dimensions can be subsumed under five factors: project meaning, structure, community, efficacy, and stress. As I will highlight later, human adaptation is enhanced to the extent that individuals are engaged in projects that, overall, are meaningful, well managed, supportable, efficacious, and not unduly stressful. If we were to calculate the mean score of Jill's projects for this month, we may find that her life is full of projects that are primarily stressful. Although the projects may be highly meaningful to Jill, she may not see them as supported by others. Jill is likely to feel conflicted and fed up with the ecosystems that are dominated by willfully thoughtless bosses and tragically uncomprehending mothers.

Conflict is also likely to accrue from another consequence of the volitional nature of projects. Apart from those who are cursed or blessed to pursue only One Project, most people, in their quotidian pursuits, are engaged in multiple projects, and conflict both within and between project systems is almost inevitable. We tap into this theme by asking individuals to complete cross-impact matrices in which they appraise directly the positive or negative implications of each of their projects for all the others. We use joint cross-impact matrices to examine the reciprocal facilitation and frustrations characterizing the projects of two or more individuals. Luke may find that he is able to do his homework while casually "minding" Jack, but he feels only Luke-warm about the homework and Jack-minding projects because it means he has to stay home while his friends are practicing slam dunks down the street.

The final assumptive theme is that of *consiliency,* a belief that measurement operations in personality and developmental science can provide a framework through which diverse sources of influence on development can be appraised and integrated. Unlike our earlier work, in which we appraised the affective, cognitive, and behavioral components of specialized orientations through *different* instruments, PPA provides simultaneous access to the cognitive representations of what we "think we are doing," the affective appraisals of them, and the behavioral acts through which they are actually carried out and, if the vicissitudes of environments allow, completed.

Another consilient theme is the provision of ways of jointly accessing the individual level and normative levels of measurement. For example, we can use scores on the various project appraisal dimensions as the equivalents of normative measures of individual differences by taking the mean score on each dimension for each individual and running measures of association with relevant outcome measures, such as subjective well-being or depression. Such normative measurement is the most frequently used approach in the published literature. However, PPA also affords the opportunity for the intensive study of a single case. Here, correlations are run within the single project matrix between dimensions (across the individual's 10 projects). Thus for one individual the correlation between project stress and control may be significantly positive, whereas for another person the same scales may be significantly negatively related. The comparability of data structures gathered at the normative and ipsative levels of analysis raises a number of intriguing psychometric and statistical issues, including that of Simpson's paradox, which warns of potential incommensurabilities between these levels of analysis, and the ecological and individual difference fallacies, which make similar claims (for more details, see Little, in press-c).

Gee (1998) has made a detailed and persuasive case that there is a high degree of similarity or consiliency between personal project measures gathered at the individual level and those gathered at normative levels. The practical implication of this is that there is some solid psychometric grounding for theoretical interplay between clinicians with intensive knowledge of individuals and research developmentalists who are more concerned with normative measurement.

Social Ecology, Channelization, and Well-Being

At about the same time as we were working on the methodological and quantitative aspects of personal projects analysis, we formulated a social ecological model of human development that had as its core concern the systematic examination of personal, contextual, and transactional influences upon human adaptation and well-being. We formalized the model in a commissioned report intended to serve as a guide to policy analysis within the area of child and adolescent development (Little & Ryan, 1979). The model, subsequently expanded to include the full life span, is based on 12 guiding propositions, each of which generates a research agenda and a set of policy implications. For the purposes of this chapter, I wish to consider one of those propositions that bears most directly upon this volume's concern with self-development and action across the life span: the channelization proposition.

The channelization proposition posits that individuals can be conceived of as personal systems whose processes and development are channelized in dynamic relation to the environmental systems impinging upon them. The prime function of personal systems is the *integration* of these impinging systems, which include biological, social, cultural, physical-environmental, and historical influences. The form that such integrative activities take changes radically during the course of development. For Jack, the biological imperatives of digestive discomfort, the well-intentioned but relatively meager social support he is provided, and the noise level of a house near a freeway means that he has had to learn ways of balancing and integrating these disparate sources of influence: He yells like hell until someone picks him up and changes him. Luke's challenges are more subtle; he needs to balance and integrate, with appropriate weighting, the social demands of his peer group, his growing conception of self as a basketball star (perhaps reflecting the cultural ideals available to him), and the biological perplexities of growing 4 inches physically over the course of a summer, but in doing so shrinking a foot in his motor coordination and social skills.

Jill's integrative demands are more subtle still. Her ability to integrate most of her biological demands has become routinized sufficiently that these demands require little conscious formulation, although she has conspired with her hairstylist to take care of those growing hints that gray matter has become a *top*-of-the-head phenomenon for her. But her social demands are complex; she has given over her life to her profession and has had two failed intimate relationships that continue to weigh heavily on her mind.

She is a systems engineer in a large engineering practice and has found the demands that have been placed upon her in recent years to be demeaning and dispiriting. A rather introverted, analytic engineer, she was the enthusiastic beneficiary of a historical context that actively promoted women's access to engineering schools. But she now finds, 10 years later, that she is expected to be the token "mother figure" in the practice, offering solace and advice to those who are having interpersonal problems and being the "front" person for consulting contracts with high-profile clients. Meanwhile, her substantive project contributions seem continually to be patronizingly praised and then set aside. She has just come back from a meeting where once again the senior partner has asked her to dine out with a client to discuss a proposal that was not even her own, but the inferior product of a superior twit.

PERSONAL PROJECTS ACROSS THE LIFE SPAN: MEANING, STRUCTURE, AND COMMUNITY IN SELF-DEVELOPMENT

Project Meaning: Having Worthwhile Pursuits

To be engaged in a meaningful project is to be pursuing something that is estimable and worthwhile. In PPA we ask individuals to rate each of their projects on the extent to which they are enjoyable, self-expressive, important, and value congruent. In early development, project pursuit is meaningful primarily to the extent that it generates positive affect and could perhaps best be captured linguistically with labels such as *fun* and *enjoyable*. Although most people retain the capacity for enjoyment throughout life, there are other dimensions of meaning that become salient at different stages of development.

One of the PPA dimensions is of particular interest for our understanding of the role of the self in human development—the extent to which individuals appraise their projects as high in self-identity. By this we mean the extent to which projects are self-expressive, ones in which individuals feel particularly "themselves." Unlike those who posit identity formation as a global developmental achievement, we see the self as *distributed* in projects that vary in their degree of "fit" with a prototypical self (Little, 1993). Luke, for example, may feel most himself when on the basketball court. Jill may feel most herself when she is working on a challenging design project. Ada may experience this feeling when she is "minding" Jack.

Our empirical research over the years has shown that, with the exception of project enjoyment, the other "meaning" dimensions in PPA are not strong predictors of subjective well-being (SWB), certainly when compared with other dimensions that tap into perceptions of efficacy or (the lack of) stress, which have, in meta-analyses, shown consistently strong relationships with well-being (e.g., Wilson, 1990). However, recent research has shown that project meaning has a more nuanced role to play in the prediction of well-being. First, as mentioned above, SWB needs to be differentiated into separate measures of happiness and of purpose in life or life meaning. When these more "serious" aspects of SWB are used as criterion measures, project meaning is a significant predictor (McGregor & Little, 1998).

In addition, project meaning plays an important role as a moderator of the effects of other project dimensions in predicting a broad spectrum of well-being indices, including those that are more purely affective in nature. For example, Sheldon and Elliot (1998) have shown that project efficacy is a predictor of well-being only to the extent that the projects are also appraised as being "autonomous" (Deci & Ryan, 1991), in the sense of their being self-initiated rather than imposed pursuits. Thus Jill's efficacy in the social projects thrust upon her by her firm does not contribute to her sum of happiness one bit, although she begrudgingly admits that it does mean that the firm lands contracts that keep the whole enterprise afloat. Ada has reached the point in life in which self-expression has taken a backseat to something more like a combination of Eriksonian generativity and integrity. She is happy and finds life most meaningful when she is contributing to the well-being of others, and sometimes this requires her to be somewhat more disingenuous than a younger Ada would have tolerated. She has to bite her tongue to keep from voicing concern about her daughter and new son-in-law, who have "taken off" once again and seem to care little for Jack. Their self-absorption makes them oblivious to the small acts of compassion going on just beyond their peripheral vision by a gangly teenager and an arthritic old woman.

Project Structure: Having Manageable Pursuits

However meaningful an individual's pursuits might be, if they are unmanageable or chaotic, that person's well-being is likely to be compromised. One of the theoretically most important dimensions in PPA is personal project control. Project control has been found to be a consistent predictor of SWB and is closely related to other dimensions, such as efficacy and a sense of competency. Control appears to be intimately related to the scope or scale of an individual's personal projects. Small-scale projects afford more control, generally speaking, than do larger-scale pursuits.

One of the most interesting developmental findings in our early research with personal projects was that older persons (ranging in age from mid-60s to 90s), compared with middle-aged and younger persons, were significantly more likely to be engaged in projects that were more meaningful, more manageable, more efficacious, more supported by others, and less stressful. We suggest that the key factor here relates to project scale and the control that is afforded by the reduction of the scope of projects undertaken (Little, 1989). As Brandtstädter has shown, one of the hallmarks of successful aging is the flexible strategy in which one accommodates to shifts in competency levels by undertaking more appropriate goals (see, e.g., Brandtstädter & Wentura, 1995).

It is important to be clear about our conclusion related to the scale of projects undertaken by the elderly. We are not saying that older persons are "selling out" or "giving up" on their cherished dreams. More likely, they formulate their dreams in a flexible rescaling that leads to greater likelihood of success. In this respect they are tacitly adopting the strategy of "small wins" advocated in organizational theory by Weik (1984), who shows that in social movements it is often beneficial to shift major aspirations to smaller goals linked to those aspirations. One consequence of this is that the occasional failures and frustrations of projects are easier to handle if they are relatively small in scale. It appears that the older subjects in our studies with personal projects have been accruing such wisdom in the course of their life experiences (or reading Weik behind our backs).

Another of the propositions in our social ecological model, the control proposition, emphasizes that adaptation is enhanced to the extent that individuals have a sense of control *based on an accurate reading of their ecosystem resources and constraints.* This proposition, in one respect, appears to contrast with the highly influential perspective of Taylor and Brown (1988), who make a strong case that a certain degree of self-delusion is necessary to sustain well-being and happiness. We emphasize, in contrast, the need for an accurate reading of the nature of one's ecosystem and hence a veridical, not distorted, picture of one's control over valued courses of action. Are these seemingly conflicting views reconcilable? Partially.

Note first that we postulate that accurate perception of control is needed for successful *adaptation,* not necessarily happiness. The concept of adaptation is more temporally extended than happiness. Although we do not gainsay the desirability of happiness and its salutary effect, we observe that illusory control can lead to action that may range from charming imprudence to tragically bad judgment. Also, by locating our construct of control in people's ongoing personal action, we avoid some of the problems attending interpretation of control either as a fixed trait or as the result of an experimental manipulation.

One consequence of adopting a personal projects approach to examining control, then, is that we can discover, in the individual case, projects that a person perceives as completely under his or her control and others that he or she sees as subject to the whims of fortune, fancy, or the good moods of bad bosses. It is quite appropriate for some projects in our system to be given an illusory spin for the purposes of sustaining our happiness in a sometimes wearisome world. For other pursuits, however—what we call *core projects*—the potential cost of illusory control becomes too high (Little, 1998). Such projects ought not be taken lightly but appraised as realistically as possible in a world of imperfect knowledge of the future course of events.

Finally, and relatedly, personal projects are in themselves temporally extended sets of action, thus they afford us the possibility of looking at the stage of a project as a moderator of the salutary effect of distortions. Taylor and Gollwitzer (1995) carried out an intriguing study in which they were able to show that it is at the earliest stages of project formulation, during which the individual is deliberating as to whether or not to undertake the project, that he or she is most likely to be veridical in perceptions of control and efficacy. However, when the individual is engaged in the implementation stage of a project, distortion is more likely to occur. This "implemental mind-set," in Gollwitzer's (1990) terms, is motivating precisely because it sustains the illusion of more control or efficacy than might be warranted.

This conclusion is not at all inconsistent with the social ecological view that control should be *based* upon accurate readings. Subsequent distortions, within the range of what Baumeister (1991) calls the "optimal zone of illusion" during the hot pursuit of project goals, may well be adaptive. Indeed, we see this as confirmation of Mark Twain's aphoristic advice on effective reporting: "I want the facts first; then I can distort them."

Luke's aspirations to become a basketball superstar, Jill's passing thought that she ought to begin her own engineering firm, and Ada's even more fleeting thought that she might live to see a cure for arthritis all need to be entered into with a perception of manageability as veridical as possible. Although it is tempting to say "Go for it!" to those we love, this would likely be more helpful advice after commitments have been made and the project is launched than when they are entertaining the possibility of a course of action that may have unanticipated consequences for their own lives and those of others.

Project Community: Having Sustainable Pursuits

Projects are typically, although not inevitably, social phenomena. They often derive from social expectations, particularly those that are regarded as normatively required age-graded "life tasks" (Cantor, 1990). Even those that are most deeply personal are often shared with intimate others. In PPA three dimensions tap into a sense of project community: visibility of projects, others' view of the importance of projects, and support given by others to the projects. The empirical evidence suggests that the higher the scores on these project community dimensions, the more likely the individual is to experience higher levels of well-being.

But there are, again, subtleties across the life span, this time relating to gender. We have some evidence suggesting that, although visibility of projects is salutary for women, it may be anxiety producing for younger men (Little, 1998). For women, well-being is enhanced to the extent that stressful projects are made visible to others; for males well-being is reduced if stressful projects are also visible ones. The reasons for this are still to be explored, but one possibility is that, for women, making a project visible increases the likelihood of support from others, whereas for men, making a project visible increases the likelihood of criticism or censure.

There is empirical evidence that there are individual differences in the extent to which people are able to solicit support for their projects. Extraverts, for example, experience greater efficacy in their project pursuits, particularly in those involving interpersonal activity and, even more specifically, in projects involving groups of others rather than dyadic relationships. Extraverts, in short, appear to thrive on making their projects visible to a larger array of individuals, whereas more introverted individuals restrict their project visibility to more intimate others (Little, Lecci, & Watkinson, 1992).

In some of our recent research with senior managers in the public and private sectors, we have found that women managers are more likely to be given more responsibility for "developing people" projects in their workforces. Yet they are not provided with sufficient support to bring these projects to successful fruition (Phillips, Little, & Goodine, 1996). I will revisit this issue later in the chapter as yet another hill that Jill must climb.

THREE TIERS FOR DEVELOPMENTAL SCIENCE: THE HAVINGS, DOINGS, AND BEINGS OF DEVELOPING SELVES

Personality psychology, in recent years, has been flourishing. McAdams (1996) has pointed to three particularly active areas of research that operate at different levels of analysis. I have depicted these as three tiers of personality research, concerned, in ascending order, with relatively stable traits, personal action constructs, and life stories (Little, 1996). Cantor (1990), invoking terms used earlier by Gordon Allport, has referred to traits and action constructs as the "havings" and "being" of personality. To sustain the gerund form, I think of the third, narrative tier, as concerned with the "beings" or selves that we create as we narrate our life stories to ourselves and others.

I believe this three-tier structure also is a helpful framework for exploring aspects of developmental science, and I wish to illustrate this by providing three examples from recent research. Although drawn primarily from our social ecological framework and projects research, the topics also incorporate contemporary research in areas that have, until recently, proceeded in isolation from one another. Together these examples illustrate some of the questions being explored and the provisional answers that have been forthcoming in the study of developing selves across the life span. Given their recency, I advance them primarily to stimulate further inquiry.

Tier 1 ("Havings"): Free Traits, Core Projects, and Acting Out of Character

Much of the discourse in developmental psychology and developmental science, more generally, has centered on questions of whether human nature is primarily plastic and mutable or fixed and frozen (Lerner, 1984). As in the field of personality psychology, some of the debate has centered on whether the notions of relatively stable traits or temperamental dispositions are viable constructs. In both personality and developmental psychology, recent scholarship has taken a turn toward acceptance of the notion of relatively enduring stable structures of personality that persist across the life span. More contentiously, some would argue that such fixity may be due to the genetic origin of the trait or temperamental dispositions. Perhaps this is captured most vividly in Costa and McCrae's (1994) invoking of William James's contention that after age 30 personality is "fixed like plaster." Under such a view, the remaining life trajectories of Jill and Ada are, to a substantial degree, shaped by the "fixed traits" that each of them "has" as a relatively invariant feature of self. Our own view, however, is that a stronger case can be made for seeing Jill and Ada as only half-plastered (Little, in press-a).

At the core of our view is the notion of "free traits" (Little, 1996). Indeed, I believe that in developmental science we need a "free trait agreement." It goes like this. Consider a trait such as extraversion, which, under Eysenck's (1970) model, is genetic in origin with a neuropsychological base (although compare Gottlieb, 1992). Extraverts have a resting state of neocortical arousal that is under the optimal level and that impels them to seek out stimulation in order to move up to more optimal processing. Such stimulation can come from environmental engagement in pursuits that are arousing, such as a game of pickup basketball or a social function with gregarious clients. Optimal arousal may also be achieved through direct action upon the central nervous system and the increased neocortical arousal caused by the ingestion of stimulants, such as caffeine.

But extraverted conduct is not just a neuropsychological predisposition, it is also a well-understood social script; we know what is involved in extraverted conduct, and we may find ourselves, unwillingly or not, for good reasons or poor, to be acting in an extraverted fashion. If a "naturally" introverted person engages in such extraverted conduct, we might say that he or she is a "pseudoextravert," and that, in a sense, he or she is acting rather disingenuously. But we might also say that such a person is acting "out of character," and I mean that description to be explicitly ambiguous.

In one sense, "out of character" entails acting in ways that are unnatural or unexpected, as when we say that Ada's reticence was "out of character" (i.e., *against* her character) at the birthday party. But the phrase is also invoked when we say that we did things because we valued them, on the basis of our deep convictions—we acted out of character (i.e., on *behalf* of our character). I believe that much of the perplexity of conduct such as Jill's depicted in this chapter can be explained if we think of individuals as acting in a "free-traited" manner. Such behavior is not necessarily phony. On the contrary, it may be in the service of the individuals' most cherished core projects.

But protractedly acting out of character, I propose, may exact a cost; it may put a person at risk for emotional burnout. Jill can be a pseudoextravert for a few hours every week because, despite her growing frustration, a core-valued project for her is "honoring my obligations to the firm." We can speculate on some of the factors that might increase the risk of burnout when an individual engages in free-traited behavior. Certainly being forced or coerced to engage in such behavior rather than its stemming from more autonomous choice will increase the likelihood of its leading to burnout.

In the case of Jill's pseudoextraversion, there is an additional twist. As a "true" introvert, Jill has a need for lower-than-normal levels of stimulation in order to work most effectively on her engineering tasks. To the extent that she is engaged in the highly evocative and overarousing social functions that have been thrust upon her, she is likely to be overstimulated neocortically. But she is also likely, because of the loose coupling between neocortical and autonomic arousal, to experience signs of anxiety and increased physiological markers of stress.

What can be done to mitigate the effects of free-traited behavior? One suggestion is that individuals might find restorative niches in which they can seek respite from overstimulation by escaping to places of lesser intensity (Little, in press-a). Clearly the affordance structure of Jill's office environment is critical here. If there is literally no place to which she can escape (a closed door being an invitation to others to rush in with tongues clicking), a long-term toll may become inevitable.

I suspect that free-traited behavior emerges in the course of identity formation and is one of the more subtle ways in which self-development proceeds. Theoretically, each of the currently influential Big Five factors of neuroticism, extraversion, openness, conscientiousness, and agreeableness (and their contrasting poles) can be engaged in a free-traited fashion. It should be noted that by invoking core projects as the justification for acting "out of character," I have linked Tier 1 for a developmental science with Tier 2. It is to this level that we now ascend.

Tier 2 (Action): Personal Projects and Probable Selves— Wisdom, Ripeness, and the Temporal Ecology of Self-Focus

Tier 2 research in both personality and developmental psychology is concerned with dynamic, contextually sensitive units of analysis. McAdams (1996) refers to these units as *personal concerns*; others prefer the term *goal units* (e.g., Nurmi, 1993). My own preference is to regard these units as *personal action constructs* (PAC units), a term that underscores the "personal" aspect common to both personal constructs and personal projects and the natural affinity that such research has with action theory (Little, 1987).

I have already discussed personal projects in detail; I want to focus here upon two issues of direct concern to the overall theme of this book. First, I will examine a particularly interesting category of project that was anticipated in the discussion of free traits at Tier 1: These are what we call *intrapersonal projects*. They are a relatively frequent kind of project, particularly among university students, annd they concern explicit attempts to change the self, to influence one's own psychological dispositions.

Examples of intrapersonal projects are "be more outgoing with my clients," "try not to get angry at the kids for being away all the time," and "be more open to others." They are perhaps the best example of projects as "carrier units" for identity and self-development. The correlates of generating a relatively high frequency of intrapersonal projects show two interesting, divergent patterns. On the one hand, research in our own laboratory as well as in Helsinki (Salmela-Aro, 1992; Salmela-Aro & Nurmi, 1996) has shown that a high frequency of intrapersonal projects is associated with depressive affect. On the other hand, a high frequency of such projects has also been shown to correlate with creativity (see Little, 1998). This raises the important question of what characteristics differentiate intrapersonal self-focused projects that are depressogenic from those that lead to greater self-exploration.

Although we do not have empirical evidence on this point as yet, I suspect that whether the project was initiated by self or others will be critical in determining whether it will have a positive or negative impact on well-being. Jill's self-initiated attempt to be more outgoing in the service of a core project might well represent her creative openness to expanding her self into an area she has shied away from in her younger years. If the project is laid down by others as a condition of continued employment, one can see how it could lead to ruminative worry and apprehension. Intrapersonal projects are likely to be successful, we anticipate, when they occur as personal experiments with the self rather than as begrudging attempts to change one's nature at the behest of others.

A second theme relates to the conjoint use of different PAC units, specifically personal projects and Markus and Nurius's (1986) "possible selves." In one of our studies with university students, we first elicited a description by each student of a "desired possible self" set 5 years into the future. Each student then completed a PPA matrix containing, on top of the standard dimensions, an ad hoc column labeled "possible self facilitation." It asked the respondent to rate each personal project on the extent to which that project helped facilitate the acquisition of the possible self he or she had previously listed. We anticipated that well-being measures would correlate significantly with the extent to which students indicated that their current projects were facilitating the acquisition of their desired possible selves. This was confirmed (Goodine, Little, & Sourani, 1993).

However, there was an instructive age effect that moderated the results. The linkage of current projects to possible selves (5 years in the future) was particularly strongly related to well-being for the younger, typically first-year students. However, for older students, typically those returning to university after being in the workplace for a period of time, there was no relationship. Rather, the best predictor of well-being for this group was the extent to which their current projects were high on *self-identity*.

It appears that there are temporal ecological factors at work here. For the younger students, hitching their projects to their future selves was salutary. For the older students, their current selves (perhaps the possible selves of 5 years ago) were most salient. It is as though they were, like Jill, saying, "If I'm not finally being myself now, maybe I'd better get out of here." Ripeness and readiness, key Shakespearean themes, thus appear to be similarly central in the lives of our students. At a certain point in adult development, the time for testing the fidelity of the self comes due, and the distant future becomes a distracting diversion.

Tier 3 (Life Stories): Personal Contexts and the Larger Picture—Images and Idio-Tapes

In both personality and developmental psychology, narrative accounts, with the life story as the central organizing theme, have come to play an influential role (e.g., McAdams, 1996; Sarbin, 1996). It is at this level that the processes of self-formation and identity are of focal, rather than peripheral or derivative, interest. I wish to make some observations about this level of analysis designed to contribute to its continued development, but critical of one of its drawbacks.

Even since my first year of teaching, I have used personal sketches in my courses in personality and developmental psychology. On the first day of the course, students choose pseudonyms and produce two-page single-spaced typed life stories that capture what, to them, are the most salient images of their lives (the students are warned to conceal any identifying information). On the second day of class these life stories are distributed to all students, with the pseudonyms protecting anonymity. The results are almost invariably dramatic. Other class members become something more than background shadows. They become central characters with stories to tell that are as various as the selves that created them—some tragic, some hilarious, many poignant. During the courses in which sketches are used, students create journals in which they apply the lecture and reading material to their own sketches, often going back and revisiting earlier entries as their knowledge of human development becomes more sophisticated. I have managed to keep copies of most of these narrative sketches gathered over the years. Apart from their value as personal documents and as pedagogical tools, they also leave a rich trace of the historical record of the time.

What becomes clear, in reading them, is that they provide a framework for discussing the *personal contexts* of students' lives at different stages of development. Although McAdams (1996) has provided a rich framework through which life stories can be evaluated, there is one problem that we have had in trying to study personal sketches, and that is the tendency for a large number of the sketches to depict very similar thematic plots. The possibility that this represents stylistic convention rather than idiosyncratic portrayal of individuals' life contexts suggests that we may need alternative ways of capturing these stories without resorting to formal essays. In addition, there is the problem of sheer volume and the intensive parsing and coding required to study identity through the open-ended narrative form. In short, there is a winnowing problem: From the abundance of themes that might be depicted, can we provide a lens through which we can view only the most evocative and defining ones?

We have begun to explore one way of dealing with this winnowing problem. We call it the *idio-tape technique.* We ask individuals to imagine that they have video cameras through which they are going to "shoot" their most important personal images. There are no restrictions on the nature of the images; they may be images of themselves, of their loved ones, or of historic events with which they have identified—even purely imaginary images, as long as they are personally evocative for them and help convey a sense of their identities. Each image, which now serves as the winnowed-down unit of analysis, can then be rated on relevant dimensions, such as how enjoyable it is and how "far away" the image is (from up close to quite distant). Also, it is possible to juxtapose idio-tape images with units gathered at the other two levels of analysis and ask a respondent to describe the relationships between them. (Further details on this method are provided in Little, 1998, in press-a.)

Perhaps the most important additional information that is generated by this technique relates to images of intimate relationships with others. Were we to ask Ada to tell us her personal projects, she may not include anything specifically relating to Jack, or her cat, feeling that these are too fleeting and insubstantial to qualify as "projects." However, as idio-tape images such pictures often play a central role, suggesting the technique may provide important information complementing that gathered in research with the other tiers.

Finally, Sarbin (1996) has written eloquently about what he calls the "poetics" of identity, in which historical myths and cultural scripts transmitted generationally become major instigators of personal action. Various forms of criminal and terrorist activity often reflect, in considerable detail, the scripts that have been transmitted in narrative form through children's stories and popular accounts of heroes and villains.

From Personal Projects to Social Policy:
Gender, Climate, and the Community

We have recently expanded our research on human development and personality into the domain of organizational analysis and social policy in a study of the personal projects of senior-level managers in the public and private sectors (Phillips, Little, & Goodine, 1996, 1997). Some of the most important findings relate to gender and organizational life.

First, we found clear evidence that women are expected to undertake "managing people" projects more often than are their male counterparts, but they are not provided the organizational support they need to carry these projects through to completion. In short, the scenario with which we began, with Jill feeling imposed upon to be the "designated person specialist" in her organization, was not an arbitrary image. It appears to be a common feature of the life of many organizations.

Second, there is very clear, indeed striking, evidence that there are major gender differences in the extent to which senior managers see their personal projects as linked with their organizational climates. When linkage is measured as the degree of association between ratings of one's projects and ratings of one's departmental climate, we found that the linkage for women was threefold higher than that for men. For these women, personal project appraisals were intimately linked with their perceptions of the microclimates within which they unfolded. For men, these appraisals were essentially independent.

There are several possible explanations for this. The effect was found first in the Canadian public service and was replicated with even stronger results in the private sector companies. However, it was not detected in municipal-level government agencies. It may well be that this is not a gender effect, as such, but the adaptive scanning of the milieu by individuals who are marginalized (perhaps by being members of a minority group) in a large organization. This explanation is consistent with the fact that in the municipal sample there was virtual gender parity and the greatest gender discrepancy was in the private sector domain, where there are fewer women in management positions.

Finally, when we probed the links between respondents' personal projects and their possible selves "5 years from now," one of the most pervasive themes we found for women was their desire to get involved in voluntary activities. They saw themselves as becoming active in their communities and as expecting to gain considerable pleasure from doing so. We are currently interviewing these subjects, 5 years later, to see if their strong desires to contribute to community action have had a chance to materialize. Interestingly, the other theme that showed up frequently in plans for retirement among these senior managers (as well as in their current project lists) was gardening. It might be suggested that both volunteering and gardening represent nurturing activities; perhaps these individuals felt that such nurturing had been stifled in their work organizations, and they now see such activities as viable possible projects.

We have made policy recommendations that organizations in public service provide greater opportunities for staff to become engaged in voluntary activities (Phillips et al., 1997). The increase in "social capital" provided by such activities redounds to everyone's benefit, and the research investment from our university in monitoring the effectiveness of these pursuits is consistent with other innovations that link the needs of children, organizations, and universities (e.g., Lerner & Galambos, 1998).

So, to round out the narrative. I would like to think that Jill has been struggling with a number of issues highlighted in this chapter. She has been asked to play the role of a pseudoextravert in social activities that are overstimulating and more manipulative than nurturing. I have had word that she has indeed switched companies and is working for a smaller firm in which there are more women and a clear expectation of shared responsibilities among all staff for all of the major tasks. Competent, analytic, and discerning, Jill still has needs for intimate exchanges that don't involve the playing of games and a tacit agenda of "selling us to the client." I like to imagine that she sees an advertisement for a Volunteer Home Visiting program across town. In my idio-tape version of the conclusion, I see images of her meeting a rambunctious kid named Jack, a decreasingly gangly teenaged Luke, and a wise grandmother who knows her physical limitations and welcomes this kind stranger into their home. Given the vicissitudes of life and the chaos involved in local prediction, however, Jill may simply plant a garden. In either case, new life is nurtured and at least one self is enhanced.

REFERENCES

Baumeister, R. F. (1991). *Meanings of life.* New York: Guilford.

Brandtstädter, J., & Wentura, D. (1995). Adjustment to shifting possibility frontiers in later life: Complementary adaptive modes. In R. A. Dixon & L. Bäckman

(Eds.), *Compensating for psychological deficits and declines: Managing losses and promoting gains* (pp. 83-106). Mahwah, NJ: Lawrence Erlbaum.

Breed, R. L., & Emmons, R. A. (1996, April). *Personal goals and bereavement: Coping with the loss of a loved one.* Paper presented at the annual convention of the Western Psychological Association, San Jose, CA.

Bruner, J. (1990). *Acts of meaning.* Cambridge, MA: Harvard University Press.

Cantor, N. (1990). From thought to behavior: "Having" and "doing" in the study of personality and cognition. *American Psychologist, 45,* 735-750.

Chambers, N. (1997). *Personal projects analysis: The maturation of a multi-dimensional methodology.* Unpublished manuscript, Carleton University, Ottawa.

Costa, P. T., & McCrae, R. R. (1994). Set like plaster? Evidence for the stability of adult personality. In T. F. Heatherton & J. L. Weinberger (Eds.), *Can personality change?* (pp. 21-40). Washington, DC: American Psychological Association.

Deci, E. L., & Ryan, R. M. (1991). A motivational approach to self: Integration in personality. In R. Dienstbier (Ed.), *Nebraska Symposium on Motivation: Vol. 38. Perspectives on motivation* (pp. 237-288). Lincoln: University of Nebraska Press.

Eysenck, H. J. (1970). *The structure of human personality.* London: Methuen.

Gee, T. L. (1998). *Individual and joint-level properties of personal project matrices: An exploration of the nature of project spaces.* Unpublished doctoral dissertation, Carleton University, Ottawa.

Gollwitzer, P. M. (1990). Action phases and mind-sets. In E. T. Higgins & R. M. Sorrentino (Eds.), *Handbook of motivation and cognition: Vol. 2. Foundations of social behavior* (pp. 53-92). New York: Guilford.

Gottlieb, G. (1992). *Individual development and evolution: The genesis of novel behavior.* New York: Oxford University Press.

Goodine, L. A., Little, B. R., & Sourani, L. (1993). *Possible selves and personal projects: A time perspective on the distributed self.* Paper presented at the annual meeting of the Canadian Psychological Association, Montreal.

Kelly, G. A. (1955). *The psychology of personal constructs.* New York: Norton.

Lerner, R. M. (1984). *On the nature of human plasticity.* New York: Random House.

Lerner, R. M., & Galambos, N. L. (1998). Adolescent development: Challenges and opportunities for research, programs, and policies. *Annual Review of Psychology, 49,* 413-446.

Little, B. R. (1968). Psychospecialization: Functions of differential interest in persons and things. *Bulletin of the British Psychological Society, 21,* 113.

Little, B. R. (1972). Psychological man as scientist, humanist and specialist. *Journal of Experimental Research in Personality, 6,* 95-118.

Little, B. R. (1976). Specialization and the varieties of environmental experience: Empirical studies within the personality paradigm. In S. Wapner, S. B. Cohen, & B. Kaplan (Eds.), *Experiencing the environment* (pp. 81-116). New York: Plenum.

Little, B. R. (1983). Personal projects: A rationale and method for investigation. *Environment and Behavior, 15,* 273-309.

Little, B. R. (1987). Personality and the environment. In D. Stokols & I. Altman (Eds.), *Handbook of environmental psychology* (pp. 205-244). New York: John Wiley.

Little, B. R. (1989). Personal projects analysis: Trivial pursuits, magnificent obsessions, and the search for coherence. In D. M. Buss & N. Cantor (Eds.), *Personality psychology: Recent trends and emerging issues* (pp. 15-31). New York: Springer-Verlag.

Little, B. R. (1993). Personal projects and the distributed self: Aspects of a conative psychology. In J. Suls (Ed.), *Psychological perspectives on the self* (Vol. 4, pp. 157-181). Hillsdale, NJ: Lawrence Erlbaum.

Little, B. R. (1996). Free traits, personal projects and idio-tapes: Three tiers for personality research. *Psychological Inquiry, 8,* 340-344.

Little, B. R. (1998). Personal project pursuit: Dimensions and dynamics of personal meaning. In P. T. P. Wong & P. S. Fry (Eds.), *The human quest for meaning: A handbook of research and clinical applications* (pp. 193-235). Mahwah, NJ: Lawrence Erlbaum.

Little, B. R. (in press a). Free traits and personal contexts: Expanding a social ecological model of well-being. In W. B. Walsh, K. H. Craik, & R. Price (Eds.), *Person environment psychology* (2nd ed.). New York: Guilford.

Little, B. R. (in press b). Personality and motivation: Personal action and the conative evolution. In L. A. Pervin & O. P. John (Eds.), *Handbook of personality theory and research* (2nd ed.). New York: Guilford.

Little, B. R. (in press c). Persons, contexts and personal projects: Assumptive themes of a methodological transactionalism. In S. Wapner, J. Demick, H. Minami, & T. Yamamoto (Eds.), *Theoretical perspectives in environment-behavior research: Underlying assumptions, research problems and methodologies.* New York: Plenum.

Little, B. R., Lecci, L., & Watkinson, B. (1992). Personality and personal projects: Linking Big Five and PAC units of analysis. *Journal of Personality, 60,* 501-525.

Little, B. R., & Ryan, T. J. (1979). A social ecological model of development. In K. Ishwaran (Ed.), *Childhood and adolescence in Canada* (pp. 273-301). Toronto: McGraw-Hill Ryerson.

Markus, H., & Nurius, P. (1986). Possible selves. *American Psychologist, 41,* 954-969.

McAdams, D. P. (1996). Personality, modernity, and the storied self: A contemporary framework for studying persons. *Psychological Inquiry, 7,* 295-321.

McGregor, I., & Little, B. R. (1998). Personal projects, happiness, and meaning: On doing well and being yourself. *Journal of Personality and Social Psychology, 74,* 494-512.

Nurmi, J.-E. (1993). Adolescent developments in an age-graded context: The role of personal beliefs, goals, and strategies in the tackling of developmental tasks and standards. *International Journal of Behavioral Development, 16,* 169-189.

Phillips, S. D., Little, B. R., & Goodine, L. (1996). *Organizational climate and personal projects: Gender differences in the public service.* Ottawa: Canadian Centre for Management Development.

Phillips, S. D., Little, B. R., & Goodine, L. (1997). Reconsidering gender and public administration: Five steps beyond conventional research. *Canadian Public Administration, 40,* 563-581.

Salmela-Aro, K. (1992). Struggling with the self: The personal projects of students seeking psychological counselling. *Scandinavian Journal of Psychology, 33,* 330-338.

Salmela-Aro, K., & Nurmi, J.-E. (1996). Depressive symptoms and personal project appraisals: A cross-lagged longitudinal study. *Personality and Individual Differences, 21,* 373-381.

Sarbin, T. R. (1996). *The poetics of identity.* Henry Murray Award Address, presented at the annual meeting of the American Psychological Association, New York.

Sheldon, K. M., & Elliot, A. (1998). Not all personal goals are personal: Comparing autonomous and controlled reasons for goals as predictors of effort and attainment. *Personality and Social Psychology Bulletin, 24,* 546-557.

Taylor, S. E., & Brown, J. D. (1988). Illusion and well-being: A social psychological perspective on mental health. *Psychological Bulletin, 103,* 193-210.

Taylor, S. E., & Gollwitzer, P. M. (1995). Effects of mindset on positive illusions. *Journal of Personality and Social Psychology, 69,* 213-226.

Weik, K. E. (1984). Small wins: Redefining the scale of social problems. *American Psychologist, 39,* 40-49.

Wilson, D. A. (1990). *Personal project dimensions and perceived life satisfaction: A quantitative synthesis.* Unpublished master's thesis, Carleton University, Ottawa, ON.

8

LIFE PLANNING

Anticipating Future Life Goals and Managing Personal Development

Jacqui Smith

Why do individuals actively anticipate and make plans about future life events or life goals? Motivational theories suggest that anticipatory planning serves several purposes. It reduces uncertainty, helps the individual to get over initial problems in starting work on a goal, establishes a mind-set conducive to achieving the goal, and helps to minimize stress for the individual and others (e.g., Aspinwall & Taylor, 1997; Buehler, Griffin, & MacDonald, 1997; Gollwitzer, 1996). Planning also provides the individual with a means of testing alternative actions without actually evoking the physical resources or social and personal costs necessary to engage in the action (Austin & Vancouver, 1996). Furthermore, once a plan is created and stored for multiple access in long-term memory, cognitive capacity can be focused on directing and monitoring on-line behavior. People generally agree that the motives behind engaging in planning are worthwhile and feel satisfied that having plans assists them in working toward future life goals.

There is, however, some debate about the actual effectiveness of planning. On the one side, work on proactive coping, mental simulation, and successful major life change suggests that anticipatory planning is beneficial (e.g., Aspinwall & Taylor, 1997; Heatherton & Nichols, 1994; Taylor, Pham, Rivkin, & Armor, 1998). People who mentally simulate future events report less stress and more positive affect, and are more likely to use effective problem-solving strategies compared with people who do not simulate. On the other hand, social psychologists have long documented evidence of the so-called planning fallacy. This refers to observations that plans are often not the best predictors of what actually happens. Planned personal and institutional projects are seldom finished on time or within anticipated financial budgets (e.g., Buehler, Griffin, & Ross, 1994; Kahneman, Slovic, & Tversky, 1982).

There thus appears to be a mismatch between our beliefs and theories about the benefits of anticipatory planning and our skills in carrying out such planning. Although most people have personal stories of planning to do something in the future and either not managing to do it or underestimating what was really involved in working toward the goal, they nevertheless regularly engage in making new life plans and in advising others to do the same. There are strong expectations in Western cultures that government bodies and private industry invest much time and effort in planning for the future. Indeed, social institutions (e.g., political parties) are often judged on their proposed long-term plans of action and are periodically evaluated as to how well they have kept to those plans.

Several strands of information are required if we are to begin to understand why this mismatch occurs between beliefs about future planning and behavior. First, we need to examine the *beliefs and social expectations* about life planning that form the context for people's engaging in it and evaluating the results. Second, we need to have models of the *process* of planning life goals in order to understand the complexity of anticipating the future course of an individual's life. Further, this information about beliefs and processes also has to be combined with research that looks at age-related and individual differences in life-planning performance. The identification of specific characteristics of effective and less effective life plans and planners in terms of process and outcome would help to clarify whether the difficulties people appear to have with life planning are a function of their lack of skill or the sheer complexity of the task.

In this chapter, I describe four general organizational skills assumed to be associated with the planning of life goals (see Smith, 1996): time management, resource management, interpersonal management (the ability to use a social network to achieve goals), and self-management (the capacity to arrange a motivation system geared to working on goals). I set out a framework for examining beliefs about the use of these four components of life planning, and I propose that the effectiveness (or success) of planning in terms of achieving or avoiding life goals or minimizing the stress of challenging anticipated events depends on two aspects: (a) selection of the appropriate mix of these four components for the life task context and goals, and (b) the skill of the planner in recognizing, creating, and implementing the mix.

Of course, the ultimate success of life planning in terms of personal development depends not only on the effective implementation and coordination of these four organizational planning components but on the individual's choice of life goal(s). In principle, an ill-chosen life goal could be effectively planned and attained yet not contribute to personal development in a desirable way. If a mind-set of the type described by Gollwitzer (1990, 1996) is firmly established for an ill-chosen life goal, for instance, it would be very difficult for the person to disengage from that goal. However, it is presumed that this latter scenario is probably a rare case. It could be that effective mind-sets are never established for ill-chosen goals. Furthermore, poor selection of life goals would probably be linked with ineffective (unskilled) planning strategies and poor organizational skills, which would result in nonattainment of the goal(s). Before describing the present framework and the four components in more detail, I provide in the next section some background about the concept of life planning, general processes of planning, and elements of a social cognitive and life-span perspective on life planning.

LIFE PLANNING: SETTING FUTURE LIFE GOALS AND PLANNING HOW TO REACH THEM

The Concept

Life planning involves an individual's thinking about the possible future content, course, and purpose of his or her life (Smith, 1996). A life plan is best thought of as a complex network of ideas about future goals and strategies for attaining these goals. These goals and strategies are constructed from a person's extensive social and personal knowledge system, and they in turn guide the person's actions. A life plan includes parts that are hierarchically organized (e.g., central goals and the various subgoals associated with them, strategies and their sequence of tactics) as well as parts that have equal status (e.g., various central goals with equal importance or alternative strategies with equal preference). This organization can change as one life goal becomes more salient or context-specific aspects afford the use of one strategy over another.

A life plan encompasses guiding aphorisms and long-range timetables as well as the dynamic processes related to devising ways to attain, maintain, monitor, and update life goals and schedules. In addition to procedural information, the content of a life plan also reflects the motivational system of the individual. Engaging in life planning implies that the individual believes that he or she can, to some degree, control (direct or manage) his or her own future development.

The knowledge-based and motivational conception of a life plan adopted here is derived primarily from the work of Schank and Abelson (1977) and subsequent work on case-based reasoning (Riesbeck & Schank, 1989). These authors make the important point that there are differences between routine plans of action that are linked to scripts for everyday behavior and plans for novel events. Plans for novel events (e.g., life goals in the distant future) evolve along the way. Life planning does not simply involve retrieving a stored routine plan from long-term memory (see Smith, 1996).

Life plans are constructed from individuals' knowledge of life situations, persons, and themselves. Knowledge about planning a life is an aspect of cognition that is socialized, applied, and challenged throughout the life course (see Berger, Berger, & Kellner, 1967; Brim, 1992; Rawls, 1971). An individual might use such knowledge to plan his or her own life, construct and guide the life plans of others (e.g., as a parent or mentor), or participate in the collaborative development of joint life plans (e.g., with friends and partners). Evidence for different usages of knowledge about life planning can be found in everyday understanding and conversations about life matters (e.g., Schank & Abelson, 1977; Stein, 1988; Wilensky, 1983), in judgments we make about the life choices and life courses of ourselves and others (e.g., Cantor & Kihlstrom, 1987; Heckhausen & Schulz, 1995; Smith & Baltes, 1990a, 1990b; Smith, Dixon, & Baltes, 1989), in reflections about the future self (Brandtstädter & Greve, 1994; Brandtstädter, Wentura, & Schmitz, 1997; Markus & Ruvolo, 1989; Raynor & Entin, 1982), and in behavior patterns and attributions (Cantor & Kihlstrom, 1987; Johnson & Sherman, 1990).

Because life plans are derived from socially shared general knowledge, there is a degree of consensus about the strategies and tactics that are linked to particular goals and that are means to reaching those goals. At the same time, there are likely individual variations in the selection and modified expression of goals and strategies. Furthermore, across the life span individuals may focus more or less on the selection of new life goals or on devising plans that include strategies to optimize goal attainment or to compensate for personal constraints (see also in this volume Brandtstädter, Wentura, & Rothermund, Chapter 13; Freund, Li, & Baltes, Chapter 14).

Processes of Life Planning and Everyday Planning: Similarities, Differences, and Heuristics

Any model of the processes involved in life planning needs to be explicit about aspects that are common to everyday planning and aspects that distinguish instances of life planning. In general, planning activities (both everyday and in relation to life goals) can occur on many levels of behavior, from micro to meta (Scholnick & Friedman, 1987, 1993; Wilensky, 1983). In all of these contexts, processes associated with planning involve the generation, selection, and coordination of goals and strategies for implementing decisions and obtaining these goals. In a general sense, planning has been described in the literature as a form of mental simulation (see Taylor et al., 1998) and as the process of linking goals to various behavioral scripts, tactics, and alternative strategies (Austin & Vancouver, 1996; Carver & Scheier, 1990). In a narrower sense, cognitive researchers studying processes involved in the solution of laboratory problems have defined planning as "the predetermination of a course of action aimed at achieving some goal" (Hayes-Roth & Hayes-Roth, 1979, pp. 275-276). Motivational theorists view planning as the step that prepares goal intentions for action (e.g., Bratman, 1987; Gollwitzer, 1996; Heckhausen & Gollwitzer, 1987).

Much experimental psychological research has focused on the micro level of planning. Studies describe planning strategies devised to attain a single concrete goal (usually predetermined by the experimenter) in a short-term context. Work within the cognitive science perspective best illustrates this approach (e.g., Hayes-Roth & Hayes-Roth, 1979; Riesbeck & Schank, 1989; Schank & Abelson, 1977; Scholnick & Friedman, 1987; Wilensky, 1983). Cognitive researchers strive to understand the knowledge and processes involved in (a) problem representation, (b) goal organization, (c) strategy activation and execution, and (d) outcome evaluation. For this purpose, they typically examine planning problems and tasks for which all (or almost all) parameters are known and for which there are accepted best solutions, so that they can introduce experimental manipulations and test hypotheses about processes. In some laboratories, this approach has been extended to investigate everyday instances of planning (e.g., planning to complete a list of shopping errands, to get to work on time, or to complete a college assignment). These tasks usually involve recalling and implementing standard "scripts" for the concrete event and action sequences (see Schank & Abelson, 1977; Scholnick & Friedman, 1987). Life-span studies within this approach have described developmental changes in problem representation, planning, and decision-making strategies (e.g., Friedman, Scholnick, & Cocking, 1987).

Life planning differs from the planning of everyday and single concrete events in several respects. At a general level, the goals and domains of life planning are typically more complex, abstract, vague, and open-ended and less able to be routinized than those of everyday problems (Smith, 1996). Although models of life planning encompass the same basic processes as models of general planning (i.e., the generation, selection, and coordination of goals and strategies for implementing decisions and actions to obtain these goals), the components have far less certainty of definition and involve more complexity. As outlined in this chapter, part of the complexity involves the individual's organization of time, resources, him- or herself, and others (see Smith, 1996).

Another obvious difference between a life plan and an everyday plan is the time frame involved. Whereas an everyday plan may specify a concrete sequence of decisions and actions aimed at the quick achievement of a short-term goal, more often than not the outcome of life planning is a vague intention for the distant future (see Berger et al., 1967; Brim, 1992; Rawls, 1971). A life plan evolves over an extended period of time, increasing in clarity of final goal(s) and precision of detail. Thus at different single time points during the generation process, an individual's life-planning strategy might well be characterized as "muddling through" (chaotic) or "straight down the middle" (highly organized). The time and interpersonal management skills required for life planning involve the individual's coordination of his or her own life schedule with the life schedules of others and his or her estimation of the time required for an array of different tasks. The individual applies self-regulation and resource management skills to keep track of long-term perspectives in the face of multiple short-term diversions and to assure that sufficient resources are invested in the long-term goals.

A further important difference between everyday planning and life planning is that the outcome of the latter cognitive activity is likely to have substantially greater long-term repercussions. Whereas the efficiency of planning for the completion of an errand (e.g., Hayes-Roth & Hayes-Roth, 1979) or the organization of a dinner menu (e.g., Byrne, 1977) may produce short-term frustration or happiness, planning to begin parenthood and to raise a child can have lifetime implications. The organization of resources has to go hand in hand with strategies of interpersonal management and self-regulation. Life plans are intimately linked to social, interpersonal, and emotional dimensions of the self (Cantor & Kihlstrom, 1987; Emmons, 1989).

Several heuristics of planning have been identified that apply equally to life planning and the planning of everyday activities (Buehler et al., 1997; Hayes-Roth & Hayes-Roth, 1979; Payne, Bettman, & Johnson, 1993). A central one is the principle of least effort. Planning is supposed to minimize time spent on a task, the energy expended, or the distance to reach the goal. Furthermore, if there are a large number of alternative pathways by which an individual might reach a goal, then simplifying heuristic rules are used, such as satisficing (Kahneman et al., 1982; Payne et al., 1993). Cognitive researchers report that people tend to be flexible, adaptive, and opportunistic in their planning. During planning, people change back and forth between different levels of abstraction and opportunistically reorder the direction of anticipated actions as they engage in the task (Hayes-Roth & Hayes-Roth, 1979). A good plan is generally thought to be one that allows room for some changes during implementation. Plans are conceived to be dynamic rather than static. Planning also appears to be biased in a generally positive and optimistic direction. For instance, people tend to underestimate the time required to execute actions and to believe that their own projects will proceed as planned even though the majority of similar plans made by others run late (i.e., the planning fallacy; Buehler et al., 1994; Kahneman et al., 1982).

Social Cognitive and Life-Span Perspectives on Life Planning

Questions about life planning can be addressed from many perspectives. This chapter draws on two: a social cognitive perspective and a life-span perspective. The social cognitive perspective emphasizes the social context of planning and the importance of knowledge and belief systems in determining planning performance over and above the operation of basic cognitive processes. The life-span perspective addresses age-related and individual differences in the structure and application of personal knowledge systems and in the life tasks that individuals plan.

Combined, these two approaches can help us to understand individual and age-related differences in the anticipation and planning of future life events and developmental goals. In particular, these approaches suggest that in the study of planning it is important to consider (a) the age of the planner, (b) the social and objective constraints associated with planning in different life domains, (c) knowledge and belief systems about planning strategies, and (d) individual differences in planning and organizational skills.

These four aspects influence the amount of life planning that an individual reports and his or her planning performance. So, for example, the different social-structural opportunities, constraints, and expectations faced by young, middle-aged, and older adults in various life domains may contribute to age differences in the amount of reported life planning. According to life-course theories of the social clock and compartmentalization of life tasks (Hagestad & Neugarten, 1985; Riley & Riley, 1994), older adults are expected to make few new plans regarding work and family, whereas young adults are expected to make many. In general, compared with young adults, older adults may consider fewer life domains as available or open for future planning. Age may also influence the profile of life planning in that it influences motives for engaging in new activities, maintaining familiar activities, or reengaging in activities started previously but never strongly pursued. Furthermore, there may be age differences in knowledge and beliefs about the use of planning strategies. I will describe initial findings about beliefs regarding planning across the life span later in this chapter.

FOUR ORGANIZATIONAL
COMPONENTS OF LIFE PLANNING

At the beginning of this chapter I suggested that, in addition to the choice of life goals relevant to the individual's competencies, effective life planning involves the appropriate mixture and skilled use of four organizational components: time management, resource management, interpersonal management, and self-management. Figure 8.1 depicts the combination of the four organizational components we apply to manage our lives and to attain

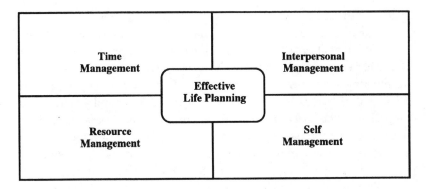

Figure 8.1. The Four Organizational Components of Effective Life Planning

the life goals for which we strive. Much work has already been devoted to describing the selection of life goals and life tasks (for reviews, refer to various chapters in this book); the present framework focuses instead on the organizational strategies associated with the selected life goals. It suggests that in order to begin to evaluate planning about life matters, we need to know how each of these components is incorporated in an overall plan and how skillfully each is applied in the course of the individual's working toward a goal. For instance, we would need to evaluate whether the weight given to the consideration of each component is appropriate and whether the component-specific strategies are relevant. Life plans could further be evaluated in terms of how well the components are synchronized (e.g., whether time is managed in such a way as to facilitate self- and interpersonal management). It is also important to understand beliefs about these four organizational skills with regard to different life goals. The priorities expected to be given to the various components may indeed differ by life domain.

Specific criteria for evaluating effective planning are likely to vary by life task. In general, however, a plan will be viewed as effective if it ensures that (a) a project is completed (a desired goal achieved or an undesired scenario avoided), (b) completion is within the estimated time period, (c) completion involves the least amount of effort, (d) any stress to the individual or others and difficulties involved in the project are minimized, and (e) in the end the individual is satisfied with the result (i.e., he or she perceives a positive balance of benefits over costs).

A mixture or combination of the four planning components will likely be appropriate and effective if it is tailored to the task domain and the capacity of the individual involved. Not all four components will be equally important in planning for goals in different life domains. Some planned activities and goals may require attention to one component more than to others. For example, planning for the goal "to stay healthy" may focus on coordinating strategies to manage oneself (e.g., motivation, persistence) and manage time for exercise, instead of on the resource and social network components. The goal to have a 3-month break from work to visit a different country, in contrast, requires close attention to planning and managing financial resources in preparation for the future event. Other life goals and tasks are so complex that they require the coordination of all four components. Planning to move with one's family to begin a job in another city in the next 6 months is a good illustration of a life goal that requires equal attention to time, resource, interpersonal, and self-management. Life goals that can be attained only over long periods of time require repeated updates of planning strategies and reorganization of the priorities given to the four components. The long-term life goal to coordinate family and work careers would involve much revision of planning strategies over time.

There are likely individual and age-related differences in the skilled knowledge and application of the four organizational components of life planning. Young, middle-aged, and older adults may consider different profiles of planning strategies and components as useful. Individual differences in future orientation and preferences for time use and structure could also influence the selection of new undertakings and beliefs about useful planning strategies. Furthermore, criteria for evaluating effective planning may differ by domain and age. I discuss some findings from an exploratory study about individual and age differences later in this chapter (Smith, 1998). That study examined social expectations and beliefs regarding life-course differences in the amount of activities that require planning. Young, middle-aged, and older adults estimated the number of things to be planned at ages 20 to 90 in seven life domains: family, friends, work, finances, leisure, health, and housing. The study also examined personal preferences for specific planning strategies and age differences in priorities given to time, resource, interpersonal, and self-management in different life domains.

Background material about the nature of the four organizational components of life planning and their role is reviewed below. Information about these components comes from diverse sources in the literature. On the basis of this literature, I offer a collection of exemplary strategies associated with each component as ways of investigating preferences for the organizational aspects of life planning (see Table 8.1). Initial findings about the preferences

TABLE 8.1 The Four Components of Planning: Examples of Organizational Strategies

Time Management	*Resource Management*	*Interpersonal Management*	*Self-Management*
Make lists	*Materials:* e.g., finances, cost-benefit analysis	Persuasian tactics	Self-monitor
Estimate time needed for each task and decide deadlines	*Skills:* acquire oneself or find others with them	Try to avoid the involvement of others	Establish a mind-set
Arrange sequence and devise a schedule or routine	*Knowledge:* selectively collect	Communication and discussion style	Use strategies that help to initiate work
Leave room for spontaneity	*Allocation of energy and effort:* least-effort principle	Foster reciprocal support	Foster persistence
Prioritize tasks for importance		Simply expect others to accommodate	
Develop strategies to avoid diversions		Engage in negotiation and collaboration	
Synchronize time plan with energy rhythms			

of persons ages 18 to 80 are summarized below (Smith, 1998). Participants in the study recognized that the strategies and tactics listed in Table 8.1 are potentially useful for life-planning tasks but also indicated personal preferences for particular strategies. Beliefs about the relative importance of time, resource, interpersonal, and self-management in the life planning of different age groups and in different life domains are also reported below.

Time Management

Time is a limited resource, and one over which individuals inherently can have no control. Nevertheless, people do use several strategies that help them feel as though they can control and manage their time. In particular, individuals devise means to create a sense of order, to make time concrete, and to give time a structure. Having done this and assigned concrete cues and symbols to measure time, they can then estimate how much time they will need to do something and evaluate whether the time they spent on a task was used efficiently.

Perceptions of psychological and personal time are social cognitive constructions. Individuals differ in their preferences for regularity (daily routine), need to know the time of day, orientation to the future, and desire to reduce the inherent uncertainty of the future. Different cultural groups have different temporal emphases (e.g., focus on past, present, or future), preferences for pace of life, and values for punctuality (e.g., Block, Buggie, & Matsui, 1996). On a societal and cultural level, groups structure life and time in terms of seasons, work, and rites of passage. Societal groups also evolve normative expectations about the benefits of planning about the future.

Clearly, calendars and clocks standardized to Greenwich mean time are obvious means for measuring and dividing physical time into concrete units. It has long been known, however, that humans are poor judges of such standardized time intervals (e.g., Fraise, 1981). Time appears to pass quickly or slowly depending on the activities in which we are involved. We experience time as passing quickly when we are busy or doing something that we find pleasant or interesting. We perceive time to pass slowly during periods when there is little activity, when we are involved in unpleasant tasks, and when the environment does not change.

Given that people are inexpert judges of physical time intervals, what strategies do individuals use to help them feel as though they can manage time? The traditional advice of time management specialists is to make lists of things that need to be done, estimate the time required to complete each task, prioritize tasks, and devise an overall schedule to order tasks efficiently and make the best use of time. Many individuals report using list making and prioritizing strategies. Use of these strategies alone, however, may not be sufficient. To begin, lists and priorities may not be drawn up skillfully. Researchers report that managers, for example, often become addicted to shorter, simpler tasks and repeatedly ask themselves, "Where did the day go?" (e.g., Kuhlenschmidt & O'Conner, 1995). Even if skillfully constructed, time management plans may break down because they fail to include periods of time not filled with activity (e.g., spare time for spontaneity or to adjust to unforeseen events).

Seven strategies for dealing with time management (time allocation and investment, and timing of actions) are listed in the first column of Table 8.1. These strategies are sufficiently general to be applied to all aspects of life. Little research has examined individual or age-related preferences or use of these or other organizational strategies in the context of life planning. There has been much work done, however, on individual and age-related differences in future time perspective (e.g., Brandtstädter et al., 1997) and in the ways that individuals prefer to structure the days of their lives with different activities (e.g., Bond & Feather, 1988; Bruno, 1996; Frese, Stewart, & Hannover, 1987). Individuals score differently on scales assessing the desire for purposive activities and structure in daily life. They differ in the amount of time allocated to being together with others versus being alone and in preferences for nondirected use of time (e.g., filling, killing, passing time with the motive to be entertained). Frese et al. (1987) suggest that individuals also differ in the extent to which they prefer to focus on goals or on the means to achieve goals (planfulness). Kuhl and Kraska (1989) have demonstrated that people differ in the extent that they are oriented to the environment (to taking action) or to reflection on internal states (rumination, introspection).

Because of age-specific life tasks and roles, people of different ages have varying amounts of daily time that can be described as "free" to arrange as they wish. Whereas children, adolescents, and older adults have much "free" time to invest in friends and leisure, most hours in the adult's day are spent in activities determined by work and family roles. Successfully managing and coordinating the time demands of work and family is a complex task that requires some skill. For example, Hessing (1994) interviewed 51 women clerical workers about their use of time at work and at home. The women described strategies of setting work time as the top priority (primarily because it is usually a rigid schedule) and manipulating or synchronizing home time to meet the externally determined schedule. One common strategy was to devise a routine. These women saw sticking to a regular established workday rhythm as a means of easing organizational stress and "freeing" up quality time for family activities. Having a standard routine also freed up cognitive load so that the women could deal with unforeseen needs and tasks. The creation of personal daily and monthly routines is an important life task after retirement or (for younger people) during periods of unemployment. Whereas work is an external constraint for personal time management, individuals not involved in work have the difficult task of devising their own schedules. Devising an everyday routine that achieves a mixture of engaging activities and interests, health promotion, and personal maintenance maybe a route to successful aging (Rowe & Kahn, 1997).

Another dimension that is expected to show age-related differences is the temporal extension of a future plan. Whereas young adults can normatively expect many years of life and a long sequence of long-term life tasks to master (Hagestad & Neugarten, 1985), older adults face the reality of death and dying. This obvious change in the perception of personal time-left-to-live over the life course might be expected to have some impact on the types of personal goals selected in later life and their temporal extension (e.g., Brim, 1992; Carstensen, 1993; Levinson, 1978; Thomae, 1989; see also Freund, Li, & Baltes, Chapter 14, this volume). Older individuals may selectively invest their reduced time-left-to-live in personal projects that can be completed in limited periods and are associated with specific sources of personal meaning and emotional support. Some support for this suggestion can be seen in the findings from a 4-year longitudinal study of 896 people aged 54 to 78 years completed by Brandtstädter et al. (1997). Although they found that chronological age played a role in predicting changes in future time perspectives toward more abstract and definite goals, the researchers discovered that perceived life expectancy was also a unique predictor.

Strategic selection of life goals and reduction in temporal horizon in old age need not necessarily result in a reduction of the variety of life goals, however (Thomae, 1989). Nor do they mean that older adults do not think about the future or have complex and dynamic self-concepts (Markus & Ruvolo, 1989; Rakowski, 1979).

Findings from the Berlin Aging Study (BASE), a longitudinal study of a heterogeneous sample of men and women ages 70 to 100 years, support this view. Although there were negative age differences in responses to questions about having plans for the future and feeling optimistic about the future, the current self-definitions of participants included, on average, seven different domains and had a relatively positive tone (Freund & Smith, 1999). More pertinent to issues about future orientation, 94% of the BASE participants, when asked about their hoped-for and feared future possible selves, responded with a large variety of scenarios (Smith & Baltes, 1999). The most prominent themes were hopes and fears about personal characteristics and health (e.g., "I would like to be someone who can be of help to lots of people"; "I don't ever want to have to be nursed"). Whereas activities and interests had predominated in current self-definitions, goals of self-acceptance, maintenance of autonomy, and continued positive social relations with others were prominent themes in the future plans of the old and very old. Furthermore, the central motives underlying hopes for the future were the achievement of something new and the opportunity to reexperience something (e.g., "I would like to go on a long trip again . . . two or three months . . . anywhere, I don't care where"). This was contrary to our expectations that in old age individuals' motives shift toward a focus on maintaining their current life situations. Certainly, desires for maintenance were linked to the health domain, but these desires were extended by achievement motives in other domains. These possible selves exhibited both stability and change over a period of 4 years (Smith, Freund, & Hauschild, 1998). It seems then that in very old age, as in younger years, the motivational systems underlying individuals' scenarios about themselves in the future are dynamic, responsive to life circumstances, and generally oriented toward ensuring positive future change.

Resource Management

Time is such a fundamental dimension of behavior that it requires special attention in planning. However, many other resources are also critical to life planning. Some are listed in the second column of Table 8.1, specifically money, skills, and knowledge, as well as physical energy and strength. Attention to resource management is something that has been described primarily in planning exercises done by private companies and social institutions. The preparation of financial budgets and cost-benefit analyses are key features of plans devised in these settings. Private companies and institutions also regularly assess whether they have on their staffs people with the skills and experience needed to complete their projects or whether they need to bring in others with the appropriate skills.

Individuals also need to consider whether their personal finances and personal competencies (i.e., skills, knowledge, energy) are sufficient to attain their chosen goals or whether they need to acquire or obtain these resources from others. In essence, life planning involves estimating the amount of resources required and calculating a cost-benefit analysis with regard to using one's own competencies or finding resources elsewhere. Baumeister (1994) argues that, rather than material or actual cost-benefits, we typically rely on subjective cost-benefit appraisals. How accurate are these subjective estimates? Much of the work on individuals' choices and decision behavior with regard to the allocation and management of resources has focused on illustrating people's judgmental inaccuracy and on systematically mapping the deviations of actual decisions from those predicted by rational models (Kahneman et al., 1982). Researchers have described the many simplifying judgment heuristics individuals use to trade off cognitive effort and overcome the limits of their cognitive resources. One common example is the availability heuristic, which refers to the fact that we tend to estimate the frequency or probability of an event by the degree to which instances of that event are readily accessible in memory (Tversky & Kahneman, 1973).

Another bias that has important implications for decisions about resource management included in life plans concerns people's propensity to overestimate their own abilities (e.g., skill levels or amount of knowledge, energy, or strength). To the extent that individuals believe that they have sufficient knowledge and energy to complete a task, they may not include strategies for acquiring information or reserving energy in their plans. These and other judgmental heuristics color the way people think about the future and make plans to attain future goals.

Decisions about life goals are usually emotion laden. This factor also influences the ways in which resources are allocated and managed. Some individuals respond to negative emotional tasks by simply avoiding the relevant decisions, procrastinating, or shifting responsibility for planning to others (e.g., Janis & Mann, 1977). Others cope with emotion-laden tasks by choosing alternatives that minimize likely regret and guilt (e.g., Gilovich & Medvec, 1995). Tasks with a very positive valence, on the other hand, may be planned in an unrealistically optimistic way that fails to consider prospects of failure or requirements of extra effort (Colvin & Block, 1994).

Interpersonal Management

The creation of a life plan could not be complete without consideration of how others are involved—as active players in working toward the goal, as sources of support or hindrance, or as passive participants. To this end, in making a plan an individual must give much attention to the management of interpersonal relations—to negotiating schedules and resource use with others, to persuading others to assist, to managing a social support network, and to maintaining a cooperative atmosphere of mutual understanding and support (see the third column in Table 8.1). An important part of planning for life goals, for example, involves communicating the ideas to others (tactical communication). Life planning can also involve influencing others through the use of power plays, manipulation, or ingratiation, compliance-gaining, negotiation, and persuasion tactics (for a review of these strategies, see Cody & McLaughlin, 1990).

Individuals not only think about themselves, they also think about significant others in their lives and construct life plans for others. In many instances, plans about life and the future first arise through the interaction, discussions, and negotiations of two or more persons. Couples discuss, develop, and revise (often heatedly and over long periods) plans for children, family management, and partnership goals (Ickes, 1985). Moreover, they attempt (more or less successfully) to convince others to follow these plans, either through dialogue or by deliberately setting up (or closing off) environmental structures that guide the other's life choices in a prescribed direction. So, for instance, parents make plans for their children's futures (Goodnow & Collins, 1990), mentors create scenarios about the future development and potential of their students or protégés (Kram, 1985; Levinson, 1978), and individuals reflect about the future goals and directions of new relationships. On a macro level, community leaders, politicians, managers, and administrators devise institutional plans that create opportunity structures and place constraints on the future lives of others (e.g., Mintzberg, 1994).

Negotiation becomes a necessary strategy when what one wants is possible or available only at the cost (or with the assistance) of someone else. This is an essential organizational strategy for anyone who must interact with other people to accomplish a life goal or task. Negotiation has been defined as a process by which parties attempt to reach an accord that specifies how they will act toward one another and distribute scarce and valued resources (e.g., Roloff & Jordan, 1992). The process often involves making concessions and demanding them of the other parties. Negotiation is presumed to function best when it serves as a method for discovering mutual interests and joint payoffs (Roloff & Jordan, 1992).

People negotiate with each other for a variety of resources: tangible goods such as money and commodities, and intangible goods such as services, information, relationship goals, personal rights, prestige, and self-identity (Thompson, 1990). Negotiation about commodities is initiated when resources (such as money, goods, services, and information) fall below an optimal level.

Not all negotiations are successful. Neale and Bazerman (1991) report that high-quality negotiation may be a matter of chance (the person just happens on an appropriate suggestion), may be due to individuals' prior experience in a particular context, or may be a function of individuals' having learned strategies that can be applied generally. Experience improves the ability of negotiators to judge the interests of other parties accurately (i.e., recognize differences in priorities) but does not influence decisions about the application of particular bargaining strategies (soft-nosed, hard-nosed, principled, or tit-for-tat; see Thompson, 1990).

Individuals also engage in negotiation of their personal images (face making). They focus on building personal impressions that enhance the credibility of their ideas and the usefulness of their capacities in the eyes of others. They also negotiate images about their right and capacity to plan life goals. Within an interpersonal relationship, mutual understanding is developed over the history of the relationship about what may be planned and decided by the parties together versus alone and how third parties might also be involved in planning processes. Interactions in initial friendships and partnerships may require intensive periods of the actors' planning future goals and activities together, so that the life themes and narratives of the relationship are defined and perceived as being the joint possession of the separate actors (Duck, 1993). In long-standing relationships, there may be more division of labor with regard to who plans what, when, and who has responsibility for what, when. Indeed, the inability of long-standing partners to take initiative about future goals and make decisions on behalf of and in the interests of each other may, in some instances, be viewed as a sign of immaturity or maladaptive functioning.

The use of persuasion as a strategy of influence in plans has received much attention in many areas of the literature for many years (e.g., Roloff & Jordan, 1992; Schank & Abelson, 1977). Schank and Abelson (1977), for example, introduced a package of *persuade scripts* in their model of planning that was to be used whenever a plan called for a change of goals in interpersonal relationships. They categorized the scripts as useful for (a) acquiring information, (b) gaining control of an object, (c) gaining social control (power or authority), and (d) getting a target person to act on behalf of source. Other researchers have attempted to define a taxonomy of general goals of persuasion and the tactics applied (e.g., Dillard, 1990; Rule, Bisanz, & Kohn, 1985). The list includes such goals as gain permission, gain assistance, give advice, change opinion, share activity, convince a third party to elicit support, enforce an obligation, protect a right, and change a relationship.

Particular types of influence and persuasion goals appear in different situations and relationships. Dillard (1990) suggests, for example, that influence goals can be categorized in terms of their situational use: whether they benefit the source, the target, or a group; how public the persuasion is and how much normative pressure is involved; whether the strategy is voluntary or nonvoluntary; whether it aims for relationship growth, maintenance, and or dissolution. Persuasion tactics used with friends (intimate companions) are different from those used with others. Studies on influence goals indicate that nearly all requests for favors, for example, are made of friends and family members (Cody & McLaughlin, 1990). In their study of requests for favors, Roloff and Jordan (1992) examined how often persuasive requests were elaborated with apologies, explanations, inducements, and contingencies. They found that requests to intimates contained relatively few elaborations; the requesters offered the minimum of information needed to induce compliance. Requests to strangers, on the other hand, needed to contain some justification for the requests.

Mutual understanding is rare and must be strived for. Conflict, on the other hand, is seen as an important dynamic in either facilitating or hindering planning processes over time (Janis & Mann, 1977). Sternberg and Dobson (1987) found that the people in their sample varied in their conflict resolution styles but were generally consistent in their preferences for ways to resolve conflict across different interpersonal relationships. These researchers argue that the strategies can be described on two dimensions: in terms of the behavior involved (active-passive) and in terms of the impact (intensify-mitigate). Active strategies involve physical force or verbal arguments. Examples of passive strategies include "wait and see" and withholding. Most of the people in Sternberg and Dobson's study considered that strategies that involve some give-and-take and minimal physical or verbal force are effective in resolving most conflict situations.

Self-Management

There is an extensive literature on the ways in which individuals monitor and regulate their own behavior, beginning from early childhood. Many of the chapters in this book review this literature, so I will not repeat that information here (see also Higgins, 1987; Mischel, Cantor, & Feldman, 1996; Schlenker, Britt, & Pennington, 1996). Central self-regulation strategies focus on personal motivation, emotion regulation, self-protection, goal selection, and action self-monitoring.

One set of strategies relevant to life planning involves self-presentation. These strategies serve to establish an impression with others, to protect the self from threats, and to motivate the self to change. Publicly disclosing desires to change and declaring a commitment to change have also been found to be important indicators of individuals' actually working on making proposed changes (Heatherton & Nichols, 1994; Stall & Biernacki, 1986). Baumeister (1994) found that once people decide to make changes in their lives, they start ignoring the positive aspects of their current situations and focus on the negative aspects. Life change is also perceived to be easier by people who report that they initially work on creating a new sense of identity by introducing new activities and new people in their lives or by moving to live in a new location.

For long-term projects, individuals may seek to initiate behaviors strategically, with the intention of making the activities more positive to perform. The more successful they are at this, the more persistent they will be in working on the projects. Sansone and Harackiewicz (1996) suggest that the phenomenal experience of interest in working on a project ("feeling like it") is as intrinsically motivating as the desire to have the outcome (outcome-derived motivation). They and others argue that all of us have learned how to regulate our own motivation (e.g., Baumeister & Heatherton, 1996; Deci & Ryan, 1991; Higgins, 1987). We have a repertoire of specific strategies and know how and when these strategies are most effective. We apply this idiosyncratic knowledge about interest-enhancing actions in situations where it is clear that there is a need for self-regulation—primarily when we find our current activities uninteresting but have sufficient reason to persist at those uninteresting activities (Sansone & Harackiewicz, 1996).

Age Differences in Life Planning: Goals, Expectations, and Strategies

The developmental and life-span literature points to age differences in several aspects of life planning. During childhood there is a growth in understanding the concept of planning as well as actual planning skill. By 5 years of age, most children understand the notion of planning for everyday routines (Brown & DeLoache, 1978; Kreitler & Kreitler, 1987; Rogoff, 1991; Scholnick & Friedman, 1993) and can devise plans and strategies to fill in time in a task requiring delay of gratification (Mischel & Patterson, 1978). In terms of life planning, several studies report that children and adolescents certainly think about their future roles in life and, at least by late adolescence, are aware of the importance and difficulties of planning in advance for a path toward achieving these goals (Nurmi, 1991; Russell & Smith, 1979; Smith & Russell, 1984). Fingerman and Perlmutter (1995) propose that throughout adulthood and into old age there may be few age differences in the amount of time spent thinking about the future. They found that all age groups reported thinking most about the near future. Young adults did report thinking more about the distant future (e.g., 10 years hence) than did older people, but at the same time indicated that they really spent very little time doing this. Fingerman and Perlmutter suggest that the age differences found in sense of time are a function of the life events and developmental tasks of individuals and are not due to developmental changes in future time perspective.

Goals and Expectations

The motives underlying the use of planning and the life goals planned for also change with age. During adulthood and into old age, the complexity and frequency of planning and the temporal extension of plans vary as a function of domain, life context, and personal preferences. Furthermore, at different points in the life course, individuals are expected to plan for different life goals in accord with the social clock and beliefs about prescriptive age norms (Hagestad & Neugarten, 1985; Peterson, 1996; Smith, 1996). Dreher and Oerter (1987), Nurmi (1991, 1993), Evans and Poole (1991), and Pulkkinen (1982) have reported that the life goals of adolescents focus on the domains of education, future occupation, material gains, and beginning a partnership or family. Girls are more likely to express conflicts between career and family goals (e.g., Pulkkinen, 1982). Few adolescents nominate goals that they expect to be realized after age 30 (Nurmi, 1991). Middle-aged and older adults, on the other hand, focus on family life, personal identity issues, and health. Nurmi, Pulliainen, and Salmela-Aro (1992) found that with increasing age (from 19 to 71 years), individuals reported more interest in planning for things over which they thought they had little control (namely, their own health) and less interest in aspects of life over which they considered they had much control.

In order to gain some information on social expectations about life planning, we asked young ($M = 25$ years), middle-aged ($M = 45$ years), and older adults ($M = 72$ years) to estimate the number of projects that people plan at different periods over the life span (age decades from 20 to 90; Smith, 1998). In addition, we asked about expectations in seven life domains: family, friends, leisure, finances, work, living conditions, and health. Theory suggests that age may interact with planning in different life domains. We asked about expectations for new projects and projects ended, because planning is necessary for both instances. Our findings are illustrated in Figure 8.2.

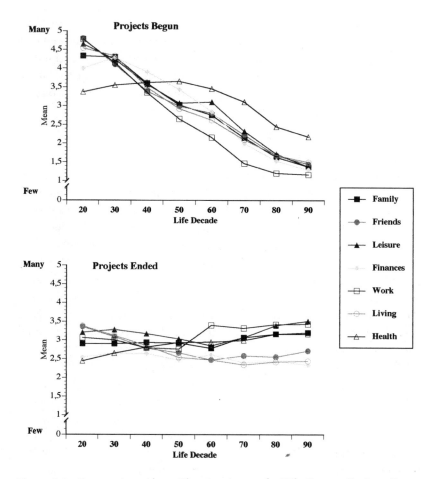

Figure 8.2. Expectations About Planning Across the Life Course: Projects Begun and Ended in Seven Domains

Overall, there was consensus that more projects were begun at ages 20 and 30 than in the decades thereafter. This pattern was true for all domains except health. In the domain of health, new projects were expected to be begun up to the 70s. People in their 80s and 90s were expected to begin a few new projects in health, but were expected to do little planning for something new in other domains. As can be seen, the pattern of expectations about planning associated with projects that are ended was similar across the age decades. Young people were expected to end as many projects as middle-aged and older adults. In terms of a balance between projects begun and ended, it seems that younger adults were expected to begin more projects than they end, older adults were expected to end more than they begin (except in the domain of health), and middle-aged adults were expected to begin and end similar numbers of projects. There were few age differences in expectations, and when they did occur it was in beliefs about the number of projects ended and when. For example, young adults thought that many projects about family and friends ended in the 20s, whereas older adults considered the 60s (family) and 90s (friends) to be age periods when more projects were ended.

Strategies

The developmental literature suggests that there should be age-related differences in strategies of planning and their effective use. Simons and Galotti (1992) asked young adults (18-20 years) to describe what planning "means to you." They found that students with better grades and better planners defined planning more in terms of achieving satisfaction, organizing activities, or breaking down goals into more manageable subgoals and that they were less likely to think of planning as constraining activities to a set of predetermined decisions. Students with higher grades were also less likely to describe planning in terms of reducing stress. Britton and Tesser (1991) similarly found that university students with better grades reported greater use of short-range planning strategies (e.g., making lists, setting priorities) and more positive attitudes toward time.

In relation to everyday tasks and planning to solve laboratory problems, there are reports that older adults are not as proficient as young adults (Chalmers & Lawrence, 1993) but that they benefit from working with others or using external aids (Adams & Rebok, 1982-1983; Chalmers & Lawrence, 1993). A different picture regarding age-related decline emerges concerning planning tasks that require planners to use their personal experiences, knowledge of life, or occupational expertise (Baltes & Smith, 1990; Smith & Baltes, 1990b; Smith, Staudinger, & Baltes, 1994). Here, having more domain-specific experience and being older can have benefits. With regard to life planning, Smith and Baltes (1990b; Smith et al., 1989, 1994) found that commentaries from older adults about life dilemmas of late adulthood were rated as showing greater wisdom-related knowledge than were commentaries from young adults. Older managers (often operating in a committee context) frequently make more pragmatic and realistic

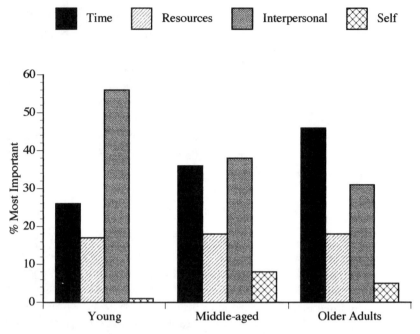

Figure 8.3. Age Differences in the Components of Life Planning Ranked as Most Important

suggestions about future company directions than do young executives (Birren, 1980; Bromley, 1969). Prognoses of older clinicians based in intuition acquired during years of professional practice often prove to be just as accurate as (if not better outcome predictors than) the laboriously developed proposals of young colleagues (Dowie & Elstein, 1988). Clearly, there are extensive individual differences among adults. Indeed, Featherman, Smith, and Peterson (1990) found that even within one professional group (namely, engineers), individuals with similar managerial positions showed different degrees of flexibility and reflection in planning tasks.

To examine age differences in strategies of life planning, we asked young ($M = 25$ years), middle-aged ($M = 45$ years), and older adults ($M = 72$ years) to rank the relative importance of the four organizational components for life planning in general (Smith, 1998). Overall, the majority of participants viewed time and interpersonal management as more important for the effectiveness of planning than resource management. Self-management was rarely endorsed as first choice. As can be seen in Figure 8.3, there were some interesting age differences in beliefs. Whereas 56% of young adults ranked interpersonal management as the most important of the four components, only 38% of the middle-aged and 30% of the older adults agreed. The proportion of people who instead ranked time management as the most important component was higher in the older group (44%) than in the younger group (26%). An equal proportion of the middle-aged participants ranked time and interpersonal management as most important.

Age differences in reported importance of the four components also differed by life domain. There were significant age-by-component interactions in the domains of leisure, housing, and finances. For leisure, young adults considered that resource management was less important than did older adults, and older adults thought that self-management was less important than did young adults. In the domain of housing, older adults thought that time and self-management were more important than did young adults.

Although, in general, the organization of time and interpersonal relationships were ranked as the most important considerations in life planning, individuals' reports of how often they used particular organizational strategies revealed a different picture (strategies listed in Table 8.1; profile of strategies in Figure 8.4). The most frequently used strategies were reported to be balancing finances, collecting information (resource management), setting priorities (time management), and self-monitoring (self-management). Here, too, there were some age differences in the reported use of time management and self-management strategies. With regard to time management, the young adults reported less use of strategies designed to synchronize action with energy levels and strategies that left time for spontaneity. Older adults more than young adults said that they tried to include strategies that helped them to avoid diversions. Older adults also reported greater use of self-monitoring and mind-set inducement strategies than did young adults.

CONCLUSION AND OUTLOOK

In this chapter I have outlined a framework for investigating four organization strategies associated with life planning: time management, resource management, interpersonal management, and self-management. I have proposed that the effectiveness of a life plan with regard to personal development might be evaluated in terms of the selection, coordination, and implementation of these strategies. The framework is set in a social cognitive and life-span perspective. Planning about life takes place in

Figure 8.4. Profile of Planning Strategies

different contexts for people of different ages, and there are age-related and social-normative expectations about age-appropriate planning activities. A research program to investigate social and cultural expectations about who should plan what, when, and with whom would contribute much to our understanding of the role of life goals in personal development.

REFERENCES

Adams, C. C., & Rebok, G. W. (1982-1983). Planfulness and problem-solving in older adults. *International Journal of Behavioral Development, 16,* 271-282.

Aspinwall, L. G., & Taylor, S. E. (1997). A stitch in time: Self-regulation and proactive coping. *Psychological Bulletin, 121,* 417-436.

Austin, J. T., & Vancouver, J. B. (1996). Goal constructs in psychology: Structure, process, and content. *Psychological Bulletin, 120,* 338-375.

Baltes, P. B., & Smith, J. (1990). Toward a psychology of wisdom and its ontogenesis. In R. J. Sternberg (Ed.), *Wisdom: Its nature, origins, and development* (pp. 87-120). New York: Cambridge University Press.

Baumeister, R. F. (1994). The crystallization of discontent in the process of major life change. In T. F. Heatherton & J. L. Weinberger (Eds.), *Can personality change?* (pp. 281-297). Washington, DC: American Psychological Association.

Baumeister, R. F., & Heatherton, T. F. (1996). Self-regulation failure: An overview. *Psychological Inquiry, 7,* 1-15.

Berger, P. L., Berger, B., & Kellner, H. (1967). *The homeless mind: Modernization and unconsciousness.* New York: Random House.

Birren, J. F. (1980). Age and decision strategies. In A. T. Welford & J. E. Birren (Eds.), *Decision making and age* (pp. 23-26). New York: Arno.

Block, R. A., Buggie, S. E., & Matsui, F. (1996). Beliefs about time: Cross-cultural comparisons. *Journal of Psychology, 130,* 5-22.

Bond, M. J., & Feather, N. T. (1988). Some correlates of structure and purpose in the use of time. *Journal of Personality and Social Psychology, 55,* 321-329.

Brandtstädter, J., & Greve, W. (1994). The aging self: Stabilizing and protective processes. *Developmental Review, 14,* 52-80.

Brandtstädter, J., Wentura, D., & Schmitz, U. (1997). Veränderungen der Zeit- und Zukunftsperspektive im übergang zum höheren Alter: Quer- und längschnittliche Befunde. *Zeitschrift für Psychologie, 205,* 377-395.

Bratman, M. E. (1987). *Intention, plans, and practical reason.* Cambridge, MA: Harvard University Press.

Brim, O. G. (1992). *Ambition: How we manage success and failure throughout our lives.* New York: Basic Books.

Britton, B. K., & Tesser, A. (1991). Effects of time-management practices on college grades. *Journal of Educational Psychology, 83,* 405-410.

Bromley, D. B. (1969). Studies of intellectual function in relation to age and their significance for professional and managerial functions. *Interdisciplinary Topics of Gerontology, 4,* 103-126.

Brown, A., & DeLoache, J. (1978). Skills, plans, and self-regulation. In R. Siegler (Ed.), *Children's thinking: What develops?* (pp. 3-35). Hillsdale, NJ: Lawrence Erlbaum.

Bruno, J. E. (1996). Time perceptions and time allocation preferences among adolescent boys and girls. *Adolescence, 31,* 109-126.

Buehler, R., Griffin, D., & MacDonald, H. (1997). The role of motivated reasoning in optimistic time predictions. *Personality and Social Psychology Bulletin, 23,* 238-247.

Buehler, R., Griffin, D., & Ross, M. (1994). Exploring the "planning fallacy": Why people underestimate their task completion times. *Journal of Personality and Social Psychology, 67,* 366-381.

Byrne, R. (1977). Planning meals: Problem-solving on a real data-base. *Cognition, 5,* 287-332.

Cantor, N., & Kihlstrom, J. F. (1987). *Personality and social intelligence.* Englewood Cliffs, NJ: Prentice Hall.

Carstensen, L. L. (1993). Motivation for social contact across the life-span: A theory of socioemotional selectivity. In J. E. Jacobs (Ed.), *Nebraska Symposium on Motivation: Vol. 40. Developmental perspectives on motivation* (pp. 205-254). Lincoln: University of Nebraska Press.

Carver, C. S., & Scheier, M. F. (1990). Principles of self-regulation: Action and emotion. In E. T. Higgins & R. M. Sorrentino (Eds.), *Handbook of motivation and cognition: Vol. 2. Foundations of social behavior* (pp. 3-52). New York: Guilford.

Chalmers, D., & Lawrence, J. A. (1993). Investigating the effects of planning aids on adults' and adolescents' organisation of a complex task. *International Journal of Behavioral Development, 16,* 191-214.

Cody, M. J., & McLaughlin, M. L. (Eds.). (1990). *The psychology of tactical communication.* Clevedon, UK: Multilingual Matters.

Colvin, C. R., & Block, J. (1994). Do positive illusions foster mental health? An examination of the Taylor and Brown formulation. *Psychological Bulletin, 116,* 3-20.

Deci, E. L., & Ryan, R. M. (1991). A motivational approach to self: Integration in personality. In R. Dienstbier (Ed.), *Nebraska Symposium on Motivation: Vol. 38. Perspectives on motivation* (pp. 237-288). Lincoln: University of Nebraska Press.

Dillard, J. P. (1990). The nature and substance of goals in tactical communication. In M. J. Cody & M. L. McLaughlin (Eds.), *The psychology of tactical communication* (pp. 70-90). Clevedon, UK: Multilingual Matters.

Dowie, J., & Elstein, A. (Eds.). (1988). *Professional judgment: A reader in clinical decision making.* New York: Cambridge University Press.

Dreher, M., & Oerter, R. (1987). Action planning competencies during adolescence and early adulthood. In S. L. Friedman, E. K. Scholnick, & R. R. Cocking (Eds.), *Blueprints for thinking: The role of planning in cognitive development* (pp. 321-355). New York: Cambridge University Press.

Duck, S. (Ed.). (1993). *Individuals in relationships.* Newbury Park, CA: Sage.

Emmons, R. A. (1989). The personal striving approach to personality. In L. A. Pervin (Ed.), *Goal concepts in personality and social psychology* (pp. 87-126). Hillsdale, NJ: Lawrence Erlbaum.

Evans, G., & Poole, M. (1991). *Young adults: Self perceptions and life contexts.* London: Falmer.

Featherman, D. L., Smith, J., & Peterson, J. G. (1990). Successful aging in a post-retired society. In P. B. Baltes & M. M. Baltes (Eds.), *Successful aging: Perspectives from the behavioral sciences* (pp. 50-93). New York: Cambridge University Press.

Fingerman, K. L., & Perlmutter, M. (1995). Future time perspective and life events across adulthood. *Journal of General Psychology, 122,* 95-111.

Fraise, P. (1981). Cognition of time in human activity. In G. D'Ydewalle & W. Lens (Eds.), *Cognition in human motivation and learning* (pp. 233-259). Hillsdale, NJ: Lawrence Erlbaum.

Frese, M., Stewart, J., & Hannover, B. (1987). Goal orientation and planfulness: Action styles as personality concepts. *Journal of Personality and Social Psychology, 52,* 1182-1194.

Freund, A. M., & Smith, J. (1999). Content and function of the self-definition in old and very old age. *Journals of Gerontology: Psychological Sciences, 54B,* 55-67.

Friedman, S. L., Scholnick, E. K., & Cocking, R. R. (Eds.). (1987). *Blueprints for thinking: The role of planning in cognitive development.* New York: Cambridge University Press.

Gilovich, T., & Medvec, V. H. (1995). The experience of regret: What, when, and why? *Psychological Review, 102,* 379-395.

Gollwitzer, P. M. (1990). Action phases and mind-sets. In E. T. Higgins & R. M. Sorrentino (Eds.), *Handbook of motivation and cognition: Vol. 2. Foundations of social behavior* (pp. 53-92). New York: Guilford.

Gollwitzer, P. M. (1996). The volitional benefits of planning. In P. M. Gollwitzer & J. A. Bargh (Eds.), *The psychology of action: Linking cognition and motivation to behavior* (pp. 287-312). New York: Guilford.

Goodnow, J. J., & Collins, W.A. (1990). *Development according to parents: The nature, sources, and consequences of parents' ideas.* Hillsdale, NJ: Lawrence Erlbaum.

Hagestad, G. O., & Neugarten, B. L. (1985). Age and the life course. In R. H. Binstock & L. George (Eds.), *Handbook of aging and the social sciences* (pp. 35-61). New York: Van Nostrand Reinhold.

Hayes-Roth, B., & Hayes-Roth, F. (1979). A cognitive model of planning. *Cognitive Science, 3,* 275-310.

Heatherton, T. F., & Nichols, P. A. (1994). Personal accounts of successful versus failed attempts at life change. *Personality and Social Psychology Bulletin, 20,* 664-675.

Heckhausen, H., & Gollwitzer, P. M. (1987). Thought contents and cognitive functioning in motivational versus volitional states of mind. *Motivation and Emotion, 11,* 101-120.

Heckhausen, J., & Schulz, R. (1995). A life-span theory of control. *Psychological Review, 102,* 284-304.

Hessing, M. (1994). More than clockwork: Women's time management in their combined workloads. *Sociological Perspectives, 37,* 611-633.

Higgins, E. T. (1987). Self-discrepancy: A theory relating self and affect. *Psychological Review, 94,* 319-340.

Ickes, W. J. (Ed.). (1985). *Compatible and incompatible relationships.* New York: Springer-Verlag.

Janis, I. L., & Mann, L. (1977). *Decision making: Psychological analysis of conflict, choice, and commitment.* New York: Free Press.

Johnson, M. K., & Sherman, S. J. (1990). Constructing and reconstructing the past and the future in the present. In E. T. Higgins & R. M. Sorrentino (Eds.), *Handbook of motivation and cognition: Vol. 2. Foundations of social behavior* (pp. 482-526). New York: Guilford.

Kahneman, D., Slovic, P., & Tversky, A. (Eds.). (1982). *Judgment under uncertainty: Heuristics and biases.* New York: Cambridge University Press.

Kram, K. E. (1985). Phases of the mentor relationship. *Academy of Management Journal, 26,* 608-625.

Kreitler, S., & Kreitler, H. (1987). Conceptions and processes of planning: The developmental perspective. In S. L. Friedman, E. K. Scholnick, & R. R. Cocking (Eds.), *Blueprints for thinking: The role of planning in cognitive development* (pp. 205-272). New York: Cambridge University Press.

Kuhl, J., & Kraska, K. (1989). Self-regulation and metamotivation: Computational mechanisms, development, and assessment. In R. Kanfer, P. L. Ackerman, & R. Cudeck (Eds.), *Abilities, motivation, and methodology* (pp. 343-374). Hillsdale, NJ: Lawrence Erlbaum.

Kuhlenschmidt, S. L., & O'Conner, J. (1995). Where does the day go? Addiction to 5-minute tasks and management by crisis. *Psychology: A Journal of Human Behavior, 32,* 27-34.

Levinson, D. J. (1978). *The seasons of a man's life.* New York: Alfred A. Knopf.

Markus, H., & Ruvolo, A. (1989). Possible selves: Personalized representations of goals. In L. A. Pervin (Ed.), *Goal concepts in personality and social psychology* (pp. 211-241). Hillsdale, NJ: Lawrence Erlbaum.

Mintzberg, H. (1994). *The rise and fall of strategic planning: Reconceiving roles for planning, plans, and planners.* New York: Free Press.

Mischel, H. N., & Patterson, C. J. (1978). Effective plans for self-control in children. In W. A. Collins (Ed.), *Minnesota Symposium on Child Psychology* (Vol. 11, pp. 199-230). Hillsdale, NJ: Lawrence Erlbaum.

Mischel, W., Cantor, N., & Feldman, S. (1996). Principles of self-regulation: The nature of willpower and self-control. In E. T. Higgins & A. W. Kruglanski (Eds.), *Social psychology: Handbook of basic principles* (pp. 329-360). New York: Guilford.

Neale, M. A., & Bazerman, M. H. (1991). *Cognition and rationality in negotiation.* New York: Free Press.

Nurmi, J.-E. (1991). How do adolescents see their future? A review of the development of future orientation and planning. *Developmental Review, 11,* 1-59.

Nurmi, J.-E. (1993). Adolescent development in an age-graded context: The role of personal beliefs, goals, and strategies in the tackling of developmental tasks and standards. *International Journal of Behavioral Development, 16,* 169-189.

Nurmi, J.-E., Pulliainen, H., & Salmelo-Aro, K. (1992). Age differences in adults' control beliefs related to life goals and concerns. *Psychology and Aging, 7,* 194-196.

Payne, J. W., Bettman, J. R., & Johnson, E. J. (1993). *The adaptive decision maker.* New York: Cambridge University Press.

Peterson, C. C. (1996). The ticking of the social clock: Adults' beliefs about the timing of transition events. *International Journal of Aging and Human Development, 42,* 189-203.

Pulkkinen, L. (1982). Self control and continuity from childhood to late adolescence. In P. B. Baltes & O. G. Brim, Jr. (Eds.), *Life-span development and behavior* (Vol. 4, pp. 63-105). New York: Academic Press.

Rakowski, W. (1979). Future time perspective in later adulthood: Review and research directions. *Experimental Aging Research, 5,* 43-88.

Rawls, J. (1971). *A theory of justice.* Cambridge, MA: Belknap.

Raynor, J. O., & Entin, E. E. (1982). *Motivation, career striving, and aging.* London: Hemisphere.

Riesbeck, C. K., & Schank, R. C. (1989). *Inside case-based reasoning.* Hillsdale, NJ: Lawrence Erlbaum.

Riley, M. W., & Riley, J. W., Jr. (1994). Age integration and the lives of older people. *Gerontologist, 34,* 110-115.

Rogoff, B. (1991). Social interaction as apprenticeship in thinking: Guided participation in spatial planning. In L. B. Resnick, J. M. Levine, & S. D. Teasley (Eds.), *Perspectives on socially shared cognition* (pp. 349-364). Washington, DC: American Psychological Association.

Roloff, M. E., & Jordan, J. M. (1992). Achieving negotiation goals: The "fruits and foibles" of planning ahead. In L. L. Putnam & M. E. Roloff (Eds.), *Communication and negotiation* (pp. 21-45). Newbury Park, CA: Sage.

Rowe, J. W., & Kahn, R. L. (1997). Successful aging. *Gerontologist, 37,* 433-440.

Rule, B. G., Bisanz, G. L., & Kohn, M. (1985). Anatomy of a persuasion schema: Targets, goals, and strategies. *Journal of Personality and Social Psychology, 48,* 1127-1140.

Russell, G., & Smith, J. (1979). Girls can be doctors can't they: Sex differences in career aspirations. *Australian Journal of Social Issues, 14,* 91-102.

Sansone, C., & Harackiewicz, J. M. (1996). "I don't feel like it": The function of interest in self-regulation. In L. L. Martin & A. Tesser (Eds.), *Striving and feeling: Interactions among goals, affect, and self-regulation* (pp. 203-228). Mahwah, NJ: Lawrence Erlbaum.

Schank, R., & Abelson, R. (1977). *Scripts, plans, goals, and understanding.* Hillsdale, NJ: Lawrence Erlbaum.

Schlenker, B. R., Britt, T. W., & Pennington, J. (1996). Impression regulation and management: Highlights of a theory of self-identification. In R. M. Sorrentino & E. T. Higgins (Eds.), *Handbook of motivation and cognition: Vol. 3. The interpersonal context* (pp. 118-147). New York: Guilford.

Scholnick, E. K., & Friedman, S. L. (1987). The planning construct in the psychological literature. In S. L. Friedman, E. K. Scholnick, & R. R. Cocking (Eds.), *Blueprints for thinking: The role of planning in cognitive development* (pp. 3-38). New York: Cambridge University Press.

Scholnick, E. K., & Friedman, S. L. (1993). Planning in context: Development and situational considerations. *International Journal of Behavioral Development, 16,* 143-167.

Simons, D. J., & Galotti, K. M. (1992). Everyday planning: An analysis of daily time management. *Bulletin of the Psychonomic Society, 30,* 61-64.

Smith, J. (1996). Planning about life: Toward a social-interactive perspective. In P. B. Baltes & U. M. Staudinger (Eds.), *Interactive minds: Life-span perspectives on the social foundation of cognition* (pp. 242-275). New York: Cambridge University Press.

Smith, J. (1998). *Strategies of life planning: Age differences in expectations.* Unpublished manuscript, Max Planck Institute for Human Development, Berlin.

Smith, J., & Baltes, P. B. (1999). Trends and profiles of psychological functioning in very old age. In P. B. Baltes & K. U. Mayer (Eds.), *The Berlin Aging Study: Aging from 70 to 100* (pp. 197-226). New York: Cambridge University Press.

Smith, J., & Baltes, P. B. (1990a). A life-span perspective on thinking and problem-solving. In M. Schwebel, C. A. Maher, & N. S. Fagley (Eds.), *Promoting cognitive growth over the life span* (pp. 47-70). Hillsdale, NJ: Lawrence Erlbaum.

Smith, J., & Baltes, P. B. (1990b). Wisdom-related knowledge: Age/cohort differences in response to life-planning problems. *Developmental Psychology, 26,* 494-505.

Smith, J., Dixon, R. A., & Baltes, P. B. (1989). Expertise in life planning: A new research approach to investigating aspects of wisdom. In M. L. Commons, J. D. Sinnott, F. A. Richards, & C. Armon (Eds.), *Adult development: Vol. 1. Comparisons and applications of developmental models* (pp. 307-331). New York: Praeger.

Smith, J., Freund, A. M., & Hauschild, C. (1998, November). *The dynamics of possible selves in very old age.* Paper presented at the 51st Annual Meeting of the Gerontological Society of America, Philadelphia.

Smith, J., & Russell, G. (1984). Children's beliefs and sex differences. *Sex Roles, 11,* 1111-1115.

Smith, J., Staudinger, U. M., & Baltes, P. B. (1994). Occupational settings facilitating wisdom-related knowledge: The sample case of clinical psychologists. *Journal of Clinical and Counseling Psychology, 62,* 989-999.

Stall, R., & Biernacki, P. (1986). Spontaneous remissions from the problematic use of substances: An inductive model derived from a comparative analysis of alcohol, opiate, tobacco, and food/obesity literatures. *International Journal of the Addictions, 21,* 1-23.

Stein, N. L. (1988). The development of children's storytelling skill. In M. B. Franklin & S. Barten (Eds.), *Child language: A reader* (pp. 282-297). New York: Oxford University Press.

Sternberg, R. J., & Dobson, D. M. (1987). Resolving interpersonal conflicts: An analysis of stylistic consistency. *Journal of Personality and Social Psychology, 52,* 794-812.

Taylor, S. E., Pham, L. B., Rivkin, I. D., & Armor, D. A. (1998). Harnessing the imagination: Mental simulation, self-regulation, and coping. *American Psychologist, 53,* 429-439.

Thomae, H. (1989). Veränderungen der Zeitperspektive im höheren Alter. *Zeitschrift für Gerontologie, 22,* 58-66.

Thompson, L. (1990). An examination of naive and experienced negotiators. *Journal of Personality and Social Psychology, 59,* 82-90.

Tversky, A., & Kahneman, D. (1973). Availability: A heuristic for judging frequency and probability. *Cognitive Psychology, 5,* 207-232.

Wilensky, R. (1983). *Planning and understanding: A computational approach to human reasoning.* Reading, MA: Addison-Wesley.

9

THE PROCESS OF MEANING CONSTRUCTION

Dissecting the Flow of Semiotic Activity

Ingrid E. Josephs
Jaan Valsiner
Seth E. Surgan

The process of construction and reconstruction of meanings is at the core of any analysis of the self and its development. The human self is a semiotic construct, created through acting in the sphere of meanings. In this chapter, we narrow down the general topic of the present volume: From a microgenetic perspective, we analyze the process of construction and reconstruction of meaning in depth.

The construction of meaning—*meaning making*—is certainly not a new domain of interest invented by the 1990s narrative turn in psychology (Bruner, 1990). In the first decade of the century, the largely forgotten so-called Würzburg school in Germany, constituted by Oswald Külpe and Karl Bühler, among others, tried to analyze (experimentally and introspectively) the process of construction and reconstruction of complex meanings (e.g., Bühler, 1908/1951). Carl Gustav Jung's (1910) work on association and Heinz Werner's (e.g., 1954) comparative approach to the construction and transformation of meaning also proceed in a similar direction.

THE PROCESS OF SIGN CONSTRUCTION: MEANING MAKING VERSUS MEANACTING

A person creates signification by way of a sign in a here-and-now-to-future context. The sign, as constructed here and now, has two functions. First, it represents something in the here-and-now context—a function that is well-known through the analyses of signs in semiotics. However, the sign has also a second function that goes hand in hand with the first: It orients the sign constructor (user) toward the immediately potential future. The sign prepares the person for new encounters with the world that might happen, but that are not to be taken for granted.

Construction of signs is thus in part the *action* of preadaptation. It is a process that proceeds as an inseparable part of the "stream of conscious-ness" (James, 1890). This processual nature of sign constructing is not well captured by the usual reference to signs as meanings as if these were fixed, objectlike tools that are just utilized as givens in psychological functioning. Hence we refer to this process as *meanacting* ("acting toward creating meaning"). We offer this purposefully artificial technical term in order to overcome the essential, product notion of meaning that is entailed in the more common concept of *meaning making*. The latter term implies that meanings are products or fixed outcomes, whereas *meanacting* focuses on the process of acting-to-mean something on the basis of something else. This meanacting orientation entails *directionality*—a created sign reflects what is in conjunction with the person's expectations of what might (or ought to) become.

However, our coverage in this chapter is limited to elucidation of the basic processes of meanacting. We attempt to expand upon a "dialogical approach" to meanacting. We demonstrate how our theoretical scheme of meanacting works on the simplest possible sign material (word meaning construction) in the intrapersonal realm; subsequently, we provide empiri-cal data about similar (yet more complex) phenomena of persons' meaning construction about their own selves in interpersonal contexts. Our perspec-tive allows for a reinterpretation of some old empirical data from the

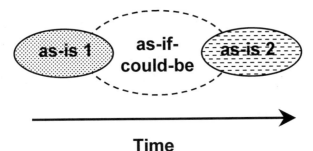

Time

Figure 9.1. The Mutual Construction of Present and Future in Irreversible Time

Würzburg school of psychology of thinking. However, we use these old data for our present theoretical purposes.

FACING UNCERTAINTY: HOW THE PRESENT IS LINKED WITH THE FUTURE

Human psychological functions involve construction (and reconstruction) of signs, through which individuals attempt to preemptively regulate their relationships with the environment (Valsiner, 1998). This necessity for preemptive regulation is guaranteed by the impending uncertainty about the immediate future. We do not live in a static "present time" but are constantly in a process of movement from the present moment toward the next moment in irreversible time.

This movement from one present to the immediately next present is a dynamic one (see Figure 9.1). Each present is already inevitably "pregnant" with the future; in other words, in the present *as-is 1* a field of *as-if-could-be* is immediately cocreated that not only transcends the present at the given moment but, more important, takes it one step further. Thus, paradoxically, the *as-if-could-be* both inevitably belongs to the present *and* transforms it in time. Out of the whole field of potentialities (the *as-if-could-be*), specific parts are "singled out" by the active meanacting person and become transformed into the immediately next present *as-is 2* (Josephs, 1998). This process of construction of potentialities and transformation of (parts of) the potential into the immediate next reality is characterized by tension and directionality.

Without tension, the person would not move at all—in other words, a quasi-stability would be reached. The embeddedness in the context-in-time guarantees continuous challenges to any quasi-stable state of the person, creating disequilibria. Directionality of meanacting is given due to the fact that it is the active person who constructs the transformative move from the *as-is 1* to the next moment in time (*as-is 2*) in a nonarbitrary way. The *as-if-could-be* is not another name for pure fantasy or "anything goes": It is a person-centered field—constructed in relation to the person's here-and-now future-oriented point of view. If the personal point of view changes, so necessarily does the *as-if-could-be*.

Adaptation as Preadaptation to Uncertainty

From this angle of dynamic construction of present and future, Darwinian notions of adaptation (to the *given* environmental condition) are not applicable, because no conditions are ever *given*. Instead, the conditions result from the process of the organism's facing the immediate next future. All conditions are permanently in the process of becoming, including the present state of affairs and their linked set of immediate future possibilities. Henri Bergson's (1907/1911) concept of adaptation as oriented toward an immediate and indeterminate future is a fitting replacement for the Darwinian notion. The latter has been abandoned also in economics (see Herbert Simon's [1957] concept of *satisficing* and the contemporary focus on hypergame modeling; e.g., Harsanyi & Selten, 1988). It can be said that the uncertainty of the future has been taken into account in those areas of human existence that are of social relevance (economic processes), whereas the relevance of real-life potential downfalls has been avoided in psychological theorizing in its self-protected belief in "prediction" and "control." In its pure conceptual form, however, any perspective on development is necessarily faced with the need to recognize some form of uncertainty of the future.

Acceptance of indeterminacy has not been an easy task for scientists (Fogel, Lyra, & Valsiner, 1997; Valsiner, 1997), yet there exist some positive examples. The notion of dynamic linking of the present and the future has been at the foundation of the concept of *zone of proximal development* (Valsiner & Van der Veer, 1993). The potential future conditions (which cannot be known before the future becomes present) and current conditions form a complex that is in principle indeterminable at any moment in time.

If adaptation is always oriented toward the future, it becomes a task that can never be solved in full. Only approximate solutions are possible. Yet looking for exact and unitary solutions is inevitable, because organisms cannot avoid the uncertainties of living. In the human case, efforts to solve this insoluble task entail construction of signs (and hierarchies of signs) that prepare the person for the future. Thus, for the human species, the emergence of semiosis (construction of signs) opened new possibilities for preadaptation. From the world of goals-oriented behavior (of other species), *Homo sapiens* moved to the construction of meaningful goals and semiotically regulated acting toward those goals.

MEANACTING AS DIALOGICAL PROCESS

Within our dialogical approach (Josephs & Valsiner, 1998), signs are conceptualized in terms of opposites. In Wilhelm Wundt's classificatory system of the logic of social sciences, this approach belongs to the class of dialectical methods—more specifically, to the subclass of *antithetical concept formation*. Antithetical concept formation entails the creation of a pair of oppositions (if a meaning, *A,* emerges, its oppositional counterpart, *non-A,* creates the tension between the two opposites; Wundt, 1921, p. 671). Theoretical efforts of this kind have been used in contemporary dialogical approaches to psychological processes (Hermans & Kempen, 1993; Marková, 1990, 1994; Rychlak, 1995). Researchers of actual dialogical phenomena—conversations between persons—have also recognized the oppositions involved (e.g., Linell, 1995). Such a look at communication recognizes the uncertainty of any communication situation (Bühler, 1934/1990; Rommetveit, 1992, 1998; Schegloff, 1987). Inferencing from the utterance is the process by which the person links the present (utterance) with the future (answer to the utterance).

Meanings as Bipolar Wholes: Sign and Countersign

When humans construct meaning to relate with their world, the field of opposites is automatically implied at every moment. Meaning arises in the form of complexes of united opposites, and the opposition between them is the basis for its change. A sign that is constructed immediately co-constructs its opposite—a countersign. Parallel examples to this theoretical notion can be discovered elsewhere (role and counterrole; see Oliveira & Valsiner, 1997). This focus on figure/ground unity in allowing meanings to become specified follows the general epistemological direction of cogenetic logic (Herbst, 1995) as well as of efforts to rescue dialectical thought from the perils of vagueness of expression (Rychlak, 1995). The issue of contrast between object and its negation has puzzled scholars in a philosophical framework (on the indeterminacy of "nothing," see Bergson, 1906; on Sartre on the "unreal," see Casey, 1981, p. 154).

We can trace the origin of conceptualizing meanings in terms of constructed opposites back to the philosophical approach to assumptions by Alexius Meinong, who established the foundations of Gestalt thought in Graz (Austria) in the 1880s. Meinong (1902/1983) claimed:

> As I am apprehending an A, I also apprehend a non-A in some sense. So we have to do with a difference regarding what is apprehended . . . a difference regarding what stands opposite [*gegenübersteht*] each intellectual experience as its object [*Gegenstand*]. . . . In the non-A, then, there is a further objective factor, the "non," as it were, supervening on the A. (pp. 14-15)

Meinong understood the basic asymmetry between the two components of representation: The *non-A* operates as *negativum* in relation to *A*. *Negativum* is always built on the basis of the positive concept (the *inferiora*). Thus it is not possible to think of "nonred" without having a notion of "red" on the basis of which the *negativum* is built up. Furthermore, the *negativum* emerges not only on the basis of the *inferiorum*, but in between that and a wide-open field of possible objects that are clearly different from it. As Meinong (1902/1983) explained:

> The idea of the *negativum* does not develop originally from the A alone; instead, there is also given an X, of which it may be or at least is asserted that it is not A, in quite the same way that the similarity must, to begin with, be established between A and some other, second object, Y. And just as abstraction then sets to work on the special complex AY formed by means of comparison—so that from the idea "Y similar to A" there is formed the idea "similarity to A" or "similar to A"—so too might an abstract representation "something that is not A" or simply non-A develop out of a complex of another sort, AX, or out of the idea "X is not A." Along with the original duality of the *fundamenta*, the matter of the producing activity is also settled: What is accomplished by comparison in the other case is here accomplished by judgment—negative judgment, naturally. (p. 16)

Meinong's insights into the processes of meanacting can be extended in our contemporary efforts. The opposition *A versus non-A* grows by the

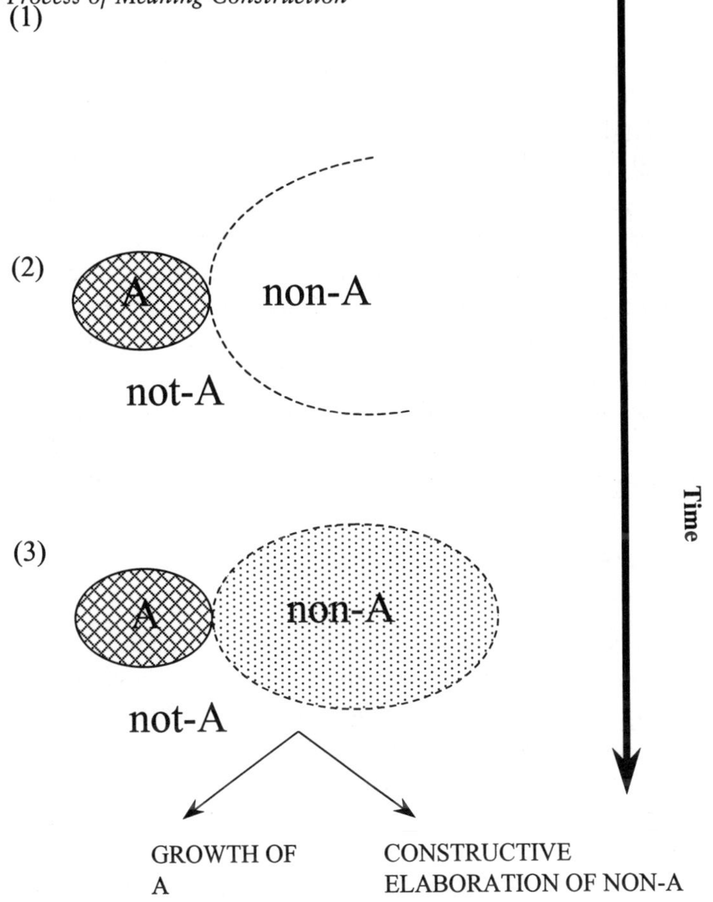

(1)

Figure 9.2. Emergence of Meaning Complexes

"positive comparison" (of similarities to *A*) and "negative judgment" (contrast with *not-A*). We will set these processes up in a microgenetic frame.

Our starting point of meanacting is *nothingness* (see Figure 9.2, step 1), or, in other words, the *universe of undifferentiated everything.* If a person relates to the world or him- or herself through constructing meaning, two mutually related fields (*A* and *non-A*) are immediately constructed and foregrounded against the universe of everything else; that is, the {*A & non-A*} complex becomes differentiated from *not-A* (steps 2 and 3). *Not-A* is conceptualized as an unbounded field of heterogeneity that is not related to by the person (see the parallel in this differentiation to Bateson's [1971] reasoning about class inclusion).

Non-A is the countersign to the sign *A*. This relationship is further specified as an *oppositional complex* in which it is possible to specify the meaning of *A* through *non-A* (but not vice versa—see Meinong's examples, above). Both parts of the duality emerge together (in accordance with cogenetic logic; Herbst, 1995) and are mutually deterministic (*A* cannot exist without *non-A,* and *non-A* cannot exist without *A*). The two poles in this theoretically created opposition are not equal. One is describable in discrete terms (as a single word, with all of its semantic field, e.g., this word means this or that, and the meaning can be expressed by similar synonyms *X, Y, Z*), whereas the other is describable in terms of partial fit of the opposites, quasi-words, subfields of feeling (e.g., "not really *A, X, Y, Z,* but something else . . . can't describe it"). Thus the {*A & non-A*} duality is more strictly given on the side of the *A* field and purposefully fuzzy on the other.

The Organization of the A Field

However, both *A* and *non-A* parts of the complex can be considered as fields (rather than as entities). As is obvious from Meinong's examples, the two fields are different in their organization. *A* as a field consists of all versions of the sign that are *similar* to *A* (*a', a'', a''',* and so on). This similarity is a personally constructed one—that is, we can never know in full what persons consider to be similar and what they do not (*internal indeterminacy*).

However, sign construction is not a completely individualistic activity. We can (and do) involve others in our meanacting—in the sense that we can (and do) communicate with each other. So we can speculate that similarity can be of three kinds (beyond the ones we cannot know; see above): First, similarity can be based on *taxonomic classification.* In that case, the field of *A* includes synonyms of the given meaning. The move from "car" to "automobile" in a person's meaning construction can be described entirely within the *A* field. Likewise, the emergence of general categories is possible within the field of *A* (e.g., "vehicle" to include "car," "automobile," and so on). Second, similarity within the field of *A* can be based on *functional* relationships (e.g., "horse" and "rider"; see Scheerer, 1959, who regards a functional relationship as one way among others of constituting a *sphere of meaning*). In short, what is ordinarily considered to take place in the act of classification (by educated or illiterate persons; Luria, 1976) belongs to the dynamic processes within the *A* field. Third, similarity can be based on the usage of *qualifiers.* Thus *A* (e.g., a person claiming that he is "stingy") could embrace *a'* ("kind of stingy"), *a''* ("very stingy"), *a'''* ("not so stingy"), and so on. Finally, *personally constructed similarity,* which does not follow the three ways outlined here, remains to be explained. The process involved here entails the construction of *higher-level signs* that focus on certain parts of the given totality and create *belongingness* (and in that sense similarity) between meanings (Liepmann, 1904). The specific outcome of this *general* process cannot, of course, be known by anyone other than the person him- or herself.

The Organization of the Non-A Field

The field of *non-A* is characterized by its contrasting indeterminacy (*external indeterminacy*). It is an unstructured, or quasi-structured, field that gradually comes into emergence (see the move from step 2 to step 3 in Figure 9.2) together with the *A* field. It includes all versions of signs that do not belong to the similarity set for *A* and those that do not belong to the (infinitely large) set of undoubtedly *not-A*. The field of *non-A* is a boundary zone between *A* and *not-A,* and as such is defined as fuzzy from the outset.

The Organization of the Relation Between A and Non-A

Meaning is given through the presence of "internal" and "external" fields of indeterminacy. In other terms, *A* is "foregrounded" and *non-A* becomes "backgrounded" (Linell, 1992). As our mental processes seem (to us) to operate with unipolar terms (e.g., "This is *A,* no doubt"—from here come the axioms of Boolean logic, *A or non-A*), from a dialogical perspective the certainty and determinate nature of *A* are a result of contextual foregrounding of *A* in relation to (including the overlook of) its contextual background.

It is further posited that the indeterminate and purposively fuzzy part (*non-A*) of the dual system {*A & non-A*} is the locus within which major transformation of the meaning takes place. This is in line with the location of developmental processes in not-yet-structured areas (or time periods) of phenomena (see Valsiner, 1997, pp. 115-120; on the indeterminacy of the zone of proximal development, see Valsiner & Van der Veer, 1993).

Non-A is paradoxically not only immediately cocreated *in parallel* with *A* as a field of meanings, but it implies a yet-to-be-differentiated field of *meanings-to-be* or a *meaning potentiality.* In this sense, *non-A* links the present to the future. We can map the notion of the relation of *"as-is—as-if-could-be"* transformation elaborated above on the {*A & non-A*} duality. Here the understanding of *non-A* goes along with the *as-if-could-be* potentiality.

TRANSFORMATION OF MEANINGS

Once an {*A & non-A*} complex is constructed, it is not to be stable. Over the course of microgenetic meanacting, novelty emerges because of the person's activity and the open, complex structure of meaning-in-context. Renegotiation of the {*A & non-A*} complex can take place interpersonally (in actual dialogues between persons) or intrapersonally (in the form of a "dialogue with oneself"—or *autodialogue*—where the {*A & non-A*} tensions and transformations are located within the internal psychological realm). In both cases, the theoretical questions are the same: *What are the processes involved in the transformation* of the {*A & non-A*} complex?

There are two ways in which transformation of meaning may occur: by growth and/or by constructive elaboration. *Growth* involves the further differentiation of the *A* field (see Figure 9.3). In case of further differentiation, *a* remains as the background in relation to which the new sign (*a'*) gains meaning. This putting of *a* into relation with *a'* takes place in a variety of ways. These include differentiation followed by integration, opposition (where *a* is still on a detectable level), or even "takeover" (where *a* is no longer mentioned, but is necessary as background for *a'*).

Constructive elaboration, on the other hand, is viewed as operating on the *non-A* field, bringing it to a state of differentiation, and possibly to the change of the nature of *A* (Figure 9.4). *A* is the "local point of departure" (Linell, 1992) for constructive emergence in/of *non-A.* In the tension between *A* and *non-A*, a new structure (*B*) may emerge within *non-A.* For example, the indeterminate field of "nonstingy" may include possibilities for constructing concrete new signs (e.g., "generous" = *B*, with its opposite field of *non-B*, or "nongenerous," which initially is undifferentiated). This {*B & non-B*} complex develops in the *non-A* field and can lead to the *takeover* of the *A* field, in which case the two meanings change their places: *B* ("generous") relates to *non-B* ("nongenerous"), and *A* ("stingy") and its counterpart ("nonstingy") become part of *non-B* ("nongenerous"). The takeover process (from differentiated *non-A* into *A*) could be blocked by

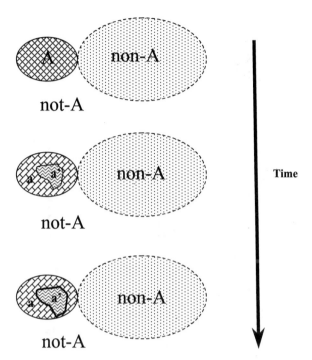

Figure 9.3. Process of Growth in the *A* Field

changes in the *A* field. For instance, growth within the *A* field could have occurred ("stingy" turning into "economical"), with the result of the grown *A* protecting the {*A & non-A*} complex against the {*B & non-B*} takeover. Takeover and the blockage of a takeover are certainly only two possible ways in which the process can move. Alternatively, *A* and *B* could, for example, also be coordinated in a harmonious, nonstressful relationship.

Our understanding of constructive elaboration of the *non-A* field, specifically the process of takeover, has a parallel to Werner's (1954) conceptualization of change of meaning through its focus on the relationships of parts and their movement within a "holophrastic complex." *Displacement* (Werner's equivalent to our takeover) is defined as a shift of one element from the central position of a holophrastic complex to a peripheral one and a peripheral part becoming focal (Werner, 1954, pp. 195 ff.). This takes the form

$$A(B) \rightarrow B(A) \rightarrow B.$$

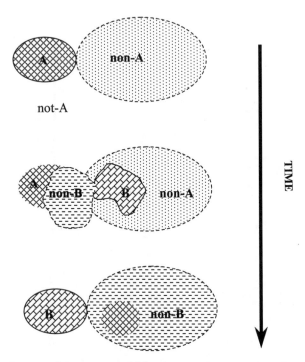

Figure 9.4. Process of Constructive Elaboration in the *Non-A* Field

Both in Werner's and in our own approach, however, change of meaning (or its maintenance) appears to entail a somewhat miraculous shift (or a similarly miraculous harmonious coexistence of, for instance, logically contradictory meaning complexes). Signs and meanings, however, are not constructed in vacuo, but are dynamically related to and embedded in a hierarchy of semiotic regulators. Circumvention strategies (elaborated below) relate these regulators to the meaning complexes. Both maintenance and change can be outcomes of this process (Josephs & Valsiner, 1998).

REVIEWING OLD EMPIRICAL EVIDENCE: INTROSPECTIONIST EXPERIMENTS— MEANACTING IN THE INTRAPERSONAL REALM

Contemporary psychology has forgotten the phenomenological richness of early work on word associations (Jung, 1910) and of the thought process analyses performed through introspectionist experimental techniques (Messer, 1906). Here we take a fresh look at some of the old data, without entering old theoretical discussions (about the reality of "imageless thought" or on the objectivity of introspectionist data; see Ogden, 1911). For our purposes, some of the data reported from these experiments reveal material that is critical for the dialogical perspective outlined here.

The specific evidence from these earlier studies that we intend to reuse comes from the work of Robert Ogden (1917), whose procedure included purposive introspective scrutiny of the process of arrival at the meaning of a stimulus word (or phrase). The observer was told:

> Close your eyes and hold yourself as passive as possible, both mentally and physically. After saying "Ready," "Now," I shall pronounce a word. Give it your immediate, full attention with the definite purpose of understanding its meaning. As soon as *you are satisfied* that the meaning has been grasped, react with "Yes." Then recount by introspection your complete experience. *Be in no hurry to react*, and let your occupation with the word be as natural as possible. (p. 79; emphasis added)

The instruction is in itself remarkable (similar ones can be found in Karl Bühler's empirical work, e.g., Bühler, 1908/1951), as the person or "subject" is taken seriously as the vantage point of the whole investigation. His or her satisfaction with the result—obtained in the time the subject regarded as adequate—is of outstanding importance for the results. But even more important is the aspect of time: Already in 1904 Liepmann from the University of Berlin analyzed "normal" thought *processes* (through an analysis of the pathological phenomenon of "flight of ideas," *Ideenflucht*). In his work he explicitly criticized the, at that time, usual association method with its instruction to produce associations in response to verbal stimuli *in the briefest possible reaction time* (which was later used by Jung). Liepmann (1904) claimed:

> One has to recognize that through that [procedure] *one artificially makes the healthy person display flight of ideas*. One *forces him or her to maximal speed* and *blocks a slowing down* that in the healthy person's natural train of thought causes the search for the fitting concept and the rejection of the nonfitting, immediately popping-up concept. One turns off the whole apparatus, which we have described above as the functioning of the *higher-level concept* [*Obervorstellung*], the selective attention and so on. (pp. 59-60; our translation)

In other words, the method itself (briefest possible reaction time) *inevitably* transforms the normal person artificially into a pathological case through the blockage of the construction of *hierarchically ordered signs* (*Obervorstellungen*), a process that needs time. We will return below to the latter aspect of sign hierarchies. In our terminology this method of producing associations as quickly as possible can at best lead to study of what we called growth in the *A* field before, but not the process of constructive elaboration. The idea of slowing down the speed of performance to study the process of emergence of meanings is similarly emphasized (and similarly forgotten)—although methodologically realized in different ways—in the work on *Aktualgenese* (microgenesis) of Friedrich Sander (1927) in Leipzig and in parallel Heinz Werner (e.g., 1927) in Hamburg and the United States.

As a result of the instructions quoted above, Ogden reported a variety of introspective accounts. Let us look closely at one of the elaborate ones—reaction by an observer to the orally presented word *pair* (our analysis, in the terminology elaborated above, is given in brackets):

[after 5.6 seconds]
1. I was waiting for the word. When it came it associated almost immediately two meanings: *pair,* as a pair of something, boots or shoes,

   [{$A = pair$ & $non\text{-}A = nonpair$}]
2. and *pear,* briefly, not visualized.

   [constructive elaboration and dominance of $B = pear \rightarrow$ {$B = pear$ & $non\text{-}B = nonpear$} in *non-A*]
3. I came back to pair which was probably present all the time.

   [immediate dominance reversal to {A & $non\text{-}A$}]
4. This experience was very active and pleasant. I resumed in a very brief thought a problem in Poincaré's book having to do with a certain theory of logic.

   [constructive elaboration of C—Poincaré's logic into *non-A* $\rightarrow$ {C & $non\text{-}C$}]
5. Lingered over the thought for a moment while some imagery developed, possibly a vague image of a printed page and the peculiar type of the French,—not visualized, I think. There was something about the appearance of the numbers,—many numbers are scattered through the book.

[growth of C]

6. With the reaction came a visual image of a *pear.*

[reemergence of B in *non-C,* dominance of {B & *non-B*}]

7. It seemed floating in the air. I could see part of the stem, like tobacco smoke, vibrating. (Ogden, 1917, p. 98)

The immediate retrospection of the introspective stream was obviously reflexive of the ambiguous stimulus word (*pair/pear*). The move from *pair* to *pear* entailed our *non-A* takeover (change from {A = *pair* & *non-A* = nonpair*} to the constructive elaboration of *pear* in *non-A,* followed by dominance of {B = *pear* & *non-B* = *nonpear*}). This dominance was reversed back to *pair* ({A & *non-A*}; note the notion of "pleasant"), only to be moved away (by constructive elaboration of C—"Poincaré's logic" in *non-A*), which took over the thought movement. The imagery of printed page (filled with numbers) would amount to growth within C. Subsequently {B & *non-B*}, *pear,* reemerged in the *non-C* and took over the dominance again. Within approximately 5 seconds, the person's meanacting process proceeded through four takeover events (including one reversal) and one growth example. The *non-A* (or *non-B* or *non-C*) fields entailed a syncretic emergence of both words and images, in different mutual configurations.

THE EMPIRICAL EVIDENCE OF MEANACTING IN THE INTERPERSONAL REALM: IMAGINING BODY MODIFICATIONS

Meanacting can take place in both the intrapersonal realm (autodialogue), as the example above shows, and interpersonal contexts. This brings us to the third type of indeterminacy associated with the co-construction of meaning in interpersonal dialogue. Every utterance is socially directed, yet the addressee need not be clearly specified. A is actively *meant* in the act of uttering by the speaker and actively understood by a listener, in a certain here and now—but the fact that listeners appeal to context to understand speakers' utterances puts the listeners' understanding outside of speakers' direct control. Although linguists argue that speakers' utterances index their context, there is always indeterminacy involved in transmission (Bühler, 1934/1990).

The excerpts that follow are taken from an interview study on the ways in which people relate modifications of their bodies (hair, tattoos, and other permanent and semipermanent modifications, each intentionally created by the person) with themselves. The starting point for the study was an elaboration of James's (1890) understanding of the *empirical self* as quasi-separate entities of social, material, and spiritual *selves*. In contrast to James, we attempted to link (theoretically and empirically) social, material, and personal (spiritual) aspects of the empirical self in time instead of looking at them as entities (Surgan, 1997).

The interview (total around 2 hours) consisted of two parts. In the first part, the interviewee was invited to select a self-relevant domain of body decoration (clothes, cosmetics, jewelry, and so on; no mention was made of tattoos). After specifying the personally relevant domain, the interviewee was asked about his or her history of feelings about that domain, social reactions by significant others, and his or her own opinions about those reactions.

The second part of the interview involved a sequence of questions about various graphic designs that could be located in different places relative to the person's body. At first, the general qualities of the designs were discussed. This was followed by discussion of the designs as located on a T-shirt. The interviewee had to elaborate why one or another design would fit (or not fit) in a specific place on a T-shirt, and was asked in which different social situations he or she would wear the T-shirt. The location of the graphic design was "moved" further toward the subject's body through the interviewer's suggestion that the interviewee draw it on his or her arm. Finally, the subject was asked about his or her previous or current feelings about tattoos, desires (or lack of them) to have tattoos crafted on different parts of his or her body, and any previous ideations around getting tattoos. At each step of this transformation, the person's aesthetic choices, changing self-feelings, and expected social reactions were assessed. The empirical project was carried out in parallel in the United States and Germany; subjects were young adults (university students).

Example From Part I of the Interview Study

In an interview with a young woman (age 24) from the German sample, the interviewee selected (actually proposed, as this was not included in our sample of objects) color as the relevant self-related domain. She described the color of clothes (and other things, such as the walls in her apartment) as extremely important to her, especially orange and a dark blue. An excerpt from the interview follows, together with the analytic interpretation (in brackets):

I: What do you want to *signal* through colors? How do *you want to be perceived by others?*

IEE: First of all, I want to say that *it is not important how others perceive me* with respect to colors.
      [*A* is suggested by interviewer and immediately rejected by the interviewee by a focus on *non-A*: {*A & non-A*} → {*A & evaluation of others*}.]

IEE: But *it is important how I perceive myself* (with respect to colors).
      [*A* is constructed in relation to *non-A*: {*Self & evaluation of others*}.]

IEE: Yes, this is *most important*. This *feeling of well-being.*
      [Growth of *A*: Perception of self is important → is most important → feeling of well-being.]

IEE: My walls at home are also orange. The windows are green, the room is totally colorful. Yet it has a *harmonious appeal*. Yes, indeed, *harmony is the key word.*
      [Further growth of *A*: Feeling of well-being → harmony.]

IEE: When something makes me feel harmonious, *I strive for that.*
      [Growth implies a future orientation: Harmony is striven for.]

IEE: It is nice, if others like that [reference of *that* is not further specified], then we have something in common. *But if others don't like, I can't help. The most important is that I like it.*
      [Loop is closed again: Return to *non-A* and previous *A*.]

In summary, a meaning is suggested to the interviewee by the interviewer and immediately rejected by her. The interviewee instead constructs her own focus (*A*), which then "grows" (*A* growth) in the process. The process of growth leads to a meaning that itself has a future orientation (striving for harmony) and through that preemptively regulates the person's future encounters with her world.

CHANGE AND MAINTENANCE OF MEANING:
THE NOTION OF CIRCUMVENTION STRATEGIES

Human meanacting is a flexible process, with both flexibility and rigidity as potential outcomes. Meanings are constructed and reconstructed immediately; some of them are overcome rather quickly (our notion of takeover), others are maintained and stay in a harmonious relationship or enter into a state of rivalry with other meaning complexes. As a result, logically mutually contradictory meanings can stay next to each other without creating any tension in the intrapersonal sphere. It is the hierarchical organization of sign construction and sign operation that allows for this flexibility. All these processes are *catalyzed* by additional semiotic devices—semiotic regulators—that can either enhance such transformation or block it (and thus maintain a moment of relative stability in the {*A & non-A*} complex).

Circumvention strategies—constructed semiotic regulators of dialogic and autodialogic relations between meaning complexes—allow for the operation of higher-level signs on the construction of meanings (Josephs & Valsiner, 1998). These strategies can reconcile otherwise contradictory complexes or, alternatively, lead to an escalation and eventual takeover. Our reasoning about circumvention strategies has its roots in Lev Vygotsky's and James Mark Baldwin's thinking. Vygotsky (1925/1971) demonstrated that in the process of understanding a short story, one word can drastically change the reader's whole feeling tone toward the story in retrospect and prospect. He also showed that human beings are not facing alternative but similar attractive meanings, like Buridan's donkey, but construct and use signs to solve otherwise unsolvable decision problems. James Mark Baldwin (1908, p. 50), on the other hand, showed in his *genetic logic* that seemingly similarly attractive decisions (or meanings, in our context) are a fiction anyway, as the person immediately constructs personal preferences, points of emphasis, or selections.

Through circumvention strategies, higher-level signs can be brought into focus and can regulate the further relationship between meaning complexes. Evaluative (moralistic) organizers of the *non-A* fields—ill-defined feelings of the opposite that may lead to tension ("I am stingy but I *should not* be"; "I am generous but I *should not* be wasting; I *should be* economical")—can both set up the tensions (contrasts, rivalries, and so on) and mediate their elimination. Different kinds of *fuzzy qualifiers* (e.g., *generally, sometimes*) are a second kind of semiotic regulator of the {*A & non-A*} complex. Different from the evaluative organizers (which work on regulating the relations of the *A* and *non-A* fields, either promoting constructive elaboration of the *non-A,* and possible takeover, or blocking the latter), fuzzy qualifiers operate upon the *A* field, relativizing the strictness of the similarity class (which the *A* field is).

The person can also short-circuit the dynamic potential of meaning complexes. This takes place when the person actively introduces contrasts within meaning complexes (through growth or constructive elaboration) and creates a relation between the oppositional parts of the system that leads to a dynamic recurrent cycle of meaning reconstruction. The person literally "goes around in circles," trying to express some meaning, but always returning to a state similar to the one from where he or she began.

On the other side, the person can avoid the entrance into meaning construction (i.e., block or suppress the emergence of {*A & non-A*} fields from the outset—"I do not want to think about that"). This amounts to "leaving the field" (in Kurt Lewin's [1927] terminology) of the ongoing meanacting process. Both the construction of "closed circles" and "leaving the field" are of great importance for human psychological adaptation. Human beings are not always creating new understanding—they may avoid being in the torturous process of doing that through circular thinking and talking or deciding not to think (and talk). Silence is often the preferred metalevel strategy for regulating human relations (for a thorough elaboration of circumvention strategies, see Josephs & Valsiner, 1998).

Example From Part II of the Interview Study

The following example, which comes from the second part of our interview with a U.S. subject (Surgan, 1997), shows how meaning is circumvented by the introduction of a higher-level organizer. The female interviewee, who has emphasized her religious background before, dislikes tattoos in total. The interview proceeds as follows:

I: Would you be okay with drawing that on your arm or hand?

IEE: Ehh . . . but I don't draw very well.

I: Do you want to give it a shot?

IEE: If you're asking me if I like it enough to just put on me, no. I would do it because it's an experiment, but just to draw or have me? No. *I don't draw things on myself, no matter what it is.* I just don't. *Same thing as I would never get a tattoo.*

I: You would never get a tattoo?

IEE: Mmm-mm. Nooo.

I: Why not?

IEE: I just don't like them.

I: Why not?

IEE: First of all, you know, it's something that I think—*first of all, it's something that I just don't like.* Other people it's fine. But I don't want to, anyway. And most importantly, I don't see how it would, in any way, glorify God. . . .

I: Even if you put like a cross or something?

IEE: Uh-huh. I know what you're saying. I mean, some Christians might choose to do that, and if they feel called and moved by God that that's what He wants them to do, that's fine, but I just wouldn't. *Unless God wanted me to.* I doubt He would want me to do something like that, *but if He wanted me to, I would.*

I: . . . What if you were having some trouble or you felt like you were losing your faith, or whatever, and you were talking about it and somebody said, "Would you consider wearing a crucifix or you should get a little golden cross on your ankle or somewhere where you could easily see it." How would you react?

IEE: Well, *I would pray about it and if God told me that He wants me to do it, I would.* I wouldn't just—they tell me that? Okay. I would pray about it. "God, do you really want me to get the tattoo?" *If He says yes, okay. Then I'll do it. I'd have a tattoo all over my body if that's what He wants me to do.*

The interviewee starts with a clear and focused {*A & non-A*} duality, {*dislike of drawing something on the arm & non-A*}, out of which the *A* part is growing {*dislike of tattoos & non-A*}, which then is firmly established by circular reasoning (I don't like it because I don't like it). The interviewer suggests a higher-level semiotic organizer (God's will), which immediately challenges the interviewee's meaning complex. This challenge does not (necessarily) imply a change of meaning (although we do not know that with certainty here) but a circumvention of it: We can assume that she would still not like to have a tattoo, but would get one anyway if this were God's will (meaning is maintained, but action can happen otherwise).

In the following elaboration she introduces another means of semiotic regulation, namely, praying (in our terminology, circumvention of meaning by symbolic action). If somebody suggested a tattoo (interpersonal realm), she would enter into an imagining interpersonal (more exactly, an intraper-sonal interpersonal) realm (asking God through praying), waiting for His answer, and only then wear a tattoo in the most general sense, namely, *all over her body.*

Thus the suggestion from the social side (both by the interviewer and by the interviewer's suggestion that the interviewee imagine a social sugges-tion from other people) is mediated by this higher-level organizer, namely, God. The latter is completely immunized toward challenges from the social and intrapersonal world—God's will stands above everything else and leads to radical changes (tattoo all over the body).

This example nicely shows that the same mechanism—operation of higher signs on the meaning complex qua circumvention strategies—entails both flexibility and rigidity as possible outcomes: The flexibility is dem-onstrated by the fact that the {*A & non-A*} complex, despite its stability, can be overcome in the action domain (eventually wearing a tattoo)—due to the catalyzing power of the organizer. The complex itself is not changed but remains—defocused through the application of the organizer—in the background. The rigidity is clearly visible in the power of the organizer itself, which eventually can become applicable in all domains (that is, the interviewee would do everything if she thinks it is in the name of God).

Here we can observe the establishment of *circular, unchallengeable loops* of semiotic organizers. It is not only the case that circumvention processes help to overcome temporary problems in meanacting; it is equally impor-tant to fixate a particular way of circumventing process through its mutually integrated loop nature (beginning → I WILL DO X IF Y → BUT Y DOES NOT HAPPEN → BUT IF IT WERE TO HAPPEN THEN → go to the beginning). Such a loop is recognizable as Möbius strip. The interior surface of that strip moves to become its exterior surface and vice versa, in a pattern that excludes innovation. Such hierarchical semiotic control loops guarantee inflexibility of thinking and (if disconnected from regulating conduct) potentially infinite cycles of talk for the sake of the talk itself. If, however, such closed loops include regulation of conduct, then we get the classic pattern of a semiotically constructed incapacity to act in any way, as has been described by Pierre Janet (1921).

The ordinary system of hierarchical semiotic regulation of course works in between the self-enclosed meanacting cycles and unregulated conduct. The constructive nature of semiosis has both remarkable speed—as it has to adjust to any new situation, preparing for future possibilities—and flexibility. Human meanacting can proceed both instantly and incredibly slowly. It can lead to consistency (as well as rigidity) and flexibility. The latter may include instant reversals of what persons mean—often to the opposites. Our view on the dialogical processes involved in meaning creation is aimed at bringing to light some of the ways in which such flexibility and inflexibility, stability and instability, may be explained.

GENERAL CONCLUSIONS

The theoretical and empirical study of meanacting implies two basic assumptions: first, the *oppositional duality* of any meaning complex, which is the condition for any process of transformation and emergence of novelty (called here constructive elaboration of the *non-A* field); and second, *the dynamic hierarchical organization* of meanings in which higher-level signs operate as catalysts on the process of meaning construction.

The notion of hierarchy of signs and their operation in "normal" thought processes was discussed in the work of Liepmann (1904) to which we referred earlier. For Liepmann, normal thought process were structured and guided through a *hierarchical organization of multiple Obervorstellungen* (higher-level signs), which focus on and single out a subwhole from the totality of experience in the here and now and give *directionality* (*richtungsgebend*; pp. 34, 37). The contrast to that would be simple *anarchy* (p. 41) of the thought process, as we can see in pathological cases of "flight of ideas." In ordered thinking parts belong to each other (*zusammengehörig*), whereas in disordered thinking parts just happen to be together (*zusammengeraten*; p. 42). This notion shows much similarity with Heinz Werner's (1957) view that every developmental process involves both differentiation and hierarchical integration.

Both basic assumptions of meanacting were clearly recognized in psychology very early in the 20th century and even before (Meinong, 1902/1983, on the oppositional duality, see above; and Liepmann, 1904, on hierarchical organization) but got lost in contemporary psychology's "romantic" understanding of meaning making. We have gone beyond the historical approaches by specifying the processes of growth and constructive elaboration, on the one hand, and by showing how higher-level signs work on meaning complexes through circumvention strategies.

The methodological implication we can draw from our work is probably a paradoxical one: The study of the messy process of meanacting requires a highly purified—for instance—experimental method, in contrast to discourse or narrative analysis. Such purification, however, does not imply the rigid application of a certain method (such as association method entailing briefest possible reaction times), but a method that is constructed to answer the very questions under consideration. This insight was probably well-known at the beginning of the century, but has been forgotten in contemporary sociocultural approaches, with their respective discursive or narrative "turns" and a moralistic contrasting of *Erklären* and *Verstehen* (explaining versus understanding)—with a clear preference for "understanding" in the domain of meaning making (e.g., Bruner, 1990). Although we used narratives in our own study, we analyzed them not as such, but as emerging constructions of meaning in time, and our goal was certainly not to understand but generally to explain psychological processes of meanacting. Further elaboration of our theory will necessarily imply an empirical return to and elaboration of the historical experimental/introspectionist methods.

Meanacting as such, it seems, is a process in which human beings are inevitably immersed. An alternative does not exist: We cannot go on in any other way. At every moment of living, we face a very wide field of next immediate possibilities. Yet the majority of these are never brought to our attention, and in the case of the relatively few that become differentiated (into our *non-A* field), we can reconstruct our reflections upon ourselves in quick and flexible ways. The most remarkable aspect of human activity is that we—easily—manage to exist, despite the inevitable uncertainty of the immediate next moment and the large sphere of possibilities.

REFERENCES

Baldwin, J. M. (1908). *Thought and things: A study of the development and meaning of thought, or genetic logic: Vol. 2. Experimental logic, or genetic logic of thought.* London: Swan Sonnenschein.

Bateson, G. (1971). The message "This is play." In R. E. Herron & B. Sutton-Smith (Eds.), *Child's play* (pp. 261-266). New York: John Wiley.

Bergson, H. (1906). L'idée de néant. *Revue Philosophique, 62,* 449-466.

Bergson, H. (1911). *Creative evolution.* New York: Henry Holt. (Original work published 1907)

Bruner, J. (1990). *Acts of meaning.* Cambridge, MA: Harvard University Press.

Bühler, K. (1951). On thought connections. In D. Rapaport (Ed.), *Organization and pathology of thought* (pp. 39-57). New York: Columbia University Press. (Original work published 1908)

Bühler, K. (1990). *Theory of language: The representational function of language.* Amsterdam: John Benjamins. (Original work published 1934)

Casey, E. S. (1981). Sartre on imagination. In P. A. Schlipp (Ed.), *The philosophy of Jean-Paul Sartre* (pp. 139-166). LaSalle, IL: Open Court.

Fogel, A., Lyra, M. C. D. P., & Valsiner, J. (Eds.). (1997). *Dynamics and indeterminism in developmental and social processes.* Mahwah, NJ: Lawrence Erlbaum.

Harsanyi, J. C., & Selten, R. (1988). *A general theory of equilibrium selection in games.* Cambridge: MIT Press.

Herbst, D. P. (1995). What happens when we make a distinction: An elementary introduction to co-genetic logic. In T. Kindermann & J. Valsiner (Eds.), *Development of person-context relations* (pp. 67-79). Mahwah, NJ: Lawrence Erlbaum.

Hermans, H. J. M., & Kempen, H. J. G. (1993). *The dialogical self: Meaning as movement.* San Diego, CA: Academic Press.

James, W. (1890). *Principles of psychology.* London: Macmillan.

Janet, P. (1921). The fear of action. *Journal of Abnormal Psychology and Social Psychology, 16,* 150-160.

Josephs, I. E. (1998). Constructing one's self in the city of the silent: Dialogue, symbols, and the role of "as-if" in self-development. *Human Development, 41,* 180-195.

Josephs, I. E., & Valsiner, J. (1998). How does autodialogue work? Miracles of meaning maintenance and circumvention strategies. *Social Psychology Quarterly, 61,* 68-83.

Jung, C. G. (1910). The association method. In *Lectures and addresses delivered before the departments of psychology and pedagogy in celebration of the 20th anniversary of the opening of Clark University* (pp. 39-89). Worcester, MA: Clark University.

Lewin, K. (1927). Gesetz und Experiment in der Psychologie. *Symposion, 1,* 375-421.

Liepmann, H. (1904). *Über Ideenflucht* [On flight of ideas]. Halle, Germany: Carl Marhold.

Linell, P. (1992). The embeddedness of decontextualization in the contexts of social practices. In A. H. Wold (Ed.), *The dialogical alternative: Towards a theory of language and mind* (pp. 253-271). Oslo: Scandinavian University Press.

Linell, P. (1995). Troubles with mutualities: Towards a dialogical theory of misunderstanding and miscommunication. In I. Marková, G. C. Graumann, & K. Foppa (Eds.), *Mutualities in dialogue* (pp. 176-213). Cambridge: Cambridge University Press.

Luria, A. R. (1976). *Cognitive development.* Cambridge, MA: Harvard University Press.

Marková, I. (1990). A three-step process as a unit of analysis in dialogue. In I. Marková & K. Foppa (Eds.), *The dynamics of dialogue* (pp. 129-146). London: Harvester.

Marková, I. (1994). Mutual construction of asymmetries. In P. van Geert & L. Mos (Eds.), *Annals of theoretical psychology* (Vol. 10, pp. 325-342). New York: Plenum.

Meinong, A. (1983). *On assumptions*. Berkeley: University of California Press. (Original work published 1902)

Messer, A. (1906). Experimentell-psychologische Untersuchungen über das Denken. *Archiv für die gesamte Psychologie, 8,* 1-224.

Ogden, R. M. (1911). Knowing and expressing. *Pedagogical Seminary, 18,* 47-53.

Ogden, R. M. (1917). Some experiments on the consciousness of meaning. In *Studies in psychology: Contributed by colleagues and former students of Edward Bradford Titchener* (pp. 79-120). Worcester, MA: Louis N. Wilson.

Oliveira, Z., & Valsiner, J. (1997). Play and imagination: The psychological construction of novelty. In A. Fogel, M. C. D. P. Lyra, & J. Valsiner (Eds.), *Dynamics and indeterminism in developmental and social processes* (pp. 119-133). Mahwah, NJ: Lawrence Erlbaum.

Rommetveit, R. (1992). Outlines of a dialogically based social-cognitive approach to human cognition and communication. In A. H. Wold (Ed.), *The dialogical alternative: Towards a theory of language and mind* (pp. 19-44). Oslo: Scandinavian University Press.

Rommetveit, R. (1998). On human beings, computers, and representational-computational versus hermeneutic-dialogical approaches to human cognition and communication. *Culture and Psychology, 4,* 213-233.

Rychlak, J. F. (1995). A teleological critique of modern cognitivism. *Theory and Psychology, 5,* 511-531.

Sander, F. (1927). Über Gestaltqualitäten. In *Proceedings and papers of the 8th International Congress of Psychology, 1926* (pp. 183-189). Groningen, Netherlands: P. Noordhoff.

Scheerer, M. (1959). Spheres of meaning: An analysis of stages from perception to abstract thinking. *Journal of Individual Psychology, 15,* 50-61.

Schegloff, E. A. (1987). Some sources of misunderstanding in talk-in-interaction. *Linguistics, 25,* 201-218.

Simon, H. (1957). *Models of man*. New York: John Wiley.

Surgan, S. E. (1997). *Constructing one's self in dialogue: Semiotic tectonics of the mind*. Chapel Hill: University of North Carolina Press.

Valsiner, J. (1997). *Culture and the development of children's action* (2nd ed.). New York: John Wiley.

Valsiner, J. (1998). *The guided mind*. Cambridge, MA: Harvard University Press.

Valsiner, J., & Van der Veer, R. (1993). The encoding of distance: The concept of the zone of proximal development and its interpretations. In R. R. Cocking & K. A. Renninger (Eds.), *The development and meaning of psychological distance* (pp. 35-62). Hillsdale, NJ: Lawrence Erlbaum.

Vygotsky, L. S. (1971). *Psychology of art*. Cambridge: MIT Press. (Original work published 1925)

Werner, H. (1927). Über pysiognomische Wahrnehmungsweisen und ihre experimentelle Prüfung. In *Proceedings and papers of the 8th International Congress of Psychology, 1926* (pp. 443-446). Groningen, Netherlands: P. Noordhoff.

Werner, H. (1954). Change of meaning: A study of semantic processes through the experimental method. *Journal of General Psychology, 50,* 181-208.

Werner, H. (1957). The concept of development from a comparative and organismic point of view. In D. B. Harris (Ed.), *The concept of development* (pp. 125-147). Minneapolis: University of Minnesota Press.

Wundt, W. (1921). *Logik der Geisteswissenschaften* (4th ed.). Stuttgart: Ferdinand Enke.

10

A MOTIVATIONAL-VOLITIONAL PERSPECTIVE ON IDENTITY DEVELOPMENT

Peter M. Gollwitzer
Ute Bayer
Michaela Scherer
Andrea E. Seifert

In this chapter we discuss identity development from a goal implementation perspective. Identity achievement is typically (e.g., Marcia, 1980) defined as a choice between options (e.g., "Should I become a physician or a pharmacist?"). This traditional perspective ignores the fact that identity choices have to be accompanied by implementational efforts.

According to self-completion theory (Wicklund & Gollwitzer, 1982), the implementation of identity goals persists over time, because identity goals cannot actually be completed. In addition, single failures do not stop their pursuit, but lead to enhanced striving for identity goals. A person spontaneously initiates this enhanced striving through compensatory efforts (called *self-symbolizing*) that focus on indicating completeness to others through the acquisition of relevant symbols of the identity aspired to (e.g., writing articles for a scientist, children's school grades for being a good mother). The person assigns to others the role of an audience that only has to take notice of the person's self-symbolizing efforts; no sensitive social interactions between the audience and the person are attempted or necessary (Wicklund & Gollwitzer, 1982).

More recent research demonstrates that self-symbolizing cannot be replaced by self-esteem-enhancing strategies (Scherer, 1999). Moreover, even simply proclaiming one's intention to acquire relevant indicators of an identity creates a sense of completeness as long as these intentions are recognized by others (Seifert, 1999). Furthermore, both easy- and difficult-to-acquire indicators of an identity are equally effective in creating a sense of possessing the aspired-to identity (Brunstein & Gollwitzer, 1996). Finally, it has been demonstrated that the cognitive orientation (mind-set) associated with merely choosing identity goals differs from the mind-set associated with actually pursuing chosen identity goals (Bayer, 1998). We discuss in this chapter the implications of these findings for personality development across the life span. We suggest that old and very old people can effectively maintain their identity claims through self-symbolizing, which is facilitated by the tendency of older individuals to reduce social contacts to a few intimate friends.

SELF-CONCEPT, SELF-ESTEEM, AND IDENTITY GOALS

Theory and research on the self have a long tradition in psychology (e.g., Allport, 1943, 1955; Baumeister, 1986, 1998; Gordon & Gergen, 1968; James, 1890/1950; Suls, 1993; Suls & Greenwald, 1983). According to James (1890/1950), the term *self* (or *identity*) refers to a cognitive structure that incorporates all of a person's answers to the question "Who am I?" Researchers organize the answers given to this question into a number of different categories. One group of answers is related to physical attributes (e.g., "I am slim"); another is related to the broader category of social identities, which includes chosen or assigned social roles of an individual (e.g., "I am a woman"; "I am a teacher"). Finally, some answers may refer to perceived traits and dispositions (e.g., "I am tolerant"), to skills and aptitudes (e.g., "I am a math whiz kid"), or to values and interests (e.g., "I love to sail").

Following William James, a research tradition developed that construes the self as something the individual needs to understand, and therefore speaks of the self or identity in terms of a *self-concept*. There are many theoretical perspectives on how the individual perceives the self (e.g,. Bem's [1972] self-perception theory; social-interactionist approaches based on Cooley [1902] and Mead [1934], e.g., Stryker & Statham, 1985). Self-concept research evidences a continuous debate about whether an individual has a single self-concept or multiple self-concepts. Most contemporary models, however, have adopted the assumption of multiple selves, which may be organized around specific contexts of life (e.g., Linville, 1985; Markus, 1977; Triandis, 1989). Several basic dimensions have been identified along which the multiple selves may vary (see Linville & Carlston, 1994). A temporal dimension is present in assumptions about past, present, and future selves (e.g., Gordon, 1968; Higgins, 1987; Markus & Nurius, 1986). A centrality dimension reflects the relative importance of different self-concepts (e.g., Gergen, 1968; Sedikides, 1995), and an evaluative dimension reflects the fact that some self-concepts are relatively positive, some are more negative, and still others are mixed (Linville, 1985, 1987; Showers, 1992).

In the self-concept research literature there are still controversies about the question of whether the self is stable or malleable (e.g., Markus & Kunda, 1986; Swann, 1983). Self-concepts maintain a certain degree of stability over time and across contexts, as people seek information that verifies their self-views and actively resist information that challenges those views (e.g., Markus, 1977; Swann, 1983). People do not use their entire repertoires of self-concepts simultaneously. Rather, specific self-aspects are activated only when they are currently relevant (e.g., Wurf & Markus, 1991), and thus their relative accessibility may change. Finally, there are discussions about whether the self is accurate or illusionary (e.g., Brown, 1991; Brown & Dutton, 1995; Taylor & Brown, 1988).

Another important branch of research focuses on how the individual evaluates his or her own self (Greenwald, 1980). This affective response is discussed in its most global form as a person's *self-esteem* (Rosenberg, 1965). It is commonly assumed that people have a pervasive need for high self-esteem, so discussion focuses on where this need comes from and how it is served. For instance, Greenberg, Pyszczynski, and Solomon (1986; Pyszczynski, Greenberg, & Solomon, 1997) suggest that the terror associated with fear of death is reduced by high self-esteem. Thus they argue that fear of death is an essential source of the need for self-esteem. Baumeister and Tice (1990; see also Baumeister & Leary, 1995) refer to the terror of social exclusion. Leary and Downs (1995), on the other hand, have proposed that self-esteem is a fundamental motive in human beings, linked inexorably to functioning in social groups.

Various other ideas have been offered to explain positive self-evaluations. Some researchers see a link to structural qualities of self-concepts (e.g., clarity of self-concept, Campbell, 1990; complexity of self-concept, Linville, 1987; compartmentalization of positive and negative self-knowledge, Showers, 1992; Showers & Kling, 1996), whereas other scholars (e.g., Higgins, 1987) point out that a person's affective responses toward the self are associated with the discrepancies that he or she experiences between so-called self-guides (i.e., the ideal self or ought self) and the actual self. Finally, researchers have analyzed how relations to others affect an individual's self-evaluations. Tesser (1988) has focused, in his self-evaluation maintenance theory, on social comparison processes, whereby basking in the reflected glory of others can enhance self-esteem. Baumeister (1982), on the other hand, points to strategic self-presentation as a means of boosting one's self-evaluation.

Research on self-esteem describes the self with regard to self-evaluation processes, adding an affective and motivational dimension to self-concept research traditionally focusing on cognitive self-aspects. What the research on positive self-evaluations has not yet captured, however, is how the desired self is achieved behaviorally. It is not enough to consider how vital diverse goals are for a person's self-esteem (e.g., being a good mother may have more influence on the self-esteem than being a good skier), one also needs to consider how identity goals are achieved successfully. This *goal perspective on the self* has been described by Wicklund and Gollwitzer's (1982) theory of symbolic self-completion, which focuses on the implementation of self-defining goals. The person is defined as an active agent (see also Baumeister, 1998; Ford & Lerner, 1992) who not only chooses among possible identity goals but also regulates the implementation of chosen goals. Self-completion theory focuses on goals that specify a person's desired self-definition: so-called identity goals. They are integrated in an individual's self-concept and have a lasting effect on behavior regulation.

Heckhausen (1989) and Gollwitzer (1990; Heckhausen & Gollwitzer, 1987) have distinguished between motivational and volitional processes of wish fulfillment. Whereas motivational processes guide a person's choices among goals, volitional processes are assumed to determine a person's goal implementation. The former relates to issues of feasibility and desirability of potential goals (i.e., wishes and desires), whereas the latter relates to the commitment to the chosen goal and to holding on to it, even in the face of difficulties. Research on the self has traditionally been concerned with motivational issues (i.e., research on the self-concept as well as self-esteem). Self-completion theory, on the other hand, is concerned with the volitional issue of implementing identity-related (self-defining) goals.

SELF-COMPLETION THEORY

Historical Roots

Self-completion theory (Wicklund & Gollwitzer, 1982) can be traced back to Lewin's (1926) and his students' research on goal-directed behavior. Lewin argues that when a person sets a goal for him- or herself, a quasi-need originates and a tension state comes into play that remains until the goal is reached. The tension state is linked to the person's commitment to reaching the goal. In support of Lewin's theory, it has been demonstrated that participants' interest in resuming a task remains high after their work on the task has been interrupted (Lissner, 1933; Mahler, 1933; Ovsiankina, 1928).

Further, the tension state can be reduced not only through the attainment of the original goal but also through the performance of alternative goal-directed activities. Following task interruption, Mahler (1933) gave some of her experimental participants a substitute task. This had a strong impact on the subsequent tendency to resume the original task; the resumption rate was rather curtailed. Mahler observed that when people's goals were to perform intellectual tasks (e.g., solving a mathematical problem), other quite different intellectual tasks (e.g., solving a puzzle) served as substitutes for goal attainment. Henle (1944) suggests that the concrete tasks in this Lewinian research were related to certain "superordinate" goals, such as creativity, intelligence, and ambition. It can be assumed that whenever participants saw a similarity between the quality of the original task and the quality of the substitute task, they were no longer inclined to return to the original task because substitute goal (e.g., to be creative) completion had occurred.

Mahler (1933) found that the resumption effect was strongest when the substitute task carried a "social reality." Only when the solution of the substitute task could be announced to the experimenter did the task have tension-reducing properties. Apparently, participants not only strove to solve the task but also wanted others to recognize their striving. Only solving the substitute tasks in a social reality situation provided the participants with a sense of having attained the self-related goal to which they aspired while working on the original task.

The Concept of Self-Defining Goals

Self-completion theory provides a theoretical framework for the analysis of striving for self-defining goals. Striving for a particular identity goal requires the execution of identity-related activities. For the self-definition of a dancer, for instance, the related activities involve a solid educational background, high-quality equipment, dancing performances, and so on. With the goal concept, the theory points to the individual's commitment to accumulating the whole set of indicators of identity attainment.

In contrast to non-self-defining goals, self-defining goals specify a desired future self or self-aspect. A non-self-defining goal (e.g., to build a tower from wooden blocks) specifies an outcome that is not related to the self. Therefore goal attainment can be judged by concrete criteria that are related to the task at hand (e.g., there are still two building stones missing). A self-defining goal, on the other hand, delineates numerous possible, culturally agreed-upon symbols. Thus progress in attaining self-defining goals (e.g., to be creative) cannot be judged by a single criterion. A common feature of self-defining goals is that they encompass a whole set of symbols that indicate progress in attaining a self-definition. This implies that when a person fails to acquire one symbol, he or she can resort to alternative routes of completing the self-definition by acquiring other symbols. In contrast, when the person tries to attain a non-self-defining goal of simply meeting the task at hand and fails, then he or she will have to complete the task by task-related means.

Indicators of Completeness and
the Importance of Social Reality

The achievement of self-defining goals implies the accumulation of various relevant indicators or symbols, as each self-definition carries a number of possible indicators. For example, one can self-symbolize through fulfilling daily duties and performances associated with a particular identity (e.g., a baker bakes bread), through the acquisition of the skills and tools associated with a specific identity (e.g., a musician acquires certain skills in order to play an instrument), by simply making a verbal claim to possess a particular identity (e.g., "I am a psychologist"), through the exercise of identity-related social influence (e.g., an academic psychologist may engage in teaching psychology), and by displaying material symbols (e.g., a pious person may wear a golden cross).

These various forms of self-symbolizing obviously differ in terms of their accessibility. For example, it is easy to show off relevant symbols one already possesses or to claim the possession of an aspired-to identity through self-description. In contrast, the actual acquisition of relevant symbols (e.g., attaining advanced education) is more difficult. From the perspective of self-completion theory, however, not only the forms of self-symbolizing that are difficult to perform but also those that are easily attainable potentially indicate to others one's claim to possess the intended self-definition. What makes a difference is whether the chosen form of self-symbolizing has become a social fact. Self-completion theory asserts that the sense of progress toward a self-defining goal depends on the acknowledgment of others. Thus the social community has to take notice of the person's possession of indicators of the particular self-definition.

The Central Hypotheses of Self-Completion

Self-completion theory can be summarized by three central hypotheses:

1. *The compensation hypothesis:* Whenever a person who strives for a self-defining goal experiences a lack of relevant symbols, a sense of incompleteness arises that elicits attempts to strive for the desired identity goal through alternative routes.
2. *The social reality hypothesis:* Self-symbolizing that becomes a social fact is likely to be particularly effective in reducing the experienced sense of incompleteness.
3. *The social insensitivity hypothesis:* Self-symbolizing individuals do not address their audiences as partners for mutual exchange but as audiences that serve the sole function of taking notice of their claim to possess the aspired-to identity.

The Compensation Hypothesis

Self-completion theory postulates that an experienced lack of relevant symbols causes a sense of incompleteness. This experience may arise when the individual receives negative feedback about identity-related performances, when the individual compares him- or herself to others, or when the individual fails to acquire a relevant symbol. When committed people experience a sense of incompleteness, they try to symbolize completeness concerning the self-defining goal through alternative routes. As identity goals commonly imply a whole array of symbols, compensatory efforts can be expressed in any of the many alternative routes of self-symbolizing.

The compensation hypothesis has been tested in a series of experiments that used the following paradigm. Participants were students committed to a certain self-definition. The researchers made half of the participants feel incomplete by pointing out that they lacked a relevant indicator ("incomplete" participants). The other half of the participants were told that they possessed this indicator ("complete" participants). Finally, in an ostensible second experiment, the participants had a chance to acquire alternative symbols. The extent to which they used this possibility was measured.

In one experiment with graduate students enrolled in a business school, a first researcher asked the participants to fill in a questionnaire to find out whether they possessed the ideal personality profile observed in successful businesspeople (Gollwitzer, 1983). In a presumably unrelated second experiment, participants were asked to play a role in a game that simulated interactional conflicts in business conference meetings. Participants could choose one of six possible roles, ranging from chair of the board to keeper of the minutes. Shortly before participants were asked to make their choices, the first experimenter disrupted the study and gave them positive or negative personality feedback. Half of the participants were told they had personality profiles similar to the ideal profile, whereas the other half were told that their personalities were dissimilar to that of a successful businessman. Participants who received negative feedback aspired to positions of higher prestige (e.g., chair of the board) more often than did people who received positive personality feedback. From the perspective of self-completion theory, these findings show that the lack of one symbol of an aspired-to identity (i.e., not matching a relevant ideal personality profile) is compensated for by self-symbolizing efforts focusing on an alternative symbol (i.e., choosing a high-prestige position).

The compensation hypothesis has been supported in numerous other studies using a variety of different self-definitional symbols, for example, influencing others (Wicklund & Gollwitzer, 1981), inventing positive self-descriptions, and refusing to admit failures (Gollwitzer, Wicklund, & Hilton, 1982). Further, incomplete participants have distanced themselves from unsuccessful people (Wagner, Wicklund, & Shaigan, 1990), displayed material symbols (Wicklund & Gollwitzer, 1982), and used prestigious tools (Braun & Wicklund, 1989).

The Social Reality Hypothesis

Self-completion theory postulates that self-symbolizing that becomes a social fact is likely to be particularly effective in reducing a sense of incompleteness. In a first experimental paradigm, participants were given the opportunity to engage in a self-symbolizing activity, either noticed or unnoticed by others (Gollwitzer, 1986b, Studies 1 and 2). Given that identity goals are located on the level of social reality, striving for an identity in front of an audience is expected to provide a stronger sense of possessing the aspired-to identity than striving in the absence of an audience. In a new situational context, participants were given a further opportunity to strive for the aspired-to identity. If self-symbolizing noticed by others provides a stronger sense of completeness than unnoticed self-symbolizing, comparatively less striving should have been observed in participants whose symbols were noticed by others.

In the first study, female college students with the identity goal of raising a family were asked to write down personal skills relevant to their succeeding as mothers (Gollwitzer, 1986b, Study 1). They were told either that these self-descriptions would be carefully studied by partner participants or that their descriptions would not become known to others. Afterward, all participants were given the opportunity to engage in further self-symbolizing by completing a personality profile that carried a sample profile representing the ideal personality of a mother. The participants who expected that their initial self-symbolizing would not be noticed by their partners felt compelled to engage in further self-symbolizing by drawing their own profiles similar to the mother's profile provided. Participants whose initial self-descriptions would be noticed by partners, however, differed more from the ideal mother profile. In a second study, following the same logic, these effects were replicated with medical students (Gollwitzer, 1986b, Study 2). Thus it has been demonstrated that a strong sense of completeness arises when the possession of indicators of an aspired-to identity is socially realized.

A second approach is based on the idea that incomplete individuals oriented toward achieving a particular identity are likely to be especially concerned with finding an audience for their identity striving. Accordingly, people's readiness to engage in identity-related goal striving needs to be manipulated (i.e., incomplete, complete), and afterward their initiative in making self-symbolizing efforts noticed by others has to be observed. In a further study, medical students with the expressed intention of becoming physicians were exposed to positive or negative personality feedback regarding their prospects as physicians (Gollwitzer 1986b, Study 3). Subsequently, these participants were given the opportunity to engage in self-symbolizing by finding solutions to a series of simple medical problems. They were allowed to submit completed sections of the assignment to the experimenter whenever they desired. More than 50% of the incomplete participants, but only 8% of the complete participants, attempted to bring their completed tasks to the experimenter's notice before they had finished the entire stack of tasks.

The Social Insensitivity Hypothesis

Knowing that self-symbolizing individuals turn to others to strengthen their sense of possessing an aspired-to identity, we have explored how self-symbolizing individuals relate to their audiences. Self-completion theory suggests that this type of relation to others is best described as a pseudo-social interaction. Self-symbolizing individuals regard their audiences as serving the sole function of taking notice of the individuals' possession of their aspired-to identities; they do not consider their audiences to be mutual exchange partners. Attributes of audiences that go beyond this purpose are largely neglected. This social insensitivity hypothesis has been tested in several experiments. Participants were told about the personal wishes and desires of their audience, posed in a way that either contradicted participants' self-symbolizing efforts or was in line with them. Afterward, it was observed how incomplete and complete participants followed the audience's wishes and desires.

Gollwitzer and Wicklund (1985) demonstrated how individuals who strive for self-completion neglect the thoughts and feelings of an audience to which their self-symbolizing efforts are directed. In one study, male undergraduates committed to various kinds of sports were first manipulated to feel either incomplete or complete through negative or positive feedback. Then they were asked to participate in a presumably second study on first impressions. The target person to be encountered was described as an attractive female undergraduate who had expressed a preference for getting to know either modest or proud people. Before participants were asked to introduce themselves to the target person through written self-descriptions of their strengths and weaknesses in their self-definitional areas (i.e., swimming, tennis, track), they rated their feelings of attraction toward this person. It was observed that incomplete participants produced more self-promoting descriptions than did complete participants, regardless of the target person's preference for meeting individuals with modest as opposed to proud self-descriptions. Moreover, self-symbolizing individuals ignored even their own interpersonal interests. Whereas complete participants followed the target person's self-presentational cue to the degree to which they felt attracted to her, incomplete participants' self-descriptions were completely unaffected by their feelings of attraction. In summary, self-symbolizing individuals do not seem to care much about their audience's interests. They focus on their self-definitional strengths whether the audience is present in person or not and whether the audience explicitly expresses its interests or not.

PROCESSES OF SELF-COMPLETION

Mutual Exchangeability of Symbols

Wurf and Markus (1991) claim, in accordance with self-completion theory, that failure in particular routes to achieve an identity striving will lead to enhanced rather than decreased striving. Further, they argue that symbolic validation of the self, such as positive self-descriptions, might be less satisfying than actual achievements. From the standpoint of self-completion theory, however, positive self-descriptions should be as effective in generating a sense of completeness as self-defining task performances when the given self-description is recognized by others, thereby becoming a social reality (Gollwitzer, 1986a).

This issue has been addressed directly in two experiments (Brunstein & Gollwitzer, 1996). In one experiment, medical students were first instructed to solve simple interpersonal problems related either to conflicts that physicians commonly experience in their profession or to problems of everyday life. Afterward, participants were asked to perform a mental concentration test (*d2* test; Brickenkamp, 1981) described as measuring a skill either relevant or irrelevant to being a physician. When participants had been given failure feedback on solving the physician-related problems (i.e., the first task) and the second task was ostensibly a physician-related skill performance, the $d2$ test performance peaked. When participants who received failure feedback on solving the physician-related problems (i.e., the first task) worked on the concentration test described as measuring a skill unrelated to physicians, test performance dropped. In the no-feedback conditions, performances on the $d2$ test were at medium level and did not differ from each other. Thus identity-relevant performances are powerful indicators that individuals possess a given identity. When such indicators are not available, individuals feel highly incomplete, which causes them to strive intensively for alternative indicators, and other non-identity-related performances are hampered.

A second study investigated whether an incompleteness experience stemming from a weak identity-related performance can also be effectively reduced through self-symbolizing based on positive self-descriptions, thereby making further self-symbolizing no longer necessary (Brunstein & Gollwitzer, 1996, Study 2). Students of computer sciences were asked to perform a concept formation test, apparently to assess a number of mental skills commonly found in successful computer scientists. After receiving failure feedback or no feedback on this first task, participants were asked to perform a second task ($d2$ test), described as measuring a skill either relevant or irrelevant to a computer scientist. Consistent with the observation made in Study 1, participants with failure feedback performed better on the $d2$ test than did participants with no feedback when the test was described as identity relevant. When the $d2$ test was described as irrelevant, comparatively worse performance was observed.

After the negative feedback on the concept formation test, half of the participants were allowed by a second experimenter to describe their personalities on a semantic differential task. When they had done so, they learned from this second experimenter that they possessed personality attributes observed in successful computer scientists. This intervention completely wiped out the performance effects of the failure feedback. Whereas no-intervention participants reduced their experienced incompleteness by stepping up their performance on the identity-related $d2$ test, incomplete participants who were told by the second experimenter that they possessed identity-relevant attributes no longer needed to do so, because their feeling of incompleteness was already reduced. This finding implies that performance-related indicators of an identity are mutually exchangeable with easily accessible indicators, such as publicly recognized positive self-descriptions.

Self-Affirmation Versus Self-Completion

Self-defining goals may differ in terms of how strongly they serve a person's need for self-esteem (e.g., being a good student may serve a particular person's self-esteem needs more than being a good gambler). In a model of self-affirmation processes, Steele (1988; Liu & Steele, 1986) argues that people's responses to events that threaten self-esteem are not confined to the domains in which the self-threats occur; rather, people strive toward a global sense of self-integrity. This superordinate motive enables individuals to engage in a variety of highly flexible compensation processes while they try to cope with self-threatening information. Incompleteness experiences regarding identity goals that are strongly linked to the superordinate goal of self-esteem protection and maintenance thus may be reduced not only through the achievement of self-symbolizing indicators but also through self-esteem-pampering maneuvers. From a pure self-completion theory perspective, however, even when an identity goal is strongly linked to self-esteem, the range of substitutability should be limited to the relevant identity symbols only, and should not encompass the region of protecting self-esteem. Whether self-esteem compensation (Steele, 1988) or self-completion compensation (Wicklund & Gollwitzer, 1982) occurs is likely to be moderated by a person's feelings of commitment to the self-defining goal in question. Effective substitution, for a highly committed individual, must involve self-symbolizing in the form of acquiring or pointing to indicators of the aspired-to self-definition. If the individual feels less committed to the self-definitional goal, however, compensatory efforts may be directed only at affirming his or her self-esteem.

This question was addressed in a recent study by Scherer (1999). Law students who were either strongly or weakly committed to the self-defining goal of becoming a successful lawyer were induced to symbolic incompleteness through negative feedback. All participants were then given, in randomized order, the opportunity to both enhance their self-esteem through self-affirmation and compensate their incompleteness through symbolic self-completion. The expectation was that highly committed students who received the incompleteness manipulation should not engage in self-affirmation, but only in self-symbolizing. Weakly committed students, however, should engage in self-affirmation and fail to self-symbolize.

In the first part of the experiment, the law students' commitment to the goal of becoming a successful lawyer was measured using a questionnaire. A few weeks later, highly and weakly committed law students were contacted again by the experimenter and asked for an appointment. The participants were made to feel incomplete in relation to the goal of becoming a successful lawyer with the help of negative feedback. After they had filled in a questionnaire containing 10 scenarios about interpersonal conflicts in the life of a lawyer, the experimenter told them that they had solved only very few of the problems in a competent manner and that the average lawyer was much better in solving social conflicts.

After this negative feedback, all participants were given the opportunity to both enhance their self-esteem through positive self-affirmation and reach symbolic self-completion. In the self-affirmation task, participants were asked to choose their most important value out of a list (e.g., aesthetics, politics) and to write as much or as little as they wanted about why this value was so important to them. The writing was later analyzed by two independent raters with regard to different dimensions (e.g., positivity of self-presentation, self-disclosing) and an overall score for self-affirmation was formed (Tesser, Martin, & Cornell, 1996). In the symbolic self-completion task, participants had to draw their personality profiles into a questionnaire with 10 different personality dimensions (e.g., rigid, suspicious). Before they began, the experimenter put an already finished profile of an ostensible lawyer next to the participants on the desk, telling them this was an ideal profile of a successful lawyer. Later, the similarity of the participants' profiles to the profile of the ideal lawyer was measured (Gollwitzer, 1981). The closer the students drew their profiles to that of the ideal lawyer, the more they could be considered to strive for completeness.

After the incompleteness manipulation, law students who were highly committed to the goal of becoming a successful lawyer showed a much greater approximation to the ideal lawyer's profile than did weakly committed law students. It did not matter whether or not they had a chance to enhance their self-esteem through the self-affirmation procedure. Self-affirmation was, on the other hand, observed less in highly committed than in weakly committed participants. Self-affirmation was not used by highly committed participants and thus does not seem to be an alternative way to reach symbolic self-completion. In other words, if people are highly committed and are made incomplete concerning their self-defining goals, the only way they can reach self-completion is through self-symbolizing in the form of acquiring or pointing to indicators of the aspired-to identity. On the other hand, if individuals are only weakly committed to their self-defining goal and receive negative feedback, they use self-affirmation to restore their lowered self-esteem.

Intended Behaviors as Symbols

One of the core assumptions of self-completion theory is the substitutability of indicators of completeness. Different types of symbols can be used in a flexible manner. One type of symbolizing is to engage in positive self-descriptions (Brunstein & Gollwitzer, 1996). It seems possible, therefore, that effective self-descriptions can also take the form of expressed intentions. In this case, self-descriptions would have to specify relevant behavioral goals that the person intends to realize in the future. If the behavioral goal is related to a self-definition, the social realization of the intention should lead to a less intensive subsequent execution of the intended action, however. This is because the publicly expressed intention leads to a higher state of completeness, which in turn reduces motivation to acquire additional symbols, such as to actually perform the behavioral goal. Thus the social realization of behavioral intentions related to a given self-definition should reduce the tension state that originates from the experience of incompleteness. This assumption was examined in two experiments.

In the first experiment, psychology students had to fill in several questionnaires (Dyes, 1984). The first one measured students' commitment to the self-defining goal of becoming a clinical psychologist ("clinicians" versus "nonclinicians"). A second questionnaire was aimed at the level of clinical knowledge and training, and induced a state of incompleteness by asking only questions that participants had to answer in the negative (e.g., "Do you have a therapy license?"). In a third questionnaire, participants were asked to give their opinions on different statements. In the critical statement, they had to respond on a 5-point scale to the sentence "I would like to watch therapy videos to learn more about therapy techniques." Thus the degree of an existing intention was measured, and for the rest of the study only participants with a strong intention were of interest. Finally, the intention to watch therapy videos was either acknowledged by the experimenter (social reality) or remained unnoticed (no social reality). In an ostensible second experiment, the participants' task was to observe the interaction between a therapist and a client (shown on a video), to count how often they made eye contact, and to rate the mood between therapist and client. Participants were told that their time was limited to 40 minutes, but they should feel free to finish earlier if they wanted to. The dependent measure was the time participants worked on the task.

Students committed to become therapists who had expressed the intention to analyze therapy videos and whose intention was acknowledged by the experimenter finished the task earlier than those in the no-social-reality condition (i.e., the intention was not acknowledged by the experimenter). The amount of time noncommitted students spent on the task was in between the two committed conditions, and there was no difference whether their intention was socially realized or not. Thus if a person is highly committed to a self-defining goal, the social realization of relevant behavioral intentions can entail a disinterest in pursuing the intended behavioral goal, because the tension state is reduced and the person has no need for acquiring additional symbols.

A question that comes to mind is whether the behavioral intention is translated into action despite social realization if people form implementation intentions in addition to goal intentions. The distinction between goal intentions and implementation intentions has been suggested by Gollwitzer (1993). It has been demonstrated that goal intentions ("I intend to show behavior X!") are less successful in guiding a person's actions than are implementation intentions ("I intend to initiate the goal-directed behavior X, when situation Y is encountered!"), especially when the goal is difficult to attain (Gollwitzer & Brandstätter, 1997; Gollwitzer & Schaal, 1998). Gollwitzer suggests that implementation intentions are particularly effective, because they link intended goal-directed behaviors to anticipated situational cues and thus induce direct automatic control of the intended behaviors through these cues. Thus, by forming implementation intentions, people pass on control of goal-directed activities from the self to the environment. For this reason, implementation intentions may not suffer the negative consequences that are observed with the social realization of goal intentions.

An experiment was conducted to test this assumption (Seifert, 1999). In the first part of the study, first-year law students committed to the self-defining goal of becoming a successful lawyer were asked to complete several questionnaires. In the first questionnaire their level of knowledge in law was measured and incompleteness was induced by reminding them of their deficient knowledge. Participants were then asked to give their opinions about several statements, one of them either formulated as a goal intention ("I intend to make best use of my present education") or as an implementation intention ("I intend to make best use of my present education. And each time I see an opportunity to intensify my studies, I seize it"). Again, only participants who strongly agreed with this statement were included in the analysis. Afterward, the intention was noticed by the experimenter or remained unnoticed. In a presumed second experiment, participants finally had the chance to realize their intention by solving 20 criminal law cases, which was an opportunity to improve their knowledge in law. The students were given 45 minutes to work on these cases, but they were allowed to finish earlier. The time participants spent on working was used as the measure of translating their intentions into behavior.

In the goal intention condition, the results of the first study were replicated. Participants whose intentions had become a social reality finished their work earlier than did participants whose intentions stayed unnoticed. In the implementation intention condition, social reality made no difference with respect to the time spent on solving the presented cases. Participants in both social reality conditions (i.e., participants' intentions were either noticed by the experimenter or stayed unnoticed) worked close to as long as possible, and thus did not differ from each other. This pattern of data demonstrates that the negative behavioral effects of the social realization of goal intentions vanish when goal intentions are furnished with implementation intentions. Apparently, when action control is delegated to environmental cues via implementation intentions, action is no longer affected by the reduced tension state stemming from the social realization of the respective goal intention.

Both of the two studies reported demonstrate that goal intentions that become a social fact can serve self-definitional functions. As a consequence, the person is less motivated to perform the intended behavior. However, this negative effect does not occur when a person has formed additional implementation intentions. This discovery has important implications for research on the intention-behavior relation. In his theory of planned behavior, Ajzen (1985) suggests that the strength of an intention (resulting from its feasibility and desirability) determines how well it is translated into behavior. But even a strong goal intention should fail to be implemented whenever a person has mentioned it to others and this social realization has led to completeness with respect to an identity goal to which the person feels committed. Only when additional implementation intentions are formed should the strength of the intention guarantee its translation into behavior.

From Incompleteness to Completeness: A Process Account

Participants were asked in some recent studies about their feelings after they had experienced failure on an identity-relevant task (Brunstein & Gollwitzer, 1996). They reported feeling more worried, pessimistic, dissatisfied, and blocked than after failing in an identity-irrelevant task. Frustration and ruminative self-concerns over a poor identity-relevant performance, however, changed into an energetic feeling when participants were given a second chance and when this second task was described as identity relevant. If the second task was described as identity irrelevant, however, participants continued to worry. It seems that incompleteness experiences are highly frustrating only until an opportunity for compensation arises, which immediately converts this severe burden on an individual's striving for identity into an energized feeling. Self-symbolizing, thus, is an *action-oriented* state in which attention rests solely on successful compensation.

Flüge and Gollwitzer (1986) analyzed the impulsiveness of self-symbolizers by giving incomplete and complete participants an opportunity to compensate their feeling of incompleteness immediately to an audience that was highly critical of participants' identity-related potentials or to a more accepting audience at a later point in time. They found that incomplete participants preferred to self-symbolize in front of the immediately accessible audience, whereas complete participants waited for the more accepting audience. Similarly, it has been demonstrated that even a mere goal intention, mentioned to another person (e.g., experimenter), can be a highly effective way to self-symbolize (Dyes, 1984; Seifert, 1999). Thus incomplete individuals' main interest is directed at documenting the aspired-to identity in front of others. However, one needs to keep in mind that opportunities merely to enhance self-esteem are of little use to the incomplete person. The impulsiveness of self-symbolizers does *not* lead them to engage in any possible activity that may reduce dissatisfaction. It has been documented that incomplete individuals engage only in self-enhancing activities that guarantee completeness with respect to their self-defining goals (Scherer, 1999).

The Choice of Identity Goals

In a historical analysis of human identity, Baumeister (1986) has suggested that society no longer assigns identity to its members, but instead forces individuals to create their own identities. Baumeister argues that identity achievement has become a struggle for the individual, because every person has to decide who he or she wants to be. Furthermore, to realize one's choice, willful effort is necessary. For instance, becoming an athlete, a physician, or a religious person requires a decision and necessitates acts to implement that decision.

Even though self-completion theory acknowledges the making of an identity choice as a prerequisite to diligent willful pursuit of identity, it focuses primarily on the implementation of a chosen identity goal. To describe the complete process of the willful pursuit of identity, one must definitely also address how people commit themselves to certain identities. Developmental psychologists, following Erikson's (1956) ideas on identity development, have addressed this issue. It is assumed that the experience of an identity crisis leads to vigorous deliberations (e.g., Marcia, 1966, 1967, 1980). The individual is torn between possible options and therefore continues weighing alternatives until a definite identity commitment is formed.

Ruble (1994) has analyzed identity crises in periods of change or transition (e.g., the transition to junior high school). She presents a model of transition with three different phases, each associated with a distinct orientation toward social information. In the first phase, a person faces a new situation in which old categories and expectations are no longer applicable. Therefore, the person engages in an active search among a range of possible self-constituents. As soon as the individual acquires some basic knowledge, a second phase of consolidation begins, in which the person weighs and considers consequences for his or her own ego (e.g., "What kind of a mother would I be?"). In the third phase, those new identities are integrated into the already existing self-concept. In addition, unexpected events during the life cycle (e.g., an unexpected pregnancy) make it necessary for the individual to choose among new identities (e.g., to be a mother; Lydon, Dunkel-Schetter, Cohan, & Pierce, 1996).

One of the most interesting aspects of self-completion theory is the psychological difference between individuals searching for an identity and self-symbolizing individuals (Gollwitzer, 1986b). Individuals searching for an identity display open-minded information processing. Maccoby and her colleagues found that women with babies were much more likely to read a booklet on child care that they got through the mail, to gather information, and to discuss it with others, compared with women with older children or women who did not have babies (see Maccoby, Maccoby, Romney, & Adams, 1961; Maccoby, Romney, Adams, & Maccoby, 1959).

It is assumed that a woman with a newborn is still in the process of searching for the identity of a mother. Similar conclusions concerning women's information seeking have been presented in a cross-sectional study by Deutsch, Ruble, Fleming, Brooks-Gunn, and Stangor (1988).

While an individual is searching for an identity, his or her cognitive orientation is characterized by open-mindedness. Once that person has committed him- or herself to a specific identity, however, the closed-mindedness of self-symbolizing sets in (Brunstein & Gollwitzer, 1996). Self-symbolizing individuals seem to be immune to questioning their identity choices. Identity failures lead to experiences of incompleteness associated with ruminative thoughts; however, when an opportunity to self-symbolize arises, ruminative thoughts are immediately put aside and a sole focus on performing self-symbolizing actions occurs. In this sense, the cognitive orientation of self-symbolizing individuals is comparable to the implemental mind-set (Gollwitzer, 1990; Gollwitzer & Bayer, 1999) that has been observed in individuals who plan the implementation of goal-directed actions. In an implemental mind-set, people process information on the execution of goal-directed actions more readily and effectively (Gollwitzer, Heckhausen, & Steller, 1990, Study 1). Moreover, an implemental mind-set also produces biased inferences, in the sense that people have stronger positive illusions about their personal attributes and skills (Taylor & Gollwitzer, 1995) and they experience illusionary feelings of control in uncontrollable situations (Gollwitzer & Kinney, 1989).

However, the willful pursuit of identity goals (e.g., to become a clinical psychologist) sometimes creates new occasions for deliberation (e.g., to choose among different kinds of therapies). On each of these occasions, it is important to obtain precise desirability-related and feasibility-related information (e.g., whether one's skills are sufficient). In short, a precise analysis of the diverse options is required. With regard to such deliberations, it is not useful to keep up a positive illusion about one's personal attributes and skills; rather, a realistic self-view is called for.

Bayer (1999) examined the assumption that people committed to identity goals are able to regain open-mindedness in the face of upcoming identity-related decisions. Students were confronted with the opportunity to obtain information on their possible weaknesses and strengths in both intellectual (relevant to "student" identity) and athletic (irrelevant to "student" identity) abilities. They had to indicate their interest in each piece of information by marking those questions (on a list of 14) they wanted to have answered. Prior to this, the participants took part in a presumably independent study in which different mind-sets had been established. To induce a deliberative mind-set, half of the participants had been asked to name a personal goal conflict (e.g., "Should I take part in an examination now or later?"), to list the diverse advantages and disadvantages, and to reflect on the likelihood of their occurrence. In addition, they had to think of potential difficulties that might arise. To induce an implemental mind-set, the other half of the participants were asked to name a concrete project on which they had already decided (e.g., to write a term paper) but had not yet started implementation. They were asked to describe the five most important steps toward its realization. Furthermore, they had to specify when, how, and where they would do so. It was expected that individuals in an implemental mind-set would prefer information about their strengths in order to create a positive self-description for their student identity. It was assumed that participants in a deliberative mind-set, in contrast, would attain accurate self-evaluations by choosing, in an evenhanded manner, positive and negative information about their identity-relevant abilities.

Participants' searches for information depended on their mind-sets. They wanted to know more about the strengths than the weaknesses of their intellectual abilities when they were in an implemental mind-set. Participants in a deliberative mind-set, on the other hand, were interested in information on both strengths and weaknesses alike. The tendency toward positively distorted information processing in order to create an identity-relevant positive self-description (as evidenced in the implemental mind-set) was replaced by an open-minded, well-balanced search for information in a deliberative mind-set. These differences concerning the positivity of the preferred information were observed only with regard to intellectual abilities (relevant to "student" identity), however. All students displayed open-mindedness in looking for information concerning identity-irrelevant abilities (athletics). Positively distorted information processing was observed with regard to identity-relevant abilities only in an implemental mind-set. But a deliberative mind-set managed to interfere with this tendency and led to a balanced search for information concerning identity-relevant abilities.

In general, identity choices are associated with a cognitive orientation of open-mindedness, whereas identity pursuit is characterized by a closed-mindedness that favors a self-serving search for information about relevant self-aspects. But even if a person is strongly committed to his or her identity goal, open-minded information processing seems possible if needed (e.g., for choices between different implemental routes). The individual has only to develop a deliberative mind-set.

LIFE-SPAN PSYCHOLOGY

The Endurance of Self-Defining Goal Pursuit

An identity goal is probably best described as a claim to possess a designated identity that is indicated by the possession of relevant symbols (e.g., owning status symbols, being able to execute relevant actions). Thus realizing an identity goal implies a continued accumulation of relevant indicators, and its pursuit is not finished simply because a powerful indicator has been acquired. Self-symbolizing becomes necessary again as soon as the lack of other alternative indicators becomes salient. Even when a person possesses extremely powerful symbols, such as many years of experience in a given field, he or she can easily be made to feel incomplete, as demonstrated by many self-completion experiments (see Wicklund & Gollwitzer, 1982).

There are many factors that cause a constant striving for identity goals. When people progress with respect to the pursuit of an identity goal, they gain increased competence in a given field, and new horizons with a host of new, more sophisticated indicators open up. Most professional identities include arrays of symbols associated with different sections of the life course, and social and physical surroundings change while the person progresses in his or her field (e.g., the identity of a scientist is defined differently during the phases of university training, an assistant professor position, and full professorship). In addition, the social community defines the indicators for a certain identity and thus guides individuals in their goal pursuits. But from time to time such definitions are also modified (e.g., 20 years ago a person could easily indicate the identity of a scientist without having to refer to a laboratory filled with computers, but today this hardly seems possible). Finally, even an age-related decline in skills and resources (Baltes & Baltes, 1990) is not likely to stop a person's identity striving. Older self-symbolizers can refer to performances achieved in the past through positive self-descriptions (i.e., engage in easily accessible, "accommodated" self-symbolizing; Brandtstädter & Greve, 1994). This allows them to remain in the field without giving up their aspired-to identities. Brunstein and Gollwitzer (1996) have demonstrated that this kind of easily accessible self-symbolizing is as successful as self-symbolizing that is based on skillful performance.

Under certain circumstances, people do give up on identity goals. In their notion of contingent action path, Raynor and Entin (1982) have suggested that a person can move on to the next step of the path only when he or she has been successful in a more immediate step. Raynor (1982, pp. 287-288) points out that self-relevant failure in a contingent path not only means a negative identity achievement and a feeling of incompleteness, it also reduces options to acquire further indicators of the aspired-to identity (e.g., when a law student fails to earn his diploma and therefore cannot move along the path of striving for his chosen professional career). Under such circumstances, failure might prompt a reappraisal of identity goals and instigate disengagement.

Moreover, when the social surroundings of people do not support their self-symbolizing as a claim to possess given identities, self-symbolizing will not become a social fact and, consequently, will not be very effective (e.g., when a young lawyer who comes from a family of artists arrives home for a family event in his three-piece suit, the relatives may fail to recognize its symbolic character and focus instead on the aesthetic quality of the fabric). However, the symbolic world of most self-definitions involves culturally shared knowledge, and self-symbolizing is usually successful. Accordingly, failure to attain social reality is more likely to occur when self-definitions are shared only within certain narrowly defined subcultures (e.g., Hare Krishnas).

Conflict between identity goals seems to be the most powerful force for disengagement processes, such as the conflict that women experience when they are torn between the roles of mother and professional (Barnett & Baruch, 1985; McBride, 1990). Identity goals conflict when they compete for one and the same opportunity to acquire relevant symbols. For example, a free Saturday afternoon is highly conducive not only to a person's finishing a scientific manuscript but also to her playing with her children. If she constantly chooses to play with her children, the female professional is likely to begin to disengage from her identity goal of being a professional.

A key factor for people's disengagement from identity goals seems to be a lack of access or a refusal to make use of opportunities to acquire relevant symbols; frequent experiences of incompleteness would seem to be less relevant. In the face of failure, committed individuals are oriented toward symbolizing the possession of the aspired-to identity and focus on effective acquiring and pointing to alternative indicators of completeness, rather than being concerned with negative outcome expectations. However, individuals sometimes need to be discouraged in their pursuit of self-definitions, and it is necessary to direct them away from self-symbolizing (e.g., a youngster with no mathematical talents who wants to become a physicist). Oettingen (1996) suggests that people start to consider negative expectations of success when they are made to mentally contrast their positive fantasies of the future with negative aspects of the present reality that stand in the way of their reaching this positive future (see also Oettingen, Chapter 11, this volume).

Compensating for Age-Related Declines

In life-span psychology, the different ways older people deal with age-related deficits leading to a skill-demand mismatch have been described (e.g., Bäckman & Dixon, 1992; Brandtstädter, Wentura, & Greve, 1993). The "selective optimization with compensation" model presented by Baltes and Baltes (1990; Marsiske, Lang, Baltes, & Baltes, 1995) portrays life-span development as a dynamic interaction between gains and losses. When the skill-demand mismatch exceeds a certain threshold, the aging person may begin to select and thereby narrow the range of domains or goals for continued development. Second, the person may try to optimize his or her performances within this narrow domain through training, practice, and motivational enhancement. As a last resort, due to compensation strategies, the person may minimize age-related losses and limits by relying on alternative internal or external resources. For instance, a scientist suffering age-related losses of memory may first try to ameliorate the skill-demand mismatch by limiting his research to certain themes that are very familiar. Then he may attempt to acquire and maximize mnemonic skills that are particularly conducive to his field of interest. Finally, he may even actively compensate for the memory deficits by employing all kinds of substitutes, such as a skilled research assistant.

This model's implications for self-completion processes extend to the notion of gains and losses. The losses of compensation, not addressed in self-completion theory so far, become immediately apparent when one considers, for example, a person who focuses primarily on positive self-descriptions. This person fails to develop his or her identity-related performance potential. On the other hand, self-completion theory has implications for understanding the compensation notion prevalent in life-span psychology, by stressing the distinction between the inner goal of the self-symbolizing individual and the outer goal considered by researchers. For an individual's inner goal, it does not matter whether positive self-descriptions or self-definitional performances are used. The person advances equally well with respect to the inner goal of indicating the possession of an identity to others. For a life-span psychologist who considers the outer goal of attaining an identity, however, the self-symbolizer who employs only self-descriptions and no actual achievement does not advance at all.

Social Contact Across the Life Span

Carstensen (1992, 1998) postulates in her theory of socioemotional selectivity that people's reasons for social contact change during the life span. In infancy, and again in old age, people pursue emotional experiences and regulation in their social contacts. In adolescence and middle age, social contact serves the purpose of people's learning more about the self, the world, and other people. These different reasons for contact have consequences for the kinds of social encounters a person prefers. Because emotional regulation and satisfaction are more easily achieved if one is surrounded by a few intimates, Carstensen suggests that older people are likely to engage in social contact with a few intimate friends rather than get to know new people.

It could be demonstrated (see above) that the social contacts of the self-symbolizer serve the purpose of social recognition of the possession of an aspired-to identity. Social psychologists have observed that people in general prefer to abstain from conveying negative feedback to others (Blumberg, 1972; Tesser & Rosen, 1975). Strangers, however, may tend to challenge an individual's sense of self-definitional completeness (e.g., out of ignorance) and are thus a potential source of incompleteness experiences. Compared with strangers, a person's intimates should know the self-definitions the person aspires to and thus should refrain from questioning his or her possession of a particular self-definition. In addition, intimates know about the self-definitional indicators the individual has acquired in the past. This knowledge allows the self-symbolizer to refer to these achievements in positive self-descriptions if incompleteness experiences should arise.

It appears, then, that intimate friends provide a narrow and stable social reality that makes it easy to self-symbolize effectively. For older individuals who have a rather low sense of completeness due to age-related declines in skills and resources, the tendency to focus on a narrow and stable social reality is likely to be particularly pronounced. In other words, older people may focus their social contacts on a few intimate friends not only for reasons of enjoyment and more effective emotion regulation (Carstensen, 1992), but also because this allows them to maintain the identities to which they have aspired throughout their lives, despite age-related declines in relevant skills and resources.

SUMMARY AND CONCLUSION

In this chapter we have described the ongoing, goal-oriented processes directed toward attaining a self-definition (e.g., being a successful business-person, a good mother, a lawyer). From the perspective of self-completion theory, these processes consist of the continuous accumulation of relevant symbols or indicators (e.g., positive self-descriptions, relevant perfor-mances, possession of relevant status symbols) of goal attainment. We have presented research that reveals the basic principles that govern this goal pursuit. We have demonstrated that one symbol can compensate for the lack of another symbol in the sense that the various symbols of any given self-definition relate to each other as substitutes (compensation principle). We have also pointed out that others play a crucial role with respect to the effectiveness of self-symbolizing (social reality principle). Furthermore, we have documented that self-symbolizing individuals ignore their audiences' interests (social insensitivity principle). Self-affirming strategies have been shown to fail to substitute for self-symbolizing efforts because the latter require the acquisition of identity-related symbols. In addition, we have demonstrated that positive self-descriptions and the expression of identity-related behavioral intentions can serve as symbols when they become noticed by others, thus impairing effective task pursuit. This negative effect can be eliminated, however, through the formation of implementation intentions. Moreover, we have pointed out that the choice of self-defining goals is governed by principles that are quite different from those that govern the pursuit of these goals.

Finally, we have discussed the implications of self-completion theory for life-span psychology. Old and very old people may turn to easily accessible forms of self-symbolizing (e.g., referring to relevant successes in the past) and forget about less accessible forms (e.g., demonstrating identity-relevant skills), as both forms of self-symbolizing tend to be equally effective. This allows old and very old people to feel still in possession of their aspired-to identities despite age-related declines in performance. Furthermore, the social reality principle suggests that reducing social contacts to a few intimate friends makes it easier for older people to self-symbolize effectively and thus to maintain their claims of possessing their aspired-to identities.

REFERENCES

Ajzen, I. (1985). From intentions to actions: A theory of planned behavior. In J. Kuhl & J. Beckmann (Eds.), *Action control: From cognition to behavior* (pp. 11-39). New York: Springer.

Allport, G. W. (1943). The ego in contemporary psychology. *Psychological Review, 50,* 451-478.

Allport, G. W. (1955). *Becoming.* New Haven, CT: Yale University Press.

Bäckman, L., & Dixon, R. A. (1992). Psychological compensation: A theoretical framework. *Psychological Bulletin, 112,* 259-283.

Baltes, P. B., & Baltes, M. M. (1990). Psychological perspectives on successful aging: The model of selective optimization with compensation. In P. B. Baltes & M. M. Baltes (Eds.), *Successful aging: Perspectives from the behavioral sciences* (pp. 1-34). New York: Cambridge University Press.

Barnett, R. C., & Baruch, G. K. (1985). Women's involvement in multiple roles and psychological distress. *Journal of Personality and Social Psychology, 49,* 135-145.

Baumeister, R. F. (1982). A self-presentational view of social phenomena. *Psychological Bulletin, 91,* 3-26.

Baumeister, R. F. (1986). *Identity: Cultural change and the struggle for self.* New York: Oxford University Press.

Baumeister, R. F. (1998). The self. In D. T. Gilbert, S. T. Fiske, & G. Lindzey (Eds.), *Handbook of social psychology* (Vol. 2, pp. 680-740). New York: McGraw-Hill.

Baumeister, R. F., & Leary, M. R. (1995). The need to belong: Desire for interpersonal attachments as a fundamental human motivation. *Psychological Bulletin, 117,* 497-529.

Baumeister, R. F., & Tice, D. M. (1990). Anxiety and social exclusion. *Journal of Social and Clinical Psychology, 9,* 165-195.

Bayer, U. (1999). *Der Einfluss der Bewußtseinslage des Abwägens und Planens auf die soziale Urteilsbildung.* Unpublished doctoral dissertation. Universität Konstanz, Germany.

Bem, D. J. (1972). Self-perception theory. In L. Berkowitz (Ed.), *Advances in experimental social psychology* (Vol. 6, pp. 1-62). San Diego, CA: Academic Press.

Blumberg, H. H. (1972). Communication of interpersonal evaluations. *Journal of Personality and Social Psychology, 23,* 157-162.

Braun, O. L., & Wicklund, R. A. (1989). Psychological antecedents of conspicuous consumption. *Journal of Economic Psychology, 10,* 161-187.

Brandtstädter, J., & Greve, W. (1994). The aging self: Stabilizing and protective processes. *Developmental Review, 14,* 52-80.

Brandtstädter, J., Wentura, D., & Greve, W. (1993). Adaptive resources of the aging self: Outlines of an emerging perspective. *International Journal of Behavioral Development, 16,* 232-349.

Brickenkamp, R. (1981). *Test d2* (4th ed.). Göttingen, Germany: Hogrefe.

Brown, J. D. (1991). Accuracy and bias in self-knowledge. In C. R. Snyder & D. R. Forsyth (Eds.), *Handbook of social and clinical psychology: The health perspective* (pp. 158-178). New York: Pergamon.

Brown, J. D., & Dutton, K. A. (1995). Truth and consequences: The costs and benefits of accurate self-knowledge. *Personality and Social Psychology Bulletin, 21,* 1288-1296.

Brunstein, J. C., & Gollwitzer, P. M. (1996). Effects of failure on subsequent performance: The importance of self-defining goals. *Journal of Personality and Social Psychology, 70,* 395-407.

Campbell, J. D. (1990). Self-esteem and clarity of the self-concept. *Journal of Personality and Social Psychology, 59,* 538-549.

Carstensen, L. L. (1992). Social and emotional patterns in adulthood: Support for socioemotional selectivity theory. *Psychology and Aging, 7,* 331-338.

Carstensen, L. L. (1998). A life-span approach to social motivation. In J. Heckhausen & C. S. Dweck (Eds.), *Motivation and self-regulation across the life-span* (pp. 341-364). New York: Cambridge University Press.

Cooley, C. H. (1902). *Human nature and the social order.* New York: Scribner.

Deutsch, F. M., Ruble, D. N., Fleming, A., Brooks-Gunn, J., & Stangor, C. S. (1988). Information-seeking and maternal self-definition during the transition to motherhood. *Journal of Personality and Social Psychology, 55,* 420-431.

Dyes, A. (1984). *Effekte sozialer Realisierung einer Intention auf ihre Ausführung.* Unpublished master's thesis, Ruhr-Universität Bochum, Germany.

Erikson, E. H. (1956). The problem of ego-identity. *Journal of the American Psychoanalytic Association, 4,* 56-121.

Flüge, R., & Gollwitzer, P. M. (1986, April). *Volitionale Aspekte der Selbstergänzung.* Vortrag auf dem 3. Workshop der Fachgruppe Sozialpsychologie, Erlangen, Germany.

Ford, D. H., & Lerner, R. M. (1992). *Developmental systems theory: An integrative approach.* Newbury Park, CA: Sage.

Gergen, K. J. (1968). Personal consistency and presentation of self. In C. Gordon & K. J. Gergen (Eds.), *The self in social interaction* (Vol. 1, pp. 299-308). New York: John Wiley.

Gollwitzer, P. M. (1981). *The social reality of self-symbolizing: Winning completeness through others.* Unpublished doctoral dissertation, University of Texas at Austin.

Gollwitzer, P. M. (1983, July). *Audience anxiety and symbolic self-completion.* Paper presented at the International Conference on Anxiety and Self-Related Cognition, Berlin.

Gollwitzer, P. M. (1986a). The implementation of identity intentions: A motivational-volitional perspective on symbolic self-completion. In F. Halisch & J. Kuhl (Eds.), *Motivation, intention, and volition* (pp. 349-369). Heidelberg: Springer.

Gollwitzer, P. M. (1986b). Striving for specific identities: The social reality of self-symbolizing. In R. F. Baumeister (Ed.), *Public self and private self* (pp. 143-159). New York: Springer-Verlag.

Gollwitzer, P. M. (1990). Action phases and mind-sets. In E. T. Higgins & R. M. Sorrentino (Eds.), *Handbook of motivation and cognition: Foundations of social behavior* (Vol. 2, pp. 53-92). New York: Guilford.

Gollwitzer, P. M. (1993). Goal achievement: The role of intentions. *European Review of Social Psychology, 4,* 141-185.

Gollwitzer, P. M., & Bayer, U. (1999). Deliberative versus implemental mind-sets in the control of action. In S. Chaiken & Y. Trope (Eds.), *Dual-process theories in social psychology* (pp. 403-422). New York: Guilford.

Gollwitzer, P. M., & Brandstätter, V. (1997). Implementation intentions and effective goal pursuit. *Journal of Personality and Social Psychology, 73,* 186-199.

Gollwitzer, P. M., Heckhausen, H., & Steller, B. (1990). Deliberative and implemental mind-sets: Cognitive tuning toward congruous thoughts and information. *Journal of Personality and Social Psychology, 59,* 1119-1127.

Gollwitzer, P. M., & Kinney, R. F. (1989). Effects of deliberative and implemental mind-sets on illusion of control. *Journal of Personality and Social Psychology, 56,* 531-542.

Gollwitzer, P. M., & Schaal, B. (1998). Metacognition in action: The importance of implementation intentions. *Personality and Social Psychology Review, 2,* 124-136.

Gollwitzer, P. M., & Wicklund, R. A. (1985). Self-symbolizing and the neglect of others' perspectives. *Journal of Personality and Social Psychology, 48,* 702-715.

Gollwitzer, P. M., Wicklund, R. A., & Hilton, J. L. (1982). Admission of failure and symbolic self-completion: Extending Lewinian theory. *Journal of Personality and Social Psychology, 43,* 358-371.

Gordon, C. (1968). Self-conceptions: Configurations of content. In C. Gordon & K. J. Gergen (Eds.), *The self in social interaction* (Vol. 1, pp. 115-136). New York: John Wiley.

Gordon, C., & Gergen, K. J. (Eds.). (1968). *The self in social interaction.* New York: John Wiley.

Greenberg, J., Pyszczynski, T., & Solomon, S. (1986). The causes and consequences of a need for self-esteem. In R. F. Baumeister (Ed.), *Public self and private self* (pp. 189-212). New York: Springer-Verlag.

Greenwald, A. G. (1980). The totalitarian ego: Fabrication and revision of personal history. *American Psychologist, 35,* 603-618.

Heckhausen, H. (1989). *Motivation und Handeln.* Berlin: Springer.

Heckhausen, H., & Gollwitzer, P. M. (1987). Thought contents and cognitive functioning in motivational versus volitional states of mind. *Motivation and Emotion, 11,* 101-120.

Henle, M. (1944). The influence of valence on substitution. *Journal of Psychology, 17,* 11-19.

Higgins, E. T. (1987). Self-discrepancy: A theory relating self and affect. *Psychological Review, 94,* 319-340.

James, W. (1950). *The principles of psychology* (Vol. 1). New York: Dover. (Original work published 1890)

Leary, M. R., & Downs, D. (1995). Interpersonal functions of the self-esteem motive: The self-esteem system as a sociometer. In M. Kernis (Ed.), *Efficacy, agency, and self-esteem* (pp. 123-144). New York: Plenum.

Lewin, K. (1926). Vorsatz, Wille und Bedürfnis. *Psychologische Forschung, 7,* 330-385.

Linville, P. W. (1985). Self-complexity and affective extremity: Don't put all your eggs in one cognitive basket. *Social Cognition, 3,* 94-120.

Linville, P. W. (1987). Self-complexity as a cognitive buffer against stress-related illness and depression. *Journal of Personality and Social Psychology, 52,* 663-676.

Linville, P. W., & Carlston, D. E. (1994). Social cognition of the self. In P. G. Devine & D. Hamilton (Eds.), *Social cognition: Impact on social psychology* (pp. 143-193). San Diego, CA: Academic Press.

Lissner, K. (1933). Die Entspannung von Bedürfnissen durch Ersatzhandlungen. *Psychologische Forschung, 18,* 218-250.

Liu, T. J., & Steele, C. M. (1986). Attributional analysis as self-affirmation. *Journal of Personality and Social Psychology, 51,* 531-540.

Lydon, J., Dunkel-Schetter, C., Cohan, C. L., & Pierce, T. (1996). Pregnancy decision making as a significant life event: A commitment approach. *Journal of Personality and Social Psychology, 71,* 141-151.

Maccoby, E. E., Maccoby, N., Romney, A. K., & Adams, J. S. (1961). Social reinforcement in attitude change. *Journal of Abnormal and Social Psychology, 63,* 109-115.

Maccoby, N., Romney, A. K., Adams, J. S., & Maccoby, E. E. (1959). "Critical periods" in seeking and accepting information. *American Psychologist, 14,* 358.

Mahler, W. (1933). Ersatzhandlungen verschiedenen Realitätsgrades. *Psychologische Forschung, 18,* 27-89.

Marcia, J. E. (1966). Development and validation of ego-identity status. *Journal of Personality and Social Psychology, 3,* 551-558.

Marcia, J. E. (1967). Ego-identity status: Relationship to change in self-esteem, general maladjustment, and authoritarianism. *Journal of Personality, 35,* 119-133.

Marcia, J. E. (1980). Identity in adolescence. In J. Adelson (Ed.), *Handbook of adolescent psychology* (pp. 159-187). New York: John Wiley.

Markus, H. (1977). Self-schemata and processing information about the self. *Journal of Personality and Social Psychology, 35,* 63-78.

Markus, H., & Kunda, Z. (1986). Stability and malleability of the self-concept. *Journal of Personality and Social Psychology, 51*, 858-866.

Markus, H., & Nurius, P. (1986). Possible selves. *American Psychologist, 41*, 954-969.

Marsiske, M., Lang, F. B., Baltes, P. B., & Baltes, M. M. (1995). Selective optimization with compensation: Life-span perspectives on successful human development. In R. A. Dixon & L. Bäckman (Eds.), *Compensating for psychological deficits and declines: Managing losses and promoting gains* (pp. 35-79). Mahwah, NJ: Lawrence Erlbaum.

McBride, A. B. (1990). Mental health effects of women's multiple roles. *American Psychologist, 45*, 381-384.

Mead, G. H. (1934). *Mind, self, and society: From the standpoint of a social behaviorist.* Chicago: University of Chicago Press.

Oettingen, G. (1996). Positive fantasy and motivation. In P. M. Gollwitzer & J. A. Bargh (Eds.), *The psychology of action: Linking cognition and motivation to behavior* (pp. 236-259). New York: Guilford.

Ovsiankina, M. (1928). Die Wiederaufnahme unterbrochener Handlungen. *Psychologische Forschung, 11*, 302-379.

Pyszczynski, T., Greenberg, J., & Solomon S. (1997). Why do we need what we need? A terror management perspective on the roots of human social motivation. *Psychological Inquiry, 8*, 1-20.

Raynor, J. O. (1982). A theory of personality functioning and change. In J. O. Raynor & E. E. Entin (Eds.), *Motivation, career striving, and aging* (pp. 249-302). Washington, DC: Hemisphere.

Raynor, J. O., & Entin, E. E. (1982). Theory and research on future orientation and achievement motivation. In J. O. Raynor & E. E. Entin (Eds.), *Motivation, career striving, and aging* (pp. 13-82). Washington, DC: Hemisphere.

Rosenberg, M. (1965). *Society and the adolescent self-image.* Princeton, NJ: Princeton University Press.

Ruble, D. N. (1994). A phase model of transitions: Cognitive and motivational consequences. In M. Zanna (Ed.), *Advances in experimental social psychology* (pp. 163-214). New York: Academic Press.

Scherer, M. (1999). *Selbstergänzung vs. Selbstwerterhöhung.* Unpublished master's thesis, Universität Konstanz, Germany.

Sedikides, C. (1995). Central and peripheral self-conceptions are differentially influenced by mood: Tests of the differential sensitivity hypothesis. *Journal of Personality and Social Psychology, 69*, 759-777.

Seifert, A. (1999). *Effekte sozialer Realisierung von Absichten und Vorsätzen auf ihre Ausführung.* Unpublished master's thesis, Universität Konstanz, Germany.

Showers, C. J. (1992). Compartmentalization of positive and negative self-knowledge: Keeping bad apples out of the bunch. *Journal of Personality and Social Psychology, 62*, 1036-1049.

Showers, C. J., & Kling, K. C. (1996). Organization of self-knowledge: Implications for recovery from sad mood. *Journal of Personality and Social Psychology, 70,* 578-590.

Steele, C. M. (1988). The psychology of self-affirmation: Sustaining the integrity of the self. In L. Berkowitz (Ed.), *Advances in experimental social psychology* (Vol. 21, pp. 261-302). New York: Academic Press.

Stryker, S., & Statham, A. (1985). Symbolic interaction and role theory. In G. Lindzey & E. Aronson (Eds.), *Handbook of social psychology* (Vol. 1, pp. 311-378). New York: Random House.

Suls, J. (Ed.). (1993). *Psychological perspectives of the self* (Vol. 4). Hillsdale, NJ: Lawrence Erlbaum.

Suls, J., & Greenwald, A. G. (Eds.). (1983). *Psychological perspectives of the self* (Vol. 2). Hillsdale, NJ: Lawrence Erlbaum.

Swann, W. B., Jr. (1983). Self-verification: Bringing social reality into harmony with the self. In J. Suls & A. G. Greenwald (Eds.), *Psychological perspectives of the self* (Vol. 2, pp. 33-66). Hillsdale, NJ: Lawrence Erlbaum.

Taylor, S. E., & Brown, J. D. (1988). Illusion and well-being: A social psychological perspective on mental health. *Psychological Bulletin, 103,* 193-210.

Taylor, S. E., & Gollwitzer, P. M. (1995). The effects of mind-sets on positive illusions. *Journal of Personality and Social Psychology, 69,* 213-226.

Tesser, A. (1988). Toward a self-evaluation maintenance model of social behavior. In L. Berkowitz (Ed.), *Advances in experimental social psychology* (Vol. 21, pp. 181-227). New York: Academic Press.

Tesser, A., Martin, L. L., & Cornell, D. P. (1996). On the substitutability of self-protective mechanisms. In P. M. Gollwitzer & J. A. Bargh (Eds.), *The psychology of action: Linking cognition and motivation to behavior* (pp. 48-68). New York: Guilford.

Tesser, A., & Rosen, S. (1975). The reluctance to transmit bad news. In L. Berkowitz (Ed.), *Advances in experimental social psychology* (Vol. 8, pp. 193-232). New York: Academic Press.

Triandis, H. C. (1989). The self and social behavior in differing cultural contexts. *Psychological Review, 96,* 506-520.

Wagner, U., Wicklund, R. A., & Shaigan, S. (1990). Open devaluation and rejection of a fellow student: The impact of threat to a self-definition. *Basic and Applied Social Psychology, 11,* 61-76.

Wicklund, R. A., & Gollwitzer, P. M. (1981). Symbolic self-completion, attempted influence, and self-deprecation. *Basic and Applied Social Psychology, 2,* 89-114.

Wicklund, R. A., & Gollwitzer, P. M. (1982). *Symbolic self-completion.* Hillsdale, NJ: Lawrence Erlbaum.

Wurf, E., & Markus, H. (1991). Possible selves and the psychology of personal growth. In R. Hogan (Series Ed.) & D. J. Ozer, J. M. Healy, & A. Stewart (Vol. Eds.), *Perspectives in personality: Self and emotion* (Vol. 3A, pp. 39-62). London: Kingsley.

11

FREE FANTASIES ABOUT THE FUTURE AND THE EMERGENCE OF DEVELOPMENTAL GOALS

Gabriele Oettingen

Action-theoretical models and research provide a new framework for analyzing questions of human development across the life span (Brandtstädter, 1998). Action theories as introduced by psychologists of motivation, social psychologists, and personality psychologists (for summaries, see Gollwitzer & Bargh, 1996; Locke & Latham, 1990; Pervin, 1989) focus on how people's goals guide their actions. More specifically, action theories analyze such phenomena as the monitoring of goal pursuit (Carver & Scheier, 1998), the evaluation of goal attainment (Bandura, 1991), the mastery of increasing difficulties (Wright & Brehm, 1989), and the responding to and coping with failure (Bandura, 1991; Carver & Scheier, 1981, 1982, 1998; Taylor & Brown, 1988; Wicklund & Gollwitzer, 1982). Two types of goal theories have been suggested to explain these phenomena (Gollwitzer & Moskowitz, 1996). Goal content theories point to the importance of goal content (Dweck, 1996; Deci & Ryan, 1991) and goal framing (Bandura & Schunk, 1981; Higgins, 1996; Locke & Latham, 1990), whereas self-regulation theories of goal pursuit focus on the role of planning and other self-regulatory strategies for successful goal pursuit (Friedman & Scholnick, 1997; Gollwitzer, 1996; Kuhl & Beckmann, 1994).

Developmental action theories address additional issues of goal pursuit, such as the ontogeny of intentional action (Lütkenhaus & Bullock, 1991), the development of a sense of control and personal agency (Oettingen, Little, Lindenberger, & Baltes, 1994; Skinner, Chapman, & Baltes, 1988), and the development of the self-system (Harter, 1983) as prerequisites of effective self-regulation. Moreover, developmental psychologists have started to map out the content of people's personal goals (or current concerns, Klinger, 1987; personal projects, Little, 1983; personal strivings, Emmons, 1986; life tasks, Cantor & Kihlstrom, 1987) across the life span (Nurmi, 1992; Ogilvie & Rose, 1995; Rapkin & Fischer, 1992), whereby the interrelations and the hierarchical structure of goals are also investigated. More recently, researchers have analyzed how various aspects of personal goals, such as goal content (materialistic versus autonomous; Kasser & Ryan, 1993), goal framing (concrete versus abstract; Emmons, 1996), goal attainability (Brunstein, 1993), social support (Brunstein, Dangelmayer, & Schultheiss, 1996), and the matching of goal content with the person's needs (Brunstein, Schultheiss, & Grässmann, 1998), affect life satisfaction and thus the person's adaptation to the demands posed by the various stages of life.

The dynamic issue of what kinds of psychological processes account for strong and weak goal commitment has been mostly neglected, however. This neglect holds for general as well as for developmental theorizing and research on goals. There is an exception with respect to the decay of goal commitment. Brandtstädter and Rothermund (1994; see also Brandtstädter, Wentura, & Greve, 1993) have analyzed the psychological processes that account for the weakening of goal commitment (i.e., accommodative processes that lead to the adjustment of goals in response to a reduction of action resources in old age). With respect to the emergence of goal commitment, however, there is still a lack of ideas and research, even though the goal literature acknowledges that people are producers of their own development. Goal striving does not end when people achieve their goals; rather, they commit themselves to new goals (regarding proactive goals, see Bandura, 1991; on developmental system theory, see Ford & Lerner, 1992). It is assumed that whether a new goal is chosen depends on the level of respective efficacy expectations (Bandura, 1991) and whether the new goal fits into the hierarchy of existing goals (Emmons, 1996). No effort has been made, however, to delineate the psychological processes leading up to individuals' readiness to set themselves binding action goals. In this chapter, I present a theory of fantasy realization (Oettingen, 1996, 1997b) that accounts for people's readiness to set themselves developmental goals in terms of their free fantasies about their personal futures.

FANTASY REALIZATION THEORY

It is possible to distinguish between two forms of thinking about the future: expectations and free fantasies (Oettingen, 1996, in press). *Expectations* are judgments of how likely it is that certain future outcomes or behaviors will occur. Expectations are based on a person's experiences in the past and therefore reflect his or her performance history. *Free fantasies* about the future, on the other hand, are thoughts and images that depict future outcomes or behaviors in the mind's eye, independent of the likelihood that these events will actually occur. In free fantasies about the future, a person can envision a desired future event even though he or she judges the actual occurrence of that event to be unlikely. For example, despite judging that her chances of successfully entering the job market are slim, a graduate student can indulge in positive fantasies about being offered the perfect position.

The theory of fantasy realization specifies three ways in which an individual might deal with fantasies about the future and relates these to the individual's readiness to act toward fantasy realization. One results in an expectancy-based readiness to act; the other two create a readiness to act that is unrelated to the person's expectations.

The first way a person might deal with positive fantasies about the future is to contrast them mentally with negative aspects of the impeding reality. This mental contrasting transforms the desired future into a future that needs to be attained and the impeding reality into a reality that needs to be changed. The experienced necessity to act leads to the question of whether the reality can be changed into the fantasy. Thus the person's expectations of successfully attaining his or her fantasies become activated, and they are used to answer this question (Oettingen, in press). If the individual's expectations of success are high, he or she will commit to behavioral goals that serve fantasy fulfillment; if the individual's expectations of success are low, he or she will refrain from commitment to behavioral goals geared toward fantasy fulfillment.

Second, a person may merely indulge in positive fantasies and disregard the impeding reality. This indulgence in positive fantasies seduces to consummate and consume the envisioned desired events in the mind's eye. Accordingly, the individual experiences no necessity to act, and therefore relevant expectations of success are not activated and used. The readiness to act toward fantasy fulfillment should reflect solely the positive incentive value of the desired events imagined in the individual's fantasies. The individual's commitment to relevant behavioral goals should therefore be moderate and independent of his or her perceived chances of success (i.e., expectations). As a consequence, the level of goal commitment is either too high (when expectations are low) or too low (when expectations are high).

Third, a person may merely dwell on the negative aspects of the impeding reality and thus disregard his or her positive fantasies about the future. The individual experiences no necessity to act, as no fantasies about the future point to the direction in which to act. Again, expectations of success are not activated and used. Commitment to relevant behavioral goals should be based solely on the negative incentive value associated with the negative aspects of the impeding reality. As with indulging in positive fantasies about the future, dwelling on the negative reality should thus lead to a moderate, expectancy-independent level of commitment, which is inadequate in the sense that it is too high (when expectations are low) or too low (when expectations are high).

With respect to the emergence of developmental goals, it is hypothesized that positive fantasies surrounding a pending developmental task (e.g., starting a family) lead to different outcomes depending on how the individual deals with these fantasies. Indulging in positive fantasies about the future and dwelling on the negative aspects of the impeding reality should lead to inadequate goal commitment. People in this category stay passive even when probabilities of success are high and become active even when probabilities of success are low.

Mentally contrasting the positive future with negative aspects of the impeding reality, however, should lead to strong goal commitments, given that expectations of success are high; when expectations of success are low, people should refrain from respective goal commitments. Both committing oneself in light of high probabilities of success and holding back in light of low probabilities of success are functional for mastering developmental tasks. In the first case, goal attainment with respect to the chosen goal is more or less guaranteed, whereas in the second case goal attainment with respect to alternative goals in the service of other developmental tasks becomes more likely, as one's resources are not wasted on a lost cause. Goal attainment can be attempted more effectively at a later point in time or in a different situational context or else is given up altogether in favor of alternative developmental tasks.

DEVELOPMENTAL TASKS AND THE EMERGENCE OF BEHAVIORAL GOALS

Fantasy realization theory offers not only hypotheses on when and how people set themselves developmental goals, but also a new perspective on the concept of developmental tasks. According to Havighurst (1948/1972), a developmental task "arises at or about a certain period in the life of the individual, successful achievement of which leads to his happiness and to success with later tasks, while failure leads to unhappiness in the individual, disapproval by the society, and difficulty with later tasks" (p. 2).

Research on developmental tasks has been concerned with identifying critical tasks for the various stages of life-span development (infancy and early childhood, middle childhood, adolescence, early adulthood, middle age, and later maturity), thereby pointing to their biological, psychological, and cultural bases. Moreover, characteristics of developmental tasks such as cultural relativity, recurrent versus nonrecurrent tasks, relations between achievement of earlier and later developmental tasks, and the role of their institutional backups (e.g., family, school, church) have been discussed (Dreher & Dreher, 1985; Dreher & Oerter, 1986; Havighurst, 1948/1972; Oerter, 1986).

So far, theorizing and research on developmental tasks has apparently focused on structural aspects, such as what kinds of tasks go with which stages of life-span development and what features characterize different developmental tasks. The dynamic question of which psychological processes make people take on pending developmental tasks and commit themselves to respective behavioral goals, thus promoting the mastery of the task, has been neglected. It is still an open question what makes people face up to developmental tasks and form respective behavioral goals.

Fantasy realization theory helps to answer this question and thus adds a dynamic perspective to the analysis of developmental tasks.

A line of experimental research has investigated whether and how various ways of dealing with fantasies about the future facilitate the mastery of developmental tasks of middle childhood, adolescence, and early adulthood (e.g., Oettingen, 1996, in press; Oettingen, Hönig, & Pak, 1999). The developmental tasks chosen for analysis have pertained to the achievement domain (e.g., developing fundamental skills in school, preparing for an occupation), the interpersonal domain (e.g., achieving mature relationships with peers and emotional independence from parents and other adults, finding a partner), and the domain of life management (e.g., starting a family, achieving economic and emotional independence). All of these experiments (save one) have established at least three experimental groups: a fantasy-reality contrast group, a positive fantasy only group, and a negative reality only group. We assessed as dependent variables whether participants had committed themselves to behavioral goals that serve the mastery of the respective developmental tasks and whether they had already evinced respective goal-directed behaviors. The dependent variables were assessed some time after the experiment had taken place (from 7 to 14 days later), as vital goal commitments are assumed to persist over time (Lewin, 1926).

Developmental Fantasies in the Achievement Domain

Fifth graders ages 10 to 12 years participated in the first experimental study on the developmental task of acquiring fundamental skills in school (Oettingen et al., 1999). More specifically, the skill of interest was the acquisition of a second language, as the native German speaking children had just started to learn English in school. We first assessed the children's expectations of succeeding in their new subject by asking them how well they thought they would do in English. Then we established the three experimental groups: the mental contrast group, in which participants had to elaborate positive aspects of the future as well as negative aspects of the impeding reality; the positive fantasy only group, in which participants had to elaborate only positive aspects of the future; and the negative reality only group, in which participants had to elaborate only negative aspects of the impeding reality.

Children in the *mental contrast* group had to name a positive aspect of succeeding in learning English and to elaborate this aspect in free thoughts or images developing in their mind's eyes; children named aspects such as "My daddy would be so happy" or "I could talk to the Back Street Boys." Subsequently, the children had to name and mentally elaborate a negative aspect of reality that stands in the way of their succeeding in English. Children named aspects such as "I am distracted by my classmates" or "Sometimes I am too lazy to study." Children in the *positive fantasy only* group, in contrast, had to name and mentally elaborate two positive aspects of succeeding in English, whereas the children in the *negative reality only* group had to name and mentally elaborate two negative aspects of the reality that stand in the way of their succeeding in English. All of these mental elaborations had to be reported in writing.

In order to assess whether participants had formed behavioral goals that serve the task of excelling in English, we asked the children 2 weeks after the experiment how well they had prepared for their English classes (in comparison to other classes and in comparison to their classmates). Moreover, we inquired how much leisure and pleasure they had forgone to do their homework in English.

Children in both the positive fantasy only and the negative reality only groups showed a medium level of study effort and of forgoing leisure that was independent of their expectations of succeeding in English. Not so the children in the mental contrast group: They evinced much study effort and forgoing of leisure when they perceived their chances of success to be high; when they perceived their chances of success to be low, they showed little study effort and little forgoing of leisure. In line with fantasy realization theory, contrasting positive fantasies about the future with negative aspects of the impeding reality turned out to be a prerequisite of high commitment to behavioral goals. With merely indulging in positive fantasies or solely dwelling on the negative reality, high levels of commitment were not observed even when expectations of success were high.

This pattern of data also emerged for the children's actual performance in the form of course grades given by the teachers 2 weeks after the experiment. When their expectations of success were high, participants who mentally contrasted their positive fantasies with negative aspects of the impeding reality scored almost two course grades higher than those who had only indulged in positive fantasies, and almost one course grade higher than those who had dwelled on the negative reality. When their expectations of success were low, participants in the mental contrast group scored half a grade and one and a half course grades lower than participants in the other two groups.

In other words, when their expectations of success were high, participants in the mental contrast group successfully acted toward fantasy fulfillment—they did very well in English. When their expectations of success were low, participants did not excel in fulfilling their future dreams—they did not do well in English at all. Participants in the fantasy only and reality only groups ranged in the middle. They got fairly good grades, and this was true irrespective of whether they expected to do well or poorly in English.

These findings were recently replicated by Brinkmann, Holder, Hurler, and Schultz-Gambard (1998), who tested young adults who participated in a vocational training program geared to educating social workers. The researchers assessed students' expectations using questions such as how likely it is that they possess the necessary skills to master their profession. Two experimental groups were established: the mental contrast group and the positive fantasy group. Participants in the *mental contrast* group had to first name and elaborate six positive aspects of successfully entering their occupation and then name and elaborate six negative aspects of reality that stand in the way of their realizing this fantasy. Participants mentioned positive aspects such as "financial improvement" and "self-actualization" and negative aspects such as "current economic depression" and "no time for my children." Participants in the *positive fantasy only* group had to name and elaborate only positive aspects of successfully starting their occupation.

Two weeks after the experiment, Brinkmann et al. (1998) asked participants how frequently they had interacted in a constructive way with their colleagues and clients during the past fortnight. Participants in the mental contrast group interacted constructively most often of all participants when their expectations of success were high, and least often when their expectations of success were low. Participants in the positive fantasy group, in contrast, reported a frequency of constructive interactions that ranged in between and was independent of their perceived chances of successfully starting their occupation as a social worker.

The same pattern of results emerged even when the quality of the participants' interactions was rated by external raters blind to the hypotheses. Two weeks after the experiment, participants were also confronted with scenarios depicting typical conflicts between a social worker and his or her clients or colleagues. The participants had to find constructive solutions for these interpersonal conflicts, and these solutions were later examined by the independent raters. The solutions of high-expectancy participants in the mental contrast group were rated as being more to the point and more constructive than those of all other participants, whereas the solutions of low-expectancy participants in the mental contrast group were rated as least to the point and least constructive. The participants in the positive fantasy only group fared in between, no matter whether they perceived the chances of success as high or low.

In sum, positive fantasies surrounding developmental tasks in the achievement domain—in the cases presented above, acquiring critical academic skills in middle childhood and getting started in one's occupation in young adulthood—serve an important motivational function when they are mentally contrasted with negative aspects of the impeding reality. Only under contrasting conditions do optimistic expectations lead to strong respective goal commitments, whereas pessimistic expectations suppress them. When people indulge in positive fantasies about successfully mastering pending developmental tasks or dwell on negative aspects of the impeding reality, they show medium levels of commitment, no matter whether they perceive their chances of success as high or low. This pattern of results emerged for all dependent variables no matter whether they were assessed through self-reports or external observations. Moreover, the pattern of results held true for both studies, even though there were a number of differences between the two (e.g., the developmental tasks pertained to different stages of life-span development). As convincing as the results of the reported studies are for the achievement domain, we wondered whether developmental fantasies play the same role for critical developmental tasks in the interpersonal domain.

Developmental Fantasies in the Interpersonal Domain

The first experimental study in the interpersonal domain addressed the developmental tasks of achieving mature relationships with peers and emotional independence from parents and other adults (Oettingen et al., 1999). In a sample of university students, each participant was asked to report his or her most important interpersonal issue, no matter whether that issue pertained to a peer, a partner, or a family member, and then to indicate the perceived likelihood of whether that interpersonal issue would have a happy ending. The issues named included, for example, "to get to know better someone I like" and "to get along with my mother." Thereafter, each participant was asked to list positive aspects pertaining to a happy ending of the interpersonal issue. Such positive aspects as "not being lonely anymore" and "being needed" were listed. Finally, each participant had to list negative aspects of the impeding reality that appeared to stand in the way of a happy ending. The negative aspects listed included "feelings of unattractiveness" and "being insecure."

We established three experimental conditions. In the *mental contrast* group, participants first had to select two of the listed positive and two of the listed negative aspects. To achieve a fantasy-reality contrast, we asked participants to alternate in their mental elaboration between the two positive aspects of a happy ending and the two negative aspects of the impeding reality, beginning with a positive aspect. In the *positive fantasy only* group, participants were asked to elaborate only four positive aspects of a happy ending. In the *negative reality only* group, participants were asked to elaborate only four negative aspects of the present reality.

As a first dependent variable we measured participants' readiness to act right after the experiment by their reports of how energetic and active they felt. Participants who had to contrast their positive fantasies mentally with negative aspects of the impeding reality showed the highest readiness to act, when their expectations were high. When their expectations of success were low, they were the least ready to act. The positive fantasy and the negative reality groups, in contrast, showed a medium readiness to act that was independent of whether their expectations of success were high or low.

The same pattern of data emerged for the second dependent variable, immediacy of relevant action, operationalized as the number of days participants waited before starting to implement their fantasies. Two weeks after the experiment, we asked participants at what point in time they had initiated relevant actions. Participants in the mental contrast group who perceived a happy ending as likely acted almost 8 days earlier than those who merely indulged in positive fantasies, and almost 5 days earlier than those who solely brooded over the negative reality. In contrast, when they perceived a happy ending as unlikely, participants in the mental contrast group acted at least 3 days later than those in the positive fantasy only and the negative reality only groups.

Feeling energized and acting without delay can be interpreted as indications of strong goal commitment (Gollwitzer & Moskowitz, 1996). Taking the results of both dependent variables together, therefore, indicates that mentally contrasting positive developmental fantasies with the negative aspects of the impeding reality leads to the emergence of binding action goals that serve the achievement of the respective developmental task, given that the chances of mastering the developmental task are perceived as being high. The present study also allowed us to rule out the possibility that the effects of the contrasting procedure are based on a change in participants' level of expectations. The levels of participants' expectations as assessed before and after the experimental instructions did not differ among the three groups.

We replicated the reported pattern of results in a further experiment that focused on the developmental task of finding a partner (Oettingen, in press). More specifically, participants were confronted with the presumed possibility of getting to know an attractive stranger. Getting to know an attractive person is a topic about which it is easy to stir up fantasies. Attractive individuals are perceived not only as exciting, but also as interpersonally and intellectually competent (Eagly, Ashmore, Makhijani, & Longo, 1991). Moreover, when in the company of attractive people, one can also feel attractive (Geiselman, Haight, & Kimata, 1984).

Female college students were told that the study was about thoughts and images of getting to know a stranger. They were then shown a picture of an attractive young man, supposedly a doctoral student working at our laboratory, with the name of Michael S. Participants first had to indicate the subjective likelihood that they would get to know Michael S. if they came across him. Then they had to name positive aspects of getting to know the attractive stranger and negative aspects of the impeding reality. Finally, the three familiar experimental groups were established. As in the previous experiment, participants in the *mental contrast* group alternated in elaborating positive aspects and negative aspects in their mind's eyes, whereas participants in the *positive fantasy only* group had to elaborate only positive aspects of getting to know the attractive stranger and the participants in the *negative reality only* group had to elaborate only negative aspects of the impeding reality.

One week after the experiment, we assessed participants' commitment to act toward getting to know the attractive stranger. First, we asked various questions pertaining to how badly they wanted to get to know the attractive stranger. Second, we more indirectly inquired about participants' commitment to act by asking questions pertaining to how much they would mind if they got to know the attractive stranger only in their thoughts.

Participants who had mentally contrasted their positive fantasies with aspects of the negative reality showed the strongest commitment to act when their expectations of success were high. When their expectations of success were low, participants in the mental contrast group were the least committed. The other two groups again evinced medium levels of commitment, and this independent of their expectations. This pattern of results was observed for the direct as well as for the more indirect measure of commitment to act.

In sum, mental contrasting is essential for mastering developmental tasks not only in the achievement domain, but also in the interpersonal domain. Even though the two studies reported show a number of differences (the developmental tasks under scrutiny were dissimilar; the dependent variables in the first study included measures of actual behavior, whereas the second study assessed commitment to act through self-reports; participants in the first study named their own interpersonal issues, whereas participants in the second were confronted with the same interpersonal issue presented by the experimenter), the patterns of results were similar. Apparently, positive developmental fantasies are critical for mastering developmental tasks, not only in the achievement domain but also in the interpersonal domain. However, we wondered whether developmental tasks that directly touch issues of life management (e.g., combining work and family life) are similarly affected by people's dealing with their developmental fantasies. People may be especially defensive when it comes to issues of life management, where the feelings of being one's own agent of personal development are particularly strong (Taylor, 1989).

Developmental Fantasies and Life Management

Life management is an area of increasing importance for personality development. This is true especially in the Western, more individualist cultures, where individuals are largely responsible for their own livelihood and well-being, as cultural norms and interpersonal principles regulate people's actions to a lesser and lesser extent (Markus & Kitayama, 1991; Oettingen, 1997a; Triandis, 1995). The first of the two studies on life management pertained to the combining of two seemingly contradictory life domains: professional work and starting a family life (Oettingen, in press). In Germany, where we conducted the study, only 58% of mothers with children under 18 years participate in work life (Statistisches Bundesamt, 1992), and 89% of working mothers report that they often have problems with combining work and family life (Hegner & Lakemann, 1989). The numbers look particularly grim when the percentage of women in German academics is considered. Even though 45% of dissertations are written by female doctoral students, only 5.3% of the associate professorships and 5.7% of the full professorships are held by women ("Frauen-förderung in der MPG," 1995).

We therefore conducted the present study with female doctoral students who were on average over 30 years old and had no children yet. Thus they were approaching a critical time with respect to family planning. To establish the three forms of thinking about the future, we used a different paradigm from that in the previously reported experiments. First, all participants were asked to generate positive fantasies about their professional and private lives 10 years from now, to see these images in their mind's eyes, and to report about their streams of thought in writing. Participants who in their positive fantasies mentioned having a professional career and a family had to indicate how hopeful they were that they could successfully combine work and family life for themselves. Then they were confronted with the impeding reality (i.e., the difficulties and problems in combining work and family life). The difficulties and problems were presented in the form of reports supposedly taken from interviews with working mothers. In the *mental contrast* condition, participants had to elaborate on these reports by producing free thoughts and images. This way, the production of positive fantasies about combining work and family life was brought into contrast with mental elaborations on the impeding reality. In the *positive fantasy only* condition, we prevented this contrast experience by having participants downplay the difficulties reported by the working mothers. Participants were told that the interviewed mothers had reported these difficulties in self-defense to hide other underlying personal or professional problems. The participants had to detect and mentally elaborate on these underlying problems. In the *negative reality only* condition, we focused participants exclusively on the difficulties of combining work and family life. They were asked to discover those difficulties and problems alluded to in the mothers' reports that so far had made them refrain from having children.

Two weeks after the experiment, we explored participants' commitment to relevant behavioral goals in both a more direct and a less direct way. Participants had to indicate how much they intended to do in order to combine professional life and a child in their personal future and how hard it would be for them if they never had a child. Although this study used a different procedure to establish the three experimental groups, the pattern of results remained the same. No matter how commitment to behavioral goals was assessed, the highest scores were observed in the mental contrast condition in participants who held high expectations of success, whereas the lowest scores were observed for participants in the same condition with low expectations of success. Commitment to behavioral goals was at a medium level in the positive fantasy only and the negative reality only groups. This was true for participants with both high and low expectations of success.

The second study in the area of life management referred to the developmental task of achieving assurance of economic and emotional independence (Janetzke, 1999). The study used the reinterpretation paradigm described in the previous experiment. The participating university students (freshmen) were told that the study would be conducted for the purpose of evaluating a new training program called Self-Efficacy Training, or SET. First, participants were shown a leaflet describing SET as a dynamic training program that helps to create self-assurance, independence, calmness, joy, and self-actualization. Then participants were asked for their expectations that they would benefit from participating in a training program such as SET. Thereafter, all participants had to fantasize positively about how their futures would look like if they had successfully participated in SET. Participants fantasized, for instance, about mastering life as a self-confident and assertive lawyer and about succeeding in their university education.

In establishing the three experimental groups, we confronted participants with 12 statements that supposedly came from interviews with persons who already had participated in SET. The statements were complaints about the hardships of SET (e.g., "Sometimes I had to prepare for SET until late in the evening!"). In the *mental contrast* group, participants were asked to free-associate to each of these statements. In this way, mental elaborations about negative aspects of the impeding reality were forced upon participants who beforehand had generated positive fantasies about their lives subsequent to SET. In the *positive fantasy only* group, participants' attention was directed away from the negative reality. We induced participants to trivialize the complaints of the presumed prior participants by suggesting that each of the complaints about the hardships of SET was simply a self-protective excuse for an underlying personal problem. We asked the participants to discover the problems that the excuses were intended to cover up. In the *negative reality only* group, we asked participants to spell out those thoughts and images that had made them refrain from participating in similar training programs in the past. In this way, participants' thoughts were directed away from a positive future after SET and solely linked to negative aspects of the impeding reality.

Two weeks after the experiment, participants were asked whether they would be interested in enrolling in SET. Moreover, they had to indicate how much money they would be willing to pay and how far they would be willing to travel to attend SET. Finally, we wanted to know if participants would be willing to forgo invitations to interesting parties or getting together with friends in order to attend. For all of these measures, we observed the familiar pattern of results. Participants in the mental contrast condition reported the strongest willingness to exert behaviors in favor of attending SET when their expectations of success were high, and they reported the weakest willingness when their expectations of success were low. Commitment to relevant behavioral goals, however, was at a medium level in the positive fantasy only and the negative reality only groups, irrespective of whether participants' expectations were high or low.

In sum, positive fantasies about the future lead to the adoption of binding behavioral goals also in developmental tasks pertaining to life management, given that the fantasies are mentally contrasted with negative aspects of the impeding reality and that chances of success are perceived as promising. This pattern of results held true for both developmental tasks investigated (i.e., combining work and family life as well as gaining and keeping financial and emotional independence), no matter how commitment to relevant behavioral goals was measured.

THEORETICAL AND APPLIED IMPLICATIONS

Research on developmental tasks has so far neglected the psychological processes that underlie getting started with task achievement. The present theorizing and the results of the reported research suggest that the achievement of developmental tasks begins with commitment to behavioral goals. The emergence of behavioral goals requires that people mentally contrast their fantasies of achieving pending developmental tasks with the impeding reality. When an individual's expectations of success are high, strong goal commitments can be expected that will in turn guide that person's behaviors. Strong goal commitments cannot develop on the basis of a person's indulging in positive future fantasies or dwelling on the impeding reality. If anything, a medium level of commitment originates that keeps a person's fantasies or ruminations alive.

In the experiments discussed above, the focus was on fantasies about a positive future that are mentally contrasted with negative aspects of the impeding reality and thus on the emergence of approach goals. One wonders whether the observed processes of goal emergence apply analogously to the emergence of avoidance goals. In respective experiments, fantasies about a negative future (i.e., aspects of having failed on a pending developmental task) would have to be contrasted mentally with positive aspects of the impeding reality (i.e., aspects that might prevent failure on the pending developmental task). For example, a person who is plagued by negative fantasies about failing at the job market would have to contrast these negative fantasies mentally with thoughts about her strong educational background. Given that the person's expectations to avoid the negative future (i.e., failure at the job market) are high, mental elaborations on both the negative future and the positive reality should create binding avoidance goals.

Expectancy Effects on Behavior

An ever-increasing body of research demonstrates that people's subjective expectations about their future predict their behavior and performance (Bandura, 1997; Scheier & Carver, 1992; Seligman, 1991; Taylor & Brown, 1988). Irrespective of whether expectations are operationalized as efficacy expectations (i.e., expectations of whether one can perform a certain behavior necessary for a desired outcome; Bandura, 1977), outcome expectations (i.e., expectations of whether a certain behavior will lead to the desired outcome; Bandura, 1977), or generalized expectations (i.e., expectations of whether a certain outcome will occur; Heckhausen, 1991; Oettingen, 1996), optimistic expectations promote persistence, effort, and successful performance in various life domains. Further, expecting a positive future in general (as measured by the Life Orientation Test; Scheier & Carver, 1987) is associated with positive outcomes such as in the health domain with physical recovery in coronary heart patients (Scheier & Carver, 1992) and psychological recovery in women suffering from postpartum depression (Carver & Gaines, 1987). In the achievement domain, efficacy and outcome expectations regarding future success in mathematics predict both the willingness to enroll in mathematics courses and the actual success measured by course grades (Lent, Lopez, & Bieschke, 1993). And in the interpersonal domain, optimistic expectations about finding a romantic partner have been shown to promote actual success (Oettingen, 1998).

The positive relation between expectations and performance is based on a number of cognitive, motivational, and affective processes that foster performance. For instance, people with high self-efficacy expectations are known to apply analytic strategies more effectively (Wood & Bandura, 1989), to adopt more challenging goals (Bandura & Cervone, 1983) as well as fewer distal goals (Bandura & Schunk, 1981), to be more successful in selecting and pursuing rewarding career paths (Betz & Hackett, 1983), and to show less physiological arousal during problem-solving tasks (Bandura, Cioffi, Taylor, & Brouillard, 1988) than people with low self-efficacy expectations.

It is not only these mediational processes that account for the positive relation between expectations and performance, but also the fact that expectations reflect a person's past. There are four principal sources of information that are relevant for appraising an individual's expectations. Next to vicarious experiences, verbal persuasion, and relevant physiological and affective states, people in particular base their performance-related expectations on their achieved performances and experienced outcomes of the past (Bandura, 1986, 1997). Accordingly, expectations reflect a person's past behavior, which should also boost the expectancy-behavior link, as past behavior predicts future behavior through multiple processes (e.g., habits or intentions; for summaries, see Ouelette & Wood, 1998; Triandis, 1977, 1980).

Even though demonstrating the expectancy-behavior relation and explaining its mediational processes has received much scientific interest in recent years, questions of when expectations fail to exert their influence on behavior have received less attention. This is surprising in light of the fact that the search for moderators of expectancy effects on *cognitive* variables has a strong tradition. For example, Stangor and McMillan (1992) have reviewed 54 experiments on the memorability of information that is either consistent or inconsistent with expectations, trying to distill relevant moderator variables.

The research presented here suggests a powerful moderator variable of expectancy effects on behavior. Whether expectations will translate into behavior depends on the person's mode of thinking about the desired future. Merely indulging in fantasies about a desired future or solely dwelling on the impeding reality will rob expectations of their action-guiding function. The individual does not experience a necessity to act and thus expectations do not become activated and used. A necessity to act is experienced, however, when positive fantasies about a desired future are mentally contrasted with negative aspects of the impeding reality. When they perceive their probabilities of success to be high, contrasting individuals set out to actualize their desired futures; when they see their probabilities of success as low, they start to disengage from fantasy realization.

The Optimism Versus Realism Debate

There are two opposing sides in the recent debate on whether illusory positive thinking about the future fosters or defeats successful personality development. Experimentally oriented social psychologists (Taylor & Brown, 1988, 1994) suggest that a positive view of the self and the world, even if illusory, is a clear asset, whereas personality psychologists (Colvin & Block, 1994) often favor a realistic view of the self and the world. So far, methodological arguments focusing on how illusory optimism and its consequences are correctly assessed have dominated the controversy (Asendorpf & Ostendorf, 1998; Colvin & Block, 1994; Colvin, Block, & Funder, 1995; Shedler, Mayman, & Manis, 1993).

The present theorizing and experimental evidence suggest a conceptual solution to this debate. One needs to differentiate two forms of thinking about the future: expectancy judgments and free fantasies (Oettingen, 1996, in press). The proponents of the realism position could advance more persuasive arguments if, instead of questioning the validity and reliability of the findings reported in the illusory optimism literature, they pointed to the irrational behavior that results from indulging in positive fantasies (i.e., too much investment in light of low, and too little investment in light of high, probabilities of success).

The proponents of the illusory optimism position, on the other hand, could offer more consistent evidence if they recognized that expectancy effects on behavior are affected by moderator variables. The desired future has to be contrasted mentally with the impeding reality for expectancy effects on behavior to occur. If an individual only indulges in fantasies of the desired future or only dwells on the impeding reality, the potentially beneficial effects of optimistic expectations are wasted.

Dreaming Your Life Away

If a person indulges in positive fantasies about the mastery of a developmental task, relevant expectations of success do not affect his or her respective actions. As expectations reflect a person's experience and thus the context in which he or she is embedded, indulging in positive fantasies disconnects the person from that context and thereby from the biological, cultural, and nonnormative influences that are supposed to determine growth across the life span (Baltes, Lindenberger, & Staudinger, 1998; Havighurst, 1948/1972). This has important consequences for successful personality development.

A prototypical example of ignoring expectations that are based on *biological* influences is a person of middle age who fails to adjust her professional and personal activities to her expectations of decreasing physical and mental strengths. Indulging in positive fantasies of keeping the stamina of a youngster hinders her searching for means to optimize her remaining resources (e.g., to develop effective mnemonic strategies) or to compensate for failing resources (e.g., to delegate responsibilities to co-workers, to lecture with the help of a microphone). This is because indulging in positive fantasies prevents both the disengagement from the idea of possessing the old stamina (despite low expectations) and the commitment to optimization and compensation goals (Baltes & Baltes, 1990), even though in the latter case expectations for goal attainment are high. Accordingly, indulging in positive fantasies hampers the individual's mastery of the developmental task of "adjusting to the physiological changes of middle age" (Havighurst, 1948/1972). The same should be true for dwelling on negative aspects of the impeding reality (e.g., decreasing physical strengths), as such ruminations also promote the disregard of expectations.

Second, ignoring expectations determined by *sociocultural* factors can also be problematic for personality development. For example, a person socialized in a sociocultural context that affirms values of large power distance (i.e., a large power differential is readily accepted by the people of the culture; Hofstede, 1991) who fantasizes about attaining personal freedom of action will not activate and use respective expectations. Accordingly, he will halfheartedly commit himself to attaining freedom of action despite low chances of success and fail to disengage from the idea of reaching full discretion. Disengagement, however, would be prerequisite to a reorientation (e.g., emigration or retreat to more liberal niches of the culture). This person will stay in his sociocultural context and will thus fail to achieve the developmental task of "taking on civic and social responsibility" (Havighurst, 1948/1972). Again, analogous consequences are to be expected for people who keep dwelling on the negative aspects of the cultures in which they are embedded.

Third, ignoring expectations that are determined by individual, *nonnormative* factors might also hurt personality development. A young adult who, for example, indulges in fantasies about becoming a violin soloist will fail to consider her low expectations of success based on the fact that she has not played the violin from earliest childhood on and thus lacks the expertise to become a star. By still pursuing a career as a violin soloist (albeit halfheartedly), she will forgo opportunities to commit herself to behavioral goals in the service of entering more mundane occupations (e.g., as a music teacher). She might recognize too late that the chances to prepare for other occupations are lost and that she has failed the developmental task of successfully "getting started in an occupation" (Havighurst, 1948/1972).

But indulging in dreams about illustrious professions (and dwelling on the impeding reality) should also hurt those individuals who do possess the necessary education and talent, because they do not commit themselves to respective behavioral goals to the degree that is suggested by their high expectations of success. Clearly, this line of thought also applies to high expectations based on biological and sociocultural factors.

Ignorance of expectations caused by indulging in positive fantasies about the future or by dwelling on the negative reality, however, does not have to hamper successful personality development under all circumstances. There seem to be developmental tasks that benefit from individuals' ignoring probabilities of success. Such developmental tasks are characterized by hopelessness in the sense that they can be neither mastered nor given up—for example, when a person is told that he suffers from a terminal disease. In this detrimental situation, mental contrasting of positive fantasies (e.g., living through the next summer, traveling abroad) with negative aspects of the impeding reality (e.g., increasing frailty, chronic pain) will only focus the person on the bleak prognosis. Activating and using this prognosis for making behavioral decisions would lead to the individual's giving up life. Indulging in positive fantasies, in contrast, should allow him to continue life and to develop his remaining resources (Taylor, 1989).

Educational Implications

In his analysis of developmental tasks, Havighurst (1948/1972) also discusses educational issues: What are the responsibilities of general education for assisting people in accomplishing one or the other developmental task? How are these responsibilities met? How can the educational system improve in helping with such tasks? The answers Havighurst offers to these questions relate to aiding people in their acquisition of relevant knowledge, values, and attitudes as well as providing the necessary opportunities for such learning to occur. The theorizing and research presented above suggest in addition that people have a better chance to succeed at pending developmental tasks if they are taught to contrast their developmental fantasies mentally with the impeding reality. When their expectations of success are high, people's willingness to commit themselves to relevant behavioral goals is increased. As a consequence, they may more readily accomplish pending developmental tasks.

But offering mental contrasting as a self-regulatory tool does not suffice for people who entertain low expectations of realizing their developmental fantasies. Educators have to bear in mind that the mental contrasting of developmental fantasies will lead to disengagement from the respective developmental tasks when expectations of success are low. Therefore, whenever educators suggest the mental contrasting procedure as a self-regulatory tool, they first have to make sure that the person's relevant expectations of success are high. If this is not the case, they need to work to strengthen those expectations beforehand. Bandura (1997) lists a number of very powerful interventions that have been shown to increase a person's expectations of success (e.g., pointing to successful models or to relevant strengths, but also providing relevant knowledge and teaching necessary skills).

Finally, the many interventions and training programs geared toward promoting expectations of success (Hackett, 1995; Schunk, 1989; Schwarzer, 1992; for a summary, see Bandura, 1997) have to be taken with a grain of salt, as this educational strategy seems incomplete. Elevating a person's expectations of success leads to strong goal commitments only if the person mentally contrasts his or her desired future with the impeding reality. If the individual only indulges in the positive future or dwells on the impeding reality, the painfully achieved strengthening of expectations is wasted—no matter whether it was acquired through an increase in knowledge and skills, through the observation of effective models, or through persuasive efforts of therapists, parents, friends, teachers, or the individual him- or herself.

SUMMARY AND CONCLUSION

Modern theorizing on goals emphasizes the analysis of goal implementation and thereby neglects the analysis of conditions and processes that stimulate the setting of goals. In this chapter I have presented a theory of fantasy realization that attempts to ameliorate this neglect. I have suggested that both indulging in positive fantasies about the future and dwelling on negative aspects of the impeding reality hinder the formation of strong goal commitments. People need to contrast mentally their positive fantasies about the future with negative aspects of the impeding reality to experience a necessity to act, which in turn leads to the formation of binding behavioral goals when expectations of success are high.

Experimental research on the mastery of developmental tasks across the life span supports these hypotheses. No matter whether fantasies related to developmental tasks of childhood, adolescence, or young adulthood were analyzed, and no matter whether these tasks belonged to the achievement domain, the interpersonal domain, or the realm of life management, the pattern of results always turned out to be the same: For participants who held high expectations of success, contrasting positive developmental fantasies with negative aspects of the impeding reality led to strong commitments to behavioral goals in the service of achieving the developmental tasks in question. In contrast, both indulging in positive future fantasies and dwelling on the negative reality failed to create strong goal commitments, even when expectations of success were high.

The theoretical implications of these findings pertain to expectancy effects on behavior. I have argued that expectancy effects on behavior are not as pervasive as assumed in the relevant literature. For expectancy effects to occur, people need to give up on indulging in positive fantasies or dwelling on the negative reality and instead engage in mentally contrasting their positive fantasies with negative aspects of the impeding reality. Furthermore, fantasy realization theory offers a conceptual solution to the optimism versus realism debate, as it distinguishes between two forms of thinking about the future: expectancy judgments and free fantasies.

With respect to the applied implications, I have provided examples of how indulging in positive fantasies and dwelling on the negative reality hinder successful personality development. People turn blind to their expectations of success and thereby become disconnected from the biological, sociocultural, and individual (nonnormative) factors influencing personal growth. Finally, I have pointed out that the common educational interventions geared toward promoting the mastery of developmental tasks are incomplete, as they predominantly focus on strengthening relevant expectations. Complementing these interventions, educators should encourage people to contrast their developmental fantasies mentally with aspects of the impeding reality in order to ensure that they commit themselves to relevant behavioral goals and thus actively approach the mastery of pending developmental tasks.

REFERENCES

Asendorpf, J. B., & Ostendorf, F. (1998). Is self-enhancement healthy? Conceptual, psychometric and empirical analysis. *Journal of Personality and Social Psychology, 74,* 955-966.

Baltes, P. B., & Baltes, M. M. (1990). Psychological perspectives on successful aging: The model of selective optimization with compensation. In P. B. Baltes & M. M. Baltes (Eds.), *Successful aging: Perspectives from the behavioral sciences* (pp. 1-34). New York: Cambridge University Press.

Baltes, P. B., Lindenberger, U., & Staudinger, U. M. (1998). Life-span theory in developmental psychology. In W. Damon (Series Ed.) & R. M. Lerner (Vol. Ed.), *Handbook of child psychology: Vol. 1. Theoretical models of human development* (5th ed., pp. 1029-1143). New York: John Wiley.

Bandura, A. (1977). Self-efficacy: Toward a unifying theory of behavioral change. *Psychological Review, 84,* 191-215.

Bandura, A. (1986). *Social foundations of thought and action: A social cognitive theory.* Englewood Cliffs, NJ: Prentice Hall.

Bandura, A. (1991). Self-regulation of motivation through anticipatory and self-reactive mechanisms. In R. Dienstbier (Ed.), *Nebraska Symposium on Motivation: Vol. 38. Perspectives on motivation* (pp. 69-164). Lincoln: University of Nebraska Press.

Bandura, A. (1997). *Self-efficacy: The exercise of control.* New York: W. H. Freeman.

Bandura, A., & Cervone, D. (1983). Self-evaluative and self-efficacy mechanisms governing the motivational effects of goal systems. *Journal of Personality and Social Psychology, 45,* 1017-1028.

Bandura, A., Cioffi, D., Taylor, C. B., & Brouillard, M. E. (1988). Perceived self-efficacy in coping with cognitive stressors and opioid activation. *Journal of Personality and Social Psychology, 55,* 479-488.

Bandura, A., & Schunk, D. H. (1981). Cultivating competence, self-efficacy, and intrinsic interest through proximal self-motivation. *Journal of Personality and Social Psychology, 41,* 586-598.

Betz, N. E., & Hackett, G. (1983). The relationship of mathematics self-efficacy expectations to the selection of science-based college majors. *Journal of Vocational Behavior, 23,* 329-345.

Brandtstädter, J. (1998). Action perspectives on human development. In W. Damon (Series Ed.) & R. M. Lerner (Vol. Ed.), *Handbook of child psychology: Vol. 1. Theoretical models of human development* (5th ed., pp. 807-863). New York: John Wiley.

Brandtstädter, J., & Rothermund, K. (1994). Self-percepts of control in middle and later adulthood: Buffering losses by rescaling goals. *Psychology and Aging, 9,* 265-273.

Brandtstädter, J., Wentura, D., & Greve, W. (1993). Adaptive resources of the aging self: Outlines of an emergent perspective. *International Journal of Behavioral Development, 16,* 232-349.

Brinkmann, J., Holder, C., Hurler, A., & Schultz-Gambard, J. (1998). *Positive Zukunftsphantasien und berufliches Engagement* [Positive fantasies and professional engagement]. Poster presented at the 41st Congress of the German Psychological Society, Dresden.

Brunstein, J. C. (1993). Personal goals and subjective well-being: A longitudinal study. *Journal of Personality and Social Psychology, 65,* 1061-1070.

Brunstein, J. C., Dangelmayer, G., & Schultheiss, O. C. (1996). Personal goals and social support in close relationships: Effects on relationship mood and marital satisfaction. *Journal of Personality and Social Psychology, 71,* 1006-1019.

Brunstein, J. C., Schultheiss, O. C., & Grässmann, R. (1998). Personal goals and emotional well-being: The moderating role of motive dispositions. *Journal of Personality and Social Psychology, 75,* 494-508.

Cantor, N., & Kihlstrom, J. F. (1987). *Personality and social intelligence.* Englewood Cliffs, NJ: Prentice Hall.

Carver, C. S., & Gaines, J. G. (1987). Optimism, pessimism, and postpartum depression. *Cognitive Therapy and Research, 11,* 449-462.

Carver, C. S., & Scheier, M. F. (1981). *Attention and self-regulation: A control-theory approach to human behavior.* New York: Springer.

Carver, C. S., & Scheier, M. F. (1982). Outcome expectancy, locus of attribution for expectancy, and self-directed attention as determinants of evaluations and performance. *Journal of Experimental Social Psychology, 18,* 184-200.

Carver, C. S., & Scheier, M. F. (1998). *On the self-regulation of behavior.* New York: Cambridge University Press.

Colvin, C. R., & Block, J. (1994). Do positive illusions foster mental health? An examination of the Taylor and Brown formulation. *Psychological Bulletin, 116,* 3-20.

Colvin, C. R., Block, J., & Funder, D. C. (1995). Overly positive self-evaluations and personality: Negative implications for mental health. *Journal of Personality and Social Psychology, 68,* 1152-1162.

Deci, E. L., & Ryan, R. M. (1991). A motivational approach to self: Integration in personality. In R. Dienstbier (Ed.), *Nebraska Symposium on Motivation: Vol. 38. Perspectives on motivation* (pp. 237-288). Lincoln: University of Nebraska Press.

Dreher, E., & Dreher, M. (1985). Entwicklungsaufgaben im Jugendalter: Bedeutsamkeit und Bewältigungskonzepte [Developmental tasks in adolescence: Importance and coping]. In D. Liepmann & A. Stiksrud (Eds.), *Entwicklungsaufgaben und Bewältigungsprobleme in der Adoleszenz* (pp. 56-70). Göttingen, Germany: Hogrefe.

Dreher, E., & Oerter, R. (1986). Children's and adolescents' conceptions of adulthood: The changing view of a crucial developmental task. In R. K. Silbereisen, K. Eyferth, & G. Rudinger (Eds.), *Development as action in context* (pp. 109-120). Berlin: Springer.

Dweck, C. S. (1996). Implicit theories as organizers of goals and behavior. In P. M. Gollwitzer & J. A. Bargh (Eds.), *The psychology of action: Linking cognition and motivation to behavior* (pp. 69-90). New York: Guilford.

Eagly, A. H., Ashmore, R. D., Makhijani, M. G., & Longo, L. C. (1991). What is beautiful is good, but . . . : A meta-analytic review of research on the physical attractiveness stereotype. *Psychological Bulletin, 110,* 107-128.

Emmons, R. A. (1986). Personal strivings: An approach to personality and subjective well-being. *Journal of Personality and Social Psychology, 51,* 1058-1068.

Emmons, R. A. (1996). Striving and feeling: Personal goals and subjective well-being. In P. M. Gollwitzer & J. A. Bargh (Eds.), *The psychology of action: Linking cognition and motivation to behavior* (pp. 313-337). New York: Guilford.

Ford, D. H., & Lerner, R. M. (1992). *Developmental systems theory: An integrative approach.* Newbury Park, CA: Sage.

Frauenförderung in der MPG: Aus dem Bericht des Vorsitzenden des Wissenschaftlichen Rates. (1995). *MPG-Spiegel, 2,* 18-20.

Friedman, S. L., & Scholnick, E. K. (Eds.). (1997). *The psychology of planning: Why, how, and when do we plan?* Mahwah, NJ: Lawrence Erlbaum.

Geiselman, R. E., Haight, N. A., & Kimata, L. G. (1984). Context effects in the perceived physical attractiveness of faces. *Journal of Experimental Social Psychology, 20,* 409-424.

Gollwitzer, P. M. (1996). The volitional benefits of planning. In P. M. Gollwitzer & J. A. Bargh (Eds.), *The psychology of action: Linking cognition and motivation to behavior* (pp. 287-312). New York: Guilford.

Gollwitzer, P. M., & Bargh, J. A. (Eds.). (1996). *The psychology of action: Linking cognition and motivation to behavior.* New York: Guilford.

Gollwitzer, P. M., & Moskowitz, G. B. (1996). Goal effects on action and cognition. In E. T. Higgins & A. W. Kruglanski (Eds.), *Social psychology: A handbook of basic principles* (pp. 361-399). New York: Guilford.

Hackett, G. (1995). Self-efficacy in career choice and development. In A. Bandura (Ed.), *Self-efficacy in changing societies* (pp. 232-258). New York: Cambridge University Press.

Harter, S. (1983). Developmental perspectives on the self-system. In P. H. Mussen (Series Ed.) & E. M. Hetherington (Vol. Ed.), *Handbook of child psychology: Vol. 4. Socialization, personality, and social development* (4th ed., pp. 275-385). New York: John Wiley.

Havighurst, R. J. (1972). *Developmental tasks and education.* New York: David McKay. (Original work published 1948)

Heckhausen, H. (1991). *Motivation and action.* Heidelberg: Springer.

Hegner, F., & Lakemann, U. (1989). Familienhaushalt und Erwerbstätigkeit [Family life and gainful employment]. In R. Nave-Herz & M. Markefka (Eds.), *Hand-*

buch der Familien- und Jugendforschung, Band 1: Familienforschung (pp. 491-511). Neuried, Germany: Luchterhand.

Higgins, E. T. (1996). Ideals, oughts, and regulatory focus. In P. M. Gollwitzer & J. A. Bargh (Eds.), *The psychology of action: Linking cognition and motivation to behavior* (pp. 91-114). New York: Guilford.

Hofstede, G. (1991). *Cultures and organizations: Software of the mind.* London: McGraw-Hill.

Janetzke, H. (1991. *Das phantasierte Selbst and seine Verwirklichung* [The fantasized self and its realization]. Unpublished master's thesis, Technical University. Berlin, Germany.

Kasser, T., & Ryan, R. M. (1993). A dark side of the American dream: Correlates of financial success as a central life aspiration. *Journal of Personality and Social Psychology, 65,* 410-422.

Klinger, E. (1987). Current concerns and disengagement from incentives. In F. Halisch & J. Kuhl (Eds.), *Motivation, intention, and volition* (pp. 337-347). Berlin: Springer.

Kuhl, J., & Beckmann, J. (Eds.). (1994). *Volition and personality: Action versus state orientation.* Seattle, WA: Hogrefe & Huber.

Lent, R. W., Lopez, F. G., & Bieschke, K. J. (1993). Predicting mathematics-related choice and success behaviors: Test of an expanded social cognitive model. *Journal of Vocational Behavior, 42,* 223-236.

Lewin, K. (1926). Vorsatz, Wille, und Bedürfnis [Intention, will, and need]. *Psychologische Forschung, 7,* 330-385.

Little, B. R. (1983). Personal projects: A rationale and method for investigation. *Environment and Behavior, 15,* 273-309.

Locke, E. A., & Latham, G. P. (1990). *A theory of goal setting and task performance.* Englewood Cliffs, NJ: Prentice Hall.

Lütkenhaus, P., & Bullock, M. (1991). The development of volitional skills. In M. Bullock (Ed.), *The development of intentional action: Cognitive, motivational, and interactive processes* (pp. 14-23). Basel: Karger.

Markus, H. R., & Kitayama, S. (1991). Culture and the self: Implications for cognition, emotion, and motivation. *Psychological Review, 98,* 224-253.

Nurmi, J.-E. (1992). Age differences in adult life goals, concerns, and their temporal extension: A life course approach to future-oriented motivation. *International Journal of Behavioral Development, 15,* 487-508.

Oerter, R. (1986). Developmental tasks through the life-span: A new approach to an old concept. In P. B. Baltes, D. L. Featherman, & R. M. Lerner (Eds.), *Life-span development and behavior* (Vol. 7, pp. 233-271). Hillsdale, NJ: Lawrence Erlbaum.

Oettingen, G. (1996). Positive fantasy and motivation. In P. M. Gollwitzer & J. A. Bargh (Eds.), *The psychology of action: Linking cognition and motivation to behavior* (pp. 236-259). New York: Guilford.

Oettingen, G. (1997). Culture and future thought. *Culture and Psychology, 3,* 353-381.

Oettingen, G. (1998). *Positive thinking about the future and its impact on health and love.* Manuscript submitted for publication.

Oettingen, G. (in press). Expectancy effects on behavior depend on self-regulatory thought. *Social Cognition.*

Oettingen, G., Hönig, G., & Pak, H. (1999). *Fantasy realization theory: Self-regulation of goal-directed behavior.* Manuscript in preparation.

Oettingen, G., Little, T. D., Lindenberger, U., & Baltes, P. B. (1994). Causality, agency, and control beliefs in East versus West Berlin children: A natural experiment on the role of context. *Journal of Personality and Social Psychology, 66,* 579-595.

Ogilvie, D. M., & Rose, K. M. (1995). Self-with-other representations and a taxonomy of motives: Two approaches to study persons. *Journal of Personality, 63,* 643-679.

Ouelette, J. A., & Wood, W. (1998). Habit and intention in everyday life: The multiple processes by which past behavior predicts future behavior. *Psychological Bulletin, 124,* 54-74.

Pervin, L. A. (Ed.). (1989). *Goal concepts in personality and social psychology.* Hillsdale, NJ: Lawrence Erlbaum.

Rapkin, B. D., & Fischer, K. W. (1992). Framing the construct of life satisfaction in terms of older adults' personal goals. *Psychology and Aging, 7,* 138-149.

Scheier, M. F., & Carver, C. S. (1987). Dispositional optimism and physical well-being: The influence of generalized outcome expectancies on health. *Journal of Personality, 55,* 169-210.

Scheier, M. F., & Carver, C. S. (1992). Effects of optimism on psychological and physical well-being: Theoretical overview and empirical update. *Cognitive Therapy and Research, 16,* 201-228.

Schunk, D. H. (1989). Self-efficacy and cognitive skill learning. In C. Ames & R. Ames (Eds.), *Research on motivation in education: Goals and cognitions* (Vol. 3, pp. 13-44). San Diego, CA: Academic Press.

Schwarzer, R. (1992). Self-efficacy in the adoption and maintenance of health behaviors: Theoretical approaches and a new model. In R. Schwarzer (Ed.), *Self-efficacy: Thought control of action* (pp. 217-243). Washington, DC: Hemisphere.

Seligman, M. E. P. (1991). *Learned optimism.* New York: Alfred A. Knopf.

Shedler, J., Mayman, M., & Manis M. (1993). The illusion of mental health. *American Psychologist, 48,* 1117-1131.

Skinner, E. A., Chapman, M., & Baltes, P. B. (1988). Control, means-ends, and agency beliefs: A new conceptualization and its measurement during childhood. *Journal of Personality and Social Psychology, 54,* 117-133.

Stangor, C., & McMillan, D. (1992). Memory for expectancy-congruent and expectancy-incongruent information: A review of the social and social developmental literatures. *Psychological Bulletin, 111,* 42-61.

Statistisches Bundesamt. (1992). Bevölkerung und Erwerbstätigkeit [Population and gainful employment], Serie 1, Reihe 3. In *Veröffentlichungen des Statistischen Bundesamtes.* Stuttgart: Kohlhammer.

Taylor, S. E. (1989). *Positive illusions: Creative self-deception and the healthy mind.* New York: Basic Books.

Taylor, S. E., & Brown, J. D. (1988). Illusion and well-being: A social psychological perspective on mental health. *Psychological Bulletin, 103,* 193-210.

Taylor, S. E., & Brown, J. D. (1994). Positive illusions and well-being revisited: Separating fact from fiction. *Psychological Bulletin, 116,* 21-27.

Triandis, H. C. (1977). *Interpersonal behavior.* Monterey, CA: Brooks/Cole.

Triandis, H. C. (1980). Values, attitudes, and interpersonal behavior. In H. E. Howe, Jr., & M. M. Page (Eds.), *Nebraska Symposium on Motivation: Vol. 27. Beliefs, attitudes, and values* (pp. 195-259). Lincoln: University of Nebraska Press.

Triandis, H. C. (1995). *Individualism and collectivism.* Boulder, CO: Westview.

Wicklund, R. A., & Gollwitzer, P. M. (1982). *Symbolic self-completion.* Hillsdale, NJ: Lawrence Erlbaum.

Wood, R., & Bandura, A. (1989). Impact of conceptions of ability on self-regulatory mechanisms and complex decision making. *Journal of Personality and Social Psychology, 56,* 407-415.

Wright, R. A., & Brehm, J. W. (1989). Energization and goal attractiveness. In L. A. Pervin (Ed.), *Goal concepts in personality and social psychology* (pp. 169-210). Hillsdale, NJ: Lawrence Erlbaum.

Part III

RESILIENCE AND EFFICACY
ACROSS THE LIFE SPAN

12

PSYCHOLOGICAL CONTROL IN LATER LIFE

Implications for Life-Span Development

Helene H. Fung
Ronald P. Abeles
Laura L. Carstensen

Old age is associated with objective losses in physiological, cognitive, and behavioral functioning (for a review, see Rowe & Kahn, 1987) that are likely to weaken the perception of control (Schulz, Heckhausen, & O'Brien, 1994). In fact, many theorists and researchers hypothesize that sense of control declines in old age (e.g., Rodin, 1987; Thompson & Spacapan, 1991). Yet the overall literature on sense of control across the

AUTHORS' NOTE: Although this chapter was prepared as part of the duties of Ronald Abeles as an employee of the U.S. government, the opinions expressed are those of the authors and do not necessarily reflect the position or policy of the National Institute on Aging. Work by the third author of this chapter was supported by a grant from the National Institute on Aging (RO1-8816). We are grateful to Heather Miles for proofreading an earlier draft.

life span contains equivocal findings. There is evidence for decreasing, stable, and increasing sense of control with age (Lachman, 1986b; Rodin, Timko, & Harris, 1985). Many of these conflicting findings may stem from different definitions of *sense of control*. In this chapter, we attempt to shed light on the controversy by discussing a model that synthesizes the major components of sense of control (Abeles, 1991). We also review stability and change in sense of control in later life and speculate, based on the theoretical model, on the psychological processes that permit people to maintain a sense of control despite the many challenges to control that accompany aging.

SENSE OF CONTROL

The phrase *sense of control* is used as an umbrella to cover several related concepts, such as locus of control over reinforcements (Rotter, 1966), self-efficacy (Bandura, 1977), personal efficacy (Gurin, Gurin, & Morrison, 1978), perceived control (Skinner, Chapman, & Baltes, 1988), and learned helplessness (Seligman, 1975). Broadly speaking, *sense of control* refers to people's interrelated beliefs and expectancies about (a) their abilities to perform behaviors aimed at obtaining desired outcomes and (b) the responsiveness of the environment, both physical and social, to their behaviors. Assume that an older person wants to improve her health through a change in her diet. What role might sense of control play in her decision to engage in the behaviors necessary for changing her diet? First, she needs to know whether she is capable of performing the required steps associated with changing her eating habits (e.g., giving up favorite foods and substituting more healthy alternatives), which involves an assessment of her own abilities. Second, she needs to consider whether her husband will support and join her in making these dietary changes, which concerns her evaluations of the social environment. Thus her sense of control entails specific beliefs and expectations about herself and her environment. Note that nothing has been said about her actual skills or the true nature of the environment. Our focus in this chapter is on *subjective* as opposed to *objective* control. The differences between actual abilities and true environmental contingencies on the one hand and a person's perceptions of those abilities and environmental characteristics on the other may be reasonably distinct. In this chapter, we address the latter.

A MODEL OF SENSE OF CONTROL

Figure 12.1 illustrates a model that synthesizes the central processes described in the literature about sense of control and schematizes their interrelations (Abeles, 1991). Four points about the model are noteworthy. First, the model refers primarily to internal, cognitive structures and processes. That is, it conceptualizes control in terms of *subjective* experiences within a person's mind. It is not a model of actual control, although many presumed antecedents and consequences are indeed external to the individual. Second, sense of control is not a unitary concept, but is composed of multiple component beliefs and expectations regarding self and the environment. Third, the model postulates that the pertinent psychological processes are dynamic and dialectical, reflected in a feedback loop from outcomes back to the hypothesized antecedents of sense of control. This loop implies that accumulating experiences result in both short-term and longer-term changes in sense of control as a person undergoes development and aging. Finally, the least elaborated or specified part of the diagram refers to the hypothesized antecedents of sense of control, which reflects the relative lack of research on antecedents.

As schematized in Figure 12.1, the model portrays the components of sense of control and their roles in influencing whether people will perform particular behaviors and how the results of those behaviors in turn influence sense of control. Sense of control consists of beliefs and expectations about the *self* and about the *environment*. According to this model, people's *self-beliefs* about their own abilities (e.g., skills) and capabilities (e.g., to exert effort) combine with *task beliefs* about the nature of the task (e.g., how difficult it is, whether it requires skill or luck) to produce their *self-efficacy expectations,* a sense of whether they could successfully perform the behaviors needed to achieve the particular desired outcomes.

Beliefs about the causal nature of the environment focus on whether people perceive the environment to be governed by "lawful" or "orderly" processes such that outcomes (e.g., "success" or "failure") are "contingent" upon people's behaviors as opposed to random forces (i.e., "noncontingent"). Environmental contingency may stem from physical rules (e.g., the laws of nature) or social rules (e.g., norms). People's believing that an environment is contingent does not necessarily mean that they believe they have control, because they may perceive their own outcomes as more contingent upon the behaviors of others than upon their own efforts. Beliefs about the causal nature of the environment also combine with task

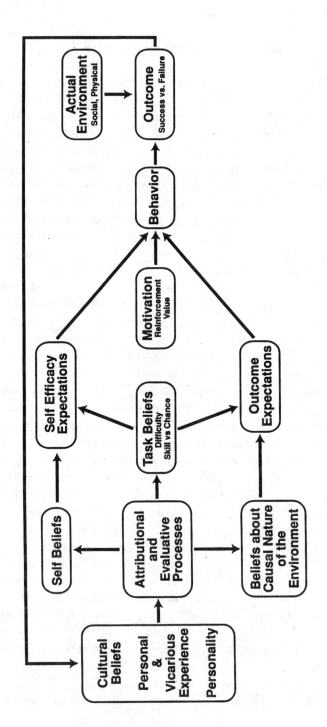

Figure 12.1. A Model of Sense of Control

beliefs to produce *outcome expectations* (i.e., whether performing action A is generally likely to result in outcome B). Thus people's sense of control consists of the complex interrelationships among their self-beliefs, self-efficacy expectations, beliefs about the causal nature of the environment, and outcome expectations.

Implicit in the model is the postulate that sense of control is modified by personal experience, as expressed by the feedback loop in Figure 12.1. Actual environment influences whether people achieve their desired outcomes, and people presumably reassess their own performance with reference to the reactions of others and to whether the desired outcomes are obtained. Such evaluative and attributional processes lead to adjustments in their sense of control through changes in beliefs and expectations about the self, the environment, or the task. Similarly, other people's experiences may affect sense of control through social comparison and reference group processes. As social psychologists have long pointed out (Festinger, 1954; Singer, 1980), people compare themselves to others in order to evaluate themselves and their performance, especially under ambiguous circumstances. For example, if other people with perceived similar levels of skill also fail, then people may be more likely to ascribe their own failure to external factors, such as the difficulty of the task or interference by powerful others. Conversely, when similar others succeed, they are more likely to interpret their own failure as reflecting something about themselves (e.g., lack of effort or skill).

Furthermore, general cultural beliefs influence the beliefs and expectations constituting sense of control (Abeles, 1990; Atchley, 1991). Cultures provide elaborate belief systems (e.g., science, religion) for explaining how both the social and physical worlds operate and about the appropriate means for achieving desired outcomes, including whether particular outcomes are contingent or noncontingent upon people's behaviors. In addition, through stereotypes, cultures also provide information about the personal characteristics of culturally defined categories of people. For example, stereotypes about people of different ages, such as ageism (Butler, 1975; Crockett & Hummert, 1987), may influence both how older people interpret and evaluate their own abilities and the interpretations and evaluations of others, which in turn may affect their sense of control.

Finally, although it may not be obvious from Figure 12.1, people may have more than a single generalized sense of control, in that they may have beliefs and expectations specific to many different behavioral domains (e.g., self-care, health, interpersonal, intellectual behaviors). One can envision reasonably independent feedback loops for specific behavioral domains, along with a generalized sense of control reflecting some sort of weighted average of the domain-specific sense of control (Paulhus & Christie, 1981).

SENSE OF CONTROL AND AGING

Age-Related Constraints on Sense of Control

Aging is related to declines in biological, cognitive, and social reserve capacity (Baltes & Baltes, 1990; Schulz, Heckhausen, & Locher, 1991). Although age may be associated with maintenance of or even gains in pragmatic knowledge (Baltes, 1993; Schaie, 1993) and emotional regulation (Carstensen, Gross, & Fung, 1997), age-related impairments (e.g., worsening eyesight and diminishing stamina) are believed to prevent older individuals from exercising control in many domains (Schulz et al., 1994). Increasing disability may lead to fewer choices in the activities that frail older people can engage in because of decreased mobility, dexterity, stamina, alertness, or social integration (Harris & Kovar, in press; Rowland, 1989). For such people, obtaining desired goals may become increasingly less contingent on their own behaviors and increasingly contingent upon the behaviors of family, friends, and health care providers. At the same time, the environment may become less sensitive to the impaired older person's desires and more responsive to those of the caretakers, who are in the position to organize the physical, temporal, and social environment according to their own needs (e.g., the scheduling of meals, baths).

In addition, the social environment may be less likely to provide constructive feedback because of diminished social contacts or because of caretakers who reinforce dependent behaviors (Baltes & Reisenzein, 1986; Baltes & Wahl, 1992a; Taylor, 1979; Timko & Rodin, 1985; Wills, 1978). Observational studies in American and German nursing homes have revealed that dependent behaviors of residents are almost always reinforced by supportive behaviors of social partners (Baltes & Reisenzein, 1986). The term *dependence support script*, a behavioral sequence in which dependence leads to social contact whereas independence does not, occurs more frequently than any other behavioral sequence. Constructively engaged behaviors of nursing home residents, such as writing letters or dressing themselves, are most frequently ignored by staff. It should be noted that these conditioning patterns are not found in homes for children, so they cannot be attributed exclusively to the rigid structure of institutional settings or needs of the residents. Even among community-dwelling older people, dependent behaviors are disproportionately reinforced by social partners (Baltes & Wahl, 1992b). Independent behaviors, in contrast, are supported only one-third of the time. Whether these patterns lead to learned helplessness (Seligman, 1975) or learned dependence (Baltes, 1995) among older people is under debate, but they certainly do not facilitate sense of control.

Moreover, ageism limits sense of control in a wide range of other settings (for a comprehensive review, see Pasupathi, Carstensen, & Tsai, 1995). Physicians show less patience and respect to their older clients in comparison with their younger clients (Greene, Adelman, Charon, & Friedmann, 1989; Greene, Adelman, Charon, & Hoffman, 1986). They direct fewer open-ended questions, give less detailed information, and provide less support to their older patients (Greene et al., 1986). Such condescending attitudes are also found among children and college students. Isaacs and Bearison (1986) asked children ages 4, 6, and 8 years to work on a jigsaw puzzle with either an older or younger confederate. They found that the children sat farther away from, made less eye contact with, spoke less to, initiated less conversation with, and asked for less help from the older confederate. Similarly, college students who were asked to explain a game to a hypothetical listener spoke fewer words when they believed that the listener was an older adult than when they believed that the listener was a younger or middle-aged adult (Rubin & Brown, 1975). Even when speaking to their own grandparents, college students have been found to use speech that was rated as of a higher pitch and more feminine, deferential, and unpleasant than when they spoke to their parents (Montepare, Steinberg, & Rosenberg, 1992).

Indeed, empirical studies suggest that the degree of sense of control supported in earlier phases of the life course may not be encouraged in late adulthood. Schulz and Hanusa (1979) provide support for this claim in their examination of the effects of competence (self-efficacy in our model) and control (outcome expectations in our model) on functioning among older adults. These researchers manipulated competence by providing positive (high competence) or ambiguous (low competence) feedback on cognitive and social tasks. They manipulated control by making (high control) or not making (low control) payment for the experiment appear to be contingent on participants' performance. Their original hypothesis was that older adults who were made to feel both competent and in control would have better functioning than those who were made to feel either competent or in control alone. This hypothesis was disconfirmed. Older adults who were made to feel *either* competent or in control had more positive changes in health status and greater staff-rated zest for life than did those who were made to feel both ways. Schulz and Hanusa explain this unexpected finding by suggesting that increasing both perceived competence and contingency may have raised sense of control to a level that the environment of older people could no longer support. To shed light on this explanation, they replicated their study with college students, a population whose environment provides many opportunities for exercising control. Indeed, college students who were made to feel both competent and in control did have better functioning than those who were only made to feel either way.

In summary, observational and experimental studies suggest that old age is associated with social conditions inconducive to a strong sense of control. With aging, forces within and outside of the person are likely to lead to a diminishing sense of control. The physical and cognitive declines that accompany old age and the internalization of negative age stereotypes are believed to attack the older person's self-beliefs and self-efficacy expectations (Lachman, 1983; Lachman & Jelalian, 1984; Lachman & McArthur, 1986). Simultaneously, interactions with health care and social service providers who reward dependent behaviors more than they do independent behaviors and with younger people who treat them as though they are less capable may undermine older persons' beliefs about the contingent nature of the environment and associated outcome expectations. It is thus not surprising that most analysts postulate that sense of control increases throughout childhood into adulthood and decreases in old age (Brim, 1974; Rodin, 1987).

Age Changes in Sense of Control

Despite strong logical and theoretical reasons for sense of control to diminish in old age, empirical evidence is equivocal. Evidence for decreasing, stable, and increasing sense of control is found in the literature (Lachman, 1986b; Rodin et al., 1985). Researchers who measure locus of control have found that people over 55 or 60 years old had lower levels of internality than did younger people (Brim, 1974; Lao, 1975). One longitudinal study also found that internality decreased with age (Gatz, Siegler, & Tyler, 1986; Siegler & Gatz, 1985). However, other studies have not found any age differences in locus of control (Brown & Granick, 1983; Hunter, Linn, Harris, & Pratt, 1980; Krantz & Stone, 1978; Kuypers, 1972; Lachman, 1986a; Nehrke, Hulicka, & Morganti, 1980). Still others have found age to be associated with increased internality (Gatz & Siegler, 1981; Rotella & Bunker, 1978; Staats, 1974; Wolk & Kurtz, 1975). Yet the only longitudinal study that has found an increase in internality with age suggests that the finding may simply reflect a time of measurement effect (Gatz & Karel, 1993).

Other researchers postulate that sense of control is a multidimensional construct and conduct studies that capture three sources of control: internal, powerful others, and chance. Findings from this approach, however, are also equivocal. Saltz and Magruder-Habib (1982) found that older people were less internal on the chance dimension than were younger people, but they found no age difference on the other two dimensions. In contrast, Lachman (1983), who measured locus of control among older people over a 2-year period, found a decline in internal control, but no change in the other two dimensions.

Apart from locus of control, age changes in other components of sense of control are less well researched, and findings from the few existing studies do not provide a coherent picture. A cross-sequential study found no age change in personal efficacy over a 4-year period, but revealed an age difference such that older adults were higher in personal efficacy than middle-aged adults (Lachman, 1985, as cited in Lachman, 1986b). In contrast, a study on attributional style found that older adults were more likely to attribute bad events to stable and specific factors than were their younger counterparts (Lachman & Leff, 1989).

In retrospect, the lack of empirical clarity should not come as a surprise. Given that sense of control is conceived as having several components and as domain specific, the reliance on generalized measures is likely to meet with failure. As the tenets of the life-course perspective remind us (Abeles, 1987; Baltes & Reese, 1984; Riley & Abeles, 1982), it is entirely possible that domain-specific sense of control may have differing age-related trajectories and that the various components of sense of control may similarly show varying patterns of change. Indeed, when findings are grouped according to domains, a more consistent pattern emerges. Compared with younger people, older people have lower internal locus of control in the physical and health domains (unidimensional, Bradley & Webb, 1976; internal control, Lachman, 1991; powerful others, Lachman, 1986a; Saltz & Magruder-Habib, 1982). In the intellectual domain, although older people maintain the same levels of internal locus of control (Bradley & Webb, 1976; Lachman & Leff, 1989), their beliefs in control by powerful others increase (Lachman & Leff, 1989). There is no age difference in locus of control in the interpersonal or political domains (Lachman, 1991).

MAINTAINING SENSE OF CONTROL

The overall impression derived from this literature is that sense of control is, for the most part, stable well into old age. It is intriguing to examine how this is accomplished in face of the "slings and arrows of outrageous fortune" that may accompany aging (Atchley, 1991). In this section, we turn to the theoretical model in Figure 12.1 for some guidance about the processes that may enable older people to maintain their sense of control.

Domain Specificity

As mentioned above, one important postulate of the model is that there is more than one generalized sense of control; rather, there are many senses of control specific to different domains. In other words, sense of control in old age may not rest on global control beliefs, but on the belief that one can obtain domain-specific desired goals (Bandura, 1997). This is particularly plausible in view of the fact that sense of control in one domain appears to be relatively independent of sense of control in other domains. Studies on sense of control in later life have found little consistency in perceived control across different event contexts (Gatz et al., 1986) and low moment-to-moment correlation of subjective control and affective states (Larson, 1989).

Moreover, sense of control is related to satisfaction in different domains among people of different ages (Huyck, 1991). For men, a general sense of control is associated with experiences in work. However, for middle-aged men, such a sense of control is related to satisfaction with health, whereas for older men it is related to both health and investment in marriage. For women, a general sense of control is correlated with satisfaction with mothering and investment in health among middle-aged women, yet it is related to satisfaction with marriage, health, and leisure among older women. Maintaining sense of control seems to rely on the individual's having satisfaction in selected domains that are central to the specific life contexts.

The self-affirmation literature provides some insight into how people can maintain a general sense of control through obtaining control in specific domains. According to self-affirmation theory, people need to feel as though they are competent and worthy individuals. When a threat to this belief occurs, a person can resolve the discrepancy by affirming self-relevant (i.e., important) aspects, even though these aspects are unrelated to the source of the threat (Steele, Spenser, & Lynch, 1993). Applying this to the control literature, it makes sense to find that people can maintain sense of control by feeling in control of a handful of important domains. In fact, many theorists define sense of control as "the perception that salient or valued aspects of life are manageable" (Wallhagen, 1992-1993, p. 219), not as feeling in control of everything. Thus, although old age is associated with many challenges that can hamper sense of control in some domains, older people can maintain their general sense of control by getting satisfaction in the handful of selected domains that are important to them. Supporting this claim, empirical findings suggest that the degree to which a domain-specific sense of control affects the general sense of control depends on the "personal importance" of that domain (Brandtstädter & Rothermund, 1994, p. 265).

Self-Beliefs, Task Beliefs, and Self-Efficacy Expectations

Old age, despite placing many constraints on control-related activities, facilitates the maintenance of control in personally important domains. Old age is a life stage in which many life tasks have been completed. Older people are freed from such social roles as full-time worker and parent. There is reduced social pressure to exercise control in areas that are not personally significant. Moreover, because time and resources are limited, older people may be motivated to concentrate on goals that truly matter, making it easier for them to achieve sense of control in those domains. This theme of selection is echoed in the literatures on possible selves, developmental tasks, and goal salience.

In general, compared with younger people, older people seem to have fewer self-facets and to care more about maintaining their current self-facets than taking up new ones. In a study in which adults were asked to describe their hoped-for and feared possible selves, Cross and Markus (1991) found that older adults had fewer hoped-for and feared possible selves than did their younger counterparts. Moreover, their hoped-for selves were centered on maintaining current levels of functioning, such as "being able to be active and healthy for another decade at least," whereas younger adults focused on more abstract and distant goals, such as "marrying the right person" (pp. 236-237). Likewise, in asking young, middle-aged, and older adults to describe their present, past, future, and ideal self-perceptions, Ryff (1989, 1991) found that older people scored lower on personal growth ("see[ing] self as growing and expanding") but higher on environmental mastery ("hav[ing] a sense of mastery and competence in managing the environment"; Ryff, 1991, p. 288). In addition, she found a closer fit between older people's ideal and present self-perceptions than between those of younger people (Ryff, 1991).

The literature on developmental tasks reaches similar conclusions. When asked to complete sentences starting with "In the coming years . . . ," older adults expressed greater concern about maintaining achieved levels of functioning and satisfaction, whereas younger adults focused more on improvements in domains such as education, career, family building, and finances (Dittmann-Kohli & Westerhof, 1997). Indeed, some researchers suggest that due to age-related losses, older people shift their concern from "transforming developmental circumstances in accordance with personal preferences" (assimilative tendency) to "adjusting personal preferences to situational constraints" (accommodative tendency) (Brandtstädter & Baltes-Götz, 1990). Consistent with this claim, empirical evidence shows that older people are less likely than younger people to exhibit tenacious goal pursuit and more likely to endorse flexible goal adjustment (Brandtstädter & Renner, 1990).

Carstensen and her colleagues explain the goal shifts in terms of changes in goal salience rather than age-related losses (e.g., Carstensen & Freund, 1994). Focusing on the social domain, Carstensen (1993, 1995, 1998; Carstensen, Isaacowitz, & Charles, 1999) proposes that the same set of essential goals operates throughout life, but the relative salience of specific goals changes as a function of a person's perception of time (as restricted or expansive), which is inextricably linked to chronological age. The theory focuses on two broad classes of social motives that follow different developmental trajectories: the knowledge trajectory and the emotion trajectory. The knowledge trajectory is future oriented and stimulates social contact most when funds of knowledge are limited and people are allocating considerable resources to maximizing preparedness for the future. The goals subsumed under the knowledge trajectory include information seeking, social comparison, identity striving, and achievement motivation. In contrast, the emotion trajectory is more present oriented. It includes motives to feel good, derive emotional meaning from life, deepen intimacy, and maintain the self. The essential premise of the theory is that people appreciate the concept of "time" and monitor the temporal course of their lives. As people grow older, events such as the birth of a grandchild and the death of a peer make them perceive time as limited, and they focus more on the here and now than on the distant future. As a result, emotional goals, given their more immediate payoffs, gain primacy over knowledge-related ones. This change in priority is reflected in many areas. In the social area, when compared with their younger counterparts, older people have social networks that are smaller but are more emotionally close (Fung, Carstensen, & Lang, in press; Lang & Carstensen, 1994; Lang, Staudinger, & Carstensen, 1998). In the cognitive area, older people remember less information overall but recollect proportionately more emotional information than do younger people (Carstensen & Turk-Charles, 1994).

Taken as a whole, the literature on self-beliefs, developmental tasks, and goals in old age suggests that older people care more about maintaining and maximizing control in a few highly important domains, such as relationships with emotionally close social partners, than about expanding their horizons. In lay terms, they may try to avoid "spreading themselves too thin" (Abraham & Hansson, 1995). This selection may be one reason older adults are, in general, able to maintain their sense of control despite age-related challenges.

Attributional and Evaluative Process, Beliefs About Causality, and Outcome Expectancies

Attempts to maintain a strong sense of control can also take place in the attributional and evaluative process. Individuals can fend off assaults against their sense of control through lesser desire for control, shifting standards of comparison, and common attributional biases, such as attributing positive outcomes to stable and internal causes and negative ones to unstable or external causes. Older people, with their greater emphasis on emotions, use these strategies more often than do their younger counterparts.

To fulfill their primary goal of emotional regulation, older people may have less desire for control in areas that are emotionally negative. In a survey conducted with community adults, Smith, Woodward, Wallston, and Wallston (1988) found that desire for health-related control was lower among older than among younger people. Similarly, a study on patients who were about to undergo medical procedures ranging from barium enemas to chemotherapy or surgery found that older adults reported less desire for control over their care and greater belief in the controlling ability of powerful others than did younger adults. Rather than lowering the general sense of control, we argue that, on the contrary, this reduced desire for control in emotion-threatening areas enables older people to gain satisfaction in the emotional domain that is of primary importance to them, and thus contributes to the maintenance of their sense of control.

Possibly because of their greater emphasis on emotions, older people have fewer negative emotional experiences and greater emotional control than do their younger counterparts (Carstensen et al., 1997; Gross et al., 1997). This age-related gain appears to protect older people from negative events that may reduce their sense of control. Taking responsibility is generally believed to be vital to a sense of control. Indeed, among the general adult population (people aged 18-85 years), feeling less responsible for good outcomes, bad outcomes, or both is associated with depression (Mirowsky & Ross, 1990). However, older people seem to be immune to this threat. Responsibility for loneliness has been found to have no relationship to the psychological well-being of older adults (Andersson, 1992). Gatz et al. (1986) also found the same results. They distinguished between two types of responsibility: *locus of control-event* (perceived responsibility for the occurrence of events) and *locus of control-handle* (perceived responsibility for the way events were coped with, managed, or handled). In a study of middle-aged and older adults, they found that the older the person, the less likely he or she was to consider perception of responsibility for negative events and perception of not being in control of negative events to have any bearing on self-evaluation of coping effectiveness.

Having greater emotional control also allows older people to gain control by carefully selecting their standards of comparison (Frey & Ruble, 1990; Taylor & Lobel, 1989). In fact, in part because people expect old age to be a time of loss, older people often see themselves as faring better than most other people or surpassing their own expectations of old age. Indeed, older people exhibit self-enhancement—seeing themselves as having more desirable and fewer undesirable attributes than most other people—to a greater extent than do their younger counterparts (Heckhausen & Krueger, 1993). They also tend to limit their standard of comparison to age peers (Gurin & Brim, 1984). This strategy is facilitated by the age-graded social system. For example, according to Gurin and Brim (1984), many athletic events have age categories that allow older age-mates to compete among themselves. A sense of efficacy is maintained as long as older people perceive themselves as relatively better off than their age-mates, even in the face of declines in actual capability (Bandura, 1997; Bandura & Jourden, 1991).

Moreover, the elderly often use strategies that regulate emotions, such as reframing events, seeing things from a positive angle, and detaching oneself from stressors, to maintain control. Secondary control (Heckhausen & Schulz, 1995; Rothbaum, Weisz, & Synder, 1982), flexible goal adjustment (Brandtstädter & Renner, 1990), and emotion-focused coping (Lazarus, 1993) reflect these strategies. Older adults are more likely to endorse items such as "I usually find something positive even after giving up something I cherish" (Brandtstädter & Renner, 1990). Older people are also more likely than younger people to use detachment as a coping strategy. They are more likely than their younger counterparts to agree with statements such as "Detachment or cool judgment is my best way to meet most life situations" (Lawton, Kleban, Rajagopal, & Dean, 1992). Empirical evidence suggests that this strategy is effective in protecting the general sense of control. A longitudinal study has shown that losses of control in a specific domain have a less adverse effect on the general sense of control when the importance of the domain is "downscaled" during the period (Brandtstädter & Rothermund, 1994, p. 265).

Furthermore, in hypothetical situations that are less instrumental and more emotionally salient, such as moving to a new town and taking care of an older parent, older adults are more likely than younger adults to use emotion-focused problem-solving styles such as "learn[ing] to live with infrequent visits" (Blanchard-Fields, Jahnke, & Camp, 1995). In fact, when coping styles were examined across a variety of stressful contexts, older people were found to report fewer confrontational coping strategies and greater distancing and positive reappraisal than their younger counterparts (Folkman, Lazarus, Pimley, & Novacek, 1987). According to Folkman and her collaborators (1987), these styles may help to "short circuit the stress process, so that incidents that might otherwise have been hassles were neutralized" (p. 182). From the perspective of sense of control, we argue that these cognitive styles may help older people maintain sense of control by neutralizing events that would otherwise be threatening.

Behavior

Of course, older people can maintain their sense of control through direct actions aimed at achieving their domain-specific goals (Bandura, 1997). This form of control is captured by constructs such as primary control (Heckhausen & Schulz, 1995), tenacious goal pursuit (Brandt-städter & Renner, 1990), and problem-solving coping (Lazarus, 1993). With the notable exception of Brandtstädter and Renner (1990), most researchers have found this type of control to be stable throughout adulthood (Blanchard-Fields et al., 1995; Heckhausen & Schulz, 1995).

In addition, older people can join together to change the aging environment, making it more conducive to sense of control (Bandura, 1997; also, A. Bandura, personal communication, April 24, 1997). Organizations such as the Gray Panthers have been founded based on this aim. The child development literature provides some clues about the environmental conditions that facilitate sense of control. Children and adolescents are likely to develop a positive sense of control when the environment is characterized as offering (a) choice as opposed to constraint and as being (b) contingent, (c) sensitive to one's goals and desires, and (d) supportive (i.e., providing constructive feedback) (Skinner, 1995). When older adults are placed in cognitive training situations with these same characteristics, they demonstrate increases in their cognitive performance and their sense of control over those cognitive tasks (Baltes & Willis, 1982; Dittman-Kohli, Lachman, Kliegl, & Baltes, 1991; Schaie & Willis, 1986).

In fact, even simple environmental improvements can increase sense of control. One must not lose sight of the fact that "disability is a gap between a person's capability and the environment's demands" (Verbrugge, 1990, p. 55). As such, functioning can be retained or improved by changes in the environment as well as in the person (Kiyak, 1992). For example, although increasing difficulties in walking may diminish an older person's feelings of self-efficacy, being provided with a cane or wheelchair or participating in a strength-building exercise program may restore some lost mobility and simultaneously provide a boost to the older person's sense of control (Spirduso & Gilliam-MacRae, 1991).

Furthermore, sense of control in old age can also be achieved through environmental selection: carefully choosing the social environments one places oneself in, so as to maximize experiences that foster sense of control and to minimize those that threaten it. Carstensen (1992) reports that aging is associated with an active pruning of the social network such that peripheral members, such as acquaintances, are dropped and core members, such as spouses and children, are retained. Lawton et al. (1992) also found that, compared with middle-aged and young adults, older adults were more likely to endorse the statement "I choose activities carefully so as to give me just the right amount of emotional stimulation, neither too much nor too little" (p. 175). In this fashion, through careful planning, older persons limit their experiences to those that are familiar, predictable, and positive, precisely those that foster sense of control. They also actively avoid experiences that are unpredictable and likely to be negative—that is, those that may threaten sense of control.

Moreover, individuals can achieve sense of control by enlisting the participation of others in their goal pursuits. Indeed, older people can maintain their sense of control by getting "those who wield influence and power to act on their behalf to effect the changes they desire" (Bandura, 1997, p. 17). This type of control is known as proxy (Bandura, 1997) or vicarious control (Rothbaum et al., 1982). In a study of nursing home residents, Shaw (1992) found that indirect actions such as getting help from family and depending on others (which she calls secondary control) had positive influence on the coping effectiveness of the residents—which, we argue, contributes to an intact sense of control.

Other evidence also suggests that older people can use this type of control without compromising their sense of control (Shapiro, Sandman, Grossman, & Grossman, 1995). Lachman and Leff (1989) found in a longitudinal study of the elderly that although beliefs in powerful others' control over intelligence increased over a 5-year period, there were no accompanying changes in generalized control beliefs, perceived internal control over intelligence, or intellectual functioning among the elderly. In the same vein, Stine, Lachman, and Wingfield (1993) found that when given the opportunity to take actual control of the input conditions of record narratives before a memory test, older people were more likely than younger people to relinquish control to the experimenter (i.e., letting the experimenter set the input conditions). Importantly, this occurred when there was only minimal age difference in perceived control, suggesting that sense of control in old age is not necessarily compromised when control is not exercised directly.

It should be noted that actions that may appear to relinquish control in one domain may achieve control in a more important domain and contribute to the general sense of control. For example, the older people in the Stine et al. (1993) study mentioned above might have been unwilling to take actual control of setting the input conditions because they attached far less importance to setting the input conditions than to avoiding negative emotions. When faced with the novel task of setting the input conditions, they might have preferred to relinquish the task and the related control to the experimenter rather than risk messing up the task and suffering the emotional costs. Because their actions (or lack of them) actually helped them to maintain control in the emotional domain that was of greater importance to them, it makes sense that their level of perceived control was maintained.

Likewise, in the face of a social environment that reinforces dependent behaviors and ignores independent behaviors (Baltes & Reisenzein, 1986; Baltes & Wahl, 1992b), it seems reasonable for those older people who value social support more than autonomy to engage in dependent behaviors. By doing so, they achieve satisfaction in a personally important domain and consequently maintain their general sense of control.

Life-span developmental theory describes such a process in eloquent terms. According to the model of selective optimization with compensation (Baltes & Baltes, 1990), selection is considered the hallmark of development. No one can control everything, and no one needs to control everything. Selection is essential in order to optimize performance. As people age, they increasingly concentrate their resources and efforts in selected domains and compensate for impairments by employing alternative means to achieve the same goals.

Bäckman and Dixon (1992) describe a similar process with the term *compensation*. To them, such a process involves responding to a discrepancy between perceived skills and environmental demands through improving existing skills, using substitute skills, and/or changing goals and aspirations. Salthouse's (1984) study of younger and older typists illustrates this process well. Salthouse found that older typists were slower in tapping rate and in reaction time, but they were not slower in the overall speed of typing. This was so because they compensated for their slower physical speed by reading further into the text before typing.

Interpreting the literature reviewed above in terms of this process, it seems plausible to suggest that people maintain a sense of control in old age by concentrating their limited resources on the few selected domains that are important to them and utilizing different means of control to achieve their desired goals in these areas.[1] Empirical findings support this claim. In a study of the job performance of middle-aged and older adults, Abraham and Hansson (1995) found that selection, optimization, and compensation through impression management were not related to performance maintenance or goal attainment (importance-weighted performance maintenance) among middle-aged workers. However, among older workers, selection and optimization were associated with maintenance and goal attainment, and compensation was related to goal attainment.

Outcome and Feedback Loop

Most important, older people may maintain their sense of control by keeping their control beliefs congruent with their environment. As we mentioned earlier, old age provides a set of conditions filled with challenges to the sense that one is in control. Older people may adapt to these conditions by defining sense of control differently from younger people. In particular, sense of control among older people does not mean that they obtain lofty goals; rather, they achieve goals within recognized boundaries (Brim, 1988). Indeed, when elderly caregivers were interviewed about what it means to feel in control, "staying within bounds" emerged as the overriding theme (Wallhagen & Kagan, 1993). Older people do not need to control all circumstances. Rather, they need to feel as though they are "on the average" in control. Larson (1989) asked people to report their subjective feelings of control at randomly selected moments. He found that although there was minimal moment-to-moment correlation of subjective control and affective states, high average daily control was associated with greater average happiness.

In fact, control beliefs may take on different meanings in old age (Blanchard-Fields & Irion, 1988). Internality is positively related to escape avoidance, hostile reactions, and self-blame among younger individuals, but is negatively related to them among older ones. Beliefs in powerful others are negatively related to planful problem solving and self-control among younger people, but positively related to them among older ones. Moreover, beliefs in chance are negatively related to distancing and self-control among younger adults but positively related to them among older adults. It seems as if various types of control beliefs can be beneficial to the elderly. The key to maintaining a sense of control in old age may be being resourceful—using different means of control according to the demands of the situation.

SUMMARY AND CONCLUSION: MORE THAN ONE ROAD LEADS TO ROME

Many roads lead to sense of control. Inconsistent findings in the literature on age changes in sense of control are probably due to the failure to assess control in domain-specific areas. The handful of domain-specific studies suggest that sense of control is largely well preserved into old age. This conclusion may seem puzzling at first glance in view of the various age-related losses that can pose challenges to sense of control. Based on a theoretical model that integrates the many components of sense of control, we have attempted to shed light on the psychological processes that enable older people to maintain control.

Sense of control in old age rests on individuals' achievement of satisfaction in important domains, not on their attainment of lofty goals. Although physical and cognitive declines, as well as ageism in society, may hamper older people's ability to achieve goals in general, these losses make older people acutely aware of the limitations of their resources and motivate them to be increasingly selective in their goal pursuits. As a result, older people in general are concerned more with maximizing goal fulfillment in a handful of personally important domains than with expanding their horizons. This selection makes maintaining control an easier task.

Like younger people, older people can maintain control directly by changing their environments, getting help, and employing compensatory devices and strategies. Such direct ways of control do not decline in old age. In addition, older individuals' better emotional control abilities (Carstensen et al. 1997; Gross et al., 1997) allow them to maximize sense of control through various alternative strategies, including lowering their goals in less personally important areas, changing standards of comparison, and reframing and detaching from negative events.

Most importantly, environment and goals change throughout life. So does the meaning of control. Actions that may signify loss of control in earlier life stages may facilitate control in old age. For example, whereas information-seeking goals are important to younger people, emotional goals are of primary importance to older people (Carstensen, 1993, 1995, 1998; Carstensen et al., 1999). Thus, although refusing to seek information about a potentially life-threatening medical condition does not match the goals of younger individuals and is detrimental to their sense of control, such an action may be in keeping with the primary goals of older people and conducive to their sense of control. Researchers need to be certain that they are assessing control over personally significant domains.

The overriding theme of this chapter is one of multidimensionality: Sense of control has many different components; the relationship between age and sense of control is different in different domains; and older people have different ways of maintaining sense of control. Recognition of domain specificity and potential goal changes across the life course is essential to an appreciation of the maintenance of sense of control throughout life.

NOTE

1. This is conceptually similar to the "learned resourcefulness" idea proposed by Rosenbaum (1983).

REFERENCES

Abeles, R. P. (1987). Introduction. In R. P. Abeles (Ed.), *Life-span perspectives and social psychology* (pp. 1-16). Hillsdale, NJ: Lawrence Erlbaum.

Abeles, R. P. (1990). Schemas, sense of control, and aging. In J. Rodin, C. Schooler, & K. W. Schaie (Ed.), *Self-directedness and efficacy: Causes and effects throughout the life course* (pp. 85-94). Hillsdale, NJ: Lawrence Erlbaum.

Abeles, R. P. (1991). Sense of control as a factor in the quality of life of the frail elderly. In J. E. Birren, J. E. Lubben, J. C. Rowe, & D. E. Deutchman (Eds.), *The concept and measurement of quality of life in the frail elderly* (pp. 297-314). San Diego, CA: Academic Press.

Abraham, J. D., & Hansson, R. O. (1995). Successful aging at work: An applied study of selection, optimization, and compensation through impression management. *Journals of Gerontology: Psychological Sciences, 50B*, 94-103.

Andersson, L. (1992). Loneliness and perceived responsibility and control in elderly community residents. *Journal of Social Behavior and Personality, 7*, 431-443.

Atchley, R. C. (1991). The influence of aging or frailty on perceptions and expressions of the self: Theoretical and methodological issues. In J. E. Birren, J. E. Lubben, J. C. Rowe, & D. E. Deutchman (Eds.), *The concept and measurement of quality of life in the frail elderly* (pp. 207-225). San Diego, CA: Academic Press.

Bäckman, L., & Dixon, R. A. (1992). Psychological compensation: A theoretical framework. *Psychological Bulletin, 112*, 259-283.

Baltes, M. M. (1995). Dependency in old age: Gains and losses. *Current Directions in Psychological Science, 4*, 14-18.

Baltes, M. M., & Reisenzein, R. (1986). The social world in long-term care institutions: Psychosocial control toward dependency? In M. M. Baltes & P. B. Baltes (Eds.), *The psychology of control and aging* (pp. 315-343). Hillsdale, NJ: Lawrence Erlbaum.

Baltes, M. M., & Wahl, H. W. (1992a). The behavior system of dependency in the elderly: Interaction with the social environment. In M. G. Ory, R. P. Abeles, & P. D. Lipman (Eds.), *Aging, health, and behavior* (pp. 83-106). Newbury Park, CA: Sage.

Baltes, M. M., & Wahl, H. W. (1992b). The dependency-support script in institutions: Generalization to community settings. *Psychology and Aging, 7*, 409-418.

Baltes, P. B. (1993). The aging mind: Potential and limits. *Gerontologist, 33*, 580-594.

Baltes, P. B., & Baltes, M. M. (1990). Psychological perspectives on successful aging: The model of selective optimization with compensation. In P. B. Baltes & M. M. Baltes (Eds.), *Successful aging: Perspectives from the behavioral sciences* (pp. 1-34). New York: Cambridge University Press.

Baltes, P. B., & Reese, H. W. (1984). The life-span perspective in developmental psychology. In M. H. Bornstein & M. E. Lamb (Ed.), *Developmental psychology: An advanced textbook* (pp. 493-531). Hillsdale, NJ: Lawrence Erlbaum.

Baltes, P. B., & Willis, S. L. (1982). Plasticity and enhancement of intellectual functioning in old age: Penn State's Adult Development and Enrichment Project (ADEPT). In F. I. M. Craik & S. E. Trehub (Eds.), *Aging and cognitive processes* (pp. 353-389). New York: Plenum.

Bandura, A. (1977). Self-efficacy: Toward a unifying theory of behavioral change. *Psychological Review, 84,* 191-215.

Bandura, A. (1997). *Self-efficacy: The exercise of control.* New York: W. H. Freeman.

Bandura, A., & Jourden, F. J. (1991). Self-regulatory mechanisms governing the impact of social comparison on complex decision making. *Journal of Personality and Social Psychology, 60,* 941-951.

Blanchard-Fields, F., & Irion, J. C. (1988). The relation between the locus of control and coping in two contexts: Age as a moderator variable. *Psychology and Aging, 3,* 197-203.

Blanchard-Fields, F., Jahnke, H. C., & Camp, C. (1995). Age differences in problem-solving style: The role of emotional salience. *Psychology and Aging, 10,* 173-180.

Bradley, R. H., & Webb, R. (1976). Age-related differences in locus of control orientation in three behavior domains. *Human Development, 19,* 49-55.

Brandtstädter, J., & Baltes-Götz, B. (1990). Personal control over development and quality of life perspectives in adulthood. In P. B. Baltes & M. M. Baltes (Eds.), *Successful aging: Perspectives from the behavioral sciences* (pp. 197-224). New York: Cambridge University Press.

Brandtstädter, J., & Renner, G. (1990). Tenacious goal pursuit and flexible goal adjustment: Explication and age-related analysis of assimilative and accommodative strategies of coping. *Psychology and Aging, 5,* 58-67.

Brandtstädter, J., & Rothermund, K. (1994). Self-percepts of control in middle and later adulthood: Buffering losses by rescaling goals. *Psychology and Aging, 9,* 265-273.

Brim, G. (1988, September). Losing and winning. *Psychology Today, 22,* 48-52.

Brim, O. G., Jr. (1974, September). *The sense of personal control over one's life.* Paper presented at the 82nd Annual Meeting of the American Psychological Association, New Orleans.

Brown, B. R., & Granick, S. (1983). Cognitive and psychosocial differences between I and E locus of control aged persons. *Experimental Aging Research, 9,* 107-110.

Butler, R. N. (1975). *Why survive? Being old in America.* New York: Harper & Row.

Carstensen, L. L. (1992). Social and emotional patterns in adulthood: Support for socioemotional selectivity theory. *Psychology and Aging, 7,* 331-338.

Carstensen, L. L. (1993). Motivation for social contact across the life-span: A theory of socioemotional selectivity. In J. E. Jacobs (Ed.), *Nebraska Symposium on Motivation: Vol. 40. Developmental perspectives on motivation* (pp. 209-254). Lincoln: University of Nebraska Press.

Carstensen, L. L. (1995). Evidence for a life-span theory of socioemotional selectivity. *Current Directions in Psychological Science, 4,* 151-156.

Carstensen, L. L. (1998). A life-span approach to social motivation. In J. Heckhausen & C. S. Dweck (Eds.), *Motivation and self-regulation across the life span* (pp. 341-364). New York: Cambridge University Press.

Carstensen, L. L., & Freund, A. (1994). The resilience of the aging self. *Developmental Review, 14,* 81-92.

Carstensen, L. L., Gross, J. J., & Fung, H. H. (1997). The social context of emotional experience. In K. W. Schaie & M. P. Lawton (Eds.), *Focus on emotion and adult development* (Vol. 17, pp. 325-352). New York: Springer.

Carstensen, L. L., Isaacowitz, D. M., & Charles, S. T. (1999). Taking time seriously: A theory of socioemotional selectivity. *American Psychologist, 54,* 165-181.

Carstensen, L. L., & Turk-Charles, S. (1994). The salience of emotion across the adult life span. *Psychology and Aging, 9,* 259-264.

Crockett, W. H., & Hummert, M. L. (1987). Perceptions of aging and the elderly. In K. W. Schaie (Ed.), *Annual review of gerontology and geriatrics* (pp. 217-241). New York: Springer.

Cross, S., & Markus, H. (1991). Possible selves across the life span. *Human Development, 34,* 230-255.

Dittmann-Kohli, F., Lachman, M. E., Kliegl, R., & Baltes, P. B. (1991). Effects of cognitive training and testing on intellectual efficacy beliefs in elderly adults. *Journals of Gerontology: Psychological Sciences, 46B,* 162-164.

Dittmann-Kohli, F., & Westerhof, G. J. (1997). The SELE-Sentence Completion Questionnaire: A new instrument for the assessment of personal meanings in aging research. *Anuario de Psicologia, 73,* 7-18.

Festinger, L. (1954). A theory of social comparison processes. *Human Relations, 7,* 117-140.

Folkman, S., Lazarus, R. S., Pimley, S., & Novacek, J. (1987). Age differences in stress and coping processes. *Psychology and Aging, 2,* 171-184.

Frey, K. S., & Ruble, D. N. (1990). Strategies for comparative evaluation: Maintaining a sense of competence across the lifespan. In R. J. Sternberg & J. Kolligan, Jr. (Eds.), *Competence considered* (pp. 167-189). New Haven, CT: Yale University Press.

Fung, H. H., Carstensen, L. L., & Lang, F. R. (in press). Age-related patterns in social networks among European-Americans and African-Americans: Implications for socioemotional selectivity across the life span. *International Journal of Aging and Human Development.*

Gatz, M., & Karel, M. J. (1993). Individual change in perceived control over 20 years. *International Journal of Behavioral Development, 16,* 305-322.

Gatz, M., & Siegler, I. C. (1981, August). *Locus of control: A retrospective.* Paper presented at the annual meeting of the American Psychological Association, Los Angeles.

Gatz, M., Siegler, I. C., & Tyler, F. B. (1986). Attributional components of locus of control: Longitudinal, retrospective, and contemporaneous analyses. In M. M. Baltes & P. M. Baltes (Eds.), *The psychology of control and aging* (pp. 237-263). Hillsdale, NJ: Lawrence Erlbaum.

Greene, M., Adelman, R., Charon, R., & Friedmann, E. (1989). Concordance between physicians and their older and younger patients in the primary care medical encounter. *Gerontologist, 29,* 808-813.

Greene, M., Adelman, R., Charon, R., & Hoffman, S. (1986). Ageism in the medical encounter: An exploratory study of the doctor-elderly patient relationship. *Language and Communication, 6,* 113-124.

Gross, J. J., Carstensen, L. C., Pasupathi, M., Tsai, J., Skorpen, C. G., & Hsu, A. Y. C. (1997). Emotion and aging: Changes in experience, expression, and control. *Psychology and Aging, 12,* 590-599.

Gurin, P., & Brim, O. G., Jr. (1984). Change in life in adulthood: The example of sense of control. In P. B. Baltes & O. G. Brim, Jr. (Eds.), *Life-span development and behavior* (Vol. 6, pp. 281-334). New York: Academic Press.

Gurin, P., Gurin, G., & Morrison, B. M. (1978). Personal and ideological aspects of internal and external control. *Social Psychology Quarterly, 41,* 275-296.

Harris, T., & Kovar, M. G. (in press). *National statistics on the functional status of older persons.* Washington, DC: National Center for Health Statistics.

Heckhausen, J., & Krueger, J. (1993). Developmental expectations for the self and "most other people": Age-grading in three functions of social comparison. *Developmental Psychology, 29,* 539-548.

Heckhausen, J., & Schulz, R. (1995). A life-span theory of control. *Psychological Review, 102,* 284-304.

Hunter, K. I., Linn, M. W., Harris, R., & Pratt, T. (1980). Discriminators of internal and external locus of control orientation in the elderly. *Research on Aging, 2,* 49-60.

Huyck, M. H. (1991). Predictors of personal control among middle-aged and young-old men and women in middle America. *International Journal of Aging and Human Development, 32,* 261-275.

Isaacs, L. W., & Bearison, D. J. (1986). The development of children's prejudice against the aged. *International Journal of Aging and Human Development, 23,* 175-194.

Kiyak, H. A. (1992). Coping with chronic illness and disability. In M. G. Ory, R. P. Abeles, & P. D. Lipman (Eds.), *Aging, health, and behavior* (pp. 141-173). Newbury Park, CA: Sage.

Krantz, D. S., & Stone, V. (1978). Locus of control and the effects of success and failure in young and community-residing aged women. *Journal of Personality, 46,* 536-551.

Kuypers, J. A. (1972). Internal-external locus of control, ego functioning, and personality characteristics in old age. *Gerontologist, 12,* 168-173.

Lachman, M. E. (1983). Perceptions of intellectual aging: Antecedent or consequence of intellectual functioning? *Developmental Psychology, 19,* 482-498.

Lachman, M. E. (1985). Personal efficacy in middle and old age: Differential and normative patterns of change. In G. H. Elder, Jr. (Ed.), *Life-course dynamics: Trajectories and transitions, 1968-1980.* Ithaca, NY: Cornell University Press.

Lachman, M. E. (1986a). Locus of control in aging research: A case for multidimensional and domain-specific assessment. *Journal of Psychology and Aging, 1,* 34-40.

Lachman, M. E. (1986b). Personal control in later life: Stability, change, and cognitive correlates. In M. M. Baltes & P. B. Baltes (Eds.), *The psychology of control and aging* (pp. 207-236). Hillsdale, NJ: Lawrence Erlbaum.

Lachman, M. E. (1991). Perceived control over memory aging: Developmental and intervention perspectives. *Journal of Social Issues, 47,* 159-175.

Lachman, M. E., & Jelalian, E. (1984). Self-efficacy and attributions for intellectual performance in young and elderly adults. *Journals of Gerontology: Psychological Sciences, 39B,* 577-582.

Lachman, M. E., & Leff, R. (1989). Perceived control and intellectual functioning in the elderly: A 5-year longitudinal study. *Developmental Psychology, 25,* 722-728.

Lachman, M. E., & McArthur, L. Z. (1986). Adulthood age differences in causal attributions for cognitive, physical, and social performance. *Psychology and Aging, 1,* 127-132.

Lang, F. R., & Carstensen, L. L. (1994). Close emotional relationships in late life: Further support for proactive aging in the social domain. *Psychology and Aging, 9,* 315-324.

Lang, F. R., Staudinger, U. M., & Carstensen, L. L. (1998). Perspectives on socioemotional selectivity in late life: How personality and social context do (and do not) make a difference. *Journals of Gerontology: Psychological Sciences, 53B,* 21-30.

Lao, R. C. (1975). The developmental trend of the locus of control. *Personality and Social Psychology Bulletin, 1,* 348-350.

Larson, R. (1989). Is feeling "in control" related to happiness in daily life? *Psychological Reports, 64,* 775-784.

Lawton, M. P., Kleban, M. H., Rajagopal, D., & Dean, J. (1992). The dimensions of affective experience in three age groups. *Psychology and Aging, 7,* 171-184.

Lazarus, R. S. (1993). Coping therapy and research: Past, present, and future. *Psychosomatic Medicine, 55,* 234-247.

Mirowsky, J., & Ross, C. E. (1990). Control or defense? Depression and the sense of control over good and bad outcomes. *Journal of Health and Social Behavior, 31,* 71-86.

Montepare, J., Steinberg, J., & Rosenberg, B. (1992). Characteristics of vocal communication between young adults and their parents and grandparents. *Communication Research, 19,* 479-492.

Nehrke, M. F., Hulicka, T. M., & Morganti, J. B. (1980). Age differences in life satisfaction, locus of control, and self-concept. *International Journal of Aging and Human Development, 11,* 25-33.

Pasupathi, M., Carstensen, L. L., & Tsai, J. L. (1995). The social construction of the disempowered elderly: Ageism in interpersonal settings. In B. Lott & D. Maluso (Eds.), *The social psychology of interpersonal discrimination* (pp. 160-182). New York: Guilford.

Paulhus, D., & Christie, R. (1981). Spheres of control: An interactionist approach to assessment of perceived control. In H. M. Lefcourt (Ed.), *Research with the locus of control construct: Vol. 1. Assessment methods* (pp. 161-188). New York: Academic Press.

Riley, M. W., & Abeles, R. P. (1982). Life-course perspectives. In M. W. Riley, R. P. Abeles, & M. S. Teitelbaum (Eds.), *Aging from birth to death: Vol. 2. Sociotemporal perspectives* (pp. 1-10). Boulder, CO: Westview.

Rodin, J. (1987). Personal control through the life course. In R. P. Abeles (Ed.), *Life-span perspectives and social psychology* (pp. 103-120). Hillsdale, NJ: Lawrence Erlbaum.

Rodin, J., Timko, C., & Harris, S. (1985). The construct of control: Biological and psychological correlates. In C. Eisdorfer, M. P. Lawton, & G. L. Maddox (Eds.), *Annual review of gerontology and geriatrics* (Vol. 5, pp. 3-55). New York: Springer.

Rosenbaum, M. (1983). Learned resourcefulness as a behavioral repertoire for the self-regulation of internal events: Issues and speculation. In M. Rosenbaum, C. M. Franks, & Y. Jaffe (Eds.), *Perspectives on behavioral therapy in the eighties* (pp. 54-73). New York: Springer.

Rotella, R. J., & Bunker, L. K. (1978). Locus of control and achievement motivation in the active aged (65 years and over). *Perceptual and Motor Skills, 46,* 1043-1046.

Rothbaum, F., Weisz, J. R., & Snyder, S. S. (1982). Changing the world and changing the self: A two-process model of perceived control. *Journal of Personality and Social Psychology, 42,* 5-37.

Rotter, J. B. (1966). Generalized expectancies for internal versus external control of reinforcements. *Psychological Monographs, 80*(1, Whole No. 609).

Rowe, J. W., & Kahn, R. L. (1987). Human aging: Usual and successful. *Science, 237,* 143-149.

Rowland, D. (1989). *Help at home: Long-term care assistance for impaired elderly people.* Washington, DC: Commonwealth Fund Commission on Elderly People Living Alone.

Rubin, K. H., & Brown, I. (1975). A life-span look at person perception and its relationship to communicative interaction. *Journals of Gerontology: Psychological Sciences, 30B,* 461-468.

Ryff, C. D. (1989). Happiness is everything, or is it? Explorations on the meaning of psychological well-being. *Journal of Personality and Social Psychology, 57,* 1069-1081.

Ryff, C. D. (1991). Possible selves in adulthood and old age: A tale of shifting horizons. *Psychology and Aging, 6,* 286-295.

Salthouse, T. A. (1984). Effects of age and skill in typing. *Journal of Experimental Psychology, 113,* 345-371.

Saltz, C., & Magruder-Habib, K. (1982, November). *Age as an indicator of depression and locus of control among non-psychiatric inpatients.* Paper presented at the annual meeting of the Gerontological Society of America, Boston.

Schaie, K. W. (1993). The Seattle longitudinal studies of adult intelligence. *Current Directions in Psychological Science, 2,* 171-174.

Schaie, K. W., & Willis, S. L. (1986). Can decline in adult intellectual functioning be reversed? *Developmental Psychology, 22,* 223-232.

Schulz, R., & Hanusa, B. H. (1979). Environmental influences on the effectiveness of control- and competence-enhancing intervention. In L. C. Perlmutter & R. A. Monty (Eds.), *Choice and perceived control* (pp. 315-337). Hillsdale, NJ: Lawrence Erlbaum.

Schulz, R., Heckhausen, J., & Locher, J. L. (1991). Adult development, control, and adaptive functioning. *Journal of Social Issues, 47,* 177-196.

Schulz, R., Heckhausen, J., & O'Brien, A. T. (1994). Control and the disablement process in the elderly. In D. S. Dunn (Ed.), Psychosocial perspectives on disability [Special issue]. *Journal of Social Behavior and Personality, 9,* 139-152.

Seligman, M. E. P. (1975). *Helplessness: On depression, development and death.* San Francisco: W. H. Freeman.

Shapiro, D. H., Sandman, C. A., Grossman, M., & Grossman, B. (1995). Age and sense of control. *Psychological Reports, 77,* 616-618.

Shaw, R. J. (1992). Coping effectiveness in nursing home residents: The role of control. *Journal of Aging and Health, 4,* 551-563.

Siegler, I. C., & Gatz, M. (1985). Age patterns in locus of control. In E. Palmore, J. Nowlin, E. Busse, I. Siegler, & G. Maddox (Eds.), *Normal aging* (Vol. 3, pp. 259-267). Durham, NC: Duke University Press.

Singer, J. E. (1980). Social comparison: The process of self-evaluation. In L. Festinger (Ed.), *Retrospections on social psychology* (pp. 158-179). New York: Oxford University Press.

Skinner, E. A. (1995). *Perceived control, motivation, and coping.* Thousand Oaks, CA: Sage.

Skinner, E. A., Chapman, M., & Baltes, P. B. (1988). Control, means-ends, and agency beliefs: A new conceptualization and its measurement during childhood. *Journal of Personality and Social Psychology, 54,* 117-133.

Smith, R. P., Woodward, N. J., Wallston, B. S., & Wallston, K. A. (1988). Health care implications of desire and expectancy for control in elderly adults. *Journals of Gerontology: Psychological Sciences, 43B*, 1-7.

Spirduso, W. W., & Gilliam-MacRae, P. (1991). Physical activity and quality of life in the frail elderly. In J. E. Birren, J. E. Lubben, J. C. Rowe, & D. E. Deutchman (Eds.), *The concept and measurement of quality of life in the frail elderly* (pp. 226-255). New York: Academic Press.

Staats, S. (1974). Internal versus external locus of control for three age groups. *International Journal of Aging and Human Development, 5*, 7-10.

Steele, C. M., Spenser, S. J., & Lynch, M. (1993). Self-image resilience and dissonance: The role of affirmational resources. *Journal of Personality and Social Psychology, 64*, 885-896.

Stine, E. A., Lachman, M. E., & Wingfield, A. (1993). The roles of perceived and actual control in memory for spoken language. *Educational Gerontology, 19*, 331-349.

Taylor, S. E. (1979). Hospital patient behavior: Reactance, helplessness, or control? *Journal of Social Issues, 35*, 156-184.

Taylor, S. E., & Lobel, M. (1989). Social comparison activity under threat: Downward evaluation and upward contacts. *Psychological Review, 96*, 569-575.

Thompson, S., & Spacapan, S. (1991). Perceptions of control in vulnerable populations. *Journal of Social Issues, 47*, 1-21.

Timko, C., & Rodin, J. (1985). Staff-patient relationships in nursing homes: Sources of conflict and rehabilitation potential. *Rehabilitation Psychology, 30*, 93-108.

Verbrugge, L. M. (1990). The iceberg of disability. In S. M. Stahl (Ed.), *The legacy of longevity* (pp. 55-75). Newbury Park, CA: Sage.

Wallhagen, M. I. (1992-1993). Perceived control and adaptation in elder caregivers: Development of an explanatory model. *International Journal of Aging and Human Development, 36*, 219-237.

Wallhagen, M. I., & Kagan, S. H. (1993). Staying within bounds: Perceived control and the experience of elderly caregivers. *Journal of Aging Studies, 7*, 197-213.

Wills, T. H. (1978). Perception of clients by professional helpers. *Psychological Bulletin, 85*, 968-1000.

Wolk, S., & Kurtz, J. (1975). Positive adjustment and involvement during aging and expectancy for internal control. *Journal of Consulting and Clinical Psychology, 43*, 173-178.

13

INTENTIONAL SELF-DEVELOPMENT THROUGH ADULTHOOD AND LATER LIFE

Tenacious Pursuit and Flexible Adjustment of Goals

Jochen Brandtstädter
Dirk Wentura
Klaus Rothermund

Human ontogeny and action stand in a reciprocal causal relation; we must pay attention to both sides of this relationship to gain an adequate understanding of development and intentional self-development in cultural contexts. Across the life span, development creates and destroys personal action potentialities; the ways in which individuals act upon, and interact

AUTHORS' NOTE: Preparation of this chapter was facilitated by a grant from the Deutsche Forschungsgemeinschaft (DFG) to Jochen Brandtstädter.

with, their environment and themselves are influenced by prior experiences and achievements, as well as by ontogenetic and age-graded change in competencies, interests, and contextual affordances. When self-definitions and identity projects become articulate during ontogeny, however, a dialectical shift occurs in the relation between development and action, and personal development increasingly becomes a target area of intentional activity. Efforts to bring the factual course of life into congruence with the normative representations that individuals have formed of their actual, present, and future selves are a basic motive of human activity and a driving force of development. Such intentional efforts can be aimed at acquiring or cultivating certain personally or socially desired skills, competencies, or ways of living; in later life in particular, they may also be aimed at maintaining desired attributes or counteracting their loss.

Humans are of course not omnipotent producers of their development; experiences of limited control over personal development constitute the dramatic twists in any life story. Developmental ecologies differ as to the developmental options they afford, and individuals tend to select or create contexts that match their interests and developmental potentials (see Bandura, 1986; Lerner, 1982; Super & Harkness, 1986)—as far as they are free to do so. Furthermore, individuals differ in regard to the degree of control they have over their development or that they ascribe to themselves; self-beliefs of high control over personally important goals tend to go with a confident and optimistic attitude toward one's life and future development (e.g., Brandtstädter, 1992; Skinner, 1995). Ontogenetic or age-related changes in social, temporal, or physical resources crucially affect the feasibility of goals and personal projects; in later life, functional losses as well as the fading of time yet to be lived often constrain goal pursuits and developmental options (see Breytspraak, 1984). Development across the life span thus involves permanent changes in the set of feasible developmental options; to attain or regain a match between personal goals and action resources is a recurring task over the life course. This task gains particular weight during later life, when action resources and "possibility frontiers" (Brandtstädter & Wentura, 1995) become narrower.

We have two main objectives in this chapter. First, we will analyze the processes and activities that may help individuals to adjust goals and ambitions to changing action resources across their life course. Second, we will spell out the implications that these processes have for issues of intentional development over the life course, and in particular for the question of how individuals can preserve personal continuity and a positive outlook on self and personal development in spite of the aversive and uncontrollable changes that often accompany the biological, social, and psychological processes of aging. The model of assimilative and accommodative coping (Brandtstädter, 1989; Brandtstädter & Renner, 1990; Brandtstädter, Wentura, & Greve, 1993) will serve as an orienting framework for these discussions.

COPING WITH AVERSIVE DEVELOPMENTAL OUTCOMES THROUGH ASSIMILATIVE AND ACCOMMODATIVE PROCESSES

Aversive developmental outcomes or experiences of loss in personally valued domains of life and functioning generally involve discrepancies between desired and actual self-states. There are different ways to reduce or neutralize such discrepancies. On the one hand, an individual may neutralize self-discrepancies by altering the actual situation as represented by the actual self. Plausibly, this tendency will prevail as long as the individual feels capable of performing the necessary corrective actions or of achieving the corresponding self-regulatory goals. The individual may still neutralize self-discrepancies that cannot be reduced through transformation of the actual situation by adjusting the desired self, that is, by modifying those preferences and priorities in relation to which the given situation is negatively valued. In other words, we can distinguish between *actional* and *mental* modes of neutralizing experiences of loss and aversive emotions.

There are possible readings of this argument that we wish to exclude. By *mental neutralization,* we do not refer to a general tendency to process self-referent information in positively biased or self-serving ways, as it has been variously postulated in social psychology and emotion research (e.g., Frijda, 1988). Rather, as we will argue in greater detail below, we assume that processes of mental neutralization arise in specified phases of coping with aversive developmental outcomes.

The model of assimilative and accommodative coping elaborates these basic assumptions within a framework that braids together action-theoretical, developmental, and self-theoretical perspectives. In terms of this model, assimilation and accommodation denote two basically different ways of achieving a match between actual developmental outcomes or prospects and personal goals and ambitions as they are represented in the individual's normative (desired, "ought") self. In the *assimilative* mode, the person actively tries to change an unsatisfying situation so that it becomes congruent or compatible with desired self-definitions or identity goals. The assimilative process thus involves an *actional neutralization* of dissatisfying developmental states in the sense given above. Assimilative activities may be motivated by self-initiated discrepancies that can arise, for example, from the individual's commitment to new, ambitious goals; they may also originate from negatively valued changes, such as the experience of functional losses and impairments in later life. In the *accommodative* mode of coping, by contrast, the individual eliminates aversive discrepancies by adjusting personal goals and preferences rather than by changing the actual situation. Accommodative processes basically tend to deactivate barren goals and projects by reducing their incentive value. This corresponds to the mental neutralization of problems as discussed above.

In contrast to assimilative activities, accommodative processes need not, and often cannot, be volitionally enacted. Although we can wish to have certain beliefs or preferences and can take measures to come to have particular mental states (e.g., by intentional forms of self-management), we cannot purposefully and intentionally originate some belief or preference (see Gilbert, 1993; Honderich, 1988). This point is of some theoretical importance: It directs our attention to the subpersonal or automatic mechanisms that subserve accommodative processes. It also sets the present theoretical approach apart from other dual-process conceptions of coping that cut across the distinction between intentional and nonintentional or automatic processes. For example, in the model of problem-focused versus emotion-focused coping (see Lazarus & Folkman, 1984), the latter category comprises strategic, intentional activities of emotion management (such as taking sedatives) along with cognitive processes (such as palliative reappraisals of the situation) that operate on nonintentional, effortless levels. According to the dual-process model espoused here, intentional techniques of emotion management would still belong to the assimilative mode, and the tendencies to use them should be particularly high when the shift toward accommodative automatisms is impeded (as may be the case, for example, if equivalent substitutes for blocked goals are not accessible to the person). Obviously, confounding intentional and automatic processes may conceal interesting interactions between these levels.

Figure 13.1 illustrates how assimilative activities and accommodative processes are intertwined in episodes of coping with crisis and loss. The diagram features a hierarchy of feedback loops. Assimilative activities originate in evaluative appraisals of personal developmental prospects and conditions, and are induced in particular when the outcome is negatively valued (1, 2[–]). The ensuing course of events crucially depends on whether or not the individual feels able to transform the situation or to enact the corresponding corrective or self-regulatory intentions; contextual as well as personal factors may intervene as moderating conditions at this juncture. Assimilative intentions will be formed if self-percepts of control are sufficiently strong and if the individual has a sufficiently differentiated representation of a viable action course (4, 5[+], 6). The implementation of assimilative intentions typically involves a sequence of intermediary levels, from planning to executing corrective actions (the diagram gives only a simplified picture at this point). When available action potentialities are insufficient for altering the situation, or turn out to be so after repeated futile attempts, auxiliary activities may be interpolated to acquire skills or knowledge that seems useful in implementing the original assimilative intentions (5[–], 7[+], 8). This subsidiary loop still belongs to the assimilative mode, but the intentional focus has shifted to intermediate compensatory objectives. When such compensatory efforts remain ineffective, assimilative efforts may shift to a secondary level of compensation; external aids or support systems may now be engaged to attain desired goals or developmental outcomes (7[–], 9[+], 10). During that stage of the coping process, self-regulatory efforts take the form of mediated "proxy control" (see Bandura, 1982) but still remain committed to the original goals and problem definitions. If instrumental efforts on these different levels of action fail and action resources are exhausted, the assimilative process reaches a critical stage that is usually considered to precipitate reactions of helplessness and depression (see Abramson, Alloy, & Metalsky, 1990; Abramson, Seligman, & Teasdale, 1978).

In contrast to prevailing cognitive or control-theoretical accounts, the present model does not consider depressive reactions as the ultimate outcome of sustained but unsuccessful efforts to achieve some desired outcome. Rather, feelings of helplessness and depression are considered as intermediate phenomena that may even promote a shift from assimilative toward accommodative processes. This partly converges with Klinger's

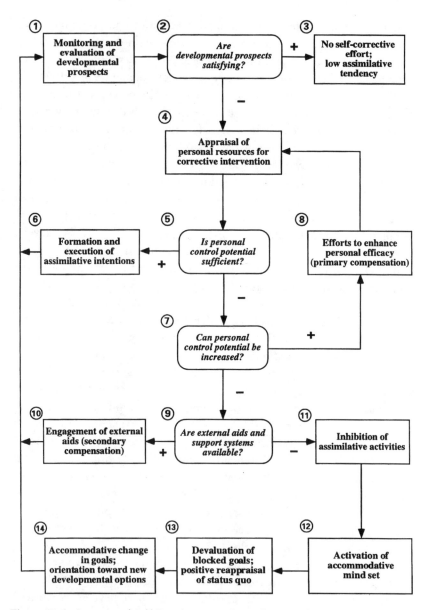

Figure 13.1. Intentional Self-Development: Assimilative and Accommodative Processes

SOURCE: Adapted from Brandtstädter (1984, 1989).

(1982) proposal that depressive reactions may support the disengagement from blocked goals and thus may instigate mechanisms that lead to recovery. In our conception, disengagement from blocked goals is a key feature of the accommodative mode of coping with losses and aversive developmental outcomes (11, 12, 13, 14). The shift from assimilative to accommodative modes of coping does not follow a fixed temporal pattern, nor does it necessarily proceed smoothly. In a later section, we will consider personal and situational factors that can impede the disengagement from blocked goals and the accommodation of preference structures.

Facets and Functions of Assimilative Coping

In principle, any domain of life or functioning that is perceived as open to intentional modification may become the target of assimilative activities. Depending on personal goals and means-ends beliefs, such activities can take various forms. To achieve or maintain some desired self-attribute or developmental goal, individuals may engage in bodily exercise, change their dieting habits, select facilitative environments, and more. They may also neutralize (or reduce the salience of) self-discrepancies by avoiding situations and contexts where self-discrepant feedback is likely to occur; such activities of "self-verification" (Swann, 1983) may be considered as a further facet of assimilative action. In later life, visions of an "undesired possible self" may feed more strongly into assimilative efforts (Cross & Markus, 1991), and assimilative activities may focus more strongly on preventive or compensatory aims. Compensatory activities can range from the use of prosthetic means to metacognitive strategies that ameliorate intellectual functioning and performance (see Bäckman & Dixon, 1992; Baltes & Baltes, 1990; Salthouse, 1987). As illustrated above (see also Figure 13.1), intentional compensatory activities form a subset of assimilative activities that characterize a given phase of self-regulation.

Assimilative activities will center particularly on life domains that are central to the individual's identity or on areas of behavior and performance where he or she must maintain some social norm or desired standard. The goals, self-definitions, and normative expectations that set the frame for assimilative efforts, however, are by no means stable over the life course; rather, they undergo change as the individual moves through the life cycle. Changes in goals, interests, and competencies result not only from the joint influence of biological changes, age-graded developmental tasks, and institutionalized role patterns, but also from accommodations to changes in personal and contextual resources that affect the feasibility of goals.

Facets and Functions of Accommodative Processes

Accommodative processes are characterized by the following functional features. First, they neutralize blocked intentions and commitments; that is, they induce a mechanism of disengagement that, in successful goal pursuit, does not occur before the intended goal is reached (see Klinger, 1982). Second, accommodative processes erode the positive hedonic difference between the current state and the intended goal state that fuels assimilative efforts. This may involve a positive reappraisal of the status quo, a negative reappraisal of formerly desired goal states, or both. As intimated above, typical outcomes of the accommodative process include the detachment from barren commitments, the rescaling of aspirations, and the activation of cognitions and meanings that render an initially aversive situation acceptable. Social comparisons that involve less demanding or "downward" perspectives can further enhance accommodative processes (see Brandtstädter & Greve, 1994; Wills, 1991).

We should distinguish among different forms of disengagement from goals in order to prevent misunderstandings. Letting go of some goal can be instrumental for the individual's attaining new developmental options that appear more attractive and promising. In such a case, disengagement can take the form of an intentional decision. This is different from cases in which uncontrolled, heteronomous influences bring about aversive changes or destroy desired options without also making possible some equivalent substitution. Such losses will at first activate a reactant tendency to undo the change; this reactant assimilative tendency reflects the individual's continuing attachment to previous goals and developmental prospects. When we speak of disengagement in the accommodative context, we refer to the dissolution of such attachments. Accommodative disengagement in this sense cannot coherently be modeled as an intentional activity or rational decision, because such a decision would seem to presuppose already what it intends, namely, an emotional detachment from the lost value.

In the assimilative mode, goals and commitments are maintained even against obstacles; the accommodative mode, in contrast, involves the flexible adjustment of goals and preferences to perceived situational constraints and changes in action resources. There is a widespread tendency to deprecate such processes as inferior modes of coping, and to align them with notions of resignation and depression. Accommodation theory posits, to the contrary, that helplessness and depression essentially stem from difficulties in relinquishing barren self-definitions and downgrading the attractiveness of blocked goals; this assumption largely coincides with clinical evidence (see Carver & Scheier, 1990). Whereas cognitive accounts of depression consider a loss of control over personally relevant goals as the prime etiological factor (see Peterson & Seligman, 1984), the present approach suggests that personal or situational factors that impede the accommodation of personal projects are equally potent risk factors for helplessness and depression.

Figure 13.2 summarizes the considerations so far. It also spells out conditions that differentially affect the strength or duration of assimilative and accommodative reactions, respectively.

DIFFERENTIAL AND MODERATING CONDITIONS

As we have mentioned, assimilative and accommodative processes function antagonistically: The assimilative mode inhibits or dampens accommodative tendencies, and vice versa. Accordingly, most of the moderating conditions listed in Figure 13.2 affect both functions in opposed ways. However, there is a particular category of influences that tend to suppress assimilative and accommodative tendencies alike. This category is referred to in Figure 13.2 as the "defensive negotiation of evidence," and we turn to it first.

Assimilative as well as accommodative processes originate in perceived discrepancies between actual and desired self-states. The self-system tends to defend itself against such discrepancies, however; this holds in particular for those parts of the self-concept that are positively valued and strongly entrenched (see Greenwald & Pratkanis, 1984). Comparable to the ways in which the core assumptions of scientific theories are defended against discrepant evidence by a "protective belt" of auxiliary assumptions (Lakatos, 1970), the theories that individuals hold about themselves engage protective processes that tend to maintain the continuity and consistency of self-definitions. Brandtstädter and Greve (1994) have distinguished two types of such protective or "immunizing" processes. A first type of process (denoted as "data-oriented" immunization) tends to handle the evidence in such a way that central self-definitions remain unaffected. For example,

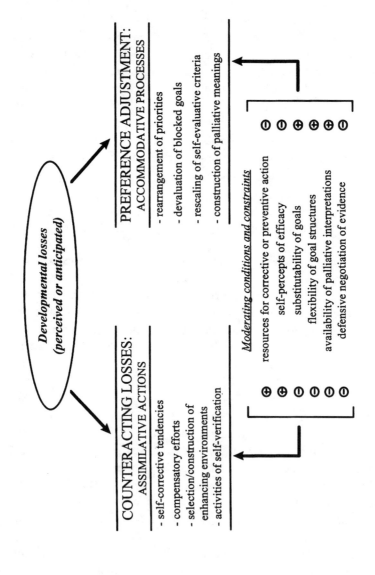

Figure 13.2. Assimilative and Accommodative Processes: Facets and Moderating Conditions

SOURCE: Brandstädter and Wentura (1995). Reprinted by permission of Lawrence Erlbaum Associates, Inc.

NOTE: Enhancing and inhibiting effects are marked by plus and minus signs, respectively.

individuals may defend their self-definitions of intellectual competence against experienced failure in competence-related tasks by attributing the results to external disturbances or handicaps. However, the evidence may become so strong that self-serving attributions can no longer be maintained. In that case, a second mode of immunizing processes ("concept-oriented" immunization) that operates on the semantic structure of threatened attributes may come into play. For example, personal concepts of intellectual competence may be reshaped so that those skills or domains of functioning where some deficiency or loss is apparent are excluded from the concept. For instance, in their personal definitions of intellectual competence, elderly persons tend to focus more strongly on such features as expertise and life experience and to de-emphasize decontextualized aspects of intellectual functioning that show age-related decline (Ryff, 1991; see also Sternberg & Wagner, 1986). The phenomenal stability of self-definitions in later life that has been documented in cross-sectional and longitudinal research (e.g., Costa & McCrae, 1994) may be due in part to such bottom-up and top-down processes of immunization (see also Greve, 1990). These processes operate on preintentional or automatic levels; although individuals may engage in "wishful thinking" and hold true what they want to be true, they cannot intentionally form or accept some belief for some self-serving purpose (see Johnston, 1995).

By reducing the salience of self-discrepant evidence, self-immunizing processes not only undermine any "assimilative" motivation to change the situation actively, they also suppress the tendency to accommodate personal preferences and goals. The important point in the present context is that perceived self-discrepancies must gain sufficient epistemic strength to override the protective or immunizing mechanisms that inherently constrain the processing of self-referential information before they can induce a correctional response.

We now turn to differential factors that affect assimilative and accommodative tendencies in opposed ways. In this regard, three groups of influences seem of particular importance (see Figure 13.2). First, assimilative activities will be enhanced (and accommodative tendencies inhibited) when the threatened goal or self-standard is central or important for the individual's self-definition. Second, assimilative tendencies will dominate over accommodative reactions as long as there is a sufficient probability of success. Within limits, the effects of goal importance may compensate those of low outcome expectancies; that is, for goals of high personal importance, even marginal chances of goal attainment may suffice to maintain assimilative efforts. A third important group of moderating conditions that feeds into the accommodative process relates to the cognitive or contextual accessibility of palliative information. We will discuss these influences in turn.

Goal Centrality and Substitutability

It is difficult and painful for individuals to relinquish goals that are fundamental to their identities or life designs and that they cannot easily replace with equally satisfying alternatives. Accordingly, it is often less difficult for individuals to disengage from lower-level, instrumental goals than from higher-level or terminal goals, except in cases where given instrumental goals are indispensable to reach the terminal goal. Due to their greater abstractness, however, higher-level goals may also provide scope for different definitions and implementations. Goal centrality and substitutability reflect the structure of the individual's goal system. A multifaceted and diversified structure of goals and life projects will generally enhance a shift from a particular barren project to other options; in fact, findings by Linville (1985) hint that low "self-complexity" raises the vulnerability for depression.

Action Resources and Self-Percepts of Control

Repeated unsuccessful attempts to achieve desired goals or developmental outcomes gradually erode self-beliefs of efficacy and control. Strong self-percepts of efficacy, whether generalized or domain linked, are more resistant to experiences of failure and will less readily give way to feelings of helplessness. Action theorists have rightly stressed the benefits of high perceived control in coping with critical events (e.g., Bandura, 1986). In irreversible or uncontrollable situations, however, strong efficacy beliefs may put the person at a disadvantage; by impeding a shift toward accommodative modes, such beliefs may lead to an exhaustion of physical resources (through persistent assimilative efforts) and increase the intensity and duration of depressive reactions. Researchers are increasingly cognizant of the potentially negative side effects of strong control beliefs (Thompson, Cheek, & Graham, 1988); particularly in contexts that are resistant to change, the presumed negative relation between measures of control and depression seems to vanish (e.g., Wolk, 1976; see also Coyne,

1992; Skinner, 1995). As outlined above, the dual-process model would predict and explain such effects.

Palliative Cognitions

As argued above, the positive valences of a blocked goal are destroyed in the accommodative mode so that further assimilative efforts are inhibited. Accommodation thus critically depends on the accessibility of information that has the potential to dampen goal attractiveness. Like the conditions considered before, palliative cognitions that foster the acceptance of an initially aversive situation may be differentially available across individuals and situations. Whether individuals can find sense and positive meaning in adversity depends on their personal knowledge, experiences, and temperaments; for example, religious beliefs or particular existential attitudes (such as the belief in a just world; e.g., Montada, 1992) may provide a resource for construing palliative meaning in situations of crisis and loss. Feeling personally responsible for a negative outcome, on the other hand, may promote negative rumination ("If I only had . . . ") and impede accommodative reappraisals (see Miller & Turnbull, 1990).

MECHANISMS UNDERLYING ACCOMMODATION

As intimated above, accommodative shifts in meanings and preferences cannot be intentionally induced. To explain such shifts, we must pass beyond an intentionalist framework and look for mechanisms that operate on subintentional or automatic levels (without necessarily proceeding outside the person's awareness, however). As we will argue below, such mechanisms are already inherent to the regulation of attention.

Accommodative Shifts in the Regulation of Attention

The deployment of attentional resources serves to specify relevant parameters for regulating an ongoing action sequence (see Neumann, 1992). During goal pursuit, mental representations of goal-relevant conditions become highly activated and primed, thus rendering goal-relevant cues more accessible (see Anderson, 1983). In initial or preparatory stages, representations of the goal state as well as of intermediary steps are formed that focus information processing during the execution phase and prevent the intrusion of distracting stimuli (see Kuhl, 1987). There is experimental evidence that judgments of control and perceived feasibility of goals tend to be positively biased during goal pursuit (Taylor & Gollwitzer, 1995).

Once a goal-directed action sequence has been launched, these supportive processes even tend to be intensified when obstacles arise that call for increased effort expenditure; within certain limits, increased difficulty of goal implementation tends to be counterbalanced by a reactant increase in goal attractiveness (Wright & Brehm, 1989). The execution phase is characterized by a tendency to ward off thoughts or arguments that would undermine the attractive valences of the goal. It would be dysfunctional, of course, if goals that have become inaccessible would further bind attentional resources and be shielded from competing action tendencies. Accommodation theory assumes that as goals drift out of the feasible range, mechanisms are engaged that withdraw them from working memory and reallocate attentional resources to new, alternative options (Brandtstädter & Renner, 1990; Wentura, 1995).

Goals that are highly important and not easily replaced by equivalent alternatives, however, may continue to bind attention even when the chances to reach them are slim. Thus accommodative processes should be further enhanced by mechanisms that destroy the incentive value of the goals and increase the salience of positive aspects of the status quo, and these mechanisms should become particularly important when the blocked goal is of high initial valence.

Deconstruction of Positive Goal Valences: The "Accommodative" Mind-Set

The attractiveness of a given goal essentially depends on the subjective meanings and consequences that are linked with the goal state. Dissociation from a barren commitment thus presupposes the deconstruction of meanings that would justify further goal pursuit. In the accommodative mode, the accessibility of cognitive content with such deconstructive potential should be enhanced. Thus the negative implications and costs of pursuing the goal that were condoned in the phase of implementation may be reconsidered, beliefs concerning the positive consequences of the goal may be discarded, and so on. We thus posit that the accommodative process involves a cognitive set that is opposed to, and overrides, the "implemental" mind-set (Gollwitzer, 1990) that supports goal pursuit in the assimilative mode. This *accommodative mind-set* would also tend to remove overly optimistic or illusionary biases in control judgments. These features are reminiscent of a cognitive-affective syndrome of "depressive realism" (Alloy & Abramson, 1979, 1988), but we do not suggest that accommodation always leads to a more "realistic" perspective. The accommodative process is not primarily geared toward greater objectivity, but rather toward alleviating emotional load and distress.

Accommodation and Conclusion-Driven Thinking

Accommodation of goals and preferences seems to be enhanced by "conclusion-driven" thinking (see Kunda, 1990). Formally, conclusions follow from given premises; conclusion-driven thinking, by contrast, selectively searches for information that would support some preferred proposition. This mode of thinking should prevail in particular when the "conclusion" in question is so attractive that the desire to be objectively correct may be compromised (see Bohner, Moskowitz, & Chaiken, 1995).

Whereas in the assimilative mode conclusion-driven thinking should gravitate toward cognitive contents that facilitate goal pursuit, in the accommodative mode it should enhance the devaluation of barren commitments and the acceptance of initially aversive developmental outcomes. Due to its positivity bias, it should likewise enhance the construction of sense and positive meaning in situations of distress. In terms of cognitive capacity and effort, conclusion-driven thinking is less demanding than systematic processing and may become more dominant when the capacity to engage in detailed elaborative processing is reduced or lacking. Age-related changes in cognitive resources—for example, neurophysiological changes leading to fuzzy activation patterns or "neural noise" (Allen, Madden, Weber, & Crozier, 1992; Cremer & Zeef, 1987)—may accentuate conclusion-driven biases in negotiating evidence (Frey, 1981; Klein & Kunda, 1993; Sanitioso, Kunda, & Fong, 1990) and thus raise the accessibility of palliative cognitions in situations of crisis and loss.

Despite these obvious supportive mechanisms, the transition from assimilative to accommodative modes of coping is not necessarily a smooth one. We have already addressed situational and personal factors that may facilitate or impede the shift toward accommodation. Rumination and depression, in our view, characterize a functional state in which assimilative tendencies are no longer strong enough to inhibit accommodation and accommodative tendencies have not yet gained sufficient strength to neutralize assimilative tendencies. Accommodation theory, however, diverges from traditional views in assuming that reactions of rumination and depression eventually mediate the shift toward accommodation and thus are inherently self-destroying. The mechanisms discussed above, for example, suggest that feelings of helplessness may be functional to eliminate blocked commitments from working memory. Furthermore, cognitions that have the potential to neutralize feelings of frustration and despair should be particularly likely to pass plausibility checks and override mood congruency effects in cognition (see Blaney, 1986).

ASSIMILATION AND ACCOMMODATION AS ADAPTIVE RESOURCES IN LATER LIFE

In its explanatory scope, the model of assimilative and accommodative coping is not limited to any particular phase of life. Empirical applications of the model, however, have been focally concerned with later adulthood and old age. In many areas of life and functioning, the processes of aging involve experiences of loss, so that the balance of positive and aversive changes tends to tip toward the negative with advancing age (see Heckhausen, Dixon, & Baltes, 1989). Role losses and bereavements, health problems, physical impairments, and the fading of remaining time to live tend to progressively constrain developmental options and resources of action. This holds all the more as age-related changes are often experienced as irreversible and tend to threaten consolidated self-definitions; negative stereotypes of aging likely further aggravate these problems. According to common clinical lore, all this should precipitate self-esteem problems, feelings of inefficacy, and depression (e.g., Seligman & Elder, 1986).

Contrary to expectations, however, there is no consistent evidence for an increased incidence of such problems in later adulthood. Despite large individual differences, elderly people on the whole are not less satisfied with themselves and their lives than are members of younger groups, and they do not show a higher vulnerability for depression, except perhaps in the terminal phases of life (see Abeles, 1991; Brandtstädter et al., 1993). Of course, some caveats have to be observed: There is the risk of confounding age and generation effects in cross-sectional investigations; moreover, relationships between age and measures of well-being may be nonlinear. Furthermore, symptoms of depression are easily misdiagnosed as age-typical somatic complaints (see Blazer, 1989; Kessler, Foster, Webster, & House, 1992). Such reservations have to be taken seriously, but they do not seem to invalidate the evidence that has accumulated over the past years; indeed, researchers are increasingly intrigued by the high degree of adaptive flexibility and stability of the self-system in later life (see Staudinger, Marsiske, & Baltes, 1995). We assume that the resilience of the aging self is rooted in the interplay of assimilative and accommodative processes, as well as in age-related shifts in the relative salience of these processes.

Assimilation, Compensation, and the Principle of Decreasing Marginal Utility

As intimated above, the prevention and active compensation of functional losses and impairments become focal themes of assimilative activity in the transition to later life. We would expect compensatory efforts to reach a maximum when losses and impairments become sufficiently clearcut to override defensive or "immunizing" processes in the above-noted sense, but still remain within margins that seem amenable to corrective intervention. As age advances, however, it may become increasingly difficult or taxing to defend self-definitions of youthful competence against discrepant evidence or feedback. Such problems may be mitigated for a while by the boosting of compensatory efforts and further optimization of the use and allocation of scarce resources (see Marsiske, Lang, Baltes, & Baltes, 1995). However, the adaptive strains of later life do not stem only from experiences of functional losses as such, but likewise from the fact that attempts to offset such losses in order to maintain prior performance standards often become increasingly costly and taxing. For example, elderly people who received mnemonic training can easily outperform younger people in particular memory tasks, but age-related losses become even more marked when the younger groups receive the same compensatory training (Kliegl, Smith, & Baltes, 1989). This highlights the fact that compensatory functional reserves may also show age-related decline, so that compensatory investments may yield diminishing returns. Accordingly, efforts to compensate for age-related loss in particular domains may show curvilinear (inverted U-shaped) regressions on age, and eventually vanish or become retargeted to new areas when the costs of compensation in a given domain outweigh the benefits (see Bäckman & Dixon, 1992; Brandtstädter & Wentura, 1995). To the same degree, accommodative processes involving readjustment of personal goals and self-evaluative standards should gain momentum. From a contextualist point of view, it should be noted that social environments differ as to the leeway they provide for the age-related accommodation of goals and performance standards. As individuals move through occupational and family cycles, they enter different informational and symbolic contexts that provide different standards and comparison perspectives for self-evaluation (see Frey & Ruble, 1990). Generally, we may assume that cultural contexts in which notions of successful aging are strongly tinged by ideals of youthful strength and efficiency will presumably put a stronger emphasis on assimilative-compensatory efforts than on accommodative adjustment of self-evaluative standards.

Assimilative Persistence and Accommodative Flexibility: Dispositional Differences

There seem to be rather stable interindividual differences in the tendency to adhere to, or disengage from, barren commitments. In our research, such dispositional differences are assessed by two scales: Tenacious Goal Pursuit (TGP) and Flexible Goal Adjustment (FGA). The TGP scale measures the tendency to maintain goals and adhere to self-evaluative standards in the face of obstacles, whereas the FGA scale taps accommodative features such as the capability to shift to new commitments and to draw sense and meaning out of aversive situations. On the dispositional level, assimilative persistence and accommodative flexibility do not form opposed poles of a unidimensional concept, but rather span independent dimensions of coping competence. Both scales show substantial positive relations with various measures of well-being and subjective life quality (e.g., Brandtstädter & Renner, 1990). In view of the cumulation of irreversible losses and the fading of action resources in later life, we would theoretically expect an increasing predominance of accommodative flexibility over assimilative persistence with advancing age. Indeed, this pattern in fact has been found repeatedly in independent studies using the TGP and FGA scales (see Brandtstädter, 1992; Heckhausen & Schulz, 1995).

The following quotations from interview studies with elderly persons may further illustrate how accommodative tendencies are expressed in self-reports (see also Brandtstädter, Rothermund, & Schmitz, 1998):

> You have to accept . . . now that doesn't mean that for instance you should give yourself over to fate, rather I'm trying to say you have to be humble enough to say: You aren't 40 anymore! Taking a break is normal! It's normal that you get more tired on some days. (male, 63 years)

When you're younger, you try to perfect your natural talents and abilities. I think that is both healthy and proper. But that feeling goes away bit by bit. You don't want to, maybe because you can't, but maybe too because it doesn't seem to make all that much sense anymore. (female, 62 years)

It's strange, like a lot of other things in life: You get used to it after a while. You regret the fact you're getting old, that your body's getting old, that you, well, don't look very attractive in a bikini anymore. But somehow, after a certain amount of time, you come to terms with it, because other things are always happening, which are nice and have little to do with your appearance. (female, 57 years)

By no means do we suggest that assimilative or compensatory efforts cease in later life. Accommodation of standards and preferences does not terminate assimilative and compensatory efforts, but establishes new reference points for such efforts, directing them to goals or standards that fit more closely with personal resources and potentialities (Rothermund & Brandtstädter, 1997). Under limited action resources, disengagement from particular goals can furthermore economize reserves that are needed for the successful attainment of assimilative objectives in other domains; for example, the fading of temporal reserves in later life often forces people to abandon some valued but time-consuming projects for the sake of other goals.

Although premature disengagement from goals clearly may have self-limiting effects (see Bandura, 1982), we consider the process of continuously readjusting goals and preferences to action reserves as crucial to the maintenance of self-esteem and even efficacy in later life. The following observations testify to this protective function of accommodative processes.

Stabilizing a Sense of Control
Through Accommodating Goals

Self-percepts of control and efficacy are generally considered to be key variables of positive aging (e.g., Baltes & Baltes, 1990). Traditionally, researchers have held the view that a gradual shrinking of physical, social, and temporal resources should go with a decreased sense of control in the elderly. However, relationships between perceived control and age are weak and inconsistent (e.g., Lachman, 1986; Rodin, 1987). This also converges with the general picture that has emerged from epidemiological research on the age-depression relation (see Blazer, 1989).

Accommodation theory offers the following rationale for these paradoxical findings. Concepts of power and control refer to the capability of reaching personally important goals; accordingly, downscaling the personal importance of goals that have drifted beyond the individual's span of control may not only mitigate frustration and emotional strain, but should likewise be functional for maintaining a general sense of personal control and efficacy (see Brim, 1992). Brandtstädter and Rothermund (1994) have reported evidence in support of this assumption. Self-ratings of general control, goal-linked control, and personal goal importance were repeatedly assessed over a longitudinal interval of 8 years. As theoretically predicted, differential decline in goal-linked control beliefs did indeed affect global or generalized control beliefs to a lesser degree when importance ratings for the given goals decreased within the same longitudinal interval. This type of interactive buffering effect emerged for a large variety of developmental goals (e.g., occupational efficiency, social recognition, physical fitness, intellectual efficiency).

Assimilation, Accommodation, and the Construal of Gains and Losses

As defined above, a core function of accommodation consists in neutralizing experiences of loss and in mitigating the emotional load that is related to such experiences. In generalized expectations and in personal experiences as well, aging connotes an increasing prevalence of negatively over positively valued changes. However, accommodative processes such as adjusting ambitions to changed resources of goal achievement, drawing sense and meaning out of initially aversive life changes, and shifting reference frames for self-evaluation should contribute to keeping the balance of gain and loss favorable. In a cross-sequential study, Brandtstädter et al. (1998) assessed differences and changes in (a) perceived distances from developmental goals as well as in (b) the personal importance of such goals. In this study, the researchers formed indicators of gain and loss by weighting longitudinal changes in goal distances (decreases or increases) by the rated importance of the respective goals and aggregating across goals. Accommodation theory suggests that goal importance ratings should be adjusted over the longitudinal interval so as to neutralize losses and emphasize gains. Consistent with this assumption, losses were less pronounced when importance ratings assessed at the end of the longitudinal interval ("postaccommodative" ratings) were used in the weighting procedure and appeared stronger when initial, "preaccommodative" importance ratings obtained at the first measurement point were used (effects for gains tended in the opposite direction, but were less marked).

Generating Palliative Cognitions: Microanalytic Studies

In our experimental research, we used a priming approach to investigate accommodative processes at the microanalytic level. A first series of experiments has focused in particular on individual differences in the availability of palliative cognitive content. Participants read brief episodes describing some stressful event. The episodes were followed by an ambivalent phrase mentioning positive as well as negative aspects of the situation (e.g., "Your husband has been in a hospital for quite some time. Living alone is very stressful, but you also realize that he has visibly improved"). After reading the episodes, subjects performed a recognition task in which the positive and negative target stimuli were preceded either by a prime stimulus denoting the stressful event (e.g., "hospital") or by a distractor. Speed of recognition as well as recognition errors were measured to assess the cognitive accessibility of positive compared with negative contents. Participants who expressed a disposition in the flexibility scale to focus on positive implications of initially aversive events were found to have enhanced access to positive or palliative aspects of the episode; this effect was especially pronounced after presentation of the prime (Wentura, Rothermund, & Brandtstädter, 1995; see also Wentura, 1995).

Another line of experiments centered on accommodative shifts in the meaning of "being old." Social stereotypes of aging are laden with deprecating connotations (e.g., Perduc & Gurtman, 1990). Accommodation theory suggests that elderly persons may shield their self-concepts from such connotations by enriching their personal notions of "being old" with positive content. To analyze such accommodative effects, we used a priming technique combined with a lexical decision task. We expected that with advancing age, the attribute "old" should have an increasingly strong priming effect on the processing of positively connoted target words (such as *good, happy, confident*) compared with control stimuli. These assumptions were tested on a sample of 120 participants ages 56 to 80 years. Lexical decision times for the positive target words in fact showed the predicted relation with the age variable (for negatively valued targets, no corresponding age effect was found). In addition, this effect was qualified by accommodative flexibility; consistent with theoretical assumptions, connotations of being old tended to become more positive for persons high in accommodative flexibility, whereas an opposite effect was observed for "inflexible" individuals (Rothermund, Wentura, & Brandtstädter, 1995; see also Wentura, Dräger, & Brandtstädter, 1997).

CONCLUSIONS

Intentional self-development over the life span is geared to the realization and maintenance of normative representations that individuals construe of themselves and their future. Goals and projects of intentional self-development, however, have to be continuously matched to actual developmental outcomes and constraints; in particular, they have to be adjusted to changes in action resources and developmental reserves over the life course. Processes of intentional self-development thus hinge on the interplay between activities through which individuals assimilate the actual course of personal development to their goals and self-definitions and processes through which goals and self-evaluative standards are accommodated to the feasible range. In this chapter we have outlined a theoretical approach that integrates these perspectives.

When the individual is confronted with aversive events or life changes that defy active, problem-solving efforts, the accommodation of preferences may be the only way to escape helplessness and depression. Through withdrawing attention from unsolvable problems and reducing the incentive values of blocked goals, accommodative mechanisms also channel resources of intentional self-development toward areas that are still open to modification and amelioration. The accommodative function becomes particularly important when action reserves and compensatory potentials narrow down, as is typically the case in later life. To date, accommodative processes have received only scant attention in action-theoretical and developmental contexts. This neglect may be due in part to the fact that accommodative shifts cannot be explained within an intentional stance (there is, however, growing consideration of nonintentional factors in intentional action and goal-directed action; see Bargh, 1990; Brandtstädter & Greve, in press).

Adaptive stress and emotional strain in later life resulting from loss and impairment in personally valued domains are further potentiated by the experience that these aversive changes are partially irreversible and that compensatory efforts yield diminishing returns. With the narrowing down of action potentials and functional reserves, the efficient deployment of scarce action resources becomes an urgent concern. The dual-process model posits that accommodative processes help elderly persons to meet these adaptive challenges. While joining with theories of control and efficacy in stressing the importance of active-offensive modes of coping with developmental loss, the model puts into question the lopsided emphasis on these modes in contemporary formulations of coping and successful aging. It cautions us that tenaciously clinging to entrenched identity goals and life designs may not only be an adaptive resource, but may also become a source of vulnerability and even depression in later life.

REFERENCES

Abeles, R. P. (1991). Sense of control, quality of life, and frail older people. In J. E. Birren, J. E. Lubben, J. C. Rowe, & D. E. Deutchman (Eds.), *The concept and measurement of quality of life in the frail elderly* (pp. 297-314). New York: Academic Press.

Abramson, L. Y., Alloy, L. B., & Metalsky, G. I. (1990). Hopelessness depression: An empirical search for a theory-based subtype. In R. E. Ingram (Ed.), *Contemporary psychological approaches to depression* (pp. 37-58). New York: Plenum.

Abramson, L. Y., Seligman, M. E. P., & Teasdale, E. J. D. (1978). Learned helplessness in humans: Critique and reformulation. *Journal of Abnormal Psychology, 87,* 49-74.

Allen, P. A., Madden, D. J., Weber, T., & Crozier, L. C. (1992). Age differences in short-term memory: Organization or internal noise? *Journals of Gerontology: Psychological Sciences, 47B,* P281-P288.

Alloy, L. B., & Abramson, L. Y. (1979). Judgment of contingency in depressed and nondepressed students: Sadder but wiser? *Journal of Experimental Psychology: General, 108,* 441-485.

Alloy, L. B., & Abramson, L. Y. (1988). Depressive realism: Four theoretical perspectives. In L. B. Alloy (Ed.), *Cognitive processes in depression* (pp. 223-265). New York: Guilford.

Anderson, J. R. (1983). *The architecture of cognition.* Cambridge, MA: Harvard University Press.

Bäckman, L., & Dixon, R. A. (1992). Psychological compensation: A theoretical framework. *Psychological Bulletin, 112,* 259-283.

Baltes, P. B., & Baltes, M. M. (1990). Psychological perspectives on successful aging: The model of selective optimization with compensation. In P. B. Baltes & M. M.

Baltes (Eds.), *Successful aging: Perspectives from the behavioral sciences* (pp. 1-34). New York: Cambridge University Press.

Bandura, A. (1982). Self-efficacy mechanisms in human agency. *American Psychologist, 37,* 122-147.

Bandura, A. (1986). *Social foundations of thought and action: A social cognitive theory.* Englewood Cliffs, NJ: Prentice Hall.

Bargh, J. A. (1990). Auto-motives: Pre-conscious determinants of social interaction. In E. T. Higgins & R. M. Sorrentino (Eds.), *Handbook of motivation and cognition: Vol. 2. Foundations of social behavior* (pp. 93-130). New York: Guilford.

Blaney, P. H. (1986). Affect and memory: A review. *Psychological Bulletin, 99,* 229-246.

Blazer, D. (1989). Depression in late life: An update. *Annual Review of Gerontology and Geriatrics, 9,* 197-215.

Bohner, G., Moskowitz, G. B., & Chaiken, S. (1995). The interplay of heuristic and systematic processing of social information. In W. Stroebe & M. Hewstone (Eds.), *European review of social psychology* (Vol. 6, pp. 33-68). Chichester: John Wiley.

Brandtstädter, J. (1984). Personal and social control over development: Some implications of an action perspective in life-span developmental psychology. In P. B. Baltes & O. G. Brim, Jr. (Eds.), *Life-span development and behavior* (Vol. 6, pp. 1-32). New York: Academic Press.

Brandtstädter, J. (1989). Personal self-regulation of development: Cross-sequential analyses of development-related control beliefs and emotions. *Developmental Psychology, 25,* 96-108.

Brandtstädter, J. (1992). Personal control over development: Some developmental implications of self-efficacy. In R. Schwarzer (Ed.), *Self-efficacy: Thought control of action* (pp. 127-145). New York: Hemisphere.

Brandtstädter, J., & Greve, W. (1994). The aging self: Stabilizing and protective processes. *Developmental Review, 14,* 52-80.

Brandtstädter, J., & Greve, W. (in press). Intentionale und nichtintentionale Aspekte des Handelns. In J. Straub & H. Werbik (Eds.), *Handlungstheorie. Begriff und Erklärung des Handelns im interdisziplinären Diskurs.* Frankfurt: Campus.

Brandtstädter, J., & Renner, G. (1990). Tenacious goal pursuit and flexible goal adjustment: Explication and age-related analysis of assimilative and accommodative strategies of coping. *Psychology and Aging, 5,* 58-67.

Brandtstädter, J., & Rothermund, K. (1994). Self-percepts of control in middle and later adulthood: Buffering losses by rescaling goals. *Psychology and Aging, 9,* 265-273.

Brandtstädter, J., Rothermund, K., & Schmitz, U. (1998). Maintaining self-integrity and self-efficacy through adulthood and later life: The adaptive functions of assimilative persistence and accommodative flexibility. In J. Heckhausen & C. S. Dweck (Eds.), *Motivation and self-regulation across the life span* (pp. 365-388). New York: Cambridge University Press.

Brandtstädter, J., & Wentura, D. (1994). Veränderungen der Zeit- und Zukunftsperspektive im Übergang zum höheren Erwachsenenalter: Entwicklungspsychologische und differentielle Aspekte. *Zeitschrift für Entwicklungspsychologie und Pädagogische Psychologie, 26,* 2-21.

Brandtstädter, J., & Wentura, D. (1995). Adjustment to shifting possibility frontiers in later life: Complementary adaptive modes. In R. A. Dixon & L. Bäckman (Eds.), *Compensating for psychological deficits and declines: Managing losses and promoting gains* (pp. 83-106). Mahwah, NJ: Lawrence Erlbaum.

Brandtstädter, J., Wentura, D., & Greve, W. (1993). Adaptive resources of the aging self: Outlines of an emergent perspective. *International Journal of Behavioral Development, 16,* 323-349.

Breytspraak, L. M. (1984). *The development of self in later life.* Boston: Little, Brown.

Brim, G. (1992). *Ambition: How we manage success and failure throughout our lives.* New York: Basic Books.

Carver, C. S., & Scheier, M. F. (1990). Origins and foundations of positive and negative affect: A control-process view. *Psychological Review, 97,* 19-25.

Costa, P. T., & McCrae, R. R. (1994). Set like plaster? Evidence for the stability of adult personality. In T. F. Heatherton & J. L. Weinberger (Eds.), *Can personality change?* (pp. 21-40). Washington, DC: American Psychological Association.

Coyne, J. C. (1992). Cognition on depression: A paradigm in crisis. *Psychological Inquiry, 3,* 232-235.

Cremer, R., & Zeef, E. J. (1987). What kind of noise increases with age? *Journal of Gerontology, 42,* 515-518.

Cross, S., & Markus, H. (1991). Possible selves across the life span. *Human Development, 34,* 230-255.

Frey, D. (1981). The effect of negative feedback about oneself and cost of information on preferences for information about the source of this feedback. *Journal of Experimental Social Psychology, 17,* 42-50.

Frey, K. S., & Ruble, D. N. (1990). Strategies for comparative evaluation: Maintaining a sense of competence across the life span. In R. J. Sternberg & J. Kolligian, Jr. (Eds.), *Competence considered* (pp. 167-189). New Haven, CT: Yale University Press.

Frijda, N. H. (1988). The laws of emotion. *American Psychologist, 43,* 349-358.

Gilbert, D. T. (1993). The assent of man: Mental representation and the control of belief. In D. M. Wegner & J. W. Pennebaker (Eds.), *Handbook of mental control* (pp. 57-87). Englewood Cliffs, NJ: Prentice Hall.

Gollwitzer, P. M. (1990). Action phases and mind-sets. In E. T. Higgins & R. M. Sorrentino (Eds.), *Handbook of motivation and cognition: Vol. 2. Foundations of social behavior* (pp. 53-92). New York: Guilford.

Greenwald, A. G., & Pratkanis, A. R. (1984). The self. In R. S. Wyer & T. K. Srull (Eds.), *Handbook of social cognition* (pp. 129-178). Hillsdale, NJ: Lawrence Erlbaum.

Greve, W. (1990). Stabilisierung und Modifikation des Selbstkonzeptes im Erwachsenenalter: Strategien der Immunisierung. *Sprache & Kognition, 9,* 218-230.

Heckhausen, J., Dixon, R. A., & Baltes, P. B. (1989). Gains and losses in development throughout adulthood as perceived by different adult age groups. *Developmental Psychology, 25,* 109-121.

Heckhausen, J., & Schulz, R. (1995). A life-span theory of control. *Psychological
Review, 102,* 284-304.

Honderich, T. (1988). *Mind and brain: A theory of determinism.* Oxford: Clarendon.

Johnston, M. (1995). Self-deception and the nature of mind. In C. Macdonald &
G. Macdonald (Eds.), *Philosophy of psychology: Debates on psychological
explanation* (Vol. 1, pp. 433-460). Oxford: Basil Blackwell.

Kessler, R. C., Foster, C., Webster, P. S., & House, J. S. (1992). The relationship
between age and depressive symptoms in two national surveys. *Psychology and
Aging, 7,* 119-126.

Klein, W. M., & Kunda, Z. (1993). Maintaining self-serving social comparisons:
Biased reconstruction of one's past behaviors. *Personality and Social Psychology
Bulletin, 19,* 732-739.

Kliegl, R., Smith, J., & Baltes, P. B. (1989). Testing-the-limits and the study of adult
age differences in cognitive plasticity of a mnemonic skill. *Developmental
Psychology, 25,* 247-256.

Klinger, E. (1982). On the self-management of mood, affect, and attention. In P.
Karoly & F. H. Kanfer (Eds.), *Self-management and behavior change* (pp. 129-
164). New York: Pergamon.

Kuhl, J. (1987). Action control: The maintenance of motivational states. In F.
Halisch & J. Kuhl (Eds.), *Motivation, intention, and volition* (pp. 279-291).
Berlin: Springer.

Kunda, Z. (1990). The case for motivated reasoning. *Psychological Bulletin, 108,*
480-498.

Lachman, M. E. (1986). Personal control in later life: Stability, change, and
cognitive correlates. In M. M. Baltes & P. B. Baltes (Eds.), *The psychology of
control and aging* (pp. 207-236). Hillsdale, NJ: Lawrence Erlbaum.

Lakatos, I. (1970). Falsification and the methodology of scientific research pro-
grammes. In I. Lakatos & A. Musgrave (Eds.), *Criticism and the growth of
knowledge* (pp. 91-196). Cambridge: Cambridge University Press.

Lazarus, R. S., & Folkman, S. (1984). *Stress, appraisal, and coping.* New York:
Springer.

Lerner, R. M. (1982). Children and adolescents as producers of their own development. *Developmental Review, 2,* 342-370.

Linville, P. W. (1985). Self-complexity and affective extremity: Don't put all your
eggs in one cognitive basket. *Social Cognition, 3,* 94-120.

Marsiske, M., Lang, F. R., Baltes, P. B., & Baltes, M. M. (1995). Selective
optimization with compensation. In R. A. Dixon & L. Bäckman (Eds.), *Com-

pensating for psychological deficits and declines: Managing losses and promoting gains (pp. 35-79). Mahwah, NJ: Lawrence Erlbaum.

Miller, D. T., & Turnbull, W. (1990). The counterfactual fallacy: Confusing what might have been with what ought to have been. *Social Justice Research, 4,* 1-19.

Montada, L. (1992). Attribution of responsibility for losses and perceived injustice. In L. Montada, S.-H. Filipp, & R. M. Lerner (Eds.), *Life crises and experiences of loss in adulthood* (pp. 133-161). Hillsdale, NJ: Lawrence Erlbaum.

Neumann, O. (1992). Theorien der Aufmerksamkeit: von Metaphern zu Mechanismen. *Psychologische Rundschau, 43,* 83-101.

Perdue, C. W., & Gurtman, M. B. (1990). Evidence for the automaticity of ageism. *Journal of Experimental Social Psychology, 26,* 199-216.

Peterson, C., & Seligman, M. E. P. (1984). Causal explanations as a risk factor for depression: Theory and evidence. *Psychological Review, 91,* 347-374.

Rodin, J. (1987). Personal control through the life course. In R. P. Abeles (Ed.), *Life-span perspective and social psychology* (pp. 103-119). Hillsdale, NJ: Lawrence Erlbaum.

Rothermund, K., & Brandtstädter, J. (1997). Entwicklung und Bewältigung: Festhalten und Preisgeben von Zielen als Formen der Bewältigung von Entwicklungsproblemen. In C. Tesch-Römer, C. Salewski, & G. Schwarz (Eds.), *Psychologie der Bewältigung* (pp. 120-133). Weinheim, Germany: Psychologie Verlags Union.

Rothermund, K., Wentura, D., & Brandtstädter, J. (1995). Selbstwertschützende Verschiebungen in der Semantik des Begriffs "alt" im höheren Erwachsenenalter. *Sprache & Kognition, 14,* 52-63.

Ryff, C. D. (1991). Possible selves in adulthood and old age: A tale of shifting horizons. *Psychology and Aging, 6,* 286-295.

Salthouse, T. A. (1987). Age, experience, and compensation. In C. Schooler & K. W. Schaie (Eds.), *Cognitive functioning and social structure over the life course* (pp. 142-150). Norwood, NJ: Ablex.

Sanitioso, R., Kunda, Z., & Fong, G. T. (1990). Motivated recruitment of autobiographical memories. *Journal of Personality and Social Psychology, 59,* 229-241.

Seligman, M. E. P., & Elder, G. (1986). Learned helplessness and life-span development. In A. B. Sørensen, F. E. Weinert, & L. R. Sherrod (Eds.), *Human development and the life course: Multidisciplinary perspectives* (pp. 377-428). Hillsdale, NJ: Lawrence Erlbaum.

Skinner, E. A. (1995). *Perceived control, motivation, and coping.* Thousand Oaks, CA: Sage.

Staudinger, U. M., Marsiske, M., & Baltes, P. B. (1995). Resilience and reserve capacity in later adulthood: Potentials and limits of development across the life span. In D. Cicchetti & D. Cohen (Eds.), *Developmental psychopathology. Vol. 2: Risk, disorder, and adaptation* (pp. 801-847). New York: John Wiley.

Sternberg, R. J., & Wagner, R. K. (Eds.). (1986). *Practical intelligence: Nature and origins of competence in the everyday world.* New York: Cambridge University Press.

Super, C. M., & Harkness, S. (1986). The developmental niche. *International Journal of Behavioral Development, 9,* 545-570.

Swann, W. B. (1983). Self-verification: Bringing the social reality in harmony with the self. In J. Suls & A. G. Greenwald (Eds.), *Psychological perspectives on the self* (Vol. 2, pp. 33-66). Hillsdale, NJ: Lawrence Erlbaum.

Taylor, S. E., & Gollwitzer, P. M. (1995). Effects of mindset on positive illusions. *Journal of Personality and Social Psychology, 69,* 213-226.

Thompson, S. C., Cheek, P. R., & Graham, M. A. (1988). The other side of perceived control: Disadvantages and negative effects. In S. Spacapan & S. Oskamp (Eds.), *The social psychology of health* (pp. 69-93). Newbury Park, CA: Sage.

Wentura, D. (1995). *Verfügbarkeit entlastender Kognitionen. Zur Verarbeitung negativer Lebenssituationen.* Weinheim, Germany: Psychologie Verlags Union.

Wentura, D., Dräger, D., & Brandtstädter, J. (1997). Alternsstereotype im früheren und höheren Erwachsenenalter: Analyse akkommodativer Veränderungen anhand einer Satzpriming-Technik. *Zeitschrift für Sozialpsychologie, 28,* 109-128.

Wentura, D., Rothermund, K., & Brandtstädter, J. (1995). Experimentelle Analysen zur Verarbeitung belastender Informationen: differential- und alternspsychologische Aspekte. *Zeitschrift für Experimentelle Psychologie, 42,* 152-175.

Wills, T. A. (1991). Similarity and self-esteem in downward comparison. In J. Suls & T. A. Wills (Eds.), *Social comparison: Contemporary theory and research* (pp. 51-78). Hillsdale, NJ: Lawrence Erlbaum.

Wolk, S. (1976). Situational constraint as a moderator of the locus of control-adjustment relationship. *Journal of Consulting and Clinical Psychology, 44,* 420-427.

Wright, R. A., & Brehm, J. W. (1989). Energization and goal attractiveness. In L. A. Pervin (Ed.), *Goal concepts in personality and social psychology* (pp. 169-210). Hillsdale, NJ: Lawrence Erlbaum.

14

SUCCESSFUL DEVELOPMENT AND AGING

The Role of Selection, Optimization, and Compensation

Alexandra M. Freund
Karen Z. H. Li
Paul B. Baltes

Most people would probably like to lead satisfying, fulfilling lives well into old age. Psychology has long been concerned with finding answers to the question of how people achieve and maintain a feeling of being satisfied and happy with their lives. What are the factors and processes that contribute to successful development and aging? We propose that three fundamental processes of developmental regulation are essential for successful development in general and successful aging in particular: selection, optimization, and compensation (the SOC model; M. Baltes & Carstensen, 1996, 1998; P. Baltes, 1997; P. Baltes & M. Baltes, 1980, 1990; P. Baltes,

Dittmann-Kohli, & Dixon, 1984; Freund & P. Baltes, in press; Marsiske, Lang, M. Baltes, & P. Baltes, 1995). The orchestration of selection, optimization, and compensation is thought to advance the maximization of gains and minimization of losses, which is one of the definitions of successful development and aging (e.g., M. Baltes & Carstensen, 1996; Brandtstädter & Wentura, 1995).

The SOC model can be operationalized, theoretically and empirically, in several ways, depending on the level of analysis, contextual conditions, and the domain of functioning under consideration. In this chapter, we take an action-theoretical perspective (Freund & P. Baltes, in press) and argue that developing and committing to a hierarchy of personal goals (*elective selection*) and engaging in goal-directed actions and means (*optimization*) are essential for the achievement of higher levels of functioning. We postulate that in order to maintain a given level of functioning in the face of loss and decline in goal-relevant means, people need to invest in compensatory means (*compensation*). When the costs for goal achievement or maintenance outweigh the gains, the SOC model posits that it is most adaptive to reconstruct one's goal hierarchy by focusing exclusively on the most important goals, developing new goals, or adapting goal standards (*loss-based selection*). Thus the SOC model conceptualizes processes that promote gains (elective selection, optimization) but also processes to counteract losses that inevitably occur in life, particularly in old and very old age (compensation, loss-based selection).

The SOC model constitutes a general model of development and applies to various domains of functioning (e.g., identity formation and maintenance, social relations, athletic performance) and to different levels of analysis (e.g., societal, group, or individual level). For instance, M. Baltes and Carstensen (1998) have shown how SOC can be conceptualized involving dyads or groups of people as a collective process of successful development (i.e., collective SOC). As an additional example, J. Heckhausen and Schulz (1995) used the SOC perspective to articulate a life-span theory of primary versus secondary control. On a more microanalytic level, SOC can also be applied to the investigation of cognitive performance in dual-task conditions (Lindenberger, Marsiske, & P. Baltes, 1998). And finally, it is possible to apply SOC-related perspectives to questions of societal functioning.

In this chapter, we apply SOC to the domain of individual successful aging. To illustrate the processes of selection, optimization, and compensation in this domain, we present three empirical illustrations that (a) support the hypothesis that SOC contributes to successful aging (Freund & P. Baltes, 1998), (b) apply SOC to the domain of identity maintenance in old age (Freund, 1995), and (c) integrate findings from the aging and cognition literature with SOC. Finally, we discuss some future directions for SOC as a model of successful aging.

BASIC ASSUMPTIONS OF HUMAN DEVELOPMENT UNDERLYING THE SOC MODEL

We begin by outlining basic assumptions about human development that underlie the SOC model as a model of successful aging (P. Baltes, 1987, 1997; P. Baltes & M. Baltes, 1990; Freund & P. Baltes, in press). We will summarize those assumptions that are most relevant to the present context: (a) Development is the interplay of individuals' proactive creation of and reaction to their environments; (b) throughout the life span, and particularly in old age, internal and external resources are limited; and (c) development is multidirectional and multifunctional—that is, it encompasses growth (gain) and decline (loss).

Development is the interplay of individuals' proactive creation of and reaction to their environments. In accordance with other life-span developmentalists, we assume that development occurs as an interaction of a person with his or her environment (e.g., M. Baltes & Carstensen, 1996; P. Baltes, Lindenberger, & Staudinger, 1998; Brandtstädter, 1998; Labouvie-Vief, 1981; Lawton, 1989; Lerner, 1991; Lerner & Busch-Rossnagel, 1981; Magnusson, Winblad, & Nilsson, 1996). People create their development by actively shaping their environments and placing themselves into certain contexts. At the same time, people also constantly react and adapt to predetermined physical, cultural, social, and historical contexts. Development evolves when an individual, with his or her specific predispositions (e.g., abilities, temperament), proactively and reactively interacts with a given context.

Throughout the life span, and particularly in old age, internal and external resources are limited. Resources can be defined as biological-genetic, social-cultural, or psychological means that support or help a person to transact successfully with his or her environment. Such internal and external resources are limited throughout the life span (e.g., nobody has unlimited physical strength). The limitation of resources increases in old age due to two factors (P. Baltes, 1997; Lerner, 1991; Staudinger, Marsiske, & P. Baltes, 1995): (a) Fewer resources are available in old age (e.g., time to death becomes shorter, cognitive and physical abilities decline), and (b) the efficiency of the available resources decreases (e.g., cognitive intervention appears to show less effect in old compared with younger adults; Kliegl, Smith, & P. Baltes, 1989). Thus the balance of gains and losses can be expected to become more negative in old age (P. Baltes, 1987; J. Heckhausen, Dixon, & P. Baltes, 1989).

Development is multidirectional and multifunctional. One of the central propositions of life-span psychology is the multidirectionality and multifunctionality of development. That is, regarding multidirectionality, development comprises not only trajectories of growth but also trajectories of decline (P. Baltes et al., 1998; Brandtstädter & Wentura, 1995; Labouvie-Vief, 1981). Multidirectionality is evident within and across domains of functioning. An example of multidirectionality *within* domains can be seen in a comparison of the knowledge-based, crystallized aspects of intelligence, which stay stable or even increase in old age, with the more biologically based, mechanical aspects of cognitive functioning, which show decline (Lindenberger & P. Baltes, 1997). An example of multidirectionality *across* domains is that most health-related measures show decline in old age (e.g., Steinhagen-Thiessen & Borchelt, 1999), whereas most self and personality measures show stability (e.g., Smith & P. Baltes, 1999).

Multifunctionality refers to the fact that developmental outcomes have multiple adaptive consequences, temporally and contextually. Examples are issues of positive and negative transfer. Stated as a proposition: Multifunctionality suggests that there is no gain without loss and no loss without gain (P. Baltes, 1987; Labouvie-Vief, 1981). This topic is similar to arguments advanced for evolutionary change.

The various age-related change trajectories combine into an overall life-span script. Although there are still trajectories that show growth in old age, on balance, the losses outweigh the gains. One of the consequences of such an unfavorable balance of gains to losses in old age is that more resources need to be invested in the maintenance of given levels of functioning (compensation) than in optimization of functioning (see J. Heckhausen, 1997; Staudinger et al., 1995). A similar perspective is contained in the life-span script of allocation of resources into three objectives/goals of development: growth, maintenance, and regulation of loss. From a primary emphasis on growth in childhood, with aging, more and more resources are allocated into processes of maintenance and regulation of loss (P. Baltes et al., 1998; Staudinger et al., 1995).

HOW CAN SUCCESSFUL DEVELOPMENT BE DEFINED?

Based on these assumptions about human development, successful development can be conceptualized as the ongoing process of the person-environment interaction that maximizes gains and minimizes losses (see M. Baltes & Carstensen, 1996; P. Baltes, 1997; Brandtstädter, 1998; Labouvie-Vief, 1981). Contrary to definitions of successful development that focus primarily on the adaptation of the individual to a given context (e.g., Havighurst, 1963), this conceptualization emphasizes the *balance* between a person's needs and competence on the one hand and environmental demands and opportunity structures on the other (Lawton & Nahemow, 1973; Thomae, 1974). Ideally, such an approach takes into consideration aspects of both the environment and the person in order to determine successful development. Further, it encompasses both objective and subjective criteria over time (M. Baltes & Carstensen, 1996; P. Baltes & M. Baltes, 1990).

The concept of successful *development* does not denote an end point that can be reached (e.g., having achieved a certain goal) but must take into account *how* people achieve certain desired states within a range of potentialities, and how these methods or strategies change with age. That is, instead of being defined as a single state, successful development should be defined as a multifaceted process (M. Baltes & Carstensen, 1996). If the cost for achieving one's goals is to suffer through years of unhappiness or frustration, this way of goal pursuit may or may not (on a subjective level) be considered successful. The gains associated with achieving desired outcomes must be balanced with the costs associated with their attainment. Such evaluations, of course, are themselves subject to developmental changes, as research on subjective "lifetime" personality suggests (Fleeson & P. Baltes, 1998).

The issue of the time window—multiple assessments of criteria of successful development over time versus "snapshots"—in which to determine successful development has not been well specified in the literature. Moreover, consensus has not been reached on the question of which criteria—objective (e.g., physical health, longevity) and subjective (e.g., self-acceptance, purpose in life)—need to be met, or what is the relative importance of each for successful development. However, much of the extant research on successful aging development has focused on *subjective* indicators (e.g., Ryff, 1989), on the basis of the assumption that a successful person-environment interaction results in subjective well-being and life satisfaction (e.g., Lawton, 1989).

SELECTION, OPTIMIZATION, AND COMPENSATION AS PROCESSES OF ADAPTIVE MASTERY

What are the factors and processes that foster successful development? In this section, we argue that selection, optimization, and compensation play key roles in successful aging. Although selection, optimization, and compensation are conceptualized as general processes of adaptive mastery across the life span, P. Baltes and M. Baltes (1980, 1990) propose that they gain importance in old age, a period in life when internal (e.g., reserve capacity) as well as external (e.g., income) resources decline and losses are more likely than in earlier phases of life.

Elective Selection

The necessity of selection is rooted in the limitation of resources and the notion that development is essentially specialization (canalization). Beginning with our sensory apparatus, we cannot perceive everything. Similar constraints apply to the amounts of time and effort available. Hence, reactively and proactively, we choose (or select) in which domains of functioning we want to focus our resources. Selection denotes narrowing the range of possible alternative options (domains of functioning, goals) that can be pursued given the internal and external resources a person has at his or her disposal. Typical instances of elective selection and some examples are given in Table 14.1.

Conceiving of humans as actors, as action theory suggests, selection then can involve (a) developing goals or targets of development, building a hierarchy of goals and preferences, and committing oneself to pursuing these goals (i.e., elective selection); and (b) restructuring one's goal hierarchy, adapting goal standards, or selecting new goals when opportunity structures change. If the change of opportunity structures is due to loss or decline in goal-relevant means, we refer to this as *loss-based selection* (see Table 14.2).

TABLE 14.1 Typical Instances of Elective Selection and Examples

Instance	Example
Specification of goals	Specifying one's area of profession (engineering) to becoming a technical engineer
Goal system (hierarchy)	Giving higher priority to raising a family than to pursuing a professional career
Contextualization of goals	Adjusting one's physical appearance (e.g., attire) to cultural customs and social contexts
Goal commitment	Feeling obligated and emotionally impelled to maintain one's friendships over time and across situations

TABLE 14.2 Organization of Selection, Optimization, and Compensation Processes in the Domain of Personal Goals

Loss of Means	Goal Setting	Goal Striving
Absent	elective selection	optimization
Present	loss-based selection	compensation

The distinction between these two forms of selection—elective selection and loss-based selection—is rooted in one of the fundamental assumptions of life-span developmental psychology outlined above, namely, that human development comprises both loss and decline. Throughout the life span, people not only electively select goals but also change their goals in response to losses in goal-relevant means. Both loss-based selection and compensation address the adaptive mastery of losses. We will discuss the function of loss-based selection and its distinction from compensation in more detail in a later section.

The most general characteristic of selection is that it implies directionality of development. If a person does not develop a hierarchy of goals or preferences and does not commit him- or herself to goals, that person's behavior is unlikely to be organized into time-extended action sequences (see Boesch, 1976, 1991; Brandtstädter, 1998; H. Heckhausen, 1989; H. Heckhausen & Gollwitzer, 1987; Oettingen, 1997). Instead, such an individual's behavior would more likely be determined by the current situation and by the person's current cognitive and individual disposition. Selection denotes not only the active choice of particular goals, but can also be located outside the individual (e.g., by parents, teachers, society). For instance, if developmental pathways are extremely normative regarding the sequence and timing of developmental tasks, active selection of personal goals might not be as important for directionality. In this case, the individual developmental pathway is highly determined by the environment (e.g., mandatory retirement) and related structures of environmental opportunities. In the end, however, a significant portion of such outside conditions and expectations are "transported" into individual minds by processes of internalization.

It has been argued that in old age the life course becomes less structured by societal demands (e.g., Atchley, 1982; Rosenmayr, 1983). Thus in old age the individual's goals and "freedom" should play a greater role in selection processes. However, there are fewer opportunity structures and internal resources available in old age (see P. Baltes, 1997), possibly leading to a narrower range of possibilities from which to select, and consequently reducing the demand to select. Empirical evidence stemming from the Berlin Aging Study (BASE; P. Baltes, Mayer, Helmchen, & Steinhagen-Thiessen, 1999) supports both the importance of selection for successful aging and the limited basis for selection in old age. Self-reported elective selection was found to be significantly associated with subjective indicators of successful aging, but at the same time appeared to be less important than optimization and compensation (Freund & P. Baltes, 1998). Also, with increasing age there was a tendency to report less engagement in elective selection. Similarly, the amount of self-reported investment across a number of goals (i.e., personal life investment) decreased in old age (Staudinger, Freund, Linden, & Maas, 1999). More important in the context of the SOC model, selectivity in life investment—selecting few domains on which to focus—proved to be particularly adaptive for older people who were confronted with constraints in resources (Staudinger & Freund, 1998).

Optimization

The SOC model posits that people need to act on their goals; that is, they need to *develop goal-relevant means* in order to optimize their level of functioning and promote successful development (P. Baltes & M. Baltes, 1990; Freund & P. Baltes, in press; Marsiske et al., 1995). Which means are best suited for achieving a given goal depends on such factors as the content of the goal, personal characteristics such as age and skills, and the given opportunity structures (see Cantor, 1994). It is possible, however, to identify general strategies of goal pursuit that foster goal achievement

TABLE 14.3 Typical Instances of Optimization and Examples

Instance	Example
Acquiring new skills/resources	Learning how to type with a 10-finger system
Seizing the right moment	Asking for a pay raise after accomplishing a major project
Persistence	Revising a manuscript until it is accepted by a good journal
Practice of skills	Practicing scales on the piano daily
Effort/energy	Thinking very hard about the solution to a mathematical problem
Time allocation	Setting aside specific times to spend with one's children
Modeling successful others	Watching videos of how professional golfers stroke the ball

independent of the factors mentioned above. Instances of such general optimization strategies are displayed in Table 14.3.

For each of the strategies listed in Table 14.3, there exists a literature showing the strategy's positive relation to goal achievement (for an overview, see Freund & P. Baltes, in press). One important aspect of optimization is the monitoring of the effects of the strategies applied. As Locke, Shaw, Saari, and Latham (1981) have shown, feedback about performance is central for goal achievement. Information about his or her progress toward a goal allows an individual to adjust his or her goal-related means to improve goal achievement or to adapt to altered circumstances (Carver & Scheier, 1995). Monitoring can take the form of external supervision (e.g., by teachers) or of the individual's conscious comparison of the distance between the actual and desired state. In many instances, however, monitoring occurs outside of awareness (Gollwitzer & Schaal, 1998; Wegner, 1992). Conscious comparison of the actual and the desired states is more likely to occur in the context of higher-order goals that require complex goal-related actions (e.g., being professionally successful). In contrast, unconscious monitoring is more likely to take place in highly routinized goal-related actions (e.g., driving to work).

Not only can monitoring occur outside of conscious awareness, but the activation of goals can also become automatic. According to Bargh and Gollwitzer's (1994) auto-motive model, the repeated activation of a goal in a certain situation leads to an association of the respective goal and situational cues. Thus situational features may automatically trigger a goal

TABLE 14.4 Typical Instances of Compensation and Examples

Instance	Example
Substitution of means	Dictating manuscripts when unable to type because of arthritis
Use of external aids/help of others	Using a wheelchair when unable to walk
Use of therapeutic intervention	Seeing a psychotherapist when personal problems become overwhelming
Acquiring new skills/resources	Getting retraining after having lost a job
Activation of unused skills/resources	Asking one's parents to baby-sit youngsters so that one may return to work
Increased effort/energy	Trying harder to run as fast as possible in a marathon after having lost 2 minutes because of a cramp
Increased time allocation	Spending more time with one's children when the relationship has deteriorated
Modeling successful others who compensate	Joining a self-help group of widowers to learn how others cope with the loss of a spouse

and activate goal-relevant actions. With increasing age, the likelihood of repeated goal activation in particular situational contexts also increases. The automatization of goal activation might free up resources that older adults can then devote to goal-related actions.

Compensation

How can people maintain a given level of functioning when loss or decline in goal-relevant means occurs? The key concept addressing the issue of overcoming mismatches between skill and demand is compensation (see Bäckman & Dixon, 1992). More specifically, in the SOC model compensation is confined to those instances of mismatch that are due to loss in goal-relevant means (P. Baltes & M. Baltes, 1990; Carstensen, Hanson, & Freund, 1995; Freund & P. Baltes, in press; Marsiske et al., 1995). Typical instances of compensation and illustrative examples are shown in Table 14.4.

In the case of optimization, means are invested in the interest of goal achievement under stable conditions of resources. In the case of compensation, means are invested in the interest of *avoiding* a loss in goal achievement (see Table 14.2). The literature on prospect theory (Tversky & Kahneman, 1981) indicates that, in general, people are highly motivated to avoid losses (see also Hobfoll, 1989): They take more risks in order to prevent losses than to make gains, and their emotional reactions to losses are stronger than their reactions to gains.

Although people of all ages appear to be motivated to engage in compensatory behavior when anticipating or experiencing loss in goal-related means and associated losses in goal achievement, this process might be of particular importance in old age. In old age, losses are prevalent in many life domains, such as health (e.g., Manton, Stallard, & Corder, 1995), sensory functioning (e.g., Marsiske et al., 1999), size of social network (e.g., Lang & Carstensen, 1994), and cognitive functioning (e.g., Lindenberger & P. Baltes, 1997). In old age, as losses of this kind are more prevalent than in younger age groups, the need for compensation might also be higher (P. Baltes, 1997; Staudinger et al., 1995) and might also increase the motivation to avoid loss. For example, in a study of appointment keeping and prospective memory in young and old adults, it was observed that to ensure that the future tasks were carried out, the old adults relied more frequently on external memory aids (e.g., calendar notation) compared with the young adults (Maylor, 1990). Furthermore, for older participants the use of memory aids was associated with more accurate prospective memory performance.

Although losses call for compensation in general, predicting a simple increase in compensatory action in response to *many* losses neglects the fact that compensation itself draws on limited resources, such as time, energy, and money (see Hobfoll, 1989; Schönpflug, 1998). In old age, then, when losses occur in a number of domains, means that can be deployed for compensation are equally scarce. Data from the Berlin Aging Study support this contention: In this sample of old and very old people, self-reported compensation was negatively associated with age (Freund & P. Baltes, 1998). This finding suggests that the compensatory efforts themselves become restricted by a limitation of internal or external resources in very old age.

Loss-Based Selection

In cases of wide-ranging resource limitations, it might be more adaptive to disengage from goals that are subject to losses than to invest resources in compensatory efforts. According to self-regulation theory (Carver & Scheier, 1981), after disruption of goal-relevant action (e.g., when a goal is blocked), individuals reassess the likelihood of goal attainment. In the

TABLE 14.5 Typical Instances of Loss-Based Selection and Examples

Instance	Example
Focusing on most important goal(s)	Giving up less important work projects and focusing on the critical ones when under time pressure
Reconstruction of goal hierarchy	Prioritizing one's daughter's career over one's own when opportunities to advance are no longer present
Adaptation of standards	Contenting oneself with being a strong amateur pianist after failing the entrance examination to a conservatory
Searching for new goals	Finding new hobbies to pursue after retirement

case of high outcome expectancies, individuals will persist in pursuing their goals (i.e., engage in compensatory strategies). In the case of low or negative outcome expectancies, however, individuals are more likely to disengage from their goals.

Disengaging from a goal that is subjected to loss is one of the facets of loss-based selection. As does compensation, loss-based selection occurs in response to decline of resources or loss of previously available goal-relevant means (see Table 14.2). Loss-based selection encompasses such strategies as reconstructing one's goal hierarchy and searching for new goals (see Table 14.5 for typical instances and examples).

Loss-based selection involves processes of developing, selecting, and setting goals as a response to loss. In contrast, compensation denotes the counteracting of loss in the service of *maintaining function* in the same domain. This distinction between compensation and loss-based selection is based on the difference between goal setting and goal pursuit (see Table 14.2), processes that involve different phases in the motivational process associated with distinct cognitive and emotional states (e.g., Gollwitzer, 1996; H. Heckhausen, 1989; H. Heckhausen & Gollwitzer, 1987).

The adaptiveness of disengagement from permanently blocked goals is also stressed by J. Heckhausen and Schulz (1995) in their life-span model of primary and secondary control (see also J. Heckhausen & Schulz, Chapter 3, this volume). In this model, downgrading of, and disengagement from, blocked goals (i.e., compensatory secondary control) buffers the negative motivational effects of failure or loss. A related concept has been put forth by Brandtstädter and his colleagues (Brandtstädter & Greve, 1994; Brandtstädter & Renner, 1990; Brandtstädter & Wentura, 1995; see also Brandtstädter, Wentura, & Rothermund, Chapter 13, this volume). Brandtstädter distinguishes between two complementary modes of coping with blocked goals: (a) assimilative coping or tenacious goal pursuit (i.e., actively shaping one's environment according to one's needs and goals), and (b) accommodative coping or flexible goal adjustment (i.e., adjusting one's goals and standards to environmental constraints). According to Brandtstädter's dual-process model of coping, when confronted with blocked goals, people first attempt to reach their goals through tenacious goal pursuit. If, despite these efforts, the goals remain blocked, flexible goal adjustment takes place (i.e., downgrading of or disengagement from blocked goals, readjustment of standards).

Consistent with this hypothesis, Brandtstädter and Renner (1990) found an age-related increase in flexible goal adjustment, supposedly because of increased losses in goal-related means. Moreover, Brandtstädter and Rothermund (1994) observed in a longitudinal study that accommodative strategies helped to maintain a sense of control when participants were faced with losses. These results suggest that downscaling the importance of a blocked goal buffers the experience of loss. As the restructuring of the goal hierarchy and the adjusting of standards as a response to loss are also facets of loss-based selection, these findings support the hypothesis that loss-based selection contributes to successful management in the face of severe and permanent losses. In old age, as losses become more severe, wide-ranging, and permanent, loss-based selection might become particularly important for developmental regulation.

THE DEVELOPMENTAL COMPOSITION AND TRANSFORMATION OF SOC

So far, we have approached the definition of SOC processes in a somewhat static manner. We have defined selection, optimization, and compensation as processes located at a particular time in a particular space of action (Boesch, 1991, 1997; Brandtstädter, 1998). Human development, however, is a temporal process in which actions combine into sequences of actions that in concert and over time result in developmental outcomes. This is accompanied by changes in the structure and function of action. Two issues arise from this developmental and combinative extension of SOC.

First, there is the issue of developmental changes in the logical status of the three component processes involved. The status of whether a given individual event signifies selection, optimization, or compensation is not fixed. In fact, change in SOC is fundamental to development (Marsiske et al., 1995). What once was treated as selection (that is, the identification of a goal) can later become a means, or what once was acquired as a compensatory means at a later point in development can function as an optimizing means. Consider the following: A person's having identified superior running ability as a goal, and then practiced to optimize performance, can at a later point become a means for that individual to achieve a more complex, higher-level goal, such as attaining physical fitness. Similarly, a widower may spend more time with his children to compensate for the loss in household assistance, but when he remarries he continues to interact with the children to optimize the development of the parent-child relationship. Because of this change in the logical status of a given event, when classifying a given event as selection, optimization, or compensation, we need to specify the history of acquisition and the functional status in a given action context.

Second, there is the issue of level of composition and the analytic decomposition of action units. This is a perennial problem of action psychology. Each action unit can be decomposed into smaller action units, and, at the same time, each action unit can be conceptualized as contributing to a larger action unit. Applying this perspective to SOC implies that each of the components (selection, optimization, and compensation) in itself can be decomposed as being constituted by the entire process of SOC. Take selection as an example: If the definition of selection implies, as action psychologists argue (Boesch, 1976, 1991; Brandtstädter, 1998; Eckensberger, 1997; Frese & Sabini, 1985; Gollwitzer & Bargh, 1996; Oettingen, 1997), that goals are not only identified but also refined and maintained over time, then that process of selection involves factors of optimization and compensation. For instance, in order to refine and maintain a specific goal, it is important to possess and employ means of attentional focus and motivational investment to implement the goal-related intention. Similarly, for the case of decomposing the process of optimization, if a person engages in refining his or her means to reach a goal such as finger agility to play the piano, this "means-oriented" activity of practicing finger motility involves turning that means into a goal. Optimization, therefore, can be decomposed into smaller action units. The same applies to the process of compensation.

These issues of action theory are unavoidable, and if SOC is approached from an action-theoretical perspective, the problems shall remain with us.

In our work, we recognize this conundrum but make an effort to treat the three components as heuristic categories that in each instance require a functional analysis of the action unit(s) involved (see also Marsiske et al., 1995). Part of this specification is the level of analysis intended. For instance, when SOC is treated as an overall theory of development, its "action focus" is on the life span as a whole, and in this instance, selection, optimization, and compensation involve temporally extended and cumulative-aggregate categories. As soon as we move into more specific contexts and temporal spans, it is the theories and research paradigms available for the categories of interest (such as subjective well-being or episodic memory) that need to be invoked to define the logical status of selection, optimization, and compensation.

EMPIRICAL ILLUSTRATIONS OF SOC

We turn now to three empirical illustrations of SOC processes and dynamics. The first concerns the subjective assessment of successful aging, the second addresses the construct of the self-definition, and the third involves the task of coordinating multiple goals.

Selection, Optimization, and Compensation in Old and Very Old Age: Evidence From the Berlin Aging Study

The central hypothesis of the SOC model is that selection, optimization, and compensation contribute to successful development. In old and very old age, when time to live becomes shorter and constraints and losses become more prevalent, these processes might contribute to sustaining a sense of well-being. We investigated this hypothesis with a subsample of the Berlin Aging Study ($N = 200$, age range = 72-103 years; Freund & P. Baltes, 1998). In this study, SOC was operationalized using a 12-item questionnaire (P. Baltes, M. Baltes, Freund, & Lang, 1995) with 3 items for each of the component processes (elective selection, loss-based selection, optimization, and compensation). Satisfaction with aging, lack of agitation, positive emotions, and absence of social and emotional loneliness served as global subjective indicators of successful aging.

As predicted, each of the components of SOC was positively related to indicators of successful aging. As was expected for a construct as complex as subjectively aging well, the magnitude of these correlations was of moderate size. It is important to note, however, that the associations between SOC and subjective indicators of successful aging were robust when various rival predictive measures of successful mastery (e.g., control beliefs, physical and mental health, neuroticism, extroversion, openness, intelligence) were controlled for, thus a unique contribution of SOC processes to successful aging is suggested.

When the relative importance of the SOC processes for aging well were compared, individual differences in self-reported selection showed the weakest associations with the outcome measures, and optimization shared as much unique variance with the indicators of successful aging they did compensation. This suggests that opportunity structures and resources are less available in old age, and this shrinkage of opportunities confines the pool of possible alternative options from which to select. With regard to the relatively greater importance of optimization and compensation, older adults seem to invest their resources in achieving positive outcomes (i.e., optimization) as much as they invest in the repair and counteracting of losses (i.e., compensation).

SOC and the Self-Definition in Old Age

Whereas the above example serves to illustrate SOC processes at a domain-general level, our second example concerns the specific domain of how people define themselves. The *self-definition* refers to a person's subjective theory about him- or herself (Epstein, 1973, 1980). It contains self-related knowledge about behaviors, goals, values, interests, and personal characteristics that is subjectively highly important, to which the individual feels committed, and that subjectively distinguishes his or her own person from that of others (Brandtstädter, 1985; Brandtstädter & Greve, 1994; Cantor & Kihlstrom, 1989; Filipp, 1980; Markus, 1983; McGuire, 1984; Wicklund & Gollwitzer, 1982).

Because of the losses in various domains of functioning accompanying old age (e.g., health, Manton et al., 1995; social network, Lang, 1994), the maintenance of the self-definition might be particularly at risk for people in this age group (Atchley, 1982, 1991; Brandtstädter & Greve, 1994; Freund, 1995; Lemon, Bengtson, & Peterson, 1971; Maddox, 1994; Rosow, 1973). For instance, reductions in mobility might prevent an elderly woman from keeping a garden and from participating in a walking group, activities that are important for her self-definition. The maintenance of the self-definition is often considered important for the maintenance of the sense of well-being in old age (e.g., P. Baltes & M. Baltes, 1990; Brandtstädter & Greve, 1994; Freund, 1995; Troll & Skaff, 1997).

One of the first personality psychologists to stress the importance of maintaining the self-definition was Lecky (1945). Similar to Lecky, Allport (1961) assumed that a sense of identify is essential for the functioning and well-being of an individual. According to Epstein (1973, 1980), structuring and organizing the many experiences individuals constantly make is the primary function of the self-definition (see also Swann, 1990; Wicklund & Gollwitzer, 1982). The self-definition offers concepts that guide behavior and provide orientation for the interaction with the environment and a sense of identity (for a more detailed discussion of the function of the self-definition, see Freund, 1995). Only temporally stable concepts can organize and structure events and experiences, extract their meaning, and guide behavior (Baars, 1988). Swann (1996) illustrates the consequences of loss of self-definition:

> Imagine waking up one morning with no idea who you are. The first thing you might notice is that nothing has any particular meaning or significance. You would not recognize the decorations on your bedroom wall, your bed-clothes, or even the person sleeping beside you. As you lay there trying to make sense of it all, you would realize that you had no idea what to do next. Lacking a sense of self, you would have no plans, no goals, and worst of all, no basis on which to fashion such plans and goals. (p. 53)

The goal, then, is to maintain one's self-definition or to transform it in acceptable ways (Wicklund & Gollwitzer, 1982). Given that older people are subjected to losses in a variety of domains (e.g., home ownership, occupation, spouse), the maintenance of the self-definition is particularly threatened in this phase of the life span. This assumption is empirically supported by the negative correlation of age with the total number of self-defining domains and their richness (number of aspects within self-defining domains) in old and very old age (Freund & Smith, 1999). This negative age correlation of self-definition is due to an increase in health-related constraints. It seems, then, that the losses that older adults experience with high likelihood do in fact pose a threat to the self-definition. Based on the SOC model, and in line with Markus and Nurius's (1986) work on possible selves, we argue that it is advantageous for the maintenance of older persons' self-definitions for those self-definitions to comprise a variety of domains. A self-definition that encompasses several different domains offers alternative sources for self-definition, thereby providing a backup supply of self-defining domains that can help to compensate for the loss of one domain (P. Baltes & M. Baltes, 1990; Brandtstädter & Greve, 1994; Freund, 1995; Linville, 1987; Rosenberg & Gara, 1985; Thoits, 1983).

Longitudinal studies on the role of a multifaceted self-definition for counteracting negative effects of loss and decline have revealed mixed results, however. Upon repeated testing, Linville (1987) found that a complex self-definition (i.e., a self-definition that contains a high number of distinct domains) buffers the negative effects of negative life events in young adults. Thoits (1983), on the other hand, found that a high number of social roles exacerbated the negative effects of losses. Thoits, however, did not have information about the distinctiveness of the self-defining domains, and it might well be that social roles of her middle-aged participants were highly embedded and interconnected. The loss of one self-defining domain might then have had a sweeping effect, carrying the connected domains with it. For instance, if an older man's social network is tightly interconnected with his wife's, if she was the one who made all arrangements for meeting friends and joint activities, the death of his wife might hit him doubly because he has lost both "married to Jane" and "activities with friends" as domains. Similarly, Donahue, Robins, Roberts, and John (1993) found a high number of unconnected domains to be detrimental rather than beneficial, underscoring the potential pitfalls of not selecting as opposed to cultivating an integrated set of domains.

The results of these studies of young and middle-aged adults, however, may not be generalizable to old age. On the one hand, because of diminishing resources, the optimal number of distinct self-defining domains might be lower among older persons than in younger age groups. On the other hand, it might be more difficult in old age to build up new self-defining domains to compensate for losses. This latter argument suggests that a high number of self-defining domains might play a more important role in counteracting the negative effects of losses in old compared with young or middle-aged adults. Results obtained in the context of the BASE suggest that the role of the number of self-defining domains might in fact be complex. Neither the cross-sectional (Freund, 1995; Freund & Smith, 1999) nor the longitudinal results (Staudinger & Freund, 1998) support the hypothesis that a higher number of self-defining domains buffers the negative effects of health-related or financial constraints for older people.

The SOC model offers some resolution of these findings. We propose that the relation between the self-definition and the number of self-defining domains might be curvilinear, with too few domains not offering a stable basis for self-definition and too many different domains overwhelming the person. The optimal number of self-defining domains depends on the person's resources and the demands with which the person is faced. Thus the optimal number of self-defining domains changes across the life span. In adolescence and young adulthood, it is important for individuals to build up their identities (e.g., Damon & Hart, 1982; Erikson, 1959; Marcia, 1980). In order to prevent foreclosure by premature selection of domains, young people need to explore alternatives to determine the best fit of personal needs and abilities to environmental demands.

This phase of exploring and testing alternative self-definitions, however, needs to be modulated with the selection of certain domains of functioning to ensure the possibility of optimizing functioning in these domains (see Archer, 1989; Ball & Chandler, 1989). Thus in middle adulthood, the optimal number of self-defining domains is expected to be relatively stable and confined to the most important domains of functioning. Commitment to, and persistence in, pursuing these self-defining domains is central for the elaboration, refinement, and optimization of the self-definition. Such a well-elaborated and refined self-definition can then be a powerful structure supporting the organization and guidance of goals and actions, thereby ensuring that development is directed rather than diffuse. Of course, as internal and external demands change across adulthood—for instance, from raising a family to (re)defining the partnership not primarily as parents but as a couple—self-defining domains will change accordingly in content, emphasis, and importance. This process of adaptation will result in a certain degree of variability in the self-definition across time. According to the SOC model, however, it might not be adaptive for individuals to invest their resources primarily in building up new domains of functioning instead of optimizing domains they have already successfully built up in the process of interacting with their environments. During adulthood, there is a high degree of interconnectedness of self-definitions.

In old age, interindividual differences in the development of the self-definition might be more pronounced because of the heterogeneity of older people and the multidirectionality of development, as well as the lack of institutional regulation. On the one hand, older persons have more freedom regarding social roles (Atchley, 1982; Riley, 1987). This freedom might offer possibilities for building up new self-defining domains (Waterman & Archer, 1990) that might even lead to what L'Écuyer (1990) calls a renewal of the self-definition. This process might lead to an increase in the number of self-defining domains that reflect best the opportunity structures of this phase in life. On the other hand, as outlined above, old age is also characterized by diminishing resources and increasing losses (P. Baltes, 1997) that can threaten the maintenance of the self-definition. The SOC model suggests that diminished resources call for higher selectivity—that is, focusing on those domains of functioning that are of central importance for the self-definition. Therefore, a smaller number of self-defining domains might be more adaptive for persons who are confronted with declining resources (Staudinger & Freund, 1998). Similarly, in the case of loss, compensatory efforts might be more successful if they are concentrated on few rather than diffused among many domains of functioning (P. Baltes & M. Baltes, 1990; Freund & P. Baltes, in press; Marsiske et al., 1995). Thus, on the basis of the SOC model, it seems crucial to go beyond the simple question of the adaptiveness of the number of self-defining domains in old age. Instead, it might be more fruitful to investigate the optimal range and contextual adaptivity of self-defining domains (i.e., under which conditions is a multifaceted self-definition a resource for compensating losses, and under which conditions is selection of self-defining domains most adaptive?).

The On-Line Assessment of SOC Processes Using a Dual-Task Approach

In general, a major issue of SOC-related conceptions is the lack of conceptual and empirical work that has as an explicit focus the parallel operation of more than one goal-directed action. Our third empirical illustration of SOC concepts, therefore, draws from the field of cognitive psychology—more specifically, from research on aging and dual-task performance. We see dual-task research as a laboratory analogue of life management situations in which multiple roles or goals must be coordinated. Consider the dual goals of raising a family and launching one's career: One must establish and maintain a balance of the two goals in the face of limitations in resources such as time, energy, ability, and expertise.

Borrowing from, and extending, standard dual-task methodology, therefore, may provide a promising avenue for the study of the interactive dynamics of selection, optimization, and compensation in an on-line fashion. Following a brief introduction to dual-task methodology and measurement, we review below the current findings as they relate to the

SOC framework and suggest ways in which the dual-task paradigm might be extended to investigate SOC processes more directly.

The general approach to studying dual-task performance is to assess task performance under both single- and dual-task instructions (e.g., McDowd & Craik, 1986; Salthouse, Rogan, & Prill, 1984; for a methodological review, see Wickens, 1991). For example, McDowd and Craik (1986) compared young and older adults on a divided attention paradigm requiring the coordination of auditory and visual categorization tasks of varying complexity. In general, dual-task studies require participants to devote equal emphasis to each task, although several studies have systematically varied the ratio of emphasis (e.g., 25:75, 50:50) to determine whether the ability to allocate attention flexibly is impaired with advancing age (e.g., Kramer, Larish, & Strayer, 1995). One can then ascertain the drop in performance in a given task after a secondary task is added (dual-task cost) by computing either absolute or proportional differences. In SOC terms, the measurement of dual-task costs in each task domain gives some indication of how individuals are able to optimize their task performance relative to their individual baseline, single-task levels.

Additional information is gained through assessment of the performance of Task A in relation to Task B. The performance operating characteristic (POC) curve method allows one to determine whether an individual is biasing performance toward one task in particular, irrespective of task emphasis instructions (see Figure 14.1). Using standardized measures of task performance, one can plot Task A performance as a function of Task B performance, with the top right corner of the POC space signifying perfect cost-free performance (i.e., both tasks are performed at levels comparable to their respective single-task levels, despite the requirement to perform both together).

The extent to which data points deviate from a symmetrical curve on the diagonal indicates whether individuals are biased in their task emphasis (symmetrical performance is depicted in the top panel of Figure 14.1; biased performance is shown in the bottom two panels). In SOC terms, the presence of task bias suggests that despite the instruction to emphasize both tasks equally, participants are using selection processes to manage the two tasks. Particularly for older adults, bias might be indicative of loss-based selection. We now illustrate with some research findings.

A recent large-scale training study was designed to ask whether younger and older adults can be trained to balance two tasks effectively with equal

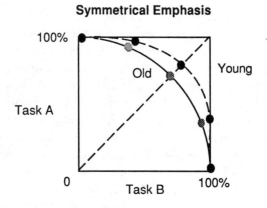

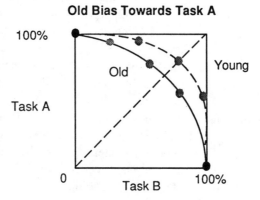

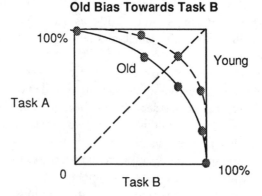

Figure 14.1. Assessing the Performance of Task A in Relation to Task B

NOTE: On each function,, the points represent dual-task performance under varying emphasis conditions (e.g., 100-0%, 25-75%, 50-50%).

priority (Kramer et al., 1995). Using a monitoring task combined with an alphabet-arithmetic task, the researchers found that after multiple sessions of training under both single- and dual-task conditions with variable emphasis instructions, young and old adults were equally successful in balancing the two tasks and in flexibly allocating attention with varying ratios. In SOC terms, this finding indicates that, through training, both age groups were able to optimize their dual-task performance, although in early stages of training, old adults showed more of a "selection" bias toward one task than did young adults.

Even more interesting is the finding that, across all emphasis conditions, old adults began the training study with a bias toward one task, suggesting evidence for loss-based selection. Kramer et al.'s (1995) results join many others in the aging and dual-task literature (e.g., Anderson, Craik, & Naveh-Benjamin, 1998; Brébion, Smith, & Ehrlich, 1997; Park, Smith, Dudley, & Lafronza, 1989; Ponds, Brouwer, & van Wolffelaar, 1988) in showing that particularly for old adults, dual-task costs in one task are greater than in the other task, and that old adults selectively drop tasks instead of attempting all in multiple-task situations (Salthouse, Hambrick, Lukas, & Dell, 1996).

An imbalance in task emphasis appears to be a prevalent finding, then, in the cognitive aging literature, although one that is rarely discussed in terms of strategic allocation of attention, and even more rarely in a priori terms. There are some notable exceptions, however. For example, Brébion et al. (1997) found that older adults *outperformed* younger adults on one task but performed less well on the secondary task (see also Ponds et al., 1988). They discuss the possibility that because of cognitive slowing, the older adults used a different strategy than the young, in which they seemed to give up on one task in order to optimize the second task. In contrast, the young adults, who did not show such cognitive limitations, attempted to maintain a balance between the two tasks (for work on young adults, see Damos, Smist, & Bittner, 1983).

What more can be learned from the dual-task literature? At present we have only indirect evidence of SOC processes (compensation, loss-based selection) at work. Future questions include asking whether task imbalances that old adults display are a compensatory response to age-related losses in functioning. Recent dual-task research suggests that with advancing age, cognitive resources are enlisted to compensate for losses in sensorimotor ability (e.g., Lindenberger et al., 1998; Maylor & Wing, 1996). This is supported by the finding that dual-task costs for these two tasks increase with aging. To obtain further support for this perspective, future studies could systematically impose and then remove simulated losses, and then observe dual-task performance as a response to these changes. Another potential line of inquiry would concern what factors determine the selection of goals. As previously mentioned, the notion of estimated outcome expectancies serves as a promising lead: Is it the case that when given instructions to choose freely which task to give highest priority, individuals always choose the one that they feel will yield the greatest gain? The dual-task paradigm offers a potentially rich avenue for the continued investigation of SOC dynamics.

SUMMARY AND CONCLUSIONS

In this chapter, we have expanded on earlier work and outlined a model proposing three fundamental processes of developmental regulation, namely, selection, optimization, and compensation. These processes are conceptualized as universal developmental processes that can be applied to various levels of analysis and various domains of functioning. The specific approach we have chosen to explicate SOC is action-theoretical. By embedding SOC in an action-theoretical framework, we have focused on processes of goal selection as well as goal pursuit and maintenance. In this framework, the selection of goals and their life-span transformations is a key concept for understanding directionality in development.

Goals direct behavior into particular pathways and exclude alternative developmental pathways. By selecting personal goals, an individual actively shapes his or her development while at the same time reacting to the opportunity structures of a given society and culture. Selecting goals that best fit one's personal needs and changing opportunity structures implies the accessibility of internal and external resources, thus making the careful selection of goals critical for the success of goal pursuit. Further, goal commitment in the face of losses in goal-relevant means is a requirement for the maintenance of a given level of functioning.

In old age, as resources become increasingly limited, selection should be of particular importance for developmental regulation. In the Berlin Aging Study, however, we found that the contribution of optimization and compensation to subjective indicators of successful aging was stronger than the contribution of selection (Freund & P. Baltes, 1998). It might be, however, that this study underestimated the importance of selection because the relevant choices had already been made earlier in life. As a consequence, older adults reported strategies that focused on those processes (optimization, compensation) that are required for goal attainment. Future longitudinal research is needed to investigate the possible long-term and cumulative effects of goal selection on subsequent optimization and compensation.

In this chapter, we have focused primarily on selection, optimization, and compensation as *single* processes of developmental regulation. To gain theoretical clarity at present, it is necessary to decompose developmental regulation into single processes. When we know enough about the single processes, we can proceed to the next step and investigate how these processes interact in the development of an individual over time. For instance, we assume that selection contributes to successful life management only if the means for achieving the selected goals are available and utilized. In line with this hypothesis, Brunstein (1993) found that goal commitment per se was unrelated to subjective well-being. High goal commitment showed positive effects on subjective well-being only when associated with goal attainment; in contrast, high goal commitment was negatively related to well-being when goals were not attained. Although the mere presence of personal goals might contribute to a sense of meaning in people's lives (e.g., Cantor & Fleeson, 1994; Klinger, 1977), the main purpose of such goals lies in their guiding action for achieving higher levels of functioning and maintaining function in the face of loss or decline (Freund & P. Baltes, in press; Kruglanski, 1996). Notably, successful goal selection requires more than simply choosing priorities; it is important that an individual develops and sets goals in domains of functioning that best match his or her opportunity structures (Freund, 1997). That is, a person should select those domains for which he or she has (actual and latent) resources and that best match his or her needs and environmental demands.

Related issues for future consideration include the unit of analysis and the time window to be observed. The adaptiveness of SOC processes depends partly on the level of goals or action units considered. On the level of single goals, successful SOC can be defined as the degree of achievement in the respective goal domain. High achievement in one goal domain, however, might be accomplished at the expense of other important goals. Thus, taking the entire goal system into account rather than only one goal, success has to be defined as the ratio of number of important goals achieved to those that were not achieved. The length of time in which a goal is pursued also invites future investigation: Focusing on only the most promising and important goals for a short period of time might be highly adaptive (e.g., studying for final examinations) but may be maladaptive if carried out for too long and at the expense of other goals (overselection). Overselection (see Freund & P. Baltes, in press; Marsiske et al., 1995) compromises one of the basic tenets of life-span psychology, namely, that a certain degree of diversity and variability is essential for continued growth and development (see J. Heckhausen, 1998). As we have pointed out in the context of the self-definition, it is important to move beyond simple hypotheses that link the number of goals or self-defining domains to indicators of successful aging. The available research indicates that such relationships are more complex than that, and are mediated by factors such as the number of available resources.

Finally, this dynamic interplay among SOC processes can be examined in the future with adaptations of the dual-task paradigm. By systematically varying task priorities, simulating losses, and providing compensatory aids, we can study, on-line, the ways in which selection, optimization, and compensation processes work in concert to produce adaptive functioning. This research direction not only serves to complement the ongoing research on SOC processes in larger contexts (e.g., successful aging, self-definition, group functioning), but also offers a potential means for enriching our understanding of phenomena within specific fields such as aging and cognition.

REFERENCES

Allport, G. W. (1961). *Patterns of growth in personality*. New York: Holt, Rinehart & Winston.

Anderson, N. D., Craik, F. I. M., & Naveh-Benjamin, M. (1998). The attentional demands of encoding and retrieval in younger and older adults: 1. Evidence from divided attention costs. *Psychology and Aging, 13*, 405-423.

Archer, S. L. (1989). The status of identity: Reflections on the need for intervention. *Journal of Adolescence, 12*, 345-359.

Atchley, R. C. (1982). The aging self. *Psychological Theory, Research, and Practice, 19*, 338-396.

Atchley, R. C. (1991). The influence of aging or frailty on perceptions and expressions of the self: Theoretical and methodological issues. In J. E. Birren, J. E. Lubben, J. C. Rowe, & D. E. Deutchman (Eds.), *The concept and measurement of quality of life in the frail elderly* (pp. 207-225). San Diego, CA: Academic Press.

Baars, B. J. (1988). *A cognitive theory of consciousness*. Cambridge: Cambridge University Press.

Bäckman, L., & Dixon, R. A. (1992). Psychological compensation: A theoretical framework. *Psychological Bulletin, 112,* 1-25.

Ball, L., & Chandler, M. (1989). Identity formation in suicidal and non-suicidal youth: The role of self-continuity. *Development and Psychopathology, 1,* 257-275.

Baltes, M. M., & Carstensen, L. L. (1996). The process of successful aging. *Aging and Society, 16,* 397-422.

Baltes, M. M., & Carstensen, L. L. (1998). Social psychological theories and their application to aging: From individual to collective social psychology. In V. L. Bengtson & K. W. Schaie (Eds.), *Handbook of theories of aging: In honor of Jim Birren* (pp. 209-226). New York: Springer.

Baltes, P. B. (1987). Theoretical propositions of life-span developmental psychology: On the dynamics between growth and decline. *Developmental Psychology, 23,* 611-623.

Baltes, P. B. (1997). On the incomplete architecture of human ontogeny: Selection, optimization, and compensation as foundation of developmental theory. *American Psychologist, 52,* 366-380.

Baltes, P. B., & Baltes, M. M. (1980). Plasticity and variability in psychological aging: Methodological and theoretical issues. In G. E. Gurski (Ed.), *Determining the effects of aging on the central nervous system* (pp. 41-66). Berlin: Schering.

Baltes, P. B., & Baltes, M. M. (1990). Psychological perspectives on successful aging: The model of selective optimization with compensation. In P. B. Baltes & M. M. Baltes (Eds.), *Successful aging: Perspectives from the behavioral sciences* (pp. 1-34). Cambridge: Cambridge University Press.

Baltes, P. B., Baltes, M. M., Freund, A. M., & Lang, F. R. (1995). *Measurement of selective optimization with compensation by questionnaire.* Berlin: Max Planck Institute for Human Development and Education.

Baltes, P. B., Dittmann-Kohli, F., & Dixon, R. A. (1984). New perspectives on the development of intelligence in adulthood: Toward a dual process conception and a model of selective optimization with compensation. In P. B. Baltes & O. G. Brim, Jr. (Eds.), *Life-span development behavior* (Vol. 6, pp. 33-76). New York: Academic Press.

Baltes, P. B., Lindenberger, U., & Staudinger, U. M. (1998). Life-span theory in developmental psychology. In W. Damon (Series Ed.) & R. M. Lerner (Vol. Ed.), *Handbook of child psychology: Vol. 1. Theoretical models of human development* (5th ed., pp. 1029-1143). New York: John Wiley.

Baltes, P. B., Mayer, K. U., Helmchen, H., & Steinhagen-Thiessen, E. (1999). The Berlin Aging Study (BASE): Sample, design, and overview of measures. In P. B. Baltes & K. U. Mayer (Eds.), *The Berlin Aging Study: Aging from 70 to 100.* New York: Cambridge University Press.

Bargh, J. A., & Gollwitzer, P. M. (1994). Environmental control of goal-directed action: Automatic and strategic contingencies between situations and behavior. In W. D. Spaulding (Ed.), *Nebraska Symposium on Motivation: Vol. 41. Integrative views of motivation, cognition, and emotion* (pp. 71-124). Lincoln: University of Nebraska Press.

Boesch, E. E. (1976). *Psychopathologie des Alltags* [Psychopathology of everyday life]. Bern, Switzerland: Huber.

Boesch, E. E. (1991). *Symbolic action theory and cultural psychology.* Heidelberg: Springer.

Boesch, E. E. (1997). The story of a cultural psychologist: Autobiographical observations. *Culture and Psychology, 3,* 257-275.

Brandtstädter, J. (1985). Entwicklungsprobleme des Jugendalters als Probleme des Aufbaus von Handlungsorientierungen [Developmental problems in adolescence as problems in building action orientation]. In D. Liepman & A. Stiksrud (Eds.), *Entwicklungsaufgaben und Bewältigungsprobleme der Adoleszenz* [Developmental tasks and problems of coping in adolescence] (pp. 5-12). Göttingen, Germany: Hogrefe.

Brandtstädter, J. (1998). Action perspectives on human development. In W. Damon (Series Ed.) & R. M. Lerner (Vol. Ed.), *Handbook of child psychology: Vol. 1. Theoretical models of human development* (5th ed., pp. 807-863). New York: John Wiley.

Brandtstädter, J., & Greve, W. (1994). The aging self: Stabilizing and protective processes. *Developmental Review, 14,* 52-80.

Brandtstädter, J., & Renner, G. (1990). Tenacious goal pursuit and flexible goal adjustment: Explication and age-related analysis of assimilative and accommodative strategies of coping. *Psychology and Aging, 5,* 58-67.

Brandtstädter, J., & Rothermund, K. (1994). Self-percepts of control in middle and late adulthood: Buffering losses by rescaling goals. *Psychology and Aging, 9,* 265-273.

Brandtstädter, J., & Wentura, D. (1995). Adjustment to shifting possibility frontiers in later life: Compensatory adaptive modes. In R. A. Dixon & L. Bäckman (Eds.), *Psychological compensation: Managing losses and promoting gains* (pp. 83-106). Mahwah, NJ: Lawrence Erlbaum.

Brébion, G., Smith, M. J., & Ehrlich, M.-F. (1997). Working memory and aging: Deficit or strategy differences? *Aging, Neuropsychology, and Cognition, 4,* 58-73.

Brunstein, J. C. (1993). Personal goals and subjective well-being: A longitudinal study. *Journal of Personality and Social Psychology, 65,* 1061-1070.

Cantor, N. (1994). Life task problem solving: Situational affordances and personal needs. *Personality and Social Psychology Bulletin, 20,* 235-243.

Cantor, N., & Fleeson, W. (1994). Social intelligence and intelligent goal pursuit: A cognitive slice of motivation. In W. D. Spaulding (Ed.), *Nebraska Symposium on Motivation: Vol. 41. Integrative views of motivation, cognition, and emotion* (pp. 125-179). Lincoln: University of Nebraska Press.

Cantor, N., & Kihlstrom, J. F. (1989). Social intelligence and cognitive assessments of personality. In R. S. Wyer & T. K. Srull (Eds.), *Advances in social cognition* (Vol. 2, pp. 1-59). Hillsdale, NJ: Lawrence Erlbaum.

Carstensen, L. L., Hanson, K. A., & Freund, A. M. (1995). Selection and compensation in adulthood. In R. A. Dixon & L. Bäckman (Eds.), *Compensating for* psychological deficits and declines: Managing losses and promoting gains (pp. 107-126). Mahwah, NJ: Lawrence Erlbaum.

Carver, C. S., & Scheier, M. F. (1981). *Attention and self-regulation: A control-theory approach to human behavior.* New York: Springer-Verlag.

Carver, C. S., & Scheier, M. F. (1995). *On the self-regulation of behavior.* Cambridge: Cambridge University Press.

Damon, W., & Hart, D. (1982). The development of self-understanding from infancy through adolescence. *Child Development, 52,* 841-864.

Damos, D. L., Smist, T. E., & Bittner, A. C., Jr. (1983). Individual differences in multiple-task performance as a function of response strategy. *Human Factors, 25,* 215-226.

Donahue, E. M., Robins, R. W., Roberts, B. W., & John, O. P. (1993). The divided self: Concurrent and longitudinal effects of psychological adjustment and social roles on self-concept differentiation. *Journal of Personality and Social Psychology, 64,* 834-846.

Eckensberger, L. H. (1997). The legacy of Boesch's intellectual oeuvre. *Culture and Psychology, 3,* 277-298.

Epstein, S. (1973). The self-concept revisited: Or a theory of a theory. *American Psychologist, 28,* 404-416.

Epstein, S. (1980). The self-concept: A review and the proposal of an interpreted theory of personality. In E. Straub (Ed.), *Personality, basic aspects and current research* (pp. 81-132). Englewood Cliffs, NJ: Prentice Hall.

Erikson, E. H. (1959). *Identity and the life cycle.* New York: International Universities.

Filipp, S.-H. (1980). Entwicklung von Selbstkonzepten [Development of self-concepts]. *Zeitschrift für Entwicklungspsychologie und Pädagogische Psychologie, 12,* 105-125.

Fleeson, W., & Baltes, P. B. (1998). Beyond present-day personality assessment: An encouraging exploration of the measurement properties and predictive power of subjective lifetime personality. *Journal of Research in Personality, 32,* 411-430.

Frese, M., & Sabini, J. (1985). Action theory: An introduction. In M. Frese & J. Sabini (Eds.), *Goal-directed behavior: The concept of action in psychology* (pp. xvii-xxv). Hillsdale, NJ: Lawrence Erlbaum.

Freund, A. M. (1995). *Die Selbstdefinition alter Menschen: Inhalt, Struktur und Funktion* [The self-definition of older persons: Content, structure, and function]. Berlin: Ed. Sigma.

Freund, A. M. (1997). Individuating age salience: A psychological perspective on the salience of age in the life course. *Human Development, 40,* 287-292.

Freund, A. M., & Baltes, P. B. (in press). The orchestration of selection, optimization, and compensation: An action-theoretical conceptualization of a theory of developmental regulation. In W. J. Perrig & A. Grob (Eds.), *Control of human behavior, mental processes, and consciousness.* Mahwah, NJ: Lawrence Erlbaum.

Freund, A. M., & Baltes, P. B. (1998). Selection, optimization, and compensation as strategies of life-management: Correlations with subjective indicators of successful aging. *Psychology and Aging, 13,* 513-543.

Freund, A. M., & Smith, J. (1999). Content and function of the self-definition in old and very old age. *Journals of Gerontology, 54,* P55-67.

Gollwitzer, P. M. (1996). The volitional benefits of planning. In P. M. Gollwitzer & J. A. Bargh (Eds.), *The psychology of action: Linking cognition and motivation to behavior* (pp. 287-312). New York: Guilford.

Gollwitzer, P. M., & Bargh, J. A. (Eds.). (1996). *The psychology of action: Linking cognition and motivation to behavior.* New York: Guilford.

Gollwitzer, P. M., & Schaal, B. (1998). Metacognition in action: The importance of implementation intentions. *Personality and Social Psychology Review, 2,* 124-136.

Havighurst, R. J. (1963). *Successful aging, process of aging: Social and psychological perspectives* (Vol. 1, pp. 299-320). New York: Atherton.

Heckhausen, H. (1989). *Motivation und Handeln* [Motivation and action]. Berlin: Springer.

Heckhausen, H., & Gollwitzer, P. M. (1987). Thought contents and cognitive functioning in motivational versus volitional states of mind. *Motivation and Emotion, 11,* 101-120.

Heckhausen, J. (1997). Developmental regulation across adulthood: Primary and secondary control of age-related challenges. *Developmental Psychology, 33,* 176-187.

Heckhausen, J. (1998). *Developmental regulation in adulthood: Age-normative and sociostructural constraints as adaptive challenges.* New York: Cambridge University Press.

Heckhausen, J., Dixon, R. A., & Baltes, P. B. (1989). Gains and losses in development throughout adulthood as perceived by different adult age groups. *Developmental Psychology, 25,* 109-121.

Heckhausen, J., & Schulz, R. (1995). A life-span theory of control. *Psychological Review, 102,* 284-304.

Hobfoll, S. E. (1989). Conservation of resources: A new attempt at conceptualizing stress. *American Psychologist, 44,* 513-524.

Kliegl, R., Smith, J., & Baltes, P. B. (1989). Testing-the-limits and the study of adult age differences in cognitive plasticity of a mnemonic skill. *Developmental Psychology, 25,* 247-256.

Klinger, E. (1977). *Meaning and void: Inner experience and the incentives in people's lives.* Minneapolis: University of Minnesota Press.

Kramer, A. F., Larish, J. F., & Strayer, D. L. (1995). Training of attentional control in dual task settings: A comparison of young and old adults. *Journal of Experimental Psychology: Applied, 1,* 50-76.

Kruglanski, A. W. (1996). Goals as knowledge structures. In P. M. Gollwitzer & J. A. Bargh (Eds.), *The psychology of action: Linking cognition and motivation to behavior* (pp. 599-618). New York: Guilford.

Labouvie-Vief, G. (1981). Proactive and reactive aspects of constructivism: Growth and aging in life-span perspective. In R. M. Lerner & N. A. Busch-Rossnagel (Eds.), *Individuals as producers of their development: A life-span perspective* (pp. 197-230). New York: Academic Press.

Lang, F. R. (1994). *Die Gestaltung informeller Hilfebeziehungen im hohen Alter— Die Rolle von Elternschaft und Kinderlosigkeit* [Social support management in late life: The role of parenthood and childlessness]. Berlin: Ed. Sigma.

Lang, F. R., & Carstensen, L. L. (1994). Close emotional relationships in late life: Further support for proactive aging in the social domain. *Psychology and Aging, 9*, 315-324.

Lawton, M. P. (1989). Behavior-relevant ecological factors. In K. W. Schaie & C. Schooler (Eds.), *Social structure and aging: Psychological processes* (pp. 57-78). Hillsdale, NJ: Lawrence Erlbaum.

Lawton, M. P., & Nahemow, L. (1973). Ecology and the aging process. In C. Eisdorfer & M. P. Lawton (Eds.), *The psychology of adult development and aging* (pp. 619-674). Washington, DC: American Psychological Association.

Lecky, P. (1945). *Self-consistency: A theory of personality.* New York: Island.

L'Écuyer, R. (Ed.). (1990). Le développement du concept de soi de 0 à 100 ans: Cent ans après William James [The development of the self-concept from 0 to 100 years: 100 years after William James] [Special issue]. *Revue québécoise de psychologie.*

Lemon, B. W., Bengtson, V. L., & Peterson, J. A. (1971). An exploration of the activity theory of aging: Activity types and life satisfactions among in-movers to a retirement community. *Journal of Gerontology, 27,* 511-523.

Lerner, R. M. (1991). Changing organism-context relations as the basic process of development: A developmental contextual perspective. *Developmental Psychology, 27,* 27-32.

Lerner, R. M., & Busch-Rossnagel, N. A. (1981). Individuals as producers of their development: Conceptual and empirical bases. In R. M. Lerner & N. A. Busch-Rossnagel (Eds.), *Individuals as producers of their development: A life-span perspective* (pp. 1-36). New York: Academic Press.

Lindenberger, U., & Baltes, P. B. (1997). Intellectual functioning in old and very old age: Cross-sectional results from the Berlin Aging Study. *Psychology and Aging, 12,* 410-432.

Lindenberger, U., Marsiske, M., & Baltes, P. B. (1998). *Dual-task costs in sensorimotor and intellectual functioning: Increase from early adulthood to old age.* Manuscript submitted for publication.

Linville, P. W. (1987). Self complexity as a cognitive buffer against stress related illness and depression. *Journal of Personality and Social Psychology, 52,* 663-676.

Locke, E. A., Shaw, K. N., Saari, L. M., & Latham, G. P. (1981). Goal setting and task performance: 1969-1980. *Psychological Bulletin, 90,* 125-152.

Maddox, G. L. (1994). Lives through the years revisited. *Gerontologist, 6,* 764-767.

Magnusson, D., Winblad, B., & Nilsson, L.-G. (Eds.). (1996). *The lifespan development of individuals: Behavioral, neurobiological, and psychosocial perspectives: A synthesis.* New York: Cambridge University Press.

Manton, K. G., Stallard, E., & Corder, L. (1995). Changes in morbidity and chronic disability in the U.S. elderly population: Evidence from the 1982, 1984, and 1989 National Long Term Care Surveys. *Journals of Gerontology: Psychological Sciences, 50B,* S194-S204.

Marcia, J. E. (1980). Identity in adolescence. In J. Adelson (Ed.), *Handbook of adolescence* (pp. 159-187). New York: John Wiley.

Markus, H. R. (1983). Self-knowledge: An expanded view. *Journal of Personality, 51,* 543-565.

Markus, H. R., & Nurius, P. (1986). Possible selves. *American Psychologist, 41,* 954-969.

Marsiske, M., Delius, J., Maas, I., Lindenberger, U., Scherer, H., & Tesch-Römer, C. (1999). Sensory systems in old age. In P. B. Baltes & K. U. Mayer (Eds.), *The Berlin Aging Study: Aging from 70 to 100.* New York: Cambridge University Press.

Marsiske, M., Lang, F. R., Baltes, M. M., & Baltes, P. B. (1995). Selective optimization with compensation: Life-span perspectives on successful human development. In R. A. Dixon & L. Bäckman (Eds.), *Compensation for psychological defects and declines: Managing losses and promoting gains* (pp. 35-79). Mahwah, NJ: Lawrence Erlbaum.

Maylor, E. A. (1990). Age and prospective memory. *Quarterly Journal of Experimental Psychology, 42A,* 471-493.

Maylor, E. A., & Wing, A. M. (1996). Age differences in postural stability are increased by additional cognitive demands. *Journals of Gerontology: Psychological Sciences, 51B,* P143-P154.

McDowd, J. M., & Craik, F. I. M. (1986). Effects of aging and task difficulty on divided attention performance. *Journal of Experimental Psychology: Human Perception and Performance, 14,* 267-280.

McGuire, W. J. (1984). Search for the self: Going beyond self-esteem and the reactive self. In R. A. Zucker, J. Aronoff, & A. I. Rabin (Eds.), *Personality and the prediction of behavior* (pp. 73-120). New York: Academic Press.

Oettingen, G. (1997). Culture and future thought. *Culture and Psychology, 3,* 353-381.

Park, D. C., Smith, A. D., Dudley, W. N., & Lafronza, V. N. (1989). Effects of age and a divided attention task presented during encoding and retrieval on memory. *Journal of Experimental Psychology: Learning, Memory, and Cognition, 15,* 1185-1191.

Ponds, R. W. H., Brouwer, W. H., & van Wolffelaar, P. C. (1988). Age differences in divided attention in a simulated driving task. *Journals of Gerontology: Psychological Sciences, 43B,* P151-P156.

Riley, M. W. (1987). On the significance of age in sociology. *American Sociological Review, 52,* 1-14.

Rosenberg, S., & Gara, M. A. (1985). The multiplicity of personal identity. In P. Shaver (Ed.), *Review of personality and social psychology* (Vol. 6, pp. 87-113). Beverly Hills, CA: Sage.

Rosenmayr, L. (1983). *Die späte Freiheit: Das Alter–ein Stück bewußt gelebten Lebens* [Late freedom: Old age—a phase of consciously lived life]. Berlin: Servin & Siedler.

Rosow, I. (1973). The social context of the aging self. *Gerontologist, 13,* 82-87.

Ryff, C. D. (1989). In the eye of the beholder: Views of psychological well-being among middle-aged and older adults. *Psychology and Aging, 4,* 195-210.

Salthouse, T. A., Hambrick, D. Z., Lukas, K. E., & Dell, T. C. (1996). Determinants of adult age differences on synthetic work performance. *Journal of Experimental Psychology: Applied, 2,* 305-329.

Salthouse, T. A., Rogan, J. D., & Prill, K. (1984). Division of attention: Age differences on a visually presented memory task. *Memory & Cognition, 12,* 613-620.

Schönpflug, W. (1998). Improving efficiency of action control through technical and social resources. In M. Kofta, G. Weary, & G. Sedek (Eds.), *Personal control in action: Cognitive and motivational mechanisms* (pp. 299-314). New York: Plenum Press.

Smith, J., & Baltes, P. B. (1999). Trends and profiles of psychological functioning in very old age. In P. B. Baltes & K. U. Mayer (Eds.), *The Berlin Aging Study: Aging from 70 to 100* (pp. 197-226). New York: Cambridge University Press.

Staudinger, U. M., & Freund, A. M. (1998). Krank und arm im hohen Alter und trotzdem guten Mutes? [Ill and poor in old age—but still in a good mood?] *Zeitschrift für Klinische Psychologie, 27,* 78-85.

Staudinger, U. M., Freund, A. M., Linden, M., & Maas, I. (1999). Self, personality, and life regulation: Facets of psychological resilience in old age. In P. B. Baltes & K. U. Mayer (Eds.), *The Berlin Aging Study: Aging from 70 to 100.* New York: Cambridge University Press.

Staudinger, U. M., Marsiske, M., & Baltes, P. B. (1995). Resilience and reserve capacity in later adulthood: Potentials and limits of development across the life-span. In D. Cicchetti & D. Cohen (Eds.), *Developmental psychopathology: Vol. 2. Risk, disorder, and adaptation* (pp. 801-847). New York: John Wiley.

Steinhagen-Thiessen, F., & Borchelt, M. (1999). Morbidity, medication, and functional limitations in very old age. In P. B. Baltes & K. U. Mayer (Eds.), *The Berlin Aging Study: Aging from 70 to 100.* New York: Cambridge University Press.

Swann, W. B., Jr. (1990). To be adored or to be known; The interplay of self-enhancement and self-verification. In R. M. Sorrentino & E. T. Higgins (Eds.), *Motivation and cognition* (Vol. 2, pp. 408-448). Hillsdale, NJ: Lawrence Erlbaum.

Swann, W. B., Jr. (1996). *Self-traps: The elusive quest for higher self-esteem.* New York: W. H. Freeman.

Thoits, P. A. (1983). Multiple identities and psychological well-being: A reformulation and test of the social isolation hypothesis. *American Sociological Review, 48,* 174-187.

Thomae, H. (1974). Anpassungsprobleme im höheren Alter—Aus psychologischer Sicht [Problems of adjustment in old age: From a psychological perspective]. *Aktuelle Gerontologie, 4*, 649-662.

Troll, L. E., & Skaff, M. M. (1997). Perceived continuity of self in very old age. *Psychology and Aging, 12*, 162-169.

Tversky, A., & Kahneman, D. (1981). The framing of decisions and the psychology of choice. *Science, 211*, 453-458.

Waterman, A. S., & Archer, S. L. (1990). A life-span perspective on identity formation: Developments in form, function, and process. In P. B. Baltes, D. L. Featherman, & R. M. Lerner (Eds.), *Life-span development and behavior* (Vol. 10, pp. 29-57). Hillsdale, NJ: Lawrence Erlbaum.

Wegner, D. M. (1992). You can't always think what you want: Problems in the suppression of unwanted thoughts. In M. P. Zanna (Ed.), *Advances in experimental social psychology* (Vol. 25, pp. 193-225). San Diego, CA: Academic Press.

Wickens, C. D. (1991). Processing resources and attention. In D. L. Damos (Ed.), *Multiple-task performance* (pp. 3-34). London: Taylor & Francis.

Wicklund, R. A., & Gollwitzer, P. M. (1982). *Symbolic self-completion.* Hillsdale, NJ: Lawrence Erlbaum.

15

EMOTIONAL LEARNING AND MECHANISMS OF INTENTIONAL PSYCHOLOGICAL CHANGE

Karen S. Quigley
Lisa Feldman Barrett

Appraisal theory is currently one of the most influential psychological theories of emotion (Parkinson, 1997). According to most versions of appraisal theory, emotional experience stems from an evaluative inter-action between person and environment. An individual evaluates or ap-praises the qualities of an object, person, or event and an emotional experience results. Lazarus (1968, 1991, 1993; Lazarus & Folkman, 1984) has presented a comprehensive appraisal theory of emotion based on a central tenet: One must consider both environmental presses and attempts to cope with those presses to understand fully the nature and intensity of emotional experience. *Primary appraisal* refers to the individual's evalu-ation of whether a situation has relevance for his or her personal well-being, and is an assessment of whether or not a threat is present in the environment. Threat is defined by the presence of cues indicating imminent damage or harm (either physical danger or danger to the individual's self-worth or self-esteem; Eysenck, 1989; Paterson & Neufeld, 1987). *Secondary appraisal* refers to the individual's evaluation of available resources, and is an assessment of whether he or she has the resources to cope with the threat, should it materialize. The specific emotional response is thought to result from a combination of primary and secondary appraisal processes. Most appraisal theories of emotion emphasize the association between the content of secondary appraisal processes and the specific emotional experience (such as sadness, fear, or anger).

In this chapter, we focus on a signal detection framework to describe how multiple experiences with threat in early life will lead to an automatic judgment strategy designed to minimize misses, a "zero-miss strategy," later in life. We suggest that a zero-miss strategy is related to enhanced emotional responsivity and is extremely difficult to change in adulthood because it is deployed without awareness. Furthermore, we argue that the only way to change this strategy is through the development and deployment of intentional strategies that can be learned in adulthood, and we consider the psychotherapeutic context as one place where this intentional self-development can take place. We then review evidence for these ideas from learning and neurobiological research. In addition, we make some prescriptive suggestions for the psychotherapeutic change process based on this research.

We begin by drawing on signal detection theory (SDT) to explain how primary appraisal patterns, and thus emotional reactivity, are developed and maintained over the life span with little attentional effort. Using the concepts of sensitivity and bias, we suggest that a person's previous learning history can decrease sensitivity to threat cues (i.e., reduce accurate detectability of threat) and/or increase response bias, thereby producing a zero-miss judgment strategy and enhanced emotional responsivity. This can be adaptive or maladaptive, depending on environmental contingencies. We then argue that the zero-miss strategy and the associated emotional consequences are automatically deployed and therefore resistant to change, primarily because of previous emotional learning that is well entrenched. Next, we present evidence from neurobiological and learning studies of emotional conditioning in animals and humans in support of our framework. Based on this evidence, we suggest that individuals must develop and deploy new judgment strategies in a deliberate, intentional fashion to overcome their previous emotional learning history, but only when emotional relearning is targeted and skills for the management of negative affect are taught. Finally, we suggest that psychotherapy is only one potential context in which this intentional self-development can take place.

PRIMARY APPRAISAL OF THREAT
AND ENHANCED EMOTIONAL RESPONSE

An Overview of Signal Detection Theory

Signal detection theory was originally designed to assess an observer's behavior when attempting to detect weak psychophysical signals (Green & Swets, 1966/1974; McNicol, 1972). Considerable evidence suggests that SDT provides a good framework for investigating a wide range of human judgment behavior, including judgments of subtle, covert psychological experiences (e.g., pain, distress, fear, and memory), judgments of ambiguous social information (Grossberg & Grant, 1978; Harvey, 1992; Swets, 1986), and, most recently, primary appraisals of threat (Feldman Barrett, 1996; Feldman Barrett & Fong, 1996). A primary appraisal of threat is a judgment of a high subjective probability that danger to the self will develop (Milburn & Watman, 1981). The harm can be either psychological or physical. Psychologically, threat typically consists of negative evaluations of the self, which can cause lowered self-esteem or negative affect (Feldman Barrett & Williams, 1998).

SDT's most significant theoretical contribution lies in its ability to separate an observer's behavior into two components: sensitivity and response bias (Harvey, 1992). *Sensitivity* has been defined as an observer's ability to detect accurately the presence or absence of target information. Sensitivity may vary because of differences in perceptual abilities or because of the properties of the stimulus. Any stimulus that has a high probability of occurrence, is intense, or is imminent (i.e., the proximity to danger is near) will be less ambiguous and therefore easier to detect (McNicol, 1972; Miller, 1979; Paterson & Neufeld, 1987). Threat cues, because of their social nature, are often difficult to interpret and identify, making them highly ambiguous (Fiske & Taylor, 1991; Paterson & Neufeld, 1987) and thereby limiting sensitivity to them.

In contrast to sensitivity, *response style* or *response bias* is defined as the observer's tendency to favor one response over another, independent of the base rate for the stimulus. Thus a response bias for threat exists when an individual judges a situation or person as threatening more or less frequently than threat objectively occurs in that environment. Of course, psychological threat is difficult to assess in many cases because the actual status of the event is ambiguous and no concrete criterion for the judgment exists. For instance, a person may appraise a situation as threatening when in fact no harm is intended. When there is no clear objective stimulus criterion, judgment accuracy is difficult to assess. There are strategies for creating a criterion where one does not exist, however. For example, a third-party observer who is independent of the situation can be used to determine the presence or absence of the stimulus criterion (i.e., whether a threat occurred or not). Although the third-party observer may have motivations that influence where he or she sets the stimulus criterion, they are not the same motivations as those of the perceiver (which constitute bias). Thus the actual absence or presence of the threat cue is decided by an external source; it is ambiguous and probabilistic, but the relativity is taken out of the hands of the perceiver, and this allows one to distinguish between the decision criterion, which is related to the perceiver's perception of the stimulus, and the stimulus criterion, which is not. This is a crucial point, because response biases are particularly likely to operate with the detection of threat: Sensitivity to threats can be limited and therefore response bias has more room to influence any given judgment. Furthermore, there is no requirement that individuals must be consciously aware of their response biases, and in fact biases typically function outside the observer's awareness (Harvey, 1992).

According to SDT, the observer perceives situationally relevant information that he or she then compares to an internal decision criterion (X_c). The location of this decision criterion determines the observer's response bias (Harvey, 1992). This process is portrayed in Figure 15.1. If the available evidence is stronger than the decision criterion, then the observer will say yes, the stimulus is present; if the evidence is weaker than the decision criterion, then the observer will say no, it is not (for discussion of responses using continuous or probability ratings, see Harvey, 1992; Macmillan, 1993). To determine the accuracy of the observer's perception, judgments are compared to a stimulus criterion (Y_c) indicating the probability that the stimulus actually did or did not occur. For a given decision criterion and stimulus criterion there are four possible judgment outcomes. A *positive hit* occurs when the observer responds yes and the target stimulus did appear; a *correct rejection* occurs when the observer responds no and the target stimulus did not appear; a *false alarm* occurs when the observer responds yes but the target stimulus did not appear; and a *miss* occurs when

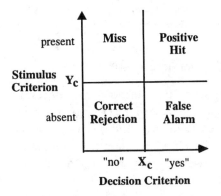

Figure 15.1. Decision Space

the observer responds no but the target stimulus did appear. Notice that as X_c increases, the observer has a higher threshold for saying no. As a result, positive hit and false alarm rates will decrease, whereas the miss and correct rejection rates will increase. As X_c decreases, the observer has a lower threshold for saying yes, so that the positive hit and false alarm rates will increase, whereas the miss and correct rejection rates will decrease.

An observer's decision criteria are influenced by three factors: (a) the observer's beliefs about the base rates of the event, (b) the goals that she or he has when making a judgment about the event (Egan, 1975; Green & Swets, 1966/1974; Healy & Kubovy, 1978), and (c) the observer's perception of the severity and consequences of a miss or false alarm (Feldman Barrett & Fong, 1996), especially when the identity of a stimulus cue is uncertain.

Evaluating the observer's hit rate in the context of the number of misses and false alarms provides information about his or her sensitivity and response bias (Harvey, 1992). Figure 15.2a presents a stimulus-response matrix for an observer with perfect sensitivity: He or she has a hit rate (positive hits + correct rejections) of 100%, with no false alarms and no misses. Figure 15.2b presents a matrix for an observer with no bias: He or she produces judgments that match the stimulus marginals (the base rate for the event). Notice that this observer also has a sensitivity greater than zero because his or her hit rate is greater than chance. Figure 15.2c presents a matrix for an observer with complete bias: He or she judges the event to occur 100% of the time. Figure 15.2d presents the most typical stimulus-response matrix: Most observers display some degree of sensitivity as well as response bias in their judgments.

Primary Appraisals of Threat From an SDT Perspective

When making judgments under uncertainty, most researchers agree that it is adaptive to use the base rates of the event (Nisbett, Krantz, Jepson, & Fong, 1982; Tversky & Kahneman, 1982). This judgment strategy allows the observer to minimize both false alarms and misses while maximizing hit rates. In general, however, people tend not to rely on base rates when making judgments in uncertain conditions (for a review, see Kahneman & Tversky, 1982). Psychologists have argued that this failure to use base rates exists for a number of cognitive reasons (e.g., people attend to the wrong information or fail to apply statistical logic).

There is also a motivational reason for not relying on base rates, namely, self-protection (Feldman Barrett, 1996; Feldman Barrett & Fong, 1996). Judgment errors (i.e., misses and false alarms) may differ in their consequences and reinforcement power, and this should in turn affect people's judgment strategies. Failing to detect a veridical threat (i.e., a miss) will cause a person to experience the full force of the threat and incur psychological or physical damage. In contrast, detecting a threat when none is there (i.e., a false alarm) will cause interpersonal disruption, behavioral restriction, and needless anxiety (e.g., Mathews & MacLeod, 1994), resulting from the erroneous perception of the self as vulnerable and of others as intending harm when this is not the case (Horney, 1950; Leary, 1957; Sullivan, 1953). We propose that because people are motivated to protect themselves, their response biases (i.e., where they locate their decision criterion, X_c) are determined by the types of errors they are trying to minimize.

The relative costs of misses and false alarms are determined by environmental conditions (Feldman Barrett & Fong, 1996). In threatening environments, when the base rate for threat is high (i.e., there is a large prior probability of threat in the environment), misses should be more costly and judgment strategies should be associated with the goal of reducing the number of misses at the expense of producing more false alarms. Consider the stimulus-response matrices in Figure 15.3 that represent an environment with a high base rate for threat. If the observer can accurately appraise the presence or absence of threat in every event (Figure 15.3a), he or she has a hit rate of 100%, with no misses or false alarms. However, considering

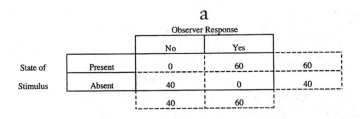

a

State of Stimulus	Observer Response			
		No	Yes	
	Present	0	60	60
	Absent	40	0	40
		40	60	

b

State of Stimulus	Observer Response			
		No	Yes	
	Present	24	36	60
	Absent	14	24	40
		40	60	

c

State of Stimulus	Observer Response			
		No	Yes	
	Present	0	60	60
	Absent	0	40	40
		0	100	

d

State of Stimulus	Observer Response			
		No	Yes	
	Present	12	48	60
	Absent	8	32	40
		20	80	

Figure 15.2. Stimulus-Response Matrices: Sensitivity and Bias

a. Perfect sensitivity and no bias.
b. Imperfect sensitivity and no bias.
c. Imperfect sensitivity and complete bias.
d. Imperfect sensitivity and some bias.

the ambiguous and inconsistent nature of most psychological threats (Fiske & Taylor, 1991; Paterson & Neufeld, 1987), it is unlikely that a person would obtain this perfect hit rate because the ambiguity and unpredictability of stimuli would reduce sensitivity. If the individual relies on base rates (Figure 15.3b), he or she will experience misses 16% of the time and false alarms 16% of the time. Thus 16% of the time the individual would face a threat unprepared because she or he failed to detect it, and 16% of the time she or he would prepare for a threat that never materialized. In a threatening environment, the individual may perceive misses to be more costly because of the magnitude or frequency of harm that is incurred. Aversive learning associated with failing to detect a threat when it is present will likely take place, and as a result the individual will minimize misses at the expense of engaging in more false alarms.[1]

To reduce the number of misses, the individual can substantially lower her or his decision criterion, thereby causing most cues to exceed threshold and be perceived as threats. Feldman Barrett and Fong (1996) call this a *zero-miss strategy*. Any cue, however weak, will exceed threshold and the individual will perceive the presence of a threat. By responding to every event as a potential threat, the individual maximizes his or her positive hit rate and minimizes misses (Figure 15.3c). In a sense, such an individual is being trained to be emotionally responsive to the environment.[2]

Each primary appraisal of threat will result in a negative emotional response that must be dealt with in some way. Individuals can protect themselves from harm (and the associated negative affect) by manipulating either their external or their internal environment (Lazarus & Folkman, 1984). They can manipulate their external environment through actions designed to decrease either the probability of the threat's occurrence or the impact of the threat once it occurs (Lazarus & Folkman, 1984). If behavioral interventions are not possible, the threatened individual can manipulate his or her internal environment through cognitive strategies and can change the meaning of the event in conscious thought (i.e., defense mechanisms; Lazarus & Folkman, 1984). In this case, the conscious construal of the event is distorted, and negative affect is damped as a result.

Although the zero-miss strategy allows the individual to avoid missing a potential threat, it has a cost because it produces an increase in the false alarm rate. For some portion of the time, individuals using a zero-miss strategy will perceive threat where the probability of danger is low or nonexistent, and there may be negative consequences associated with this form of dysregulation. Yet when the base rate for threat is high, this increase

a

		Appraisal			
		No Threat	Threat		
Reality	Threat	0	80	80	
	No Threat	20	0	20	
		20	80		

b

		Appraisal			
		No Threat	Threat		
Reality	Threat	16	64	80	
	No Threat	4	16	20	
		20	80		

c

		Appraisal			
		No Threat	Threat		
Reality	Threat	0	80	80	
	No Threat	0	20	20	
		0	100		

d

		Appraisal			
		No Threat	Threat		
Reality	Threat	0	20	20	
	No Threat	0	80	80	
		0	100		

Figure 15.3. Stimulus-Response Matrices: Strategies and Environments

a. Correct judgments in a threatening environment.
b. Use of base-rate information in a threatening environment.
c. Use of zero-miss strategy in a threatening environment.
d. Use of zero-miss strategy in a nonthreatening environment

in false alarm rates is only slight, and the emotional and possibly even physical consequences of a miss far outweigh the costs of a false alarm. As a result, the cost associated with an increased false alarm rate might be preferred over the cost of misses under these environmental conditions. Although we might not describe the zero-miss strategy as accuracy-seeking or rational (i.e., one is not using statistical information and formal logic to make primary appraisals), it is a rule learned through interactions with the environment that allows for optimal adaptation in a particular context (Einhorn, 1982). Thus false alarms can be considered "errors" in the strictest sense, but they are not mistakes with respect to a broad frame of reference, because the zero-miss strategy that produces an increase in false alarms is adaptive for individuals living in conditions of high threat (see Funder, 1987).

Thus far, we have reasoned that the perceiver adjusts the location of the decision criterion (i.e., sets his or her response bias) as a function of (a) the prior probability of psychological threat in that environment, (b) the motivation to protect the self, and (c) the relative consequences of misses and false alarms. We reason that the individual should employ a zero-miss strategy in any environment or context where a threat cue is present or in any similar context that shares cues (i.e., such as persons, objects, sounds, smells, or other sensations) with the environment in which threat was previously evoked (Bouton, 1988, 1993).

If the detection of threat is under the control of feedback and reinforcement contingencies, then the individual who habitually uses a zero-miss strategy will develop a model of the world as a highly threatening place. People learn the utility of their decision strategies on the basis of the number of positive hits (and therefore the number of misses) while generally ignoring the number of false alarms (Einhorn, 1982). Thus the individual growing up in a high-threat environment learns from experience that a zero-miss strategy produces the most beneficial effect. Furthermore, escape from threat is a negative reinforcer, the intensity of which increases with the intensity of the threat. Through feedback and reinforcement, the individual will develop cognitive structures that facilitate threat detection and set the expectancy that all experiences are potentially dangerous or harmful. As a result, the individual who lives in a threatening environment develops well-entrenched assumptions that ambiguous stimuli are threatening stimuli (Ittleson & Kilpatrick, 1951; Kahneman & Tversky, 1982). These assumptions function automatically and effortlessly (Posner, 1978) and are usually inaccessible to conscious knowledge or intention (Kahneman & Tversky, 1982). As a result, the individual may be well adapted to the conditions of the current environment, and yet may be completely unaware that he or she has been trained to be an "expert" in threat detection.

In sum, an individual may develop and maintain primary appraisal patterns over his or her life span with little attentional effort or awareness. The ambiguity typically associated with threat cues limits sensitivity. Limited sensitivity, combined with high base rates for threat in the environment, influences an individual to adopt a self-protective goal associated with a low decision criterion, X_c. The result is an individual who has developed a view of the world as threatening and dangerous, who is emotionally responsive, but who is well adapted to the conditions of a threatening environment. This same individual may be unable to calibrate his or her judgment strategies, however, when the base rates for threat change.

Failure to Calibrate to a Changing Environment

One aspect of adaptation is the ability to assess and respond to changes in the environment (Keren, 1987). When the amount of threat endemic to the environment decreases, it would be adaptive for the individual to abandon a zero-miss strategy and to calibrate his or her judgment strategy to the new environmental conditions. If the base rate for threat decreases and the individual does not adjust his or her decision criteria accordingly, that person's false alarm rate will increase substantially (e.g., comparing Figures 15.3c and 15.3d, false alarm rates increase from 20% to 80%), as will the psychological consequences associated with that type of error. As a result, the individual will appear highly emotionally reactive to the environment, often "overreacting" to cues that others would consider nonexistent (i.e., the individual will experience and express frequent and intense negative emotional responses, whether or not the environment warrants them). The negative affect that results from an excess of false alarms may be difficult to manage if the individual has not learned effective affect regulation skills. In addition, the individual may also have developed particular physiological response patterns, such as enhanced cardiovascular or gastrointestinal reactivity to threats (e.g., Krantz & Manuck, 1984), that can also heighten the negative affective experience associated with a primary appraisal of threat.

An individual with a high false alarm rate may also experience significant interpersonal disruption that results from being suspicious and expecting the worst from others, and this may actually increase the number of perceived or real threat cues in the environment. Such an individual may use offensive or preemptive strategies to avoid anticipated threats from others, which may cause disruptions in communication and may, in turn, alter other persons' behavior to produce a self-fulfilling prophecy. For example, if another person is confused, angered, or threatened by the individual's preemptive maneuver, this may lead to an even greater likelihood that he or she will pose a threat to the individual. In addition, the individual may not have significant others to rely on to help with affect management because of the difficulty of maintaining a supportive social network when one is overly vigilant to threat.

Therefore, from a number of psychological vantage points, false alarms are more costly than are misses when the base rates for threat are low. As a result, a zero-miss strategy, although adaptive in a threatening environment, is not so adaptive in a nonthreatening environment. Individuals who rely on a zero-miss strategy may have difficulty calibrating their judgments to changes in environmental conditions. Failure to adjust decision criteria in response to new base rates for threat can occur for cognitive, behavioral, and emotional reasons.

Cognitive reasons. Individuals using a zero-miss strategy may fail to detect changes in their environment because their sensitivity to the absence of threat cues is limited by cognitive bias. Previous experiences with threat produce cognitive structures that direct attention to information that is consistent with threat and filter out whatever is inconsistent (Fiske & Taylor, 1991). As a result, an individual will develop cognitive structures that (a) facilitate threat detection, (b) chronically prepare the individual to deal with ambiguous events as if they are threatening, and (c) produce the expectancy that most experiences have the potential to be dangerous or harmful. Previous research suggests that implicitly held expectancies mediate the large effects of context on recognition and exert their greatest influence on the interpretation of ambiguous stimuli (Epstein & Roupenian, 1970). Expectancies that have developed over a lifetime of previous experience not only have a profound effect on judgments, but they are usually inaccessible to conscious knowledge or intention, function automatically and effortlessly, and essentially constitute a dispositional preparedness for detecting threat (Ittleson & Kilpatrick, 1951; Kahneman

& Tversky, 1982; Posner, 1978). As a result, the individual may not be consciously aware that he or she has been "trained" to detect or avoid threat and may have limited sensitivity to the increase or decrease in threat cues in a new or changed environment. In addition, decision rules are typically learned deductively (Einhorn, 1982) and are used without intention or awareness (Lewicki, Hill, & Sasaki, 1989). These decision rules structure the encoding of ambiguous information such that it is seen as confirming evidence and thereby strengthens the further use of the rule (Kahneman & Tversky, 1982). As a result, confirmatory biases lead people to try to verify, rather than falsify, their working hypotheses about the world. In turn, individuals may suffer from the illusion of validity (Einhorn & Hogarth, 1978), causing them to be overconfident of the truth value of their judgments.

Behavioral reasons. Individuals using a zero-miss strategy may fail to calibrate to changes in the base rates for threat because of behavioral restrictions. Avoiding certain situations and certain people is one way to avoid a miss. Such avoidance prevents individuals from encountering disconfirming evidence, however, and that in turn likely contributes to the maintenance of a zero-miss strategy.

Emotional reasons. Individuals using a zero-miss strategy may fail to calibrate to a change in environmental conditions due to previous emotional learning. By *emotional learning,* we refer to an individual's ability to retain associations between specific stimuli or contexts and the emotional responses to those stimuli or contexts. Emotional learning is essentially a bottom-up phenomenon. By *bottom-up,* we mean that it occurs via processes that are quick, nonreflective, and automatic. Both the subcortical activation associated with emotion (e.g., LeDoux, 1996) and the automatically deployed appraisal processes we are describing here occur without awareness or conscious allocation of attention, and so can be considered bottom-up processes. We suspect that individuals using a zero-miss strategy are likely to have learned strong, stable associations between specific stimuli and contexts on the one hand and bottom-up processing producing negative affect, in particular fear, on the other. It is these associations that make it especially difficult for the individual to learn and maintain new associations to changed environmental contingencies. We review the evidence for this claim below.

In addition to having strong associations between fear responses and previously threat-related stimuli or contexts, the individual using a zero-miss strategy may also exhibit new learning if he or she engages in an inadvertent miss. Following a miss, not only will the individual suffer the consequences of exposure to the threatening stimulus, but he or she may recollect or even reexperience previous situations in which he or she was harmed in some way. Furthermore, the individual's perceived physiological reactivity to threats may function to heighten the intensity of negative affect associated with a miss.

Thus misses will likely retain strong motivational currency for someone using a zero-miss strategy, not only because the miss may have current negative consequences, but because it may also evoke the long-retained memories of negative emotional responses experienced in the formative environment, where misses were costly. Because judgment errors (i.e., inadvertent misses) are emotionally disruptive to the individual, they may retain strong reinforcement power and may subsequently reinforce readoption of the original zero-miss appraisal strategy.

Summary

Thus far, we have argued that a zero-miss strategy produces an emotionally responsive individual who is an expert at functioning in a threatening environment, but this strategy may leave the individual at a disadvantage when the environmental conditions change. The individual using a zero-miss strategy has a strong pattern of bottom-up activation of threat detection as well as emotional memories associated with threat, resulting in experiences of frequent and intense negative affect. The individual is also in a constant state of preparedness for threat and thus is well adapted to a threatening environment. However, the individual will have difficulty calibrating to a low-threat environment. We now turn to findings from both nonhuman animal and human studies on emotional conditioning to demonstrate that emotional learning in contexts of threat is long-lasting and relatively resistant to change.

EMOTIONAL LEARNING ABOUT THREAT-RELATED STIMULI AND CONTEXTS

Throughout the animal kingdom, the ability to learn about conditions associated with danger or threat is present (LeDoux, 1996). It has been suggested that the neural systems that permit the organism to predict and avoid threat have been necessary for survival in the course of evolution.

Those organisms that best avoided harm and could predict its future occurrence were more likely to survive to pass along their genes and raise their offspring to reproductive maturity. Moreover, nonhuman animals and humans appear to share similar physiological and subcortical responses to stimuli and contexts that predict imminent danger.[3] In the emotional learning literature, this response is generally labeled *fear*; we will use this conventional terminology in describing those findings.

Because learning about fear cues appears to be so well conserved across phyla, we have amassed considerable data on the neural mechanisms and psychological processes integral to fear learning in both human and non-human animals (for review, see LeDoux, 1996; also see Bouton, 1988). These data have provided us with some important clues about the initiation and maintenance of fear learning, as well as the difficulties inherent in "unlearning" fear responses, that are consistent with our SDT analysis. Furthermore, findings from studies of extinction and counterconditioning of fear responding suggest that humans need to develop and employ deliberate behaviors in order to calibrate intentionally to new, less threatening environments.

Initial Learning About Threat

Initial emotional learning about threat is believed to occur when cues in the environment inadvertently become paired with an occurrence of true threat or danger. Consider the case of a child living in a physically abusive environment. Abusive events (i.e., the threats) take place typically within the home context and at the hands of a particular person or persons. As a result, cues from the abusive environment, the abuser, and other seemingly irrelevant cues that are merely present during the threatening events can become associated with danger. In the future, these serve as threat cues (i.e., indications that danger is imminent).

Learning about cues predicting threat is privileged. Thus learning about events that engender threat can occur quickly, often following only a single pairing of a threat and a co-occurring cue, and this learning can be retained without degradation for relatively long periods (e.g., over years; LeDoux, 1996). Other survival-related learning, such as conditioned taste aversions, is also attained rapidly and demonstrates a remarkable stability over long periods of time. Fear cues that are learned in formative environments and are retained in later life may outlive their usefulness to the individual, however, in that they may not be reliable predictors of danger in the adult environment, where threat is likely to be less frequent. Because fear learning is so stable, associations with now irrelevant cues of threat may remain long after those cues no longer provide reliable prediction of danger. This retained fear response to cues that no longer predict threat typifies the adult using a zero-miss strategy.

Extinguishing and Counterconditioning Threat Responses

We have argued that individuals using a zero-miss strategy will find it difficult to calibrate their judgments to changing environmental conditions. Recent evidence from both learning theory and neurobiological studies of fear extinction and counterconditioning confirm that it is difficult to eliminate learned associations between true danger and potential threat cues. Since Pavlov's (1927) descriptions of spontaneous recovery, in which extinguished learned behaviors reemerged after the passage of time, we have known that neither extinction (the removal of the original learned association) nor counterconditioning (forming a new association between the learned fear cue and a nonfear response) completely removes the associations between threat cues (i.e., conditioned stimuli) and threats (i.e., unconditioned stimuli; Bouton, 1994a). Old associations are not replaced; rather, they merely coexist with new associations.

New (or counterconditioned) associations present a particular challenge to the individual using a zero-miss strategy. New associations to previous threat cues increase the ambiguity of the cues, because there are now multiple, competing associations linked to the same event. For the new associations to affect behavior, the individual must engage in considerable effortful processing and select from among the multiple associations with that cue. That is, the individual must develop and employ intentional, deliberate judgment strategies so that his or her attention and behavior are disproportionately influenced by the new association relative to the old.

Intentional, deliberate behaviors of any kind require attentional resources. Thus manifestations of the original fear learning should reemerge under circumstances in which attentional resources are limited. In situations where effortful processing is too demanding, in which the individual is under a substantial processing load or cannot effectively deploy attentional resources, or in which the new associations are less accessible, the learned fear response will reemerge because the individual cannot effectively access and use the newly learned associations to guide behavior

(Bouton, 1994a, 1994b; LeDoux, 1996, p. 250). For example, stressors can lead to the reemergence of responding to old threat cues (Jacobs & Nadel, 1985).

These hypotheses are further buttressed by neurobiological studies indicating that certain memories, particularly those related to fear, leave virtually indelible traces in the brain (LeDoux, Romanski, & Xagoraris, 1989; Quirk, Repa, & LeDoux, 1995). Such studies have shown that even after extinction of fear responses to a conditioned stimulus, an animal's brain retains changes in neuronal firing patterns (Sanghera, Rolls, & Roper-Hall, 1979) or in neuronal connections between cells (Quirk et al., 1995) that were not present prior to learning. Thus the neural traces that were strengthened during learning about threats are not eliminated by extinction, and this may help explain why the fear response can so easily reemerge. When extinction does occur, then, we cannot assume that the original learning is gone. Rather, it seems to be masked by newer learning. This masking of old responses by new learning may take place via connections from higher cortical structures, such as the medial prefrontal cortex, to subcortical areas integral to fear learning (such as the amygdala; Morgan, Romanski, & LeDoux, 1993). Moreover, the conscious apprehension of emotional states also likely requires cortical structures (such as the lateral prefrontal cortex, cingulate cortex, and orbitofrontal cortex; LeDoux, 1996, pp. 273-278). As a result, any process that limits cortical activity or requires the division of cognitive resources (e.g., increased cognitive load or multitasking that limits working memory resources) could permit a return of the initial fear response. This may explain why, when under significant stress, people experience a resurgence of the fear response. It also suggests that any interference with controlled cognitive processing may interfere with an individual's deliberate attempts to give up the zero-miss judgment strategy.

Reinstatement and Renewal of Threat Responses

Not only will stress make it difficult to access counterconditioned responses, it may provide cues similar to those in the formative environment, in effect priming old associations to the threat cue and ultimately leading to a reemergence of the learned fear response. This type of reemergence is called *reinstatement*. Reinstatement occurs when an extinguished fear response reemerges because the individual perceives a veridical threat (Bouton, 1988, 1994a; Bouton & Swartzentruber, 1991); that is, the old association is primed, and the fear response reemerges as a result. Fear can be reinstated easily—only a few exposures to a veridical threat cue are enough to prime old associations. For individuals who rely on the zero-miss strategy, reinstatement of fear could occur simply as a result of the occurrence of a few threats or stressors in the individual's home or work environment, even when the overall base rate of threat in the environment is low. Furthermore, if the individual fails to detect the veridical threat and there are adverse consequences of the miss, the result might be negative reinforcement of the zero-miss strategy.

The mere presence of a cue associated with threat also can be enough to prime old associations, especially when the individual is no longer in the context where extinction or counterconditioning occurred. This type of reemergence of the fear response is called *renewal*. Renewal occurs when cues that were associated with threat (i.e., conditioned stimuli) appear either in a new context or in the context in which the original associations were formed (Bouton, 1994a, 1994b; Bouton & Swartzentruber, 1991).[4] Thus, even if an individual using the zero-miss strategy manages to learn new associations to old threat cues and to allocate attention to employ the new judgment strategy in a particular context, fear may emerge when that stimulus is encountered in a new environmental context.

Generalization

Finally, considerable generalization in the learned fear response is likely to occur (Jacobs & Nadel, 1985). Contexts that share aspects of the original fear learning environment may renew learned fear responses. As a result, any feature of a new, benign environment that is perceptually similar to the threatening, former environment might induce an individual to readopt a zero-miss strategy. Furthermore, although initial fear learning tends to be context independent (i.e., considerable generalization occurs to other cues that come to signal threat), fear extinction is relatively context-bound and susceptible to disruption by changes from the counter-conditioned context (Bouton, 1988, 1993, 1994a, 1994b; Bouton & Swartzentruber, 1991). If, for example, the grocery store contains few cues associated with the context in which fear associations were extinguished, but does contain cues associated with the original fear context, then the similarity of cues between the old environment and the current environment (i.e., grocery store) can serve to renew fear.[5]

Can Automatic Fear Responses Be Unlearned?

Given the counterconditioning, reemergence, and generalization effects that we have just considered, it seems not only difficult for an individual to stop using a zero-miss strategy permanently when there are cues that can serve to initiate the fear response, but also unlikely that he or she will do so. Animal research provides evidence of learning and neurobiological processes that could easily support a stably maintained zero-miss strategy in humans. This evidence suggests not only that failure to calibrate completely is plausible, but that it perhaps should be expected. The only remedy for calibration seems to be the development and intentional use of deliberate judgment strategies. If the suppositions about learning processes and neuronal involvement in emotional relearning are correct, then these findings have prescriptive implications for the use of psychotherapeutic strategies for emotional relearning.

CONDITIONS FOR CHANGING
THE ZERO-MISS STRATEGY

Thus far, we have examined how a formative environment filled with threat and danger can produce an emotionally reactive threat detection expert. Judgment strategies that were automatically deployed and therefore adaptive in the initial environment leave the individual maladjusted to any environment that contains considerably less threat or danger. The bottom-up, automatic emotional learning associated with primary appraisals of threat may help to maintain the zero-miss judgment strategy. If an individual modifies this learned judgment strategy in any way, he or she will encounter more misses. Not only will the individual suffer the full consequences of a miss, but the learned fear response is likely to be reinstated. If the individual is exposed to cues that are contextually similar to those in the formative environment, the fear response may be renewed. And because misses will be emotionally disruptive to the individual, they may retain strong reinforcement power and may subsequently reinforce the readoption of the original zero-miss appraisal strategy.

Furthermore, learning studies demonstrate that associations between cues of threat and actual threat can become weakened through either extinction or counterconditioning, but that learned cues of threat likely will always retain some power to reinitiate a fear response. In part, this is due to the fact that cues of threat likely trigger very quick, nonconscious responses that, once evoked, will require the zero-miss individual to use conscious processing to deactivate or turn off the initiated fear response (LeDoux, 1996, p. 265). In addition, cues of threat learned early in development by the zero-miss individual likely have special properties, such as being relatively independent of context and being highly generalized to many other cues that have also come to evoke fear responses (Jacobs & Nadel, 1985). Thus the zero-miss individual in the adult environment, even one with few real threats, has a learning history that predisposes her or him to continue to respond to cues previously associated with threat, and it is unlikely that she or he will easily relinquish the long-standing, ingrained zero-miss strategy.

Given all of the obstacles, can an individual change his or her primary appraisal judgment strategy and the resulting level of emotional reactivity? We suggest that it depends. Calibration of judgment strategies (and the resulting decrease in emotional reactivity) requires several preconditions. First, for an individual to decrease his or her response bias (set a new decision criterion), increase sensitivity in the primary threat appraisal process, and thereby decrease his or her emotional reactivity, he or she must receive repetitive, unambiguous feedback about the outcome of judgments (see the literature on calibration in medical and weather prediction domains, e.g., Lichtenstein, Fischoff, & Phillips, 1982; Murphy & Winkler, 1971). It is very unlikely, although not impossible, that this type of information can be garnered in normal social interactions that are inherently ambiguous in meaning. This type of feedback may be available under certain social conditions, such as in interactions with close others or attachment figures, in a psychotherapeutic context, or in other training programs specifically designed to foster the development of top-down judgment strategies (i.e., processes that require attention deployment and conscious reflection).

Second, to recalibrate his or her judgment strategy (and emotional response to an occasional miss), an individual has to overcome the various cognitive, behavioral, and emotional habits that increase the likelihood of his or her making judgments of threat when in fact no threat is really there. That is, the individual must reduce cognitive bias, reduce behavioral avoidance, and learn to actively inhibit the fear response associated with actual or learned threat cues. He or she can learn to achieve the first two goals through standard psychotherapeutic interventions. To reduce cognitive bias, the individual would have to (a) make his or her judgment strategy explicit and thus accessible for conscious intervention (e.g., increase reliance on base rates for judgment) and (b) avoid confirmatory bias (i.e., learn to treat his or her view of the world as a hypothesis, rather than as a truism, and be willing to attempt to falsify this hypothesis). Such attempts at changing cognitive interpretations and bias are key to several forms of cognitive therapy (e.g., Beck, Rush, Shaw, & Emery, 1979). In addition to making cognitive changes, the individual would have to expand his or her behavioral repertoire to create a context within which to gather new information and try out new judgment strategies. The use of behavioral strategies for effecting psychotherapeutic change is typical of a variety of cognitive-behavioral approaches.

The third process, that of emotional relearning, is not so easily accomplished, as we noted above. If we take the view that both bottom-up processes (i.e., those that are quick, nonreflective, and automatic) and top-down processes (which are slower and require conscious reflection) are important to the construction of an emotional response, and if it is next to impossible to modify bottom-up processes, then the mechanisms for emotional change must focus on the development and implementation of top-down strategies. The emotional relearning aspect of emotional change has not played a major role in most psychotherapeutic modalities, however.[6] From the evidence reviewed, it is clear that although it is *necessary* for the individual to relearn new associations to cues that previously signaled threat, this relearning will likely not completely eradicate the old associations, and thus alone will *not be sufficient* to permit successful calibration. Given that a learned fear response can never be completely extinguished and can easily reemerge under various conditions, we propose that successful calibration also requires that a person (a) come to expect that the fear response will emerge at unexpected times and learn to label those responses explicitly as false alarms, (b) learn affect regulation skills that will permit him or her to tolerate the negative affect he or she will inevitably experience when occasional misses occur, and (c) develop strategies to maintain and flexibly deploy his or her attentional resources.

Prescriptions for Psychotherapy

Although calibration can occur in several contexts, people seem to gravitate to psychotherapy as a way of modifying their existing levels of emotional reactivity and associated judgment patterns. That is, people often choose therapy as a method for developing the intentional, deliberate judgment strategies that they need for behavior change. If a goal of therapy is to eliminate responding to invalid cues of threat, then therapists should consider the many ways in which fear behaviors may reemerge. Therapists could begin with the assumption that fear reemergence is likely in most, if not all, clients.[7] Rather than focusing their efforts on attempting to eliminate relapse, instead therapists should assume that clients will continue to experience fear and focus their efforts on helping clients to continue calibration efforts even in the face of recurring fear responses. Permanent calibration will require that a client learn to tolerate negative affect and the other unpleasant manifestations of fear, and that he or she learn affect regulation skills while continuing calibration efforts.

In addition to a focus on management, rather than prevention, context is paramount to understanding when relapse to a zero-miss strategy will occur. A shift from the therapeutic environment (which is, in essence, the extinction or counterconditioning context; Bouton, 1994b) to the nontherapeutic environment may result in reemergent fear because the client is exposed either to cues associated with threat (as in renewal) or to actual threats (as in reinstatement). A renewal of the fear response can occur because the current external environment contains cues that the individual associates with threat in the formative environment (e.g., the sound of a drunk yelling, which is associated with an abusive parent) or even cues that have generalized to the present environment (e.g., the sound of anyone yelling). A reinstatement of the fear response can occur when new threats materialize in the current external environment (e.g., psychosocial stressors such as divorce or loss of a loved one). Either way, the individual may reexperience fear and resort to a zero-miss strategy outside the therapeutic context, even if this strategy has been essentially extinguished inside that context.

One strategy for avoiding renewal of fear is to make the client's current context as similar to the extinction context as possible (Bouton & Swartzentruber, 1991). In fact, relapse is predicted to be most likely when the constellation of contextual cues is more similar to the original learning environment than to the therapeutic environment (Bouton, 1994b). Some of the positive therapeutic impact of such tools as a palmtop computer containing suggestions for therapy may come from the strong associations the client has formed between such tools and the therapeutic context (e.g., Newman, Consoli, & Taylor, 1997). Recent studies in animals have also demonstrated that presenting retrieval cues associated with the extinction environment just prior to presentation of cues associated with threat seems to prime the extinction associations and to reduce the renewal effect (Brooks & Bouton, 1993, 1994). Thus if therapy enables the client to recall or to have present aspects of the therapeutic context in his or her nontherapeutic environment, then the likelihood that fear will reemerge should be lessened. Based on learning theory, one also might predict that matching the extinction context to the original learning context would also maximize therapeutic success. Unfortunately, recent findings in rats demonstrate that renewal of fear can occur in a novel context even when both original learning and extinction have taken place in the same context (Bouton & Ricker, 1994).

Even if the client can retain or recall aspects of the therapeutic context, this may not preclude the reemergence of fear, because reinstatement effects also may come into play. Recall that reinstatement occurs when actual threats occur outside the therapeutic environment and fear responding reemerges (Bouton & Swartzentruber, 1991). One way to reduce reinstatement effects is to create strong associations between the nontherapeutic context and safety cues. Again, however, the practicality of this suggestion may be limited given that threats are typically present to at least some extent in the everyday environments of most people. In sum, these prescriptions for reducing the reemergence of fear lead to the inescapable conclusion that completely eliminating the possibility of relapse into fear responding may be a fruitless goal. Instead, we suggest that in addition to trying to minimize relapse, the therapist also work with the client to reduce the impact of the likely occurrence of at least some reappearance of inappropriate fear responding.

An alternative solution to the probably unrealistic goal of eliminating all real or conditioned threat cues would be to reduce the impact of such cues by teaching the client to be aware of them. If a client can identify threat cues from the original learning context or those that have generalized from the formative environment, then he or she can label the resulting fear response a "false alarm." This may be one way to break the association between the automatic fear response and the tendency to use a zero-miss strategy, thus reducing the likelihood of a relapse. Of course, in reality, it is difficult to identify these cues. Some cues are embedded in the context and, perhaps because they were learned via implicit processes, may not be accessible to conscious awareness (e.g., LeDoux, 1996). Furthermore, emotional and drug-induced states can also serve as contexts to promote renewal and may be difficult to eliminate or control (Bouton, Kenney, &

Rosengard, 1990; Bouton & Swartzentruber, 1991). Moreover, an individual who has engaged in a zero-miss strategy over a long period of time is likely to experience a higher base rate of interpersonal stressors that may serve either as cues associated previously with threat and promote renewal or as unlearned, veridical threats and promote reinstatement.

CONCLUSIONS

In sum, we suggest that therapy aimed at achieving the development of intentional self-regulation strategies, successful emotional learning, and therefore a reduction of the zero-miss strategy must include the following elements:

1. Provision of repetitive, unambiguous feedback about judgment outcomes in multiple contexts
2. Attempts to overcome cognitive bias by making judgment strategies explicit and accessible for conscious apprehension, and learning to avoid confirmatory bias
3. Prevention of behavioral avoidance and expansion of the behavioral repertoire to create a context for new learning
4. Activation of emotional networks in situ
5. Training of new affect regulation skills and tolerance of negative affect
6. Training to identify potential threat cues and to learn to label associated automatic fear responses as false alarms

None of these elements alone is sufficient for change. To the extent that any context includes all of these elements, the individual will be poised for change in both judgment strategy and emotional reactivity to the environment. Note, however, that acquisition and implementation of the skills noted above require active participation on the part of the individual. Active learning and implementation require both motivation and cognitive processing capacity. For example, it has been observed that some (if not all) therapeutic interventions require motivation. What has been less often noted, and little studied, is whether a client's cognitive capabilities influence the degree to which therapy can be successful when the therapeutic process makes intensive cognitive demands. For example, an individual requires some ability to use divided attentional processing in the event that relapse occurs; he or she needs to regulate affect, whether it is tolerating an automatically activated response or deliberately managing the cognitive construction of that response, while at the same time continuing the business of calibration, and this requires the ability to multitask. It is even conceivable that simultaneous calibration and fear management efforts require considerable working memory capacity or other mental capabilities related to intelligence, attention, and/or memory. In addition, therapy demands active inhibition of previously learned responses, which requires considerable cognitive capacity.

It is perhaps the case that some individuals do not have the requisite cognitive skills and motivation to maintain extinction of fear actively and intentionally. Moreover, tolerance of ambiguity is probably an important personal resource for those trying to change their judgment and emotional response patterns. As we have suggested above, extinction or counterconditioning procedures lead to greater ambiguity in the meaning of previously learned cues of threat. Thus an increase in the ambiguity of cues is inherent to the reduction of learned fear responses and the calibration of judgment strategies. Furthermore, when cues with a long history of association with threat become ambiguous, there remains the possibility that cues in the environment will result in relapse. Thus clients (and therapists) should consider it sufficient to provide (a) alternative interpretations of cues that were previously associated with threat, (b) explanations that fear is likely to return, and (c) affect regulation skills that will be needed when fear reemerges. Sustained emotional reactivity should not be taken as an indication that therapy is not working.

NOTES

1. In contrast, a positive-illusion strategy will develop when the base rates for threat are low, because the individual will have the goal of reducing the number of false alarms rather than minimizing misses.

2. Although a zero-miss strategy likely develops with many primary appraisals over time, one vivid miss (e.g., being a victim of a random act of violence) might be enough to shift a person's judgment strategy in a single trial. Similarly, people don't develop food aversions every time they are ill, but aversive conditioning to a particular food can occur with one vivid experience of food poisoning.

3. Several authors have argued that data derived from studies of learning in animal models are relevant for understanding human far learning and unlearning (see Jacobs & Nadel, 1985; Mineka, 1985; Shalev, Rogel-Fuchs, & Pitman, 1992).

4. Both renewal and reinstatement can occur in situations other than aversive conditioning, including both appetitive classical and instrumental conditioning, suggesting that these learning phenomena are pervasive aspects of some learning processes (for a review, see Bouton, 1993).

5. Although most of the existing learning and neurobiological data have been obtained from nonhuman animals, it appears plausible that such effects can be observed in humans. Indeed, there is some preliminary evidence that both renewal and reexposure to a phobic stimulus (i.e., reinstatement) may be related to recovery of fear responding in spider-phobic subjects (Rodriguez, 1996). Unfortunately, virtually no other studies have specifically addressed the possibility that such learning phenomena may be influential in the reappearance of fear responding in humans. Future research is needed to demonstrate the existence of these phenomena and their potential power over fear reemergence in humans.

6. Of course, there are exceptions. For a nice example of the theoretical importance of emotional processing as an active ingredient of psychotherapeutic change, see Foa and Kozak (1986). In addition, cognitive-behavioral therapists have begun to explore the importance of emotional learning and emotional experience in successful psychotherapeutic change (Castonguay, in press; Castonguay & Goldfried, 1997; Castonguay, Goldfried, Wiser, Raue, & Hayes, 1996).

7. It is clear that relapse, and reemergence of fear, is an ongoing problem for clients receiving many forms of therapy (Foa & Kozak, 1986; Jacobs & Nadel, 1985; McNally, 1995; Shalev et al., 1992).

REFERENCES

Beck, A. T., Rush, A. J., Shaw, B. F., & Emery, G. (1979). *Cognitive therapy of depression: A treatment manual.* New York: Guilford.

Bouton, M. E. (1988). Context and ambiguity in the extinction of emotional learning: Implications for exposure therapy. *Behavior Research and Therapy, 26,* 137-149.

Bouton, M. E. (1993). Context, time, and memory retrieval in the interference paradigms of Pavlovian learning. *Psychological Bulletin, 114,* 80-99.

Bouton, M. E. (1994a). Conditioning, remembering and forgetting. *Journal of Experimental Psychology: Animal Behavior Processes, 20,* 219-231.

Bouton, M. E. (1994b). Context, ambiguity, and classical conditioning. *Current Directions in Psychological Science, 3,* 49-53.

Bouton, M. E., Kenney, F. A., & Rosengard, C. (1990). State-dependent fear extinction with two benzodiazepine tranquilizers. *Behavioral Neuroscience, 104,* 44-55.

Bouton, M. E., & Ricker, S. T. (1994). Renewal of extinguished responding in a second context. *Animal Learning and Behavior, 22,* 317-324.

Bouton, M. E., & Swartzentruber, D. (1991). Sources of relapse after extinction in Pavlovian and instrumental learning. *Clinical Psychology Review, 11,* 123-140.

Brooks, D. C., & Bouton, M. E. (1993). A retrieval cue for extinction attenuates spontaneous recovery. *Journal of Experimental Psychology: Animal Behavior Processes, 19,* 77-89.

Brooks, D. C., & Bouton, M. E. (1994). A retrieval cue for extinction attenuates response recovery (renewal) caused by a return to the conditioning context. *Journal of Experimental Psychology: Animal Behavior Processes, 20,* 366-379.

Castonguay, L. G. (in press). A common factors approach to psychotherapy training. *Journal of Psychotherapy Integration.*

Castonguay, L. G., & Goldfried, M. R. (1997). Psychotherapy integration and the need for better theories of change: A rejoinder to Alford. *Applied and Preventive Psychology, 6,* 91-95.

Castonguay, L. G., Goldfried, M. R., Wiser, S., Raue, P. J., & Hayes, A. M. (1996). Predicting the effect of cognitive therapy for depression: A study of unique and common factors. *Journal of Consulting and Clinical Psychology, 64,* 497-504.

Egan, J. P. (1975). *Signal detection theory and ROC analysis.* New York: Academic Press.

Einhorn, H. J. (1982). Learning from experience and suboptimal rules in decision making. In D. Kahneman, P. Slovic, & A. Tversky (Eds.), *Judgment under uncertainty: Heuristics and biases* (pp. 268-283). New York: Cambridge University Press.

Einhorn, H. J., & Hogarth, R. M. (1978). Confidence in judgment: Persistence of the illusion of validity. *Psychological Review, 85,* 395-416.

Epstein, S., & Roupenian, A. (1970). Heart rate and skin conductance during experimentally induced anxiety: The effect of uncertainty about receiving a noxious stimulus. *Journal of Personality and Social Psychology, 16,* 20-28.

Eysenck, M. W. (1989). Personality, stress, arousal, and cognitive processes in stress transactions. In R. W. J. Neufeld (Ed.), *Advances in the investigation of psychological stress* (pp. 133-192). New York: John Wiley.

Feldman Barrett, L. (1996, June). *Primary appraisals of threat: A signal detection model.* Paper presented at the annual meeting of the American Psychological Society, San Francisco.

Feldman Barrett, L., & Fong, G. T. (1996). *Primary appraisals of threat: A signal detection model.* Unpublished manuscript.

Feldman Barrett, L., & Williams, N. L. (1998). *An analysis of defensive verbal behavior.* Unpublished manuscript, Boston College.

Fiske, S. T., & Taylor, S. E. (1991). *Social cognition.* New York: McGraw-Hill.

Foa, E. B., & Kozak, M. J. (1986). Emotional processing of fear: Exposure to corrective Information. *Psychological Bulletin, 99,* 20-35.

Funder, D. C. (1987). Errors and mistakes: Evaluating the accuracy of social judgment. *Psychological Bulletin, 101,* 75-90.

Green, D. M., & Swets, J. A. (1974). *Signal detection theory and psychophysics.* New York: John Wiley. (Original work published 1966)

Grossberg, J. M., & Grant, B. F. (1978). Clinical psychophysics: Applications of ratio scaling and signal detection methods to research on pain, fear, drugs, and medical decision making. *Psychological Bulletin, 85*, 1154-1176.

Harvey, L. O. (1992). The critical operating characteristic and the evaluation of expert judgment. *Organizational Behavior and Human Decision Processes, 53*, 229-251.

Healy, A. F., & Kubovy, M. (1978). The effects of payoffs and prior probabilities on indices of performance and cutoff location in recognition memory. *Memory and Cognition, 6*, 544-553.

Horney, K. (1950). *Neurosis and human growth*. New York: W. W. Norton.

Ittleson, W. H., & Kilpatrick, F. P. (1951). Experiments in perception. *Scientific American, 185*, 50-55.

Jacobs, W. J., & Nadel, L. (1985). Stress-induced recovery of fears and phobias. *Psychological Review, 92*, 512-531.

Kahneman, D., & Tversky, A. (1982). Variants of uncertainty. In D. Kahneman, P. Slovic, & A. Tversky (Eds.), *Judgment under uncertainty: Heuristics and biases* (pp. 509-520). New York: Cambridge University Press.

Keren, G. (1987). Facing uncertainty in the game of bridge: A calibration study. *Organizational Behavior and Human Decision Processes, 39*, 98-114.

Krantz, D. S., & Manuck, S. B. (1984). Acute psychophysiologic reactivity and risk for cardiovascular disease: A review and methodological critique. *Psychological Bulletin, 96*, 435-464.

Lazarus, R. S. (1968). Emotions and adaptation: Conceptual and empirical relations. In W. J. Arnold (Ed.), *Nebraska Symposium on Motivation* (Vol. 16). Lincoln: University of Nebraska Press.

Lazarus, R. S. (1991). *Emotion and adaptation*. New York: Oxford University Press.

Lazarus, R. S. (1993). From psychological stress to the emotions: A history of changing outlooks. *Annual Review of Psychology, 44*, 1-21.

Lazarus, R. S., & Folkman, S. (1984). *Stress, appraisal and coping*. New York: Springer.

Leary, T. (1957). Interpersonal diagnosis of personality. New York: Ronald.

LeDoux, J. E. (1996). *The emotional brain: The mysterious underpinnings of emotional life*. New York: Simon & Schuster.

LeDoux, J. E., Romanski, L., & Xagoraris, A. (1989). Indelibility of subcortical memories. *Journal of Cognitive Neuroscience, 1*, 238-243.

Lewicki, P., Hill, T., & Sasaki, I. (1989). Self-perpetuating development of encoding biases. *Journal of Experimental Psychology: General, 118*, 323-337.

Lichtenstein, S., Fischoff, B., & Phillips, L. D. (1982). Calibration of probabilities: The state of the art to 1980. In D. Kahneman, P. Slovic, & A. Tversky (Eds.), *Judgment under uncertainty: Heuristics and biases* (pp. 306-334). New York: Cambridge University Press.

Macmillan, N. A. (1993). Signal detection theory as a data analysis method and psychological decision model. In G. Keren & G. Lewis (Eds.), *A handbook for* data analysis in the behavioral sciences: Methodological issues (pp. 21-58). Hillsdale, NJ: Lawrence Erlbaum.

Mathews, A., & MacLeod, C. (1994). Cognitive approaches to emotion and emotional disorders. *Annual Review of Psychology, 45,* 25-50.

McNally, R. J. (1995). Automaticity and the anxiety disorders. *Behavior Research and Therapy, 33,* 747-754.

McNicol, D. (1972). *A primer of signal detection theory.* London: Allen & Unwin.

Milburn, T. W., & Watman, K. H. (1981). *On the nature of threat: A social psychological analysis.* New York: Praeger.

Miller, S. M. (1979). Controllability and human stress: Method, evidence, and theory. *Behavioral Research and Therapy, 17,* 287-304.

Mineka, S. (1985). Animal models of anxiety-based disorders: Their usefulness and limitations. In A. H. Tuma & J. Maser (Eds.), *Anxiety and the anxiety disorders* (pp. 199-244). Hillsdale, NJ: Lawrence Erlbaum.

Morgan, M. A., Romanski, L. M., & LeDoux, J. E. (1993). Extinction of emotional learning: Contribution of medial prefrontal cortex. *Neuroscience Letters, 163,* 109-113.

Murphy, A. H., & Winkler, R. L. (1971). Forecasters and probability forecasts: Some current problems. *Bulletin of the American Meteorological Society, 52,* 239-247.

Newman, M. G., Consoli, A., & Taylor, C. B. (1997). Computers in the assessment and cognitive-behavioral treatment of clinical disorders: Anxiety as a case in point. *Behavior Therapy, 28,* 211-235.

Nisbett, R. E., Krantz, D. H., Jepson, C., & Fong, G. T. (1982). Improving inductive inference. In D. Kahneman, P. Slovic, & A. Tversky (Eds.), *Judgment under uncertainty: Heuristics and biases.* New York: Cambridge University Press.

Parkinson, B. (1997). Untangling the appraisal-emotion connection. *Personality and Social Psychology Review, 1,* 62-79.

Paterson, R. J., & Neufeld, W. J. (1987). Clear danger: Situational determinants of the appraisal of threat. *Psychological Bulletin, 101,* 404-416.

Pavlov, I. P. (1927). *Conditioned reflexes.* New York: Dover.

Posner, M. I. (1978). *Chronometric explorations of the mind.* Hillsdale, NJ: Lawrence Erlbaum.

Quirk, G. J., Repa, J. C., & LeDoux, J. E. (1995). Fear conditioning enhances short-latency auditory responses of lateral amygdala neurons: Parallel recordings in the freely behaving rat. *Neuron, 15,* 1029-1039.

Rodriguez, B. I. (1996). Context-specificity of relapse: The effects of context and stimulus factors on return of fear following exposure treatment for specific fear (Doctoral dissertation, University of California, Los Angeles, 1996). *Dissertation Abstracts International, 57,* 9634017.

Sanghera, M. K., Rolls, E. T., & Roper-Hall, A. (1979). Visual response of neurons in the dorsolateral amygdala of the alert monkey. *Experimental Neurology, 63,* 610-626.

Shalev, A. Y., Rogel-Fuchs, Y., & Pitman, R. K. (1992). Conditioned fear and psychological trauma. *Biological Psychiatry, 31*, 863-865.

Sullivan, H. S. (1953). *Conceptions of modern psychiatry.* New York: W. W. Norton.

Swets, J. A. (1986). Indices of discrimination or diagnostic accuracy: Their ROCs and implied models. *Psychological Bulletin, 99*, 100-117.

Tversky, A., & Kahneman, D. (1982). Evidential impact of base rates. In D. Kahneman, P. Slovic, & A. Tversky (Eds.), *Judgment under uncertainty: Heuristics and biases* (pp. 153-160). New York: Cambridge University Press.

16

ACTION REGULATION, COPING, AND DEVELOPMENT

Ellen A. Skinner

An intriguing theme is emerging in the field of coping. At its core is the idea that notions of "regulation" may be useful to conceptualizations of coping. The connection between coping and regulation has crystallized most clearly in work on emotion regulation in children (Dodge, 1989; Fox, 1994; Saarni, Mumme, & Campos, 1998). Some coping researchers suggest that emotion regulation may be a form of coping. For example, Rossman (1992) states, "In the case of emotion-focused coping, emotion regulation and coping become virtually synonymous" (p. 1375). At the same time, researchers studying emotion regulation sometimes offer definitions of their phenomena that lie well within the territory usually encompassed by coping. For example, Dodge (1989) posits that emotion regulation can be understood as "coordinating responses to aversive stimuli."

AUTHOR'S NOTE: Earlier drafts of this chapter benefited from the critiques and insights of Kathleen Edge, Thomas Kindermann, and James Wellborn. Support from research grant HD19914 from the National Institute of Child Health and Human Development and from a Faculty Scholar's Award from the William T. Grant Foundation are gratefully acknowledged.

The overlap between emotion regulation and coping has been examined explicitly by several researchers (Barrett & Campos, 1991; Bridges & Grolnick, 1995; Eisenberg, Fabes, & Guthrie, 1997; Rossman, 1992).

Although perhaps not as noticeable as the burgeoning work on emotion, discussions of other kinds of regulation have also benefited conceptualizations of coping. Models of *behavioral* self-regulation have been used as a basis for theoretically derived ways of coping (e.g., Carver, Scheier, & Weintraub, 1989). *Self*-regulation has become an element in descriptions of "proactive" coping or coping that aims to prevent or prepare for stressful encounters (Aspinwall & Taylor, 1997). *Attention* regulation has been suggested as a "shuttle" between cognition and emotion regulation, and hence as a critical mediator between risk and psychopathology (Wilson & Gottman, 1996).

The connection between coping and regulation has been made in reference to almost every point in the life span. In theoretical accounts of how infants deal with interactive stress, *mutual* or interactive regulation is suggested as a key feature of coping (Gianino & Tronick, 1988). At the other end of the age continuum, descriptions of how people actively cope with the changes and losses of aging rely on notions of *developmental* regulation (Heckhausen & Schulz, 1998). Some life-span researchers have explicitly studied the functions of broad classes of coping responses, such as assimilative and accommodative coping, in intentional self-regulation of development (Brandtstädter & Renner, 1990; Brandtstädter, Rothermund, & Schmitz, 1998). Across the life span, regulatory resources, such as regulatory control, have been suggested as "highly relevant and critical to a complete understanding of individuals' responses to stressful contexts" (Fabes & Eisenberg, 1997, p. 1107; see also Block & Block, 1980; Mischel, 1983).

Taken together, variations on the theme of regulation seem to have much to offer conceptualizations of coping. Perhaps most important, the idea of regulation is consistent with the general perspective on coping that dominates the field today, namely, that posited by Lazarus and Folkman (1984). According to this definition, coping is "the process of managing demands (external or internal) that are appraised as taxing or exceeding the resources of the person" (p. 283). Some of the issues involved in "managing demands" may be further delineated using theories of regulation. As Rossman (1992) notes, both coping and regulation include processes related to "an appraisal of the significance of the environmental circumstance, the attendant emotional experience, the selection of some action to regulate the heightened emotion and perhaps alter the environment, and some kind of feedback about the success of the regulation attempt" (p. 1375).

For the field of coping, theories of regulation offer access to rich explanatory systems. These can augment more descriptive accounts of coping that tend to focus on taxonomies or categories of coping (Compas, 1998). In addition, theories of regulation are often developmental and so focus on the emergence and development of many processes that may be related to coping, such as intentionality, volition, social referencing, and the coordination of action. Adapting some of this work may guide research on both age progression and socialization of coping (Aldwin, 1994; Compas, 1998; Garmezy & Rutter, 1983; Skinner & Edge, 1998; Wolchik & Sandler, 1997).

My goal in this chapter is to make progress in using work on regulation to enrich developmental conceptualizations of coping. Toward that end, I would like to articulate a view of coping that rests on concepts of regulation, in this case the view that coping can be defined as "action regulation under stress" (Skinner, 1995; Skinner & Wellborn, 1994). After briefly arguing the merits of a conceptualization of coping that includes action, regulation, and stress, I focus on four implications of this perspective: the role of action tendencies in coping, intentionality of action, the social embeddedness of coping, and developmental processes and goals of coping. Rather than striving to be comprehensive, I have attempted to select implications that are interesting and may be mutually informative to researchers studying both coping and regulation.

MOTIVATIONAL MODEL OF COPING

The definition of coping defended in this chapter is the result of work on the development of children's motivation (Skinner & Wellborn, 1994). At the heart of this motivational model is the notion of "patterns of action," with engaged versus disaffected patterns of action as the central outcomes of motivational processes (Connell & Wellborn, 1991; Deci & Ryan, 1985; Skinner, 1995; Wellborn, 1991). According to this view, *engagement,* which refers to active, goal-directed, flexible, constructive, persistent, focused interactions with the social and physical environments, is the mechanism through which motivational processes contribute to the development of adaptive functioning. In contrast, patterns of *disaffected* action, in which individuals are alienated, apathetic, rebellious, frightened, or burned out, turn people away from opportunities for development and toward psychopathology.

Fundamental Needs

The motivational model holds that individuals at any point in the life span will be engaged in an enterprise (e.g., school, family, work) to the extent that social contexts within that enterprise allow them to meet their basic psychological needs (Connell & Wellborn, 1991; Deci & Ryan, 1985). Three needs are posited as fundamental, meaning present at birth and common to all humans. These are the needs for relatedness, competence, and autonomy (see Figure 16.1).

Relatedness refers to the need to experience oneself as connected to other people, as belonging. This need is hypothesized to underlie processes of attachment (Ainsworth, 1979; Bowlby, 1969, 1973), in which newborns show interest in other people and possess the capacity and desire to initiate contact with, respond to, enjoy, and be comforted by social partners (Papousek & Papousek, 1980). *Competence* refers to the need to experience oneself as effective in one's interactions with the social and physical environments (Harter, 1978; Koestner & McClelland, 1990; White, 1959). It is hypothesized to underlie processes of control (Bandura, 1997; Peterson, Maier, & Seligman, 1993; Seligman, 1975), in which infants manifest interest in the external world and have the ability and desire to initiate contact with, respond to, enjoy, and explore environmental events (Finkelstein & Ramey, 1977; Morgan & Harmon, 1984; Piaget, 1976, 1978; Watson, 1979). *Autonomy* refers to the need to express one's authentic self and to experience that self as the source of action. It is hypothesized to underlie processes of self-determination (Deci & Ryan, 1985, 1987, 1991, 1995), in which newborns evince interest in their own inner states and have the capacity and will to detect, express, protect, and defend their own states, desires, and preferences (Bridges & Grolnick, 1995).

Social Contexts

Social and physical contexts can be characterized by the extent to which they provide children (and people in general) with opportunities to fulfill their needs (Connell & Wellborn, 1991; Deci & Ryan, 1985; Grolnick &

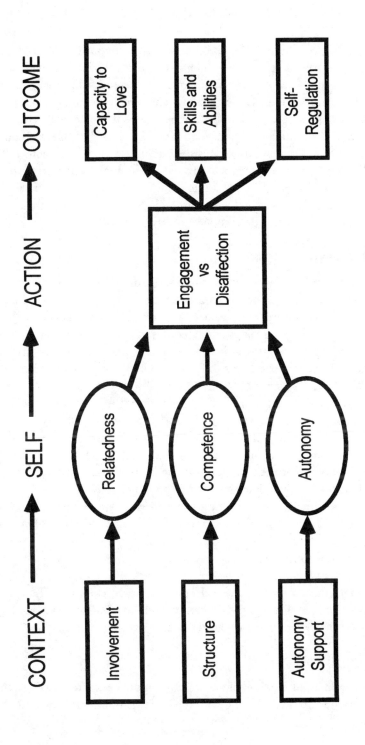

Figure 16.1. A Motivational Model of Human Development

Ryan, 1989; Skinner, 1995). Children are given opportunities to experience themselves as related and belonging when they interact with social partners who love them, who are involved and emotionally available, and who express affection, warmth, caring, and nurturance (Lamb & Easterbrooks, 1981). Children accumulate experiences of competence when they interact with contexts that respond to them and that are structured, predictable, contingent, and consistent (Gunnar, 1980; Suomi, 1980). Finally, children experience themselves as autonomous when they interact with social partners who respect them, allow them freedom of expression and action, and encourage them to attend to, accept, and value their inner states, preferences, and desires (Deci & Ryan, 1987).

Processes of Development

Mechanisms for development can also be organized with reference to the three needs. For example, based on the need for relatedness, children come with the desire and capacity to imitate others (Zeedyk, 1996). Imitation also creates feelings of relatedness in others, and so has the effect of prolonging positive social interactions. One manifestation of the need for competence is children's curiosity about exploring and operating contingencies (Watson, 1966, 1979; Watson & Ramey, 1972; White, 1959). Creating contingent effects is intrinsically enjoyable and so is responsible for prolonged bouts of interactions with social and material partners, sometimes called *practice* (Piaget, 1976, 1978). The need for autonomy can explain the infant's (and child's) intrinsic desire for and enjoyment of self-expression, for example, through play, drawing, singing, and dancing (Morgan, Harmon, & Maslin-Cole, 1990).

Taken together, imitation, curiosity, and self-expression are powerful intrinsic mechanisms for development. All three have the effect of promoting engagement on the part of the individual, and through their effects on social and material partners, they also have the effect of prolonging interactions with the environment. This pattern of constructive engagement over time contributes to learning and the development of cognitive structures, sociability and the development of attachments, and intentionality and the development of expressiveness and personality.

Self-System Processes

By-products of these experiences are children's appreciation of their relationships to the context and their views of themselves and their social/physical worlds. These are referred to as *self-system processes* (Connell & Wellborn, 1991). Early in development, they take the form of generalized expectations (e.g., Finkelstein & Ramey, 1977), but eventually they become organized and robust sets of beliefs. For relatedness, these have been studied as internal working models of attachment figures (Bretherton, 1985; Crittenden, 1990) and contain views about the self as lovable and loving and about the context as caring and trustworthy. For competence, self-system processes have been studied as perceptions of control (Abramson, Seligman, & Teasdale, 1978; Bandura, 1997; Dweck, 1991; Skinner, 1996; Weisz, 1986) and contain views about the self as able and effective and about the environment as structured and predictable.

For autonomy (which has received relatively less empirical attention than relatedness and competence), self-system processes have been studied as autonomy or goal orientations (Deci & Ryan, 1985, 1991; Dweck, 1991; Kuhl, 1987; Ryan & Connell, 1989) and contain views about the self as authentic and integrated and about the environment as accepting and supportive. Because these self-system processes serve to guide children's initiation and interpretations of interactions with the social and physical environment (e.g., Skinner, Zimmer-Gembeck, & Connell, 1998), they become one pathway by which early experience is carried forward into later development and through which children continue to be active participants in their own development.

Motivational Model of Stress

Although this motivational model was originally constructed to explain ongoing action and the development of adaptive functioning, it can also be used as a model of stress and coping (see Figure 16.2; Skinner & Wellborn, 1994). It makes strong claims about the nature of objective stress. Events and contexts are potentially stressful to the extent that they interfere with the three basic needs. Hence contexts that are negligent or hostile should thwart relatedness needs, events that are noncontingent or chaotic should tax competence, and interactions that are coercive or controlling should threaten autonomy needs. Together, these three broad categories of events explain the seemingly inherent stressfulness of a variety of specific experiences, such as separation, deprivation, or unavailability or loss of an attachment figure (instances of neglect); noncontingency, novelty, unpredictability, or failure (instances of chaos); and restraint, demands, controllingness, or pressure (instances of coercion).

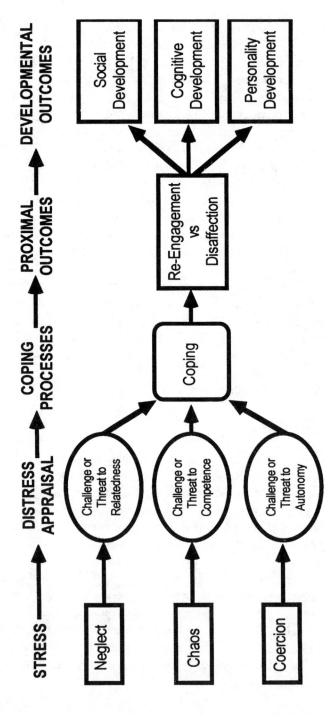

Figure 16.2. A Motivational Model Linking Stress and Coping to Development

Self-System Vulnerabilities

The motivational model also explains why certain self-system processes should render individuals more vulnerable to stressful circumstances. For example, individuals with insecure internal working models are more likely to appraise instances of separation as experiences of abandonment. Individuals with low perceptions of control tend to view difficulty and failure as evidence of incompetence. And individuals with an external autonomy orientation tend to view environmental demands as coercive. As a result, these individuals tend to experience a broader array of situations as thwarting basic needs, and hence as distressing.

Patterns of Action

Most interesting from a coping perspective are the patterns of action that are organized in response to stress (Skinner & Wellborn, 1994). Six basic patterns have been suggested, corresponding to the extent to which the event actually impinges (or is experienced as impinging) on one of the three needs (see Table 16.1). When a stress occurs in a context that the individual perceives as warm, involved, and available, a pattern of responding occurs that includes the individual's seeking out specific others for support (proximity seeking; Ainsworth, 1979; Bowlby, 1969, 1973). In contrast, if the individual expects the context to be negligent or unsafe, his or her response will be to avoid or fend off others. When the individual experiences stress in a context perceived as structured and predictable, then the response pattern will be for him or her to include information seeking and problem solving (mastery orientation; Dweck, 1991; Dweck & Leggett, 1988). On the other hand, if the individual views the context as chaotic or uncontrollable, his or her response will be confusion and withdrawal (helplessness; Seligman, 1975). Finally, if the individual sees the context as supporting autonomy, his or her response will be the assertion of preferences or flexible negotiation. If, however, the individual experiences the context as coercive or demanding, his or her response will be to fight back and oppose the source of coercion (Deci & Ryan, 1985).

Effects on Engagement

As can be imagined, these patterns of action have their own effects on the individual, the social context, and the interactions between them. For example, actively seeking attachment figures tends to demonstrate the

TABLE 16.1 Six Patterns of Action (Action Tendencies) in Coping

Psychological Need	Environmental Event/Appraisal	Action Tendency	Behavior	Emotion	Orientation
Relatedness	separation	seek proximity	go to other	yearning	make contact away (to other)
	loss	freeze	hold still	shock	disappear toward (inward)
Competence	novelty	observe	study	interest	discover toward (object)
	chaos	flee	run away	fear	escape away (outward)
Autonomy	resistance	defend	stand firm	indignation	protect away (to obstacle)
	coercion	fight	move toward obstacle	anger	attack toward (to object)

availability and caring of the social context as well as the lovability of the self. In a parallel vein, actively collecting information and problem solving tend to reveal the structure and possibilities in the environment as well as the capacities of the self. And actively asserting preferences and negotiating tend to increase the likelihood that the environment will respond supportively and grant more autonomy. All three of these patterns of action have in common their effects on engagement. They tend to prolong constructive, goal-directed, focused interactions with the social and physical environments, and, in fact, contribute to interactions in which individuals experience their needs as being fulfilled.

In contrast, the other three patterns of action tend to cut off interactions or to provoke interactions in which the individual's needs are thwarted. For example, avoiding others guarantees that the individual will be experienced as unavailable, and this prevents social partners from even being aware that he or she needs comfort. Likewise, withdrawal prevents children from discovering any strategies through which they might successfully exert control. And attacking a social partner may not only provoke more coercive reactions, it may also prevent both the attacking individual and the partner from accurately discerning what it is each other want or desire. In a fundamental sense, then, these different patterns of reactions contribute not only to the short-term resolution (or escalation) of the stressful situation, but also, through their effects on engagement and disaffection, to the individual's long-term development.

COPING AS ACTION REGULATION UNDER STRESS

The motivational model, although designed to integrate work from a number of perspectives, is based on an action-theoretical framework (Boesch, 1991; Brandtstädter, 1998; Chapman, 1984; Chapman & Skinner, 1985; Frese & Sabini, 1985; Heckhausen, 1991; Kuhl & Beckmann, 1985). Action theories are theories that in general hold that the most useful units of analysis are not sets of behaviors or emotions or cognitions, but "actions." In general, actions are considered to be goal-directed, emotion-colored behaviors that are carried out in social and cultural contexts. Actions are considered to have dynamic reciprocal relations with culture and with development (Brandtstädter, 1998, p. 808, fig. 14.1). That is, social contexts constrain and facilitate actions at the same time that actions select and provoke social contexts. Likewise, development limits and allows action, whereas actions in turn channel and shape development.

Action

An action approach, although not often mentioned in relation to theories of coping (see Brandtstädter et al., 1998; Kuhl & Fuhrmann, 1998), nevertheless seems consistent with the basic tenets of those theories. Coping theorists have a long history of expressing dissatisfaction with unidimensional descriptions of coping processes (Lazarus, Coyne, & Folkman, 1984). In current conceptualizations, coping theorists have found a central place for cognition in the concept of appraisal and a central place for motivation in such concepts as commitments and discussions of what is "at stake" for individuals in specific encounters. The insistence that a full account of coping requires consideration of behavior, emotion, cognition, *and* motivation can find a metatheoretical home in action theory.

Action as a Target of Regulation

Although many theories can be identified in which notions of regulation are central, no consensus is apparent with regard to the question of *what* exactly is regulated during stressful episodes and precisely *who* carries out the regulation (Thompson, 1994). Within coping, some definitions mention "internal and external demands" as targets of regulation, and some specify efforts aimed at the problem and at the individual's own emotional reactions to it (Lazarus & Folkman, 1984). Others suggest that coping attempts can focus on behavior, emotion, or appraisal (Pearlin & Schooler, 1978). Still others suggest that either the context or the self can be targeted (Heckhausen & Schulz, 1998; Rothbaum, Weisz, & Snyder, 1982).

Theories of emotion regulation are equally diverse in their depictions of what is regulated (Thompson, 1994). Given the label, conceptualizations naturally focus on the regulation of emotion first and foremost, but many descriptions also refer to the deployment of attention or behavior in service of emotional modulation (Barrett & Campos, 1991; Bridges & Grolnick, 1995; Kopp, 1989; Saarni et al., 1998). The same point can be made about theories of behavior, attention, and "self" regulation, namely, that although each focuses on the phenomenon identified in its label, each also includes discussion of the other aspects involved in regulation (Carver & Scheier, 1990; Kopp, 1982). In addition, most of these theories also emphasize the role of social partners, noting that (especially during childhood) people can play a role in regulating others.

Within an action theory of coping, the target of regulation is defined, not surprisingly, as action. This means that, under stress, what is coordinated, organized, or managed includes behavior, emotion, *and* attention. According to this perspective, every stressful encounter produces a set of emotional, motivational, and motor responses; the job of the individual is to regulate these. In functionalist theories, behavior, feeling state, and motivation have all been included as features of emotion itself (e.g., Campos, Campos, & Barrett, 1989). Including these all as part of a construct of emotion serves to emphasize their interrelatedness. However, according to an action perspective, it may also obscure the complexity of the task presented by regulation.

Under stress, the organism is not "merely" concerned with the expression or inhibition of emotion, even with all its social consequences. The individual must realize an entire action sequence, of which emotion is but a part. Emotion is in fact a critical and defining part, given its potential to energize and direct behavior and to mobilize and guide the actions of others. However, an action perspective insists on additional critical and defining features as well, arguing that any account of coping must include motor (or behavioral) features and attention (or motivational) features.

Regulation

Terms reminiscent of the concept of regulation are often used to describe the activities of coping. Terms such as *manage* and *deal with* are common in definitions of coping. The notion of regulation elaborates on these themes, suggesting verbs such as *modulate, initiate, energize, guide, maintain, dampen, coordinate,* and *organize* (Rothbart, 1991). The term *dysregulation* (Garber & Dodge, 1991) implies the failure to accomplish these activities or the attempt to accomplish them ineffectively, resulting in states sometimes referred to as *underregulation* and *overregulation.*

Theoretically, both coping theories and theories of regulation have acknowledged the importance of the dual processes of activation and modulation. However, careful reading of these literatures suggests a difference in emphasis. Coping theories, because they focus on external stressors, tend to emphasize the adaptive nature of activity, initiation, and approach (Roth & Cohen, 1986). Some theories of regulation, especially emotion and behavior regulation, seem to emphasize the adaptiveness of inhibiting behavior or dampening emotions, especially in relation to rule following, social relations, and optimal cognitive functioning (Kopp, 1989; Mischel, 1983).

Bringing the two perspectives together reinforces the idea (present in both frameworks) that, when dealing with stress, both energization and inhibition of action are essential. All the important questions posed in stressful situations imply answers that specify initiation *and* modulation. For example, the basic question, "What should I do?" requires answers that inform the individual not only about the actions he or she should implement but also about those actions that should be inhibited (e.g., those that will interfere with implementation and those that will make things worse). Theories of volition emphasize the notion of shielding or buffering intended actions from competing action tendencies and note the problems with regulation that result when this cannot be accomplished (Heckhausen, 1977; Kuhl, 1984, 1987).

Stress

Most theories of regulation include some notion of "demands." The central proposition is that individuals usually function well using relatively automatic processes under normal conditions (Bargh, 1997), but regulation is called for when these automatic processes are no longer able to guide behavior satisfactorily (or when individuals anticipate this state). Hence demands (internal or external) are a central condition under which regulation is called for. However, the term *stress* usually extends beyond the concept of demand to include situations in which, in the words of Lazarus and Folkman (1984), "demands tax or exceed resources."

Regulation under stress is highly interesting for two opposing reasons. The first is that stressful situations (e.g., problems, threats, potential harm) are ones that by definition require better-than-average regulation. These are situations in which the individual has something at stake, and in which the coordination and effective deployment of action should make a material difference to the individual's physical or mental well-being. However, at the same time, stress has the potential to interfere with regulation. In the very situations in which individuals need to operate at their peak, stress can interfere with access to cognitive resources, such as working memory capacity, higher-order problem-solving skills, and information about genuine goals and preferences (Kofta & Sedek, 1989; Kuhl & Fuhrmann, 1998; Sedek, Kofta, & Tyszka, 1993). Hence of interest to coping researchers are the particular processes and qualities of regulation in stressful situations— that is, in situations that both require and interfere with optimal action regulation.

IMPLICATIONS OF AN ACTION-THEORETICAL PERSPECTIVE ON STRESS AND COPING

A view of coping as action regulation under stress has many implications for the conceptualization and study of coping processes. In the remainder of this chapter, I focus on four of these implications: action tendencies in coping, the role of intentionality, the embeddedness of coping in social relationships, and the progression of coping across age. I argue that consideration of these four is essential if the contributions of regulation to work on coping are to be fully realized. I hope that some of these issues will also provoke discussion in the broader field of coping and, in particular, in theories and research on the development of coping.

Coping as Constructed on Action Tendencies

The idea of an action tendency is basic to many theories within an action perspective. It has been most fully elaborated in work on volition (Brandt-städter, 1998; Heckhausen, 1977, 1991; Kuhl & Fuhrmann, 1998) and in functionalist theories of emotion (Barrett & Campos, 1991; Frijda, 1987, 1988; Saarni et al., 1998). In general, the term *action tendencies* refers to emotionally colored flexible motor programs that are directed toward a goal. For emotion theorists, the defining features of action tendencies are emotions (Frijda, 1987, 1988; Saarni et al., 1998). However, not surprisingly, action theories focus on action and characterize action tendencies in terms of their joint properties in creating an "urge," "desire," "want," or "impulse" that is redundantly experienced as a motor program (e.g., the urge to get out of the way or hide), an emotion (e.g., fear or shock), or a goal orientation (e.g., the desire to become small or disappear).

Action tendencies are adaptive in times of stress because, on the one hand, they organize action and speed up response time and, on the other hand, they are more flexible than reflexes. Action tendencies are triggered by specific context conditions, such as novelty or restraint. They are activated by an individual's appreciation of the significance of an inter-action with the context, but they do not require representation or other higher-order forms of cognition. Over time, through their realization and refinement in interactions, action tendencies become modified, elaborated, and hierarchically organized.

Emotion theorists argue that humans come with basic action tendencies, which are hardwired to emotions (Frijda, 1987, 1988). These are sometimes referred to as *primordial emotions,* meaning emotional reactions that do not need to be acquired (Barrett & Campos, 1991). We are all familiar with three fundamental action tendencies in response to stress—fight, flight, and freeze. These three tendencies involve action (and not just behavior or emotion) because each describes a distinctive pattern of motor, emotional, *and* orienting responses. Flight, for example, includes fear, the urge to run, and an orientation away from the stressor. Fight, in contrast, includes an orientation toward the stressor or obstacle, anger, and the urge to attack or remove the stressor. These patterns make sense as basic action tendencies, because they are functional and adaptive in protecting individuals from harm. For example, if an organism freezes when its caregiver rushes away from it, then it will still be where the caregiver can find it when he or she returns.

The presence of inborn action tendencies is also posited, in some form, by many theories, including theories of attachment, temperament, competence, mastery, reactance, and helplessness. Terms such as *proximity seeking, effectance motivation, reactance, sociability,* and *contingency detection* should not disguise the fact that these organizational constructs all contain the essentials of action tendencies: appreciation of the significance of certain kinds of interactions with the context that trigger distinctive patterns of goal-directed, emotion-flavored behavior. As noted previously, the motivational model also hypothesizes three basic action tendencies based on the fundamental needs for relatedness, competence, and autonomy. These action tendencies are also adaptive because they support constructive engagement with the social and physical contexts.

Action Tendencies in Coping

An important implication of a definition of coping as action regulation is that all coping efforts are built on action tendencies. Simply stated, it could be said that all coping is an action tendency wrapped in a regulation, embedded in a set of social relationships in a particular context (see Figure 16.3). At its most basic, this definition implies that in response to environmental demands (or, more specifically, individuals' appreciation of those demands), individuals experience the urge or desire to act. If unobstructed

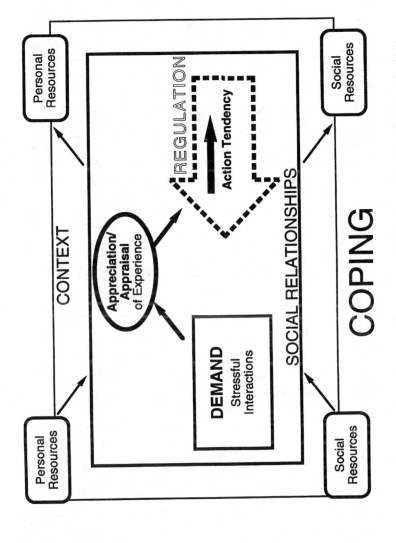

Figure 16.3. Coping Represented as Action Tendencies Wrapped in Regulation Embedded in a Set of Social Relationships in a Specific Context

by the self or the social or physical context, this urge usually is followed; in other words, the action tendency is realized—the desired action is implemented.

According to this reasoning, stressful situations trigger action tendencies. At the same time, stressful situations are likely to be ones in which action tendencies are blocked and so require regulation. From this perspective, the targets of regulation during coping episodes are always the individual's own action tendencies. In many cases, adaptive coping is possible—for example, if the individual's action tendencies are compatible with the situational demands and can be boosted enough to be effective, or if action tendencies are incompatible but can easily be diverted by the regulatory capacities available to the individual in that situation. Although developmental researchers tend to focus on action tendencies that are normative and adaptive, coping researchers are also interested in individual differences and responses to stress that are maladaptive. Maladaptive coping can occur when the action tendency is incompatible with situational or personal demands, when the tendency is intense, and when compensatory regulatory capacities are lacking or incapacitated.

Individual Differences in Action Tendencies

If coping is based on action tendencies, one important implication is the idea that individuals who show more adaptive coping are not necessarily better at regulation (in any direct sense) than people who show more maladaptive coping. Instead, it is possible that they have very different action tendencies to regulate. For example, in work on helplessness, a pattern of responding to failure and noncontingency has been identified that includes passivity, dejection, self-blame, rumination, and the desire to withdraw from the situation (Dweck, 1991). The contrasting mastery pattern, in which children improve performance under the same conditions, does not seem to be a function of the mastery-oriented children's superior regulatory skills. That is, it is not as if, when faced with failure, mastery-oriented children also ruminate and want to escape, but yet are somehow better at keeping themselves in the situation or at stopping intrusive thoughts. Instead, the action tendencies of mastery-oriented children seem to be completely different. They are *attracted* by the difficulties they encounter; they are more concentrated, focused, and involved in problem solving. These initial patterns of responding to challenge are not the result of intentional regulation; rather, they are built on relatively automatized action tendencies.

A parallel argument can be made about coping in the interpersonal domain. It is possible that aggressive-rejected children differ from socially accepted children in their basic action tendencies. When aggressive-rejected children experience an interpersonal slight, they infer hostile intentions and want to retaliate against the perpetrator (Crick & Dodge, 1994; Graham, 1998). However, in explanations of the radically different reactions of socially accepted children, it does not seem that socially accepted children experience the same urges to retaliate, but do not express them because they are able to use self-regulatory skills successfully to hold themselves back. The same objective events seem to trigger completely different action tendencies. Socially accepted children, when slighted, become more engaged, asserting their rights, soliciting information, or negotiating with the social partner.

The notion of coping as an action tendency shaped by regulation gives coping researchers several leads on how to approach coping theoretically. It allows work on temperament (Calkins, 1994; Kagan, 1998; Rothbart, 1991) to inform conceptualizations of individual differences in coping proclivities (Compas, 1998). It also describes how previous experience is carried forward in appraisals and action tendencies. It is also a beginning point for organizing the seemingly infinite ways of coping and their variations across contexts and ages. If ways of coping are all members of families of action tendencies, then they should have in common the root desire (e.g., proximity seeking or escape) but should take their *specific* form from the developmental capacities and the situational possibilities available during the stressful episode (Skinner, Edge, Altman, & Sherwood, 1998).

Intentionality in Action Regulation

As in most areas of psychology, in work on coping, concepts relating to volition have not traditionally played a central role (see Brandtstädter et al., 1998; Kuhl & Fuhrmann, 1998). Nevertheless, a few discussions have touched upon issues of intentionality. For example, definitions proposed by Lazarus and Folkman (1984) explicitly limit coping to "effortful responses" and exclude adaptational activities that are innate and temperamentally based or automatic and overlearned. It is common for descriptions of coping to reflect assumptions about coping's intentional and voluntary nature through terms such as *select* or *choose* and references to coping *efforts* or *strategies*.

Perhaps the most explicit discussion of the issues of volition in coping has been undertaken by Compas, Connor, Osowiecki, and Welch. For example, in their 1997 chapter titled "Effortful and Involuntary Responses to Stress: Implications for Coping With Chronic Stress," they lay out a framework that places the distinction between effortful and involuntary responses to stress as critical and defining features of coping. They state: "First, responses to stress can be distinguished as effortful or involuntary. This is the most fundamental distinction among stress responses and distinguishes coping (effortful responses) from other reactions to stress that are non-volitional" (p. 118).

According to this argument, coping researchers have tended to focus on effortful responses and have mistakenly included involuntary processes in discussions of coping and automatic responses in assessments of coping. Compas et al. (1997) suggest that category systems that classify responses to stress should have effortful versus involuntary responses at the top of the hierarchy—that is, as the most basic of mutually exclusive categories. This would result in classifications of ways of coping that include only effortful responses such as problem solving, information seeking, planning, help seeking, and distraction, and that exclude from coping involuntary responses to stress such as rumination, catastrophizing, denial, and venting.

From an action perspective, it does not seem like a good idea to restrict coping to effortful responses, nor does it seem desirable (or even possible) to classify in an a priori manner all potential ways of coping according to their effortfulness versus involuntariness. In fact, these suggestions would seem to be taking the field of coping in the wrong direction, if, as argued here, the roots on which all coping responses are constructed are automatic processes, namely, action tendencies.

Terms of Intentionality

Part of the difficulty is the relative immaturity of the study of volition. Theorists and researchers alike tend to use as interchangeable a variety of terms implying will, including *goal directed, intentional, volitional, voluntary, active, purposive, autonomous, self-directed, effortful,* and *conscious* (Zeedyk, 1996). As work on volition continues, the different characteristics and capabilities implied by these terms are being clarified. Some of them may be useful to distinguish in developmental accounts of coping.

From an action-theoretical perspective (and in functionalist theories of emotion), infants are born with the potential for "goal-directed" behavior, that is, with predispositions toward action. Infants are intrinsically motivated to recognize and express a variety of preferences, desires, or wants.

In simple terms, no one has to tell an infant, "Call me if you want something." From the moment of birth, based on reflexes, action tendencies, and social interactions, infants construct a repertoire of actions that not only express pleasure and pain, but are also discriminated according to the infants' experiences of a variety of objective demands. These actions are distinctive patterns of behavior, emotion, and orientation and include action tendencies such as protest to restraint, interest to novelty, disgust to unpalatable stimulation, and calming to soothing.

These patterns of expression are clear enough to allow experienced caregivers to respond to infants' actions appropriately, that is, in concert with the infants' actual desires. For example, in response to infants' gaze aversion, mothers will reduce social stimulation; in response to protest, mothers will allow more freedom of movement; in response to distress, mothers will hold, murmur, and rock. And, of course, if the caregiver's initial response does not meet the infant's need, the infant will continue to act. Social interactions in which caregivers respond to infants' expressed wants and desires (not behaving "as if" infants had intentions but actually responding to infants' expressed preferences) contribute to the emergence of coordinated action tendencies, generalized expectations of social context reactions, voluntary actions, circular reactions, and eventually representations of means and ends (Zeedyk, 1996).

Effortful and Involuntary Responses to Stress

Stress, by definition, places demands on the action system. Stress involves the blocking of goals or the experiencing of preferences that cannot be realized. Initial action tendencies are carried out until it is clear that they are not working. At this point, regulation is needed; active effort will be required if actions are to be improved enough to be effective. This coordination of responses can be called *regulation* (e.g., Dodge, 1989).

Regulation appears to be effortful in the sense that it requires and uses resources from the executive function, working memory, or ego (Baumeister, Bratslavsky, Muraven, & Tice, 1998; Kuhl & Weiss, 1994). However, it can also be argued that, although effortful, regulation does not necessarily involve voluntary processes. This is clearest in infancy, when infants have a variety of means for boosting and modulating action (such as protest, attention shifting, and proximity seeking) that, although not reflexive, do not seem to be the product of represented intentions. I would argue that effortful *and* involuntary regulation of action tendencies characterizes a wide range of coping in infants, children, and even adults.

Effortful and involuntary coping processes are most noticeable (to both the social context and the individual) when they are maladaptive. Cognitive processes such as self-denigration, intrusive thoughts, rumination, and worry seem to be effortful, in that they interfere with other energetic (attentional, behavioral, or cognitive) processes that might be used for improving action, such as strategizing or persistence. At the same time, children and adults are aware of these cognitive activities; they can be captured in talk-aloud protocols or self-reports (Diener & Dweck, 1978; Nolen-Hoeksma, 1998). However, it is hard to describe them as intentional, and they are certainly not voluntary. Adults who try to stop these processes find it very difficult (Nolen-Hoeksma, 1998). They are reminiscent of incidents in infancy in which attention is "captured" by certain environmental events and cannot be freed by the infant. In both cases, attention shifting or distraction seems to be one of the few ways of freeing attention (Nolen-Hoeksma, 1998) and hence making executive energy again available to the person.

It is likely that adaptive coping functions in a similar manner. For example, mastery-oriented children who engage in strategy generation and problem solving show many signs of having their attention captured by the difficulty of the task. They move closer to the task, narrow their focus, increase concentration, exert effort, and persist. I would argue that these are also effortful and involuntary responses, but in this case executive energy is directed toward boosting action (Kuhl, 1984). There seems to be no evidence that mastery-oriented children "decide" or "choose" to problem solve; this is their action tendency, and it is boosted by effortful regulation (Kuhl, 1984, 1987).

Voluntary Coping

At some point in the coping process, individuals can try to exert voluntary control over their actions; they attempt to regulate action intentionally. This often happens at the point when individuals experience or anticipate that their actions are not working—for example, their actions are not effective in producing the desired outcome, are not in line with their true preferences, or are upsetting a social partner. Voluntary self-control turns out to use up a great deal of energy or executive capacity (Baumeister et al., 1998) and to be relatively limited in its possible effects.

For example, as noted by volition, emotion, and coping researchers, it is difficult to change one's goals, thoughts, or emotional states voluntarily; even directing attention and behavior can be difficult.

Part of the reason is that action tendencies, by their very nature, are compelling. They are constructed from appraisals of apparent reality (Frijda, 1988), and, as mentioned previously, they are automatized and redundantly directed by behavioral, emotional, and attentional urges. For some individuals and in some situations, these action tendencies are extremely intense. Tools such as cognitively represented "wishes" or "intentions" turn out to be no match for these organized and energized action programs (Heckhausen & Kuhl, 1985). Often, the best individuals can do voluntarily is to interfere with the undesired action tendency or to rigidly contain it. This kind of regulation does not leave many resources for implementing alternative preferred action tendencies.

Self-Determined Coping

Autonomous or integrated regulation, in which the true self is experienced as the source of action, seems to produce the highest quality of action (Deci & Ryan, 1985, 1991, 1995). During autonomous regulation, action tendencies (behaviors, emotions, and orientations) work in a synergistic fashion, and executive or ego energy is available for engagement without being used for self-awareness or conscious control (Kuhl, 1984). When action tendencies are formed that are counter to the individual's actual preferences, or when regulation is used to pressure overt actions from expressing action tendencies based on genuine preferences, executive or ego resources are depleted (Baumeister et al., 1998). This results in degraded actions, for example, in which behavior and emotion are opposed (e.g., high anxiety or guilt), in which attention and behavior are not coordinated (e.g., high distractibility), or in which energy is sapped (e.g., low persistence, tiredness; Kuhl & Fuhrmann, 1998).

Intentionality in Coping

From this perspective, no action can be classified a priori as effortful or voluntary. Most actions (except reflexes) are available to many different levels of volition, for example, automatic action tendencies, effortful action regulation, intentional action regulation, and autonomous regulation. This should hold not only for maladaptive ways of coping, such as intrusive thoughts and perseverance, but also for adaptive ways of coping, such as problem solving or support seeking. Hence dimensions such as voluntary, effortful, or involuntary are not good for distinguishing *between* categories of coping. However, they do capture an important set of qualities for distinguishing *within* a family of action tendencies or coping categories. Understanding the situational, individual difference and the developmental characteristics that move actions up and down these levels—for example, that make coping available to voluntary regulation—is an important task for coping researchers and interventionists.

Social Context in Action Regulation

The role of social forces in coping has not been well-defined. On the one hand, issues of social support have been discussed continuously in work on coping (Cohen & Wills, 1985; Pierce, Sarason, & Sarason, 1996; Sarason, Shearin, Pierce, & Sarason, 1987). On the other hand, coping theories seem ambivalent about the function of social partners, pointing out that social support and help are not always supportive and that it may be maladaptive or even a marker of vulnerability for a person to seek or accept aid. Traditional perspectives have been accused of characterizing coping as largely an *individual* enterprise, with social others relegated to the roles of stressors or resources (Berg, Meegan, & Deviney, 1998).

Action theory, functional theories of emotion, and work on coping in children all converge on the view that action, regulation, and coping are socially embedded. In terms of the view of coping as action regulation presented here, several specific social functions can be highlighted. Social contexts constitute one set of demands that call up the need for regulation. As pointed out by regulation researchers, they also provide one set of affordances and limitations that influence whether the capacities of the child will be sufficient for regulation to work. For example, for young children, simple proximity to a caregiver can be sufficient to allow them access to better regulation.

Coping as Support Seeking

Thinking about coping in terms of action regulation highlights the notion that accessing other people can be an explicit goal of coping (Thompson, 1994). Attachment research is informative about the developmental steps by which the action tendency of proximity seeking is supplemented and transformed by its intentional and discretionary use (Bretherton, 1985). This work suggests several lessons for coping theories. First, it highlights the affective bond that is created and sustained by proximity seeking. Hence one condition for the intentional deployment of support seeking in new contexts (e.g., day care, school, or peer relations) should be the construction of an affective bond or attachment (Ainsworth, 1989). By the same token, an affective bond toward the child from the potentially helpful adult should also be an important precondition for providing "supportive support."

Second, this selective attachment, because it is based on a history of sensitive responsiveness of the caregiver to the child's needs, ensures that the strategy of proximity seeking will have its intended positive effect. Specifically, it means that part of adaptive support seeking is seeking comfort from the "right" social partners, namely, those upon whom one can rely for responses that are constructive and genuinely supportive. As mentioned previously, answers to all the important questions about action initiation in coping, such as (in this case), "To whom do I turn?" also imply answers to questions about action inhibition, such as (in this case), "To whom do I *not* turn?" Staying away from potentially harmful social interactions is especially important for the individual in times of stress, because both individual and action may be more vulnerable than usual to the effects of additional stressors.

Third, selective support seeking does not imply only identification of appropriate social partners, it also implies discretionary access. Specifically, adaptive support seeking accesses others only when it is clear that the individual's self-reliant attempts will not work or will be too costly in terms of resources. At young ages, certain levels of stress will almost always meet these criteria. However, as children mature, they can accomplish more and more in a self-reliant fashion, and when they seek others, they recruit those others for specific roles in action regulation (e.g., for information or advice). These processes allow social support to serve many functions: in the short term, to aid successful coping efforts and preserve social resources, but also in the long term, to build both individual regulatory capacity and close relationships.

Fourth, these interactions may also contribute to something like mutual regulatory capacity, which is sometimes experienced as "working well as a team." If both partners (or all the members of a social group) have practice working together in stressful situations, they may develop some "collective action tendencies" (such as cooperation and joint problem solving) and collective regulatory resources (such as open communication and mutual emotional availability) that will act as buffers when individuals or groups face stressful situations. These characteristics are often included in studies of family coping and resilience (e.g., McCubbin, Thompson, & McCubbin, 1996; Wills, Blechman, & McNamara, 1996).

Selective support seeking should not be confused with active attempts to avoid all social contact, such as through concealment or social isolation. These strategies cut off social avenues of regulatory support and eliminate opportunities to develop collective regulatory capacity. Such coping strategies may also be markers for other maladaptive conditions, such as unavailability of trusted social partners or the inability of the individual to benefit from the social involvement of others, for example, to derive comfort from others or to allow others to advise or help in stressful situations. The root causes of an individual's difficulty in experiencing social interactions as supportive are an important topic for research on social support at all ages.

Coping as a Social Signal

Other means of coping that are not directly aimed at recruiting or discouraging social partners may nevertheless have strong effects on them. For example, coping through opposition or escape may not only reduce the likelihood of support but may actually escalate unsupportive context reactions, such as retaliation or rejection. Interestingly, other ways of coping, such as anxiety and dependence, although they increase social involvement, may do so at the cost of individual regulation. If distress leads social partners to take over the stressful encounter (through overprotectiveness or intrusion), this kind of social involvement may interfere with the child's exercise of his or her full regulatory capacities.

An important avenue for further research involves the social consequences of different ways of coping (Skinner & Edge, 1998). Some of the more adaptive ways of coping, such as negotiation, problem solving, information seeking, and cooperation, may also have the unintended side effect of making interactions more attractive to social partners. For example, the close concentration and enthusiasm of mastery-oriented children, or the negotiation and perspective taking of socially accepted children, may have the effect of attracting others. However, in addition to increasing social involvement, these ways of coping also shape the roles of social partners so that the regulatory activities of the target individuals can still be exercised.

Expressiveness in Coping

A coping perspective also sheds light on an issue that appears from time to time in discussions of emotion and behavioral regulation. This issue centers on the goals of regulation in social contexts—that is, whether it is better for an infant (or child or adult) to modulate negative emotionality and inhibit socially proscribed behaviors or to express negative emotions or undesired action tendencies. Although the clinical utility of genuine expression of emotional states has sometimes been recognized (Cole, Michel, & Teti, 1994), the overall tone of discussion implies that social contexts will be more satisfied with lower levels of negative emotionality and higher levels of behavioral inhibition.

An action perspective on coping takes a strong position in favor of genuine expression of action tendencies. If one important function of children's coping is to inform the social context about the nature and source(s) of their distress, then genuine expression will provide the most accurate information about children's appraisals, wants, and desires. According to this perspective, children's patterns of distress and coping provide essential information to caregivers about what is wrong and how to help. Although emotion theorists correctly point out the signaling value of emotion (Saarni et al., 1998), children's behaviors and orientations provide additional diagnostic information to others. Children who, due to temperament or experience, are overreactive or inhibited pose a challenge to caregivers, not only because of the small range of situations in which their regulation can function, but because of the low diagnosticity of their action patterns.

A major goal of socialization then becomes to preserve or boost children's access to their genuine action tendencies (and emotions, desires, and preferences) while at the same time offering acceptable channels for expressing them. The prototypical shift is from expressing action tendencies in behavior to expressing them in words. This conversion makes action tendencies easier to read and more amenable to regulation. As detailed in theories of socialization of metaemotion, learning to accept and talk about feelings (and desires) may be an important part of effective action regulation (Dix, 1991; Gottman, Katz, & Hooven, 1996), perhaps in part because words provide an alternative, socially acceptable means of expressing action tendencies. At the same time, however, words help sharpen and focus the meanings of "urges," allowing them to become the objects of discussion, representation, and reflection. Continued access to one's own preferences, goals, and emotions, especially if they are in a form that can be communicated but does not overpower behavior, is an important regulatory resource throughout the life span (Deci & Ryan, 1991; Kuhl & Fuhrmann, 1998).

The Development of Action Regulation

Thinking about coping as action regulation connects conceptualizations of coping to areas of vigorous research and theorizing, not only to work on regulation in all its guises, but also to work on attachment, temperament, learned helplessness, and self-determination (Compas, 1987, 1998). Perhaps most important, it links work on coping to the development of volition (Bullock & Lütkenhaus, 1988), intentionality (Zeedyk, 1996), and ego resilience (Block & Block, 1980). These theories and bodies of research can already reveal the broad outlines of normative progression in children's coping capacities, and they provide rich explanations of the social contexts (especially parenting) that facilitate them.

Processes of Socialization

In general, coping research has focused on socialization of coping strategies through parent practices such as modeling, teaching, and coaching (Kliewer, Sandler, & Wolchik, 1994). An action perspective suggests that these activities may be a late point of entry into the social processes that influence the development of coping (Skinner & Edge, in press). Caregivers are partners in the long sequences of interactions that create action tendencies and so can be considered co-constructors of the roots of children's coping as well as of the self-system processes that shape appraisals of stressful situations. In addition, caregivers play a major role in children's acquisition of general competencies, many of which may not seem directly tied to coping but have been identified as resources for effective regulation. As mentioned previously, these include warm and loving attachments; children's access to genuine goals, preferences, and feelings; and the cognitive and motivational tools that support the development of these capacities, such as verbal ability, problem solving, and empathy.

Even when considering how parents are best able to "teach" coping in specific stressful situations, a focus on action regulation can be helpful in suggesting the kinds of parental activities, in addition to direct instruction, that might be helpful. Work on emotion regulation suggests that one important function of caregivers is to help children establish states in which optimal regulation is possible. Such states can be physiological—for example, when parents discourage regulatory activities such as problem solving when conditions are poor (e.g., when the child is tired or hungry). *State* also refers to emotion, behavior, and attention, with the notion being that when children are too upset, active, or distracted, they cannot regulate optimally. Parents use a wide array of strategies to alter children's states in ways that get them "ready for regulation." These strategies may inhibit actions that interfere with regulation (e.g., disrupting incompatible behavior, calming emotion, or distracting attention) and/or may initiate actions that facilitate regulation (e.g., bringing the child within proximity, inducing pleasant emotions such as laughter, or focusing attention). Certain strategies that do not obviously seem connected to coping, such as distraction, time-outs, or acknowledging a child's point of view, may nevertheless be handy tools for breaking up action tendencies and so may create a space within which action regulation can operate.

By the same token, parents (and other social partners) also seem to have a wide array of reactions that interfere with children's ability to regulate. In general, these include actions that overarouse children's emotions (e.g., fear, excitement, or anger) and so provoke strong action tendencies (e.g., escape or opposition) that are incompatible with the desired direction of regulation, that override autonomous regulation through coercion or pressure, or that do not require regulation that could have been successfully executed (e.g., backing down). From this perspective, an important role of the social context is to contribute to conditions in the environment and states in children that allow them the full use of their best regulatory capacities.

Development of Autonomous Action Regulation

The focus on regulation also points out that the processes through which coping is socialized matter to the quality of regulation that will develop (Deci & Ryan, 1987; Grolnick & Ryan, 1989). If parents (or others) use fear or guilt as tools to coerce children to control their actions, or if children are pressured to act against their own preferences and desires, then an external or introjected regulatory style results that uses ego energy to execute and that degrades the quality of action (Ryan & Connell, 1989). In contrast, if adults generally cooperate with children in the expression and realization of their goals and use noncoercive means to alter children's behavior through influencing the children's own goals (e.g., through empathy, induction, or reasoning about consequences), then a more integrated and autonomous style of regulation will result that is more effective in guiding and sustaining constructive action.

Interventions Into Coping Processes

An action perspective expands on the goals and processes involved in interventions aimed at supporting coping. It suggests that coping interventions that focus only on the teaching of self-regulatory skills will be of limited effectiveness and may in fact place an additional burden on already strained regulatory capacities. Instead, intervention goals should concentrate on the construction of adaptive action tendencies and effortful regulation—that is, the construction of automatic coordinated responses to stress that are adaptive. Effective interventions will work with the features of the social context and individuals' appraisals that shape the sequences of interactions responsible for the construction of action tendencies.

A key issue for interventionists is how to help children who have already formed maladaptive ways of coping. The critical task is to identify maladaptive automatic action tendencies and bring them up to be open to voluntary regulation. At this level, then, it will be possible to alter them in the direction of intentional adaptive reactions. These new action tendencies must then themselves be "sent back down" to become automatized, so they will be effortlessly deployed or effortfully boosted as the new first line of defense against stress. Lifelong lessons will include the individual's ability to modify his or her own action tendencies voluntarily and to select and create contexts, intentionally and proactively, in which stresses are manageable and optimal coping is facilitated (Aspinwall & Taylor, 1997).

CONCLUSION

Theories and research on regulation are beginning to surface in work on coping. If notions of regulation capture the imagination of coping researchers, these concepts may influence the scope, focus, and specific questions that define the area of coping. Hence, as perspectives on regulation are adopted, it is important that they also be *adapted*—that is, that they be transformed sufficiently that they are rendered useful to the particular goal: the study of coping.

In this chapter, I have explored how a definition of coping as "action regulation under stress" might serve as a bridge between work on the development of regulation and conceptualizations of coping. Most of the theories and empirical illustrations discussed here were drawn from work with infants and children. However, the perspective is intended to pertain to developments all across the life span. The use of an action-theoretical perspective suggests that at the root of all ways of coping are action tendencies that energize and direct compelling initial reactions to experienced stress. In stressful conditions, action tendencies are effortfully regulated—that is, boosted or deflected through processes that use up executive resources. However, such regulation is not always voluntary or autonomous, even in adulthood.

At all ages, action, regulation, and coping processes are embedded in social relationships (Skinner & Edge, in press). Social partners and groups play decisive roles in the co-construction of action tendencies and the self-systems involved in appraisals. Children and their parents as well as couples and their families and friends reciprocally create and buffer experiences of stress for one another (Berg et al., 1998). These close relationships facilitate and hinder regulation. A coping perspective also highlights the critical role of stress in these developments.

An action perspective makes explicit what is to be gained from coping. In the long term, the developmental goal is the construction and enhancement of individual and group regulatory capacity (Block & Block, 1980; Eisenberg et al., 1997; Fabes & Eisenberg, 1997; Mischel, 1996). Robust action regulation includes the capacity, under conditions of increasingly higher stress, to form, defend, and buffer genuine durable intentions and to coordinate actions (and their emotional, behavioral, and motivational features) sequentially in a way that allows them to become and remain organized, coherent, and meaningful and yet still flexible and responsive to changing environmental and personal demands. A key part of these processes is the capacity to maintain or boost access to all cognitive, volitional, and social resources while judiciously using as little of these as possible, in order to preserve them for future use. In a very real sense, regulatory capacity constitutes an important set of tools that allows people to shape their own actions intentionally and thereby influence their own development.

REFERENCES

Abramson, L. Y., Seligman, M. E. P., & Teasdale, J. D. (1978). Learned helplessness in humans. *Journal of Abnormal Psychology, 87,* 49-74.

Ainsworth, M. D. S. (1979). Infant-mother attachment. *American Psychologist, 34,* 932-937.

Ainsworth, M. D. S. (1989). Attachment beyond infancy. *American Psychologist, 44,* 709-716.

Aldwin, C. M. (1994). *Stress, coping, and development: An integrative perspective.* New York: Guilford.

Aspinwall, L. G., & Taylor, S. E. (1997). A stitch in time: Self-regulation and proactive coping. *Psychological Bulletin, 121,* 417-436.

Bandura, A. (1997). *Self-efficacy: The exercise of control.* New York: W. H. Freeman.

Bargh, J. A. (1997). The automaticity of everyday life. In R. S. Wyer (Ed.), *Advances in social cognition* (Vol. 10, pp. 1-61). Mahwah, NJ: Lawrence Erlbaum.

Barrett, K. C., & Campos, J. J. (1991). A diacritical function approach to emotions and coping. In E. M. Cummings, A. L. Greene, & K. H. Karraker (Eds.), *Life-span developmental psychology: Perspectives on stress and coping* (pp. 21-41). Hillsdale, NJ: Lawrence Erlbaum.

Baumeister, R. F., Bratslavsky, E., Muraven, M., & Tice, D. M. (1998). Ego depletion: Is the active self a limited resource? *Journal of Personality and Social Psychology, 74,* 1252-1265.

Berg, C., Meegan, S., & Deviney, F. (1998). A social-contextual model of coping with everyday problems across the life span. *International Journal of Behavioural Development, 22,* 239-261.

Block, J. H., & Block, J. (1980). The role of ego-control and ego-resiliency in the organization of behavior. In W. A. Collins (Ed.), *Minnesota Symposium on Child Psychology: Vol. 13. Development of cognition, affect, and social relations* (pp. 39-101). Hillsdale, NJ: Lawrence Erlbaum.

Boesch, E. E. (1991). *Symbolic action theory in cultural psychology.* Berlin: Springer.

Bowlby, J. (1969). *Attachment and loss: Vol. 1. Attachment.* New York: Basic Books.

Bowlby, J. (1973). *Attachment and loss: Vol. 2. Separation.* New York: Basic Books.

Brandtstädter, J. (1998). Action perspectives on human development. In W. Damon (Series Ed.) & R. M. Lerner (Vol. Ed.), *Handbook of child psychology: Vol. 1. Theoretical models of human development* (5th ed., pp. 807-863). New York: John Wiley.

Brandtstädter, J., & Renner, G. (1990). Tenacious goal pursuit and flexible goal adjustment: Explication and age-related analysis of assimilative and accommodative strategies of coping. *Psychology and Aging, 5,* 58-67.

Brandtstädter, J., Rothermund, K., & Schmitz, U. (1998). Maintaining self-integrity and efficacy through adulthood and later life: The adaptive functions of assimilative persistence and accommodative flexibility. In J. Heckhausen & C. S.

Dweck (Eds.), *Motivation and self-regulation across the life span* (pp. 365-388). New York: Cambridge University Press.

Bretherton, I. (1985). Attachment theory: Retrospect and prospect. In I. Bretherton & E. Waters (Eds.), Growing points of attachment theory and research. *Monographs of the Society for Research in Child Development, 50*(Serial No. 209), 3-35.

Bridges, L. J., & Grolnick, W. S. (1995). The development of emotional self-regulation in infancy and early childhood. In N. Eisenberg (Ed.), *Social development* (pp. 185-211). Thousand Oaks, CA: Sage.

Bullock, M., & Lütkenhaus, P. (1988). The development of volitional behavior in the toddler years. *Child Development, 59,* 664-674.

Calkins, S. D. (1994). Origins and outcomes of individual differences in emotion regulation. In N. A. Fox (Ed.), The development of emotion regulation: Biological and behavioral considerations. *Monographs of the Society for Research in Child Development, 59*(2-3, Serial No. 240), 53-72.

Campos, J. J., Campos, R. G., & Barrett, K. C. (1989). Emergent themes in the study of emotional development and emotion regulation. *Developmental Psychology, 25,* 394-402.

Carver, C. S., & Scheier, M. F. (1990). Principles of self-regulation: Action and emotion. In E. T. Higgins & R. M. Sorrentino (Eds.), *Handbook of motivation and cognition: Vol. 2. Foundations of social behavior* (pp. 3-52). New York: Guilford.

Carver, C. S., Scheier, M. F., & Weintraub, J. K. (1989). Assessing coping strategies: A theoretically based approach. *Journal of Personality and Social Psychology, 56,* 267-283.

Chapman, M. (1984). Intentional action as a paradigm for developmental psychology; A symposium. *Human Development, 27,* 113-114.

Chapman, M., & Skinner, E. A. (1985). Action in development/development in action. In M. Frese & J. Sabini (Eds.), *Goal-directed behavior: The concept of action in psychology* (pp. 199-213). Hillsdale, NJ: Lawrence Erlbaum.

Cohen, S., & Wills, T. (1985). Stress, social support, and the buffering hypothesis. *Psychological Bulletin, 98,* 310-357.

Cole, P. M., Michel, M. K., & Teti, L. O. (1994). The development of emotion regulation and dysregulation: A clinical view. In N. A. Fox (Ed.), The development of emotion regulation: Biological and behavioral considerations. *Monographs of the Society for Research in Child Development, 59*(2-3, Serial No. 240), 73-100.

Compas, B. E. (1987). Coping with stress during childhood and adolescence. *Psychological Bulletin, 101,* 393-403.

Compas, B. E. (1998). An agenda for coping research and theory: Basic and applied developmental issues. *International Journal of Behavioral Development, 22,* 231-237.

Compas, B. E., Connor, J., Osowiecki, D., & Welch, A. (1997). Effortful and involuntary responses to stress: Implications for coping with chronic stress. In

B. J. Gottlieb (Ed.), *Coping with chronic stress* (pp. 105-130). New York: Plenum.

Connell, J. P., & Wellborn, J. G. (1991). Competence, autonomy and relatedness: A motivational analysis of self-system processes. In M. Gunnar & L. A. Sroufe (Eds.), *Minnesota Symposium on Child Psychology* (Vol. 23, pp. 43-77). Chicago: University of Chicago Press.

Crick, N., & Dodge, K. (1994). A review and reformulation of social-information processing mechanisms in children's social adjustment. *Psychological Bulletin, 115,* 74-101.

Crittenden, P. M. (1990). Internal representational models of attachment relationships. *Infant Mental Health Journal, 11,* 259-277.

Deci, E. L., & Ryan, R. M. (1985). *Intrinsic motivation and self-determination in human behavior.* New York: Plenum.

Deci, E. L., & Ryan, R. M. (1987). The support of autonomy and the control of behavior. *Journal of Personality and Social Psychology, 53,* 1024-1037.

Deci, E. L., & Ryan, R. M. (1991). A motivational approach to self: Integration in personality. In R. Dienstbier (Ed.), *Nebraska Symposium on Motivation: Vol. 38. Perspectives on motivation* (pp. 237-288). Lincoln: University of Nebraska Press.

Deci, E. L., & Ryan, R. M. (1995). Human autonomy: The basis for true self-esteem. In M. Kernis (Ed.), *Efficacy, agency, and self-esteem* (pp. 31-49). New York: Plenum.

Diener, C. I., & Dweck, C. S. (1978). An analysis of learned helplessness: Continuous changes in performance, strategy, and achievement cognitions following failure. *Journal of Personality and Social Psychology, 36,* 451-462.

Dix, T. (1991). The affective organization of parenting: Adaptive and maladaptive processes. *Psychological Bulletin, 110,* 3-25.

Dodge, K. A. (1989). Coordinating responses to aversive stimuli: Introduction to a special section on the development of emotion regulation. *Developmental Psychology, 25,* 339-342.

Dweck, C. S. (1991). Self-theories and goals: Their role in motivation, personality, and development. In R. Dienstbier (Ed.), *Nebraska Symposium on Motivation: Vol. 38. Perspectives on motivation.* Lincoln: University of Nebraska Press.

Dweck, C. S., & Leggett, E. L. (1988). A social-cognitive approach to motivation and personality. *Psychological Review, 95,* 256-273.

Eisenberg, N., Fabes, R. A., & Guthrie, I. (1997). Coping with stress: The roles of regulation and development. In S. A. Wolchik & I. N. Sandler (Eds.), *Handbook of children's coping: Linking theory, research, and intervention* (pp. 41-70). New York: Plenum.

Fabes, R. A., & Eisenberg, N. (1997). Regulatory control and adults' stress-related responses to daily life events. *Journal of Personality and Social Psychology, 73,* 1107-1117.

Finkelstein, N. W., & Ramey, C. T. (1977). Learning to control the environment in infancy. *Child Development, 48,* 806-819.

Fox, N. A. (Ed.). (1994). The development of emotion regulation: Biological and behavioral considerations. *Monographs of the Society for Research in Child Development, 59*(2-3, Serial No. 240).

Frese, M., & Sabini, J. (Eds.). (1985). *Goal-directed behavior: The concept of action in psychology*. Hillsdale, NJ: Lawrence Erlbaum.

Frijda, N. H. (1987). Emotions, cognitive structure, and action tendency. *Cognition and Emotion, 1*, 115-144.

Frijda, N. H. (1988). The laws of emotion. *American Psychologist, 43*, 349-358.

Garber, J., & Dodge, K. (Eds.). (1991). *The development of emotion regulation and dysregulation*. New York: Cambridge University Press.

Garmezy, N., & Rutter, M. (Eds.). (1983). *Stress, coping and development in children*. New York: McGraw-Hill.

Gianino, A., & Tronick, E. Z. (1988). The mutual regulation model: The infant's self and interactive regulation and coping and defensive capacities. In T. M. Field, P. M. McCabe, & P. M. Schneiderman (Eds.), *Stress and coping across development* (pp. 47-68). Hillsdale, NJ: Lawrence Erlbaum.

Gottman, J. M., Katz, L. F., & Hooven, C. (1996). Parent meta-emotion philosophy and the emotional life of families: Theoretical models and preliminary data. *Journal of Family Psychology, 10*, 243-268.

Graham, S. (1998). Social motivation and perceived responsibility in others: Attributions and behaviors of African-American boys. In J. Heckhausen & C. S. Dweck (Eds.), *Motivation and self-regulation across the life span* (pp. 137-158). New York: Cambridge University Press.

Grolnick, W. S., & Ryan, R. M. (1989). Parent styles associated with children's self-regulation and competence: A social contextual perspective. *Journal of Educational Psychology, 81*, 143-154.

Gunnar, M. R. (1980). Contingent stimulation: A review of its role in early development. In S. Levine & H. Ursin (Eds.), *Coping and health* (pp. 101-119). New York: Plenum.

Harter, S. (1978). Effectance motivation reconsidered: Toward a developmental model. *Human Development, 21*, 36-64.

Heckhausen, H. (1977). Achievement motivation and its constructs: A cognitive model. *Motivation and Emotion, 1*, 283-329.

Heckhausen, H. (1991). *Motivation and action* (P. K. Leppmann, Trans.). New York: Springer. (Original work published 1989)

Heckhausen, H., & Kuhl, J. (1985). From wishes to action: The dead ends and short cuts on the long way to action. In M. Frese & J. Sabini (Eds.), *Goal-directed behavior: The concept of action in psychology* (pp. 134-160). Hillsdale, NJ: Lawrence Erlbaum.

Heckhausen, J., & Schulz, R. (1998). Developmental regulation in adulthood: Selection and compensation in primary and secondary control. In J. Heckhausen & C. S. Dweck (Eds.), *Motivation and self-regulation across the life span* (pp. 50-77). New York: Cambridge University Press.

Kagan, J. (1998). Biology and the child. In W. Damon (Series Ed.) & N. Eisenberg (Vol. Ed.), *Handbook of child psychology: Vol. 3. Social, emotional, and personality development* (5th ed., pp. 177-236). New York: John Wiley.

Kliewer, W., Sandler, I., & Wolchik, S. (1994). Family socialization of threat appraisal and coping: Coaching, modeling, and family context. In K. Hurrelman & F. Nestmann (Eds.), *Social networks and social support in childhood and adolescence* (pp. 271-291). Berlin: Walter de Gruyter.

Koestner, R., & McClelland, D. C. (1990). Perspectives on competence motivation. In L. A. Pervin (Ed.), *Handbook of personality: Theory and research* (pp. 527-548). New York: Guilford.

Kofta, M., & Sedek, G. (1989). Repeated failure: A source of helplessness or a factor irrelevant to its emergence? *Journal of Experimental Psychology: General, 118,* 3-12.

Kopp, C. B. (1982). Antecedents of self-regulation: A developmental perspective. *Developmental Psychology, 18,* 199-214.

Kopp, C. B. (1989). Regulation of distress and negative emotions: A developmental view. *Developmental Psychology, 25,* 343-354.

Kuhl, J. (1984). Volitional aspects of achievement motivation and learned helplessness: Toward a comprehensive theory of action control. In B. A. Maher & W. A. Maher (Eds.), *Progress in experimental personalities research* (pp. 99-171). New York: Academic Press.

Kuhl, J. (1987). Action control: The maintenance of motivational states. In F. Halisch & J. Kuhl (Eds.), *Motivation, intention, and volition* (pp. 279-291). New York: Springer.

Kuhl, J., & Beckmann, J. (Eds.). (1985). *Action control: From cognition to behavior.* New York: Springer.

Kuhl, J., & Fuhrmann, A. (1998). Decomposing self-regulation and self-control: The Volitional Components Inventory. In J. Heckhausen & C. S. Dweck (Eds.), *Motivation and self-regulation across the life span* (pp. 15-49). New York: Cambridge University Press.

Kuhl, J., & Weiss, M. (1994). Performance deficits following uncontrollable failure: Impaired action control or global attributions and generalized expectancy deficits? In J. Kuhl & J. Beckman (Eds.), *Volition and personality: Action versus state orientation* (pp. 317-328). Seattle, WA: Hogrefe & Huber.

Lamb, M. E., & Easterbrooks, M. A. (1981). Individual differences in parental sensitivity: Some thoughts about origins, components, and consequences. In M. E. Lamb & L. R. Sherrod (Eds.), *Infant social cognition: Empirical and theoretical considerations* (pp. 127-153). Hillsdale, NJ: Lawrence Erlbaum.

Lazarus, R. S., Coyne, J. C., & Folkman, S. (1984). Cognition, emotion, and motivation: The doctoring of Humpty-Dumpty. In K. R. Scherer & P. Ekman (Eds.), *Approaches to emotion* (pp. 221-237). Hillsdale, NJ: Lawrence Erlbaum.

Lazarus, R. S., & Folkman, S. (1984). *Stress, appraisal, and coping.* New York: Springer.

McCubbin, H. I., Thompson, A. I., & McCubbin, M. A. (1996). *Family assessment: Resiliency, coping, and adaptation.* Madison: University of Wisconsin Press.

Mischel, W. (1983). Delay of gratification as process and as person variable in development. In D. Magnusson & U. L. Allen (Eds.), *Human development: An international perspective* (pp. 149-166). New York: Academic Press.

Mischel, W. (1996). From good intentions to willpower. In P. M. Gollwitzer & J. A. Bargh (Eds.), *The psychology of action: Linking cognition and motivation to behavior* (pp. 197-218). New York: Guilford.

Morgan, G. A., & Harmon, R. J. (1984). Developmental transformations in mastery motivation: Measurement and validation. In R. N. Emde & R. J. Harmon (Eds.), *Continuities and discontinuities in development* (pp. 263-291). New York: Plenum.

Morgan, G. A., Harmon, R. J., & Maslin-Cole, C. A. (1990). Mastery motivation: Definition and measurement. *Early Education and Development, 1,* 318-339.

Nolen-Hoeksma, S. (1998). Ruminative coping with depression. In J. Heckhausen & C. S. Dweck (Eds.), *Motivation and self-regulation across the life span* (pp. 237-256). New York: Cambridge University Press.

Papousek, H., & Papousek, M. (1980). Early ontogeny of human social interaction: Its biological roots and social dimensions. In M. von Cranach, K. Foppa, W. Lepenies, & D. Ploog (Eds.), *Human ethology: Claims and limits of a new discipline.* Cambridge: Cambridge University Press.

Pearlin, L. I., & Schooler, C. (1978). The structure of coping. *Journal of Health and Social Behavior, 19,* 2-21.

Peterson, C., Maier, S. F., & Seligman, M. E. P. (1993). *Learned helplessness: A theory for the age of personal control.* New York: Oxford University Press.

Piaget, J. (1976). *The grasp of consciousness: Action and concept in the young child.* Cambridge, MA: Harvard University Press.

Piaget, J. (1978). *Success and understanding.* Cambridge, MA: Harvard University Press.

Pierce, G. R., Sarason, B. R., & Sarason, I. G. (Eds.). (1996). *Handbook of social support and the family.* New York: Plenum.

Rossman, B. B. R. (1992). School-aged children's perceptions of coping with distress: Strategies for emotion regulation and the moderation of adjustment. *Journal of Child Psychiatry, 33,* 1373-1397.

Roth, S., & Cohen, L. (1986). Approach, avoidance, and coping with stress. *American Psychologist, 41,* 813-819.

Rothbart, M. K. (1991). Temperament: A developmental framework. In J. Strelau & A. Angleitner (Eds.), *Explorations in temperament: International perspectives on theory and measurement* (pp. 61-74). New York: Plenum.

Rothbaum, F., Weisz, J. R., & Snyder, S. S. (1982). Changing the world and changing the self: A two-process model of perceived control. *Journal of Personality and Social Psychology, 42,* 5-37.

Ryan, R. M., & Connell, P. (1989). Perceived locus of causality and internalization: Examining reasons for acting in two domains. *Journal of Personality and Social Psychology, 57,* 749-761.

Saarni, C, Mumme, D. L., & Campos, J. J. (1998). Emotional development: Action, communication, and understanding. In W. Damon (Series Ed.) & N. Eisenberg (Vol. Ed.), *Handbook of child psychology: Vol. 3. Social, emotional, and personality development* (5th ed., pp. 237-309). New York: John Wiley.

Sarason, B. R., Shearin, E. N., Pierce, G. R., & Sarason, I. G. (1987). Interrelations of social support measures: Theoretical and practical implications. *Journal of Personality and Social Psychology, 52,* 813-832.

Sedek, G., Kofta, M., & Tyszka, T. (1993). Effects of uncontrollability on subsequent decision-making: Testing the cognitive exhaustion hypothesis. *Journal of Personality and Social Psychology, 65,* 1270-1281.

Seligman, M. E. P. (1975). *Helplessness: On depression, development and death.* San Francisco: W. H. Freeman.

Skinner, E. A. (1995). *Perceived control, motivation, and coping.* Thousand Oaks, CA: Sage.

Skinner, E. A. (1996). A guide to constructs of control. *Journal of Personality and Social Psychology, 71,* 549-570.

Skinner, E. A., & Edge, K. A. (in press). Parenting, motivation, and the development of coping. In L. J. Crockett (Ed.), *Nebraska Symposium on Motivation: Vol. 46. Motivation, agency, and the life course.* Lincoln: University of Nebraska Press.

Skinner, E. A., & Edge, K. A. (1998). Reflections on coping and development across the lifespan. *International Journal for the Study of Behavioral Development, 22,* 357-366.

Skinner, E. A., Edge, K. A., Altman, J., & Sherwood, H. (1998). *Searching for the structure of coping.* Unpublished manuscript, Portland State University.

Skinner, E. A., & Wellborn, J. G. (1994). Coping during childhood and adolescence: A motivational perspective. In D. Featherman, R. Lerner, & M. Perlmutter (Eds.), *Life-span development and behavior* (Vol. 12, pp. 91-133). Hillsdale, NJ: Lawrence Erlbaum.

Skinner, E. A., Zimmer-Gembeck, M. J., & Connell, J. P. (1998). Individual differences and the development of perceived control. *Monographs of the Society for Research in Child Development, 63*(2-3, Whole No. 254).

Suomi, S. J. (1980). Contingency, perception, and social development. In L. R. Sherrod & M. E. Lamb (Eds.), *Infant social cognition: Empirical and theoretical considerations.* Hillsdale, NJ: Lawrence Erlbaum.

Thompson, R. A. (1994). Emotion regulation: A theme in search of a definition. In N. A. Fox (Ed.), The development of emotion regulation: Biological and behavioral considerations. *Monographs of the Society for Research in Child Development, 59*(2-3, Serial No. 240), 25-53.

Watson, J. S. (1966). The development and generalization of "contingency awareness" in early infancy: Some hypotheses. *Merrill-Palmer Quarterly, 12,* 123-135.

Watson, J. S. (1979). Perception of contingency as a determinant of social responsiveness. In E. G. Thoman (Ed.), *Origins of the infant's social responsiveness* (pp. 33-64). Hillsdale, NJ: Lawrence Erlbaum.

Watson, J. S., & Ramey, C. T. (1972). Reactions to response-contingent stimulation in early infancy. *Merrill-Palmer Quarterly, 18,* 219-227.

Weisz, J. R. (1986). Understanding the developing understanding of control. In M. Perlmutter (Ed.), *Minnesota Symposium on Child Psychology: Vol. 18. Social cognition* (pp. 219-278). Hillsdale, NJ: Lawrence Erlbaum.

Wellborn, J. G. (1991). *Engaged and disaffected action: The conceptualization and measurement of motivation in the academic domain.* Unpublished doctoral dissertation, University of Rochester, New York.

White, R. W. (1959). Motivation reconsidered: The concept of competence. *Psychological Review, 66,* 297-333.

Wills, T. A., Blechman, E. A., & McNamara, G. (1996). Family support, coping, and competence. In E. M. Hetherington & E. A. Blechman (Eds.), *Stress, coping, and resiliency in children and families* (pp. 107-133). Mahwah, NJ: Lawrence Erlbaum.

Wilson, B. J., & Gottman, J. M. (1996). Attention—the shuttle between emotion and cognition: Risk, resiliency, and physiological bases. In E. M. Hetherington & E. A. Blechman (Eds.), *Stress, coping, and resiliency in children and families* (pp. 189-228). Mahwah, NJ: Lawrence Erlbaum.

Wolchik, S. A., & Sandler, I. N. (Eds.). (1997). *Handbook of children's coping: Linking theory, research, and intervention.* New York: Plenum.

Zeedyk, M. S. (1996). Developmental accounts of intentionality: Toward integration. *Developmental Review, 16,* 416-461.

Author Index

505

Subject Index

Accommodation, xiii, 356, 375-379
  and attention, 385-386
  as adaptive resource, 388-394
  mechanisms, 385-388
Accommodative flexibility, 207, 390-391
Action:
  and choice, 122
  and culture, 39
  and development, 373-374
  and intention, 39, 106, 107
  and interaction, 108
  and meaning, 107
  and rules, 44
  consequences of, 106, 111, 115
  embodied, 162
  nonintentional mechanisms, xiv, 39, 40
  phases, 91
  regulation, 139, 140, 475-479
  unintended consequences, 115-120
Action path, 305
Adaptation, 208
Affect, 154, 155. See also Emotion
Age norms, 83-85
Ageism, 349, 351
Agency, 139-146. See also Action;
  Intentionality

Agentic asymmetry, 111
Aging:
  and control, 345-364
  and dual-task performance, 420-424
  and goal-commitment, 184-185
  and memory performance, 411
  and neuronal functioning, 76
  and resources, 76-77, 362, 388,
    403-404
  and self-definition, 419
  stereotypes, 393
  "successful" aging, 391, 402
Alienation, 120-123
Appraisal theory, 435, 436
Aristotelian principle, xiii
Assimilation, 356, 375-380
  as adaptive resource, 388-395
Assimilative persistence, 390-391
Attention, 385, 421
Autodialogue, 266, 271
Auto-motive theory, 409
Autopoiesis, 41, 49

Behavioral inhibition, 491
Beliefs:

ABOUT THE CONTRIBUTORS

Ronald P. Abeles is Special Assistant to the Director of the Office of Behavioral and Social Sciences Research in the Office of the Director at the National Institutes of Health. From 1994 to September 1998, he served as the Associate Director for Behavioral and Social Research at the National Institute on Aging, where he served as the Deputy Associate Director from 1980 to 1991 and Acting Associate Director from 1991 to 1994. In 1993, he received the National Institutes of Health Award of Merit for "leadership and contributions to the advancement of behavioral and social research on aging." His 1971 doctoral degree in social psychology (with a minor in sociology) is from the Department of Social Relations, Harvard University. His experience as a Staff Associate at the Social Science Research Council (1974-1978) for the Committee on Work and Personality in the Middle Years and the Committee on Life Course Development stimulated his interest in life-course issues. He has organized several symposia at the annual meetings of professional societies, published chapters, and edited books on various aspects of life-course and aging research, most frequently in regard to the sense of control and to the interface between social structure and behavior. He is the editor of *Life-Span Perspectives and Social Psychology* (1987), coeditor of *Aging, Health, and Behavior* (1993) and *Aging and Quality of Life* (1994), and an associate editor of the fourth edition of the *Handbook of the Psychology of Aging* (1996). In addition to his duties at the National Institute on Aging, he has been instrumental in fostering behavioral and social research throughout the National Institutes of Health. From 1980 to 1993, he served as the Executive Secretary and Acting Chair of the ad hoc NIH Working Group on Health and Behavior. From 1993 to the present he has been first the Vice Chair and then the Chair of the NIH Health and Behavior Coordinating Committee and then the NIH Behavioral and Social Sciences Research Coordinating Committee, which is successor to the Working Group and is charged with coordinating behavioral and social research across the NIH and with making recommendations to the Director, Office of Behavioral and Social Sciences Research, NIH. For these activities, he received the NIH Director's Award in 1990.

Paul B. Baltes is Director of the Center of Lifespan Psychology at the Max Planck Institute for Human Development in Berlin and Professor of Psychology at the Free University of Berlin. He received his doctorate from the University of Saarbrücken (in Saarland, Germany) in 1967. Before returning to Germany in 1980, he spent 12 years as Professor of Psychology and/or Human Development at several American institutions, including Pennsylvania State University, where he directed the Division of Individual and Family Studies. He is interested in advancing a life-span view of human ontogenesis that considers behavioral and cognitive functioning from childhood into old age. Substantive topics in his research include work on historical cohort effects, cognitive development, a dual-process conception of life-span intelligence, and the study of wisdom. His interests also include models of successful development (including aging) and the cross-cultural comparative study of self-related agency beliefs in the context of child development and school performance. Together with his late wife, Margret Baltes, he proposed a systemic metatheory of ontogeny that characterizes life-span development as the orchestration of three processes: selection, optimization, and compensation. He is active in various national and international organizations, including the U.S. Social Science Research Council (where since 1996 he has served as Chair of the Board of Directors), the German-American Academy Council, the Berlin-Brandenburg Academy of Sciences, and the European Academy of Science. Regarding interdisciplinarity, he is engaged primarily in two projects: He chairs (together with Karl Ulrich Mayer) the Berlin Aging Study and, together with the sociologist Neil Smelser, he is coeditor in chief of the 26-volume

International Encyclopedia of the Social and Behavioral Sciences, which is scheduled to appear in 2001. He is author or editor of 15 books and more than 250 scholarly articles and chapters. For his work, he has been honored with numerous awards, including honorary doctorates and election as foreign member to the American Academy of Sciences and the Royal Swedish Academy of Sciences.

Ute Bayer has worked since 1993 as a Research Assistant in the Psychology Department of the University of Konstanz. She is a member of Professor Gollwitzer's team researching social psychology and motivation and has specialized on various aspects of the mind-set concept. Her doctoral thesis deals with the effects of the deliberate and implemental mind-sets on social information processing.

Jochen Brandtstädter is Professor of Psychology at the University of Trier, Germany. He received his Ph.D. in psychology from the University of Saar, Saarbrücken, Germany, and subsequently held academic positions at the University of Trier and the University of Erlangen, Germany. He has received numerous grants to support his research in developmental psychology and action theory. His current longitudinal and experimental research projects center on issues related to personal control over development in adulthood, development in partnership relations, and mechanisms of coping and adaptation in later life. His publication record is extensive, with influential contributions in the areas of adult development, action theory, psychological prevention, theoretical psychology, theory of science, and methodology. He has held editorial board positions and has served in other capacities on several journals, including *Human Development* and the *International Journal of Behavioral Development.* Since 1992, he has been a member of the Academia Europaea, London. In 1984-1985, he was Fellow at the Wissenschaftskolleg (Center for Advanced Study) in Berlin. He is currently (1998-1999) a Fellow at the Center for Advanced Study in the Behavioral Sciences, Stanford University.

Joachim C. Brunstein is Professor of Educational Psychology at the University of Potsdam in Potsdam, Germany. Prior to graduating in 1983 from the University of Giessen, he was a guest student at the University of Pennsylvania and the University of California, Santa Cruz. A Fellow of the Scholarship Foundation of the German People, he received a doctoral degree in 1986 from the University of Giessen. He then joined the Max

Planck Institute for Psychological Research in Munich, where he worked together with the late Heinz Heckhausen. Before he joined the Department of Psychology at the University of Potsdam, he was a Lecturer of Developmental and Educational Psychology at the University of Erlangen and a stand-in Professor of Educational Psychology at the University of Frankfurt. He is a member of the German Psychological Association, the American Psychological Association, and the American Educational Research Association. His research focuses on the points of intersection among motivational, developmental, and educational psychology. His primary areas of interest include helplessness and depression, volition and self-regulation of performance, cognitive and affective underpinnings of achievement motivation, personal goals and subjective well-being, life aspirations and identity commitments, and social support in close relationships.

Laura L. Carstensen is Professor and Vice Chair of the Psychology Department at Stanford University. She holds the Barbara D. Finberg Directorship of the Institute for Research on Women and Gender, and she is a Fellow of the American Psychological Association, the Gerontological Society of America, and the American Psychological Society. On two occasions she has been a Visiting Fellow at the Max Planck Institute for Human Development in Berlin. In 1994 she was President of the Society for a Science of Clinical Psychology and in 1996 served as Chair of the Behavioral Sciences Section of the Gerontological Society of America. Among her awards are the Richard Kalish Award for Innovative Research and the Dean's Distinguished Teaching Award. Her research, supported by the National Institute on Aging, focuses on life-span development, gender, and emotion.

Dale Dannefer is Professor of Education and Sociology in the Margaret Warner Graduate School of Education and Human Development, University of Rochester. He has been a Fellow of the Andrew Norman Institute for Advanced Studies, Andrus Gerontology Center, University of Southern California, and a visiting scholar at the Max Planck Institute for Human Development and Education in Berlin. His extensive writings on the life course and human development include "Differential Aging and the Stratified Life Course" (in *Annual Review of Gerontology*), "On the Concept of Context in Developmental Discourse" (in *Life Span Development and Behavior*), and "Paths of the Life Course: A Typology" (coauthored with Peter Uhlenberg, in the *Handbook of Aging Theory*). His current research examines the effects of radical social change in nursing homes on the normal trajectories of decline displayed by those who live in such facilities.

Lisa Feldman Barrett is Associate Professor of Psychology at Boston College. A psychologist whose interests span clinical, social, and personality psychology, she received a Ph.D. in 1992 from the University of Waterloo. Prior to joining Boston College, she was on the faculty at the Pennsylvania State University. She is the author of many scholarly articles and chapters that discuss the varying facets of human emotion. Her use of experience-sampling methodologies in the study of emotion is currently supported by the National Science Foundation.

Kurt W. Fischer, Professor of Education and Director of the Mind, Brain, and Education Concentration at the Harvard Graduate School of Education, is a student of human development from birth through adulthood. Before coming to Harvard, he began his career at the University of Denver, where he was Professor of Psychology. He has also been Visiting Professor or Scholar at the University of Geneva (Switzerland), the University of Pennsylvania, the University of Groningen (Netherlands), and the Center for Advanced Study in the Behavioral Sciences at Stanford University. At Harvard, he is Chair of the Department of Human Development and Psychology. His work focuses on the organization of behavior and the ways it changes, especially cognitive development, social behavior, emotions, and brain bases. In his approach, called *dynamic skill theory,* he aims to combine the many personal organismic and environmental factors that contribute to the rich variety of developmental change and learning across and within people. His research analyzes change and variation in a range of domains, including students' problem solving and co-construction, concepts of self in relationships, cultural contributions to social cognitive development, early reading skills, emotions, child abuse, and brain development. His research generally focuses on the diversity of cognitive and emotional development, including developmental variation between and within different cultural and ethnic groups. His primary research directions include dynamic growth modeling, analysis of microdevelopmental change in real-life learning situations, emotional pathways to psychopathology, brain bases of cognitive change, and pedagogical implications of knowledge about development of cognition, emotion, and brain. His cultural research focuses on the development of emotions and self in diverse nations, including Korea, China, and the United States. He is coauthor of "Dynamic

Development of Psychological Structures in Action and Thought" in the *Handbook of Child Psychology* (5th edition, Volume 1) and has written more than 200 scientific articles and nine books and monographs.

Alexandra M. Freund is currently a Research Scientist at the Max Planck Institute for Human Development in Berlin. She received her diploma in psychology in 1989 and her Ph.D. in 1994 from the Free University of Berlin. Before she took her current position at the Max Planck Institute in 1994, she was a postdoctoral fellow at Stanford University. Her dissertation was about the content, structure, and function of the self-definition in old age. This topic continues to be one of her central research interests. Her other research interests include processes of developmental regulation and motivation across the life span. Her current projects focus on the empirical investigation of selection, optimization, and compensation as processes of developmental regulation from an action-theoretical perspective.

Helene H. Fung is a fourth-year predoctoral student in personality psychology at Stanford University. She received her B.S. from the University of Washington at Seattle in 1995 and her M.A. from Stanford University in 1997. Her research interests lie in the area of sociocultural influences on adult socioemotional development. For her paper "The Influence of Time on Social Preferences: Implications for Life-Span Development" she received the 1998 Margaret Clark Award.

Peter M. Gollwitzer has held the Social Psychology and Motivation Chair at the University of Konstanz, Germany, since 1993. From 1988 to 1992 he headed the "intention and action" research group at the Max Planck Institute for Psychological Research in Munich. He studied psychology and educational sciences at the University of Regensburg and social psychology at the Ruhr University-Bochum. In 1981 he received his Ph.D. at the University of Texas at Austin. His research interests cover a broad range of issues that have broken new ground in social and motivation psychology. In his work on self-completion theory (with Robert Wicklund at the University of Texas at Austin), he discovered that people conceive of their identities (e.g., being a good father) in terms of long-term goals that in turn stimulate an ongoing and enduring pursuit of the respective identities that includes numerous different compensatory efforts (so-called self-symbolizing). In collaboration with Heinz Heckhausen at the Max Planck Institute for Psychological Research, he suggested in the mid-1980s that goal pursuit is best conceptualized in terms of a progression through four consecutive action phases: deliberation, planning, acting, and evaluating. This perspective led him to the development of two important theoretical concepts: mind-sets and implementation intentions. The mind-set concept stimulated an in-depth analysis of the type and quality of people's information processing when preparing to get started on a goal (implemental mind-set) compared with choosing a goal (deliberative mind-set). The concept of implementation intentions initiated theorizing on automatic action initiation. Peter Gollwitzer is coeditor (with John Bargh) of *The Psychology of Action* (1996) and coauthor (with Robert Wicklund) of *Symbolic Self-Completion* (1982). He is a member of the Academia Europaea and a Charter Fellow of the American Psychological Society. In 1990, he received the Max Planck Research Award.

Jutta Heckhausen is a Senior Research Scientist at the Center for Lifespan Psychology at the Max Planck Institute for Human Development in Berlin where she heads a research group on "Motivational Psychology of Ontogenesis." She received her Ph.D. in 1985 from the University of Glasgow, Scotland. Her work addresses motivational psychology and control behavior in life-span development in general and developmental regulation in particular. Together with Richard Schulz, she developed the life-span theory of control and is applying it to processes of developmental regulation at various stages in life. From 1995 to 1996, she was a Fellow at the Center for Advanced Study in the Behavioral Sciences at Stanford University. Her recent publications include "A Life-Span Theory of Control" (with Richard Schulz, *Psychological Review*), a monograph, *Developmental Regulation in Adulthood,* and a volume coedited with Carol S. Dweck titled *Motivation and Self-Regulation Across the Life Span.*

Ingrid E. Josephs was educated in psychology at the Ruhr University, Bochum, Germany, where she obtained her Ph.D. in 1993. She then worked in the Section of Developmental Psychology at the Otto von Guericke University Magdeburg. Since October 1998 she has continued her research in developmental psychology at Clark University in Worcester, Massachusetts, sponsored by a fellowship from the Alexander von Humboldt Foundation. Her main area of interest is the development of the self within a cultural psychological framework.

Richard M. Lerner holds the Bergstrom Chair of Applied Development Science at Tufts University. A developmental psychologist, he received a Ph.D. in 1971 from the City University of New York. He has been a fellow at the Center for Advanced Study in the Behavioral Sciences and is a fellow of the American Association for the Advancement of Science, the American Psychological Association, the American Psychological Society, and the American Association of Applied and Preventive Psychology. Prior to joining Tufts University, he was on the faculty and held administrative posts at Michigan State University, Pennsylvania State University, and Boston College, where he was the Anita Brennan Professor of Education. During the 1994-1995 academic year he held the Tyner Eminent Scholar Chair in the Human Sciences at Florida State University. He is the author or editor of 32 books and more than 250 scholarly articles and chapters, including his 1995 book *America's Youth in Crisis: Challenges and Options for Programs and Policies*. He edited Volume 1 of the fifth edition of the *Handbook of Child Psychology*, titled *Theoretical Models of Human Development*. He is known for his theory of, and research about, relations between life-span human development and contextual or ecological change. He is the founding editor of the *Journal of Research on Adolescence* and of the new journal *Applied Developmental Science*.

Karen Z. H. Li is currently a Postdoctoral Research Fellow at the Center for Lifespan Psychology at the Max Planck Institute for Human Development in Berlin. She completed her M.Sc. in psychology at the University of Alberta in 1991 and her Ph.D. in psychology at the University of Toronto in 1996. Prior to joining the Max Planck Institute, she spent a postdoctoral year at Duke University. As a researcher of cognition and adult development, she has investigated processes that underlie age-related change in working memory, dual-task performance, and selective attention. Her recent work includes less conventional memorial factors such as age and individual differences in circadian arousal levels and sensory acuity as possible determinants of memory and cognitive change. Her present work focuses on the integration of dual-task methodology and principles of the Baltes and Baltes framework of selection, optimization, and compensation (SOC). Using the SOC model, she aims to delineate the costs and benefits of compensatory aid use in the context of age-related losses in the sensori-motor and cognitive domains.

Brian R. Little received his early education in British Columbia and his Ph.D. from the University of California, Berkeley. He was a Commonwealth Scholar and subsequently a faculty member at Oxford University. He is currently Professor of Psychology and Director of the Social Ecology Laboratory at Carleton University in Ottawa, Ontario. In 1995, he was at McGill University as the inaugural recipient of the Royal Bank Fellowship in University Teaching. His research lies at the intersection of personality, social, and life-span developmental psychology, and his recent writing has emphasized the conative turn in psychological research. His development of "personal projects analysis" has been influential in both personality psychology and developmental science. He has been the recipient of several awards for research and teaching, and he delivered the G. Stanley Hall lectures for the American Psychological Association in 1996.

Günter W. Maier is a Lecturer of Industrial and Organizational Psychology at the University of Munich. He studied psychology at the Universities of Giessen (Germany) and Munich. After graduation in psychology in 1992 from the University of Munich he worked on a research project called "Selection and Socialization of Managerial Candidates." He received his doctoral degree in 1996. He is a member of the German Psychological Association, the American Psychological Association, the International Association of Applied Psychology, and the Academy of Management. His research focuses on motivational psychology and organizational socialization. His areas of interest include personal goals at work, self-regulation, realistic job preview, organizational citizenship behavior, team climate and team performance, and organizational learning.

Michael F. Mascolo is Professor of Psychology at Merrimack College in North Andover, Massachusetts. He received his Ph.D. from the State University of New York at Albany and performed postdoctoral work at Harvard University. He is editor (with Sharon Griffin) of *What Develops in Emotional Development?* (1998) and author of numerous articles on social constructivism, systems theory, and the development of self and emotion in sociocultural contexts.

Robert A. Neimeyer is Professor in the Department of Psychology at the University of Memphis in Memphis, Tennessee, where he also maintains an active private practice. He completed his doctoral training in clinical psychology at the University of Nebraska in 1982, and since then the majority of his research has drawn on concepts and methods in personal construct theory and related constructivist approaches to personality and psychotherapy. He has published 17 books, including *The Development of Personal Construct Psychology* (1985), *A Personal Construct Therapy Casebook* (1987), *Advances in Personal Construct Theory* (Volumes 1 through 4; 1990, 1992, 1995, 1997), and *Constructivism in Psychotherapy* (with Michael J. Mahoney; 1995). The author of more than 200 articles and book chapters, he is currently most interested in developing a narrative and constructivist framework for psychotherapy, with special relevance to the experience of loss. He is coeditor of the *Journal of Constructivist Psychology* and serves on the editorial boards of a number of other journals. In recognition of his scholarly contributions, he has been granted the Distinguished Research Award by University of Memphis (1990), designated Psychologist of the Year by the Tennessee Psychological Association (1996), made a Fellow of Division 12 (Clinical Psychology) of the American Psychological Association (1997), and received the Research Recognition Award of the Association for Death Education and Counseling (1999).

Gabriele Oettingen is a Senior Researcher at the Max Planck Institute for Human Development in Berlin. After her dissertation in behavioral biology working with I. Eibl-Eibesfeldt at the Max Planck Institute for Behavioral Physiology in Seewiesen, Germany, and Robert A. Hinde at the Medical Research Council in Cambridge, Great Britain, she did her postgraduate work at the Department of Psychology at the University of Pennsylvania in Philadelphia. Starting out with investigating the impact of educational style on peer interactions and the development of hierarchies in peer groups, she later extended this observational research to cultural contexts by observing behavioral signs of depression and analyzing explanatory style (with Martin E. P. Seligman) in various political and socio-cultural contexts. A cross-cultural focus prevailed in her analyses (with Todd D. Little and Paul B. Baltes) of the development of efficacy and control beliefs, where she and her collaborators identified relevant cultural factors that shape the appraisal of efficacy expectations. Her recent research focuses on the development and motivational function of thinking about the future. She published a monograph titled *Psychologie des Zukunftsdenkens* (Psychology of Thinking About the Future) that addresses the question of when and how people set themselves developmental tasks.

Karen S. Quigley is Assistant Professor of Psychology at Pennsylvania State University. She received her Ph.D. in psychobiology from Ohio State University and completed postdoctoral work in developmental psychobiology at Columbia University. Her primary research interests lie in understanding the cardiovascular, autonomic, and behavioral effects of threat, fear, and distress in both humans and animals. Her work in collaboration with Gary Berntson and John Cacioppo on models of autonomic control of the heart has been published in *Psychological Review, Psychological Bulletin,* and *Psychophysiology.* Her more recent work on individual differences in cardiovascular reactivity to interpersonal and physical stressors has been supported by the National Institute of Mental Health and Pennsylvania State University.

Klaus Rothermund is Research Scientist at the University of Trier, Germany, where he received his Ph.D. in 1998. He has published in the fields of development, cognition, and motivation. As a member of Jochen Brandtstädter's research group, he has been involved in the investigation of coping processes and personal control over development, primarily with regard to development in later adulthood and old age. His current research projects focus on attentional mechanisms, automatic affective processing, and motivated reasoning.

Michaela Scherer recently received her master's degree from the University of Konstanz in Germany; the topic of her thesis was self-affirmation versus self-completion. During an internship at the University of Georgia in Athens, she worked with Abraham Tesser on confluences of self-serving mechanisms and attitude change. She is now working on her doctoral degree; her dissertation will deal with how fantasies turn into binding action goals.

Oliver C. Schultheiss is currently a Fellow of the German Research Foundation (Deutsche Forschungsgemeinschaft) at the University of Potsdam in Germany. He earned both his diploma (1994) and his doctoral degree (1996) at the University of Erlangen, Germany. As an undergraduate and as a graduate student, he was awarded scholarships by the Scholarship Foundation of the German People (Studienstiftung des deutschen Volkes). In 1997, he was a Research Fellow at Harvard University, where he worked together with the late David C. McClelland. He is a member of the American Psychological Association, the German Psychological Association (Deutsche Gesellschaft für Psychologie), and the Society for Personality and Social Psychology. Although in the past he has done research on the role of goal imagery in motive-goal congruence and goal commitment, his current research focuses on the function of neuroactive hormones in implicit motivation. His primary areas of interest include biopsychological substrates and correlates of implicit motives, motivational components of implicit learning, the interplay between motivational and temperamental factors in personality functioning, and the effects of motive-goal mismatches on mental and physical health.

Richard Schulz is Professor of Psychiatry and Director of the University Center for Social and Urban Research at the University of Pittsburgh. He has spent most of his career doing research and writing on adult development and aging. He has been particularly interested in social psychological aspects of aging, including the role of control as means for characterizing life-course development; age-related changes in the experience, perception, and expression of affect; and the impact of disabling late-life disease on patients and their families. His publications include "A Life-Span Model of Successful Aging" (with Jutta Heckhausen; *American Psychologist*, 1996), *Adult Development and Aging: Myths and Emerging Realities* (1999), and *Handbook of Alzheimer's Disease Caregiver Intervention Research* (forthcoming).

Andrea E. Seifert received her master's degree in psychology from the University of Konstanz, Germany, in 1999. Her thesis deals with the effects of social reality of goal intentions and implementation intentions on their execution. She is currently working on her doctoral dissertation, which concerns the importance of future-related thinking for conflict resolution.

Ellen A. Skinner is Professor of Human Development and Psychology at Portland State University, where she has worked since 1992. She was trained as a life-span developmental psychologist at the Pennsylvania State University, from which she received her Ph.D. in human development in 1981. She spent the next 7 years as a Research Scientist at the Max Planck Institute for Human Development and Education in Berlin. In 1988, she joined the Motivation Research Group at the University of Rochester. Her research focuses on the development of children's self-system processes; how the self can exert so powerful an influence on children's motivation, ongoing engagement, and coping with challenges and failures; and the role close relationships with parents and teachers play in promoting or undermining the developing self. She has written most on perceived control and coping. In the past few years, in addition to research articles and chapters, she has published a book on control, motivation, and coping; a review article on constructs of control; and a Society for Research in Child Development monograph on individual differences and the development of control. She has also edited a special section for the *International Journal of Behavioral Development* on the development of coping across the life span. She was named a W. T. Grant Faculty Scholar and the Distinguished (Young) Researcher of the Year for 1996 by the Western Psychological Association.

Jacqui Smith is a Senior Research Scientist at the Max Planck Institute for Human Development in Berlin and has a long research collaboration with Paul B. Baltes. She is Codirector (together with Paul Baltes) of the Psychology Unit of the Berlin Aging Study, a project sponsored by the Berlin-Brandenburg Academy of Sciences. A life-span developmental psychologist, she received her Ph.D. in 1984 from Macquarie University, Sydney, under the mentorship of Jacqueline J. Goodnow. She was on the faculty at Macquarie University for 10 years before moving to the Max Planck Institute in 1984. She is the editor of four books and more than 50 scholarly articles and chapters. Her research spans cognitive, personality, and life-span psychology and includes studies on memory, wisdom, expertise, life planning, and aging. Her particular interest in the Berlin Aging Study is to examine the dynamic interdependencies of cognitive functioning, self-related processes, and social relationships in late life. In this context she has published on psychological predictors of longevity, cross-domain profiles of functioning, self-regulation processes, well-being, and gender differences in old age.

Seth E. Surgan is pursuing a doctorate in developmental psychology at Clark University in Worcester, Massachusetts, as a National Science Foundation Predoctoral Fellow. He is interested in theoretical issues within developmental cultural psychology and has done research on how self is constructed and maintained through body decoration and modification. Despite time spent in Massachusetts, he still prefers the New Jersey dialect and blue T-shirts.

Jaan Valsiner works on issues of cultural and developmental psychology. He has written a number of monographs, among which *The Guided Mind*

(1998), *Culture and the Development of Children's Action* (2nd edition, 1997), and *Understanding Vygotsky* (with Ren Van der Veer, 1991) are of notice. He is the founding editor of the journal *Culture and Psychology* (from 1995 on) and is editor of numerous volumes, including *The Individual Subject and Scientific Psychology* (1986), and of the book series Advances in Child Development Within Culturally Structured Environments. Prior to joining Clark University in Worcester, Massachusetts, as Professor of Psychology in 1997, he was a faculty member at the University of North Carolina at Chapel Hill (since 1981) and a frequent visitor to the University of Brasilia, Technical University of Berlin, Institute of Psychology of Italian Research Council (CNR), and University of Melbourne.

Ted Walls is completing his doctoral work in developmental and educational psychology at Boston College. Prior to his study at Boston College, he was a research manager at a nonprofit organizational consulting firm, where he developed methods for organizational problem solving and strategic planning. His current research interests lie in the areas of program evaluation from a developmental perspective, longitudinal study of social development, and work-based interventions for youth and families.

Dirk Wentura is Assistant Professor at the University of Muenster, Germany. He received a Ph.D. in 1994 from the University of Trier, Germany. Prior to joining the University of Muenster, he was a member of Jochen Brandtstädter's research group, with which he has been involved in the investigation of coping processes, especially in later adulthood and old age. His research interests include topics at the interface of cognitive psychology, life-span psychology, and social psychology. He has published on coping, age stereotypes, and automatic affective processes.